The Open University

The art of English:
literary creativity

Edited by Sharon Goodman and Kieran O'Halloran

Published by Palgrave Macmillan in association with The Open University

The Open University, Walton Hall, Milton Keynes MK7 6AA United Kingdom

PALGRAVE MACMILLAN, Houndmills, Basingstoke, Hampshire RG21 6XS and
175 Fifth Avenue, New York, N. Y. 10010
Companies and representatives throughout the world

PALGRAVE MACMILLAN is the global academic imprint of Palgrave Macmillan division
of St. Martin's Press, LLC and of Palgrave Macmillan Ltd. Macmillan® is a registered
trademark in the United States, United Kingdom and other countries. Palgrave is a
registered trademark in the European Union and other countries.

First published 2006

Edited and designed by The Open University.
Typeset in India by Alden Prepress Services, Chennai.
Printed and bound in the United Kingdom by Scotprint, Haddington.

This book forms part of an Open University course E301 *The art of English*. Details of
this and other Open University courses can be obtained from the Student Registration
and Enquiry Service, The Open University, PO Box 197, Milton Keynes, MK7 6BJ,
United Kingdom: tel. + 44 (0)870 333 4340, email general-enquiries@open.ac.uk
http://www.open.ac.uk
A catalogue record for this book is available from the British Library.
A catalog record for this book is available from the Library of Congress.

ISBN-13: 978-1-4039-8560-6
ISBN-10: 1-4039-8560-X

1.1

808,
042
ART

Book editors

Sharon Goodman is a lecturer in the Centre for Language and Communications at The Open University, where she has been involved in the writing and production of many of the Centre's undergraduate and postgraduate English Language courses. Her interests include stylistics, media literacy, multimodal communication, and academic writing. She co-edited *Redesigning English: New Texts, New Identities* (Routledge, 1996) and *Language and Literacy in Education: A Reader* (Trentham, 2002), and co-authored *Teaching Academic Writing: A Toolkit for Higher Education* (Routledge, 2003).

Kieran O'Halloran is a lecturer in the Centre for Language and Communications at The Open University. His research interests include critical discourse analysis and stylistics, especially the use of corpora in these areas, as well as cognitive approaches in discourse analysis. Publications include *Critical Discourse Analysis and Language Cognition* (Edinburgh University Press, 2003) and *Applying English Grammar: Functional and Corpus Approaches* (Hodder Arnold, 2004, with Caroline Coffin and Ann Hewings).

Other original contributors

Ruth Finnegan is Visiting Research Professor, Faculty of Social Sciences, The Open University. An anthropologist, her work has particularly focused on oral literature, performance and multimodal communication. Her books include *Oral Traditions and the Verbal Arts* (Routledge, 1992), *Tales of the City: A Study of Narrative and Urban Life* (Cambridge University Press, 1998) and *Communicating: The Multiple Modes of Human Interconnection* (Routledge, 2002).

Geoff Hall is a senior lecturer in the Centre for Applied Language Studies (CALS) at Swansea University, tutor on the Open University MA in Literature, and Assistant Editor of the journal *Language and Literature* (Sage). Research interests include stylistics and literature in education. His book *Literature in Language Education* was published by Palgrave Macmillan in 2005.

Theresa Lillis is a senior lecturer in the Centre for Language and Communications at The Open University. Her research interests include academic writing and the politics of knowledge production. Published works include *Student Writing: Access, Regulation, and Desire* (Routledge, 2001) and co-authored texts on sociolinguistics; *A Dictionary of Sociolinguistics* (Edinburgh University Press, 2004, with Joan Swann, Ana Deumert and Raj Mesthrie) and *Analyzing Language in Context: A Student Workbook* (with Carolyn McKinney, Trentham, 2003).

Anna Magyar is an associate lecturer at The Open University, where she is also involved in research and in producing distance learning and staff development materials. Her research interests include widening participation, academic communication, and English as an international language. She has also worked as a freelance translator and language teacher.

Janet Maybin is a senior lecturer in the Centre for Language and Communications at The Open University. Originally trained as a social anthropologist, she has written extensively for Open University courses on language, literacy and learning and also researches and writes on children and adults' informal language and literacy practices. She co-edited *Using English: From Conversation to Canon* (Routledge, 1996) and *Language, Literacy and Education: A Reader* (Trentham, 2002). Most recently she has authored *Children's Voices: Talk, Language and Identity* (Palgrave, 2005).

Michael Pearce is a senior lecturer in English Language at the University of Sunderland. He has research interests in critical discourse analysis and stylistics, and is the author of *The Routledge Dictionary of English Language Studies* (Routledge, 2006, forthcoming).

Elena Semino is a senior lecturer in the Department of Linguistics and English Language, Lancaster University. Her books include *Language and World Creation in Poems and Other Texts* (Longman, 1997) and *Corpus Stylistics: Speech, Writing and Thought Presentation in a Corpus of English Narratives* (Routledge, 2004, with Mick Short). Her research interests are in stylistics, corpus linguistics and cognitive linguistics (especially cognitive metaphor theory).

Joan Swann teaches at The Open University, where she has many years' experience producing distance-learning multimedia materials on linguistics and English language studies. She is currently Director of the Centre for Language and Communications. Her research interests include language and gender and other areas of sociolinguistics. Recent books include *Introducing Sociolinguistics* (Edinburgh University Press, 2000, with Rajend Mesthrie, Ana Deumert and William Leap), *Children's Cultural Worlds* (John Wiley, 2003, co-edited with Mary Jane Kehily) and *A Dictionary of Sociolinguistics* (Edinburgh University Press, 2004, with Ana Deumert, Rajend Mesthrie and Theresa Lillis).

Maria Thomas is an associate lecturer in the Faculty of Arts at The Open University. She has several years' experience of teaching in the Humanities, particularly on Shakespeare. She currently contributes to the Open University course *Shakespeare: Text and Performance*, where she specialises in Shakespeare's works as scripts for performance. Her research interests include the Jacobean stage, Shakespeare's *Sonnets*, and the psychological function of creativity in surviving exile/migration.

Joanna Thornborrow is a senior lecturer at the Centre for Language and Communication Research at Cardiff University, where she teaches mainly in the areas of media discourse and communication, and stylistics. Her most recent book, *The Sociolinguistics of Narrative* (co-edited with Jennifer Coates), was published by John Benjamins in 2005. Other publications include *Language Society and Power* (Routledge, 2004) and *Power Talk* (Pearson Education, 2002). She is currently Director of Postgraduate Studies in the Centre.

Contents

Introduction

What is literary creativity? What distinguishes some texts as high quality literature? Looking at the language of literary texts and the sociocultural issues around them, this book considers what happens when these texts are performed on stage or accompanied by images and sound, made to move, or created collaboratively on the internet. The role of the reader or audience of literature is also an important focus. We consider what readers do when they read literature and how this can contribute to the exploration of literary creativity.

In the late twentieth century, oppositional critique of literature (feminist, neo-Marxist, post-colonial) offered liberating reading positions in times of rapid social change. These were embraced by many literary scholars and valuable insights were afforded, but questions of creativity and literary value did not receive sustained attention. This is despite literary value being central to the writer of literature, as the literary journalist James Wood argues:

> The very thing that most matters to writers, the first question they ask of a work – is it any good? – is often largely irrelevant to university teachers.

(*London Review of Books*, 20 May 2004)

This book returns to questions of literary creativity with fresh perspectives, drawing on research that makes use of new technology to open out questions of what constitutes creativity. It explores the broader social, cultural and critical dimensions of creativity as well as the participatory nature of much text production and reception. The chapters bring different theoretical perspectives and analytical approaches to literature, drawing on insights from poetics, stylistics, sociolinguistics, literary studies, multimodal studies, corpus linguistics, drama and media studies. Examples of new and established research from these disciplines illuminate and exemplify the many different ways we can consider creativity.

Chapter 1 establishes many of the key concepts and perspectives used in the book and will enable readers to begin articulating their responses to questions of what constitutes literary creativity.

Chapter 2 has a textual focus. It starts by looking at poetic language from the perspective of Russian and Prague School Formalism and their key thinkers, Roman Jakobson and Jan Mukařovský. It then goes on to examine the distinction between the literary and non-literary in terms of a cline of core qualities.

Chapter 3 continues with a textual focus, this time looking at plot and characterisation in narrative fiction. A range of analytical tools are introduced for examining narrative fiction from both a macro- and micro-perspective.

In **Chapter 4**, the focus shifts from the primarily written texts explored in Chapters 2 and 3, to consider literature in performance. Using examples taken from drama, poetry and narrative fiction, it considers creative practices in a wide range of performances, from stage plays to oral unscripted storytelling.

Chapter 5 considers the creative processes involved in translating literary works from and into English, and questions where we can locate creativity.

Chapter 6 builds on Chapters 4 and 5, where creative texts utilising resources beyond language were introduced. It looks more closely at printed literature that uses words and images, to show some of the ways in which visual communication in literature can be seen as playful and creative.

Chapter 7 looks at the impact of technology on literature, from reworkings of canonical texts for film to the creation of new works for the internet. It builds on the multimodal themes of Chapters 4, 5 and 6 but moves further away from the text in considering how meanings are activated in the reading and viewing of texts.

In **Chapter 8**, the relationship between literary creativity and the reader is explored further but this time from a cognitive perspective. In what ways might the effects on readers' minds in reading a poem be different to the reading of an advert, for example?

Chapter 9 considers empirical research into how readers respond to literary texts, and the social practices through which readers engage with literature. It then goes on to consider how literary writers view their own creativity, as well as examining work which challenges the dichotomy of reading/writing.

Each chapter is structured in the form of teaching text divided into sections, followed by three or four associated **readings**. The **activities** provide guidance on the readings or tasks to stimulate further understanding of the topic.

Boxed text contains illustrative material or definitions.

Key terms are set in bold type at the point when they are explained; they also appear in bold in the index for easy location in the text.

Marginal notes are used for brief explanations, cross-references and editorial notes on the readings.

The section containing **colour illustrations** is located between pages 214 and 215. These illustrations are referred to in the text as 'Colour Figures'.

Literature and creativity in English

Janet Maybin and Michael Pearce

1.1 Introduction

What makes a text literary? Why are some creative texts seen as high-quality literature and others dismissed as of little lasting value? Is what we value as 'literariness' located inside a text, or does it reside in the ways in which poetry, drama and fiction are read and used? This chapter introduces a variety of approaches to defining, analysing and valuing literary texts in English. This exploration of the nature and functions of literary creativity will continue in subsequent chapters, where we will look at how creativity works within a wide range of genres – from traditional narrative fiction, poetry and drama to more recent electronic forms and media texts. Throughout this book, we use 'literary', 'literature' and 'literariness' as a family of related terms, but you will find that they are defined somewhat differently according to whether we are examining creativity in the language of poetry, fiction or drama, the effect of such creativity on readers and audiences or whether a culture regards such language as valuable.

But first, how do you recognise creativity in the English language?

ACTIVITY 1 Creativity and literature

Allow about 30 minutes

- Which of the texts overleaf would you see as creative? In what ways are they creative? Which would you also identify as 'literature'? What criteria are you using?

- We recommend that you do this exercise first without necessarily knowing where these texts are from. Then think about the texts again when you know their origins (see 'Comment').

1

Ariell Song. Full fadom fiue thy Father lies,
Of his bones are Corrall made :
Those are pearles that were his eies,
Nothing of him that doth fade,
But doth suffer a Sea-change
Into something rich,& strange:
Sea-Nimphs hourly ring his knell.
       Burthen: ding dong.
Harke now I heare them, ding-dong bell.

2

simpology:
the perfect balance between
simplicity and techn**ology**

3

The Unknown

As we know,
There are known knowns.
There are things we know we
know.
We also know
There are known unknowns.
That is to say
We know there are some things
We do not know.
But there are also unknown
unknowns,
The ones we don't know
We don't know.

4

I lost my own father at 12yr. of age and know what it is to be raised on lies and silences my dear daughter you are presently too young to understand a word I write but this history was for you and will contain no single lie may I burn in Hell if I speak false.

God willing I shall live to see you read these words to witness your astonishment and see your dark eyes widen and your jaw drop when you finally comprehend the injustice we poor Irish suffered in this present age. How queer and foreign it must seem to you and all the coarse words and cruelty which I now relate are far away in ancient time.

Your grandfather were a quiet and secret man he had been ripped from his home in Tipperary and transported to the prisons of Van Diemen's Land. I do not know what was done to him he never spoke of it.

5

**More spinned
against than
spinning**
Nick Cohen on Mandy's
big mistake, page 11

6

XXXII.

OF DISCOURSE.

SOME in their *Discourse*, desire rather Commendation of Wit, in being able to hold all Arguments, then of Judgment, in discerning what is True: As if it were a Praise, to know what might be Said, and not what should be Thought. Some have certaine Common Places, and Theames, wherein they are good, and want Variety: Which kinde of Poverty is for the most part Tedious, and when it is once perceived Ridiculous. The Honourablest Part of Talke, is to give the Occasion; And againe to Moderate and passe to somewhat else; For then a Man leads the Daunce. It is good, in *Discourse*, and Speech of Conversation, to vary, and entermingle Speech, of the present Occasion with Arguments; Tales with Reasons; Asking of Questions, with telling of Opinions; and Jest with Earnest: For it is a dull Thing to Tire, and, as we say now, to Jade, any Thing too farre. As for Jest, there be certaine Things, which ought to be priviledged from it; Namely Religion, Matters of State, Great Persons, Any Mans present Businesse of

7

And now we're walking down the street
Wid a brand new pride
A spring inna de step
Wid our heads held high
Young Asian brothers and sisters
Moving forward, side by side
Naya Zindagi Naya Jeevan
New Way New Life

Comment

How you responded to this task depends, of course, on what you understood by the terms 'creative' and 'literature'. Much of the rest of this chapter is concerned with exploring these terms, so keep your responses to Activity 1 in mind as you read on.

1   Ariel's song 'Full fathom five' from Shakespeare's *The Tempest*, I, ii (1611). There is manipulation of the language to produce rhyme, rhythm, alliteration, imagery and the overall structure of the song (on the stage, the use of music and performance is as important as the words). If you recognised the source as Shakespeare, you may have automatically defined the extract as literature. Well-established texts in the English literature canon seem unequivocally literary, but where would you place the boundary around what counts as literature outside the canon?

2   Text from a brochure for a Nissan Micra car. Advertising and promotional texts often manipulate language to produce striking and memorable effects. But are they literary?

3   A 'poem' by Hart Seely (2003), created from US Secretary of Defense Donald Rumsfeld's Department of Defense news briefing to journalists on US operations in Afghanistan (22 February, 2002). Do you see creativity as residing in Rumsfeld's original turn of phrase or in Seely's structuring of it in a literary form, to parody a poem?

4   From 'Parcel 1' of Peter Carey's novel *True History of the Kelly Gang* (the story of Ned Kelly, the nineteenth-century Australian cattle-thief, which won the Booker Prize in 2001). Carey uses non-standard grammar and punctuation to create a distinctive narrator's voice. Each chapter is represented as a 'found document' and headed with summary notes in the nineteenth-century style.

5   This *Guardian* newspaper headline contains a playful intertextual reference to Shakespeare's *King Lear*. After Lear has been cast out of his daughters' houses, he laments that he is 'a man more sinned against than sinning' (III, ii). (Mandy is the nickname of the British politician, Peter Mandelson.) Notice the coining of 'spinned' to create the parallel alliterative echo with the Shakespeare text. Does the ephemerality and brevity of creative wordplay and intertextual referencing in newspapers exclude these texts from 'literature'?

6   The opening paragraph from Essay XXXII 'Of discourse' by Francis Bacon (1625). History, essays and other forms of 'polite letters' were included in the seventeenth-century conception of literature as 'polite learning through reading', and Bacon's elegant writing is still on the syllabus of some university English literature courses.

7   Extract from 'New way, new life' (Asian Dub Foundation, 2000). This Jamaican-style rap sung by British musicians from a South Asia background mixes styles, ethnicity and languages creatively. Can art forms which are popular rather than classic, and performed rather than read, ever count as 'literature'?

The notes above suggest a variety of ways in which texts can be creative; they also raise questions about what makes creative texts into literature. In this chapter, we will focus on three important approaches, which reflect different views of the nature of literature and of how creativity works (Carter, 1999):

1   The 'inherency approach' treats artistry as residing within creative uses of language intrinsic within the text.

2   The 'sociocultural approach' explores social and ideological factors around the concept of 'literature'.

3   The 'cognitive approach' shifts the focus onto the ways in which readers engage with literary, as opposed to other kinds of, texts.

Initially, we stay fairly close to texts traditionally defined as literature, but we raise questions about change, diversity and new forms of verbal art towards the end of the chapter.

1.2 Creativity as inherent in the text

We begin with the inherency approach, which defines creativity at the level of language itself. It focuses on the writer's skill in manipulating the sounds, words, phrases and overall linguistic form of the text. Scholarly approaches to literature which pay attention to the relationship between linguistic form and creativity can be traced back to the classical period, in particular to Aristotle (384–322 BC). In his *Poetics*, Aristotle applied the 'scientific' method of analysis (which he had invented) to literary works, identifying and systematically describing their distinctive features. The body of ideas, however, with the most profound influence on current thinking about creativity in literary language (and which laid the foundations for the linguistic analysis of literature known as 'stylistics') was developed by academics working in Moscow, Leningrad and Prague in the early twentieth century: the Russian Formalists and the Prague School Structuralists.

Stylistics is the analysis of formal features in the text to show how they function in its interpretation and in the production of literary effects.

These scholars (most active in the years between the two world wars) advocated, like Aristotle, a 'scientific' approach to literature. They viewed literary works as self-contained aesthetic objects. Biographical, historical, sociological or psychological dimensions were irrelevant to their main objective, which was to identify and define the form of literary language. The early Formalists focused on how poetic devices in literature produce an effect which they called *ostraneniye* ('making strange'), or **defamiliarisation**, in which our routine ways of seeing and thinking are disrupted; our perceptions freshened; and our awareness of the world heightened (Shklovsky, in Hawkes, 1977, p. 62). Their ideas were developed by scholars within the Prague School who analysed literature through drawing on the discipline of linguistics.

Through the work of Roman Jakobson (a central figure in both Formalism and the Prague School), the Formalists were concerned with what became known as the *poetic* function of language. They saw this as closely connected to 'literariness', which they defined as the special properties of language that could be located in literary texts.

Jakobson developed an influential typology of language functions:

Jakobson's language functions

- The **referential** function is associated with the *context* of the message. It focuses on conveying information about the world beyond the communicative event itself.

- The **emotive** or expressive function is associated with the *speaker/ writer*. It focuses on their attitude toward what they are speaking about, which may be expressed through a particular choice of words, grammar, or tone of voice.

- The **conative** function is associated with the *hearer/reader*. It is concerned with aspects of language designed to affect or influence the hearer/reader in some way. This function may be expressed through features such as requests and commands.

- The **phatic** function is associated with the *contact*. It is fulfilled by language which is addressed at initiating, sustaining or closing the channel of communication, e.g. 'Well, here we are chatting away at last' or by ritualised formulas, e.g. 'Lend me your ears'.

- The **metalingual** function is associated with the *language code* itself. An utterance performs a metalingual function when it refers to the code and how the code works. For example, whenever interactants need to check up on their mutual comprehension of the code they are using, they focus on this function of language, asking questions such as 'Do you know what I mean?' or 'What do you mean by "ritualised formulas"?'

- The **poetic** function is associated with the *message*. It focuses on the message for its own sake, emphasising the linguistic qualities of words themselves rather than any other factors in the situation.

(Adapted from Jakobson, 1960, p. 356)

All utterances perform at least one of these functions; but most are multifunctional. For example, when a TV weather forecaster says *Hold onto your hats! It's a breezy one today*, one function of the utterance is **referential** – the speaker is conveying information about the world. However, if a viewer then rams his hat more firmly on his head before going out, a **conative** function is present, because the forecaster's utterance is influencing his thoughts and behaviour in some way. Further, if the statement is delivered with an elongated vowel in *breezy* (i.e. *breeeezy*), the utterance could perform an **expressive** function – in English, exaggerated prosodic patterns like this are used to convey emotion. Finally, a **poetic** function is present: the repetition of the /h/ initially in the stressed syllables is a prominent piece of phonetic patterning.

As the weather forecaster example demonstrates, the poetic function is not unique to literature. It is a feature of many 'everyday' texts too. Conversely, literary texts perform other functions alongside the poetic. But, according to Jakobson (1960, p. 356), it is the *dominant* function of poetry, 'whereas in all other verbal activities it acts as a subsidiary, accessory constituent'. The poetic function involves the language drawing attention to its own form in some way; it then becomes especially prominent and is therefore **foregrounded** in the mind of the reader. Foregrounding is achieved through stylistic choices that either depart from the norms of everyday language ('**deviation**'), or which set up noticeable patterns of repetition ('**parallelism**'). Because poetic uses of language involve the highlighting and, in a sense, distortion of its 'natural' characteristics, Jakobson suggests that literature, especially poetry, can be seen as 'organized violence committed on ordinary speech' (quoted in Eagleton, 1983, p. 2).

Deviation

Deviation is present when words, phrases and grammatical structures draw particular attention to themselves by 'deviating' from what is expected. Deviation can occur at the level of **phonology**, **graphology** (the writing system including punctuation, layout, size and typeface), grammar or lexis and meaning, and often at a number of these levels simultaneously.

- Graphological deviation is closely linked to phonological deviation, because authors sometimes use unusual forms of writing to provide information about how something sounds when spoken aloud. In *Ulysses*, for example, James Joyce (1986, p. 627) wrote the drawn-out sound of a train as: 'Frseeeeeeeeeeeeeeeeeeeefrong'. This can be seen as a graphological deviation since we don't normally expect to see 20 letter 'e's together in a written word. Graphological deviation from standard English can also capture the regional and social origins of a speaker: for instance, in Zadie Smith's (2000, p. 25) *White Teeth*, she represents the speech of a nineteen-year-old woman 'from Lambeth (via Jamaica)': 'Man ... dis life no easy'.

- Writers also manipulate a wide variety of **grammatical** structures. For example, in the above example, Smith uses features associated with Jamaican Creole, such as a zero copula (there is no *is* linking the subject and its complement), and the invariant negator *no*.

- Deviation at the level of **words and meaning** includes rare, dialect or foreign words which stand out from the surrounding text, and neologisms (e.g. Joyce's word for the train sound is also a neologism). Semantic deviation is associated with figurative language, particularly metaphor and simile.

- Finally, texts sometimes display **genre deviation**: words, grammatical features, and so on, which we typically associate with one type of speech and/or writing are deployed in another genre (for example, when an advertisement is written in the form of a sonnet). Such 'intertextuality' is often related to the kinds of deviation outlined above.

Parallelism

Whereas deviation might be characterised as 'unexpected irregularity' in a text, parallelism is 'unexpected regularity' (McIntyre, 2003, p. 4), involving prominent patterns of repetition at the level of sound, grammatical structure or meaning.

- Phonological parallelism is the combining of the same or similar sounds. Alliteration results from the repetition of word-initial consonants; the repetition of similar vowel sounds produces assonance. Rhyme is present when similar syllables are repeated, and the repetition of rhythmic patterns produces metre.
- Grammatical parallelism is the repetition of phrase and/or clause structure.
- Semantic parallelism involves the repetition and sometimes extension of the meaning of words, phrases and images. For example, 'The voice of the LORD is over the waters;/the God of glory thunders/the LORD thunders over the mighty waters' (Psalm 29: 3–5) combines semantic and grammatical parallelism.

ACTIVITY 2   **Organised violence on ordinary speech**

Allow about
30 minutes

Identify examples of deviation and parallelism in the Activity 1 texts.

Comment

Here are some of the most prominent examples that you might have identified. There are, of course, many more.

Deviation

Foregrounded spelling and graphology: Text 2 illustrates graphological deviation. Usually, bold font is used to make whole words stand out from the surrounding text, but here, in order to draw attention to the constituent components of the neologism, bold is used to emphasise parts of the words: *simpl*icity and techn**ology**. We also find an instance of graphological deviation in Text 4, where the absence of punctuation at certain sentence and clause boundaries is used to represent the unsophisticated writing style of a man with very little formal education.

Foregrounded grammatical structure: In Text I the first line shows an order of clause elements different from the canonical English pattern: *Full fadom [fathom] five* (adverbial of place) *thy Father* (subject) *lies* (verb). In English (even in the early seventeenth century) the most common position for circumstance adverbials (such as adverbials of place) is at the end of the clause. The 'unmarked' order then, is *thy Father* (subject) *lies* (verb) *full fathom five* (adverbial of place). Further syntactic deviation occurs in the second line: *Of his bones are Corrall [coral] made*. Here, we might 'normally' expect *coral are made of his bones*. Such re-orderings can also occur at phrase level, as in *full fathom five*. These are examples of a type of syntactic 'creativity' which is common in English poetry.

Foregrounded meaning relations: In Text 4, the character Ned Kelly claims that he was *raised on lies and silences*. This metaphor involves conceptualising abstract phenomenon (*lies and silences*) as having 'nutritional' value in child rearing, in the same way that food does. Semantic deviation can also take the form of the juxtaposition of words which do not normally occur together. For example, in Text 3 the noun phrases *known knowns*, *known unknowns* and *unknown unknowns* seem to be designed to draw attention to their paradoxical nature.

Foregrounded word choice: One of the most obvious forms of lexical deviation is when a writer invents a new word (Short, 1996, p. 46). For example, in Text I Shakespeare seems to have coined the noun *sea-change*. In the context of the extract, this is a term to describe the transformation of a human body wrought by the sea, but it is now used more widely to describe any kind of dramatic change. In Text 2, we have the coinage *simpology*, which draws attention to the process of its own formation: as a combination, apparently, of simplicity and technology.

Genre deviation: In Text 2 the conventions of a dictionary definition are deployed in a promotional text, and in Text 4, apparently factual documents are presented as a fictional novel.

Parallelism

We find parallelism at the level of sound, such as the alliteration (**F**ull **f**athom **f**ive thy **f**ather lies), and rhymes in Text I; the repeated /ɑɪ/ in Text 7 (*pride, high, side, life*) or the alliterative parallel intertextual echo in *more* **sp**inned *against than* **sp**inning. We also find repetition of individual words, and many of these repetitions occur in parallel structures: *There are known knowns/There are things we know we know*; *Wid a brand new pride … Wid our heads held high*; in Text 6, *It is good … to vary, and entermingle Speech, of the present Occasion with Arguments; Tales with Reasons; Asking of Questions, with telling of Opinions; and Jest with Earnest.'*

Influential as the work of Jakobson and other Formalists has been, the suggestion that literary creativity is mainly a product of linguistic deviation and parallelism at the level of the text is often difficult to sustain, largely because 'deviation' can be difficult to measure. As the literary critic Terry Eagleton (1983, p. 5) points out, 'one person's norm may be another's deviation'. Some of the Activity 1 texts illustrate this. For example, a modern reader faced with unusual word forms, such as *Honourablest* and *Theames* (Text 6), might find these 'deviant', but they would have been unremarkable to early seventeenth-century speakers of English, or to an academic with a research interest in the period. Similarly, although many readers might have found the code-switching (between English and Hindi/Urdu) and non-standard spelling of the Asian Dub Foundation lyric 'deviant', others more familiar with this kind of music would see this as typical of groups in the genre, and these linguistic features unremarkable and expected.

So, there are difficulties associated with how deviation is measured. Moreover, claims that deviation and parallelism are the *defining* features of prose literature are also difficult to sustain. For example, it is not immediately obvious how the poetic function is 'dominant' in, say, the essays of Francis Bacon or George Orwell – works generally regarded as having literary merit.

Code-switching is dealt with in more detail in the companion volume, **Maybin and Swann (2006)**.

1.3 A sociocultural approach to what counts as literature

There is obviously something more to literature, then, than the poetic uses of language defined by Jakobson, important as these may be for catching our attention and leading us into new ways of seeing and thinking about the world. Literary authors are commonly seen as writers who draw substantially upon their imaginations. Is it then the imaginative nature of literary writing which makes it different? Terry Eagleton, whose sociocultural arguments about literature have been a rather different kind of influential force within literary theory, argues volubly against this suggestion. He points out that in the seventeenth and eighteenth century 'literature' meant 'polite writing' and essays (like Bacon's quoted in Activity 1), sermons, philosophy and history have all been included, at times, in the English literary canon.

Furthermore, while not all literature is imaginative, neither is all imaginative writing (for example, in pulp novels) literature. Alternatively, is there something about true literature which evokes a particular quality of aesthetic response in the reader? Eagleton (1983, p. 9) rejects this suggestion as well, arguing that any piece of writing can be read poetically: 'If I pore over the railway timetable not to discover a train connection but to stimulate in myself general reflections on the speed and complexity of modern existence', then the structure of the timetable could be said to have a poetic function. Similarly, as we saw in Activity 1, a news briefing in certain circumstances can be read as a poem.

In fact, Eagleton argues that there is no common factor nor intrinsic essence to 'literature'. Rather, we need to take social and ideological factors into account, in order to understand the role of literature in society. For Eagleton (1983, p. 11), literature consists of those works of writing which are valued and revered in a society for particular social and historical reasons – the so-called literary canon is not inherently great, nor even a stable entity, but has been 'fashioned by particular people for particular reasons at a particular time'. This 'sociocultural' concept of literature explains why a piece of writing which starts off life as history or philosophy can later come to be ranked as literature. Eagleton (1983, p. 9) argues that 'What matters may not be where you come from but how people treat you. If they decide that you are literature, then it seems that you are, irrespective of what you thought you were'. For Eagleton, the decision about what counts as literature is ideological – it is taken within 'an often invisible network of value categories', connected, together with particular 'modes of feeling, valuing, perceiving and believing', to the power structure and power relations of the society in which we live.

How do you react to this statement? Are there examples of literature which you feel are simply great writing, no matter how they are treated? If so, what is it about them that makes them great? To what extent does Eagleton conflate literature with the *use* of literature?

ACTIVITY 3   Literature as ideology (Reading A)

Please turn to Reading A by Terry Eagleton: 'The rise of English'. Here, Eagleton uses English literature as a kind of case study to test out his theory about how particular kinds of writing come to be defined as literature.

- What role does he see literature playing in society?
- How convincing do you find his argument that 'literature is an ideology'?

Comment

Eagleton sees the concept of literature in England as relating closely to the needs of the times and the priorities of powerful social groups within society. Literature embodies social values and it also helps to disseminate them. For example, in the eighteenth century the polite manners and taste in literature helped to bind the middle and upper classes after a period of civil war. In the nineteenth century, ideas about the organic unity, spontaneity and creativity of literary imagination offered an alternative ideology to the wage slavery and alienation of early industrial capitalism in Britain. Eagleton claims that the concept of literature which we now take for granted emerged only in the early nineteenth century, out of the revolutionary Romantic period. Its revolutionary, transformative vision was, however, muted by writers turning aside from the dominant ideology of philistine utilitarianism into an alternative, more appealing world of imagination and aesthetics. Then, in Victorian times, Eagleton (p. 29 of this volume) argues that the religion which had provided an effective ideological control over the working classes was waning and literature took its place as a body of shared and revered ultimate truths about life, beauty and moral ideals which would 'save our souls and heal the state'.

In suggesting that literature is an ideology, Eagleton addresses the issue of quality and value from a more sociological perspective than the Formalists, or the Prague School. Thinking back to my (JM's) schooldays, the literature I read certainly conveyed particular values (e.g. of 'virtue rewarded' and the importance of loyalty to one's country) and Shakespeare and the Bible were equally revered. Historians have shown that English literature was clearly connected with the emergence of England as a nation and with defining what counted as 'standard English' (Bailey, 1992; Leith and Graddol, 1996), and the ideological function of teaching English literature in British colonies has been well documented (e.g. Brathwaite, 1981; Viswanathan, 1989). But is Eagleton's sociocultural explanation of what counts as literature any more comprehensive than the Formalists' account of its linguistic devices? Eagleton, for instance, doesn't explain why some works of literature have been valued so consistently across history, somehow able to escape the conditions within which they were written or intended to be performed. Eagleton's theory is, as he acknowledges in his 'Afterword' to the 1996 second edition of *Literary Theory*, very much linked to its own historical context, that of Europe and North America in the 1960s and 1970s. Writing just after the 1960s' period of 'social hope, political militancy and high theory' Eagleton deconstructs the concept of 'literature' using the Marxist and poststructuralist theory which was influential at the time. Over twenty years later, at the beginning of the twenty-first century, people are more likely to describe themselves as post-modern than post-Romantic, and the concept of English literature is problematised more through globalisation and technology than theory. But that, perhaps, proves Eagleton's point about the sociocultural nature of literature and its uses.

1.4 Literature in the mind of the reader

So far we have looked at two ways of thinking about how we identify literature. The Formalist account defines it in terms of features inherent in the text, focusing on specific patterns of language such as deviation and parallelism. For Jakobson, texts may be categorised according to which 'function' is dominant. In texts most readily identifiable as 'poetic', the poetic function comes at the top of the hierarchy (but remember that Jakobson stresses that 'poetic' language is not limited to poetry). The sociocultural approach moves beyond the text itself and defines literature as an ideological discourse with a particular political purpose; it shows how texts may undergo processes of recategorisation and re-evaluation, irrespective of their original role.

In Section 1.4 we shall be considering a third way of arguing for the distinctiveness of literature, the 'cognitive approach' (see p. 6). Since the 1990s, stylistics has taken a cognitive turn. Drawing on insights from psychology and artificial intelligence, scholars have been exploring the processes which take place in readers' minds as they engage with literary texts, arguing that what distinguishes the literary from the non-literary is not so much the way the *writer* writes, but the way the *reader* reads.

ACTIVITY 4   From transcript to poem

Allow about
20 minutes

In Activity I you looked at a 'poem' created from a news briefing to journalists in early 2002 by the US Secretary of Defense (Donald H. Rumsfeld). Now look at this section of a transcript of the event, which was archived on the US Department of Defense website:

> **Question**: In regard to Iraq weapons of mass destruction and terrorists, is there any evidence to indicate that Iraq has attempted to or is willing to supply terrorists with weapons of mass destruction? Because there are reports that there is no evidence of a direct link between Baghdad and some of these terrorist organizations.

> **Rumsfeld**: Reports that say that something hasn't happened are always interesting to me, because as we know, there are known knowns; there are things we know we know. We also know there are known unknowns; that is to say we know there are some things we do not know. But there are also unknown unknowns – the ones we don't know we don't know. And if one looks throughout the history of our country and other free countries, it is the latter category that tend to be the difficult ones.

Did you read the poem and the transcripts in different ways? What characterises these ways of reading? What features of the text and the broader contexts in which the texts are situated motivate these contrasting reading strategies?

Comment

Textual features mark this out as belonging to an identifiable, culturally specific language event – a particular kind of **speech genre** with distinctive content matter, style and evaluative perspective according to typical situations of speech communication (Bakhtin, 1986, p. 87). As competent members of a discourse community, we are able to recognise the textual features of different speech genres, and the recognition of text-type motivates a particular way of reading. The genre on the website is 'news briefing/press conference', and once we have identified the genre we begin to read in a particular way.

See also Chapter 6
in the companion
volume, **Maybin
and Swann (2006)**.

Both participants in the sequence of speech recorded in the transcript are playing a part determined by a number of social, cultural and institutional factors. Some things are allowable in this genre; others are not. The journalists, politicians and military spokespeople in the briefing have particular institutionalised speaker rights. The journalist has the right to ask questions; Rumsfeld is obliged to answer them (or at least give reasons for not answering). Contextual factors determine other features of the language – level of formality, features of structure (questions, answers, requests for clarification). Furthermore, there is an external 'real-world' context to which these words refer. Rumsfeld – in spite of his highly abstract language – is not indulging in general epistemological speculation. His comments refer to a context in which there are things military intelligence knows about; other areas where they realise there is something they do not know (which it would be useful to know). And then there are the complete mysteries – things which come out of the blue. If he were at liberty he could, presumably, illustrate these points with real-world examples, and we could check up on them.

How differently did you approach the 'poem' version in Activity 1? As with the news briefing, the recognition of genre provokes a particular way of reading. In this version we recognise it as a poem primarily by its layout on the page. There is a title, followed by 12 lines. The lines do not go all the way to the right-hand margin and each begins with a capital. Because this is a culturally sanctioned text-type called a 'poem', we approach it differently from the news briefing. The way in which we read poetry depends on upbringing, education, disposition – but most of us are used to seeking for 'meaning' in poetry, beyond the 'surface impression' of the words. Faced with Rumsfeld's original comments in the briefing, we look for meaning with reference to an external, 'real-world' context. And we do this with all non-literary texts. But in the poem, these same words do not point to a wider social context at all. There is no way of knowing precisely what the 'known knowns' refer to. The poem – and by extension, all 'literature' – is designed to provoke us into constructing an *imaginary* context.

ACTIVITY 5   Literature as enclosure (Reading B)

Please read the extract from 'Critical practices: on representation and the interpretation of text' (Reading B). In the reading, Widdowson's argument for the distinctiveness of literature is based on a number of characteristics which literary texts have, but which non-literary texts do not. What are these differences? How far do you agree with Widdowson's suggestion that a literary text 'floats free in a state of vacant possession for readers to appropriate and inhabit'? How convincing do you find his arguments?

An important part of Widdowson's argument refers to Grice's maxims (see box below).

Grice's maxims

The English philosopher Paul Grice (1975) argued that all conversation is founded on the 'co-operative principle', an unspoken agreement between participants in a conversation. This assumes that speakers are generally following these rules (or maxims):

Don't give too much information or too little information. (Quantity)

Don't lie or mislead. (Quality)

Don't be irrelevant. (Relation)

Don't be unclear, disorderly, ambiguous and obscure. (Manner)

Comment

Widdowson suggests that when we read 'non-literary' 'conventional', 'normal' texts (these are all Widdowson's terms), we use the language as a set of directions which points us towards an external, verifiable reality. These texts can be re-ordered or reformulated without changing their meaning substantially, since they will still refer indexically. On the other hand, if aspects of textual design get altered in a literary text, substantial alterations of meaning result. This is because literary texts do not refer to an external reality; they create in interaction with the mind of the reader their own imaginary context, their own representations. A reader of non-literary texts ignores those aspects which do not seem to serve a pragmatic purpose, and the reader's attention is drawn away from the text. Conversely, in literary texts our attention is drawn into the text itself – significance is sought in features of textual patterning which might only be a distraction in non-literary texts.

In non-literary texts, participants are bound by the cooperative conditions of conventional communication: we can ask whether the events referred to are true, are being presented according to normal expectations of economy and clarity, are relevant to the previous utterance or to the context. But it simply doesn't make sense to ask these questions when faced with a literary text. Widdowson claims that in literary texts these maxims are not being followed (and indeed, readers aren't expecting them to be followed). Literature doesn't have to be true: it just has to carry conviction; it doesn't have to be relevant, but consistent and coherent in its own terms. As he puts it in the reading, literary texts are:

> of their nature untrue, uninformative, irrelevant and obscure. The maxims of quality, quantity, relation and manner are consistently denied, and consequently literary texts give rise to complex and irresolvable implicatures on a vast scale. It is this which constitutes their aesthetic effect.
>
> (p. 36–7 of this volume)

The lack of direct referential connection with the readers' concerns, the flouting of Gricean maxims, produces what Widdowson calls the 'enclosing effect', which he claims is a characteristic feature of all literature.

Like the Russian Formalists, Widdowson concentrates mainly on poetry – he chooses to exemplify what is 'special' about literature by looking at a Wordsworth lyric. He acknowledges that the enclosing effect of secondary patterning is most obvious in this genre. But he also says that it is 'a defining feature of all literature'. Are *all* literary texts as capable of generating this 'enclosing' effect as poetry? Do you think this argument is equally applicable to the novel or drama, for example? Another aspect of the reading which you might want to interrogate is the fact that Widdowson's examples are drawn from canonical literary texts (Wordsworth, Hemingway); but his 'definition' of literature is in fact much wider than he seems to imply here. According to Widdowson's criteria, non-referential use of language is 'literary'. But this definition seems far too broad in comparison with what is generally labelled 'literature'. As we have seen, jokes, word-play, and so on are prototypically excluded from the category, yet these are all non-referential uses of language. So what people generally say is literature is not actually captured in his definition. Widdowson (unlike Eagleton) seems unwilling to engage with the notion of value (even though, in general use, literature is often an evaluative term).

For more discussion on jokes and word-play, see Chapter 1 in the companion volume, **Maybin and Swann (2006)**.

While Widdowson focuses on individual acts of reading, it could be argued that texts are sometimes read within the context of particular institutional practices where specific kinds of readings and interpretations are valorised. Within the fields of education, literary criticism and publishing, some approaches to reading are constructed as more authoritative than others and there certainly are penalties for 'getting it wrong' (such as failing an examination). Thus, it could be argued that while the textual design closes the text off in one sense, some readings of texts cannot be so readily cut off from their *context*, or from the social and institutional values associated with it.

Widdowson's (p. 36 of this volume) main concern is not about what 'the writer meant by the text, but what the text means, or might mean, to the reader'. This interest in the construction of individual 'readings' – what happens in people's heads when they read literature – is further developed in cognitive poetics. This is a relatively new approach to literary studies which draws on insights from the cognitive sciences (e.g. artificial intelligence, psychology, cognitive linguistics) in an attempt to relate texts 'to their presumed or observed psychological effects' (Steen and Gavins, 2003, p. 1). These psychological effects are produced in the interaction between the text and 'the past knowledge and experience' stored in the mind of the reader (Culpeper, 2001, p. 28). Unlike the Formalists, practitioners of cognitive poetics do not see 'literariness' as a property of the text. But they do share with the Formalists the belief that 'deviation' is often a characteristic of texts widely regarded as literary. However, it is a different kind of deviation from those we have been considering so far.

ACTIVITY 6   Literature as schema refreshing (Reading C)

Please read 'Cognitive poetics', by Elena Semino (Reading C). Then consider the following questions:

- What is 'discourse deviation' and how is it different from the kind of deviation outlined in Section 1.2? Is all literature 'schema refreshing'?
- How does cognitive poetics deal with the notion of literary 'value'?

Comment

In Reading C, Semino refers to influential work by Guy Cook, who argues that what distinguishes literary from non-literary texts is not *linguistic* deviation on its own, but **discourse deviation**. Cook (1994) argues that readers approach a text with certain background knowledge and expectations about 'objects, people, situation, and events', and that these expectations are disrupted by literary discourse so that the reader's schemata are challenged and changed to produce **schema refreshment**. Cook uses the term 'discourse' in 'discourse deviation' firstly to refer to the patterning of language at the linguistic level and the level of the text structure (both of which are addressed in textual approaches discussed in Section 1.2). However, for Cook, the term 'discourse' refers not only to the language but also to the world it creates within the literary work, for instance the personal world created by Plath in 'Tulips'. He is most interested in the interaction between the existing worldview of the reader, and the language and worldview of the text.

Semino herself focuses on how metaphors in the Plath poem result in discourse deviation where the normal positive and negative expectations of a particular situation and objects are reversed. Semino points out, while the tulips are personified/animised (usually in 'unpleasant' terms), the poem's *persona* (i.e. its 'voice') represents herself as an inanimate object. This reversal of usual expectations results in schema refreshment, and is therefore an example of discourse deviation. Texts, such as an advert or a newspaper headline, may be full of linguistic deviation, but they are unlikely to challenge a reader's way of looking at the world; indeed, they are more likely to reinforce 'conventional' ways of thinking. Semino emphasises the 'less elitist' approach of cognitive poetics in viewing literary and non-literary language on a continuum in terms of creativity, and in the analysis of popular as well as canonical texts. 'Value', in cognitive poetics, appears to be related to the artfulness and significance of the schema refreshment.

While Semino acknowledges that background knowledge and the possibilities for schema refreshment vary from reader to reader, this has not been enough to ward off criticisms of cognitive poetics for a lack of attention to contextual issues. Jeffries (2001) argues that literature does not always have to be 'schema refreshing', because readers from minority social groups may experience literary impact when their point of view and experience is actually represented and reinforced. Furthermore, she argues that a model of the cognitive aspects of reading literature needs to incorporate the possibility of meanings derived from multiple group identities, so that an individual may be reading from a number of (possibly conflicting) viewpoints at any one time.

1.5 Creativity, hybridity and new language arts

An elitist canon?

Literary texts in English have traditionally been valued in relation to criteria set up in the canon, that body of authoritative 'great works' which are seen as the finest examples of writing in English, and which still form the backbone of university courses in English. Yet, as Jakobson demonstrated, poetic uses of language are not confined to high art. From a different point of view, Eagleton argued in Reading A that Literature with a capital 'L' has no special intrinsic quality, but is composed of works which have come to be highly valued for historical and ideological reasons. Alongside its deconstruction by Eagleton, the canon has also been critiqued from other directions. Feminists argue that the small number of women writers represented is related to the traditional monopoly of men over poetry writing (because this grew out of the classical education which before the twentieth century was mainly only available to boys), and over drama (because theatres were associated with 'disreputable' women). They point out that the dominance of male writing in these two genres has been matched by the domination of men and masculine perspectives in publishing and literary criticism (Showalter, 1986; Birch, 1992). The canon has also been attacked as elitist and entrenched within the British class system, both through the values expressed in canonical texts and in the way in which the canon functions in education at all levels. Literary criticism, it has been argued, is still influenced by the English literary critic F.R. Leavis' belief that we have to look to the past for truly great literary uses of the English language and that true literary value can only be appreciated by a small cultural elite.

Challenges to the canon

A particularly strong challenge to the traditional canon of English literature has come from writers in countries that were formerly part of the British empire. These 'postcolonial' writers began to develop new ways of using the English language and literary forms, attempting in some cases to decouple the language from its past associations (Achebe, 1988), and in others abandoning it altogether (Ngugi, 1986). The first wave of postcolonial writers (e.g. Achebe, Brathwaite, Narayan, Ngugi, Thumboo) wrote with the weight of the 'English literature' which had formed the mainstay of their education on their shoulders, in the context of growing nationalist–independence movements. A subsequent generation of writers reflect a rather different context of local 'counter-traditions' (Lim quoted in Pennycook, 1994, p. 287) and global migratory patterns (e.g. Indian diaspora writers like Rushdie, Ondaatje and Mistry).

By the turn of the twenty-first century, the increasing use of English in global communication has loosened the original close connection between the English language, English literature, and England as a nation state. In addition, the rapidly changing global communication technologies and the hybrid cultural practices emerging from the mixing of traditions and experience through migration are producing new kinds of creative practices in English and new kinds of literary and popular creative texts.

Pennycook (2003) suggests that the global spread of English is usually seen either as a swallowing up of local languages and cultural practices into one global market (the 'homogeny position') or as a process of local adaptation and appropriation, leading to 'Indian English', 'Singapore English' and so on (the 'heterogeny position'). He argues, however, that current creative uses of English in different parts of the world are more complex than either of these two positions would suggest. Pennycook is particularly interested in the cultural dynamics of popular verbal forms in global youth culture, which he focuses on in Reading D.

ACTIVITY 7   **New English arts: hybridity and identity (Reading D)**

Please read Alistair Pennycook's 'Beyond homogeny and heterogeneity' (Reading D). In what ways is he arguing that hip-hop, as a creative language form, cannot be understood in terms of either linguistic and cultural homogenisation or linguistic and cultural adaptation?

Having completed the reading, think about ways in which the spread of art forms like hip-hop might, if at all, challenge the value of more traditional forms of English literature.

Comment

Within local histories, Pennycook suggests, the grand designs of expansionist projects like British colonialism have not been either taken on completely wholesale, or simply adapted and accommodated. Rather, there has been a continuing interaction between global forms with their ideological and commercial freight, and local intermixed forms with their own complex history. For Pennycook, different uses of hip-hop around the world exemplify how writers and performance artists are using both the English language, and its historical and ideological connotations, to produce new cultural forms and meanings within contexts with both local and global dimensions. Pennycook suggests that hip-hop is used at a local level for creative and sometimes subversive purposes. He argues that through rap and hip-hop young people celebrate pride in their own cultural heritage, whether London South Asian or Fijian–Australian, they challenge and resist the status quo and they make links with other young people worldwide. In using English, sometimes in connection with other languages, they not only take hold of the language and its artful verbal forms, but combine forms and ideas in new ways to keep their own cultural history moving along, to express an identity within a rapidly changing, culturally hybrid world.

If a 'fluid mixture of cultural heritage ... and popular culture' (p. 46 of this volume) is currently more significant to the spread of English than the formal teaching of English language and literature, then it could be argued that the majority of English speakers worldwide in the future might draw on a multicultural range of verbal art forms and performances for their creative experience and own use of the language, rather than on a single authoritative English literature tradition. The popularity of these new forms among young people globally, and the proliferation of multimodal practices in the world of entertainment, may reduce the reading of the canonical texts of English literature to a minority activity practised only by serious scholars. In the context of the new global order, it might be that the idea of 'English' literature is too closely connected with English nationalism and colonialism to still provide the authoritative reference point for writers and artists using English worldwide. Thus the historical forces which Eagleton traces in the development of 'English literature' could now be moving in directions which will lead to its demise. Or do you consider that English literature still remains institutionally secure enough, or flexible enough, or just simply of such enduring artistic and intellectual quality, that it will always retain its position and value above and apart from more popular verbal art among English-speaking people, wherever they are?

One of the striking differences between English literature and the popular forms described by Pennycook is the **multimodal** and improvisational nature of art in hip-hop, where a hybrid poem/song may be combined with music and dance thus mixing different modes: verbal, visual, sound and movement. Artists can move rapidly from one generic form to another; for instance in 2004 the rap and hip-hop artists of Asian Dub Foundation were commissioned by the English National Opera to produce a multi-media opera with a political theme (Denselow, 2004). In contrast, English literature, especially within educational contexts, tends to remain within its relatively fixed traditional generic forms. Apart from a small number of experimental novels on the internet which incorporate email, instant-messaging and websites (Baer, 2004), writers like Zadie Smith may depict their characters using the kind of popular oral creativity which Pennycook describes, but this remains a written representation within a creative work which is clearly structured as a novel.

Outside literature, there are an increasing number of examples of 'high culture' art which mix words with other modes and use intertextuality, recombination and performance to produce creative effects. In 2004, the American artist Bruce Nauman's exhibition *Raw Materials* in the Turbine Hall at London's Tate Modern Gallery (a former power station) included 22 spoken texts taken from his previous sound and video pieces which were projected in bands of sound across the otherwise empty hall through 18 parallel pairs of speakers. The levels of the voices were adjusted to create a 'sound sculpture', so that the visitor walked through waves of greetings, statements, poems, pleas, propositions and jokes which whispered, shouted, chanted and echoed across the hall, ranging in tone from clear to indistinct and from tender to abusive, melancholy to sinister. These words mingled with the new sounds of visitors' voices. Nauman's ideas for the exhibition were inspired by the constant low hum in the hall from the electricity sub-station which still occupies part of the former power station, and the echoing voices of parties of schoolchildren visiting the gallery: he selected and arranged the texts, from his previous work, by rhythm and emotional content rather than according to their original meaning (Higgins, 2004).

ACTIVITY 8   Poetic sounds

Allow about 20 minutes

Thinking back to Section 1.2, can you identify any examples of parallelism and deviation in the box below? How might these contribute to the effects of the 'sound sculpture' on the audience?

Words and phrases in *Raw Materials*

'Thank you thank you thank you thank you thank you ...'

'Pete and Repeat are sitting on a fence. Pete falls off. Who's left? Repeat. Pete and Repeat ...'

'Work work work work work work work work ...'

'Live and die, die and die, shit and die, piss and die, fail and live, smile and live, think and live, pay and live ...'

'I'm having fun, you're having fun, we are having fun. This is fun. I'm bored, you're bored. We're bored, life is boring. I'm boring, you're boring, we're boring, this is boring ...'

'Get out of my mind, get out of this room ...'

'His precision and acuity left small cuts on the tips of my fingers or across the backs of my hands without any need to sit or otherwise withdraw ...'

'Feed me, eat me, anthropology ... help me, hurt me sociology ... feed me, help me, eat me hurt me' ...

(Nauman, 2004)

Comment

Nauman is fascinated by the effects of repetition, and the differences in meaning and effect which even a small change within repeated patterns can produce. He repeats words and phrases to create rhythmic patterns which also convey ideas, for instance the tyranny of work, the frustration of an endless loop between question and answer. Repetition raises questions about changed meaning and causal relationships across parallel structures. The possible connections between having fun, being bored and being boring, the irrevocable connection between feeding and eating (and, by implication, between helping and hurting) and the reduction of life to failing, smiling, thinking and, after thinking, paying, could have a cumulative discomforting, disorientating effect on the audience. An immediately powerful use of deviation in Nauman's work is at the level of artistic form, in his play with the boundaries between process and product, the new and the old, the audience and the exhibit, and his 'medium-crossing' in using the spatial dimension of sound to create a hybrid 'sound sculpture'. In this sense the exhibition could be seen as 'schema refreshing', in its disruption of background knowledge and expectations.

Nauman, like the rappers discussed by Pennycook, makes use of sophisticated sound recording and transmitting equipment to produce innovative art forms. New forms of technology are clearly encouraging new types of creativity, as well as challenging established notions of the language arts. But how are we to judge the quality of such contemporary forms, which may require different kinds of criteria and analytic tools? And how novel are they, really? Do they still draw on the kinds of linguistic creativity identified by the Formalists, within contemporary media, framed ideologically as 'art'? Or will the possibilities of technology and the internet generate new kinds of creative genres (remember, as Eagleton points out, that the novel was once seen as an upstart form)?

1.6 Conclusion

In this chapter we have introduced three influential approaches to analysing literary creativity; an inherency approach (associated with Formalism and the work of Roman Jakobson), a sociocultural approach (argued by Terry Eagleton) and recent work focusing on cognitive aspects of language, creativity and literature which includes cognitive poetics. We finished by looking briefly at new emerging forms of creativity in English in the global culture of speakers of English worldwide and in hybrid art forms, at the beginning of the twenty-first century. We have examined different criteria for what counts as literature and poetic language; criteria relating to ways of 'making language strange', foregrounding through deviation and parallelism, criteria relating to the ideological function of literature within society, the argument that literary texts are 'enclosed' and draw the reader's attention inside the text, and the concepts of 'discourse deviation' and 'schema refreshment'. In the final section we looked briefly at some transnational multimodal art forms which cross and play with cultural boundaries and hybridity, and at the use of language in a medium-crossing sound sculpture. New cultural landscapes and new technologies raise questions about the form and the role of English literature, and about our criteria for analysing and valuing language creativity. These questions about literature, literariness and value will be explored and revisited in different ways in the chapters which follow.

READING A: Extract from 'The rise of English'

Terry Eagleton

In eighteenth-century England, the concept of literature was not confined as it sometimes is today to 'creative' or 'imaginative' writing. It meant the whole body of valued writing in society: philosophy, history, essays and letters as well as poems. What made a text 'literary' was not whether it was fictional – the eighteenth century was in grave doubt about whether the new upstart form of the novel was literature at all – but whether it conformed to certain standards of 'polite letters'. The criteria of what counted as literature, in other words, were frankly ideological: writing which embodied the values and 'tastes' of a particular social class qualified as literature, whereas a street ballad, a popular romance and perhaps even the drama did not. At this historical point, then, the 'value-ladenness' of the concept of literature was reasonably self-evident.

In the eighteenth century, however, literature did more than 'embody' certain social values: it was a vital instrument for their deeper entrenchment and wider dissemination. Eighteenth- century England had emerged, battered but intact, from a bloody civil war in the previous century which had set the social classes at each other's throats; and in the drive to reconsolidate a shaken social order, the neo-classical notions of Reason, Nature, order and propriety, epitomized in art, were key concepts. With the need to incorporate the increasingly powerful but spiritually rather raw middle classes into unity with the ruling aristocracy, to diffuse polite social manners, habits of 'correct' taste and common cultural standards, literature gained a new importance. It included a whole set of ideological institutions: periodicals, coffee houses, social and aesthetic treatises, sermons, classical translations, guidebooks to manners and morals. Literature was not a matter of 'felt experience', 'personal response' or 'imaginative uniqueness': such terms, indissociable for us today from the whole idea of the 'literary', would not have counted for much with Henry Fielding.

It was, in fact, only with what we now call the 'Romantic period' that our own definitions of literature began to develop. The modern sense of the word 'literature' only really gets under way in the nineteenth century. Literature in this sense of the word is an historically recent phenomenon: it was invented sometime around the turn of the eighteenth century, and would have been thought extremely strange by Chaucer or even Pope. What happened first was a narrowing of the category of literature to so-called 'creative' or 'imaginative' work. The final decades of the eighteenth century witness a new division and demarcation of discourses, a radical reorganizing of what we might call the 'discursive formation' of English society. 'Poetry' comes to mean a good deal more than verse: by the time of Shelley's *Defence of Poetry* (1821), it signifies a concept of human creativity which is radically at odds with the utilitarian ideology of early industrial capitalist England. Of course a distinction between 'factual' and 'imaginative' writing had long been recognized: the word 'poetry' or 'poesy' had traditionally singled out fiction, and Philip Sidney had entered an eloquent plea for it in his *Apology for Poetry*. But by the time of the Romantic period, literature was becoming virtually synonymous with the 'imaginative': to write about what did not exist was somehow more soul-stirring and valuable than to pen an account of Birmingham or the circulation of the blood. The word 'imaginative' contains an ambiguity suggestive of this attitude: it has a resonance of the descriptive term 'imaginary', meaning 'literally untrue', but is also of course an evaluative term, meaning 'visionary' or 'inventive'.

Since we ourselves are post-Romantics, in the sense of being products of that epoch rather than confidently posterior to it, it is hard for us to grasp just what a curious historically particular idea this is. It would certainly have seemed so to most of the English writers whose 'imaginative vision' we now reverently elevate above the merely 'prosaic' discourse of those who can find nothing more dramatic to write about than the Black Death or the Warsaw ghetto. Indeed it is in the Romantic period that the descriptive term 'prosaic' begins to acquire its negative sense of prosy, dull, uninspiring. If what does not exist is felt to be more attractive than what does, if poetry or the imagination is privileged over prose or 'hard fact', then it is a reasonable assumption that this says something significant about the kinds of society in which the Romantics lived.

The historical period in question is one of revolution: in America and France the old colonialist or feudalist regimes are overthrown by middle-class insurrection, while England achieves its point of economic 'take-off', arguably on the back of the enormous profits it has reaped from the eighteenth-century slave trade and its imperial control of the seas, to become the world's first industrial capitalist nation. But the visionary hopes and dynamic energies released by these revolutions, energies with which Romantic writing is alive, enter into potentially tragic contradiction with the harsh realities of the new bourgeois regimes. In England, a crassly philistine Utilitarianism is rapidly becoming the dominant ideology of the industrial middle class, fetishizing fact, reducing human relations to market exchanges and dismissing art as unprofitable ornamentation. The callous disciplines of early industrial capitalism uproot whole communities, convert human life into wage-slavery, enforce an alienating labour-process on the newly formed working class and understand nothing which cannot be transformed into a commodity on the open market. As the working class responds with militant protest to this oppression, and as troubling memories of revolution across the Channel still haunt their rulers, the English state reacts with a brutal political repressiveness which converts England, during part of the Romantic period, into what is in effect a police state.[1]

In the face of such forces, the privilege accorded by the Romantics to the 'creative imagination' can be seen as considerably more than idle escapism. On the contrary, 'literature' now appears as one of the few enclaves in which the creative values expunged from the face of English society by industrial capitalism can be celebrated and affirmed. 'Imaginative creation' can be offered as an image of non-alienated labour; the intuitive, transcendental scope of the poetic mind can provide a living criticism of those rationalist or empiricist ideologies enslaved to 'fact'. The literary work itself comes to be seen as a mysterious organic unity, in contrast to the fragmented individualism of the capitalist marketplace: it is 'spontaneous' rather than rationally calculated, creative rather than mechanical. The word 'poetry', then, no longer refers simply to a technical mode of writing: it has deep social, political and philosophical implications, and at the sound of it the ruling class might quite literally reach for its gun. Literature has become a whole alternative ideology, and the 'imagination' itself, as with Blake and Shelley, becomes a political force. Its task is to transform society in the name of those energies and values which art embodies. Most of the major Romantic poets were themselves political activists, perceiving continuity rather than conflict between their literary and social commitments.

Yet we can already begin to detect within this literary radicalism another, and to us more familiar, emphasis: a stress upon the sovereignty and autonomy of the imagination, its splendid remoteness from the merely prosaic matters of feeding one's children or struggling for political justice. If the 'transcendental' nature of the imagination offered a challenge to an anaemic rationalism, it could also offer the writer a comfortingly absolute alternative to history itself. Indeed such a detachment from history reflected the Romantic writer's actual situation. Art was becoming a commodity like anything else, and the Romantic artist little more than a minor commodity producer; for all his rhetorical claim to be 'representative' of humankind, to speak with the voice of the people and utter eternal verities, he existed more and more on the margins of a society which was not inclined to pay high wages to prophets. The finely passionate idealism of the Romantics, then, was also idealist in a more philosophical sense of the word. Deprived of any proper place within the social movements which might actually have transformed industrial capitalism into a just society, the writer was increasingly driven back into the solitariness of his own creative mind. The vision of a just society was often enough inverted into an impotent nostalgia for the old 'organic' England which had passed away. It was not until the time of William Morris, who in the late nineteenth century harnessed this Romantic humanism to the cause of the working-class movement, that the gap between poetic vision and political practice was significantly narrowed.[2]

It is no accident that the period we are discussing sees the rise of modern 'aesthetics', or the philosophy of art. It is mainly from this era, in the work of Kant, Hegel, Schiller, Coleridge and others, that we inherit our contemporary ideas of the 'symbol' and 'aesthetic experience', of 'aesthetic harmony' and the unique nature of the artefact. Previously men and women had written poems, staged plays or painted pictures for a variety of purposes, while others had read, watched or viewed them in a variety of ways. Now these concrete, historically variable practices were being subsumed into some special, mysterious faculty known as the 'aesthetic', and a new breed of aestheticians sought to lay bare its inmost structures. It was not that such questions had not been raised before, but now they began to assume a new significance. The assumption that there was an unchanging object known as 'art', or an isolatable experience called 'beauty' or the 'aesthetic', was largely a product of the very alienation of art from social life which we have already touched on. If literature had ceased to have any obvious function – if the writer was no longer a traditional figure in the pay of the court, the church or an aristocratic patron – then it was possible to turn this fact to literature's advantage. The whole point of 'creative' writing was that it was gloriously useless, an 'end in itself' loftily removed from any sordid social purpose. Having lost his patron, the writer discovered a substitute in the poetic.[3] It is, in fact, somewhat improbable that the *Iliad* was art to the ancient Greeks in the same sense that a cathedral was an artefact for the Middle Ages or Andy Warhol's work is art for us; but the effect of aesthetics was to suppress these historical differences. Art was extricated from the material practices, social relations and ideological meanings in which it is always caught up, and raised to the status of a solitary fetish.

At the centre of aesthetic theory at the turn of the eighteenth century is the semi-mystical doctrine of the symbol.[4] For Romanticism, indeed, the symbol becomes the panacea for all problems. Within it, a whole set of conflicts which were felt to be insoluble in ordinary life – between subject and object, the universal and the particular, the sensuous and the conceptual, material and spiritual, order and spontaneity – could be magically resolved. It is not surprising that such conflicts were sorely felt in this period. Objects in a society which could see them as no more than commodities appeared lifeless and inert, divorced from the human subjects who produced or used them. The concrete and the universal seemed to have drifted apart: an aridly rationalist philosophy ignored the sensuous qualities of particular things, while a short-sighted empiricism (the 'official' philosophy of the English middle class, then as now) was unable to peer beyond particular bits and pieces of the world to any total picture which they might compose. The dynamic, spontaneous energies of social progress were to be fostered, but curbed of their potentially anarchic force by a restraining social order. The symbol fused together motion and stillness, turbulent content and organic form, mind and world. Its material body was the medium of an absolute spiritual truth, one perceived by direct intuition rather than by any laborious process of critical analysis. In this sense the symbol brought such truths to bear on the mind in a way which brooked no question: either you saw it or you didn't. It was the keystone of an irrationalism, a forestalling of reasoned critical enquiry, which has been rampant in literary theory ever since. It was a *unitary* thing, and to dissect it – to take it apart to see how it worked – was almost as blasphemous as seeking to analyse the Holy Trinity. All of its various parts worked spontaneously together for the common good, each in its subordinate place; and it is therefore hardly surprising to find the symbol, or the literary artefact as such, being regularly offered throughout the nineteenth and twentieth centuries as an ideal model of human society itself. If only the lower orders were to forget their grievances and pull together for the good of all, much tedious turmoil could be avoided.

To speak of 'literature and ideology' as two separate phenomena which can be interrelated is, as I hope to have shown, in one sense quite unnecessary. Literature, in the meaning of the word we have inherited, *is* an ideology. It has the most intimate relations to questions of social power. But if the reader is still unconvinced, the narrative of what happens to literature in the later nineteenth century might prove a little more persuasive.

If one were asked to provide a single explanation for the growth of English studies in the later nineteenth century, one could do worse than reply: 'the failure of religion'. By the mid-Victorian period, this traditionally reliable, immensely powerful ideological form was in deep trouble. It was no longer winning the hearts and minds of the masses, and under the twin impacts of scientific discovery and social change its previous unquestioned dominance was in danger of evaporating. This was particularly worrying for the Victorian ruling class, because religion is for all kinds of reasons an extremely effective form of ideological control. Like all successful ideologies, it works much less by explicit concepts or formulated doctrines than by image, symbol, habit, ritual and mythology. It is affective and experiential, entwining itself with the deepest unconscious roots of the human subject; and any social ideology which is unable to engage with such deep-seated a-rational fears and needs, as T.S. Eliot knew, is unlikely to survive very long. Religion, moreover, is capable of operating at every social level: if there is a doctrinal inflection of it for the intellectual elite, there is also a pietistic brand of it for the masses. It provides an excellent social 'cement', encompassing pious peasant, enlightened middle-class liberal and theological intellectual in a single organization. Its ideological power lies in its capacity to 'materialize' beliefs as practices: religion is the sharing of the chalice and the blessing of the harvest, not just abstract argument about consubstantiation or hyperdulia. Its ultimate truths, like those mediated by the literary symbol, are conveniently closed to rational demonstration, and thus absolute in their claims. Finally religion, at least in its Victorian forms, is a *pacifying* influence, fostering meekness, self-sacrifice and the contemplative inner life. It is no wonder that the Victorian ruling class looked on the threatened dissolution of this ideological discourse with something less than equanimity.

Fortunately, however, another, remarkably similar discourse lay to hand: English literature. George Gordon, early Professor of English Literature at Oxford, commented in his inaugural lecture that 'England is sick, and ... English literature must save it. The Churches (as I understand) having failed, and social remedies being slow, English literature has now a triple function: still, I suppose, to delight and instruct us, but also, and above all, to save our souls and heal the State.'[5] Gordon's words were spoken in our own century, but they find a resonance everywhere in Victorian England. It is a striking thought that had it not been for this dramatic crisis in mid-nineteenth century ideology, we might not today have such a plentiful supply of Jane Austen casebooks and bluffer guides to Pound. As religion progressively ceases to provide the social 'cement', affective values and basic mythologies by which a socially turbulent class-society can be welded together, 'English' is constructed as a subject to carry this ideological burden from the Victorian period onwards.

Notes

1   See E.P. THOMPSON (1963) *The Making of the English Working Class*, London and E.J. HOBSBAWM (1977) *The Age of Revolution*, London.

2   See R. WILLIAMS (1958) *Culture and Society 1780-1950*, London, esp. Chapter 2, 'The Romantic artist'.

3   See J.P. TOMPKINS (1980) 'The reader in history: the changing shape of literary response', in J.P. TOMPKINS (ed.) *Reader-Response Criticism*, Baltimore and London.

4   See F. KERMODE (1957) *The Romantic Image*, London.

5   Quoted by C. BALDICK (1981) 'The social mission of English studies' (unpublished D. Phil thesis, Oxford 1981), p. 156. I am considerably indebted to this excellent study, published as *The Social Mission of English Criticism* (London, 1983).

Source: EAGLETON, T. (1983) *Literary Theory: An Introduction*, Oxford, Blackwell, pp. 17–24.

READING B: Extracts from 'Critical practices: on representation and the interpretation of text'

Henry Widdowson

[A]s far as Eagleton is concerned, so-called 'Literature' is simply a discursive practice like any other: just a label that people stick on certain kinds of writing for some obscure reason or other, signifying nothing. It is a name, not a concept, and what's in a name? There is, nevertheless, a curious contradiction here. The use of the *term* 'literature' is itself a discursive practice and it is precisely the purpose of critical analysis to infer what its use might signify. The point repeatedly made by sociolinguists [...] is that there is good deal in a name: that the way things are labelled marks sociopolitical values. They are not just randomly attached. So if people identify something as distinctive, then it *is* distinctive. If, for example, they say that what they speak is a distinct language, then that defines it as a language and there is no point in the linguist insisting that it is a dialect. By the same token, if people say that certain texts are literary, that defines them as such, no matter what literary theorists might say; and to identify texts as literary is to adopt a certain attitude to them and a certain way of reading them. So which way?

Let us enquire into the question by considering two texts. They are alike in that they are both in English and have a common topic (the death of a woman). They are comparable in length (both about 80 words) and in each case the text is vertically rather than horizontally aligned – that is to say, it does not extend over the whole page but is confined in a column of print.

Text A

Annabella, film actress,
died on September 18
aged 87, she was born on
July 14, 1909

Even from earliest childhood Annabella
had a passion for cinema. As a child
playing in the garden of her family
home near Paris, the chicken shed out
in the yard became her imaginary
studio where, lost in a world of
imagination, she would act out scenes
from the films she had watched, taking
upon herself the roles of director,
cameraman and leading lady all at
once.

(From *The Times* 23.9.96)

Text B

She dwelt among the untrodden ways

1   She dwelt among the untrodden ways
2   Beside the springs of Dove,
3   A Maid whom there were none to praise
4   And very few to love.

5   A violet by a mossy stone
6   Half hidden from the eye!
7   – Fair as a star, when only one
8   Is shining in the sky

9   She lived unknown, and few could know
10   When Lucy ceased to be;
11   But she is in her grave, and, oh,
12   The difference to me!

(From William Wordsworth, *Collected Poems*)

We readily identify these texts as different in genre: the first as a newspaper obituary, the second as a poem. One immediate consequence of this is that we disregard the vertical arrangement in Text A as a feature of no significance. We know that columns of print are conventionally used in newspapers to save on space, or to provide convenient blocks of text for easy reading when folded. In Text B, on the other hand, we recognise that we do not just have an expedient disposition of print, but a pattern of metrically regular lines which are intrinsic to the text itself. Identifying the first text as a conventional obituary also leads us to overlook other textual features. We recognise that its purpose is to provide information about a particular person and that the language is effective to the extent that it succeeds in doing that. In other words we use the language indexically as a set of referential directions, and ignore any textual features which are not referentially functional. So it is that while we take note of structural features, we attach no particular importance to their sequential realisation. Consider the consequence of making *structural* changes to the heading of the text so that it read:

> *Annabella, film actress,*
> *was born on September 18*
> *aged 87, she died on*
> *July 14, 1909*

The text now fails in its indexical function: it directs the reader to a referentially impossible world. But a *sequential* alteration has no such referential effect. The sequence, we might say, has no consequence:

> *Film actress, Annabella,*
> *was born on July 14, 1909*
> *died on September 18 aged 87*

Similarly, the structural change:

> From earliest childhood
> Annabella even had a passion
> for cinema

completely alters the referential meaning and makes it presuppositionally dependent on some non existent context of shared knowledge. Not so with a sequentially different version:

> Annabella had a passion for
> the cinema even from earliest
> childhood.

So it would seem that Text A can be reformulated in different versions without changing its meaning in any substantial way. The differences do not matter and this suggests that there are features of conventional texts which readers edit out as of no pragmatic importance. What matters is that the texts should indexically refer, and this means that they should effectively refer readers to some context of situation that they can recognise in their world. Even structurally defective texts can be pragmatically effective. It is unlikely, for example, that newspaper readers would be disturbed by the dangling participle in Text A: *As a child … the chicken shed.* It is not the chicken shed that is playing in the garden. This is nonsense as grammatically signified; but it is nonsense that, pragmatically speaking, does not signify. None of the people to whom I have given the text to read (even abstracted from its normal appearance on the newspaper page) has noticed the structural non-sequitur.

It is a pragmatic truism that readers normally proceed on a least effort principle, and treat language in a fairly cavalier fashion: they pay attention to it only to the extent that it makes a satisfactory indexical connection for them. Writers also, of course, design their texts accordingly, assuming, for their part, that the Gricean co-operative principle is in place (Grice, 1975) and that readers will not perversely dissect their texts and analyse the entrails. They assume that they are writing for readers not analysts. […]

As I have already mentioned, in identifying [Text B] as a poem, we recognise that its actual physical shape is intrinsically a part of the text. It is a series of metrically regular lines, which are ordered in a rhyme scheme. There is here a patterned texture, a secondary arrangement of language which is not informed by the requirements of the language code itself. There is significance here in the textual design which is not simply a matter of what the linguistic elements signify. With Text A you can meddle with sequence without altering the referential functioning of the text. Meddling with Text B, however, is a very different matter, for in so doing you inevitably alter the second order textual design.

1/2	She dwelt beside the Springs of Dove,
1	Among the untrodden ways,
3	A Maid whom there were none to praise,
4	And very few to love.

3/4	A Maid whom there were very few to love,
3	And none to praise,
1	Dwelt among the untrodden ways
2	Beside the Springs of Dove.

So why then should it matter if the textual design gets changed? If it does not affect referential functioning in Text A, why should it do so here? My answer would be that there *is* no referential functioning in Text B, and that the textual design in effect closes the text off from contextual connection. Thus although both texts are about women, their mode of existence is quite different. The description of Annabella in the obituary corresponds to a factual counterpart. She has independent existence quite apart from the text, and we could, if we chose, check up on the accuracy of the information we are given about her. The text is organised to achieve this referential purpose as effectively as possible. Thus Annabella is named at the start, and information about her is provided to establish her as the topic, and the pronoun *she* then functions anaphorically for subsequent reference in the normal co-operative way. But Lucy has no separate existence outside the poem: she is created in its very design. And so it is that her first appearance is not as a person at all but as a pronoun, a pro-person, and we are kept in the dark about who she is until the last verse, and even then we get only a name. Her identity is traced only in the patterns of negative phrases: *untrodden, none, very few, only one, few, unknown, ceased to be.* The language itself *represents* who she is.

I suggest, then, that the secondary patterns of language in the poem close it off from context and, in so doing, set up conditions for representation rather than reference. It would follow that if you wanted to be referential, you would avoid such patterns. And here one might cite the example of William Whewell, author of a learned work (published in 1819) entitled *Elementary Treatise on Mechanics* (quoted in Butler and Fowler, 1971, Text 23). In it Whewell wrote the sentence: *There is no force, however great, can stretch a cord, however fine, into a horizontal line that is accurately straight.* It was pointed out to him that he had thereby produced inadvertent verse, the pattern of which could be made more evident by vertical alignment thus:

> There is no force, however great,
> Can stretch a cord, however fine,
> Into a horizontal line,
> That is accurately straight.

Whewell rightly assumed that the secondary patterning would be a distraction, and restored normal referential conditions by deleting the offending sentence in the next edition of his book. Where such patterning is apparent, the reader will, I argue, read the text as representation rather than reference. So, if we were to modify Text A in only quite minor ways to provide it with such patterning (changing the way the text is disposed on the page and giving metrical regularity to the lines of print), it would, even though its content remains essentially the same, no longer be read as an obituary, but as a poem, and Annabella would accordingly, like Lucy, be closed off within it, and take on a different existence.

> Even from her earliest childhood
> Annabella had a passion
> For the cinema and she
> As a child and playing in

> The garden of the family home
> The chicken shed out in the yard
> Became her studio and there,
> Lost in her imagined world,
>
> She acted out the scenes from films
> She had watched, while taking on
> In turn the different roles herself
> of film director, cameraman
> And leading lady all at once.

I would not claim much merit for this as a specimen of verbal art. It may not be adjudged to be a very good poem, but it is read as a poem nevertheless, and so understood quite differently from the way the original Text A is understood. You do not treat it indexically by using it as a set of directions for engaging some existing reality. In the reading of normal conventional texts your attention is directed *away* from the text and you take note of its linguistic features to the extent that they are referentially effective. But in reading a poem, your attention is directed *into* the text, and you seek significance in the very textual pattern. So, to take just one example, in the Annabella obituary, it does not matter in what sequence the noun phrases (*director*, *cameraman*, *leading lady*) occur. In the Annabella poem, it does: you read significance into the sequence. And it matters too that the last of them has a line all to itself.

The literary texts we have been concerned with so far take a poetic form, and here, of course, the secondary patterning and its enclosing effect are particularly apparent. But I believe that enclosure is a defining feature of all literature. So I would argue still (as I have argued with stubborn persistence ever since Widdowson, 1975) that if you read something as literature, you recognise that it does not have any direct referential connection with your concerns. The text is essentially parenthetical and unpractical, and you are relieved of any obligation to take it seriously. It would not matter if you did not read it at all. Literature is an optional extra. It represents an alternative reality in parallel, which co-exists with that of the everyday world, *corresponds* with it in some degree, but does not *combine* with it. You do not have to act upon it, or incorporate it into the continuity of your social life, or make it coherent with conventional modes of thought. You do not have to worry about whether your interpretation corresponds with the author's communicative intention. You assume that the very existence of the text implies intentionality, some claim to significance, but you are free to assign whatever significance suits you. There is no possibility of checking out whether your understanding matches what the author meant, and no penalties for getting it wrong. In this respect, the literary text is in limbo: there is authorship but no ownership. As the French poet Paul Valery observed: 'There is no true meaning for a text. No author's authority.

Whatever he may have wanted to say, he has written what he has written'
(quoted in Butler and Fowler, 1971, Text 542).

In literature, the text does not mediate between first and second person
parties. It floats free in a state of vacant possession for readers to appropriate
and inhabit. The reader engages *with* the text but cannot participate in
interaction with the writer *through* the text. Literary interpretation, therefore,
is not concerned with what the writer meant by the text, but what the text
means, or might mean, to the reader. One might indeed hazard the
proposition that what defines a literary text is that it is essentially vacuous, in
the sense that it creates a vacuum for the reader to fill. Here, for example, is
the beginning of Hemingway's story 'The short but happy life of Francis
Macomber':

> It was lunch time and they were all sitting under the double green fly
> of the dining tent pretending that nothing had happened.

Here a scene is textually set, with time and place location linguistically
specified. The definite article signals shared contextual knowledge, but there
is no shared contextual knowledge. The pronoun *they* presupposes that we
know who the referents are, but we don't: the specification leads to no
identification. They are pretending that nothing has happened, and this
presupposes something *had* happened, a previous event to which this text
refers, and that we are in the know. But we are not in the know, and there is
no previous event. In short, the text creates the illusion of contextual space,
a referential vacuum which the reader is drawn into to give imaginative
substance to. It is this being drawn into a different contextual reality, being
absorbed into a different order of things that is, I think, the essence of
aesthetic experience. In this way, readers make the literary text their own. [...]

The general point, then, is that a literary text is different because it does
not mediate between first- and second-person parties as other texts do. This
means therefore that Grice's co-operative principle, the normal contract
between parties which enables them to converge on agreed meaning, is
necessarily in abeyance. However, literature is not normal communication.
We assume intentionality, but there is no way of assigning intentions. It
makes no sense to ask whether the events are being presented as true, or
according to normal expectations of economy or clarity of expression, or as
relevant to what has been previously said or to the immediate context. We do
not require of literature that it should be true, but only that it should carry
conviction; we do not require of it that it should be relevant, but only that it
should be consistent and coherent on its own terms and in its own terms.
There is no point in trying to trace what is being referred to, because the
point of literature is that it does not refer to actual worlds, but represents
imaginary ones. Literary texts are not bound by the co-operative conditions
of conventional communication because they are disconnected from the
social contexts in which those conventions operate. They are of their nature
untrue, uninformative, irrelevant and obscure. The maxims of quality,

quantity, relation and manner are consistently denied, and consequently literary texts give rise to complex and unresolvable implicatures on a vast scale. It is this which constitutes their aesthetic effect.

References

BUTLER, C. and FOWLER, A. (eds) (1971) *Topics in Criticism*, London, Longman.

EAGLETON, T. (1983) *Literary Theory: An Introduction*, Oxford, Basil Blackwell.

GRICE, H.P. (1975) 'Logic and conversation', in P. COLE and J.L. MORGAN (eds) *Syntax and Semantics 3: Speech Acts*, New York, Academic Press.

WIDDOWSON, H.G. (1975) *Stylistics and the Teaching of Literature*, London, Longman.

Source: SARANGI, S. and COULTHARD, M. (eds) (2000) *Discourse and Social Life*, Harlow, Pearson, pp. 155–69.

READING C: Cognitive poetics

Elena Semino

What is cognitive poetics?

'Cognitive poetics' is an approach to the study of literature that combines linguistic analysis with insights from cognitive science in order to explain the relationship between the language of texts and readers' responses to texts. Cognitive poetics is not a single, unitary theory or analytical framework, but rather a broad and developing area which includes different theoretical and analytical traditions (you may wish to compare, for example, Tsur, 1992, with Stockwell, 2002, and the different chapters included in Semino and Culpeper, 2002).

Literary language and creativity

Although different practitioners of Cognitive Poetics will have different views of the relationship between literary and non-literary language, they mostly share the following assumptions: first, that texts that are regarded as 'literary' exploit the same linguistic and cognitive resources as texts that are regarded as 'non-literary'; second, that there is a continuum between literary and non-literary language, especially as far as 'creativity' is concerned; third, that literary texts are characterised by particularly novel and creative uses of the linguistic and cognitive resources used in everyday communication. As a consequence of these assumptions, it has been claimed that Cognitive Poetics is part of a general contemporary tendency to make the study of literature 'less elitist' [...]

(Steen and Gavins, 2003, p. 1).

Much of the work that is done in cognitive poetics is concerned with linguistic creativity in literature, whether it be the creative exploitation of conventional metaphors (Lakoff and Turner, 1989) or the strategies used in meditative poetry to disrupt readers' 'ordinary' sense-making processes in order to enable them to perceive altered states of consciousness (Tsur, 1992, pp. 411ff.). Canonical works and authors are often discussed alongside non-canonical texts, including 'popular' fiction and non-literary writing (see, for example, Emmott [2002] on the linguistic construction of 'split-selves' in fiction and autobiography, and Steen [2003] on the interpretation of 'love stories' in canonical poetry and rock lyrics).

An example of analysis

The best way to give you an idea of the nature of that work is to demonstrate some aspects of cognitive poetics with reference to a particular literary text. I have chosen the poem 'Tulips' (Plath, 1965), which was inspired by some tulips Sylvia Plath received while she was in hospital recovering from an appendectomy (Hughes, 1970). If you are familiar with Plath's poetry, you will recognise some of the central themes and concerns of her work: a deep sense of unease with life, an attraction for death (or death-like states), a difficult relationship with one's own identity, a problematisation of the role of wife and mother, and so on. Here I will only quote the most relevant extracts of the poem for the purposes of my analysis.

The text world: schema instantiation and potential schema refreshment

A basic assumption of cognitive science is that comprehension crucially depends on the availability and activation of relevant background knowledge. The term 'schema' is traditionally used to refer to a portion of background knowledge that contains generic information about objects, people, situation, and events (e.g. a schema for a visit to a supermarket) (see Eysenck and Keane, 2000, pp. 252ff.). Consider the first stanza of 'Tulips':

The tulips are too excitable, it is winter here.
Look how white everything is, how quiet, how snowed-in.
I am learning peacefulness, lying by myself quietly
As the light lies on these white walls, this bed, these hands.
I am nobody; I have nothing to do with explosions.
I have given my name and my day-clothes up to the nurses
And my history to the anaesthetist and my body to surgeons.

In order to begin to understand what the poem is about and to construct a coherent text world, readers will need to activate and instantiate (i.e. apply) their 'schema' for hospitals.[1] The activation of this schema is likely to be triggered by textual references to whiteness, and, more explicitly, to 'this bed', 'the nurses', 'the anaesthetist' and 'surgeons'. The information and expectations provided by the schema are essential for readers to arrive at some crucial inferences, such as that the first-person speaker in the poem is a patient in a hospital and that she has recently received a bunch of tulips from a visitor (presumably as a conventional expression of sympathy and good wishes).

The way in which the hospital setting and staff are described in the poem is likely to be broadly compatible with the expectations generated by most readers' hospital schema (e.g. the nurses are described as tending to the patient and frequently passing by her bed). In contrast, the *persona*'s perception and evaluation of herself and her surroundings may well clash with readers' expectations about hospital patients. Here are some particularly salient extracts, from the third and fifth stanzas respectively, which you can consider alongside stanza one above:

Now I have lost myself I am sick of baggage –
My patent leather overnight case like a black pillbox,
My husband and child smiling out of the family photo;
Their smiles catch onto my skin, little smiling hooks.
[...]
I didn't want any flowers, I only wanted
To lie with my hands turned up and be utterly empty.
How free it is, you have no idea how free –
The peacefulness is so big it dazes you,
And it asks nothing, a name tag, a few trinkets.
It is what the dead close on, finally;

The poetic *persona* appears to welcome and enjoy the very aspects of hospitalisation that we normally expect people to find uncomfortable: anonymity, lack of activity and isolation from loved ones. Similarly, while hospital patients normally find comfort in any reminders of life outside the hospital, the poetic speaker appears to resent the presence of the tulips, and gives a rather negative description of the family photograph at her bedside.

These attitudes are conveyed by a wide range of linguistic choices. For example, in the expression 'too excitable' in the first line of the poem, the tulips are simultaneously personified and negatively evaluated. A few lines later, they are implicitly associated with (metaphorical) 'explosions', which the poetic speaker disassociates herself from. In the third stanza of the poem, the speaker's husband and child are negatively evaluated via the conventional metaphorical expression 'baggage', and by the more novel metaphorical description of their smiles in the family photograph as 'little smiling hooks' that 'catch onto' the speaker's skin. In contrast, many conventionally negative experiences are associated with welcome sensations of peacefulness and freedom, and therefore positively evaluated: this applies, for example, to the white and impersonal hospital setting (which, in the first stanza, is metaphorically described as winter), and to the states metaphorically described as 'being nobody', having 'lost' oneself, being 'utterly empty', and so on. As a consequence of these and many other linguistic choices in the poem, readers will probably perceive the *persona* as a rather unusual, non-prototypical hospital patient, and see her idiosyncratic world-view as a reflection of Plath's own complex and ambivalent relationship towards life and death (which is also expressed in other poems).

Overall, the poem can be said to project a novel, somewhat 'strange' view of a relatively familiar scenario, in which readers' conventional expectations of positive versus negative experiences are turned on their heads. This may, for some readers, lead to what Cook (1994) has called 'schema refreshment' – the modification of existing schemata as a consequence of processing a (textual) input that deviates from expectations in some way. In the case of 'Tulips', some readers may, for example, reconsider their default perception and evaluation of the experience of being hospitalised, and recognise that, for some people at least, some aspects of this experience may be more welcome and positive than they previously assumed. Cook uses the term 'discourse deviation' for the phenomenon whereby linguistic or text-structural deviation (e.g. the novel metaphorical expressions in 'Tulips') 'interacts with the reader's existing schemata to cause schema refreshment' (Cook, 1994, p. 198). Cook claims that the occurrence of discourse deviation is an essential characteristic of literature as a type of discourse. In contrast, Cook argues, other types of discourse which make frequent use of linguistic deviation, such as advertising, normally confirm rather than challenge their audiences' expectations, and are not therefore characterised by discourse deviation.

A schema theory approach, and Cook's approach in particular, can be useful in accounting for readers' interpretations of texts, and for interpretative differences among readers. Because background knowledge varies from reader to reader, for example, a text may be schema refreshing for some readers and not for others, or it may be schema refreshing in different ways for different readers. As a consequence of this variation, Cook points out, the claim that literature is an essentially schema-refreshing discourse does not mean that every literary text is schema refreshing for every individual reader (Cook, 1994, p. 192). Cook also suggests that the potential for schema refreshment may account for why some (literary) texts are more highly valued than others, even though this will not necessarily apply to all individual texts and readings (Cook, 1994, pp. 191–2). Some readers may well be put off by highly estranged world-views such as that of 'Tulips' and may attribute higher value to the experience of reading more reassuring texts, that broadly confirm rather than challenge their expectations. In spite of these caveats, you may still wish to reflect on whether Cook's approach accounts equally well for all types of literary texts, periods and reading experiences.

Some examples of metaphor in the poem

In the case of 'Tulips', I would argue that the text's idiosyncratic world-view and schema refreshing potential are largely due to the use of creative and often striking metaphorical expressions to construct and contrast the main elements of the poem's text world: the tulips, the poetic *persona*, the hospital setting and staff, and the *persona*'s relationship with the world outside the hospital. In the terms used within Cognitive Metaphor theory (Lakoff and Johnson, 1980, 1999; Lakoff and Turner, 1989), these elements are the 'target domains' in a series of metaphors involving a range of different 'source domains'.

For more discussion on cognitive metaphor theory, see the companion volume, **Maybin and Swann (2006)**.

A close look at the metaphorical expressions in the complete poem (Plath, 1965) reveals the presence of a number of metaphorical patterns. The majority of the metaphors where the tulips function as target involve personification (e.g. 'I could hear them breathe/Lightly, through their white swaddlings, like an awful baby'), or, minimally, the description of the tulips in animate terms (e.g. 'now I am watched' and 'the tulips should be behind bars like some dangerous animals'). Generally, this can be seen as a reflection of a cognitive tendency to make sense of inanimate aspects of experience 'in terms of human motivations, characteristics, and activities' (Lakoff and Johnson, 1980, p. 33). However, as far as the tulips are concerned, the specific aspects of people or animals that are picked out tend to be unpleasant (e.g. 'like an awful baby') or threatening (e.g. 'like dangerous animals'). In addition, the tendency to personify or 'animise' the tulips contrasts with the poetic speaker's tendency to describe herself in inanimate terms (e.g. as 'a pebble', 'a thirty-year-old cargo boat', or 'a cut-paper shadow'). Taken together, these two general patterns emphasise the speaker's perception of herself as inert and helpless, and her perception of the tulips as potentially dangerous agents. This is one of the many reversals that contribute to the strangeness of the world-view projected by the poem.

In 'Tulips', the personification of the tulips in line 1 ('too excitable') metaphorically attributes to the flowers the potential for excessive emotions. Later in the same stanza, the expression 'explosions' in the statement 'I have nothing to do with explosions' can be interpreted as a creative exploitation of conventional conceptual metaphors such as EMOTION IS HEAT (OF FIRE) or INTENSITY OF EMOTION IS HEAT. More specifically, by referring to a possible extreme consequence of excessive heat when applied to certain objects (i.e. explosions), the *persona* seems to suggest that the tulips' presence on the ward has caused a dangerous and unwelcome increase in emotional intensity.[2]

In the same stanza, the (white) hospital setting (and the speaker's own emotional state) are metaphorically described in terms of winter and snow, which are, of course, strongly associated with low temperatures ('it is winter here./ Look how white everything is, how quiet, how snowed-in.'). These metaphorical expressions are quite novel, but, because of the conventional association between emotional intensity and temperature, they are likely to be interpreted as references to the lack of (intense) emotion in the hospital setting and in the speaker herself. In Lakoff and Turner's (1989, pp. 67–9) terms, the use of the specific images of winter and snow to refer metaphorically to the absence of intense emotion is a case of 'elaboration' of a conventional conceptual metaphor: an element from the source domain of a conventional conceptual metaphor ('low temperature', in this case) is realised in a new non-conventional way (i.e. by referring to winter and snow). Contrary to the prevalent negative evaluation of lack of emotion, however, the speaker in 'Tulips' appears to welcome and enjoy the hospital's emotional winter, and explicitly associates it not with total lack of emotion, but with a controlled and moderate emotional state ('quiet', 'peacefulness' in lines 1 and 2).

A similar analysis of how Plath exploits conventional conceptual metaphors creatively can be applied to other metaphorical expressions in the poem. In some cases, however, the novelty of Plath's specific choices is more striking and potentially disturbing than is the case with the temperature-related metaphors I have just discussed. In the third stanza, for example, the poetic speaker refers to her husband and child who are 'smiling out of the family photograph' as part of the 'baggage' she is 'sick of', and goes on to say: 'Their smiles catch onto my skin, little smiling hooks'. The use of conventional metaphorical expression 'baggage' here can be related to the conventional conceptual metaphor DIFFICULTIES ARE BURDENS (Lakoff and Turner, 1989, p. 25). The inclusion of close family members as part of this metaphorical 'baggage' is also not particularly novel (even though we might expect hospital patients to have a more nostalgic and benevolent attitude towards their families, due to their enforced isolation).

The metaphorical description of the husband's and offspring's smiles as 'little smiling hooks' that 'catch onto' the speaker's skin is much more novel and striking, however. On the one hand, most readers will interpret these expressions as suggesting that, when she looks at the photograph, the *persona* is inevitably reminded of her responsibilities and feelings for her family, in spite of herself. This basic interpretation can be explained in relation to conventional conceptual metaphors such as (FAMILY) RELATIONSHIPS ARE PHYSICAL LINKS (e.g. 'family ties', 'family connections') and LOVE IS A BOND (e.g. 'There is a strong tie between them') (see Kövecses, 2000, pp. 26, 94). On the other hand, however, the specific choice of 'little hooks' as the instrument causing the physical connection results in a number of potential contrasts, namely between the shape of smiles and the shape of hooks, flesh and metal, affection and coercion, and so on. The source image of hooks catching onto skin also presents the feelings and thoughts that the speaker experiences at the sight of the photograph in terms of physical pain. So, although it has a conventional basis, the 'hooks' metaphor is strikingly novel, and potentially disturbing, because of the specific choice of type of 'physical link' to evoke an emotional relationship (this is another case of what Lakoff and Turner call 'elaboration').

Tsur, the founder of an important tradition in Cognitive Poetics, states that, when metaphors emphasise the *incongruity* between source and target (like Plath's 'little smiling hook'), they have a 'split focus', and are often perceived as witty, ironical or far-fetched. This contrasts with metaphors that emphasise the *congruity* between source and target, which have an 'integrated focus' and tend to be perceived as elevated or sublime (Tsur, 1987, p. 7). Tsur's distinction can account for some of the potential effects of the 'hooks' metaphor as I have described them above.

Overall, a cognitive poetic approach inspired by Lakoff and Turner (1989) emphasises the connections between poetic language and everyday language. It also helps us to explain how writers may strike a balance in their works between two central but opposed goals of art: being original on the one hand, and being comprehensible on the other. By creatively exploiting conventional conceptual metaphors, writers achieve originality while at the same time relying on well-established conceptual (and linguistic) associations. It is also the case, however, that cognitive metaphor theorists such as Lakoff and Turner do not sufficiently recognise the ways in which individual uses of metaphor in individual texts often lead to unique, distinctive effects, that cannot be assimilated to the many other examples that rely on the same conceptual metaphor. Similarly, cognitive metaphor theory has paid little attention to the possibility for (poetic) metaphor to be entirely novel, both linguistically and conceptually. Nevertheless, cognitive poetics has started to make a significant contribution to the study of literature, and is likely to continue to grow as a field in the decades to come.

Notes

1   The notion of 'schema' is a convenient abstraction for talking about how background knowledge is organised in long-term memory. It is more precise to say that a 'schema' corresponds to particular patterns of activity in our brains' neural networks.

2   Other conventional conceptual metaphors may also be relevant here, such as those whereby excessive emotions are constructed in terms of the overflowing of hot fluids from containers (e.g. Kövecses, 2000, pp. 148–9).

References

COOK, G. (1994) *Discourse and Literature: The Interplay of Form and Mind*, Oxford, Oxford University Press.

DEIGNAN, A. (1995) *English Guides: Metaphor*, London, HarperCollins.

EMMOTT, C. (2002) '"Split selves" in fiction and in medical "life stories": cognitive linguistic theory and narrative practice', in E. SEMINO and J. CULPEPER (eds) *Cognitive Stylistics: Language and Cognition in Text Analysis*, John Benjamins.

EYSENCK, M.W. and KEANE, M.T. (2000) *Cognitive Psychology: A Student's Handbook*, 4th edn, Hove, East Sussex, Psychology Press.

GAVINS, J. and STEEN, G. (eds) (2003) *Cognitive Poetics in Practice*, London, Routledge.

HUGHES, T. (1970) 'The chronological order to Sylvia Plath's poems', in C. NEWMANN (ed.) *The Art of Sylvia Plath: A Symposium*, London, Faber and Faber.

KöVECSES, Z. (2000) *Metaphor and Emotion*, Cambridge, Cambridge University Press.

KöVECSES, Z. (2002) *Metaphor: A Practical Introduction*, Oxford and New York, Oxford University Press.

LAKOFF, G. and JOHNSON, M. (1980) *Metaphors We Live By*, Chicago, Chicago University Press.

LAKOFF, G. and JOHNSON, M. (1999) *Philosophy in the Flesh: The Embodied Mind and its Challenge to Western Thought*, New York, Basic Books.

LAKOFF, G. and TURNER, M. (1989) *More than Cool Reason: A Field Guide to Poetic Metaphor*, Chicago, Chicago University Press.

PLATH, S. (1965) 'Tulips', in *Ariel: Poems by Sylvia Plath*, London, Faber and Faber.

SEMINO, E. and CULPEPER, J. (eds) (2002) *Cognitive Stylistics: Language and Cognition in Text Analysis*, Amsterdam, John Benjamins.

STEEN, F. (2003) '"Love stories": cognitive scenarios in love poetry', in J. GAVINS and G. STEEN (eds) *Cognitive Poetics in Practice*, London, Routledge.

STEEN, G. and GAVINS, J. (2003) 'Contextualising cognitive poetics', in J. GAVINS and G. STEEN (eds) *Cognitive Poetics in Practice*, London, Routledge.

STOCKWELL, P. (2002) *Cognitive Poetics: An Introduction*, London, Routledge.

TSUR, R. (1987) *On Metaphoring*, Jerusalem, Israel Science Publishers.

TSUR, R. (1992) *Toward a Theory of Cognitive Poetics*, Amsterdam, Elsevier (North Holland) Science Publishers.

Source: commissioned for this volume.

READING D: Extracts from 'Beyond homogeny and heterogeny'

Alastair Pennycook

[Note: Pennycook uses the term 'rap' to refer to a genre of African-American music emerging in the 1980s, in which rhyming lyrics are chanted to a musical accompaniment. He defines hip-hop as a collection of cultural practices: rap, DJ-ing, break-dancing, graffiti-art associated with styles of clothing, talking and acting which have local variations across the world (Pennycook, 2003).]

New Englishes, hybridity and popular culture

If we are looking for new Englishes, we could do worse than starting with Asian Dub Foundation's CD *Community Music* (2000, London Records 90), even if (or especially since) Jamaican-style rap sung by young British men of South Asian background is not often deemed to be a standard form of new English. As they sing in their song 'New Way, New Life':

> And now we're walking down de street
> Wid a brand new pride
> A spring inna de step
> Wid our heads held high
> Young Asian brothers an sisters
> Moving forward, side by side
> Naya Zindagi Naya Jeevan
> New Way New Life

The phrase 'Naya Zindagi Naya Jeevan'[1] means 'new way, new life' in Hindi and Urdu. It was the title of a BBC programme in the UK in the 1970s aimed at Indian and Pakistani immigrants. Here these second-generation South Asians recall how this programme 'Kept our parents alive/Gave them the will to survive/Working inna de factories/Sometimes sweeping de floor'. But now a new generation has arrived:

> And we're supposed to be cool
> Inna de dance our riddims rule
> But we knew it all along
> Cos our parents made us strong
> Never abandoned our culture
> Just been moving it along
> Technology our tradition
> Innovation inna the song
> Now de struggle continues
> To reverse every wrong
> New heroines an heroes

> Inna de battle we belong
> When we reach de glass ceiling
> We will blow it sky high
> Naya Zindagi Naya Jeevan
> New Way New Life

What is interesting, it seems to me, is the mixtures and ironies here. While their parents kept them strong, never abandoning their culture, they have been moving it along – indeed, not just shifting it along, but rather shifting it into a quite different space, an African–Caribbean rap celebration of the new life of second-generation South Asian youths in London, a space that their factory-working parents who watched *Naya Zindagi Naya Jeevan* on TV in the 1970s might find it hard to accept as an extension of the cultures they have maintained. This fluid mixture of cultural heritage (a transformed version of South Asian cultures) and popular culture (an appropriated style of London-Caribbean but also global rap), of change and tradition, of border crossing and ethnic affiliation, of global appropriation and local contextualization, is in many ways what the new global order is about. This is neither homogenization nor heterogenization.

Similar contexts can be found in Zadie Smith's novel *White Teeth*. As Millat and Majid, the twin sons of Bengali parents, walk down a street, they start 'taxing' objects as they pass:

> Millat and Majid jumped into action. The practice of 'taxing' something, whereby one lays claims, like a newly arrived colonizer, to items in a street that do not belong to you, was well known and beloved to both of them. '*Cha*, man! Believe, I don't want to tax dat crap,' said Millat with the Jamaican accent that all kids, whatever their nationality, used to express scorn.

> (Smith, 2000, p. 145)

Later, Smith describes *Raggastanis* who

> spoke a strange mix of Jamaican patois, Bengali, Gujarati and English. Their ethos, their manifesto, if it could be called that, was equally a hybrid thing: Allah *featured*, but more as a collective big brother than a supreme being, a hard-as-fuck *geezer* who would fight in their corner if necessary; Kung Fu and the works of Bruce Lee were also central to the philosophy; added to this was a smattering of Black Power (as embodied by the album *Fear of a Black Planet*, Public Enemy); but mainly their mission was to put the Invincible back in Indian, the Bad-aaaass back in Bengali, the P-Funk back in Pakistani.

> (Smith, 2000, p. 200)

[...] From a cultural-imperialist framework, the global spread of rap and hip-hop is clearly orchestrated by the major recording companies, even if the sentiments of rap music may run counter to larger cultural and political agendas. A closer look at contexts of its spread and use, however, suggests a more complex picture. As Bent Preisler points out, although it may have been true in the past, it is no longer the case in many EFL contexts that English is learned only through formal, classroom contexts. Rather,

> informal use of English – especially in the form of code-switching – has become an inherent, indeed a defining, aspect of the many Anglo-American-oriented youth subcultures which directly or indirectly influence the language and other behavioural patterns of young people generally, in Denmark as well as in other EFL countries. It is impossible to explain the status of English in, and impact on, Danish society (as this is reflected, for example, in advertising and other areas of the Danish media) without understanding the informal function of the English language, and indeed its sociolinguistic significance, in the Anglo-American-oriented subculture.
>
> (Preisler, 1999, p. 244)

[...] As an example, he lists the vocabulary of a group of Danish hip-hop 'street dancers', which includes techniques and styles of break-dancing (electric boogie, windmills etc.), rap and DJ (ragamuffin, scratch etc.), graffiti (tag, bombing etc.) and hip-hop mythology (battle, biting etc.) [...]

These Danish kids have mastered a domain of international English that indeed puts them in touch with other kids around the world. Global rap/hip-hop language is a form of international English.[2] [...]

Awad Ibrahim's (1999) research on the ways in which African students studying in a Franco-Ontarian school in Canada identify with forms of hip-hop adds another dimension to this picture. As he shows, these students, entering the racialized world of North America, 'become Black' and start to redefine their identities in terms of the available social and cultural categories on the new continent. In doing so, they increasingly identify with forms of black culture and black language, particularly hip-hop and Black English. Rap and hip-hop, he shows, are 'influential sites in African students' processes of becoming Black, which in turn affected what and how the students learned' (Ibrahim, 1999, p. 364). The choice of these cultural forms and the position on the margins associated with being black was 'simultaneously an act of investment, an expression of desire, and a deliberate counterhegemonic undertaking'. Rap, he goes on to suggest, 'must be read as an act of resistance' (pp. 365–6) [...]

Meanwhile back in Australia, MC Trey (*Island Rappers*, SBS, 4 June 1999), a Fijian-Australian rapper, explains that:

> I'm into hip-hop because it has all those elements that you can express yourself, you know, like in Fiji, they have, you know, their art and their dancing, and their music, you know, and I feel that hip-hop has that. It's

one of the only modem art forms where you've got, you know, your breaking, your DJ-ing, graffiti, your MC-ing, you know, your story-telling.

She goes on:

> I feel that MC-ing is definitely an extension of oral tradition, like just in the islands they used to sit around the Kuva Bowl, and their story-telling, you know, a lot of it was passed down through word of mouth, they didn't have much documentation.

It is worth dwelling on the significance of these arguments for a moment. Here we have hip-hop in English being claimed as akin to a form of cultural maintenance or revival. This is a form of hip-hop that reflects the oral traditions of Fiji, the art and carving (via graffiti), the dancing and the music. As with the Asian Dub Foundation, this pride in a cultural heritage is one that may be hard for a previous generation to identify with: South Asian cultures being moved along through Jamaican rap; Fijian cultures being extended through hip-hop. Once again, there is no space here for either a simple homogenizing thesis or a simple heterogenizing thesis. This is a far more complex space.

Notes

1   Bhaskaran Nayar has informed me that it should be 'Nayi Zindagi, Naya Jeevan' (since *Zindagi* is feminine, it has to take the feminine form of the adjective). I am also indebted to Bhaskaran for explaining some of the multiple layers of meaning in this phrase.

2   It also occurs in other languages and in quite similar hybrid ways, as in current French rap with its mixture of French, North African Arabic, and Caribbean creoles.

References

ASIAN DUB FOUNDATION (2000) *Community Music* (CD), London, London Records 90.

IBRAHIM, A.M. (1999) 'Becoming black: rap and hip-hop, race, gender, identity, and the politics of ESL learning', *TESOL Quarterly*, **33**, pp. 349–70.

PREISLER, B. (1999) 'Functions and forms of English in a European EFL country', in T. BEX and R.J. WATT (eds) *Standard English: The Widening Debate*, London, Routledge.

SMITH, Z. (2000) *White Teeth*, Harmondsworth, Penguin.

Source: adapted from MAIR, C. (ed.) *The Politics of English as a World Language*, pp. 9–14, Amsterdam/New York, Rodopi.

Poetic language

Joanna Thornborrow

2.1 Introduction

In Chapter 1, you saw the terms literature, literary and literariness being used across a number of perspectives and a number of different genres. In this chapter, I will look at one type of literariness – **poetic language** – a type of language commonly associated with one type of genre, that of poetry. In Chapter 1, you were also introduced to three perspectives for looking at literariness – inherency, cognitive and sociocultural. In order to explore what constitutes poetic language, an inherency perspective, such as Formalism, would look at the formal organisation of words on a page; for example, something might be seen as poetic because it is written in lines and arranged in verse or because it rhymes. (Although just because we recognise a text as intrinsically poetic does not mean we might regard it as any good.) We could also think about poetic language in terms of its effect on us, whether we are moved or stimulated – whether we think a piece of language has quality because of its cognitive effect. Moreover, in line with a sociocultural perspective, we might also recognise that what gets regarded as poetic can change over time and will probably continue to do so.

ACTIVITY 1   Which is more poetic?

Allow about 10 minutes

To start you thinking about what constitutes poetic language, which do you consider to be more poetic, Text 1 or Text 2 (Text 2 orthographically represents the sound of a marked Glaswegian accent)? Why?

Text 1

> Shall I compare thee to a summer's day?
> Thou art more lovely and more temperate:
> Rough winds do shake the darling buds of May,
> And summer's lease hath all too short a date;

Text 2

> yir eyes ur
> eh
> a mean yir
> pirrit this
> wey
> ah think yir
> byewtifl like ehm

Comment

Text 1 is the opening four lines from Shakespeare's 'Sonnet 18', while Text 2 is the first six lines from 'A summer's day' by Tom Leonard, from a collection published in 1984. Both texts initially seem to carry the same 'message' but in two very different forms. The sonnet was a conventional poetic way of expressing love and admiration for someone in the sixteenth century, and Shakespeare uses the formal conventions of rhythmical structure (iambic pentameter, i.e. lines of ten syllables with an unstressed/stressed beat) and rhyme scheme in this poem, as well as metaphorical language, where human beauty is compared to the warmth of summer, but also subject to the passing of seasons. In the second text, Leonard draws on the first, borrowing his title from the first line of the sonnet, as well as taking up the theme. But unlike the first, the second text uses a non-standard language which is not generally recognised as conventionally 'poetic'. By using non-standard language, and by representing the hesitancy of natural speech, the stumbling presentation of the message in Leonard's text stands in marked contrast to the polished eloquence of the message in Shakespeare's. In this text, Leonard seems to me to be drawing attention to the forms of poetic language, and challenging the status of standard and non-standard varieties of English in relation to literary convention. The 'message' in this poem, then, may in the end be making a rather different point to the 'message' of Shakespeare's sonnet.

Even though much recent and contemporary poetry may no longer conform to a stereotypical idea of what a poem looks like, nevertheless a concern with *form* and *meaning* remains a central characteristic of poetic language. The selection and combination of linguistic material and the use of these materials to make patterns via lines, which in turn produce particular meanings, are what constitute the literariness of verse from an inherency perspective. Chapter 2 will explore poetic language largely from this perspective. This chapter also looks at the relationship between poetic language and the kind of literariness found in richly descriptive passages in some narrative fiction, literariness that can be regarded as in a sense poetic despite the absence of formal line arrangements. I will consider too how poetic language can be judged as having aesthetic value. I start by looking at the issue of poetic language by developing the treatment from Chapter 1 of the theories of the Russian Formalist, Roman Jakobson.

2.2 Parallelism and the poetic function

In this section, we discuss how the Swiss linguist Ferdinand de Saussure's concepts of 'paradigm' and 'syntagm' can help clarify the role of parallelism in the poetic function. (You met the concept of parallelism in Chapter 1.) You will recall that the goal of Formalists, such as Roman Jakobson, was to identify literariness, and that much of the focus was on identifying literariness in poetry, in other words, poetic language. In Chapter 1, you saw that there were six functions of communication proposed by Roman Jakobson (referential, emotive, conative, phatic, metalingual and poetic).

The key function for discussion of poetic language is the poetic function, which is evident when a text emphasises the linguistic properties of the words themselves. In Jakobson's (1960) 'Closing statement: linguistics and poetics', a seminal paper which has acted as one of the cornerstones of modern stylistics, he illustrates his idea of the poetic function with the example, *I like Ike*, a political slogan for the then American presidential candidate, General Dwight Eisenhower. Jakobson puts forward an explanation of how this or any piece of language functions poetically, one which is rooted in Saussure's approach to language.

Saussure: paradigms and syntagms

For Saussure (1915), as speech unfolds in time, there are two ways of meaning being created. The first is where signs create meaning in relation to their place in a **syntagm**. A syntagm is a rule-governed combination of signs. *Ike likes me* and *I like Ike* are different syntagms (they follow the rule of subject-verb-object order). Because the combination of signs is different, we have different **syntagmatic** meanings for *like(s)* in these two examples.

The second way of creating meaning is in relation to a **paradigm**. A paradigm is a group of words which have something in common, words which potentially can be selected for the same slot in a syntagm. For example, *prefer* or *support* could be selected instead of *like* in the syntagm, *I like Ike*. *Prefer, favour* and *like* can thus be seen as belonging to the same paradigm (see Table 2.1). For Saussure, a sign also gets meaning because of what it is *not*, i.e. it is not the other signs in the relevant paradigm. So in addition to syntagmatic meaning, *like* gets **paradigmatic** meaning in *I like Ike* because it is not *favour, prefer*, etc. The ideas of paradigm and syntagm, as well as others in Saussure (1915), laid the foundation for an approach to studying literature (as well as history, anthropology, etc.) known as **structuralism**, which reached a peak in the 1960s. In structuralism, interest focuses not so much on evaluating literary texts but rather on exploring their structural patterns. Structuralism was influenced by both Russian and Prague School Formalism and so Jakobson's work provides a kind of bridge between these traditions.

You will return to Saussure in Chapter 6.

In order to illustrate why Jakobson regards *I like Ike* as poetic, let me start with a syntagm which Jakobson would not recognise as poetic, *I support General Eisenhower*. In this syntagm, there has been a selection of *support* from a paradigm of semantically related verbs (*choose, favour,* etc.) and *General Eisenhower* from a paradigm of possible names for this former presidential candidate (*Dwight, Ike,* etc.) (see Figure 2.1).

PARADIGM	Subject	Verb	Object	[aɪ]	[aɪk]
	I	chose	Dwight	cry	dyke
		favour	General Eisenhower	die	Ike
		like	Ike	I	like
		prefer	Mr Eisenhower	Ike	Mike
		support	the Republican Presidential candidate	like	pike
		vote for		tide	tyke
SYNTAGM	I	like	Ike		
	Monosyllabic	Monosyllabic	Monosyllabic		
	[aɪ]	[aɪk]	[aɪk]		

Figure 2.1   Paradigms from which the syntagm *I like Ike* is selected.

In the verb and the object paradigms, the terms are **equivalent**. By 'equivalent', Jakobson does not mean identical but substitutable. So the names *Dwight, Ike, General Eisenhower* can be used to refer to the same person and thus are all substitutable by each other.

So why is *I like Ike* poetic for Jakobson but *I support General Eisenhower* not? Equivalence is a concept normally associated with a paradigm. As can be seen from Figure 2.1, *I, like* and *Ike* have 'vertical' equivalence. This is because as well as *like* and *Ike* belonging to different semantic paradigms, *like, Ike* and *I* also simultaneously come from phonetic paradigms. They come from a paradigm of one syllable words containing the sound [aɪ] (see the [aɪ] column in Figure 2.1). Furthermore, *like* and *Ike* also come from yet another phonetic paradigm, that of one syllable words ending in the sound [aɪk] (see the [aɪk] column in Figure 2.1). When the signs *I, like* and *Ike* are combined in *I like Ike*, that is, arranged in a syntagm, the 'vertical' equivalences become 'horizontal'. In other words, paradigmatic equivalences of sound become syntagmatic ones.

When 'vertical' equivalences become 'horizontal' ones, repetition of sound and other parallelisms can occur. As Jakobson (1960, p. 358) puts it 'The poetic function projects the principle of equivalence from the axis of selection [paradigm] into the axis of combination [syntagm].' That is why we get the rhyme between *like* and *Ike* – the poetic function is active. In contrast, *I support General Eisenhower* would not be poetic for Jakobson since the signs, *I*, *support* and *Eisenhower* do not share paradigms. This is why the syntagm *I support General Eisenhower* does not function poetically.

As I said, when a syntagm functions poetically, it draws attention to itself. Readers are thus invited to make meaning on the basis of parallelism or equivalences in the syntagm. What meanings emerge from the poetic *I like Ike* for you ? For me, the concentration of monosyllabic sounds, when uttered repeatedly, would evoke political tribalism. Moreover, with the use of the first person and the short alternative name, repeated utterance of *I like Ike* could suggest Dwight Eisenhower is not a remote politician from the people.

The dominance of the poetic function in poetry

The poetic function is active in *I like Ike* but it can hardly be said to be a poem. So when is a poem a poem for Jakobson? The answer is when the poetic function *dominates* over other Jakobsonian functions, for instance, the referential function (the use of language to refer to a context) and the conative function (the use of language to persuade a hearer or reader). The poetic function does not dominate in *I like Ike* because it also has an important referential function – it refers to the candidate, Dwight Eisenhower. In addition, it has a conative function – it reminds voters of Eisenhower and is thus part of a strategy to influence voting behaviour. Though the poetic function of *I like Ike* draws attention to the message and we are invited to infer extra meanings, these inferences will be made in relation to the referential and conative functions, and possibly to others. With a poem, for Jakobson, the poetic function is much more dominant over other functions. As a result, we infer much more from how a poem draws attention to itself, its 'self-referentiality'.

The extract in the box below is taken from Jakobson's 'Closing statement: linguistics and poetics' (1960), where he first set out this definition of the poetic function:

The poetic function of language

The [...] focus on the message for its own sake, is the poetic function of language [...] Any attempt to reduce the sphere of the poetic function of poetry or to confine poetry to the poetic function would be a delusive oversimplification. [The] poetic function is not the sole function of verbal art but only its dominant, determining function, whereas in all other verbal activities it acts as a subsidiary, accessory constituent [...]

What is the empirical linguistic criterion of the poetic function? In particular, what is the indispensable feature inherent in any piece of poetry? To answer this question we must recall the two basic modes of arrangement used in verbal behavior, selection and combination. If 'child' is the topic of the message, the speaker selects one among the extant, more or less similar nouns like child, kid, youngster, tot, all of them equivalent in a certain respect, and then to comment on this topic, he may select one of the semantically cognate verbs – sleeps, dozes, nods, naps. Both chosen words combine in the speech chain. The selection is produced on the basis of equivalence, similarity and dissimilarity, synonymy and antonymy, while the combination, the build-up of the sequence, is based on contiguity. The poetic function projects the principle of equivalence from the axis of selection into the axis of combination. Equivalence is promoted to the constitutive device of the sequence.

(Jakobson, 1960, pp. 356–9)

ACTIVITY 2 **The poetic function's invitation to make extra meanings**

Allow about
30 minutes

Read the following texts.

Lexis is another
word for
vocabulary.

- Note all the repeated or parallel elements (sound, rhythm, grammar, lexis).

- In reading each text, do you find you are being invited to make meaning differently?

- In what ways, if any, does the poetic function in these texts relate to Jakobson's conative and referential functions?

Text 1

It's midday spin you lose I win
I'm back and that's a fact
When I say it's twelve-oh-one it means we're gonna have some fun
twelve-oh-two means great Scotsman how are you?
twelve-oh-three we're on a spree
twelve-oh-four we're gonna walk right out the door with some fantastic sounds
twelve-oh-five time to come alive
twelve-oh-six that don't rhyme not overtime
twelve-oh-seven we're in heaven
twelve-oh-eight we can't hesitate we can't wait
twelve-oh-nine make you feel mighty fine
twelve-ten we're gonna hear from Big Ben

(BBC Radio One, *Emperor Rosko*, 1970s' jingle)

Text 2

Paper and sticks and shovel and match
Why won't the news of the old world catch
And the fire in a temper start

Once I had a rich boy for myself
I loved his body and his navy blue wealth
And I lived in his purse and his heart

(Dylan Thomas, 1974)

Comment

In Text 1, there is a rhyme in *spin/win*, a half-rhyme in *back/fact*, and the ensuing sequence of rhymes which are generated in response to the sounds of the minutes moving on: *Twelve-oh-one means we're gonna have some fun*; *Twelve-oh-three we're on a spree*. Even in the line which does not follow the pattern, *Twelve-oh-six that don't rhyme not overtime*, the first rhyming word is pushed further into the line: *rhyme/overtime*. Although this is a radio jingle which I encountered first as a spoken, indeed even a 'sung', text rather than written one, in representing it in written form I have automatically arranged it in lines like a poem, rather than prose. This is probably because of its rhythmical structure; there is a strong beat in each line which triggers a natural break between each rhyming unit, and this again tends to be a feature of poetry, not of prose. Apart from the parallelisms of sound, there are parallelisms of syntax, for example, we+verb, and so on. A line like *twelve-oh-eight we can't hesitate we can't wait* demonstrates especially how equivalence in a paradigm of words (i.e. containing the last sound [eɪt]) is projected into a syntagm. However, one line is markedly irregular with a prepositional phrase following the internal rhyme, *twelve-oh-four we're gonna walk right out the door with some fantastic sounds*. Is this internal deviation significant for you?

Text 2 consists of the two opening stanzas from the Dylan Thomas poem, 'Paper and sticks'. There is a clear rhyme pattern at the end of each line, which can be represented as aab (*match/catch/start*), ccb (*myself/wealth/heart*). Although the 'c' sounds do not make a full rhyme, they are closely related in the way they are produced. There is also a strong metrical beat in the first stanza: four main beats in the first two lines and three in the last in each case:

[**/** represents a stressed syllable; . represents an unstressed syllable]

```
/  .    .    /   .   /   .   .   /
Paper and sticks and shovel and match
 /   .    .   /   .  .  /   .   /
Why won't the news of the old world catch
  .   .   /   . . /  .    /
And the fire in a temper start
```

The second stanza is not identical in metrical pattern though. On my analysis, the first two lines of stanza 2 are less regular than the first two lines of stanza 1. The third lines of each stanza are largely parallel; there is an extra syllable in the last line of stanza 2. What is also parallel is that there are fewer stressed syllables in the last lines of each stanza than in the preceding two lines.

```
 /   / . . /  /  .  .  /
Once I had a rich boy for myself
/ /    . /  . . . / . .   /
I loved his body and his navy blue wealth
  . . /  .  . /  .  .  . /
And I lived in his purse and his heart
```

Apart from the end rhymes, we can find many other parallel or repeated elements within the extract, for example, *wont/old; rich/sticks/lived*.

How then does the poetic function in these texts relate to Jakobson's conative and referential functions? Text 1 is a jingle from a popular British radio station (BBC Radio One). The function of a jingle is to act as a mnemonic tag for a particular programme so that listeners are occasionally reminded of what station and programme they are tuned into. The literariness of the jingle is angled towards making the message stick with the audience. So the poetic function is not dominating over the referential function (the jingle tells us what we are listening to) or the conative function (the jingle tries to persuade us to keep on listening). In contrast, in Text 2, we do not have an obvious referential or conative function. The poetic function dominates – the text is self-referential.

As I said above, readers are likely to infer meanings and thus seek significance from texts where the poetic function is being expressed. *How* they will infer meanings is different when the poetic function is the dominant function. For Jakobson:

> ... the supremacy of the poetic function over the referential function does not obliterate the message but makes it ambiguous. The double sensed message finds correspondence in a split addresser, in a split addressee, as well as in a split reference.
>
> (Jakobson, 1960, p. 371)

What Jakobson means here is that when the poetic function is dominant, a text is 'split' off from the normal relationship between language and context. Because we do not have this normal language–context relationship, ambiguity can arise. With the appropriate referential context a sentence such as, *Once I had a rich boy for myself* may be someone bemoaning the loss of their financially well-endowed lover. Without an obvious referential context as in the Dylan Thomas poem, it exhibits the 'Jakobsonian split' where signs are less directly connected to a referent. As a result, the possibilities of what this line means and in relation to the rest of the poem are opened up. Likewise, because the poetic function is dominant, a reader is likely to seek significance in the similarities and differences of rhythm between the stanzas of 'Paper and sticks'. In contrast, because the poetic function is not so dominant in the radio jingle, a reader is less likely to seek significance in the anomalously lengthy line, *twelve-oh-four we're gonna walk right out the door with some fantastic sounds.*

Jakobson's Formalist ideas on literariness in the text itself laid the foundation for stylistics. Indeed, his ideas can be seen in the reading in Chapter 1 by the stylistician, Henry Widdowson. Widdowson (page 35 of this volume) says for example 'I would argue ... that if you read something as literature, you recognise that it does not have any direct referential connection with your concerns.' Widdowson's purpose is to indicate that literary reading is different in kind to non-literary reading. He did not interpret the Wordsworth poem, i.e. he did not focus on how its poetic function invited him to form an interpretation, to say what the poem means to him. Similarly in the last activity, while you saw that there were parallelisms in the Dylan Thomas poem, I did not ask you to say what the two stanzas mean to you. You will see, in Reading A, how parallelisms in a poem invite a particular reader to seek meaning. In it, Walter Nash analyses the form of a poem by Cecil Day Lewis, entitled 'Last words', and relates his analysis to what the poem means to him. We will come to Nash's analysis and interpretation of the poem in a moment. First, I would like you to read the poem, 'Last words' and think about what it means to you.

ACTIVITY 3   'Last words'

Allow about
40 minutes

Look through the poem for parallelisms of sound, rhythm, grammar, meaning and formal arrangement (either at the level of the sentence or verse).

- How do these parallelisms relate (or not) to each other?
- In what ways do you link these parallelisms in your interpretation of the poem?

Last words

Suppose, they asked,
You are on your death-bed (this is just the game
For a man of words),
With what definitive sentence will you sum
And end your being? ... Last words: but which of me
Shall utter them?

– The child, who in London's infinite, intimate darkness
Out of time's reach,

Heard nightly an engine whistle, remote and pure
As a call from the edge
Of nothing and soon in the music of departure
Had perfect pitch?

– The romantic youth
For whom horizons were the daily round,
Near things unbiddable and inane as dreams,
Till he had learned
Through his hoodwinked orbit of clay what Eldorados
Lie close to hand?

– Or the ageing man seeing his lifelong travel
And toil scaled down
To a flimsy web
Stranded on two dark boughs, dissolving soon,
And only the vanishing dew makes visible now
Its haunted span?

Let this man say,
Blest be the dew that graced my homespun web,
Let this youth say,
Prairies bow to the treadmill: do not weep.
Let this child say,
I hear the night bird, I can go to sleep.
(Day Lewis, 1957, cited in Nash, 1993, p. 47)

ACTIVITY 4   The lyrical game (Reading A)

Please turn to Reading A and then consider the question below. Nash links his analysis to an interpretation, outlining what 'Last words' means to him. His analysis is a detailed one and may contain some linguistic terms that you are unfamiliar with (some of these are glossed in the margins).

- Focus in your reading on how he links parallelisms in the poem to his interpretation. Does your interpretation differ from his?

Comment

Nash finds shifts in sound, rhythm, grammar, meaning and line-lengths, all of which support his interpretation that the persona in the poem moves from 'talkative hesitation' and doubt, to a 'reassured harmony' or 'epigrammatic certainty' in the 'decisive assertions of its close'. In coming to this interpretation Nash discerns, for example, that stanzas 2 and 5 are mirrors of one another in terms of line-lengths – a form of parallelism. For Nash, this mirroring reinforces 'the impression of an ending, of reaching a goal'. Moreover, the parallelisms inside stanza 5 (*let this man/youth/child say*) produce a more concentrated regularity which further evokes a sense of decisiveness and harmony.

Unlike Nash, I do not read stanza I as 'hesitant mumbling'. This perspective relies on Nash's interpretation that the persona is talking to himself at the start of the poem. But it could be read that the *they*, his friends, family, colleagues, etc., did suppose the question. In other words, the interrogative *... with what definitive sentence will you sum and end your being?* could be a representation of direct speech by others. However, I have of course no reference to a context where I could find out whether this was a man hypothesising his own question or musing on a question that his friends or family might have offered. From a Jakobsonian perspective, the poem is 'split' off from a referential context and thus ambiguity arises. Given this increased potential for meaning making, how individual readers focus in on elements of a poem, and link them together to make an interpretation, is likely to vary.

You are familiar now with Jakobson's idea of the 'split' from context and thus how the meaning potential of a poem can open out, which in turn accounts for why interpretations of a poem vary. However, *analysis* of the stylistic content of a poem can vary too. For Jakobson (1968) a 'total' and unbiased analysis of a poem is possible. But what if different analysts use different systems of linguistic description to analyse the same poem? This is likely to result in different analyses. Furthermore, linguistic descriptive systems are usually continually refined, made richer and more delicate. So even if stylisticians are from the same linguistic tradition, they may have different analyses of a poem depending on the level of the descriptive system they work with. The more refined a descriptive system is, the more refined an analysis of a poem can become. All these points create tensions for the prospect of an objective or 'total' analysis in a Jakobsonian sense but they do not rule out the prospect that stylisticians cannot reach much agreement on the stylistic content of a poem, once the system and level of analysis is made clear. This is because many linguistic categories are relatively stable ones. All the same, this does not stop a critic of stylistics, Stanley Fish (1980), from going as far as to say that the linguistic facts that a stylistician finds in a poem, such as parallelism, are in fact interpretations by a stylistician. You might want to ponder on the validity of this perspective in relation to how both you and Walter Nash located parallelism in 'Last words'.

I now leave the concept of parallelism and return to other Formalist concepts you met in Chapter 1: deviation and foregrounding.

2.3 Deviation and foregrounding

The early years of Formalism, between 1915 and 1920, are associated with the work of Russians such as Jakobson and Shklovsky. In 1920 Jakobson moved to Prague, and in 1926 was one of the founding members of the Prague School of Linguistics. Another key member of this school was Jan Mukařovský. Like Jakobson, Mukařovský viewed poetic language as being essentially different from non-poetic, ordinary language, and he developed the concept of 'deviation' to explain that difference. He describes poetic language as a *deviation from the standard* – or what he calls an 'aesthetic intentional distortion' from conventional language use. Dylan Thomas' poem 'Paper and sticks' deviates from the standard through, for example, the presence of the unusual expression, 'navy blue wealth'. For Mukařovský, 'navy blue wealth' would function poetically because the deviant use of language is foregrounded: it is made to stand out.

In the box below you will see how Mukařovský conceived of the notions of deviation and foregrounding. Notice too the similarities between his vision and Jakobson's.

Deviation and foregrounding

... for poetry, the standard language is the background against which is reflected the aesthetically intentional distortion of the linguistic components of the work, in other words, the intentional violation of the norm of the standard. Let us, for instance, visualise a work in which this distortion is carried out by the interpenetration of dialect speech with the standard; it is clear then that it is not the standard which is perceived as a distortion of the dialect, but the dialect as a distortion of the standard, even when the dialect is quantitatively preponderant. The violation of the norm of the standard, its systematic violation, is what makes possible the poetic utilisation of the language; without this possibility there would be no poetry. [...]

The function of poetic language consists in the maximum foregrounding of the utterance. [...] Foregrounding is, of course, common in the standard language, for instance, in journalistic style, even more in essays. But here it is always subordinate to communication: its purpose is to attract the reader's (listener's) attention more closely to the subject matter expressed by the foregrounded means of expression. [...] In poetic language foregrounding achieves maximum intensity to the extent of pushing communication into the background as the objective of expression and of being used for its own sake; it is not used in the services of communication, but in order to place in the foreground the act of expression, the act of speech itself.

(Mukařovský, 1970, pp. 41–4)

Use of deviant language for Mukařovský draws our attention to a text or, to use Jakobson's terminology, to the form of the 'message'. Mukařovský, like Jakobson, is aware that foregrounding also occurs in non-literary texts but that this does not dominate over other functions of language. In a poem, foregrounding becomes the most important, dominant aspect.

Let us now apply the concepts of deviation and foregrounding to analyse a poem.

ACTIVITY 5 **'love is more thicker than forget'**

Allow about
30 minutes

The following poem by e e cummings contains many instances of linguistic deviation. Make a note of where you think the poet is deviating from the standard, and think about what kind of linguistic rules he is breaking in this text. In what ways does the foregrounding of deviant language invite you to make an interpretation? In other words, what does the poem mean to you?

love is more thicker than forget
more thinner than recall
more seldom than a wave is wet
more frequent than to fail

it is most mad and moonly
and less it shall unbe
than all the sea which only
is deeper than the sea

love is less always than to win
less never than alive
less bigger than the least begin
less littler than forgive

it is most sane and sunly
and more it cannot die
than all the sky which only
is higher than the sky

(cummings, 1958)

Comment

In this text, cummings breaks the grammatical rule for forming comparative structures in English, *x is more y* (~~more~~ *y+er*) *than z*, by doubling the comparative. He uses expressions that are semantically unusual in standard English: we say, for instance, *love is blind*; we do not say *love is thick/thin*. *Love is less always* is deviant because *less* cannot modify the time adverbial *always* in standard English. His text is also morphologically deviant: words such as *unbe*, *sunly* and *moonly*. Furthermore, he makes comparisons between non-comparable phenomena, for example, *love* and *forget*; nouns (*love*) are usually compared to other nouns, not to verbs (*forget*).

The effect of foregrounding this amount of deviation makes me think about love in new and unusual ways. The Russian Formalists called this process, where a text disturbs the way we perceive of a phenomenon, defamiliarisation (*ostraneniye*), a concept you met in Chapter 1. To me, the link between linguistic form and textual meaning in cummings' poem can be found in the relationship between the theme of the poem, love, and the unruliness of the language used to describe it. On my interpretation, cummings is saying that 'love breaks rules', that it is in many ways indescribable and confusing, that it brings together impossible things and cannot be understood according to the norms and conventions of ordinary language.

Ellipsis – where clause or phrase elements are omitted.

In Chapter 1, you saw some problems with the notion of deviation; for example, spellings such as 'deserveth' would not have been deviant in the seventeenth century but would be to a modern reader. Another objection is that there is never only one norm. Mukařovský, in the box above, speaks of the norm of the standard but what exactly is that? Any language is made up of different **genres**, uses of language for particular purposes, for instance, informal conversation and academic writing. Because genres have different uses there will naturally be some differences between them as to norms of grammar and lexis. For example, it is common in conversation for grammatical subjects to be **ellipted** such as in *Must be some narky bastards in the rugby club* (Biber et al., 1999, p. 1105). Academic English is not marked by ellipsis of subjects. And so on. Nevertheless, with certain texts such as cummings' poem, a number of its deviations would be recognised as deviant from standard English as a whole. But it is difficult to say *how* deviant they are. Another problem with the 'deviation from the standard' argument is that deviant language is also used in non-literary texts, for example, newspaper headlines or advertisements. This could then mean that if we included advertisements and headlines in a non-literary norm, our norm would contain elements of the 'deviant'. Given this, it is better to think of norms in terms of statistical probabilities. In recent years, with the development of computational search techniques and the capacity for computer storage, large databases of languages have been assembled. Such a database is known as a **corpus** (corpora is the plural). It has become possible to track which words and phrases are used regularly and thus establish an empirically based norm (as defined by a corpus of language data from a range of sources) rather than from merely an intuitive perspective. Another advantage of a corpus is that we can also say how deviant an expression is from a norm. We shall see something of this in the next section.

2.4 Levels of literariness

It is indisputable that the Formalist approach, objections notwithstanding, has spawned a large number of studies of individual works of literature in stylistics (e.g. Fowler, 1966; Fowler, 1975; Leech, 1969; Widdowson, 1975; Leech and Short, 1981; Carter, 1982; Carter and Simpson, 1989; Bex et al., 2000). The emphasis in the Formalists' work on the self-referential nature of poetry has also been a key one for stylistics. But for a number of critics, their focus has been too narrow. For Eagleton (1996, p. 5) 'to think of literature as the Formalists do is really to think of all literature as poetry'. There is truth in this criticism. Parallelism and deviation are often more apparent in poetry than in prose. But even within the genre of poetry, deviation is more apparent for certain poems, such as those by e e cummings and Dylan Thomas, than in, say, Wordsworth's *Lucy* poems, in avant-garde rather than naturalist drama, in experimental novels such as James Joyce's *Finnegan's Wake* rather than in novels by writers who favour a 'plain' style such as Ernest Hemingway.

And what if, rather than a poem, a particular passage from a novel draws attention to itself, because of its richly descriptive style, a style which may involve a degree of parallelism or even deviation? Would we want to rule out such prose passages from being referred to as poetic despite the absence of line and verse arrangement? Is the boundary between poem and non-poem always so clear cut? On this issue, here is Attridge (2004a, p. 71):

> Is poetry a definably distinctive type of literature? Much ink has been spilled on this question, and it is evident that if what is implied are intrinsic markers or clear-cut boundaries the answer is no … it will be more helpful to think in terms of the degree to which any literary work is poetic, or invites the kind of response we normally associate with poetry, rather than imagining that we can distinguish absolutely between poems and non-poems.

To substantiate his argument, Attridge (2004a, p. 72) goes on to give the example of Charles Dickens, a writer who produces 'prose works which yield to a "poetic" reading'. This is because much of his work 'exploits the sonic and rhythmic properties of English in a manner that can be most fully enjoyed in reading aloud'.

Building on the work of the Formalists, in Reading B Ronald Carter aims to provide a set of inherency-based criteria to enable a broader specification of literariness, one which would include poetic language in passages of narrative fiction. Jakobson supplied no clear criteria for ascertaining the degrees of literariness between non-literary and literary texts – he only specified that the poetic function was more dominant in verbal art. Another of Carter's aims is to plug this gap in supplying criteria to determine degrees of literariness between non-literary and literary texts and thus provide a basis for saying one text is more or less 'literary' than another. In providing this basis, Carter is unconcerned with the relationship between literariness and literary value.

You will explore stories by Hemingway and Joyce in detail in Chapter 3.

A C T I V I T Y 6   Levels of literariness (Reading B)

Please read Reading B. Carter uses three texts which relate to Malaysia in different ways.

- While reading, note the different criteria that Carter uses to determine why Text C has a greater degree of literariness than the other texts.
- Where does Carter subsume Jakobson's and Mukařovský's poetic criteria/ concepts for determining literariness?
- Do you think Carter's criteria for literariness can be discussed without invoking the concept of literary value?

Comment

Carter has discussed the cline of literariness in relation to 'literary' forms in everyday conversation. This is addressed further in the companion volume, **Maybin and Swann (2006)**.

Carter's argument is based on a **cline of literariness**. He identifies six features and claims prototypical literary texts possess most of them, i.e. medium independence, genre-mixing, polysemy, displaced interaction, text patterning as well as high semantic density produced through the interaction of linguistic levels. Furthermore, a prototypically literary text would include more of these features than a non-literary text. Carter's focus in this extract is largely an inherency-based one and he subsumes a number of Formalist poetic criteria/ concepts. The focus on text patterning (akin to parallelism) could be construed as Jakobsonian, as could the focus on interactive repetitive patterning (semantic density) at the levels of syntax, lexis, phonology. When Carter says 'a displaced interaction in a text allows meanings to emerge indirectly and obliquely', this is redolent of Jakobson's argument about 'split' reference when the poetic function dominates. For Jakobson, when a text is 'split' off from the normal relationship between language and context, ambiguity can arise. Moreover, Carter uses Mukařovský's concept of deviation in his analysis of IT'S ALL HERE IN MALAYSIA. He also employs Mukařovský's term 'foregrounding' in relation to interactive patterning in Text C. So from Carter's analysis, a prototypically literary text, such as the Burgess extract, will include poetic elements even if it is not a poem. Lastly, his notion of genre-mixing has echoes of Mukařovský's 'interpenetration of dialect speech with the standard interpenetration'. Though dialect and genre are not the same, the principle – mixing different varieties of a language – is.

Carter indicates that literariness is not just about formal features but also how these set up oblique or indirect meanings, the text's 'unstated content', or how a text 'reinforces content'. For example, Carter infers that the genre-mixing in the literary extract serves to satirise travel brochure prose as 'comically inappropriate to a world which is much more heterogeneous and resistant to external ordering or classification'. For this to occur, the text requires the reader not just to skim the 'surface' of a text but to involve themselves in the generation of such indirect meanings. And for this to happen effectively, literariness in the text needs to be achieved *skilfully* by the author. Carter's inherency focus is ostensibly unconcerned with literary value. But it would seem implicit in his account that the high degree of literariness in the Burgess extract relates to its literary craft in terms of the kinds of indirect meanings likely to be generated by a reader and thus in turn the value of this literary text. In other words, although Carter keeps the issue of literary value in abeyance in his use of the six criteria, it is implicit in his analysis of Text C. Anthony Burgess is indeed valued by many as a serious literary author. In contrast, one could imagine a similar-sized extract from a Barbara Cartland popular romance novel which has a high degree of inherent literariness but which does not lead to such a richness of indirect meanings in reading and thus is not so valued as a result. One can also imagine a similar-sized extract from an Ernest Hemingway novel where the style is 'plain', and thus where the degree of inherent literariness is less than the Burgess extract, but nevertheless where the richness of indirect meanings is as great.

> You will be asked to look in more detail at Barbara Cartland's writing in Reading C.

It would be unfair, however, to criticise Carter's cline of literariness as not being useful for showing differences in value between different literary texts; this is not its purpose. It is useful from an inherency perspective for showing that there is no sharp cut-off between literary and non-literary texts and that prototypical literary texts, even if not poems, contain poetic elements. Also from an inherency perspective, the cline of literariness can account for why certain works of non-fiction can be seen as literary, works such as Milton's or Donne's prose works and Orwell's essays or Francis Bacon's 'elegant writing' in 'Of discourse' mentioned in Chapter 1. In other words, these texts are non-prototypically literary in possessing only some of Carter's criteria, (e.g. semantic density).

You now have an opportunity to apply Carter's criteria yourselves.

ACTIVITY 7   Little Italy, New York City

> Allow about 40 minutes

Below are two text extracts, of almost the same length, which refer to a district in New York City known as 'Little Italy'.

- Using Carter's criteria, decide which one has more literariness.
- Guided by your application of Carter's criteria, what kinds of indirect meanings are generated by you from these two texts?

Text 1

About Little Italy NYC

Walking beside the narrow, cobblestoned streets beneath the fire escapes of turn-of-the-century tenements, you're tempted by the sights, sounds and smells of Italian cuisine and culture emanating from the restaurants surrounding you at every step.

Here at Little Italy NYC, we're bringing it all to you! See our **restaurant list and map** to visit many of these restaurants online. Get an idea for the restaurant that's right for you and your family and friends. And when you arrive in Little Italy, you can say *'you've been here before.'*

Text 2

Local rumour maintains that Little Italy is one of the cleanest and safest enclaves in Manhattan. Any junkie or Bowery red-eye comes limping down the street, then five sombre fatboys with baseball bats and axe-handles stride out of the nearest trattoria. Well, Little Italy just felt like more Village to me. The zeds of the fire-escapes looked as through they were used in earnest twice a week – they were grimed to a cinder. In these clogged defiles they could never wash off all the truck-belch and car-fart bubbling upwards in vapours of oil and acid and engine coolant.

Comment

The first text is from a promotional website (http://www.littleitalynyc.com/about.asp). There is a fair degree of sound patterning in the first sentence: the repeated consonants of *cobblestoned*, *streets*, *restaurants*, *surrounding*, *step*, *sights*, *sounds and smells*. This density of sound patterning interacts with the density of the syntactic arrangement of *sights, sounds and smells of Italian cuisine*. There would seem to be a deliberate attempt to construct text to reinforce meaning. For me these levels of phonology and syntax reinforce meaning associated with restaurants; the compact clustering of sibilants evoke the 'bustle' and 'hissing' of a restaurant kitchen. The text has semantic density. There is some text patterning too, for example, the parallelism of the imperatives *see our ...* and *get an idea*. There is also some genre-mixing in the use of the representation of direct speech (*you've been here before*) with the more 'poetic' first sentence. However, the text is explicit about its medium dependence (*see our restaurant list and map*) and facilitates this through a web-link. This is not an example of displaced interaction either, in that the text has a conative function to persuade the reader to eat in Little Italy. There is little obvious polysemy.

> **Sibilants** – hissing sounds such as the sounds in bold in **s**treet and **sh**op.

You might have found it tricky to say what the source for Text 2 is. Is it a piece of 'literary' travel journalism or perhaps an extract from a novel? The first line might come from the genre of travel journalism. The second line departs from this in aping direct speech since there seems to be some ellipsis, e.g. *if* from the start of the sentence. So there seems to be genre-mixing, using Carter's criterion, between the first and second line. The next line also evokes informal direct speech with the dysfluency of *like more*. From the point of view of standard written English it is grammatically deviant but from the norm of informal conversational English it may well not be. The next sentence *zeds of the fire-escapes ...* is not conversational and returns to standard written English. It uses a metaphor *zeds*, which introduces polysemy, and what seems to be a deviant expression, *grimed to a cinder*. Intuitively, for me, the phrase from which this is a deviation is *burnt to a cinder*. *Grimed* seems deviant too; I normally associate 'grime' with its noun form and not with its adjective or verb form (though *grimed* in *grimed to a cinder* seems more adjectival than verbal). In the next line there are semantically deviant compounds, *truck-belch* and *car-fart* which personify the pollution. By the end of the paragraph there is a fair amount of semantic density which indirectly invites me to make links between human beings, combustion (*fire* escapes and petrochemical-based vehicles), pollution and squalor. This is reinforced by the polysemy of *defiles* (the narrow pass of a fire-escape or making dirty). The 'unstated content' is for me ironic – despite having fire-escapes, one doesn't escape from the 'fire of pollution' of Little Italy. Text 2 is medium independent and characterised by displaced interaction. On Carter's cline of literariness perspective, this text would constitute a high degree of literariness, higher than the Little Italy website text. It is in fact an extract from a novel, *Money* by Martin Amis (1984, p.104).

Though Carter located deviation in the Malaysia advert, he did not in the Burgess extract from the novel *Time for a Tiger*. In the extract from *Money*, I discerned *grimed* as being deviant and *grimed to a cinder* as being a deviation from *burnt to a cinder*. But I could only claim all this intuitively speaking. At the end of Section 2.3, I said that corpora can be useful in getting a sense of how deviant a piece of language is. To get a sense of how deviant *grimed to a cinder* is, I use a 450 million word corpus known as The Bank of English. Searching for *to+a+cinder* I found 25 instances.

Figure 2.2 is known as a set of **concordance lines**, and shows 23 instances of *to+a+cinder*. These lines enable the viewer to see how *to+a+cinder* is used in texts in The Bank of English by listing each instance in turn with its surrounding text. As you can see, almost all of the lines are either explicitly *burnt/burned to a cinder* or relate to fire in some way. Drawing on evidence from this very large corpus, we can treat *grimed to a cinder* as deviant. But an advantage of using this corpus as a norm is that we can also say that *grimed to a cinder* is a deviation from a not very common expression since *burnt/burned, etc. +to+a+cinder* occurs only 25 times in a corpus of 450 million words. Let me look at *grimed* also, which intuitively I felt was deviant too. In a search for the noun, *grime*, I found 702 instances (a portion of which were names). When I searched for *grimed* (as an adjective or a verb) I only found 15 instances (Figure 2.3). So my intuition that *grimed* is more unusual than *grime* would seem to have some support. The Bank of English is made up of subcorpora of different types of text, consisting mainly of newspaper journalism, but also subcorpora of speech as well as subcorpora which consist of fiction and non-fiction books. In the Bank of English, 13 out of

battle. He grilled Mr Blair to a cinder over beef, taunting the PM over
worldcom's cooking of its books to a cinder. But nobody, beyond those who pine
if her birthday cake is burned to a cinder - she'll probably find it more
with sawdust, quickly burnt to a cinder, and Jane was left shrieking. It
my guest's pheasant was burnt to a cinder. We were bitterly disappointed. It
fire. The tracksuit was burnt to a cinder and Hartson was thrown into a
fire. The tracksuit was burnt to a cinder and Hartson was thrown into a
action other than getting burnt to a cinder. Anyway, the Hyatt Regency does
world having been burnt to a cinder, now found herself lodged in a
our clothes have been burnt to a cinder, our bones will be crushed to
Matches and ended up burnt to a cinder, as told to me by my mother when I
Republic, until it was burnt to a cinder in February 1933. The fire gave
of an Iraqi soldier burnt to a cinder by Allied bombardment in the Gulf
announced, 'So. Atlanta's burnt to a cinder and all the explosives is blown sky
half and hour. When burnt to a cinder, or still pink inside, stick in a
My method of disposal ... Burnt to a cinder. This cinder to be deposited in my
Was burned, poor fellow, to a cinder. Whether or nor Jane Apreece had
they did not fear being fried to a cinder? Possibly. But I have done too
nice." Before bbc1 burned him to a cinder, of course. That'll teach him to
nice." Before bbc1 burned him to a cinder, of course. That'll teach him to
no thunderbolt to blight him to a cinder simply by hoping for it. The rank
car. We followed the pounding to a cinder block classroom at Our Lady of Lord'
the bulk of the UK was reduced to a cinder". The prior question was: "How

Figure 2.2   Concordance lines for *to a cinder* from The Bank of English.

of peace in this clamorous, dust-grimed city. A deranged woman attempts to
the huge, empty space, so faded and grimed that it is almost impossible to
splashed with winter road mud, hands grimed, faces streaked with dirt. They
on a coal wharf but never washes his grimed face - - though he operates a
complexion and hands perpetually grimed from reading too much newsprint.
it out and the derelict took it, his grimed hand like a claw. Scabs of dirt
of socialism and commerce. The grimed compartment where Deacon finally
entrance here at seven." He put a grimed forefinger on the spot, then turned
dropping a penny into the man's dirt-grimed hand. The student stopped and
as the coach jolted through the soot-grimed orchards and vegetable fields about
of fire on bare chests and sweat-grimed faces, the harsh crackling and the
moonlight, filtering in through dust-grimed windows. Another set of doors
was there too, his face adn clothes grimed from his expedition down the shaft.
rucksack's flap. The rucksack was grimed with dried mud. They didn't open
just a small and musty larder with grimed gauze over the window, a couple of

Figure 2.3   Concordance lines for *grimed* from The Bank of English.

the 15 instances of *grimed* come from fictional sources. The other two are from
journalistic sources.

By having a norm like the Bank of English divided into subcorpora, it is
possible to be more discerning as to judgements of deviation. Judged against
grime in the whole of the Bank of English, *grimed* is highly deviant. But
judged against a subcorpus which consists in part of fiction, it is less deviant.
It might be said on the basis of the above evidence that *grimed* is a modern
literary word analogous to *twain* and *verdure* mentioned in Reading B.

With the compiling of larger corpora of fiction, such claims can receive more substantiation.

I provided above a brief analysis of the Amis literary extract. But in line with comments I made about objectivity of analysis at the end of Section 2.2, there may well be levels of meaning that I did not pick up upon. But even if I had described the text exhaustively in a Jakobsonian sense, and let us suppose that this can be achieved, would I have been accounting for all of its literariness? We return to the issue that, while an analyst may lay out many of the ingredients of literariness in the text, what a reader does with those ingredients will differ. Literariness is not just text-inherent properties but about how the craft of a text leads readers to infer unstated content. Carter recognises this in Reading B when he says that 'activation of meanings must be dependent on a reader whose literary competence permits "reasonable" correlations of linguistic forms and semantic functions'. In bringing in the concept of literary competence (characterising someone who is practised in reading literature), Carter thus introduces an element of reader dependency which is not part of traditional Formalism. What a reader picks up on in a text could also vary socioculturally (you will recall Eagleton's argument in Chapter 1) which would move the focus further away from the Formalist concern with the language itself. For example, a Malay speaker reading the Burgess extract from *Time for a Tiger*, will recognise that *Tahi Panas* means *hot shit* and could then potentially link this into an interpretation that a non-Malay speaker would most likely not.

We have seen in this section and the previous ones that Carter's criteria are useful in helping us judge literariness in both literary and non-literary texts. We have also seen that they usefully go beyond the Formalist emphasis that literariness is the language of poetry. But as has been pointed out, saying a poem has a high degree of literariness is a different thing to saying it has literary value. (The issue of literary evaluation was not something that Jakobson and Formalism generally were especially concerned with.) How we might go about assessing whether a poem or a passage of prose has literary value is the topic of the last section.

The relationship between literariness and the reader is explored in Chapters 7, 8 and 9.

2.5 Assessing literary value

Probably the most celebrated bad poet in the English language is the Scot, William McGonagall. He is associated with a subgenre, doggerel, or very bad poetry. This is because although he uses rhyme and verse forms, they would seem to have little purpose in his poems. You will come across a poem by McGonagall in Reading C. Despite his low standing as a poet, an article on stylistics by Paul Werth (1976) argues that a Jakobsonian stylistic methodology reveals levels of literariness in a McGonagall poem that would be found in a Shakespeare sonnet. It would be unthinkable, though, that a skilled and experienced reader of literature would regard McGonagall as the better poet. Following this argument through, there would seem to be no correlation between the level of literariness in a poem and its value. So why might one poem be regarded as better than another? The answer, as was hinted at in the last section, is connected in part with how a text is crafted to guide the reader to link levels of literariness and then go on to infer 'unstated content'.

Richard Bradford (1997) argues that it is possible to use stylistic analysis to enable judgements as to why one text carries more literary value than the other.

ACTIVITY 8   Evaluative stylistics (Reading C)

Read the extract from Bradford's chapter, 'Evaluative stylistics' (Reading C).

- What is the 'double-pattern' and why does Bradford think it is significant for judgements of literary value?
- In what ways do you think the double-pattern relates to Carter's cline of literariness?
- Are you convinced by Bradford's argument and the evaluative analyses he offers?

Comment

In order to assess a literary work, Bradford seeks out the double-pattern in it – the relationship between its literary form (e.g. lines in a poem) on the one hand and its non-literary form and content on the other. Bradford argues that the quality of a literary work should be judged in relation to the balance between these two dimensions. In the Adcock poem, there is constant interference between the literary features of the text and its topic, perhaps female masturbation, although the topic is never revealed explicitly. As a result, for Bradford the poem resists closure; he says, for example, the poem might be about 'savouring one's own company'. In contrast, the Cartland extract encourages closure; there is no tension between elements of the double-pattern. Bradford uses 'resistance to closure' as a criterion to evaluate Adcock's literary text as better than Cartland's. I agree this criterion can distinguish between literary texts in terms of value. If a literary work is polysemic to different people across time and space, it has more value than one which is monosemic. Lastly, as Bradford argues, and reiterating the above, the use of poetic devices in McGonagall's poem seems to have no purpose other than make it *sound* and *look* like a poem.

There are connections with Carter's cline of literariness in Bradford's argument. Clearly, for Bradford there is no such thing as a literary language either–literary texts are composed of both literary elements (e.g. lines in a poem) and elements that non-literary texts possess. The notion of the double-pattern also links to Carter's criterion of genre-mixing, where a non-literary genre can be mixed in with a literary text for particular effects.

Another reason that Bradford regards the Adcock poem as better is because it unsettles 'familiar patterns of reality'. Interestingly, this other criterion for judging the Adcock poem is a classically Formalist one since Bradford is essentially saying the poem is defamiliarising. However, while the poem may be defamiliarising for a male reader, would it necessarily be for a female reader? For Jeffries (2001), 'Against coupling' is not defamiliarising since it affirms an aspect of female experience that is often not discussed.

You first met the concept of defamiliarisation in Chapter 1. Let me dwell a little more on it. For Bradford, Cartland is as good as Jane Austen in her narratorial skill. But how might the ending of Jane Austen's novel, *Pride and Prejudice*, compare to 'Against coupling' in terms of its capacity for defamiliarisation? It would not be controversial to see *Pride and Prejudice* at the high end of romantic fiction and thus see it as better than Barbara Cartland's *The Naked Battle*. But it is hardly defamiliarising in that it produces the expected happy ending of romantic fiction. On Bradford's rationale, the defamiliarising Adcock poem would seem to be better than the ending of *Pride and Prejudice*. Faced with such a comparison, one starts to see potential problems in making comparative judgements of literary quality between texts from different genres. Besides, do good literary texts really have to be defamiliarising? Attridge (2004a, p. 39) takes issue with Formalism when he contends that literary experience as being characterised by defamiliarisation is 'far from the whole story'. Literary creativity, for him, does not so much shatter our familiar perceptions of reality as open us up to **otherness** – 'a truth, a value, a feeling, a way of doing things, or some complex combination of these, that has been historically occluded and whose emergence or re-emergence is important for a particular time and place'. Jeffries' (2001) reading of 'Against coupling' would seem to be one of experiencing otherness since female masturbation has traditionally been an 'occluded' topic. And, in relation to *Pride and Prejudice* (with its non-defamiliarising ending), Attridge (2004a, pp. 21–2) argues that Austen was profoundly aware of the 'impossibilities, the exclusions and prohibitions' that limited the novel of the time; it is out of her profound awareness of these which 'emerges the otherness' that makes *Pride and Prejudice* a fiction of 'extraordinary richness and subtlety'. Thus, if valued literary texts are not necessarily experienced as defamiliarising (and we will return to this issue in Chapter 8), the following could be argued: it is better to use the double-pattern only to see whether a literary text encourages or resists closure. In any case, as argued above, it is better to make comparative judgements of literary quality between texts from the same genre.

ACTIVITY 9 **'Death-bed confessions'**

Allow about 40 minutes

Read the following poem, 'Death-bed confessions', an alternative to Cecil Day Lewis' 'Last words'. Which poem has the most literary value for you? Think about this issue by exploring how each poem's literariness relates to the topic of a man being asked about his last words. Draw on stylistic concepts and criteria introduced in this chapter and Chapter 1 in exploring the literariness of the two poems. (Draw on Nash's analysis of 'Last words' if you think it appropriate to do so.)

Death-bed confessions

'You are a man of words', they said;
'Suppose your pulse is growing weak;
Which of your former selves should speak
For you upon your dying bed?'

'Perchance that inner voice you'll hear
Will tell of childhood, how at night
An engine-whistle soothed your fright
And seemed to make the future clear?'

'Or else – maybe! – the appropriate word
Belongs to your high-flying youth,
Circling for honour, freedom, truth,
Like some great predatory bird?'

'This aged man, it might befall,
Just half alive, still not quite dead,
Whose days draw out like spider's thread,
Can speak the speech that says it all?'

'Who knows? Confess! Which self to keep?
Greybeard submission, meek and mild?
Youth's lofty pride? Or else that child,
Tucked up in bed, and half-asleep?'

Comment

'Death-bed confessions' has for the most part a very regular rhythm (known as iambic tetrameter):

```
    .    /    .   /    .     /   .  /
'Who knows? Confess! Which self to keep?
```

The regular rhythm and divisions into lines and stanzas would place this text into the genre of poetry, as would the regular rhyme scheme (a-b-b-a – s**aid**/ w**eak**/sp**eak**/b**ed**). From a Jakobsonian perspective, this poem is dense with parallelisms of sound and metre. But does this regularity relate successfully to the topic of the poem – a man being asked about what his dying words may be? Reading stanza 1, there would seem to be a tension between the jaunty regularity and such sombre content. Initially, I thought this might be deliberate so as to produce ironic effect. Then I read stanza 2, which relates to a child.

The jaunty regularity for stanza 2 could be said to be more appropriate in echoing a children's song perhaps – so there would be no irony there. But if the poem moves from irony to non-irony, this would seem to indicate that my initial analysis was misplaced. In other words, stanzas 1 and 2 signal to me that the writer is not spending effort in linking literariness and content. And the more one explores the regularity of the poem, its rhymes, its metre, the more one realises there is little purpose for this regularity other than to signal the text is a poem. 'Death-bed confessions' in this respect is quite McGonagallesque. As I go further through the poem I get a better sense that it is not suggesting 'unstated content' through its use of rhyme, its parallelisms, etc. 'Death-bed confessions' has archaic literary words such as *perchance* and *befall*. These are similar to the words *twain* and *verdure* which Carter mentioned in Reading B. Like the rhymes and metre, their function in the poem seems only to make it sound 'literary'.

In contrast, in 'Last words' there is much 'interference of device and meaning' (as there was for Bradford in Adcock's poem). There is, in Carter's terms, genre-mixing – the move from conversational tone at the start of the poem to what I infer as unstated content – the religious solemnity (*let this x say*) of the last stanza, last words as 'last rites'. In his analysis of 'Last words', Nash points out that the rhyme scheme is subtle and complex throughout the poem, an 'acoustic progression' leading to the powerful connection established by the full rhyme in the last stanza between *weep* and *sleep*. I could not make the same claim about 'Death-bed confessions' or more particularly, *which self to keep/half asleep*.

Nash also examines the complex semantic relationships in 'Last words', particularly its polysemy, or what he calls the 'transmutations' in the text. For example, Day Lewis uses the word *hoodwinked* in stanza 3 which means 'deluded' and is also associated with falconry. It is in these semantic relationships that 'Last words', for me, more obviously resists closure. In contrast, the language of 'Death-bed confessions' is very literal; only one simile is retained from the first text – *days draw out like spider's web* – and the metaphors tend towards the clichéd, for example, *high flying youth*, *greybeard submission*, *youth's lofty pride*. Polysemy and thus ambiguity is less apparent in 'Death-bed confessions' which in turn encourages closure.

I don't find 'Last words' particularly defamiliarising – I would expect a 'man of words' on his death-bed to reflect on his former selves as well as to want to leave this world sententiously. Nevertheless, in terms of the relationship between the poem's literariness and content, in how it sets up readers to infer unstated content, and because it has elements that resist closure, 'Last words' is the more successful and so has more literary value. ('Death-bed confessions' is in fact a deliberately bad poem written by Walter Nash.) Finally, on Carter's criterion, 'Death-bed confessions' does not have as much interaction of levels of meaning as 'Last words', that is, it does not have as much semantic density. Given also its greater amount of polysemy and genre-mixing, 'Last words' has more literariness than 'Death-bed confessions'. So in this instance, there really is a correlation between level of literariness and literary value.

2.6 Conclusion

We have looked in this chapter at how two Formalists of the Russian and Prague Schools, Roman Jakobson and Jan Mukařovský, characterised poetry from an inherency perspective. While the Formalists introduced useful concepts and techniques of analysis which have been drawn upon extensively in stylistics, their relevance is more often than not to poetry and particular examples of it. But, as we have seen in this chapter, poetic language in poems is not the only form of literariness. The chapter extended the scope of inherency analysis, so as to account for poetic literariness in certain passages of narrative fiction, by drawing on Ronald Carter's cline of literariness. Moreover, we saw that literariness is not just about examining text-intrinsic properties. It is also about how the craft of a text leads readers to infer unstated content. Finally, the chapter looked at the issue of literary value.

Earlier in the chapter, you came across the issue of exhaustability of analysis. It may be possible to exhaustively describe a short passage from a novel using one linguistic descriptive system and at a specified level of analysis. But this would not be readily achievable for a *whole* novel. Given this, there would seem to be limits on how a stylistic analysis of literariness can ultimately key into assessments of whether a novel has literary value. Indeed, once we get beyond the genre of poetry into narrative fiction, other phenomena, such as plot and characterisation, will feed into assessments of quality. The next chapter moves the discussion of literariness and literary value further by looking at plot and characterisation in narrative fiction. But in line with the limits of stylistic analysis, it necessarily has its major focus on a particular subgenre of narrative fiction – the short story.

READING A: Extracts from 'The lyrical game: C. Day Lewis's "Last words"'

Walter Nash

I

'Last words' is a subtle and in some respects complicated poem. Its playfulness is complex. Rereadings bring out eccentricities of form, of content, of syntax and semantics, until it seems to the reader that the words 'just the game' are indeed applicable to these verses; though whether we are entitled to describe them as 'just *a* game' is another matter.

II

Prosody – patterning of sound and rhythm in verse.

Its prosodic form, at first glance quite regular in broad outline, is notably eccentric in two respects. The first of these is its rhyme-scheme, for it is indeed a rhyming poem of sorts. In each six-line stanza, the first, third, and fifth lines are unrhymed, while lines two, four, and six rhyme – or rather 'chime', with half-rhymes [...] . Thus in stanza 1 we find 'game', 'sum', 'them'; in 2, 'reach', 'edge', 'pitch'; in 3, 'round', 'learned', 'hand'; in 4, 'down', 'soon', 'span'. In 5, there is at first a half-rhyme, 'web' – 'weep', but then the poem concludes with its one and only full rhyme, 'weep' – 'sleep'. This full rhyme obviously communicates a sense of ending, and of positive ending at that; we close the poem on a major, reassuring, conciliatory harmony, after all the preceding [...] uncertainty.

[...] In each rhyming trio it is the consonantal element that is the most obvious: the nasal /m/ in stanza 1 [e.g. **m**an, su**m**], the affricates /ʧ/, /ʤ/ in 2 [e.g. **ch**ild, e**dg**e], the nasal+stop cluster /nd/ in 3 [e.g. rou**nd**, ha**nd**], the nasal /n/ in 4 [e.g. ma**n**, spa**n**], the stops /b/ and /p/ in 5 [e.g. **b**lest, wee**p**]. The accompanying vowels, it might almost seem, are merely there to shape the syllable. They do, however, make interesting acoustic progressions as we follow them through each stanza – progressions from length to shortness, or from greater to lesser sonority. The progressive diminution of sonority is quite evident in stanza 1, where the vowel-length of 'game' is drastically shortened in 'sum', and where the [...] vowel of 'sum' gives place to a vowel of even lower resonance in 'them'. [...] In stanza 2 the progression runs from the long vowel of 'reach' to the shorter vowels of 'edge' and 'pitch'; in stanza 3, the diphthong of 'round' is followed by the long vowel of 'learned' and then by the short vowel of 'hand'; and in 4 there is a similar acoustic progression from diphthong ('down') to long vowel ('soon') to short vowel ('span'). Only in the last stanza is the general progression from greater to lesser sonority reversed; there, the short 'web' is followed by the long 'weep' in preparation for the full, concluding sonority of 'sleep'. [...]

Is it then fanciful to suggest a connection between such recurrent shifts of vowel quantity or quality and the prevalent 'mood' or 'feeling' of the poem,

Sonority – describes the strength and length of a sound.

Diphthong – where two vowels have been glided into one, e.g. 'cry' which consists of the glided vowels, **a:** (as in P*a*) and **I:** (as in m*e*).

its conveyed sense of a talkative hesitation and doubt turning at last to epigrammatic certainty? We here confront the problem that so often vexes beginners in the art of literary stylistics: how can we be sure that the writer *intended*, or indeed was aware of, the 'effects' which we as readers are so ready to perceive? But creativeness – as the teacher must repeatedly tell his pupils – trades between levels of conscious awareness and a deep, instinctual feel for the right choice, the true harmonic. In 'Last words' the full rhyme at the close no doubt occurred in clear consciousness as a matter of purposeful design, but the drifting half-rhymes of the preceding stanzas need not have been so deliberately worked out; they suggest a feeling for 'the true harmonic', grounded in instinct, confirmed in effect.

III

The second respect in which the form of 'Last words' is eccentric is in the pattern of varying line-lengths from stanza to stanza. [...] No two stanzas follow quite the same pattern, as the following representation of the scheme will show [short (S) and long lines (L)]:

	1	2	3	4	5	6
Stanza 1	S	L	S	L	L	S
Stanza 2	L	S	L	S	L	S
Stanza 3	S	L	L	S	L	S
Stanza 4	L	S	S	L	L	S
Stanza 5	S	L	S	L	S	L

We might see this simply as an instance of the poet varying the form to amuse himself. Nevertheless, it prompts interesting speculations about relationships between line-length, stanza pattern, and poetic perspective. For instance, the poem begins with a short, syntactically incomplete line ('Suppose, they asked') and ends with a line that is long and syntactically self-contained ('I hear the night bird, I can go to sleep'). The final stanza, indeed, is the only one to end on a long line. That might suggest the following relationship: a short line links to lack of resolution of the question of what the persona's last words should be; a long line links to resolution. But although it is arguable that the fluctuations of line-length do indeed trace some such course from questioning to certainty – corresponding to changes noted above in the acoustic and emotional character of the rhyme-words – it is not quite so simple or banal (or demonstrably fruitless) as trying to say what the short line 'equals' or what the long line 'connotes'. The significance of the long–short variations is best considered with reference to the total shape of the poem.

Of the five stanzas, the first has a question; [...] the last offers a resolution; and the stanzas in the intervening group present three [...] related 'arguments' [as to who should utter the last words, the child, the romantic youth or the ageing man]. This resembles the standard lay-out of Graeco-Roman rhetoric, with an introduction, a narration, and a conclusion. We must notice, however, the quite striking stylistic contrast between the introduction, which is conversational, musing, *pre-poetic*, the evocation of a man talking to himself, and the rest of the poem, which is unabashedly *poetic*, rhetorical, or even – if one wished to suggest an adverse criticism – high-flown. But there is a further internal contrast, between the style of the narration, with its three arguments, each filling the stanza with a different syntactic scheme, and that of the conclusion with its three concise, syntactically parallel declarations, each contained in a short–long pair of lines.

In their alternations of line-length, two stanzas have a mirror-relationship with each other: stanza 2, the first of the arguments, and stanza 5, the conclusion. Stanza 2 has L—S—L—S—L—S, and stanza 5 supplies the reverse pattern with S—L—S—L—S—L. If we accept that the poem proper begins with the attempt to resolve the question of who should utter the last words and thus with stanza 2, then the mirror turnabout in the patterning of the final stanza must reinforce the impression of an ending, of reaching a goal.

... Stanzas 3 and 4 (the 'romantic youth', the 'ageing man') seem at first glance to be haphazardly regulated in their divisions of long and short, but they too make a symmetrical pair. In their first four lines they mirror one another. Stanza 3 begins S—L—L—S; stanza 4 has L—S—S—L. In the last two lines they are not mirrors but parallels: each ends L—S.

Four stanzas of a poem in which the management of line-length is apparently random, or possibly geared to syntactic requirements, thus turn out to have recursive symmetrical relationships in their prosodic design, like patterns in wallpaper or carpeting. Only the first stanza, it appears, has no design partner; but this is the odd item out, not only in the numerical sense (there are five stanzas in the poem, and two pairs leave one over), but also in the rhetorical-poetic sense, the first stanza being the prefatory mulling over of a proposition roughly paraphrasable as 'let's write a poem'. It is external to the symmetry which contains the rest of the poem, a symmetry leading, in the final stanza, to a prosodic mirror which is also a mirror of content; for the 'child', 'youth', and 'ageing man' of the narration appear in reverse order in the conclusion, as 'man', 'youth', and 'child'.

Once again, those old questions of intentionality arise. Here we have what seems to be a very ingenious control of prosodic design, linking the management of line-length with the very movement and meaning of the poem, its progression from the hesitant mumbling of its opening to the decisive assertions of its close. Is this a clear case of a poet knowing and consciously choosing?; or of what might be called the permutations of instinct?; or simply of a reader seeing what a reader wishes to find? It is in the nature of things poetic that we cannot be wholly certain about such matters; nevertheless, this text presents more than one instance of the ostensibly casual choice that must in fact be the product of an inherent, controlling intelligence.

IV

There is, for example, the matter of the poem's syntax in relationship to its prosody and to its overall design in the phases of introduction, narration, and conclusion. The first and the last stanzas, are, so to speak, structurally fragmented, albeit in significantly different ways. Stanza 1 rambles over its six lines, but the ramble is interrupted by marks suggesting the vocal features of an 'aside' (the parenthesis), a pause (the dots), a colloquial musing (signalled with a colon after 'Last words'). The syntax, the dynamics of punctuation, the breaking of lines and overrunning of line-ends, collectively suggest talk, and talk of a hesitant and somewhat muted kind. This is in contrast with stanza 5, which is divided, or 'portioned', rather than 'fragmented'. The portions are of equal size, are parallel syntactic/rhetorical structures, and suggest, unlike the 'talk' of stanza 1, that the poem's persona is now convinced of the rightness of his oration. [...]

These 'fragmented' and 'portioned' outer stanzas are to be contrasted with the interior group of three making up the narration. Here in each case there is an elaborate syntactic structure filling the whole stanza, without breaking or portioning. These are ... structures which develop their initial headwords ('the child', 'the romantic youth', 'the ageing man') through qualifying ... clauses ('who ... heard', 'for whom horizons were' ... , 'seeing his lifelong travel ... '). These qualifying clauses are in each case extended by additional clauses expressing, in some way, a sense of the unfolding of time. Thus, in stanza 2, 'Heard nightly ... and *soon* ... had perfect pitch'; in 3, 'were the daily round ... *till* he had learned'; and in 4, 'seeing his ... toil scaled down to a flimsy web ... dissolving *soon*, and only the ... dew makes visible *now* its haunted span'.

> **Clause**: a grammatical unit built around a verb.

[...] Stanzas 2 and 3 are perspectives on the past, but 4 tells us emphatically that the standpoint of the story is *now*; which explains [...] why what we read is not '*the* man', suggesting an objective distance, as in 'I am not the man I was', but '*this* man'. Furthermore, 'this man' is emphatically identified with 'this youth' and 'this child'. The question is no longer 'which of me'? The answer is 'each and all of me' – even though it is the child who is given the last tender word.

V

This is a poem of transmutations, not least in the lexicon, where there are shifts of meaning – or perhaps shifts of shades of meaning – comparable with the shiftiness of the acoustic colouring, the prosodic design, and the syntax. Anyone generally acquainted with Day Lewis's work will be aware of his liking for what might be called the serious pun, the play on words that significantly enriches an image. There are several examples of this in 'Last words'. 'Hoodwinked' is an instance of a word with a dual relationship, referring on the one hand to 'orbit', via the implied image of falconry, and on the other to the notions of 'deception', 'delusion', commonly associated with this term. 'Travel' in stanza 4 is a manifest etymological play on 'travail', a reminder of the close association between journeying, labour, and suffering. 'Stranded' puns on the senses 'stretched out like a strand, or thread', and 'left in helpless isolation'. It is generally characteristic of this poet that the overt allusion to some kind of *fact* is accompanied by a veiled, transmuting reference to a state of mind or *feeling*.

In the cases quoted, the transmutation takes place within a single word; the receptive reader takes these ambiguities into immediate account. But there is another device of transmutation, spanning the poem, linking the three arguments of the narration with the three declarations of the conclusion. This lexical scheme runs as follows:

'an engine whistle'	becomes	'the night bird'
'hoodwinked orbit'	becomes	'treadmill'
'flimsy web'	becomes	'homespun web'

Each of these implies a psychological change for the better, though that might not seem immediately obvious from the bare examples. The instance of 'an engine whistle' – 'the night bird' is the clearest; something objective, factual, specific, *worldly*, reappears at the end as something subjective, mythical, *unworldly*. The transmutation of 'flimsy web' to 'homespun web' is also quite clearly a change towards positive affirmation. 'Homespun' suggests the strength of decent effort and craftsmanship. There is truth and honour in what is homespun; 'flimsy' may suggest hapless failure, 'homespun' does not. More puzzling is the transmutation of an 'orbit' into a 'treadmill'. Both may imply repetitive movement, vain circling – but the treadmill is surely a more painful, punitive thing than the hunting bird's orbit. This looks rather like a change for the worse until we consider the assertion that '*prairies* bow to the treadmill' – meaning that hard labour may have huge rewards; whereas the falcon's flight is an 'orbit of *clay*', a vain, hoodwinked circling over barren ground. The transmutation of 'orbit' into 'treadmill' is the change from profitless yearning to a perception of how golden attainments – Eldorados and prairies – become accessible through common repetitive toil.

VI

'Last words' is characteristic of Day Lewis's mature (or middle-aged) lyric style: a blend of modern techniques – for example, in the use of half-rhymes – with traditional or classical sentiments and topics. [...] Its strength, it may be said, is in its playfulness, the ludic spirit that almost distracts attention from the sombre question 'how should we face age, and loneliness, and death?' – and creates a poem of conciliatory elegance, most memorable in the tenderness and grace of its closing line. Just the game for a man of words – but the game is serious, the words well-chosen.

Source: adapted from VERDONK, P. (ed.) (1993) *Twentieth Century Poetry: From Text to Context*, London, Routledge.

READING B: Extracts from 'Is there a literary language?'

Ronald Carter

In this reading some criteria for specifying literariness in language are proposed, criteria which go beyond the poetic ones of Russian and Prague School Formalism. The criteria, although based on those proposed in Carter and Nash (1983), are extended and modified in a number of ways. Reference to the criteria will enable us to determine what is prototypical in conventional literary language use, as far as it is understood in its standard, modern average Western conception; in other words, the criteria will assist in determining *degrees* of literariness and provide a systematic basis for saying one text is more or less 'literary' than another. The texts about Malaysia used in this discussion are labelled A–C.

Text A

Watch 'Little Asia' come alive in Kuala Lumpur, then relive the historical past of nearby Malacca.

Kuala Lumpur. Malaysia's capital city with an endless maze of colourful images. The people; the food, the sights, the sounds. All an exotic mix of European and Asian cultures. A pulsating potpourri of Malays, Chinese and Indians.

And there's more. To the south is the historic town of *Malacca*. Here, 158 km from *Kuala Lumpur*, you can step into history and relive the glorious past of this ancient port.

Fish, sail, swim or simply relax on the sandy, sun-kissed beaches of *Port Dickson*, only 100 km away from *Kuala Lumpur*.

Or take a scenic drive from the capital city to one of several hill resorts, set in the midst of lush green tropical jungles.

And it's all here in Malaysia. The country where great cultures meet, where the diversity of its history, customs and traditions is reflected in the warm hospitality of gentle, friendly Malaysians.

Come share a holiday in this wonderful land. Come to Malaysia. We welcome you now and any time of the year.

IT'S ALL HERE IN MALAYSIA

Text B

Malaysia, East, part of Federation of Malaysia: inc, Sarawak and Sabah (formerly Brit. N. Borneo); less developed than W. Malaysia; p. concentrated on cst.; hill tribes engaged in hunting in interior; oil major exp., exploration off cst.; separated from W. Malaysia by S. China Sea; a. 77,595 sq. m.; p. (1968) 1,582,000.

Malaysia, Federation of, indep. federation (1963), S.E. Asia; member of Brit. Commonwealth; inc. W. Malaysia (Malaya) and E. Malaysia (Borneo sts. of Sarawak and Sabah); cap. Kuala Lumpur; a. 129,000 sq. m.; p. (1968) 10,455,00.

Malaysia, West (Malaya), part of Federation of Malaysia; consists of wide peninsula, S. of Thailand; most developed in W.; world's leading producer of natural rubber, grown in plantations; oil palm and pineapples also grown; world's leading exporter of tin; nearly half p. Chinese; a. 50,806 sp. m.; p. (1968) 8,899,000.

Text C

Victor Crabbe slept through the *bilal's bang* (inept Persian word for the faint unheeded call), would sleep till the *bangbang* (apt Javanese word) of the brontoid dawn brought him tea and bananas. He slept on the second floor of the old Residency, which overlooked the river.

The river Lanchap gives the state its name. It has its source in deep jungle, where it is a watering-place for a hundred or so little negroid people who worship thunder and can count only up to two. They share it with tigers, hamdryads, bootlace-snakes, leeches, pelandoks and the rest of the bewildering fauna of up-stream Malaya. As the Sungai Lanchap winds on, it encounters outposts of a more complex culture: Malay villages where the Koran is known, where the prophets jostle with nymphs and tree-gods in a pantheon of unimaginable variety. Here a little work in the paddy-fields suffices to maintain a heliotropic, pullulating subsistence. There are fish in the river, guarded, however, by crocodile-gods of fearful malignity; coconuts drop or are hurled down by trained monkeys called *beroks*; the durian sheds its rich fetid smell in the season of durians. Erotic pantuns and Hindu myths soothe away the depression of an occasional *accidia*. As the Lanchap approaches the coast a more progressive civilization appears: the two modern towns of Timah and Tahi Panas, made fat on tin and rubber, supporting large populations of Chinese, Malays, Indians, Eurasians, Arabs, Scots, Christian Brothers, and pale English administrators. The towns echo with trishawbells, the horns of smooth, smug American cars, radios blaring sentimental pentatonic Chinese tunes, the morning hawking and spitting of the *towkays*, the call of the East. Where the Lanchap meets the Sungai, Hantu is the royal town, dominated by an Istana designed by a Los Angeles architect, blessed by a mosque as bulbous as a clutch of onions, cursed by a lowering sky and high humidity. This is Kuala Hantu.

Victor Crabbe slept soundly, drawn into that dark world where history melts into myth.

1   Medium dependence

The notion of medium dependence means that the more literary a text, the less it will be dependent for its reading on another medium or media. In this respect Text B is dependent on a key to abbreviations used and on reference to a map or illustrations (e.g. inc.; indep.; a.; p.; cst; exp.; cap.).

To a lesser extent Text A could probably be said to be medium dependent in that it is likely to be accompanied by some means of pictorial supplement. By contrast, Text C is dependent only on itself for its 'reading'. It generates a world of internal reference and relies only on its own capacity to project. This is not to suggest that it cannot be determined by external political or social or biographical influences. No text can be so entirely autonomous that it refers only to itself nor so rich that a reader's own experience of the Malaysia it refers to (though, paradoxically, none of the places actually exist: there is no Kuala Hantu, etc.) cannot extend the world it creates. But the text is sovereign. Relative to the other writing about Malaysia, this text requires no necessary supplementation.

2   Genre-mixing

Genres such as legal language or the language of instructions are recognised by the neat fit between language form and specific function; but any language at all can be deployed to literary effect by the process of genre-mixing. In other words, no single word or stylistic feature or genre is barred from admission to a literary context. For example, Auden makes use of bureaucratic genres in his poem 'The Unknown Citizen'; wide use of journalistic and historical styles is made in such novels as Salman Rushdie's *Midnight's Children* (1981) and *Shame* (1983) and in numerous novels by Norman Mailer. This is, of course, not to suggest that certain stylistic or lexical features are not appreciably more 'literary' than others; but such words as 'twain', 'eftsoons', 'azure', 'steed', 'verdure', together with archaic, syntactic forms belong to a past literary domain. They are associated with what was considered to be appropriately elevated and decorous in poetic language and were automatically used as such, losing in the process any contact with a living, current idiom and becoming fossilised and restrictedly 'literary'. Genre-mixing recognises that the full, unrestricted resources of the language are open to exploitation for literary ends. Text C (the opening to Anthony Burgess' novel *Time for a Tiger*), for example, exploits the language more normally connected with travel brochure and geography book genres but redeploys it for subtle literary purposes. Here the guidebook style is regularly subverted, an ironic undercutting serving to suggest that the conventional geographical or historical presentation of the state is comically inappropriate to a world which is much more heterogeneous and resistant to external ordering or classification.

3   Interaction of levels: semantic density

This is one of the most important of defining criteria. The notion here is that a text that is perceived as resulting from the additive interaction of several linguistic levels is recognised as more literary than a text where there are fewer levels at work or where they are present but do not interact as densely. There are different linguistic levels at work in Texts A and B but in C, I would argue, we have a degree of semantic density which is different from that in the other texts and which results from an interactive patterning at the levels of syntax, lexis, phonology and text. The most prominent of these patterns is **contrast**. Contrasts exist between a simple syntax in 'The river Lanchap gives the state its name', 'This is Kuala Hantu' (both of which act as a kind of frame for the first two paragraphs, and a more complexly patterned structure involving greater clausal complexity. There are contrasts, too, on the level of lexis between words of Greek and Anglo-Saxon derivation ('accidia', 'unimaginable', 'pantheon', 'dominated', 'progressive' as opposed to 'clutch', 'hurled', 'sheds', 'smug', 'fat') which is simultaneously a contrast between mono- and polysyllabic, formal and informal lexical items. The contrast is carried further into semantic oppositions marked in the items 'inept'/'apt', 'lowering sky'/'high humidity', 'blessed'/ 'cursed', 'soothe away'/'blare' and the opposition of East and West in 'smug American cars'/ 'Los Angeles architect', 'call of the East' and 'pentatonic tunes'.

Grammar, lexis and semantics are complemented by effects at the level of phonology. Here the plosive 'b' and 'p' are predominant patterns (overlapping notably with the more formal and 'ancient' lexical items, for example bulbous, pentatonic, pullulating, pantheon, paddy-fields, pantuns, prophets); but they exist in contrast with an almost equally predominant pattern of 's' sounds (second, source, snakes, sleep, tigers, etc.). This interaction of levels, particularly in the form of contrast, serves to symbolise or represent the unstated content of the passage. For example, one of the possible functions of these linguistic contrasts is to underscore the contrast between Victor Crabbe, an idealistic colonial teacher, and an alien ex-colonial territory; but between these contrasting worlds there also subsists a less clearly marked, more heterogeneous reality to which Crabbe is directly exposed.

Text C is, however, not the only passage in which an interactive patterning of different linguistic levels is foregrounded. Text A contains many such features from the phonetic symbols of 'Fish, sail, swim or simply relax on the sandy, sun-kissed beaches of Port Dickson', or the metaphoric and phonetic constellation of: 'A pulsating potpourri of Malays, Chinese and Indians', or the almost self-referential syntactic deviation of 'IT'S ALL HERE IN MALAYSIA' or the strategic semantic reiterations of 'relive the historical past', 'relive the glorious past' and the contrasts between past and present figured in the juxtaposition of present and past, Malacca and Kuala Lumpur, the past tense and the eternal present of clauses without verbs ('The people, the food, the sights, the sounds').

Across this spectrum of texts about Malaysia it is clear that where different levels of language multiply interact, there is a potential reinforcement of meaning. More than one possible meaning is thereby represented or symbolised although any activation of meanings must be dependent on a reader whose literary competence permits 'reasonable' correlations of linguistic forms and semantic functions. In this respect Text C can be demonstrated to have greater semantic density than Text B, for example. The interesting case is Text A which, as we have seen, contains an interaction of levels. The existence of these texts illustrates one aspect of a cline of relative 'literariness' and enables us to begin to talk about one text being more or less literary than another.

4   Polysemy

Polysemy: more than one meaning.

Monosemic: only one meaning.

The main point here is one which has been widely discussed: the existence in literary texts of **polysemy**. In terms of this criterion of literariness Text B, by being restrictively and necessarily **monosemic**, sacrifices any immediate claims to be literary. The monosemy of the text is closely connected with the need to convey clear, retrievable and unambiguous information. This end is served by a number of means: the formulaic code of the headings, for example 'Malaysia, Federation of': the many abbreviations employed; the geographical and numerical explicitness and the extreme economy of presentation (giving as much information in as little space as possible). There is no indication that the text should be read in more than one way although the compositional skills which go into entries such as this in encyclopaedias and geography textbooks should not be dismissed. Polysemy is a regular feature of advertisements although there are no particular examples of this in Text A, which is perhaps best referred to as *plurisignifying* rather than polysemic in that it shares the capacity of many advertisements to be memorable and to provide a verbal pleasure which can result in frequent citation. Text C is, however, polysemic (in that individual lexical items in Text C have more than one meaning: 'call' in 'call of the East' (actual 'sound' and 'longing for'); 'smooth' in 'smooth American cars' ('surface metal' and, by extension, 'the personality of their owners') and 'dark' in 'dark world' ('lack of light and mysterious', 'uncivilised', etc.). And so on.

5   Displaced interaction

The notion of displaced interaction serves to help differentiate the suggestions for activity in Text A, in which readers, if they go on holiday, may well perform, 'fish, sail, swim, etc.', from Text C where the reader is asked to perform no particular action except that of a kind of mental accompaniment to the text in the course of which he or she interprets or negotiates what the message means. The meaning may change on rereading of course; but this is unlikely to be the case with Text B, although in the case of Text A there is some scope for taking it in more than one way and this is a function of its potential literariness. A displaced interaction in a text allows meanings to emerge indirectly and obliquely. What we conventionally regard as 'literary' is likely to be a text in which the context-bound interaction between author and reader is displaced.

6   Text patterning

Criteria for literariness discussed so far have focused mostly on effects at
sentence level. At the level of text, effects can be located which can help us
further to differentiate degrees of literariness. Space prohibits detailed analysis
at this level so the point will have to be underlined with reference to
one example.

In Text C patterning at the level of text occurs by virtue of repetition of
the particulars of place, which are concentrated in the long second
paragraph. Reference to the river and town is made as follows:

> The river Lanchap gives the state its name.
> As the Sungai Lanchap winds on ...
> As the Lanchap approaches the coast ...
> Where the Lanchap meets the Sungai, Hantu is the royal town ...
> This is Kuala Hantu

The main effect of cross-sentential repetition here, reinforced by repeated
syntactic patterns of clause and tense, is to enact the lingering presence and
progress of the river and to provide for the appearance of the town as if the
reader were actually engaged in a journey through the jungle towards the
town. The short focusing sentence 'This is Kuala Hantu' is thus textually
interconnected with a number of related patterns out of which it grows
organically and, in terms of the content of the passage, *actually* grows.
Although there is a related patterning around the word 'Malaysia' in the other
texts (especially A) the text does not reinforce content to the same extent.

7   Some conclusions

1   Literary language is not special or different, in that any formal feature
    termed 'literary' can be found in many different types of text.

2   Literary language is different from other language uses in that it functions
    differently. Some of the differences can be demarcated with reference to
    criteria such as: medium dependence; genre-mixing; semantic density
    produced by interaction of linguistic levels; displaced interaction;
    polysemy; text patterning. What is prototypically literary will be a text
    which meets most of the above criteria; a non-literary text will meet none
    or few of these criteria; that is, it will be monosemic, medium-dependent,
    project a direct interaction, contain no genre-mixings and so on.

3   The misleading absolute division into literary/non-literary or fictional/
    non-fictional can be avoided by positing a **cline of literariness** along
    which texts can be arranged.

Reference

CARTER, R. and NASH, W. (1983) 'Language and Literariness', *Prose Studies*, **6**(2), pp. 123–41.

Source: adapted from 'Is there a literary language?' in CARTER, R. (1997) *Investigating English Discourse: Language, Literacy and Literature*, London, Routledge.

READING C: Extracts from 'Evaluative stylistics'

Richard Bradford

The first of the following extracts is from Barbara Cartland's novel *The Naked Battle* (1978), which I borrow from Walter Nash's *Language in Popular Fiction* (1990), whose extensive survey of 'women's' popular fiction you should compare with my own reading. The second is Fleur Adcock's poem 'Against coupling' (1971).

> And as he kissed her, as his lips pressed themselves against her mouth, her eyes, her cheeks and the softness of her neck, Lucilla felt a fire rise within her ignited, she knew, by the fire in him.
>
> 'I love ... you ... ' she tried to say but her voice was deep and passionate and seemed almost to be strangled in her throat.
>
> 'You are mine!' Don Carlos cried. 'Mine completely and absolutely.'
>
> He kissed her again until she felt the world disappear and once again they were on a secret island of their own surrounded by a boundless sea.
>
> It was what she had felt when she was with him in the little Pavilion; but now it was more real, more wonderful, more intense.
>
> Ever since she had known him she had changed and become alive to new possibilities within herself.
>
> Now she knew she could never go back to what she was before, because she had been reborn! Reborn to a new life and above all to love.
>
> It was a love that was perfect, and Divine, a love that was not only of the body but of the soul and the spirit.
>
> 'I love you! Oh, Carlos ... I love you with ... all of me!' she whispered.
>
> He took the last words from her lips saying fiercely:
>
> 'You are mine, my beautiful, adorable wife, now and for all eternity!'

AGAINST COUPLING

I write in praise of the solitary act:
of not feeling a trespassing tongue
forced into one's mouth, one's breath
smothered, nipples crushed against the
ribcage, and that metallic tingling
in the chin set off by a certain odd nerve:

unpleasure. Just to avoid those eyes would help –
such eyes as a young girl draws life from,
listening to the vegetal
rustle within her, as his gaze
stirs polypal fronds in the obscure
sea-bed of her body, and her own eyes blur

There is much to be said for abandoning
this no longer novel exercise –
for not 'participating in
a total experience' – when
one feels like the lady in Leeds who
had seen *The Sound of Music* eighty-six times;

or more, perhaps, like the school drama mistress
producing *A Midsummer Night's Dream*
for the seventh year running, with
yet another cast from 5B.
Pyramus and Thisbe are dead, but
the hole in the wall can still be troublesome.

I advise you, then, to embrace it without
encumbrance. No need to set the scene,
dress up (or undress), make speeches
Five minutes of solitude are
enough – in the bath, or to fill
that gap between the Sunday papers and lunch.

I would argue that Adcock's poem has far more claim to the status of 'good literature' than Cartland's extract, and in order to justify this argument I shall establish my working criteria.

It is possible, with a novel or a poem, to identify two textual allegiances. One is principally stylistic, in that it involves features that the text in question shares with other texts in the same genre or sub-genre: the most obvious cases of this are the narrative structure of a novel and the division of a poem into lines. The other involves formal and referential elements that are not exclusive to literature, ranging from reported speech in novels and informal syntax in free verse to topics that are just as likely to feature in conversation, philosophic treatises or on television as in literary texts. This twin allegiance between literary form on the one hand and non-literary form/content on the other I refer to as the **double pattern**.

The quality of a literary text should be judged in relation to the balance between the two dimensions of the double pattern. This scale of stylistic criteria cannot provide an objective measure of quality: our interests, tastes, types of enjoyment and values are subjective formations and will inevitably play a part in how we distinguish between good and bad writing. What the scale can provide is a comparative index, a means of identifying the particular features of literary texts which motivate our personal judgements. For example, one might pose the question, to someone with a basic knowledge of the texts: which of Joyce three novels, *A Portrait*, *Ulysses* or *Finnegans Wake*, is his most significant contribution to literature; in short, which is the best? All manner of perspectives and criteria will influence our respondent. It could be claimed that *Finnegans Wake* is better because it is demonstrably the most experimental. Perhaps this qualifies it as the most challenging literary response to the incalculably dense, multilayered nature of twentieth-century life. It could conversely be argued that *A Portrait* and to a lesser degree *Ulysses* are better books because they maintain a level of accessibility, a narrative thread that is likely to appeal to an audience who do not have the time or inclination to ponder the relevance of formal experiments in the books they read. The criteria underpinning these two judgements are different, but both putative respondents would agree that they base them upon immutable stylistic facts: that in *Finnegans Wake* the process of mediation overwhelms and effectively obscures a clear perception of its topics, while in *Ulysses* and *A Portrait* there is a relative balance between form and topic. I shall base my evaluation of Cartland and Adcock upon this perception of the double pattern. You might well disagree with my findings but you will also see that your own judgement will rely on the same tangible stylistic phenomena.

A second, more technical, consideration in literary evaluation relates to the stylistic competence of the writer. Irrespective of whether your personal affiliations lend value to this or that dimension of the double pattern, is it possible to establish how well or how badly a writer brings the two dimensions together? Is there an objective criterion for the judgement of stylistic skill? I shall address this question to a poem by William McGonagall. But first, to Cartland and Adcock.

Cartland's passage consists in part of the following types of content: the specific [...] references to bodily contact and its immediate effect ('his lips pressed', 'Lucilla felt a fire', 'He kissed her again'); and linguistic terms which shift the perspective away from the immediate events to some other part of the narrative ('It was what she had felt when she was with him in the little Pavilion') or to a less specific spatio-temporal condition ('Reborn to a new life', 'now and for all eternity!', 'Mine completely and absolutely'). As the passage proceeds, the second type of content gradually replaces the first.

The details of lips, mouth, eyes, cheek and neck and the hesitant response of the woman ('I love … you'), in the opening two paragraphs are specific enough, but as we read on physicality is first supplemented by simile and metaphor ('seemed almost to be strangled', 'until she felt the world disappear') and eventually replaced entirely by connotative notions of possession, spiritual unity, and submission to an overarching but unspecified condition of 'love'. The passage shifts towards a pattern of behavioural codes and expectations that exist independently of the novel and are inscribed within the norms of gender relations that we might refer to as utopian or conformist. […] Its meaning and its signifying function are efficiently orchestrated to disclose a particular pattern of expectations.

By contrast, in Adcock's poem, there is a constant level of interference between device and meaning; between the literary features of the text and those which might be said to anchor it to a topic. In any attempt to make sense of this text we must return again and again to the question of what exactly is 'the solitary act', praised by the speaker? Adcock, in various ways, urges us to answer, 'masturbation'. She does so by saturating the poem with images and verbal constructions that connote the sexual act. […] Sexual activity, and its effects and resonances, are divided in a similar way to those of Cartland's extract. We begin with the specifics ('tongue', 'mouth', 'breath', 'nipples'), move towards their less physical, more figurative, correlatives ('his gaze/stirs polypal fronds;' ' "participating in a total experience" '), and on to a mildly ironic dismissal of these activities as emotive events (*The Sound of Music* and *A Midsummer Night's Dream*) transformed into hollow, ritualistic habits.

How these elements seemingly relate to a topic is supplemented by a subtle interplay of line structure and syntax that seems to generate a mood of control and submission. The major verb phrases either occur at the end of the line and cause us to push forward to a point of syntactic completion or achieve a similar effect by being cunningly (perhaps coyly) delayed until the beginning of the line ('tongue/forced', 'without/encumbrance', for example). But when we attempt to reassemble these stylistic features as a solution to … the text's meaning, our activity is disrupted. The text is dominated by verbal and adverbial negatives. Every elaborate reference to sexuality is qualified by a negative ('of not' 'abandoning' 'not "participating" '), until the final stanza when the reader is advised to 'embrace it'. The 'it', the 'solitary act', is it seems a total negation of all of the activities previously described. 'It' could well be masturbation; 'it' might just as plausibly be savouring one's own company, undisturbed by the incursions of other people, sexual or non-sexual. 'It' might even refer to the process of having bipartite sex without being too involved or concerned with the efforts of the man or with the cultural-emotional associations of the act.

Adcock's text resists closure. At a localized level we can explain and specify the stylistic devices used, but their combination within the text as a whole cannot be readily made sense of it as a single purposive meaning.

Cartland encourages closure. Her stylistic strategies are a means to an end. Cartland's text displays a kind of fantastic realism, in the sense that it promotes and discloses a form of reality that is preferable to the alternatives which might be experienced by its readers.

[...] Cartland is as narratorially adept as Jane Austen or Charles Dickens in the organization of the reader's perceptions: [...] she is particularly good at balancing the immediate features of the events described (which in real time occupy probably no more than two minutes) against a more universalized fabric of ideals, fantasies, norms and ambitions. But Cartland's narrator employs these skills as a means of satisfying the assumed fantasies of a certain kind of reader. The stylistics of fiction are being used in a way that is comparable to the stylistics of advertising. Language organizes the perception of the reader but it does so according to an assumed notion of how the reader wants them to be organized. In contrast, in Adcock's poem the complex and often conflicting aspects of the sexual act (submissive, violent, pointless, pleasurable, unpleasurable, cultural, ritualistic) are assimilated, to the equally conflicting levels of verbal style within the text itself.

In purely technical terms Adcock is not a better stylist than Cartland, but, according to these criteria of value, she is a better writer. If, as in the writing of Cartland, literary style is employed exclusively to promote a particular fantasy or belief then literature itself becomes a sub-genre to all other functional and utilitarian modes of writing. Adcock, conversely, employs literary style in order to challenge the unitary, transparent relationship between language and its referent. There are, however, literary writers whose basic command of literary style raises the question of whether there are purely technical criteria which can enable us to distinguish between good and bad style.

In a 1976 article on 'Roman Jakobson's verbal analysis of poetry', Paul Werth presents Jakobson's methods, as the embodiment of the flaws and failed objectives of textualist stylistics. He chooses as one example a poem by William McGonagall:

> All hail to the Rev. George Gilfillan of Dundee,
> He is the greatest preacher I did ever hear or see.
> He is a man of genius bright,
> And in him his congregation does delight,
> Because they find him to be honest and plain,
> Affable in temper, and seldom known to complain
> He preaches in a plain straightforward way,
> The people flock to hear him night and day
> And hundreds from the doors are often turn'd away,
> Because he is the greatest preacher of the present day.
> He has written the life of Sir Walter Scott,
> And while he lives he will never be forgot,
> Nor when he is dead,
> Because by his admirers it will be often read.

And fill their minds with wonder and delight,
And wile away the tedious hours on a cold winter's night.

Werth claims, correctly, that the application to McGonagall's poem of
Jakobson's exhaustive stylistic methodology would disclose levels of textual
complexity comparable with those that Jakobson and Jones found in a
Shakespeare sonnet. Werth's point is that Jakobson's method obscures
'a direct conflict between linguistic evidence and critical instinct', since while
it discloses technical similarities between Shakespeare's and McGonagall's
work it does not enable us to prove that 'the value of McGonagall's poem is
surely abysmally low' (1976, p. 43). This is true in the sense that Jakobson
does not supplement his analyses with evaluative comments. Such an
omission on Jakobson's part does not however disprove the thesis that we
need to be able to analyse the stylistic features of a text objectively in order
to substantiate our more subjective judgement of its quality.

McGonagall uses irregular rhythm, but so did Coleridge in 'Christabel' and
so did Blake and Whitman in their most celebrated work. His rhyme scheme
is unremitting but so is that of a vast number of regular poems. McGonagall's
failure as a poet is due to his apparent unwillingness or inability to decide
whether he is writing poetry or prose. The rhymes interfere with the progress
of the syntax, but not in a way which creates a purposive tension between
literary and non-literary features of the poem. The rhymes are found and
dumped at line endings as a duty to poetic convention, and syntax is altered
only as a concession to this convention. If we substitute non-rhyming
synonyms for the rhyme words we find a directionless, almost ungrammatical
prose style:

> He preaches in a plain straightforward style, the people flock to hear him
> day and night, and hundreds from the doors are often turn'd away,
> because he is the greatest preacher of the present time.

The formal and the referential dimensions of McGonagall's verse proceed
rather like two drunks walking home from the pub. Neither can entirely
support the other, but they are locked together in an uncertain, undignified
shuffle.

McGonagall, in his chaotic, mildly endearing way, poses a serious
question for evaluative stylistics. We may judge him to be a bad poet because
his failure to control and command the formal, literary dimension of language
compromises his ability to absorb its referential dimension and to offer the
reader an unexpected and possibly enlightening perspective on the relation
between language and perceived reality. If he had written a prose essay
about the activities and characteristics of the Reverend Gilfillan and told us
roughly the same as he does in his poem, stylistic evaluation would be
suspended. But because he uses a form in which the structural dimensions of
the text constantly interfere with its communicative purpose, we begin to ask
questions about how, and how well, he deals with this provocative merger of
style and function. In effect making sense of the poem becomes an evaluative

rather than a purely practical procedure. McGonagall, by writing a poem, provokes our wish to understand it, only to leave us disappointed. His literary style is an encumbrance, an irritation, rather than a medium which transforms or even constructs the message.

Let us now consider the role of stylistics in these evaluations of texts by Adcock, Cartland and McGonagall. Each reading has involved three levels of [...] encounter.

Level 1: [Double pattern analysis]

[...] Stylistics, with its debt both to linguistics and to literary criticism, enables me to distinguish between those elements of a text whose main allegiance is to the network of non-literary genres – e.g. syntax [...] in Adcock's and McGonagall's poems; reported speech and dialogue in Cartland's fiction – and those which are bound into a patently literary tradition – free verse and metre, respectively, in Adcock and McGonagall; narratorial control and emphasis in Cartland: the identification of the double pattern of non-literary and literary devices.

Level 2: [Making sense]

[...] Level 2 involves the identification of a tension between those elements which the text shares with non-literary genres and those that are patently literary. We make sense of each text by translating it into the terms and conditions of the former: it is effectively destylized. Making sense of Adcock's poem entails an attempt to monitor its use of literary devices to disrupt and refocus familiar contexts of domestic life and sexuality. With Cartland the stylistic devices of fiction writing are deployed to promote an idealized, fantastic model of male-female relationships. McGonagall is patently incapable of properly controlling the relation between poetic and non-poetic genres. As a consequence, what McGonagall means is of less significance than his stylistic incompetence.

Level 3: Judgement

The judgemental criteria proposed here are clear enough. Adcock is the best writer of the three. Her stylistic skill in the use of the double pattern is superior to McGonagall's. Cartland shares with Adcock a degree of technical accomplishment in the management of literary and non-literary genres. However, according to these criteria, the use of this craft to challenge and unsettle familiar perceptions of reality (Adcock) is regarded as superior to its use to project, maybe satisfy, an idealized, fantastic idea of how people should behave (Cartland).

It is not my intention to offer my criteria for good literature as official and conclusive: they are mine and they are probably symptomatic of my various sociocultural affiliations. More significant is my use of the three levels of [...] encounter; the first two incorporating the disciplines of stylistics, the third relating these to a specific system of aesthetic, perhaps ideological, values.

We need to be reasonably competent in the first two to confidently articulate our experience of the third, which involves everything from the specialized polemic of academic criticism, through book reviewing to personal taste and reading habits.

References

NASH, W. (1990) *Language in Popular Fiction*, London, Routledge.

WERTH, P. (1976) 'Roman Jakobson's Verbal Analysis of Poetry', *Journal of Linguistics*, **12**, pp. 21–73.

Source: BRADFORD, R. (1997) *Stylistics*, **London, Routledge.**

Plot and characterisation

Kieran O'Halloran

3.1 Introduction

Like poetry and drama, narrative fiction is a key literary genre, taking on many different forms: the epic, the novel, the novella, short story, the comic, etc. It can be subdivided further in terms of content: detective, fairy tale, romance, thriller and so on. Major components of narratives are **characterisation** (how characters are set up and developed) and **plot** (how the actions and events unfold). These are the elements of narrative central to this chapter.

I will be mainly using the form of a short story to get some understanding of how plot and characterisation are configured for literary effect; I shall also explore the relationship between plot, characterisation and literary value.

You will learn more stylistic techniques of analysis – these will show you how to articulate literary creative skill you perceive in how characters and plots are developed. In addition, you will see how quantitative methods of analysis can be used alongside qualitative methods to analyse a text.

In this chapter, we move away then from a focus on poetic language. But this is not to say that we cannot have a poetic take on narrative, and you will see some threading through of the work on poetic language that you encountered in Chapter 2.

3.2 Heroes and villains

For a focus on everyday conversational narrative, see Chapter 2 in the companion volume, **Maybin and Swann (2006)**.

One of the most influential scholars of narrative is Vladimir Propp, his academic reputation deriving from his claim to have found structural elements common to the Russian folk-tale. Propp's (1928) *Morphology of The Folk Tale* is a study of 115 Russian folk-tales. His focus was on the structure of events that take place in folk-tales and he claimed to have found 31 such event types which were underlying bases for them. With such an emphasis on the underlying structures of narrative, Propp's work thus has an inherency perspective. In the folk-tales, there are 'heroes' and 'villains'. Here are some of these event types Propp identified in the Russian folk-tale:

- The HERO is commanded not to do something.
- The HERO is tested, interrogated, attacked, etc., which prepares the way for his receiving either a magic thing or helper.
- The HERO acquires the use of a magic object or power.
- The HERO and the VILLAIN join in direct combat.

With such a strong focus on actions and events in Russian folk-tales, Propp paid much less attention to character. So while Propp isolated 31 event types, in contrast he singled out only seven basic character types which he also regarded as common to these tales:

1   HERO
2   VILLAIN
3   PRINCESS
4   DISPATCHER
5   DONOR
6   HELPER
7   FALSE HERO

HERO, VILLAIN and PRINCESS should be self-explanatory. The other Propp roles will need a little explanation. The DISPATCHER sends the HERO on his mission. The DONOR is someone in the story who provides the HERO with a magic object which helps in vanquishing the VILLAIN. The HELPER in contrast provides *human* assistance for this goal. The FALSE HERO is someone who might be seen as the authentic HERO when this is in fact not really the case.

Do Propp's seven character roles seem at all familiar? It is quite astonishing how many of these roles show up more generally in popular fantasy/adventure narratives across different genres such as novels and films, for example *James Bond*, *Lord of the Rings*, *Star Wars*. Let us take one of the best-regarded of James Bond stories, *Goldfinger*, to illustrate the point. I chose the film version (1964) since it is more widely known than the novel (1959). Below are the central characters of *Goldfinger* partnered with Propp's seven character roles:

HERO:	James Bond
VILLAIN:	Auric Goldfinger, Oddjob (Goldfinger's henchman)
PRINCESS:	Pussy Galore
DISPATCHER:	M
DONOR:	Q
HELPER:	Pussy Galore
FALSE HERO:	Pussy Galore

James Bond is the obvious HERO in the films. But a James Bond story always needs a VILLAIN – in this case Auric Goldfinger, whose plan is to radioactively contaminate the US gold reserves in Fort Knox, Kentucky. To accomplish this, Goldfinger receives help from the Communist ('Red') Chinese who supply the expertise to build an atomic device. In each James Bond mission, the British spy is dispatched by 'M', his boss in the British secret service. Bond also has a DONOR, 'Q', a British secret service boffin who supplies a particular gadget which enables Bond to ease himself out of scrapes technologically. As in one of Propp's event types above, it is a fairly 'magic' gadget in that it either probably does not exist in real life or, if it did, it would be hugely expensive. In *Goldfinger*, one magic object is an Aston Martin DB5 that fires off smoke screens, punctures the tyres of other vehicles on the chase, and boasts an ejector seat. James Bond also receives help in the form of 'Bond girls'. These, as is the case in *Goldfinger*, often work for the VILLAIN. The PRINCESS is the principal 'Bond girl', often one that Bond saves. In *Goldfinger*, the PRINCESS who Bond 'saves', by turning her against Goldfinger, is Pussy Galore. Persuaded by Bond, Pussy alerts the CIA and Pentagon to Goldfinger's plan which leads to it being foiled. She is then also a HELPER. But she is also something of a FALSE HERO. Despite her assistance in thwarting Goldfinger's plan, she still helicopters Goldfinger away from Fort Knox before he can be apprehended by the CIA and US soldiers. Fort Knox having been saved, Bond steps aboard a plane to take him to the White House where he is to be feted. But Goldfinger emerges once the plane is airborne, the plane being piloted by Pussy Galore ...

The novel and film, *Goldfinger*, has attracted the interest of literary scholars such as Roland Barthes (see Barthes, 1977). Umberto Eco (1979), another literary scholar, is concerned with Ian Fleming's James Bond novels more generally. For Eco, the novels are constructed of a series of oppositions (e.g. Bond versus M; Bond versus VILLAIN; 'Free World' versus 'Communism'). The narrative skill of the novels is in their capacity to immerse a reader in a game where he or she knows 'the pieces and the rules – and perhaps the outcome – and draws pleasure simply from following the minimal variations by which the victor [Bond] realises his objective' (Eco, 1979, p. 160). This is not to say that for Eco this narrative skill translates into literary value:

> ... the work of Fleming represents a successful means of leisure, the result of skilled craftsmanship. To the extent that it provides to anyone the thrill of poetic emotion, it is the last *avatar* of Kitsch; to the extent that it provokes elementary psychological reactions in which ironic detachment is absent, it is only a more subtle, but less mystifying, example of soap opera.
>
> (Eco, 1979, p. 172)

Let me return to Propp. Although his analysis was of the Russian folk-tale, the basic HERO/VILLAIN narrative can be taken as a cultural universal while not necessarily following exactly the 31 event types that Propp finds. In the Indian epic, *The Ramayana*, the HERO Rama defeats the ten-headed demon Ravan. In Japanese Kabuki theatre, 'supermen' heroes defeat 'men whose villainy is complete and unmitigated' (Bowers, 1974, p. 132). The Iroquois Native Americans describe the victory of Good Twin over Evil Twin at the beginning of the world (Rosenberg, 1994, pp. 509–17). And so on. Some theorists go even further than just arguing for the universality of the HERO/VILLAIN narrative across different cultures. They provide an evolutionary biological basis for this universality (e.g. Carroll, 1999); our attribution of an evil essence to a VILLAIN supposedly reflects the tendency to demonise people who are in competition with us.

Clearly, given this universality (cultural or biological or both), journalists often have a straightforward task in cuing a HERO/VILLAIN framework when readers are engaged with another narrative genre – the popular tabloid story. This can render the contents of the story more dramatic. The following comes from a popular British tabloid newspaper story (this part of the story appears on the second page of the newspaper). It is a narrative by a man called Sam Latifi who is recounting the events of the previous evening. Since this narrative is told from his perspective, it is known as a **first-person narrative**. The 'poor woman' referred to is the British actress, Liz Hurley:

> This poor woman came up to my window in distress and signalling for me to stop. She said she had been attacked by four girls and she was very frightened. She wasn't screaming or crying but she was talking very fast and was out of breath. She pointed to the girls who were walking away. I got hold of the biggest one and another came towards me shouting abuse and I grabbed her as well. I tried to hold them, then another one came at me shouting, 'I'll kill you if you don't let go.' She looked very threatening as though she might hit me, which made me let go of the two I had. One girl then threw a bottle at me which luckily missed because I ducked. The littlest one then took a knife out of her back pocket and passed it to another girl who lunged at me. It caught me slightly and there was some bleeding.

(*The Sun*, 25 November, 1994, p. 2)

ACTIVITY 1   'I saved Hurley from 4 burly girlies'

Allow about
20 minutes

Now look at the text which appeared on the front page of the tabloid newspaper (see how it was printed in Colour Figure 1). This is a journalist's report of what happened and so is a **third-person narrative**:

- In what ways has Sam's first-person narrative been transformed in line with the HERO/VILLAIN framework?

  1   I SAVED HURLEY FROM 4 BURLY GIRLIES.

  2   A HANDSOME hat seller last night revealed he was the have-a-go hero who saved lovely Liz Hurley from a gang of four girl muggers.

  3   Fitness fan Sam Latifi, 30, chased the teenage gang after they held a knife to the terrified actress's throat and stole £10.

  4   He was SLASHED on the hand and PELTED with bricks and bottles before cornering the girls with police.

  5   Grateful Liz – girlfriend of film heart-throb Hugh Grant – rewarded him with a big kiss.

6   As he got a 'well done' hug from his pretty girlfriend Lorraine Lever
     last night, brave Sam said: 'I'd have done the same for anyone.'

('I Saved Hurley from 4 Burly Girlies', *The Sun*, 25 November 1994, p. 1)

Comment

In the journalist's third-person narrative, we might assume that Sam's chasing
of the muggers immediately followed the holding of the knife to Liz Hurley's
throat and thus prevented the actress from being harmed. The headline and
first sentence, with the use of 'saved', would seem to reinforce this
assumption – Sam as HERO, burly girlies as VILLAINS, Liz Hurley as PRINCESS. But
from Sam's first-person narrative, he did not save the actress at all in this
sense. This is because the four muggers had already left the victim by the time
Sam entered the scene. So the front page strongly suggests the reader should
see Sam's actions as more heroic than was actually the case. Indeed, this is
reinforced by the third-person narrative presenting a headline from the first
person ('I saved Hurley ...'), as though Sam actually uttered these words. This
third-person *transformed* narrative takes up most of the front page; the more
dramatic the story, the more impact it has. For Fairclough (1995), this kind of
narrative transformation is consonant with the marketability of the story.

We have seen that narrative universals (HERO, VILLAIN, etc.) are apparent in
the folk-tale and also show up in other popular narrative forms. But what
of texts which are seen as *centrally* literary – texts that form part of a
contemporary canon of English literature because they are deemed to have
literary value? Could Propp's scheme be applied to these texts as well in
order to illuminate plot or character? There is not space in this chapter to test
this question out on a large number of literary narratives or even on one
novel. So I chose one short story – James Joyce's 'Eveline', which centres on
the life of a young woman of the same name. 'Eveline' comes from Joyce's
short story collection of 1914, *Dubliners*. It has been the subject of many
analyses (e.g. Attridge, 2004b; Chatman, 1969; Culler, 1975a; Hart, 1969;
Toolan, 2001; Stubbs, 2001). Since Joyce is a key twentieth-century author,
and 'Eveline' is indeed a valued piece of literature for critics, it is safe to
regard this story as canonical. Leonard (2004, p. 94), for example, refers to
'Eveline' as 'so apparently simple, and yet so wondrously complex'.

You will recall that
the 'canon', and
associated
problems with how
it is defined, are
discussed in
Chapter 1.

ACTIVITY 2   'Eveline' (Reading A)

While reading 'Eveline', see if you can isolate within it the Propp character
roles that you were introduced to. Is this an easy thing to do? Whether it is or
not, think about why this might be the case. Try seeing if any of the four
Proppian event types you met above can also be applied.

Comment

As Chatman (1969, p. 3) says, this narrative is a *psychological* one. Because of its psychological nature, it is less obviously plot driven than an action-based narrative like *Goldfinger.* This makes it difficult to find blatant instantiations of HERO, VILLAIN, etc. Initially, we might think Eveline's father is something of a VILLAIN in that he makes violent threats to Eveline. But his status as VILLAIN in 'Eveline' is rather unstable. This is because Eveline seems to change her mind about her father. So, for example, in lines 105–110, she finds that he is not so bad after all. Perhaps, though, we can ascribe one particular Propp character role with more confidence – the role of HERO to Frank. Indeed, 'Frank would save her' (line 129) rather chimes with the 'heroic' tabloid article headline you saw earlier. With Frank as HERO, Eveline would nicely slot into the Propp character role of PRINCESS. But how heroic is Frank actually in terms of action? He doesn't 'save' Eveline in the action narrative sense – his role seems to be more a HELPER ('after all he had done for her', line 144).

Going beyond an inherency perspective to a sociohistorical one, Frank's status as HERO or HELPER is in doubt. Hugh Kenner (see Hodgart, 1978, p. 46) puts forward an interpretation of Frank based on knowledge of the time *Dubliners* was written. Atlantic liners, apparently, did not sail then from Dublin but instead from British ports such as Liverpool. The ship Frank and Eveline would have boarded together would not have been heading straight to Buenos Aires. Kenner deduces that Frank merely wants Eveline to go with him to a British port where he will most likely seduce her. Indeed, it does seem a very long way for Frank to go for a 'holiday' in the early twentieth century. And why would he be 'lodging' (which implies rented accommodation for a longish period) if he is on 'holiday'? So then is Frank a FALSE HERO or a VILLAIN? And if Frank is not all he seems, perhaps Eveline's father is the HERO for warning her about Frank. Or maybe Eveline is the HERO, rather than 'Frank's PRINCESS' because she comes to her senses. She is initially portrayed as a callow, unworldly woman: 'when he [Frank] sang about the lass that loves a sailor, she always felt pleasantly confused' (lines 86–7). Later the story suggests she is not actually so naïve about Frank: 'he [Frank] would give her life, *perhaps love, too*', (my emphasis) (lines 129–30). So she is not going blindly into an elopement with Frank. Eveline's HERO status might be seen to fit with one of Propp's event types that I mentioned earlier (*the HERO is commanded not to do something*) since her father forbids her to say anything to Frank (lines 95–7). But if Eveline really is HERO and her father the VILLAIN, there is no Proppian show-down between them (*the HERO and the VILLAIN join in direct combat*).

It would seem that 'Eveline' is too mercurial for application of the HERO/ VILLAIN framework. Toolan notes:

> [...] while Propp's fairytales proceed through developmental actions, 'Eveline' is very largely a mental projection, both forward to possible future events and backward to actual past ones [...] as we read this story we are not entirely sure whether we should – as normally – be looking for incidents, or instead, attend to character.
>
> (Toolan, 2001, pp. 20, 31)

It could be argued that a hallmark of literariness that is valued is a significant level of interconnectedness of plot and characterisation. Plot and characterisation would seem to have a higher level of interdependency in 'Eveline' than in a narrative such as *Goldfinger* which follows a plot formula in which the characters fill ready-made slots. Henry James (another writer whom many literary scholars would consider a part of a canon of English literature) offers the following dictum: 'What is character but the determination of incident? What is incident but the illustration of character?' (James, 1948, p. 13). Toolan (2001, p. 30) accords with this when he says 'in the case of literary narrative fiction perhaps more than elsewhere, the force of James' famous observation seems especially telling'. Moreover, Bennett and Royle (2004, p. 60), also quoting James' dictum, say the following: 'Indeed, the novels and plays we respond to most strongly almost invariably have forceful characters as well as an intriguing plot. Our memory of a particular novel or play often depends as much on our sense of a particular character as on the ingenuities of the plot.'

To understand how 'Eveline' 'works' as a successful literary narrative, it would be a useful exercise to try to tease apart aspects of it which are more salient to plot than characterisation. Using Propp's scheme, however, to provide this illumination is not going to get us very far. Propp's event types are based on a *separation* between seven distinct character types and 31 event types. And so naturally, they become less useful when a story makes close connections between plot and characterisation. Given that Propp's general categories are too blunt for the job, we need more precise instruments of analysis. Using stylistic analysis to try to locate aspects of a literary story which are salient to plot is the focus of the next section.

3.3 Focus on plot

In Reading B, Michael Toolan uses a close stylistic analysis of the first 24 sentences of 'Eveline' to try to decide which sentences are more likely to be key to plot. For Toolan, plot is primarily about change over time. He employs in part a concept from traditional grammar – **finiteness**. Verbs in **finite** form, such as 'she *stands*' or 'he *ran*', carry, in part, information about time (present or past tense). Verbs in **non-finite** form such as 'She saw Frank *standing* on the quayside' do not carry information about time. (The concept is explained in more detail in Reading B.) For Toolan, the use of finite verb forms in the past (particularly when these are verbs of action) may indicate moments of a narrative which are crucial to plot. This is because finite verb forms when used in the past can indicate change over time. However, change over time can be indicated in other ways, as you will see in Reading B.

ACTIVITY 3   In search of plot structure (Reading B)

Please now turn to Reading B and consider the following questions:

- Do you agree with Toolan that out of the first 24 sentences in 'Eveline' it is really only sentences 16 and 24 that have high plot-status?

- Are sentences 16 and 24 only plot devices and so reveal no information about character?

Comment

Like Toolan I would argue that the plot status of sentences 16 and 24 ('Now she was going to go away like the others, to leave her home' and 'She had consented to go away, to leave her home') has much to do with the near repetition. Information in sentence 24 is then foregrounded with this parallelism. This not only makes the proposition of Eveline's departure salient, but through this foregrounding, allows us to recognise readily some development in plot – presumably she was going away with someone else who has initiated the idea. But who or even what did she consent to? The plot develops because suspense is generated – as readers we may well be asking these 'who' or 'what' questions.

You explored parallelism in Chapters 1 and 2.

Having said this, and despite what Toolan says about finite verbs, right at the start of the story you might have felt that the non-finite 'watching the evening invade the avenue' is important to the plot in creating a sense of Eveline being alone and gazing out into the street, waiting for some kind of sign to tell her what to do. Moreover, the references to events long ago might be seen as crucial to building up the sense of suspended animation which could also be seen as central to the plot of 'Eveline'. Indeed, both of these facets of the story in the opening 24 sentences provide information on Eveline's character as well.

Sentences 16 and 24 do not initially seem to provide so much information on Eveline's character. But with these sentences, we are near the start of the story; if plot and characterisation are really interconnected in 'Eveline' we might expect meaning potential in these sentences in relation to character to be released retrospectively. (Correspondingly, Toolan does concede that plot assessment may need rethinking after the whole story has been read.) Having read all of 'Eveline', it should be apparent that foregrounding via parallelism in sentences 16 and 24 potentially seeds information about characterisation that becomes evident later in the story. Eveline seems not to know her own mind when she aborts her own escape; she seems not to have a strong enough desire to leave Dublin. So retrospectively, since Eveline 'consented' to Frank to leave Dublin, we can see that it was not first and foremost a strong desire of *hers*.

Sources of evidence do not just have to be inherency-based ones; indeed, a stylistic approach to a story will not reveal everything about plot, nor characterisation for that matter. We can also take, for example, a more sociocultural or sociohistorical perspective. When 'Eveline' was written, Ireland was part of the United Kingdom, and governed from London. Those who thrived economically in Ireland were more likely to be Protestants, mainly people with allegiance to the London government. The greatest concentration of Protestants is in the north of Ireland where Belfast is situated. Dwellers in Dublin (in Ireland's south) who had no wealth were likely to be Catholic. So the property developer from Belfast who bought the field (lines 8–10) is likely to be a Protestant and so somewhat 'alien' to Eveline. This 'alien' figure effectively prevents children playing in the field, the same field that Eveline used to play in. In the same second paragraph, her father also prevents her and the other children from playing in the field. Thus, the 'alien' man from Belfast and her father produce parallel effects. Her father is implicitly 'alien' by association, via this 'sociocultural parallelism', which seeds for Eveline wanting to escape.

The parallelism between sentences 16 and 24 is an example of poetic literariness (see Chapter 2). But it is not the only example of poetic literariness in 'Eveline' achieved via the device of repetition with differences. Consider the following:

> Lines 1–3: She sat at the window watching the evening invade the avenue. Her head was leaned against the window curtains and in her nostrils was the odour of dusty cretonne.

'Cretonne' is a type of fabric used for furnishing.

> Lines 111–13: Her time was running out but she continued to sit by the window, leaning her head against the window curtain, inhaling the odour of dusty cretonne.

This is an interesting repetition since it 'poetically' marks off Eveline's weighing-up of her situation, this cogitation constituting most of the story. Shortly after lines 111–13, Eveline seemingly decides to take action and escape with Frank.

The purpose of the next activity is to see whether Joyce might be using this second key moment of poetic literariness to communicate information around plot only.

Plot and further parallelism in 'Eveline'

In line with the inherency perspective of Chapter 2, literary significance could be sought in the patterns of repetition of lines 1–3 in lines 111–13.

- What, for you, is being signalled about development in plot by this poetic device of repetition with differences? Is anything being communicated about character by this poetic device? Focus on grammar, including finite/non-finite verb forms where appropriate and lexis (vocabulary).

Toolan suggests that ultimately one should use a holistic perspective in assessing the plot status of sentences in a literary work. In your judgements of both plot and characterisation, relate your analysis of lines 111–13 to preceding text.

Comment

Here is my analysis of lexis and grammar, followed by my interpretation. How do your analysis and interpretation differ from mine?

Firstly, a focus on lexis. In lines 111–13, Eveline is inhaling the odour of dusty cretonne where previously it was only 'in her nostrils'. With 'time running out', information which tells us the plot is moving along, the inhalation of cretonne suggests to me deeper breathing induced by growing anxiety. I make a connection with previous text where Eveline suffers *palpitations* induced by her father's violence or at least violent threats (line 50); she is weary from squabbling with her father (line 58), and presumably as well from his gross unfairness (lines 60–5), her hard life (line 72), her father forbidding her to say anything to Frank (lines 96–7); moreover, as revealed via the 'sociocultural parallelism' (lines 8–10), her father is implicitly 'alien' to Eveline. For me, Joyce is delicately suggesting in lines 111–13 that Eveline is actually dwelling on her father, a cause of her anxiety. (I produce more evidence later for this indirect meaning in 'Eveline'.) So, I would argue that as the plot develops ('time running out'), so too does characterisation.

What about a grammatical focus? Toolan argues that in the repetition with differences of sentences 16 and 24, it is verbs of action in finite form which are propelling the plot. However, what is really interesting in the sentence of lines 111–13 is that we have a change from finite verb forms to *non-finite* verb forms. The finite past tense forms *sat* and *leaned* in lines 1–2 are no longer finite in lines 111–12 (*to sit, leaning*). For Toolan, plot development is more likely to be realised through finite verb forms. So if this is the case, paradoxically Joyce is 'slow-motioning' the plot with the change to non-finite forms, whilst accelerating it with 'time running out'. This skilfully suggests to me not only something about character (Eveline is becoming more static) but also plot in the *future* – Joyce is hinting that Eveline will not actually leave her home.

Taking the lexical and grammatical information together, I am beginning to formulate an interpretation that Eveline's inability to leave derives from how her father has treated her. Of course, this is only my inchoate interpretation and yours is no doubt different. While the above grammatical *analysis* can be replicated by others because the above grammatical concepts are stable ones, an objective and replicable *interpretation* cannot be read off from grammar. We are all different and so what we bring to a literary narrative in terms of our life experience and sympathies will vary. Interpretations are then likely to vary too. Moreover, what we choose to focus on stylistically in even a short story will vary as well. But the more sources of evidence we can draw upon, the more likely our interpretation is likely to carry conviction.

We have seen that, through a good level of interdependency of plot and characterisation, indirect meanings can be cued. Just as you saw in Chapter 2, literariness is not just about linguistic properties but also about the crafting of language to give rise to indirect meanings. Cueing such indirectness is consonant with the adage given to aspiring fiction writers – *show don't tell* (Burroway, 2002). Showing in detail a character doing (or not doing) something, such as we have with lines 1–3 and lines 111–13 of 'Eveline', rather than telling the reader explicitly what is going on in a character's mind, constitutes an element of literariness in narrative fiction. This is because this 'showing' facilitates more reader involvement in attempting to trace reasons why a character acts in the way they do. A more engaged process of reading is afforded, which in turn *can* lead to the reader having a richer experience of fictional characterisation. I stress *can* since there is no necessary link between literary value and literariness in narrative fiction which cues such indirect meanings. However, that Joyce is able to allow me to register a subconscious which is jarring with a conscious mind in the above fragments and, as I will argue, does the same elsewhere in the story, marks 'Eveline' out for me as possessing a prized literariness.

It would be useful to complement the previous section's focus on plot with one on character. That is, with a focus this time on teasing apart characterisation from plot in a literary work, we could 'from the opposite end' also potentially pinpoint and illuminate literary skill in the weaving of the two. Complementing Toolan's 'principles' for guiding a reader's real-time processing of text in search of plot, in the next section you will be looking at some 'principles' for guiding real-time processing of character.

3.4 Focus on character

Greimasian analysis

As I said in Section 3.2, in Propp (1928) character is very much subordinate to analysis of events, with 31 event types but only seven character roles. Work in the study of narrative which contrasts sharply with Propp's is that of the Lithuanian linguist, Algirdas Greimas. This is because in Greimas' (1983) analytical scheme in *Structural Semantics*, events are subordinate to character. Like Propp, Greimas is another investigator of the 'deep structures' of narrative, i.e. from an inherency perspective. Greimas' aim was to give a richer analytical framework to account for characterisation in a narrative by homing in on relationships of desire, power and communication between characters. What Greimas did was to take Propp's seven character roles (HERO, VILLAIN, PRINCESS, DISPATCHER, DONOR, HELPER, FALSE HERO) and reconfigure them into six roles:

1 SUBJECT	4 OBJECT
2 OPPONENT	5 HELPER
3 SENDER	6 RECEIVER

Greimas (1983) calls these six roles **actants** (or **actantial roles**). Crucially for Greimas, these actants are described in terms of the *relationships* between them, something that receives less emphasis in Propp's scheme. Because Greimas' focus was character, he wanted also to make his scheme less restrictive than Propp's character roles, such as Propp's use of 'HERO' or 'VILLAIN'. As a result, Greimas introduced more generic roles such as SUBJECT and OBJECT. Another reason for doing this was so his scheme could more richly account for character perspectives other than that of HERO. To show the advantages of Greimas' scheme more clearly, let us return to *Goldfinger* but (1) move away from Bond's perspective and look at things from Goldfinger's and (2) see how Greimas' scheme can accommodate relationships of desire, power and communication between Goldfinger and other main characters.

Relationship of desire

When the narrative focus is on Goldfinger's desire, when he is SUBJECT, his wish is the nuclear contamination of Fort Knox (OBJECT) (indicated in the diagram below by the direction of the arrow). OBJECT then in Greimas' scheme is not necessarily a person: it can be a thing which is desired. The more generic role of OBJECT, rather than a 'sought-after-person' such as PRINCESS in Propp's scheme, allows more flexibility in accounting for the narrative structure:

Greimas' actant, SUBJECT, is not to be confused with the grammatical subject of a clause as mentioned in Reading B. The same applies for the actant OBJECT and the grammatical object.

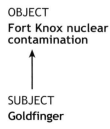

OBJECT
Fort Knox nuclear contamination

↑

SUBJECT
Goldfinger

Relationship of power

So that Goldfinger can achieve his desired OBJECT, he entrusts his dirty work to Oddjob, someone he has power over, his HELPER, who has the deadly weapon of a projectile steel-rimmed hat. The HELPER assists in trying to remove impediments to the OBJECT being realised. The chief impediment is Bond who in relation to Goldfinger's perspective is his OPPONENT:

HELPER ———————▶ SUBJECT ◀——————— OPPONENT
Oddjob   Goldfinger   Bond

Relationship of communication

So that Goldfinger can achieve his aims, he is in communication with the 'Red Chinese'. The 'Red Chinese' (SENDER) provide the necessary 'atomic device' for Goldfinger (RECEIVER) to contaminate Fort Knox. Goldfinger in turn is then in a position to realise his aim to make his own gold more valuable once the explosion is communicated to 'The West'. Economic chaos in 'The West' would ensue (also satisfying the desires of the 'Red Chinese'):

SENDER ———————▶ OBJECT ———————▶ RECEIVER
'Red Chinese'   Fort Knox nuclear   Goldfinger
                       contamination   'The West'

For Greimas, these three relationships of desire, power and communication can be combined into one scheme:

Relationship of communication

'Red Chinese'   Fort Knox nuclear   Goldfinger
                       contamination   'The West'

SENDER ———————▶ OBJECT ———————▶ RECEIVER

▲
| Relationship
| of desire

HELPER ———————▶ SUBJECT ◀——————— OPPONENT
Oddjob   Goldfinger   Bond

Relationship of power

As I said, an advantage of having more generic character roles is that we are better able to take account of the perspectives of different characters in a narrative; this can also be done at different moments in the narrative. So for example, the balance of power in the relationship between HELPER, SUBJECT and OPPONENT shifts at different points in the story. Early in the narrative Bond has the upper hand. Later, though, he is in Goldfinger's power, strapped to a table while a laser beam of gold gets closer and closer to the British secret service's top gadget. In the next activity, you are going to change perspective and look at the main climactic scene of *Goldfinger* from Bond's point of view.

ACTIVITY 5   **Defusing the atomic device in *Goldfinger***

Allow about
10 minutes

Having handcuffed Bond to the atomic device in Fort Knox, Goldfinger intends him to die in the explosion. Bond, however, escapes his shackles but then has to contend with Oddjob whom he defeats through electrocution. (You read earlier that Pussy Galore had turned against Goldfinger and had contacted the CIA and the Pentagon. They in turn dispatch agents and soldiers.) Outside Fort Knox, US soldiers do battle with Goldfinger's men, gain entry to Fort Knox, and allow CIA agents in as well. But Bond does not know how to defuse the atomic device and there are only seconds left for him to do so. It is left to a CIA agent to arrive in the nick of time. Fort Knox and the western economy is saved.

Fill in the actants with the appropriate characters, etc. from *Goldfinger* to produce a Greimasian representation of the main climactic scene from Bond's perspective.

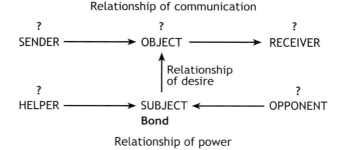

Comment

I analyse the actants as follows:

SENDER:	CIA; The Pentagon.
OBJECT:	defuse atomic device; more generally, to defeat Goldfinger.
RECEIVER:	'The West' (threat to economic stability removed); more particularly, Bond (since he receives the help of the CIA agent, etc.).
HELPER:	CIA agent; US soldiers; Pussy Galore.
OPPONENT:	Goldfinger; Oddjob; Goldfinger's men.

You have seen something of how using Greimas' actant scheme can give a richer account of characterisation than Propp's scheme. Can you, though, see a problem with such analysis – a problem that ultimately bedevils any narrative analytical scheme?

Here is the problem as I see it: it is one thing to analyse narratives into actants; it is another to assume that viewers or readers do in fact organise their understanding of a fictional narrative such as *Goldfinger* via the above actants. The literary theorist Jonathan Culler (1975b, p. 235) argues that it is actually plausible that readers of a fictional narrative do understand characters in terms of actants and the relationships between them. Nevertheless, there is little in Greimas to indicate *how* readers (or viewers) might do this.

Functional grammatical (transitivity) analysis

In Reading C, which you will come to shortly, Martin Montgomery aims to show how readers might understand actants in their reading of a literary story (by Ernest Hemingway), a story where the characterisation has the kind of ambiguity often not so prominent in fantasy/adventure narratives like *Goldfinger*. Montgomery aims to show this by drawing on a type of grammar developed by the British linguist, Michael Halliday. This is known as **functional grammar** (see Halliday and Matthiessen, 2004). Montgomery also aims to show how Hallidayan functional grammar can precisely reveal ambiguity of characterisation in a literary short story. Let me give you some basics of functional grammar to set you up for doing the reading.

Though linguistic **form** and linguistic **function** are different types of phenomena, analysis of either is from an inherency perspective. So a focus on linguistic form or function is not primarily concerned with what sociocultural knowledge or sociohistorical knowledge a reader would draw on in understanding a text.

Traditional grammar is to a large extent concerned with **linguistic form**. To go back to Reading B for a moment, we saw how Toolan makes use of a traditional grammatical term, 'finiteness'. Finiteness is a formal property of a verb – whether a verb carries endings which signal tense (e.g. she *plays/played*) or not (e.g. she saw him *playing*). Functional grammar is, on the other hand, much more concerned with **linguistic function**. It is concerned with how grammatical form works (functions) to make meaning. To illustrate this idea, consider the following:

Eveline continued to sit by the window

We have two verbs, 'continued' and 'to sit'. At the level of linguistic form, we can say that 'continued' is finite, and 'to sit' is non-finite. But how are these verb forms functioning in the sentence to lead us to make meaning in our heads? If we imagine Eveline here we do not think of two different actions, 'continuing' and 'sitting', that she is performing. In understanding the meaning here, we think instead of one **process**. In the functional grammar devised by Michael Halliday, this would be referred to as one process realised by two verb forms (though processes may also be realised by one verb):

FUNCTION		← PROCESS →	
	(Eveline)	continued	to sit
FORM		VERB 1	VERB 2

The process 'continued to sit', Halliday would refer to as a **material action** process. These are processes which involve physical activity and are concerned with who (or what) does an action (to whom). In Reading C, you will come across other processes: **mental** processes, **verbal** processes and **relational** processes. Reading C will explain what these are.

In Halliday's grammar, processes are accompanied by different 'roles' which have different functions. In:

He chased the burly girlies

and:

He was slashed by the burly girlies

the subject, 'he', is the same. It is the third-person, masculine subject pronoun. In other words, the subject has the same grammatical form in both these clauses. But does it have the same grammatical function? In the first sentence above, 'he' is doing the chasing; the grammatical form of the masculine subject pronoun is realising the role of AGENT:

FUNCTION	AGENT	
	He	(chased the burly girlies)
FORM	masculine subject pronoun	

But 'he' has a different function in the second sentence:

FUNCTION	AFFECTED	
	He	(was slashed by the burly girlies)
FORM	masculine subject pronoun	

'He' now is not the AGENT – the burly girlies are. 'He' is being done to and is thus functioning as a different role, the role of AFFECTED.

Roles such as AGENT and AFFECTED which function at the level of the clause are known in Hallidayan functional grammar as **participant roles**. There are other types of participant role for other processes, which you will find out about in Reading C.

In unpacking the relationships between the processes and the participant roles above, I have been performing what Halliday calls a **transitivity** analysis. Transitivity analysis is usually performed on clauses in texts rather than just single clauses. If you think about it, this analysis has parallels with Greimasian analysis of the relationships between actants. Greimasian analysis, being at the level of plot, is a macro-level analysis of relationships between characters in a narrative. When focusing on characters, Hallidayan transitivity analysis of narrative is a micro-level analysis of relationships between characters in a clause.

Understanding actants in a Hemingway short story (Reading C)

Turn now to Reading C. While you are reading, think about the following questions:

- What is the application of Halliday's functional grammar able to reveal precisely about ambiguity in Hemingway's character, 'The Revolutionist', in relation to Greimas' scheme?

- Does Montgomery's analysis help show why the character of the revolutionist is intriguing and prompts interpretation? Do you feel his analysis helps reveal literary skill and thus perhaps a certain literary value?

- What problems might there be with Montgomery's argument that functional grammatical analysis can reveal how readers understand actants?

Comment

Montgomery initially produces a Greimasian actant representation of characters in the Hemingway story. This is a macro-level representation, at the level of plot, of relationships between the revolutionist and other characters in the story. However, with Halliday's functional grammar, he is able to produce a participant role analysis which is both qualitative and quantitative. It is *qualitative* in that it reveals particular types of participant role for the revolutionist. Since it is also *quantitative*, we can compare different numbers of participant roles. As a result, we are able to see that the revolutionist is a SENSER and a SAYER in roughly equal proportions to instances where he is an AGENT. With the functional grammatical analysis, and thus micro-level of analysis of narrative, it becomes clear that Hemingway has produced a reasonably balanced set of participant roles. He has produced an ambiguous character. Unlike an obvious hero in a very plot-driven narrative such as *Goldfinger*, who would automatically slot into SUBJECT position on Greimas' scheme, Montgomery shows that it is difficult to ascribe the actant of SUBJECT to the revolutionist. Because Greimas' actants are organised dynamically along axes, we are able to think of these axes as continua. So the revolutionist can be placed *between* SUBJECT and OBJECT on the axis of desire. Thus, Montgomery shows that Greimas' scheme is usefully plastic in that it nicely accommodates ambiguity in characterisation. The ambiguity of characterisation here could not be accommodated in Propp's scheme.

From a Formalist poetic point of view (as you will recall from Chapter 2), the Hemingway story is seemingly not so interesting. There is little use of poetic literariness. Literariness instead derives from the choice of participant roles, which create ambiguity of character. But for there to be successful literariness for a reader, and thus for a reader to ascribe value to a story, he or she needs to be intrigued, in part, by the characterisation, spending time for instance in trying to resolve any ambiguity. From a physical perspective, the boy is a revolutionist, in the sense of 'revolving', since he is being passed from one set of people to another.

This seems to reflect that he is still reeling from the brutality he has suffered at such a young age under Horthy. His psychological damage means he fails to realise himself as a man of action in keeping with the title. (If the story were really about a stereotypical revolutionist, I would expect a greater proportion of material action processes with the boy, as AGENT, consistently operating on AFFECTED participant roles, including human ones, rather than the other way round.) I have merely the beginnings of an interpretation here – you may have a different one of course or perhaps you were not intrigued by the ambiguity of Hemingway's characterisation and for you the story has little skill or value.

It must be said, though, that my interpretation has an inherency basis only. In line with what Montgomery says, it might be possible to make inferences about the painters referred to in the story on the basis of sociocultural knowledge, and this may also provide insights into the revolutionist's character. Would the knowledge that the boy does not like Mantegna but likes Giotto, Masaccio and Piero della Francesca lead an Italian Renaissance art enthusiast to discern something about the boy's psychology that I would not, and thus potentially fill in actants in a different way to how Montgomery assumes readers would? It might also be possible to make inferences on the basis of sociohistorical knowledge just as I did for 'Eveline' in Section 3.3. A reader who, unlike myself, is very aware of the post-World-War I Hungarian political context may well project this understanding on to the boy's situation. Therefore, how this type of reader would realise actants could be affected by this knowledge; the results could be different to what Montgomery proposes. In the end, it is because I do not possess enough of either type of contextual knowledge that I am in a position to accept Montgomery's argument that patterns of transitivity in a text will affect how I 'fill in' actants in my reading. As a corollary, though, the extent of a reader's sociocultural or sociohistorical knowledge may affect how they understand actants in other fictional narratives.

ACTIVITY 7   Understanding 'Sam' as an actant in *The Sun* story

Allow about 15 minutes

To throw into relief aspects of characterisation of the 'hero' of the above literary text, let us go back to another short narrative, *The Sun*'s third-person narrative. Overleaf you will see a Hallidayan functional analysis of the processes and participant roles which describe Sam Latifi. Go back to earlier in Section 3.4 and Reading C, if you wish, to make sure you are happy with how the participant roles and processes are described.

- What does this functional grammatical description tell you at a micro-level about how a reader might understand Sam as an actant?
- How does characterisation in this text compare with that of the revolutionist in the Hemingway story?

1	I AGENT	saved MATERIAL ACTION	(Hurley)
2	A handsome hat seller SAYER	revealed VERBAL	
3	He CARRIER	was RELATIONAL	(the have-a-go hero who saved lovely Liz Hurley)
4	[He] AGENT	saved MATERIAL ACTION	(lovely Liz Hurley)
5	Sam Latifi, 30 AGENT	chased MATERIAL ACTION	(the teenage gang)
6	He AFFECTED	was slashed MATERIAL ACTION	(on the hand)
7	[He] AFFECTED	[was] pelted MATERIAL ACTION	(with bricks and bottles)
8	[He] AGENT	cornering MATERIAL ACTION	(the girls)
9	(Grateful Liz)	rewarded MATERIAL ACTION	him BENEFICIARY
10	He BENEFICIARY	got MATERIAL ACTION	(a 'well done' hug)
11	Sam SAYER	said: VERBAL	(I'd have done the same for anyone.)

BENEFICIARY is another participant role for use with MATERIAL ACTION processes. It is a person or thing which receives something.

Comment

You will see that most of the processes are MATERIAL ACTION processes; Sam is predominantly AGENT (four instances). Though there are two instances of SAYER, there are also two instances of AFFECTED and the same for BENEFICIARY. The overall picture is of Sam doing or being done to; he is in the thick of action or being rewarded for his actions. Unlike the Hemingway story, there are no examples of mental processes and thus no examples of SENSER or PHENOMENON participant roles. So there is little evidence of reflection on his actions or of feeling afraid, for example. Yet in Sam's first-person narrative (as you saw in Section 3.2), we know that he did feel threatened at one point. And even though Sam is an AFFECTED in being slashed and pelted, he turns the situation around by cornering the girls, that is, acting as an AGENT. The impression created for me is that Sam is being configured to be read by a *Sun* reader as fairly heroic, as a fairly prototypical SUBJECT actant, and thus not mid-placed being SUBJECT and OBJECT like the revolutionist. As I noted in Section 3.2, an ambiguous hero is a less marketable one.

In Reading B, the first 24 sentences of 'Eveline' were focused upon by mainly looking at verb forms. The purpose of this was to find clauses/sentences where plot was more obviously being moved forward. But with Halliday's functional grammar, we simultaneously look in a clause at functional processes which might describe an event, *and* participant roles which might relate to character. In other words, to go back to Henry James' dictum, where incident and character are woven together such as in 'Eveline', transitivity analysis can help to reveal such weaving.

We return to 'Eveline'. By focusing on repetition with differences (lines 111–13), I argued in Section 3.3 that Joyce employs parallelism to hint at why Eveline is feeling static. Narrative fiction, however, does not commonly richly sustain such use of poetic device across entire works, and this is particularly the case with 'Eveline'. Indeed, Attridge (2004b, p. 4) writes in reference to lines 74–87 of 'Eveline' that 'what is most remarkable about this writing is its unremarkableness; it hardly seems to be "literary" language at all. But that does not mean that it is a mode of writing which is completely transparent...'. In Section 3.5, you will see how transitivity analysis can be used to enable articulation of meanings that are cued indirectly across 'Eveline', meanings which are not so 'transparent' due to the fact that they are not, in the main, realised poetically. In turn, I shall continue to argue that these indirect meanings contribute to its literariness, and indeed for me a valued literariness. I will supplement this with insights on the story afforded by corpus methods.

In Chapter 2 Ronald Carter (Reading B) calls these indirect meanings 'unstated content'.

3.5   Further literariness in 'Eveline'

Much of 'Eveline' involves her trying to weigh up her current situation against eloping with Frank to Argentina. This is not done by Eveline as a first-person narrator. Rather, a third-person narrator is representing Eveline's thinking about the future. Such tracing of thought about the future in a fictional narrative is often accomplished with the use of 'would' by a third-person narrator. Here is a concordance of the instances of 'would' with Eveline weighing up her future before she decides to 'escape':

> the dust came from. Perhaps she would never see again those familiar ob
> the house and at business. What would they say of her in the Stores whei
> as a fool, perhaps; and her place would be filled up by advertisement. M:
> ok lively, Miss Hill, please." She would not cry many tears at leaving the
> ntry, it not be like that. Then she would be married - she, Eveline. People
> be married--she, Eveline. People would treat her with respect then. She v
> l treat her with respect then She would not be treated as her mother had
> oming old lately, she noticed; he would miss her. Sometimes he could be

The notion of concordance lines was introduced in Chapter 2.

Figure 3.1   Concordance lines for Eveline's thinking represented via *would* until the 'escape'.

Below is a participant role analysis of 'Eveline' around 'would' in the above:

Lines 25–6	She SENSER	(would never see again those familiar objects)		
Line 38	What [VERBIAGE]	(would they say)	of her	(in the Stores) VERBIAGE
Line 40	Her place AFFECTED	(would be filled up by advertisement)		
Line 45	She SENSER	(would not cry many tears at leaving the Stores)		
Line 47	she CARRIER	(would be married)		
Lines 47–48	People	(would treat)	her AFFECTED	(with respect)
Lines 48–49	She AFFECTED	(would not be treated as her mother had been)		
Line 104	He	(would miss)	her PHENOMENON	

If you wish to, go back to Section 3.4 and Reading C to make sure you are happy with these descriptions of participant roles.

ACTIVITY 8   **Eveline's 'weighing up'**

Allow about 30 minutes

For you, what insights (if any) might the above participant role analysis provide about what 'lies beneath' Eveline's conscious thinking?

Comment

I make the following interpretation. Given that Eveline is musing on her future, there is little here about what she would actively do in her new life. There are no instances of Eveline as an AGENT. Rather she is SENSER, AFFECTED, CARRIER, PHENOMENON and part of VERBIAGE.

The lack of AGENT participant roles for someone who is supposedly about to leave Dublin and start a new life reinforces the interpretation in Section 3.3 that Eveline is not going to leave her home. Again, for me, what Joyce is effecting is a delicate tension between what Eveline's conscious mind is telling us and what her subconscious mind is intimating. As I said before, such indirect meanings contribute to the literariness of 'Eveline' in that it can lead to the literary effect of richer, more satisfying characterisation. Moreover, this literariness as revealed by transitivity analysis over a large stretch of narrative is not the kind of poetic literariness you encountered in Chapter 2.

Using corpora to analyse text

Throughout 'Eveline', Joyce is making different grammatical choices with regard to characterisation, not just those in relation to transitivity. (You will see in a moment choices of pronouns in 'Eveline' for male and female characters.) With some idea of linguistic norms, we could quantitatively compare the distribution of grammatical selections in 'Eveline' and thus potentially attach greater significance to the choices Joyce makes. To get some idea of linguistic norms, we need a large corpus, which was first mentioned in Chapter 2. We also need computational means for comparing one text with a corpus. When a corpus is used for purposes of computational comparison, it is known as a **reference corpus**.

So far there has been a focus on the first 24 sentences of 'Eveline' and then on Eveline's weighing up whether to leave. In Reading D, by Michael Stubbs, you are going to go further and look across the *whole* of the story at certain grammatical selections. Stubbs draws upon large corpora of English to illuminate these grammatical choices through comparison. Moreover, and again in relation to the whole of 'Eveline', you will see how Stubbs uses computational software to reveal how Joyce's lexical selections relate to its narrative structure.

ACTIVITY 9   **Exploring 'Eveline' with computational methods (Reading D)**

Please now turn to Reading D. As you are reading, consider the questions below:

- What differences is Stubbs able to find in the usage of English in 'Eveline' and usage generally?
- How do these differences feed into his interpretations of 'Eveline'?
- How might the Youmans' software be limited as to what it can reveal about key narrative boundaries in 'Eveline'?

Comment

You saw that while in 'Eveline' *he* is more common than *him/his*, it is the opposite for *she* and *her*. This is significant in comparison with the LOB reference corpus. Stubbs interprets this as follows: 'This is a story in which Frank wants Eveline to act, but in the end she cannot act (as he wishes).'

Another interesting observation that the corpus comparison brings to light is with regard to *would*. Instances of *would* are significantly higher in 'Eveline' than in the 2.5 million word reference corpus. For Stubbs, this is evidence of the intensity of Eveline's mental projection: 'Eveline' is 'a story about a young woman thinking about – but in the end failing to act on – hypothetical possibilities for her future.' (That *would* is a keyword supports the focus on it in the previous activity.)

Finally, through replication of the Youmans' software, Stubbs shows how the introduction of new lexis in the story signals key narrative phases in 'Eveline' and substantiates Hart's (1969) reading. Joyce's skill here, as made easier to see with Youmans' software, is in effecting a sudden eruption of lexical diversity in relation to what has preceded.

There are, though, limitations with the analyses, as Stubbs (2001) acknowledges. For instance, the analyses all assume that lexical units are single word forms, for example, *window*. But there are lexical units in 'Eveline' which contain more than one word form, e.g. *call out* (line 16). When Joyce (line 87) writes '[Frank] used to call her Poppens', he is using again the lexical item *call*, but with a different meaning. The software Stubbs used would pick up on the repetition of lexis but not on meaning differences. This in turn may mean more generally that key *lexical* boundaries in 'Eveline' found by the software will closely, but not exactly, map on to key *semantic* boundaries. Where meaning is to be interpreted, humans will be required; computer software is limited in this regard.

You saw in Section 3.4 that, because it involves looking at both participant roles and processes, transitivity analysis helps us to illuminate aspects of a narrative where plot and characterisation are interconnected. As such, it is useful in revealing something of Joyce's skill in cueing indirect meanings which contribute to the literariness of the story. Activities 4 and 8 got you to look at the first phase of 'Eveline' where she thinks about her past and possible future. Activity 10 will ask you to think about the story's second and third phases. I said in Section 3.3 that having other sources of support for an interpretation means it is more likely to carry conviction. Activity 10 will ask you, in part, about whether any observations that Stubbs provides, with the use of computer software, might bolster insights about indirect meanings and literariness in 'Eveline'.

A C T I V I T Y   1 0   'Eveline's decision and failure to escape

Allow about 40 minutes

Have a look at the concordance of *would* (6 instances) in 'Eveline' to express her thoughts after she decides to escape (lines 128–9). Using Halliday's functional grammar, perform a participant role analysis of Eveline (as represented by *she* or *her*) in these concordance lines.

- What, for you, might the analysis say indirectly about Eveline's evolving mental state after she has decided to escape?
- Which (if any) insights that Stubbs provides complement your interpretation of Eveline's evolving mental state?
- Does the literariness of the climax to 'Eveline' translate into literary value for you?

Escape! She must escape! Frank would **save her. He would give her life,**
scape! Frank would save her. He would **give her life, perhaps love, too. B**
e had a right to happiness. Frank would **take her in his arms, fold her in l**
lis arms, fold her in his arms. He would **save her. She stood among the sw**
e mist. If she went, tomorrow she would **be on the sea with Frank, steamil**
[e was drawing her into them: he would **drown her. She gripped with bot**

Figure 3.2 Concordance lines for *would* in 'Eveline' after the 'escape' moment.

Comment

I offer my interpretation below. To what extent does your own interpretation
concur with mine?

Via the use of computer software, Stubbs isolates the beginning of a burst
of new lexis shortly after lines 111–13, the repetition with difference, where
the type–token ratio starts to slope upwards. Much of the preceding text has
seemed to consist of carefully considered mental reflection (*she tried to weigh
each side of the question*, line 35). The burst of new lexis is coincident with an
acceleration of plot, that is when Eveline decides to escape. This
burst suggests to me that Eveline is not in the end leaving because of her
well-pondered 'weighing up' in the first phase of the story but because
of an explosive emotional impulse. In line with my previous interpretation
(Section 3.3) of a key repetition with differences in lines 111–13, I would
argue the following: her decision to escape at that moment (lines 128–9) is, at
least in part, because Eveline has been thinking about her father's very poor
treatment of her. Her memory of her mother would also seem to contribute
to her decision, though in a less suggestive way.

At this very point of deciding to take action, we would expect even more
that Eveline would function as an AGENT, in the sense of thinking about what *she*
would now do. Instead, she is an AFFECTED (*Frank would save her*, line 129).
Indeed, Eveline continues not to be realised as an AGENT around any of the
remaining instances of *would*, that is, in expressions of her thoughts for the future:

Line 129	(Frank	would	save)	her AFFECTED	
Line 129	(He	would	give)	her BENEFICIARY	(life)
Line 131	(Frank	would	take)	her AFFECTED	(in his arms)
Line 132	(He	would	save)	her AFFECTED	
Line 142	She CARRIER	(would	be	on the sea	with Frank)
Line 149	(He	would	drown)	her AFFECTED	

As can be seen in the above, Eveline is an AFFECTED or BENEFICIARY for five instances, signalled with the grammatical form, *her*; the one instance of *she* is realising a CARRIER. All this takes on greater value given what was found to be significant in Stubbs' corpus comparison: that *would* is a keyword and there are more instances of *her* than *she* in the story (in the LOB corpus they are in equal proportions). So while it might seem 'on the surface' that Eveline is taking action for herself, I make the interpretation that actually she is feeling deep down that she is someone else's OBJECT in Greimas' terms. Once more, plot and characterisation are woven together. This greater tension between the 'surface' of the text and cueing of indirect meanings at this point of the narrative in turn intensifies literariness. The literary effect for me is that I now feel the 'agitated stasis' in Eveline's psychology more keenly. As Eveline takes action, she is actually paralysed mentally – indeed more clues that she is not going to leave Dublin. Overall, in Greimas' terms, I interpret Eveline as a passive-active SUBJECT whose own OBJECT she cannot strongly define. This is because she is 'drowning' as the OBJECT of one SUBJECT (Frank) and was too much the OBJECT of another SUBJECT (her father).

As you saw in Chapter 2, literariness does not necessarily translate into literary value. But from Stubbs' corpus insights, and what has been revealed via Hallidayan functional grammar, I would argue that Joyce *does* sustain literary skill into the final sections. Especially for me, in the final part of the narrative, the success of literariness in 'Eveline' is in the following: how it is able to rapidly intensify the cueing of indirect meaning and thus provide a rich sense of Eveline's desperate paralysis, and through the story's indeterminacies, space for us as readers to find possible reasons for it, as the plot accelerates.

3.6 Conclusion

In this chapter, I have explored characterisation and plot in a number of different narratives. You saw the limitations with Propp's framework for dealing with subtle linking of plot and characterisation. To capture this subtlety, you saw how Greimas' framework can be usefully supplemented by analysis at clause level. Literariness within 'Eveline', I have argued, derives from the following: indirect cuing of Eveline's deeper thoughts which thus enriches characterisation. The capacity of such literariness to excite a reader into engagement, and which in a sense allows the reader to contribute to the enrichment of characterisation, is a literary effect which I would also argue contributes to any story's literary value. I have contended that optimum conditions for such literariness are when plot and characterisation have some interdependency. To show such interdependency, I have mostly used an inherency perspective in this chapter but I have also indicated how a sociocultural (sociohistorical) perspective could be used. Indeed, a purely grammatical focus is unlikely to reveal plot and characterisation comprehensively. You will no doubt have found other aspects of 'Eveline' which contribute to its plot and characterisation, its religious imagery for example.

You have seen how stylistic analysis of narrative can draw on a number of tools for studying linguistic form and function. And you have gained a sense of how these tools are useful for helping to articulate how a good literary writer draws a reader into a story through tensions, indeterminacies and ambiguities in plot and characterisation. So you now have some useful tools with which to trace literary craft in other fictional narratives as well as to articulate the quality of this craft. You have also seen how a corpus comparison with a literary story is a way of increasing the power of an inherency-based analysis. So far you have dealt with aspects of two key literary genres: poetry and narrative fiction. In the next chapter the focus is on the third key literary genre – drama.

READING A: 'Eveline'

James Joyce

1   SHE sat at the window watching the evening invade the avenue. Her head was leaned against the window curtains and in her nostrils was the odour of dusty cretonne. She was tired.

Few people passed. The man out of the last house passed on his
5   way home; she heard his footsteps clacking along the concrete pavement and afterwards crunching on the cinder path before the new red houses. One time there used to be a field there in which they used to play every evening with other people's children. Then a man from Belfast bought the field and built houses in it—not like their
10   little brown houses but bright brick houses with shining roofs. The children of the avenue used to play together in that field—the Devines, the Waters, the Dunns, little Keogh the cripple, she and her brothers and sisters. Ernest, however, never played: he was too grown up. Her father used often to hunt them in out of the field with
15   his Blackthorn stick; but usually little Keogh used to keep *nix* and call out when he saw her father coming. Still they seemed to have been rather happy then. Her father was not so bad then; and besides, her mother was alive. That was a long time ago; she and her brothers and sisters were all grown up; her mother was dead. Tizzie Dunn was
20   dead, too, and the Waters had gone back to England. Everything changes. Now she was going to go away like the others, to leave her home.

Home! She looked round the room, reviewing all its familiar objects which she had dusted once a week for so many years, wonder-
25   ing where on earth all the dust came from. Perhaps she would never see again those familiar objects from which she had never dreamed of being divided. And yet during all those years she had never found out the name of the priest whose yellowing photograph hung on the wall above the broken harmonium beside the coloured print of the
30   promises made to Blessed Margaret Mary Alacoque. He had been a school friend of her father. Whenever he showed the photograph to a visitor her father used to pass it with a casual word:

—He is in Melbourne now.

She had consented to go away, to leave her home. Was that wise?
35   She tried to weigh each side of the question. In her home anyway she had shelter and food; she had those whom she had known all her life about her. Of course she had to work hard, both in the house and at business. What would they say of her in the Stores when they found out that she had run away with a fellow? Say she was a fool, perhaps;
40   and her place would be filled up by advertisement. Miss Gavan would be glad. She had always had an edge on her, especially

whenever there were people listening.

—Miss Hill, don't you see these ladies are waiting?

—Look lively, Miss Hill, please.

45 She would not cry many tears at leaving the Stores.

But in her new home, in a distant unknown country, it would not be like that. Then she would be married—she, Eveline. People would treat her with respect then. She would not be treated as her mother had been. Even now, though she was over nineteen, she

50 sometimes felt herself in danger of her father's violence. She knew it was that that had given her the palpitations. When they were growing up he had never gone for her, like he used to go for Harry and Ernest, because she was a girl but latterly he had begun to threaten her and say what he would do to her only for her dead mother's sake.

55 And now she had nobody to protect her. Ernest was dead and Harry, who was in the church decorating business, was nearly always down somewhere in the country. Besides, the invariable squabble for money on Saturday nights had begun to weary her unspeakably. She always gave her entire wages—seven shillings—and Harry always

60 sent up what he could but the trouble was to get any money from her father. He said she used to squander the money, that she had no head, that he wasn't going to give her his hard-earned money to throw about the streets, and much more, for he was usually fairly bad of a Saturday night. In the end he would give her the money and ask

65 her had she any intention of buying Sunday's dinner. Then she had to rush out as quickly as she could and do her marketing, holding her black leather purse tightly in her hand as she elbowed her way through the crowds and returning home late under her load of provisions. She had hard work to keep the house together and to see that

70 the two young children who had been left to her charge went to school regularly and got their meals regularly. It was hard work—a hard life—but now that she was about to leave it she did not find it a wholly undesirable life.

She was about to explore another life with Frank. Frank was very

75 kind, manly, open-hearted. She was to go away with him by the night-boat to be his wife and to live with him in Buenos Ayres where he had a home waiting for her. How well she remembered the first time she had seen him; he was lodging in a house on the main road where she used to visit. It seemed a few weeks ago. He was standing

80 at the gate, his peaked cap pushed back on his head and his hair tumbled forward over a face of bronze. Then they had come to know each other. He used to meet her outside the Stores every evening and see her home. He took her to see *The Bohemian Girl* and she felt elated as she sat in an unaccustomed part of the theatre with him. He

85 was awfully fond of music and sang a little. People knew that they were courting and, when he sang about the lass that loves a sailor, she always felt pleasantly confused. He used to call her Poppens out

of fun. First of all it had been an excitement for her to have a fellow and then she had begun to like him. He had tales of distant countries.
90   He had started as a deck boy at a pound a month on a ship of the Allan Line going out to Canada. He told her the names of the ships he had been on and the names of the different services. He had sailed through the Straits of Magellan and he told her stories of the terrible Patagonians. He had fallen on his feet in Buenos Ayres, he said, and
95   had come over to the old country just for a holiday. Of course, her father had found out the affair and had forbidden her to have anything to say to him.

—I know these sailor chaps, he said.

One day he had quarrelled with Frank and after that she had to
100   meet her lover secretly.

The evening deepened in the avenue. The white of two letters in her lap grew indistinct. One was to Harry; the other was to her father. Ernest had been her favourite but she liked Harry too. Her father was becoming old lately, she noticed; he would miss her.
105   Sometimes he could be very nice. Not long before, when she had been laid up for a day, he had read her out a ghost story and made toast for her at the fire. Another day, when their mother was alive, they had all gone for a picnic to the Hill of Howth. She remembered her father putting on her mother's bonnet to make the children
110   laugh.

Her time was running out but she continued to sit by the window, leaning her head against the window curtain, inhaling the odour of dusty cretonne. Down far in the avenue she could hear a street organ playing. She knew the air. Strange that it should come that very
115   night to remind her of the promise to her mother, her promise to keep the home together as long as she could. She remembered the last night of her mother's illness; she was again in the close dark room at the other side of the hall and outside she heard a melancholy air of Italy. The organ-player had been ordered to go away and
120   given six pence. She remembered her father strutting back into the sickroom saying:

—Damned Italians! coming over here!

As she mused the pitiful vision of her mother's life laid its spell on the very quick of her being—that life of commonplace sacrifices
125   closing in final craziness. She trembled as she heard again her mother's voice saying constantly with foolish insistence:

—Derevaun Seraun! Derevaun Seraun!

She stood up in a sudden impulse of terror. Escape! She must escape! Frank would save her. He would give her life, perhaps love,

130   too. But she wanted to live. Why should she be unhappy? She had a
right to happiness. Frank would take her in his arms, fold her in his
arms. He would save her.

.   .   .   .

She stood among the swaying crowd in the station at the North
Wall. He held her hand and she knew that he was speaking to her,
135   saying something about the passage over and over again. The station
was full of soldiers with brown baggages. Through the wide doors of
the sheds she caught a glimpse of the black mass of the boat, lying in
beside the quay wall, with illumined portholes. She answered nothing. She felt her cheek pale and cold and, out of a maze of distress,
140   she prayed to God to direct her, to show her what was her duty.
The boat blew a long mournful whistle into the mist. If she went,
to-morrow she would be on the sea with Frank, steaming towards
Buenos Ayres. Their passage had been booked. Could she still draw
back after all he had done for her? Her distress awoke a nausea in her
145   body and she kept moving her lips in silent fervent prayer.
A bell clanged upon her heart. She felt him seize her hand:
—Come!
All the seas of the world tumbled about her heart. He was drawing
her into them: he would drown her. She gripped with both hands at
150   the iron railing.
—Come!
No! No! No! It was impossible. Her hands clutched the iron in
frenzy. Amid the seas she sent a cry of anguish!
—Eveline! Evvy!
155   He rushed beyond the barrier and called to her to follow. He was
shouted at to go on but he still called to her. She set her white face to
him, passive, like a helpless animal. Her eyes gave him no sign of
love or farewell or recognition.

**Source: JOYCE, J. ([1914]2000) 'Eveline', *Dubliners*, pp. 25–29,
New York/Oxford, Oxford University Press.**

READING B: In search of plot structure

Michael Toolan

The aim of this reading is to offer some simple principles which may guide a reader's 'real time' processing of text in the search for plot. I try to uncover links between stylistic information and plot, in the conviction that such links quite typically do exist. While the folk-tales that Propp focused on proceed through developmental actions, 'Eveline' is very largely a mental projection, both forward to possible future events and backward to actual past ones. The main complication that 'Eveline' presents is that as we read this story we are not entirely sure whether we should – as normally – be looking for incidents, or, instead, attend to character. But let us proceed by trying to see why, as many analysts (e.g. Culler, 1975a, p. 129) claim:

> She had consented to go away, to leave her home. (sentence 24 – line 34)

is one of the more important disclosures of plot in the story. In thinking about whether sentence 24 has high plot status, we should first compare it to the 23 sentences that precede it.

To establish whether these sentences are crucial to plot or not I am going to principally look at verbs in these sentences. To begin with I will draw on the grammatical concept of finiteness. Have a look below at the first three sentences from 'Eveline' and you will see a number of verbs underlined. They have a number of things in common:

> She <u>sat</u> at the window watching the evening invade the avenue. (1) Her head was <u>leaned</u> against the window curtains and in her nostrils <u>was</u> the odour of dusty cretonne. (2) She <u>was</u> tired. (3)

All of these underlined verbs carry information about time – they are in the past tense. When verbs are being used to communicate information about time, they are said to be used in a finite way. Now have a look at sentence 1 again. This time you will see different verbs underlined:

> She sat at the window <u>watching</u> the evening <u>invade</u> the avenue. (1)

'Watching' and 'invade' do not communicate information about time (past or present) through their verb endings. When verbs are not communicating information about time, they are said to be used in a non-finite way.

The story is clearly about Eveline. And so we would expect Eveline to occur frequently as a grammatical subject such as in sentence 1 ('*she* sat...'). Since non-finite verb forms, such as 'watching' and 'invade' in sentence 1, do not attach to/do not agree grammatically with subjects, and the story is about Eveline, my expectation would be that information about plot is more likely to be communicated via finite verb forms.

Finiteness is a property of a verb form. 'Leaned' is finite in sentence 2 but much later in the story (line 112) is being used in a non-finite way, i.e. 'leaning'.

Accordingly, and while mindful that my assessment could change in light of later text, I calculate that, for example, the non-finite clause 'the evening invade the avenue' does not express a crucial plot event.

Since plot is about movement and change over time, clauses most central to a plot are more likely to be realised through verbs which express action. But in sentences 1, 2 and 3 from 'Eveline', even the verbs of action (*sit*, *lean*) are used in static ways. This fact then reduces the prospect that the first three sentences, despite incorporating finite verb forms, are so crucial to plot. The text continues:

Clause: a grammatical unit built around a verb. There are two clauses in the following sentence (lexical verbs underlined): Now she was <u>going</u> away like the others (1), to <u>leave</u> her home (2).

> Few people passed. (4) The man out of the last house passed on his way home; she heard his footsteps clacking along the concrete pavement and afterward crunching on the cinder before the new red houses. (5) One time there used to be a field there in which they used to play every evening with other people's children. (6)

What of sentence 4? Are there any grounds for doubting its importance to plot? Perhaps only if we compare it with the nearly synonymous:

> A few people passed.

The latter could be used to describe the passage of a particular group of pedestrians (e.g. 'A few nuns passed'), where we can respond by wondering 'What sort of people?' This is not true of the 'Few people passed' in 'Eveline', i.e. without an indefinite article. 'People' is one of a group of general items (others include 'thing', 'person', 'stuff'). We are likely, then, to demote (rather than promote) sentence 4 as a candidate for having high plot status. In spite of the verb of action ('passed') being used in a finite way, 'people' is too non-specific.

By contrast the next sentence (sentence 5) does exhibit what I have argued is characteristic of clauses which are more central to plot, particularly in its definite description of a specified individual:

> The man out of the last house passed on his way home. (5)

The use of a finite verb form which expresses action, 'passed', means this incident *could* be crucial in the plot. However, there are two counter-signals:

1   In none of the following sentences is the man named
2   Important characters and their important actions are not usually mentioned and then immediately discarded.

The following sentences, then, revert to the distant past:

> One time there used to be a field there in which they used to play every evening with other people's children. (6) Then a man from Belfast brought the field and built houses in it – not like their little brown houses but bright brick houses with shining roofs. (7) The children of the avenue used to play together in that field – the Devines, the Waters, the Dunns,

little Keogh the cripple, she and her brothers and sisters. (8) Ernest, however, never played: he was too grown up. (9)

There are basically two grounds for discounting most of this material as crucial to plot in 'Eveline': one is the frequent emphasis on events which would have happened on many occasions, an emphasis that becomes pronounced in the following sentence:

> Her father used often to hunt them in out of the field [...] but usually little Keogh used to keep *nix* ... (10)

The second ground which suggests these are not contributing to the plot is the following: sentences 6–10 are remote from Eveline's current situation. This is especially communicated through words and expressions such as *one time, there, then, that* also seen in sentences 11 and 12:

> Still they seemed to have been rather happy then. (11) Her father was not so bad then; and besides, her mother was alive. (12)

Indeed, the above sentences do not imply events have taken place anyway since their main verbs express states rather than actions. The text continues:

> That was a long time ago; she and her brothers and sisters were all grown up; her mother was dead. (13) Tizzie Dunn was dead, too, and the Waters had gone back to England. (14) Everything changes. (15) Now she was going to go away like the others, to leave her home. (16)

Again, we have a series of descriptions of states rather than actions (sentences 13 and 14), closing with an event which took place in the past, and a sentence (15) which does not indicate a specific time.

Only with sentence 16 do we encounter an utterance quite different with regard to time from all those preceding. Introduced by 'Now', in striking contrast to all the previous instances of 'then', it is oriented to Eveline's present, with an explicit verb of action ('going'). Not only is the utterance oriented to Eveline's present, it expresses an intended future course of action. The links between sentence 16 and the surrounding text are plentiful which again marks it out; some of these may be briefly listed, making reference to phrases here shown in italics:

> *Now* she was going to *go away* like *the others*, to leave her *home*. (16)

The 'Now' links by contrast with the 'then' of times past, recounted in the foregoing sentences; the 'go away' is lexically related to the 'gone back' of sentence 14; the 'others' in 'like the others' is linked to the previously-mentioned brothers and sisters, or the Waters, or possibly even her dead mother and Tizzie Dunn, or any combination of these. But all such links do nothing to detract from the narrative distinctiveness of sentence 16 in terms of its use of a verb of action which expresses a clear change of state.

What I have done for these first two paragraphs could be done for the third paragraph, leading up to sentence 24 – 'She had consented to go away, to leave her home' – which analysts agree is important to plot. Briefly, paragraph 3 displays many of the same low plot status characteristics as the previous two, particularly using either verbs expressing states rather than actions or at least ones implying no change of state:

> She looked round the room ... Perhaps she would never <u>see</u> again those familiar objects ... He had <u>been</u> a school friend ... 'He <u>is</u> in Melbourne now'.

Other low plot status characteristics that paragraph 3 contains are actions which can be taken as occurring regularly and thus not specific to the plot:

> which she had <u>dusted</u> once a week for so many years ... Whenever he <u>showed</u> the photograph ... her father <u>used</u> to pass it.

or:

> from which she had never <u>dreamed</u> of being divided ... during all those years she had never <u>found</u> out the name of the priest.

Again, by sharp contrast with these examples of regular occurrences, and now with the additional impact of being a near-repetition of sentence 16, comes sentence 24:

> She had consented to go away, to leave her home.

But it is, note, a repetition with some changes, which makes it all the more salient to plot. For while sentence 16 can be read as the expression of Eveline's purely personal decision to act, it now emerges that another party is involved, and has proposed a course of action to which Eveline has agreed.

I have offered some simple principles which may guide a reader's 'real time' processing of text in the search for plot. But my argument is in terms of preferences, expectations, and tendencies (we expect main events to come in main verbs, we expect main characters to be designated – recurrently – in individualizing ways, and so on). It must be conceded then that this whole exercise of provisional plot-assessment sometimes needs radical recasting after the act of reading, when a perspective on a *whole* story can be adopted.

Reference

CULLER, J. (1975a) 'Defining narrative units', in R. FOWLER (ed.) *Style and Structure in Literature*, Oxford, Blackwell.

Source: adapted from TOOLAN, M. (2001) *Narrative: A Critical Linguistic Introduction*, 2nd edn, Section 2.5, London, Routledge.

READING C: Understanding actants in a Hemingway short story

Martin Montgomery

Introduction

> What is character but the determination of incident?
> What is incident but the illustration of character?
>
> (Henry James, 1888)

In narrative theory, character has received relatively little systematic attention. In this reading, it is argued that the comparative neglect of character in the systematic treatment of narrative stems from emphasising what is done rather than who is doing it; and that Hallidayan functional linguistics may provide a way of integrating both foci. I will show this through using a functional analysis of transitivity – the relationship between the kind of process encoded by the verb and the accompanying participant roles. Halliday's account of transitivity (or variants of it) has been used in the stylistic analysis of literary text (see for example Halliday, 1996; but only obliquely has its use been linked to literary construction of character in a theoretical way – the work of Toolan (2001) being a particular exception. As an account of the grammatical options expressing 'who does what to whom and how' at the level of the clause, we shall see that transitivity blends considerations of both role and event within a single framework of analysis in line with the dictum of Henry James above. Moreover, if as Culler (1975b) argues, interpreters of narrative make use of some general hypotheses concerning Greimas' actants (Greimas, 1983), we need a more developed account of what kinds of textual cues guide readers in apportioning characters to actants. I argue also that the Hallidayan concept of transitivity can do just that.

In this reading, I will first briefly discuss Hemingway's story, 'The Revolutionist' and then perform a Greimasian actant analysis of it. I go on to outline Halliday's framework for transitivity analysis. I show how a transitivity analysis illuminates the kinds of textual cues which guide readers in apportioning characters to actants as well as more precisely revealing ambiguity in the character of the revolutionist.

Analysing actants in Hemingway's 'The Revolutionist'

The title of Hemingway's short story 'The Revolutionist' identifies its central figure by its title and hardly a sentence of text fails to refer to him in one way or another, usually by the pronouns *he* or *him*, which refer back ultimately to the title itself. Although other people are intermittently referred to (Horthy's men, the Whites, the people, the train men, the Swiss, etc.), and although a first person narrator surfaces near the mid-point of the text, no other figure is subject to the same degree of repetitive reference or receives the same degree of narrative attention. The title itself, however, can be seen as something of a misnomer – if by 'revolutionist' is designated 'one who seeks to bring about radical social change'. To a European or North American readership, attributes which would stereotypically be associated with such activity may include idealism but would also conventionally include traits such as 'heroism', 'energy', 'ruthlessness' and 'single-mindedness'. And yet, if such traits are signalled by the title, they are scarcely supported by the text. Instead, rather atypical descriptors are attached to him – principally shyness and youth, as we can see in lines 5, 6 and 17 of the story, reprinted below:

THE REVOLUTIONIST

In 1919 he was travelling on the railroads in Italy, carrying a square of oilcloth from the headquarters of the party written in indelible pencil and saying here was a comrade who had suffered very much under the Whites in Budapest and requesting comrades to aid him

5   in any way. He used this instead of a ticket. He was very shy and quite young and the train men passed him on from one crew to another. He had no money, and they fed him behind the counter in railway eating houses.

He was delighted with Italy. It was a beautiful country, he said.

10   The people were all kind. He had been in many towns, walked much, and seen many pictures. Giotto, Masaccio, and Piero della Francesca he bought reproductions of and carried wrapped in a copy of *Avanti*. Mantegna he did not like.

He reported at Bologna, and I took him with me up to the

15   Romagna where it was necessary I go to see a man. We had a good trip together. It was early September and the country was pleasant. He was a Magyar, a very nice boy and very shy. Horthy's men had done some bad things to him. He talked about it a little. In spite of Hungary, he believed altogether in the world revolution.

20   'But how is the movement going in Italy?' he asked.

'Very badly,' I said.

'But it will go better,' he said. 'You have everything here. It is the one country that everyone is sure of. It will be the starting point of everything.'

25   I did not say anything.

At Bologna he said good-bye to us to go on the train to Milano and then to Aosta to walk over the pass into Switzerland. I spoke to him about the Mantegnas in Milano. 'No,' he said, very shyly, he did not like Mantegna. I wrote out for him where to eat in Milano and
30   the addresses of comrades. He thanked me very much, but his mind was already looking forward to walking over the pass. He was very eager to walk over the pass while the weather held good. He loved the mountains in the Autumn. The last I heard of him the Swiss had him in jail near Sion.

Producing a Greimasian actant scheme for the relationships in the story between the revolutionist and other characters, etc., I get the following:

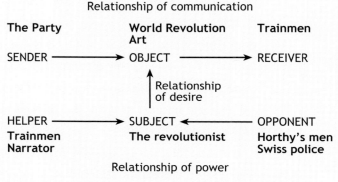

Figure 1   Greimasian representation of Hemingway's 'The Revolutionist'.

It is the revolutionist who is *sent* (by the headquarters of the Party, whose message he carries), *received* (by the trainmen, who pass him from one crew to another), *helped* (by the comrades, who are requested to aid him, and by the narrator) and *opposed* (by Horthy's men, who have done bad things to him, and by the Swiss police, who put him in jail). The revolutionist does not seem then like a very active SUBJECT. Nevertheless, the revolutionist does desire OBJECTS – 'World Revolution' and 'Art'. That the revolutionist desires two very different things would point to ambiguity in his character. But how can we more precisely account for this ambiguity than can be seen in a Greimasian scheme? How can we get a better sense of the detail of the revolutionist's character? I will show that this can be done through using a transitivity analysis using Halliday's functional grammar (Halliday and Matthiessen, 2004). Before I start the analysis, let me outline what transitivity is.

Transitivity and the clause: outline of a Hallidayan approach

Transitivity relations in the English clause can be understood in terms of the relationship between the kind of process encoded by the verb and the accompanying participant roles. Four fundamental types of process may be distinguished:

	Material	*They fed him behind the counter*
TRANSITIVITY	Mental	*He did not like Mantegna*
	Verbal	*He talked about it a little*
	Relational	*The people were all kind*

1   *Material action processes* (realised by verbs such as *break, wipe, dig, unbolt*) are processes concerned with physical activity. They are associated with participant roles such as an AGENT (someone or something to perform the action), and AFFECTED (someone or something on the receiving end of the action):

Jane	broke	the lock	
AGENT	PROCESS	AFFECTED	
They	fed	him	(behind the counter)
AGENT	PROCESS	AFFECTED	

2   *Mental processes* (realised by verbs such as *know, feel, think, believe*) are naturally not concerned with physical activity. So we need different participant roles to describe what is happening. In Halliday's functional grammar, mental processes are associated with participant roles such as SENSER (the one who performs the act of 'knowing', 'thinking' or 'feeling') and PHENOMENON (whatever is 'known', 'thought' or 'felt' by the SENSER):

He	loved	the mountains
SENSER	PROCESS	PHENOMENON
She	believed in	the world revolution
SENSER	PROCESS	PHENOMENON
The message	amazed	me
PHENOMENON	PROCESS	SENSER

3   *Verbal processes* are different altogether. These are processes expressing the communication of something and come in many forms, not just those

related to speech, for example *promise, enquire, tell, write, scribble*. Because verbal processes are very different from material action processes and mental processes, again we need different participant roles. Typical ones are SAYER (who is doing the communicating), VERBIAGE (what is being said), and RECIPIENT (who is being communicated to):

I	said	it was time to leave	
SAYER	PROCESS	VERBIAGE	

'No',	he	said	
VERBIAGE	SAYER	PROCESS	

I	wrote out	for him	where to eat in Milano
SAYER	PROCESS	RECIPIENT	VERBIAGE

4   *Relational processes* are not concerned with physical or mental activity or with communication. In their simplest form, they involve some entity which is identified by reference to an attribute of someone or something. The process may be realised by verbs such as *become, seem, be,* and *have.* Once more, we need different participant roles. Typical ones are CARRIER (e.g. a person) and ATTRIBUTE (e.g. a quality describing a person):

He	was	very shy
CARRIER	PROCESS	ATTRIBUTE

Other important roles are those of POSSESSOR and POSSESSED as in:

He	had	no money
POSSESSOR	PROCESS	POSSESSED

Transitivity analysis of 'The Revolutionist'

Having laid out the four basic processes and their typical participant roles, I perform a transitivity analysis to show how a reader could well fill in actants in an Ernest Hemingway story. I want to suggest that this can be done by inspecting clauses where the revolutionist figures as a participant role with respect to a process. These are listed below with both the process type and the participant role identified being given in each case.

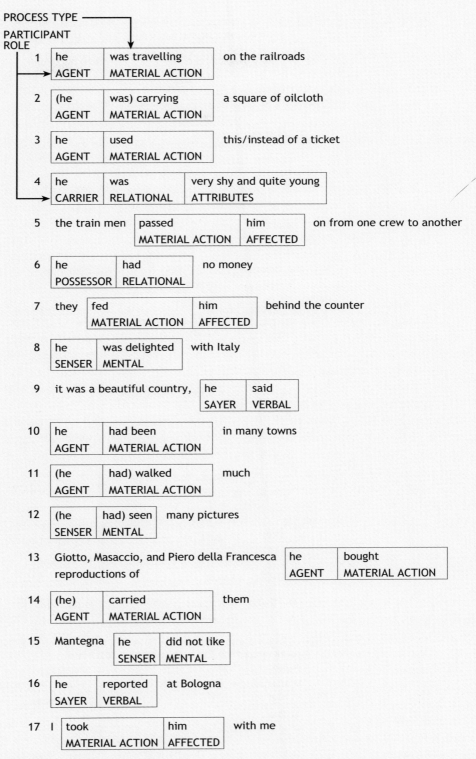

PROCESS TYPE
PARTICIPANT ROLE

1   he | was travelling | on the railroads
    AGENT | MATERIAL ACTION

2   (he | was) carrying | a square of oilcloth
    AGENT | MATERIAL ACTION

3   he | used | this/instead of a ticket
    AGENT | MATERIAL ACTION

4   he | was | very shy and quite young
    CARRIER | RELATIONAL | ATTRIBUTES

5   the train men | passed | him | on from one crew to another
    MATERIAL ACTION | AFFECTED

6   he | had | no money
    POSSESSOR | RELATIONAL

7   they | fed | him | behind the counter
    MATERIAL ACTION | AFFECTED

8   he | was delighted | with Italy
    SENSER | MENTAL

9   it was a beautiful country, | he | said
    SAYER | VERBAL

10 he | had been | in many towns
    AGENT | MATERIAL ACTION

11 (he | had) walked | much
    AGENT | MATERIAL ACTION

12 (he | had) seen | many pictures
    SENSER | MENTAL

13 Giotto, Masaccio, and Piero della Francesca reproductions of | he | bought
    AGENT | MATERIAL ACTION

14 (he) | carried | them
    AGENT | MATERIAL ACTION

15 Mantegna | he | did not like
    SENSER | MENTAL

16 he | reported | at Bologna
    SAYER | VERBAL

17 I | took | him | with me
    MATERIAL ACTION | AFFECTED

Figure 2   Hallidayan participant role and process analysis of Hemingway's 'The Revolutionist'.

18

he	was	a Magyar, a very nice boy and very shy
CARRIER	RELATIONAL	ATTRIBUTES

19 Horthy's men

had done	some bad things	to him
MATERIAL ACTION		AFFECTED

20

he	talked
SAYER	VERBAL

about/it/a little

21

he	believed
SENSER	MENTAL

altogether/in the world revolution

22

he	asked
SAYER	VERBAL

23

he	said
SAYER	VERBAL

24 at Bologna

he	said
SAYER	VERBAL

good-bye/to us

25 I

spoke	to him
VERBAL	RECIPIENT

about the Mantegnas in Milano

26

he	said
SAYER	VERBAL

27

he	did not like
SENSER	MENTAL

Mantegna

28 I

wrote out	for him
VERBAL	RECIPIENT

where to eat in Milano

29

he	thanked	me
SAYER	VERBAL	

very much

30

he	was	very eager
CARRIER	RELATIONAL	ATTRIBUTE

31

he	loved
SENSER	MENTAL

the mountains/in the Autumn

32 the Swiss

had	him
RELATIONAL	POSSESSED

in jail/near Sion

This analysis can be summarised in the following chart, which displays proportionally the participant roles into which the revolutionist is inscribed.

	Material			*Mental*	
AGENT	✔✔✔✔✔✔✔	(7)	SENSER	✔✔✔✔✔✔	(6)
AFFECTED	✔✔✔✔	(4)		*Relational*	
	Verbal		CARRIER	✔✔✔	(3)
SAYER	✔✔✔✔✔✔✔✔	(8)	POSSESSOR	✔	(1)
RECIPIENT	✔✔	(2)	POSSESSED	✔	(1)

Figure 2 (continued)

On the basis of the chart, we can make the following observations. First of all, when we consider the processes associated with the revolutionist, we discover that the largest portion turns out to be of the material action type. We should note immediately, however, that just over one-third of these figure the revolutionist as AFFECTED rather than AGENT. In these cases he is on the receiving end of activity, rather than the source of it:

> The train men fed him ...
> I took him with me.
> Horthy's men had done bad things to him.

And when we turn to those cases where the revolutionist is inscribed into the role of AGENT, it is noticeable either that the activity is not associated with any AFFECTED entities:

> he was travelling ...
> he had ... walked much

or, alternatively, the AFFECTED entity is of an inanimate, non-human type:

> he was carrying a square of oilcloth
> he bought reproductions of (painters).

So, the revolutionist is on the receiving end of actions done to him by others and his own actions are not associated with other human figures as AFFECTED entities; when he occurs as an AGENT, it is of a limited and circumscribed nature.

Second, he is, in any case, slightly more often inscribed into the role of SAYER than that of AGENT. Thus:

> he talked about it a little
> he said good-bye to us
> 'No', he said very shyly.

Finally, we may note that he is almost equally as often inscribed into the role of SENSER as that of SAYER and AGENT. 'He believed altogether in the world revolution', we are told; and that 'he did not like Mantegna', but that 'he loved the mountains in the Autumn.'

The relationship between participant roles and actants

The inscription of the revolutionist into a particular configuration of participant roles at a micro-level analysis of the narrative may be seen as cues as to how readers understand the revolutionist in terms of a macro-level Greimasian actant. The revolutionist is a SAYER, SENSER and AGENT in roughly equal proportions. In other words, he is not behaving as a stereotypical 'HERO', which we might imagine from the title of the story, and thus where we would expect many more AGENTS than SAYERS and SENSERS. We might imagine, on the basis of the micro-level analysis, that readers would not readily ascribe the ACTANT of SUBJECT to the revolutionist. And we also need to consider the number of times he features as an AFFECTED. Propp's scheme as well as Greimas' is constructed in part to take account of 'magic objects' which are sent or donated to the HERO (Propp)/RECEIVER (Greimas). But it is the revolutionist who is sent and received when he is passed from one crew to another.

With the transitivity analysis, we can also grasp more clearly the nature of the ambiguity of his OBJECT. Given the title, we might expect it to be revolution. Certainly the narration tells us that 'he believed altogether in the world revolution.' But when we inspect the other clauses in which he occurs as SENSER, we discover two broad classes of phenomenon: the countryside (he loved the mountains in the Autumn; he was delighted with Italy); and art (he did not like Mantegna). 'Beauty', we might say, figures more often for him than 'political change'.

By looking at the transitivity in the story, we get a micro-analysis of the character of the revolutionist in relation to the other ACTANTS in the story. Because Greimas' actants are organised dynamically along axes, we are able to think of these axes as continua. Given that the above micro-level analysis reveals more precisely the ambiguity in the character of the revolutionist, it would seem more appropriate to place him in between SUBJECT and OBJECT along the axis of desire.

Conclusion

A central contention of this reading is that transitivity as a domain of linguistic choice is strongly implicated in the construction of character. This is because the set of meanings modelled in the transitivity network combines role with process or action, thus making it possible to re-integrate linguistically the notion of character with the notion of event. If we accept Culler's (1975b) claim that as readers 'we do, presumably, make use of some general hypotheses concerning possible roles', then what I have displayed analytically in the case of the revolutionist are the kind of cues which a reader may tacitly be drawing upon in understanding a character via actants.

Of course, in this respect transitivity choices are not the only source of textual cues. For a short text 'The Revolutionist' contains a high proportion of reference by proper noun (Budapest, Italy, Bologna, Horthy, Giotto, Massacio, Aosta). But it is noticeable that this practice is avoided in the case of the revolutionist himself. Instead, the only definite reference is provided by the title. This has the paradoxical effect of signalling the relevance of a stereotype, even when the specific choices of the text run counter to it. The story, therefore, could be seen as built upon an ironic tension between the expectations of the title and the linguistic choices that accumulate around the pronouns that refer back to it.

We must also recognise that not all information about the revolutionist is explicitly encoded in the text. Some aspects of the character of the revolutionist will be recovered through inferences. For example, readers habitually infer things about him from his dislike of Mantegna, though what precisely is inferred depends upon knowledge of Italian Renaissance painting and it is difficult to identify which background assumptions about such painting are most relevant in this context. Detailed readings of the story often invoke interpretative activity of this type. These, however, lie somewhat outside the scope of the present reading, designed as it is not to offer a definitive interpretation of the character of the revolutionist, but to delimit the framework within which such interpretations take place. This is in the belief that the key goal of linguistic criticism is to elucidate the process of reading rather than to provide substantive readings in themselves. If as Culler (1975b, p. 230) argues 'for many readers character serves as the major totalizing force in fiction – everything in the novel exists in order to illustrate character and its development', then it is important to discover how characters are constructed and on the basis of what kinds of linguistic choices.

References

CULLER, J. (1975b) *Structuralist Poetics: Structuralism, Linguistics and the Study of Literature*, London, Routledge.

GREIMAS, A. (1968) *Structural Semantics*, English edn (1983), Lincoln, University of Nebraska Press.

HALLIDAY, M. (1996 [1971]) 'Linguistic function and literary style: an inquiry into the language of William Golding's 'The Inheritors', in WEBER, J.J (ed.) *The Stylistics Reader: From Roman Jakobson to the Present*, London: Routledge.

HALLIDAY, M. and MATTHIESSEN, C. (2004) *An Introduction to Functional Grammar*, 3rd edn, London, Edward Arnold.

JAMES, H. (1948 [1888]) 'The art of fiction', in *The Art of Fiction and Other Essays,* New York, Oxford University Press.

TOOLAN, M. (2001) *Narrative: A Critical Linguistic Introduction*, 2nd edn, London, Routledge.

Source: adapted from MONTGOMERY, M. (1993) 'Language, character and action: a linguistic approach to the analysis of character in a Hemingway short story', in J. SINCLAIR, M. HOEY and G. FOX (eds) *Techniques of Description: Spoken and Written Discourse*, pp. 127–142 London, Routledge.

READING D: Exploring 'Eveline' with computational methods

Michael Stubbs

Introduction

The main aim of this reading is to show how computer-assisted methods can be used to study grammatical and lexical patterns and how these patterns can in turn help in the literary interpretation of a short story. The main data are taken from James Joyce's 'Eveline', and as comparative data I use two different reference corpora of one million and two and a half million words respectively. Computer-assisted methods of text analysis cannot interpret texts for us, but they can provide, for subsequent human interpretation, new kinds of evidence.

I will show that quantitative methods provide: i) ways of studying the grammatical and lexical patterns in a text that may not be obvious to the naked eye; ii) an empirical basis for textual interpretation.

Pronouns

Linguists draw a basic distinction between vocabulary or **lexical words** and **grammatical words**. Lexical words (e.g. *dog, quickly, run*) are an open set – each year more and more lexical words enter a language. Grammatical words (e.g. *the, him, she, a, of, in*) are, on the other hand, a closed set. Relative to lexical words, there are only a small number of such words. However, because these words are basic to the structure of phrases and clauses, they are usually common in a text.

An essential starting point for many quantitative text analyses is a word frequency list. Even the frequencies of the most common grammatical words in a text can be revealing if they are compared with the most frequent words in general use. The ten most frequent words in the LOB corpus of one million words of written English, and in 'Eveline', in descending frequency, are:

LOB stands for Lancaster-Oslo-Bergen, the universities where the scholars who worked on the construction of the corpus were based. It consists of one million words of British English which were published in 1961.

[1]   LOB: the of and to a in that is was it

[2]   'Eveline':   the her she to had of and he a was

The most frequent word in both corpus and text is *the*. This is only to be expected: it is usual to find that the single word *the* makes up a relatively large percentage of many texts. However, there are pronouns which occur in [2], but not in [1]: *her, she,* and *he*. This shows simply that these three words occur higher in the frequency list for 'Eveline'. The difference in relative frequencies for these pronouns becomes more striking if we compare their frequencies to the most frequent word, *the*. Thus, for example, we can take the frequencies, in the text and in the corpus, of the words *her* and *the*, and calculate one as a percentage of the other. For 'Eveline', we have 96 instances of *her* and 103 of *the*. So *her* occurs 93% as frequently as the commonest word. We can do the same for LOB.

[3]   LOB: her 6%, she 6%, he 13%

[4]   'Eveline':   her 93%, she 81%, he 44%

The story is about a young woman and so it is not surprising that there are many more instances of *her* and *she* in 'Eveline' than in LOB.

However, there is a comparative pattern which is more surprising as we will see in the following. [3] and [4] contain three third-person singular pronoun forms: *her, she, he*. We might wonder whether completing the pattern, by looking at the other third-person masculine singular pronouns, *him/his*, would also be revealing. As percentages of *the*, they are:

[5]   LOB: him/his 13% [he 13%]

[6]   'Eveline':   him/his 19% [he 44%]

In 'Eveline' the relative frequency for *he* (44%) is much greater than *him/his* (19%) as compared with LOB where the frequencies are the same (*he* 13%; *him/his* 13%). Just looking at 'Eveline' itself, there are more instances of the male subject pronoun *he* (45) than *him/his* (18); but there are fewer instances in 'Eveline' of the female subject pronoun *she* (83) than *her* (96). That, in 'Eveline', *she* is less frequent than *her*, but *he* is more frequent than *him/his*, is highly significant in comparison with their equal frequencies in the reference corpus, LOB (*her* 6%, *she* 6%; *he* 13%, *him/his* 13%). What interpretation do we then place on this quantitative evidence? This is a story in which Frank wants Eveline to act, but in the end she cannot act (as he wishes).

Would

So far, I have made simple comparisons between word frequencies in the text and a corpus. It is also possible to compare a text with a reference corpus in order to see which words occur *significantly more frequently* (according to standard statistical tests) in the text than in the corpus. Such words are known as **keywords**. This type of analysis is proposed by Scott (1997b) and it can be carried out using software which he has written (Scott, 1997a).

Using this software, I compared 'Eveline' with a different corpus of around 2.5 million words of written British English, both fiction and non-fiction. The comparison showed the following words to be significantly more frequent in the story. (The probability of error was less than one in a million for all items):

[7]   her, she, had, Frank, Ernest, Ayres, Harry, he, home, Buenos, father, avenue, mother's, used, would

As Scott (1997b, p. 51) points out, such keywords usually 'give a reasonably good clue to what the text is about'. As here, proper nouns will often be frequent in a specific text, but rare in a large corpus (Ernest and Harry are Eveline's brothers.)

One word which has been picked out by the keywords procedure, in [7], is *would*. It occurs 18 times, and in the context of the story, it does indeed seem to be significant. This significance, revealed via comparison with a reference corpus, reinforces 'Eveline' as a story about a young woman thinking about – but in the end failing to act on – hypothetical possibilities for her future. Examples from the text (emphasis added) are:

[8]   Perhaps she *would* never see again those familiar objects ... Frank *would* save her. He *would* give her life, perhaps love, too.

So far we have found through the use of corpus comparison that the pronoun pattern and use of *would* in 'Eveline', which would not be so apparent to the naked eye, are significant. We have though been looking at frequencies of words in the whole text, but not how word selections change *within* the story. In turn, this could provide insight into key narrative boundaries in 'Eveline'.

Key narrative boundaries in 'Eveline'

A powerful method, described by Youmans (1991), is capable of tracking changes in word selections across the text, and can therefore tell us about its overall structure. This in turn can provide insight into key boundaries in a text. This method makes use of the distinction between (word-) **types** and (word-) **tokens**, and of a statistic known as the **type–token ratio**. When we say that a story is 1800 words long, we are referring to word-tokens, but the story will not consist of 1800 different words, since some words will be repeated. When we are talking of the number of different words in a text, we are referring to word-types. So, if the word *home* occurs ten times in the story, then this is ten word-tokens, but only one word-type.

As a text becomes longer, the type–token ratio generally speaking becomes lower. This is because the number of word-tokens continues to rise at a constant rate, but the number of word-types rises more and more slowly, since words tend to get repeated more and more often. If the text was very long indeed, the speaker or writer would eventually run out of new words: everyone's vocabulary is finite. So eventually, there would be no new types, only new tokens. The type–token ratio is, then, a measure of how varied vocabulary is across a text.

As the text gets longer, the probability of new words steadily decreases. The speaker-writer is under two opposing pressures. New words are needed in order to develop and broaden the topic, otherwise the same things are being continually repeated. Old words are needed in order to make the text cohesive, otherwise the text will become impossibly diverse and incomprehensible. There are different limits for lexical and grammatical words, however. As a text gets longer, the number of different lexical word-types gets larger, subject to the constraint of what the text is about, and subject to the ultimate constraint of the size of the author's vocabulary. On the other hand, the number of grammatical word-types is limited and quite small. Although 30 to 40 per cent of words in written texts are likely to be grammatical word-tokens, these will be realizations of a small set of word-types which keep recurring.

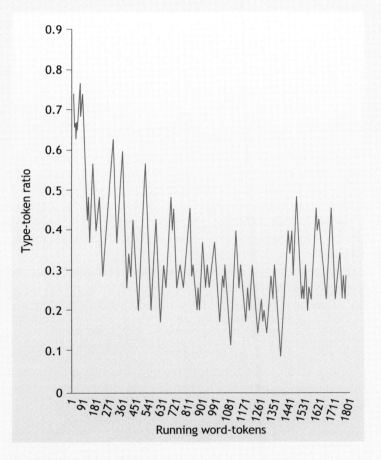

Figure 1   Type–token ratios in 'Eveline' for span 35.

Youmans (1991) has proposed a computational method of text analysis based on these ideas. Usually, the type–token ratio is calculated as a single statistic for whole texts, but Youmans' software calculates the type–token ratio separately for different segments of text. The software identifies points in the text at which words are used for the first time, by sampling the type–token ratio with a moving span of running word-tokens. The moving span proceeds token-by-token through the text: for example, from word 1 to 35, 2 to 36, 3 to 37, and so on. The program keeps track of all word-types in the text so far. For each new span, it checks whether the words in the current span have already occurred earlier in the text (old words), or whether they are occurring here for the first time (new words). The span size can be altered to any value, and a larger span will show broader patterns across a longer text. Within the span, it calculates the ratio of new words to old words.

I will illustrate the power of the technique to identify significant boundaries in 'Eveline'. Output from runs of a similar program to Youmans' on 'Eveline' are shown in Figures 1 and 2, with the span set at 35 and 151 words respectively. The curves start high: at the beginning of the text all words occur for the first time. The smaller span in Figure 1 shows more jagged ups and downs, and, as Youmans (1991, p. 783) points out, it shows quite regular peaks where new vocabulary is introduced every 100 words or so. The larger span in Figure 2 shows more clearly the overall structure: a steady down-slope, with small intervening peaks, until three-quarters of the way through the story, where there is the longest up-slope in the whole curve.

Up-slopes are the points at which new lexis is being used for the first time (Youmans 1991, p. 77). If a prominent up-slope occurs late in the text, then this is likely to signal a major boundary. The new words have, as it were, had the chance to occur during the whole story so far, but they have not occurred till now. Although late in the text, perhaps a burst of new vocabulary is introducing a new turn in the story. I will concentrate on the lowest point in Figure 2 together with what follows: the single most prominent rise in the curve.

A feature of the text which would surely not be missed by any alert reader is that Joyce uses almost identical lexis at two points in the story: in the opening sentences and towards the end, as Eveline's time is 'running out':

[token 1] She sat at the window...Her head was leaned against the window curtains and in her nostrils was the odour of dusty cretonne.

[token 1316] Her time was running out but she continued to sit by the window, leaning her head against the window curtain, inhaling the odour of dusty cretonne.

Up to this point in the story, there has been no external action. Eveline has been sitting at the window, remembering incidents from her childhood and the more recent past with her father and Frank. Now she hears a street organ outside and this reminds her of a street organ playing on the night of her mother's death. The curve starts to rise, as her mother's death scene is described:

[token 1358] Strange that [the street organ] should come that very night to remind her of the promise to her mother, her promise to keep the home together as long as she could. She remembered the last night of her mother's illness; she was again in the close dark room...

The curve continues to rise to high points between tokens 1430 and 1480, the point in the story which describes her mother's final madness and death:

> [token 1431] She remembered her father strutting back into the sickroom saying: 'Damned Italians! Coming over here!' As she mused the pitiful vision of her mother's life laid its spell on the very quick of her being – that life of commonplace sacrifices closing in final craziness. She trembled as she heard again her mother's voice saying constantly with foolish insistence: 'Derevaun Seraun! Derevaun Seraun!'

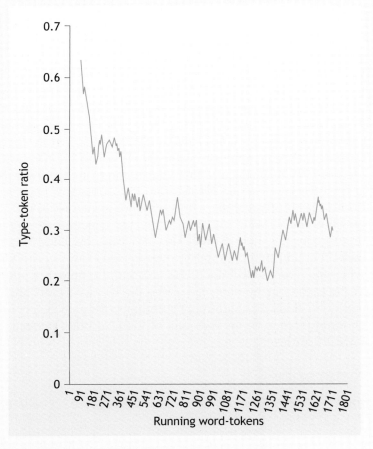

Figure 2   Type–token ratios in 'Eveline' for span 151.

Here the curve is higher than it has been since around token 735. The story has reached a lexical high point. The curve remains high, as the text continues with Eveline's first physical action in the whole story:

> [token 1493] She stood up in a sudden impulse of terror. Escape! She must escape! Frank would save her.

The curve dips slightly, but stays high as she goes to the harbour, and meets Frank. The peak reaches its highest point between tokens 1590 and 1620, where she sees the boat which is to take her to South America, and between 1630 and 1680, where her indecision reaches its climax:

> [token 1594] Through the wide doors of the sheds she caught a glimpse of the black mass of the boat, lying in beside the quay wall, with illumined portholes. She answered nothing. She felt her cheek pale and cold and, out of a maze of distress, she prayed to God to direct her, to show her what was her duty. The boat blew a long mournful whistle into the mist. If she went, tomorrow she would be on the sea with Frank, steaming towards Buenos Ayres. Their passage had been booked. Could she still draw back after all he had done for her? Her distress awoke a nausea in her body and she kept moving her lips in silent fervent prayer.

In a literary critical interpretation, Hart (1969) identifies 'three main parts' in the story: a long first part in which Eveline thinks about the past and possible future; a second 'brief interlude', in which she 'reasserts her decision to choose life'; and a third part which ends in her 'psychological failure'. These three parts correspond astonishingly closely to the troughs and peaks identified by the program. In addition, the evidence from the program can at least partially explain Hart's otherwise subjective impression of a 'general flatness both of vocabulary and sentence-structure' in the first section, which contrasts with 'the almost frenzied conclusion'. The literary critic's impressions are quite correct, but they can now be given an objective textual basis. It is important, though, to distinguish between the formal features which the computer finds in the text and the human reader's interpretation of the text. Only humans can assess the literary significance of what the computer finds. The computer's findings (frequencies, comparisons) are not an interpretation of the meaning of the text, but a presentation of some of its formal features.

References

HART, C. (1969) 'Eveline', in C. HART *James Joyce's 'Dubliners'*, London, Faber and Faber.

SCOTT, M. (1997a) *Wordsmith Tools*, version 2.0 [Computer Software], Oxford, Oxford University Press.

SCOTT, M. (1997b) *Wordsmith Tools Manual*, Oxford, Oxford University Press.

YOUMANS, G. (1991) 'A new tool for discourse analysis: the vocabulary management profile', *Language*, **67**, 4, pp. 763–89.

Source: adapted from STUBBS, M. (2001) *Words and Phrases: Corpus Studies of Lexical Semantics*, Chapter 6, Oxford, Blackwell.

Text and performance

Joan Swann

4.1 Introduction

Chapters 2 and 3 showed how stylistic analysis can be used to address the question of what constitutes literary creativity in poems and narrative fiction. So you looked at how literariness in a poem can involve parallelism and deviation, or how literariness in a short story can involve choices of how to represent characters in terms of their agency or lack of agency. Importantly, these chapters suggested that literariness is not just about the formal properties of a text, but also about the capacity to suggest extra meanings, which can in turn give value to a literary work.

In this chapter, I shall look at texts designed for performance and also at dramatic performance itself. To open the debate over what might constitute literary creativity and literary value in relation to literature in performance, this chapter starts by taking an inherency approach, exploring stylistic features of texts designed for performance. But it then goes beyond this, by taking account of aspects of the context of performance and the performance itself.

Performance does not simply represent a change of mode from writing to speech. Any consideration of literature in performance needs to take account of *how* the text is performed, and this brings into play a range of factors such as manner of delivery, facial expression and body movement, dress, possibly scenery and lighting effects, that work alongside the verbal text and contribute to the meaning and literary value of the performance. There are also long traditions of oral literature that preceded more recent written genres, and contemporary literature may also be spoken in performance rather than represented on the page.

Analyses of text in performance tend to be multimodal, looking at the combination of different verbal and nonverbal elements in the creation of meaning. Such analyses also take account of the role of the audience in any performance event. They represent, therefore, a relatively contextual approach to the study of literature, going beyond the purely verbal text.

The next section discusses the stylistic analysis of dramatic texts and, in this sense, it complements the analysis of poetry and narrative you met in Chapters 2 and 3. Sections 4.3 and 4.4 focus more closely on plays, narrative and poetry in performance.

This is the first of a set of chapters that begins to go beyond verbal texts. Multimodality is considered further in Chapters 6 and 7, and readers and writers of literary texts are considered in Chapter 9.

A note on terms: text, production and performance

In this chapter I shall make a conventional distinction between literary text, **production** (e.g. a particular production of a play) and **performance**. In the case of drama, a production will offer a certain interpretation of a play, but each performance of that production will also differ from others to some extent. 'Text' tends to be found in one of two senses: first, text considered outside of a particular performance. The object of analysis here is usually a play script, or any other written text such as a poem, story, and so on. This may have been written to be performed, or it may have developed out of performance. Second, there is the text as uttered as part of the performance itself, whether or not this is pre-scripted. I shall try to make it clear, on any occasion, which type of text I am referring to. To make things more complicated, analyses of performance sometimes refer to a 'performance text' – performance is seen as a composite text that includes verbal and nonverbal elements.

4.2 The text's the thing

Stylistic analysis of dramatic texts suggests that it is possible to gain a great deal from the analysis of a text outside of any performance of that text. This argument is made explicit in a discussion of dramatic text and performance by the stylistician Mick Short. Short (1998, p. 7) argues that 'sensitive understandings of plays can be arrived at through "mere reading"' and, furthermore, that 'dramatic texts contain very rich indications as to how they should be performed'. It is possible, therefore, to understand how a play works as a piece of literature from close scrutiny of the play script.

ACTIVITY 1   *Fawlty Towers*: the value of 'mere reading'

Allow
10–15 minutes

As an initial illustration of this argument, Short discusses a brief extract from the British TV comedy series *Fawlty Towers*, first broadcast in the 1970s. The series was set in a hotel in Torquay, on the south-west coast of England. The extract comes from the beginning of an episode entitled 'Communication problems'. Basil is Basil Fawlty, the hotel manager, and Sybil his wife who also works in the hotel. Polly is another member of the hotel staff:

*[The hotel lobby. Things are busy; Sybil and Polly are dealing with
guests; Basil is finishing a phone call. He goes into the office.
Mr Mackintosh comes to the reception desk.]*

MACKINTOSH: *[to Polly]* Number seventeen please.
SYBIL: *[to her guest]* Goodbye. Thank you so much. *[He moves off ...]*

(Cleese and Booth, 1998, p. 161)

How much can you infer about the performance of this extract from the
printed text (dialogue plus stage directions)?

Comment

Short argues that, while stage directions are performance instructions to actors
and directors, considerably more can be inferred about the performance than
is given in the stage directions above. This includes features of the setting:
whether or not you are familiar with *Fawlty Towers,* you would for instance be
able to draw on your general knowledge of hotel lobbies to picture a
reception desk with the hotel staff behind it, and with Basil moving into an
office further behind the desk. *Things are busy* suggests there will be guests
moving around, and that Sybil and Polly will be talking to guests at the desk. It
is likely that Mr Mackintosh will have walked from the main entrance to the
desk, since guests habitually leave their keys at the desk when they go out of
the hotel. Short also suggests we can infer something of the characters and
their demeanour – Mr Mackintosh's *please,* suggests that his facial expression
and gestures will also be polite. Written features such as punctuation also
provide clues about how words will be uttered. Giving *Goodbye* a sentence of
its own suggests it will need to be said fairly loudly and with quite a wide
range of pitch movement.

How far do you agree with Short's interpretation? You may have thought
of other performance features – the examples above are by no means
exhaustive. And there are several performance features that cannot be inferred
from this text. It is likely that Sybil and Polly will be dressed smartly, but we
do not know what they are wearing, or much else about their physical
appearance. We cannot predict Sybil's exact tone of voice, which would give
further clues to her character (though we would be able to infer more of this
from reading the whole episode). Short's argument is not that we can
construct all of performance from dramatic text, but that the text permits
some aspects of performance and rules out others, or at least makes them
unlikely. For Short (1998, p. 13) 'the script still has a massive effect in
predisposing production and performance decisions'.

ACTIVITY 2   *Fawlty Towers*: an illustration

Allow
5–10 minutes

Figure 4.1 below is a still from *Fawlty Towers* at the time the dialogue above took place. Spend a few minutes looking at it. How much does it add to your interpretation of the sequence? Bear in mind that this is only a tiny fragment (0.04 seconds): it provides additional visual information, but is not an adequate representation even of this very brief sequence.

Figure 4.1   The Fawlty Towers lobby: Sybil thanks her guest.

It seems to me that, in *Fawlty Towers*, Short has selected quite a strong test of his argument about the value of 'mere reading'. The script of *Fawlty Towers* is freely available, and anyone may choose to perform this. It was written as a television series, however, and has a single widely recognised performance that is also freely available as a recording. It is likely that most people who read the script will be familiar with this performance. It may therefore be harder to separate this kind of script from its (televised) performance than it is to consider independently a play produced for the theatre, and which will have many different performances.

   Short's discussion, however, applies to drama in general. He acknowledges that readers need to know something of theatrical conventions to understand a play text. With this caveat in mind, he lists the following points in support of his argument about the value of studying dramatic text independently of performance:

1   Directors and actors need to read and understand a script before performing it; if an understanding of drama were restricted to performance, the logical consequence of this would be that scripted plays could not be performed.

2   Each production of a play can be seen as the play plus an interpretation of it (in which certain elements are emphasised, etc.).

3   If plays could only be understood in the theatre, it would be problematical to have any discussion of a play except by people who had seen the same production.

4   Different productions of the same play do not necessarily constitute different interpretations – in many cases they are better seen as variations on the same interpretation (i.e. differences are not always as great as may be imagined).

5   There is pressure on modern directors and actors to 'do something different' with plays that have been put on many times before: this can mean texts are treated in a cavalier fashion.

6   There are further problems in restricting analysis/discussion to performance, since each performance of the same production of a play will differ in some respects from other performances. Short prefers to see these as different instantiations of the same production, to emphasise the fact that there is usually a great deal of commonality between performances.

7   Even if you haven't seen or read a play before it is possible, in many respects, to distinguish the contribution of the playwright from the contributions of those involved in the production of the play. An audience can decide: (a) whether the production was a reasonable rendering of the play; (b) whether the play was a good play; (c) whether the theatrical experience was good or not.

8   There are advantages and disadvantages both in reading and watching plays – e.g. in reading a play you can imagine and try out different interpretations; this isn't possible in watching a performed play, but the performance itself (acting, lighting, etc) can provide a more vivid experience of the play.

(Adapted from Short, 1998, pp. 8–9)

How far do you agree with Short's arguments? These seem to apply particularly to pre-scripted plays (where the script precedes performances rather than vice versa). All the points made by Short assume it is possible to distinguish the scripted text of a play from its production and performance, and that study of the text alone is worthwhile and productive. Short also notes that it is possible to make judgements of value separately about plays and their production/performance (you can distinguish a bad production from a good play, or vice versa). His argument suggests that play scripts impose constraints on production and performance, although these may be disregarded – it is possible to have a 'reasonable' rendering of a play, or to treat texts in a 'cavalier' fashion. Faithfulness to the text is not necessarily directly related to the perceived value of a performance, however – for instance, Short gives an example of a production of Shakespeare's *King John* in which the actors pretended to be puppets – clearly 'cavalier' but, for Short (1998, p. 9), still 'an interesting and enjoyable theatrical experience'.

The notion of faithfulness to the text is discussed in Chapter 5 in relation to translation, and further in Chapter 7, with regard to adaptation of literature from one medium to another.

Reading A provides an example of a study that focuses on the analysis of a dramatic text, and will allow you to consider some of these issues further. In this reading, Vimala Herman analyses an extract from John Osborne's play *Look Back in Anger*. It is possible to analyse the poetic literariness of dramatic texts, or the construction of plot in drama; Herman, however, focuses on a more obviously 'dramatic' property of drama – the dialogue. To do this, she borrows from research on spoken interaction – and specifically from **conversation analysis**.

Conversation analysis

Conversation analysis (CA) is a tradition of enquiry concerned with the empirical study of 'naturally occurring' spoken interaction (and not just informal conversation, as the name may imply). CA grew out of ethnomethodology, an area of sociology developed during the 1960s and 1970s, with a primary interest in people's everyday activity. In CA, speech is viewed as a form of activity, and analysts investigate how participants 'get things done' interactionally (e.g. how they open and close conversations, manage the smooth exchange of speaking turns and carry out activities such as giving and accepting or rejecting an invitation). Conversation analysts are interested in the overall structure of conversation, its sequential organisation, and how this is cooperatively managed by participants.

(Adapted from Swann et al., 2004)

ACTIVITY 3   **Turn-taking in *Look Back in Anger* (Reading A)**

Herman's analysis in Reading A looks at how turn-taking is organised between the different characters in Osborne's play. Please now work through the reading, noting the aspects of turn-taking Herman identifies and how she relates these to the characters and their relationships.

- How far do you agree with Herman's interpretations?
- How convincing do you find this analysis of dramatic text?
- How useful do you find this sort of analysis for ascribing literary value to texts ?

Look Back in Anger

The play *Look Back in Anger*, by John Osborne, was first produced by the English Stage Company at the Royal Court Theatre on 8 May 1956 (published 1957). It proved a landmark in the history of the theatre, a focus for reaction against a previous generation and a decisive contribution to the corporate image of the 'Angry Young Man'.

The action takes place in a Midlands town, in the one-room flat of Jimmy and Alison Porter, and centres on their marital conflicts, which appear to arise largely from Jimmy's sense of their social incompatibility: he is a jazz-playing ex-student from a 'white tile' university, she is a colonel's daughter. Jimmy is by turns violent, sentimental, maudlin, self-pitying and sadistic, and has a fine line in rhetoric. The first act opens as Alison stands ironing the clothes of Jimmy and their lodger Cliff. In the second act, Alison's friend Helena attempts to rescue her from her disastrous marriage; Alison departs with her father, and Helena falls into Jimmy's arms. The third act opens with Helena at the ironing board; Alison returns, having lost the baby she was expecting, and she and Jimmy find a manner of reconciliation through humiliation and game-playing fantasy.

(Adapted from Drabble and Stringer, 1996)

Comment

Herman's main point is that turn-taking patterns tell us something about speakers, and therefore about characters in a play – for instance, a speaker who is consistently interrupted and unable to gain the floor may be seen as less powerful than other speakers. Other patterns may indicate ineffectuality, boredom or other attributes.

In *Look Back in Anger*, Herman focuses on four aspects of turn-taking: 'turn-grabs', 'turn allocation', 'turn order', and 'turn size and texture'. The points she makes about these – e.g. how Helena's and Cliff's turn-grabs deflect Jimmy's barbs from their intended victims; how turn allocation, or selecting the next speaker, is used by Jimmy to taunt Alison or Helena; how turn order revolves round Jimmy – seemed to me to be convincing and to provide insights into characterisation and, more generally, how the play text works. I was also interested in the ambiguities pointed out by Herman – for example, how Alison's silence may indicate either vulnerability or resistance. Kieran O'Halloran argued in Chapter 3 that such ambiguities may enrich our encounter with a text and lead us to ascribe literary value to it. To what extent do you agree, with regard to *Look Back in Anger*?

While Herman's analysis is primarily textual, when discussing Alison's silence she introduces elements of performance. On the page, Alison's silence is ambiguous, but this could be portrayed differently in different performances – as relatively passive, allowing others to speak for her; or as withholding a response, which would convey a more powerful position. These possible portrayals still derive from the text, however. For instance Herman notes that a stage direction has Alison carrying out 'stage business' rather than responding to Jimmy's question at Turn 14. This provides a sanction for portraying the silence as a turn lapse (non-compliance), rather than simply not speaking and being protected by Helena's intervention. Other aspects of characterisation – e.g. Jimmy's ambivalent relationship to social class, mentioned by Herman – could be pushed in one direction or another in performance by the adoption of a certain speaking style, tone of voice or accent.

In this section I've focused on what can be gained from carrying out a stylistic analysis of dramatic texts, on a par with the analysis of other literary genres such as poetry (Chapter 2) and narrative fiction (Chapter 3). Such analyses have restricted themselves to textual features but, in the case of dramatic texts, they also give rise to inferences about how the text may be performed. In the next section, I look at actual theatrical performances, and consider approaches to the analysis of texts *in* performance.

4.3 Words on stage

While it is possible to look at dramatic texts independently of performance, plays are intended to be performed, and artistic decisions need to be taken that will affect the literary value of the performance itself. Some of these relate closely to the verbal text of a play (e.g. how words are uttered, as in the case of Jimmy's accent above), but other aspects of staging (characters' actions and activities, costumes, scenery, lighting) affect how a play is received and understood, and will sometimes be more salient than the dialogue.

ACTIVITY 4   **Performing *Look Back in Anger***

Allow about
20 minutes

To start thinking about these issues, consider how you might stage the brief extract from *Look Back in Anger* discussed by Herman. Try out different ways of uttering the words (using different types of intonation, stress, accent, etc). What kinds of costumes, props and scenery might you use? How do you think your creative choices might affect the meaning of the performance?

For those interested in the analysis of theatre or performance art, the text may not be something you prioritise in analysis, but part of the overall performance. The French theatre studies researcher Patrice Pavis (1992), for instance, sees the *mise-en-scène* of a play (its production or staging) as the bringing together of different signifying systems – the text, along with costumes, lighting, and so on. The dramatic text acquires meaning in this context. For Pavis:

> *Mise en scène* tries to provide the dramatic text with a situation that will give meaning to the statements (*énoncés*) of the text. Dramatic dialogue therefore seems to be the product of (stage) utterance and at the same time the text used by the *mise en scène* to envisage a context of utterance in which the text acquires a meaning.
>
> (Pavis, 1992, p. 30)

Pavis is concerned here, like Short, with pre-scripted plays. He sees dramatic dialogue both as the dialogue that is uttered on stage and, in its scripted form, as the text that forms the basis of production. For Pavis, however, this scripted text provides the starting point for a play as a work of art, and the starting point for meanings that may be conveyed. The text only acquires full meaning in performance, after creative input from director, actors, and so on. In Pavis's conception, it would make little sense to consider the literariness of a dramatic text independently of its performance. This suggests also that meanings may change with different *mises-en-scène*; more generally, the interpretation of a play is likely to shift over time and in different social or cultural contexts. The text cannot be regarded as something central and stable that is simply 'translated' in performance. In contrast to Short, therefore, Pavis sees the idea that a production should be faithful to a scripted text as 'pointless', as it is based on the assumption that the text has an ideal and fixed meaning, free from any social, cultural or historical variations. The text and its performance are presented simultaneously on stage, and it makes as little sense to ask whether a production is faithful to the text as to ask whether the text is faithful to its production.

In referring to the signifying systems evident in theatrical productions, Pavis is appealing to a tradition of enquiry known as **semiotics**. Semiotics has been defined, very broadly, as:

Semiotics recurs in Chapter 6 of this book, with regard to the use of word and image in literary texts.

> [...] a science dedicated to the study of production of meaning in society. As such it is equally concerned with the processes of signification and with those of communication, i.e. the means whereby meanings are both generated and exchanged. Its objects are thus at once the different sign-systems and codes at work in society and the actual messages and texts produced thereby.
>
> (Elam, 2002, p. 1)

The most obvious human sign system is verbal language, but people deploy other signs as means of communication (e.g. clothing, architecture, furniture). This is exploited in adverts and other promotional material – for instance, a kitchen brochure I looked through recently informed me that 'A kitchen is a personal statement about who you are and how you live'. Within a semiotic framework these ways of communicating would all be seen as sign systems with culturally specific rules for the selection of particular items (e.g. kitchen units, items of clothing) and their combination (e.g. putting certain types of unit together, wearing a jumper with jeans).

In the everyday choice of items of clothing the communication of meaning may sometimes be incidental or at least not thought about very carefully. Theatrical performances, however, are the result of a whole set of production decisions regarding the choice of costumes, lighting effects, etc. Theatre semioticians such as Keir Elam would see performances as carefully contrived 'performance texts' in which different sign systems work together to create meaning.

Semiotics and structuralism

"Saussure's work, and the terms paradigm and syntagm were introduced in Chapter 2.

In terms of the traditions discussed in Chapters 1 and 2, semiotics has its roots in structuralism, deriving in part from the work of Ferdinand de Saussure. For instance, Saussure's notion of paradigmatic and syntagmatic structures may also be applied to nonverbal sign systems: a T-shirt, jumper and shirt may be part of the same paradigm, selected to form a syntagm with either jeans, trousers or a skirt, together with certain types of footwear. The Prague School structuralists, referred to in Chapter 1, carried out semiotic studies of the theatre, amongst other art forms. More recent theatre semioticians such as Keir Elam retained a focus on the analysis of formal structures in performance – something which has been critiqued by those who prefer a more holistic or contextualised approach.

Semiotic analysis is potentially highly complex. To give one very specific example, Aston and Savona (1991) discuss a framework devised by the Polish semiotician Tadeusz Kowzan, and apply this to an early performance of *Phaedra* by Sarah Bernhardt. Kowzan (1968) had identified the following theatrical sign systems: word, tone, mime (here, facial expression), gesture, movement, make-up, hair style, costume, props, settings, lighting, music and sound effects. Aston and Savona (1991, p. 107) consider only those systems associated with the actor. In each case they identify specific signs and their meaning. In the case of gesture, for instance, arms open signifies a declaration of love, arms clinging signifies pleading, baring of breast signifies a death wish and seizing a sword a death wish intensified. While it is possible to look at specific sign systems at this level of detail it would be unwieldy to attempt to cover all aspects of performance even for a short extract from a play. Elam himself refers to the 'baroque' complexities of traditional semiotic analysis and questions whether such analysis offers a convincing approach to the 'riches of theatrical discourse' (2002, p. 195).

Elam notes that, during the 1980s, semiotics attracted criticism from theatrical professionals – it was seen, for instance, as a 'naming of parts' that was of limited practical value. In academic terms too, there is a danger of reducing theatrical experience to a formal analysis. More recent academic approaches tend to adopt a broader framework that goes beyond formal characteristics of performance. Patrice Pavis, for instance, devised a 'questionnaire' – a checklist for the study of performance (originally published in 1985 but still cited frequently). This identifies features such as 'scenography', lighting system, stage properties, costumes, actors' performances, music and sound effects, pace of performance, text in performance, but also encourages observers to consider the kinds of production choices that have been made, ambiguities in performance and the role of the audience.

An abiding problem in the analysis of performance is that, by its very nature, performance is ephemeral. Checklists such as Pavis's questionnaire allow the description and characterisation of performances 'on the hoof', but this must necessarily be carried out at a rather general level. The existence of recorded performances, however, allows closer scrutiny of how the verbal text works alongside other performance elements. In Reading B Maria Thomas provides such an analysis of extracts from different performances of the same scripted play, Shakespeare's *Richard II*. Thomas herself is not a semiotician but came to the study of performance from a background in literature studies and an interest in Shakespearean theatre. Like Pavis, however, she identifies a range of performance elements that contribute to the meaning and literary value of a play. Her analysis also emphasises the context specific, and changing, nature of nonverbal as well as verbal meaning, and the role of the audience in the performance.

ACTIVITY 5   **Performing Shakespeare (Reading B)**

Please now work through Reading B, by Maria Thomas.

*   As you read, note how the three performances of *Richard II* differ, and what Thomas suggests the effects may be of such differences.

*   How does Thomas' approach to a dramatic text seem to you to differ from the stylistic analysis carried out by Herman in Reading A?

Comment

Thomas suggests that play texts such as *Richard II* are 'open': they may be interpreted in a variety of ways, and 'the same script will work differently in different productions and different performances of the same production'.

This is not just a matter of how the play appears on stage; it is also a matter of audience perception. Thomas points to the 'unthinkable act', when the play was first produced, of a monarch being deposed – and the potentially dangerous act of representing this on stage. Audiences for the more contemporary productions discussed by Thomas would be unlikely to find a monarch's forced abdication unthinkable, though there may be rather different political resonances.

Thomas points to the different ways Richard and Bolingbroke are performed – for example, their costume and physical appearance, stance, movement, how they speak, actions around the crown, in the case of Richard the actor's gender – and suggests these produce rather different characterisations. A still image of Richard from each of the productions is shown in Colour Figure 2. Thomas argues further that looking at performance illustrates the creative richness of the play text and illuminates its potential meanings. The 'open-ness' of the text, demonstrated by its very different renderings in performance, are perhaps key to understanding why this play is widely regarded as having high literary value.

Herman and Thomas are clearly looking at different things: Herman at a scripted verbal text and Thomas at a performance in which a range of other elements combine with the verbal text to create meaning. It seems to me however that their approaches are also underpinned by different conceptions of literary creativity. For Herman, at least in the analysis in Reading A, a considerable degree of meaning resides in the text and literary value can be deduced from this. For Thomas, meaning is not a textual given, but is produced in a particular context and in interaction between actors and audience. This assumes that audience members may bring different interpretations to a performance depending on their cultural and linguistic experience (the shocking act of deposing a monarch in sixteenth-century England). It would also be possible to consider a reading of a play text as an interpretational event – as the interaction between a reader and a text, with the reader bringing cultural experiences, etc. to bear on their interpretations, and perhaps engaging with a virtual performance (imagining a particular staging, 'hearing' certain words spoken). Herman is sometimes cautious in her phrasing, suggesting she is not trying to impose a single, incontrovertible interpretation – her comment that a speaker who is consistently interrupted 'can be interpreted as the less powerful interactant' (my italics) allows for the possibility of alternative interpretations. Her focus, however, is still mainly on the text itself, rather than how this may be read and interpreted by readers in specific contexts.

In order to make her analysis manageable, Thomas concentrates on certain aspects of the extract from *Richard II* – the position of the crown, the relationship between Richard and Bolingbroke, the delivery of parts of the dialogue. This points to a potential difficulty in delimiting performance for the purposes of analysis: what may count as relevant performance features, and what limits can you set on performance? I shall return to this issue towards the end of the chapter.

So far we have seen how perceptions of literariness can depend on the analytical approach taken – whether the perspective is textual or performance-focused. But I have been looking at performance in relation to the western literary tradition. The next section broadens our analysis of performance into African folklore, and Caribbean performance poetry. I continue to explore the issue of literariness in performance, but focus now on oral literary forms which are not necessarily pre-scripted and, as we shall see, may be written down after the performance has taken place.

4.4 Performance in context

Studies of verbal art that are primarily interested in performance tend to attach considerable importance to the context in which performances take place. 'Context' here includes the broad social, historical and cultural context within which performances, or types of performance, are located (in Reading B the different political contexts for sixteenth-century and contemporary, western performances of Shakespeare); as well as the local context of a particular performance event (the dynamic connection between actor and audience in individual staged performances). This section extends the discussion of performance in context, drawing particularly on the anthropologically oriented study of performance that began in the 1960s and 1970s, initially in research on oral literature or folklore in non-European cultures. The reading for this section, by Ruth Finnegan, has its roots in this tradition.

Although there were some exceptions, traditional (pre-1960s) approaches to folklore tended to focus on the collection and analysis of folklore texts. Richard Bauman (1986, p. 2), for instance, comments that, from the emergence of folklore in the eighteenth century, oral literature had been conceived of as 'stuff – collectively shaped, traditional stuff that could wander around the map, fill up collections and archives, reflect culture and so on'. This, however, was to abstract oral literature from the context in which it had originally been performed, leaving 'the thin and partial record of deeply situated human behavior'. Bauman himself, by contrast, was concerned with the 'ethnography of oral performance', where verbal art was analysed as a particular way of speaking within a particular cultural context.

Bauman on performance

I understand performance as a mode of communication, a way of speaking, the essence of which resides in the assumption of responsibility to an audience for a display of communicative skill, highlighting the way in which communication is carried out, above and beyond its referential content. From the point of view of the audience, the act of expression on the part of the performer is thus laid open to evaluation for the way it is done, for the relative skill and effectiveness of the performer's display. It is also offered for the enhancement of experience, through the present appreciation of the intrinsic qualities of the act of expression itself. Performance thus calls forth special attention to and heightened awareness of both the acts of expression and the performer. Viewed in these terms, performance may be understood as the enactment of the poetic function, the essence of spoken artistry.

(Bauman, 1986, p. 3)

Similarly, Dell Hymes (1975, p. 13) speaks of performance as being 'situated in a context, the performance as emergent, as unfolding or arising within that context'. This shift to performance was a radical move which, amongst other things, revalued oral literature significantly. In the case of storytelling, for instance, what had seemed like fairly simple forms (with trite plots and limited characterisation) were revealed as highly complex and creative performances: what was important was the whole performance event, and not simply the verbal text extracted from its context.

Everyday, conversational performance is considered in the companion to this volume, **Maybin and Swann (2006)**.

The approaches developed by Bauman, Hymes and others also extended the boundaries of verbal art. Bauman's definition above would include literary genres such as poetry, story and drama, but also genres not conventionally recognised as literary, such as song, stand-up comedy and even the performance of narratives or jokes in everyday conversation, and all of these may be the subject of contemporary performance studies. In this section however we remain with what are usually considered to be more obviously literary genres, and particularly with narrative and poetry.

Reading C presents an example of the performance-oriented study of verbal art. Ruth Finnegan discusses her own influential research on Limba storytelling in Sierra Leone, then moves on to a consideration of dub poetry as an example of more contemporary performance art.

ACTIVITY 6   **'It's not just the words …' (Reading C)**

As you work through Reading C, note what Finnegan has to say about the 'breakthrough into performance' in anthropology and related fields; the range of elements, verbal and nonverbal, that she sees as contributing to the performances she discusses; and the importance of audience in any performance event. How far are you convinced by Finnegan's argument?

Comment

Finnegan relates her research to the developments in anthropology and folklore mentioned above, where, in the 1960s and 1970s, the focus of attention in the study of storytelling and other forms of verbal art shifted from (transcribed) texts to contextualised performance.

She illustrates these points with examples from her early research on Limba storytelling and more recent performances of dub poetry by the Jamaican–Canadian poet Lillian Allen. In each case Finnegan attempts to convey elements of the performance: how the Limba storyteller, Dauda, constructs a vivid portrayal of the events that make up his story and how he enacts characters, conveying their personality and emotion; similarly, how the literary value of Lillian Allen's work is conveyed in the act of performance. Finnegan identifies several different elements that she sees as contributing to the value of these performances: poetic elements in the verbal text – repetition, rhyme, rhythm, etc.; paralinguistic features – pitch of voice, loudness, groans and sighs; the performer's use of the body in facial expression, gesture, and other body movements.

The role of the audience in performance is further discussed in Chapter 5.

Like Thomas, and fellow anthropologists such as Bauman, Finnegan highlights the importance of audience in performance. The audience is important in several respects. For Bauman, part of the definition of performance is that the performer assumes responsibility to an audience for a display of communicative skill. Thomas made the further point that, during the act of performance, meaning is collaboratively constructed between actor/performer and audience. However, audiences may also have a more direct effect on the nature of the performance. In the examples studied by Finnegan, the text itself is not fixed but developed in performance. The performance may be tailored to a particular audience, and the audience also participates more actively in the performance through calling out and so on – which in turn will affect the follow-up words and actions of the main speaker. Finnegan therefore sees the audience as 'co-creator' of the performance. This highly active involvement would usually be less evident in performances of scripted plays, though audience response would still play a part.

While Finnegan focuses on the analysis of particular performances, she also points to the importance of the wider cultural context in which these performances occur: 'the specificities of historical and ideological setting' such as, for Allen, the political act of using Creole, particularly when representing performed poetry in writing, in a context where standard English is the literary norm.

Finnegan tries to convey the literary quality of performance by describing aspects of the performance event, highlighting features such as Dauda's appearance and activities and Lillian Allen's mode of delivery. Other researchers, such as Elizabeth Fine, have tried to represent more closely, in transcription, the relationship between verbal and nonverbal activity in performance. Figure 4.2 overleaf is an extract from Fine's transcript of an African American story told by James Hutchinson, a student in a class on Black literature. This is the story of Stagolee, an outlaw who engages in several exploits before ending up in hell where he terrorises the devil. The extract comes from a point in the story when Death comes down to earth to collect Stagolee.

conversational— **Death got on his big white horse and <u>rode on</u>**   *mimes riding. lt. hand holds reins in front, rt. hand hits rear of horse, 3 rapid pelvic thrusts*

<u>down to Earth.</u>

[chuckles]

↕ **<u>Well Death got down there about</u>**   *hip/arm stance*

<u>twenty minutes LAter,</u>

Stagolee was still sittin' on the porch

<u>shuckin' some</u>
    hip swing

    <u>BLUES on the GUItar.</u>   *mimes playing guitar*
hip swing   *hip swing*

    <u>Stagolee looked up—</u>   *still holds guitar, disbelieving expression caused by slight head turns—*

crescendo **<u>saw this BI--G old white HO--SS</u>** ⌒   *(- - -)*

crescendo **<u>with this LI--ttle old WHI--TE MA--N</u>** ⌒   *(- - -)*

crescendo **<u>dressed in this LO--NG old WHITE</u>**   *(- - -)*

    <u>SHEE--T</u> ⌒

loud, surprised **<u>Stagolee say, "MA--N, we NEVer had no</u>**

    <u>KLANS in the DAYtime befo'!"</u>   *steps back in surprise, both hands emphasis*

[laughter]

Figure 4.2   Extract from 'Stagolee', performed by James Hutchinson (cited Fine, 1984, p. 190).

Transcription conventions:

Words in left margin describe vocal characteristics.

Words in right margin describe movements that occur with the underlined text.

'Hip/arm stance' means: left hand on hip, right arm across chest (one of two basic positions).

↑ ↑ ↟ ↟	Indicates four degrees of falsetto. / ↑ / is slight; / ↟ / is extreme
~~	Indicates a rasp, or harsh, guttural, grating quality.
ALL CAPS	Indicates words said with greater emphasis or stress.
hyphens between letters in a word	Indicate that the preceding vowel is held longer than usual.
end of line	Indicates a major pause of about three-quarters of a second.
commas, periods, exclamation marks within a line	Indicate a barely perceptible pause.
/ ⁄ / or / ? /	Indicates rising juncture; pitch on last phoneme rises slightly.
(- - -)	Indicates the same movements as the line above.

A C T I V I T Y 7   **Representing performance: 'Stagolee'**

Allow
10–15 minutes

Fine's aim in transcribing the Stagolee story was to provide a full representation of the performance. This would allow a researcher to analyse how Hutchinson achieved his effects through a range of performance devices. The transcript is meant to be complete enough to allow another person to re-create the verbal and nonverbal elements of Hutchinson's style.

- To what extent do you think this is successful?
- Try this out for yourself – do you feel able to re-create a performance from this transcript?

Comment

I find I can make a stab at the voice quality, intonation, loudness, body movements and expression transcribed by Fine, though I'm sure my performance is nowhere near as accomplished as that of Hutchinson! Not everything can be represented – I'm not sure exactly what the hip swing would look like, or the crescendo sound like, and it's not obvious how Hutchinson gets from the hip/arm stance in *Well Death got down there about twenty minutes later* to his subsequent miming of guitar playing. Fine's representation of pronunciation is also restricted to a few stereotyped forms – *sittin'*, *hoss*, etc. The transcription does, however, give a sense of Hutchinson's performance style.

One thing I find interesting in Fine's representation of the performance is that it illustrates how nonverbal elements contribute to the literariness of Hutchinson's narrative: for instance, the lexical and syntactic parallelism in *this big old white hoss*, *this little old white man* and *this long old white sheet* is supported by Hutchinson's stress patterns and by the repeated crescendo. The transcript also indicates how characterisation is achieved partly in Hutchinson's performance, e.g. like Dauda in his Limba stories, Hutchinson takes on the character of Stagolee as he mimes his actions and utters his words.

My own study of a performance by a British storyteller, Jan Blake, also attempted to capture performance elements in transcription, though in rather less detail than Fine (Swann, 2002). I analysed a performance of a Nigerian story entitled 'A Man Amongst Men'. The story concerns a powerful hunter, much respected in his village but also extremely vain. It is about how he gets his come-uppance when he encounters two giants, each much stronger than he is. During the performance, Blake encourages audience participation. Towards the beginning of the story, for instance, the audience features as villagers, ululating to welcome the hunter home. The extract transcribed (Figure 4.3) comes a little later in the performance and illustrates how Blake recounts the story and represents different characters.

	Narrator	Characters	Visual/vocal information
11	... now (.) this hunter was a very vain and boastful man and after he *heard the people singing his praises and after he heard the women ululating he would *<u>uproot young trees and hold them high above his head and he would say</u>		N addresses A; *slight hand movement to side *uprooting gesture; brandishes trees; still in N's voice.
12		**ha ha ha hhh truly I am a man amongst men**	switch to H's voice – his body, face; gaze takes in A; voice louder, speaking rate slower; Blake makes herself taller, stronger movements and gestures; embodiment outlasts spoken words;
13	<u>he would throw the tree down and he would *walk into his house and he would beat his chest</u> and he would say to his wife		looks down, throws tree; *hand moves forward, and as if pushing something to side; beats chest
14		**ha ha ha hhh I am a man amongst men**	switch to H's voice, body
15	his wife would say		
16	[laughter]	**every day it's the same thing you come home you uproot trees you frighten the children you kick the dog you come inside you make your noise *ha ha ha I am a man amongst men**	switch to HW – higher pitch; posture slightly stooped; addressing H but facing A; disparaging tone of voice; *'takes off' H

Figure 4.3   Extract from 'A Man Amongst Men', performed by Jan Blake.

Transcription conventions:

Narrator's voice is in plain text; characters' voices are in **bold**

<u>Underlining</u> = enactment of a character

* indicates a point in the transcript referred to in the visual/vocal column

A = audience; N = narrator; H = hunter; HW = hunter's wife

ACTIVITY 8   Characterisation in 'A Man Amongst Men'

Allow
5–10 minutes

In the extract in Figure 4.3, what impression do you have of the character of the hunter, and how does Jan Blake convey this?

Comment

As narrator, Blake describes the hunter as vain and boastful, and this is also evident in her account of how he displays his power by uprooting young trees and holding them above his head, and in his claim to be 'a man amongst men'. All this is part of the verbal text, but it is emphasised in performance in the way Blake takes on the character of the hunter, representing his actions, inhabiting his body and uttering his words. The hunter's pride is soon undermined by his wife, however. This comes through strongly in Blake's performance: the wife's view of her husband is evident in her mocking and dismissive tone of voice as she recounts his activities and imitates his words. This has an effect on the audience, seen in their laughter, and no doubt changes their perception of the hunter, perhaps preparing the way for his eventual downfall.

In analysing this and other narratives I became interested in the interplay between verbal and nonverbal elements of narrator and character voices, and how this contributed to characterisation: how Blake conveys aspects of the hunter in her narration and also in her enactment of the character; more subtly, how Blake conveys the hunter's wife who, in turn, becomes an ironic re-narrator of the story and, in her embedded narrative, ironically re-enacts the character of her husband. Also of interest is the way distinctions between voices sometimes become blurred: while speaking as narrator, Blake takes on an echo of the visual persona of a character; while speaking as a character she also partly orients towards the audience. Stylistic studies of written narratives have drawn attention to the phenomenon of 'free indirect speech', in which it is not clear whether the narrator, or a character is speaking (e.g. Leech and Short, 1981; Short et al., 1996). This may allow an author to play on the ambiguity between narrator and character perspectives on events. In Blake's story it is always clear, verbally, who is speaking, but nonverbal aspects of performance introduce greater complexity and give Blake the potential simultaneously to represent different (narrator and character) stances. For me, this complex interplay between voices contributes to the literary value of the performance.

If you're able to see a performance in the near future (preferably live – of a play, story or if you prefer an alternative genre such as song or stand-up comedy, or even a TV programme) try to identify different performance elements and see how, together, they contribute to the quality of the performance.

4.5 Conclusion

I began this chapter by looking at the stylistic analysis of scripted dramatic texts. While these are designed for performance, the argument here was that the literariness and literary value of a play may be appreciated by 'mere reading': the analysis of text independently of particular performances. Later sections focused on the analysis of text *in* performance – including pre-scripted dramatic dialogue and oral literature that is created in performance. Performance in this case is not some simple 'add-on' to a verbal literary text, but a range of multimodal dimensions and processes through which certain forms of literature come into being.

I have suggested that the study of performance assumes a contextualised model of literary creativity: perceptions and understandings of particular performances depend on the historical and cultural context in which the performances take place, as well as on the immediate context of performance (the performance space, audience response, etc). Such factors also play a part in the interpretation of written literary texts, of course, but they are harder to ignore in the study of performance.

A problem for analysts is that performance, as an object of analysis, is hard to pin down. Not only do performances change from one occasion to the next, it is not obvious what to count as, or exclude from, performance. The readings for this chapter have tended to focus on aspects most closely associated with the verbal text – a performer's tone of voice, gesture and stance, costume, immediate props such as the crown in *Richard II*. However lighting, scenery, and other aspects of staging may also be important. Even things that are not on stage – the nature of the theatre or other performance space, seating, curtains and other decoration – may affect the perceived quality of a performance.

Performances are also likely to be experienced differently by different audience members. Where you are sitting or standing, or what you happen to look at, will quite literally affect your view of a performance. Differing social, cultural and personal experiences will also give rise to different interpretations. The studies in this chapter suggest that the interaction between different aspects of performance are complex, work together to create meaning and contribute to whether or not a performance is highly valued. Features such as tone of voice and facial expression may, for instance, extend the verbal text, emphasising some aspect of characterisation. They also complement the verbal text, providing additional layers of meaning – for example, about a character's appearance, personality or state of mind. Different performances may offer alternative interpretations, highlighting certain potential meanings and playing down others. This complexity is hard to capture in analysis. Faced with the richness of a performance event, any attempt to analyse this is necessarily partial.

It is possible however to overplay the specificity of contextualised meanings and the diverse interpretations of individual audience members, and in practice analysts do not attempt to capture anything like this degree of variability. Thomas and Finnegan, for instance, do not analyse every single potential meaning difference – they assume some commonality of understanding amongst contemporary readers of their work. To the extent that members of an audience share cultural and linguistic backgrounds, there will be substantial overlaps in meaning.

READING A: Extracts from 'Turn management in drama'

Vimala Herman

The order of speech in dramatic texts is organized to project the order of turns to be taken by the *dramatis personae* and is in the control of the dramatist. [...] The one-speaker-speaks-at-a-time kind of [context] and the turn-management strategies that construct it are the dominant mode of organizing speech in drama. But within this overall mode, the use of turn-lapses, pauses, gaps, interruptions, overlaps, either partial or as full simultaneous speech, also make their appearance. ... Such choices bring significant elements of meaning which can condition the content and function of what is 'said' or meant by a speaker's speech. For instance, where a dramatic character is consistently interrupted and the opportunity to speak is consistently denied to one or other character, and no counter-bid to speak is successful, the interrupted speaker can be interpreted as the less powerful interactant. Similarly, when dual starts are made for a turn, and become a consistent ploy which does not succeed in gaining attention and the floor, or if turn-taking choices by-pass a character's attempts to speak, the path constructed by the use of such options can dramatize or enact the fact of a character's ineffectuality. Consistent turn-lapses on the part of a targeted other who is addressed by a speaker can signal indifference, boredom, hostility, the desire to be left in peace, opting out, etc. and import negative tones into the interaction, even in silence.

In [contexts] of this kind, the event being constructed by speech can colour the situation and interpretation of those who are jointly involved in creating it, turn by turn. The following are all variables in the system: (a) who speaks to whom, (b) who is not spoken to, (c) who listens or doesn't listen, (d) whether listeners are responsive in turn, or not, (e) whether those who respond are those targeted by the speaker or not, (f) length of speeches, (g) linguistic style and texture of a character's speech, (h) how changeovers are effected, (i) the uses of silences, either [within or between turns]. Situation, event and character thus emerge, develop, in the 'here and now' of speech as speech alternation is blocked or progresses in troubled or untroubled fashion.

In the analysis of the extract given below, the variables in the turn-taking system will be identified and the specific patterns and choices of uses will be interpreted for what they contribute to a reader's understanding of the dramatic situation they construct. This is inevitably a partial analysis, since other dimensions, like turn sequencing and pragmatics, and gender, are left out of account. The interest is in the use of the turn-taking system and the turn-management strategies used for what they contribute to the understanding of this extract. The extract itself is taken from John Osborne's *Look Back in Anger*. There are four dramatic characters – Jimmy and Alison are a married couple, whose marriage is in trouble. Cliff and Jimmy are enduring friends, but Cliff is also close to Alison and a confidant of hers. Helena, an actress, and a long-standing friend of Alison's, is visiting the couple. The turns are numbered for reference.

(1) JIMMY: Oh, yes, and I know what I meant to tell you — I wrote a poem while I was at the market yesterday. If you're interested, which you obviously are. *[To Helena]* It should appeal to you, in particular. It's soaked in the theology of Dante, with a good slosh of Eliot as well. It starts off 'There are no dry cleaners in Cambodia!'

(2) CLIFF: What do you call it?

(3) JIMMY: 'The Cess Pool!' Myself being a stone dropped in it, you see –

(4) CLIFF: You should be dropped in it, all right.

(5) HELENA: *[to Jimmy]*. Why do you try so hard to be unpleasant?

[He turns very deliberately, delighted that she should rise to the bait so soon – he's scarcely in his stride yet.]

(6) JIMMY: What's that?

(7) HELENA: Do you have to be so offensive?

(8) JIMMY: You mean now? You think I'm being offensive? You underestimate me. *[Turning to Alison.]* Doesn't she?

(9) HELENA: I think you're a very tiresome young man.

[A slight pause as his delight catches up with him. He roars with laughter.]

(10) JIMMY: Oh dear! Oh dear! My wife's friends! Pass Lady Bracknell the cucumber sandwiches, will you?

[He returns to his meal, but his curiosity about Alison's preparations at the mirror won't be denied any longer. He turns round casually, and speaks to her.]

          Going out?

(11) ALISON: That's right.

(12) JIMMY: On a Sunday evening in this town? Where on earth are you going?

(13) ALISON: *[rising]*. I'm going out with Helena.

(14) JIMMY: That's not a direction – that's an affliction.

[She crosses to the table, and sits down C. He leans forward, and addresses her again.]

          I didn't ask you what was the matter with you. I asked you where you were going.

(15) HELENA: She's going to church.

[He has been prepared for some plot, but he is as genuinely surprised by this as Cliff was a few minutes earlier.]

(16)   JIMMY: You're doing what?
                [Silence.]

                Have you gone out of your mind, or something? *[To Helena]*
                You're determined to win her, aren't you? So it's come to this
                now! How feeble can you get? *[His rage mounting within.]*
                When I think of what I did, what I endured, to get you out —

(17)   ALISON: *[recognising an onslaught on the way, starts to panic]*. Oh
                yes, we all know what you did for me! You rescued me from
                the wicked clutches of my family, and all my friends! I'd still
                be rotting away at home, if you hadn't ridden up on your
                charger and carried me off!

(Osborne, 1965 [1957], Act 1, pp. 50–l)

[Regarding turn-management in this extract], current speaker can select next, to whom turn rights pass; or next speaker can self-select, or the turn may lapse and the original speaker may incorporate the 'lapse' into their own turn as 'pause' and continue with the turn. [...] In the extract all three options are used, but with different frequencies of occurrence, and with variations on how next turns are actually taken. The two most frequent options used are current speaker selecting next and self-selection, but they often clash since the speaker selected by current speaker is not the one who speaks next, since next speaker self-selects against the rights to speak of the previously selected speaker. Jimmy is the 'dominant' character. Eight of the seventeen turns are Jimmy's and Jimmy does most of the selection. In Turn l, Jimmy chooses Helena, but Cliff takes Turn 2. Helena self-selects in Turn 5, changing the focus and direction of the talk away from Cliff to herself. After a brief exchange with Helena, Jimmy chooses Alison in mid-turn in Turn 8. But it is Helena who takes Turn 9. After a brief interchange with Alison, whom he chooses, Jimmy's address to Alison again in Turn 14 is returned by Helena. The self-selections are therefore 'turn-grabs' by unauthorized speakers who interpose themselves between Jimmy and his targets.

Turn-grabs

Turn-grabs can have different functions, since interposing oneself into an interaction uninvited and against the rights of invited speakers can be either self-orientated, to promote one's own interests, or other-orientated. It appears to be the latter here, given that Jimmy selects his targets in order to bait them in one way or another. Thus, the sarcasm directed at Helena in Turn 1, and the potential conflict it can initiate is deflected from developing by Cliff who interjects his own contribution and makes himself Jimmy's interactant rather than Helena for the next two turns. Helena, however, installs herself into the interaction, and takes her delayed turn by self-selection, and, 'rising to the bait', challenges Jimmy. After a brief exchange with her, Jimmy selects Alison, but Alison's turn lapses as Helena interposes herself between Jimmy and Alison, continuing her challenge to him. In Turn 10, Jimmy chooses Alison again, but on a change of topic – as to where she is going. A brief altercation with Alison ensues, but when it gets critical, in Jimmy's insistence to be told *where* she is going, Helena interposes herself in place of Alison again in Turn 15, powerfully sidelining Alison in her use of the third person 'she' in Alison's presence, while taking her turn. Jimmy's Turn 16 addressed to Alison chiefly, gets a collective lapse, and the silence becomes a 'gap' since nobody self-selects to answer him, and Jimmy incorporates the gap into his own turn and continues, choosing first Alison, then Helena, then an aside to himself and then Alison again in the space of one turn, leaving little room for any response. Alison cuts his turn off with an interruption and holds the floor (even though in panic, as the stage directions note) with a long turn, thus inhibiting his access to the floor.

The development of hostility reciprocally is frustrated by the others self-selecting to speak to deflect the barbs. Turn-changes in the responsive dimension are actually effected in such a way as to curtail the dominance awarded to Jimmy in the frequency of turns. Alison is the most protected in this way, usually by Helena. Cliff, too, acts on Helena's behalf, although Helena has her say, nevertheless, even in delayed mode.

Turn allocation

In defiance of canonical expectations built into turn-taking 'rules', Jimmy's turn allocation strategies via participant selection are *not* designed only to pass his turn to another. His choice of addressee is usually politic, since he targets, often midturn, the addressee most likely to be undermined by his taunts – the two women, in particular. The turn allocational strategy used first targets those he names as the butts of his speech and then the passing of turn to them is challenging, confrontational. Thus, in Turn l, Jimmy turns to Helena and selects her by gaze, and addresses the last part of his turn to her, with the sting in the tail specifically aimed at her: 'It should appeal to you, in particular. It's soaked in the theology of Dante, with a good slosh of Eliot as well ...'. Similarly, in Turn 8, having declared to Helena to whom his turn is addressed that she underestimates him, he selects Alison at the end with the challenge for confirmation 'Doesn't she?' In Turn 16, there are swift changes of addressee from Alison to Helena and back to Alison which brackets them, in his perception, as in collusion against him. The content of his turn becomes accusatory and negative. Although all three participants are addressees and part of the interactive 'floor', Cliff is generally omitted from the scope of the address, as the untargeted addressee, and the conflict and antagonism is directed specifically at one or both of the women.

Turn order

Turn order, too, reveals unequal distribution of turns among those present. The seventeen turns that constitute the extract can be subdivided into basically two-party interactions in succession, within the four-party floor. Jimmy is central to all the interactions and the participant structures in force. All present address Jimmy. He is thus the focal point of their speech. This is the 'holding forth' 'one-speaker-speaks-at-a-time' linear development of action which single floors encourage (Edelsky, 1993), which provides space for the turn-holding speaker and individuates its participatory trials and outcomes. Turn order takes up and drops participants, one at a time, in succession. Thus, Turns 1–4 have Jimmy–Cliff–Jimmy–Cliff in interaction. The pattern then changes to Helena–Jimmy until Turn 11, when it passes to Alison. Alison's selected turn at Jimmy's Turn 8 lapses as Helena proceeds. In Turn 10, Jimmy addresses Alison and the turn order takes a different course: Alison (Turn 11)–Jimmy–Alison–Jimmy. Helena takes Alison's Turn 15, and so there is yet another shift – Helena to Jimmy, but the order reverts to Jimmy–Alison. Apart from Jimmy, Helena is awarded most turns and interactive prominence in the turn distribution pattern used. Alison has to wait her turn till the last third of the extract.

Turns to speak for Alison are delayed till Turn 11. Cliff, who takes turns at the beginning of the extract, is then sidelined by the other interactions. There is a difference, however, since nobody speaks for Cliff, whereas Helena does for Alison. Nobody targets him, either, as Alison is targeted by her husband. Active measures undertaken to block the Jimmy–Alison participation marginalize Alison more, even if in her own interests, and make her the most vulnerable character in the episode. But the vulnerability can be ambiguous, and can be portrayed variously. For instance, if another option, provided by the turn-taking system but not included in the stage directions, were to be used by a director, a different interpretation of Alison's demeanour and character could be constructed. And this is dependent on the way silence is used. The above interpretation is built on the assumption that others 'turn-grab' – i.e. turns are returned with the usual split-second timing habitual in conversations. But if Alison were to play her non-responsiveness as a *turn-lapse,* so that she actively *does not answer* when addressed by Jimmy, thus intentionally and ostentatiously ignoring him and his taunts, then her performance would seem more actively resistant, even if she does not take her turn. In fact, she does perform an obvious turn-lapse to Jimmy's Turn 14 when he expresses his opinion of what he thinks of her going out with Helena: 'That's not a direction – that's an affliction.' She does not respond either in comment/comment fashion, or to the implicit demand for information as to where she is going. She indulges in stage business instead, merely crossing to the table and sitting down, which leads Jimmy to repeat his question again. The script and content of her turns does not change, but the change in the distribution of silences at [turn] junctures would make a significant difference to the kind of meaning that is conveyed. But whether

her silences are played passively, as the consequence of others' grabs, or as turn-lapses, actively, the delay of speech turns for her does contribute to the building up of tension within her, which explodes in the final confrontation with Jimmy at the end. [...]

Turn change, on the whole, is smoothly achieved. One speaker speaks, stops, and the next speaker speaks, stops, and so on. There is variation, however, in the two interruptions, both of Jimmy's turn, once by Cliff at the beginning in Turn 3, and again by Alison at the end in Turn 16. These are marked options given the dominant pattern of smooth turn change. But as mentioned above, turn-lapses could be introduced wherever there is a turn-grab, on Helena's part after Jimmy's first address to her, and again, to Alison after Turns 8 and 14. The two dominant participants, Jimmy and Helena, conduct their interactions via smooth turn change. They give each other a full hearing and exchange offences in equal measure, promptly and smoothly. Smooth turn change, paradoxically, does not produce comity, but facilitates an equality between them in the control of the conflict that is enacted between them. Cliff and Alison, on the other hand, interrupt Jimmy and attempt thereby to stem the flow of Jimmy's speech and block his access to the floor. Whereas Helena displays her ability to confront and engage with Jimmy on his terms, and he with hers, neither Cliff nor Alison have the stomach for it.

Turn size and texture

Turn size and texture also vary, but not drastically. Jimmy's turns are occasionally longer, multi-clause turns which he uses to develop or to intensify some personal point to be delivered to his interactant – to Helena in Turn 1 to mock her, or in Turn 16, to Alison, to magnify his feeling of outrage at the thought of her aligning herself with Helena in going to church. His turns can also include many questions, rather than one, or question and comment, and so on, although short, one-clause turns are also evident – to express surprise and disbelief, as in 'You're doing what?' to Alison about the imminent visit to church, or in the pretence of innocence to Helena in Turn 6 'What's that?' in response to her direct expression to him of his unpleasantness. Apart from Alison's Turn 17 at the end, when she matches his outburst with one of her own in equivalent fashion, all the rest are short turns. Helena's turns are all one-clause, the brevity emphasizing the directness of encounter – 'Why do you try so hard to be unpleasant?' or 'Do you have to be so offensive?' or 'I think you are a very tiresome young man', and later, 'She's going to church'.

Alison's turn-lengths vary – short, one clause, evasive answers to begin with but culminating in a long and desperate turn at the end. After her enigmatic silent presence for most of the extract she takes the floor with Jimmy, responding to his questions, but her answers are not satisfactory to Jimmy, who reinitiates his questions till Helena gives him the answer which Alison had withheld. The weapon of silence – *not saying* what he required of her – finds its mark far more effectively than either his spoken taunts or Helena's directness had done. Whereas his interactions with Helena's counter-insults to him were met, as the stage directions state, with 'delight' and roaring laughter, he responds to Alison with mounting 'rage'. In her last turn in this extract, Alison not only emerges into full speakerhood (hers is a turn as long as Jimmy's), but she interrupts Jimmy and reduces him to silence as well. Thus, the tables are turned, with the silent, often passive, long-suffering Alison taking centre stage, and using speech as weapon in active mode, back against Jimmy, whose speech profile has been high throughout the extract. But participatory, counter-speech with Jimmy, for better or for worse, is not her usual mode of interaction with him. Jimmy's excessive, aggressive speech tactics and Alison's silent, non-responsiveness and non-reactions, of the kind dramatized here, are part of their marital relationship, which construct a destructive pathology of speech and silence. Only at the end of the play does turn-taking in interpersonally collaborative fashion occur systematically between them, and speech and counter-speech approximates to the canonical requirement of interpersonality. Cliff uses one-liners, in laconic fashion, and then opts out.

The *linguistic style* is uniform for all of them – 'naturalistic', standard language prose, in informal, conversational idiom. Given that class is an issue – for Jimmy – in performance Alison's accent could well reflect her upper-class status, with the others distributed according to their class affiliations. Jimmy, however, in spite of his work at the market, and declared friendships with others of his origins and contempt for Alison's class, betrays his own 'upward mobility' class split – the literary allusions which pepper his speech to Helena (Dante, Eliot, Wilde) reflect his distance from the class origins he champions. His speech casts him as university-educated middle class, even in rebellion against it. Jimmy is thus a more ambivalent figure than his proclaimed class stances might lead one to believe, entrapped in, and resistant to, his class position. Although, in the 1950s, the play questioned hallowed myths regarding class, empire, etc., the sting in the social ambiguities of class, it would seem, is not easily overcome. Jimmy also has a more complex *speech style* – he can be indirect – targeting the women, while bantering with Cliff; sarcastic, especially to Helena, direct and challenging or expressive of personal outrage, and demanding in his interactions, especially with Alison. Helena is mostly direct in delivering questions, even 'face-threatening' ones, or answers to Jimmy. Alison's speech style is mostly composed of answers, delivered in minimalist mode, to Jimmy, except for the final long and sarcastic counter-turn.

Topic control is generally in Jimmy's hands, and others' turns orientate to his. Helena is the exception, since it is she who initiates the topic of his unpleasantness with which he engages, but the other topics, like his poem, and where Alison is going, are initiated by him. Neither Cliff nor Alison bother to challenge his topics, nor initiate their own. Cliff develops Jimmy's topic of his poem by requesting information about it but then interrupts him with a bantering, half-serious comment of his own. Alison is the minimal respondent when she is allowed to or bothers to answer at all. Thus both attempt either to opt out, or to stop development of the course they suspect is about to come into existence by aborting it with interruption.

Reference

EDELSKY, C. (1993) 'Who's Got the Floor?' in D. TANNEN (ed.) *Gender and Conversational Interaction*, pp. 189–227, New York and Oxford, Oxford University Press.

Source: HERMAN, V. (1998) 'Turn management in drama', in J. CULPEPER, M. SHORT and P. VERDONK (eds) *Exploring the Language of Drama*, **pp. 24–32, London, Routledge.**

READING B: Words on stage

Maria Thomas

What happens to the meaning of written text when it is performed? Words do not go on stage alone, so the answer must lie in part with those other variables besides the text which come into play: physical matters such as casting, gesture, or intonation; technical layers of lighting, costume or other design; contextual aspects such as location, time of day, or cultural expectations. A primary factor in live performance is the perception and reception of the audience. Stage performance happens now, in real time, and it makes a dynamic connection between actor and audience member. Meaning is created before our very eyes and ears, and only with our participation. It has been said that the excitement of watching a live show is in part generated by the possibility of something going wrong: however, it is equally connected with the hope that our expectations will be exceeded: that the audience will witness and participate in something uniquely valuable.

And while the end of that process of creating meaning involves collaboration between actor and audience, it must begin with another collaboration, in the rehearsal room and the technical departments, as a reading of the text on the page is arrived at. The script must be interpreted, intellectually and physically: choices must be made between all the possible ways of understanding these words, and between all the ways of demonstrating that understanding to an audience, in order to arrive at one possible presentation of the text in performance. Over a run of performances that reading may develop further, as the interpretation of the text evolves with a succession of audiences.

My intention here is to provide a comparative study of one particular piece of text, in different theatrical presentations from recent years. Although its first ever performance cannot be reconstructed I will include brief background information to encourage thinking about what might have been important considerations for its first producers. An underlying assumption is that the text is open: that the same script may work differently in different stage productions, and that, within the same production, interest and emphasis will vary to some extent between performances. For this reason the examples discussed below have all been drawn from performances which began in the theatre but were subsequently recorded on film or videotape; thus, the essential impermanence of performance has been captured and may be considered more objectively.

So, let us take an undeniably literary text, William Shakespeare's *Tragedy of King Richard II*, and see what happens to a few lines of script. *Richard II* appears to have been popular from its earliest performances in 1590s' London, during the last years of the reign of Elizabeth I. It is written in the History Play genre, which, along with romantic comedies, provided Shakespeare with his first playwriting success. It is entirely in verse, sometimes rhyming, verse so strong that extracts were appearing in anthologies within five years.[1] Yet this play was not written for the page: plays were published after their initial success on stage, and then usually for financial rather than literary reasons.[2] Elizabethan audiences went to 'hear' a play, a play that they could not have read in advance. Indeed, we can assume that, given the social diversity of playgoers in Elizabethan London, a good proportion of the original audience would not have been able to read at all.

Apart from the strength of the writing, *Richard II* has fascinating political resonances which may have contributed to its success. Although the author avoided censorship by re-telling a story which was two hundred years old, the play is concerned with England's dilemma when God's anointed ruler turns out to be bad for the country. The deposition of a reigning monarch – an unthinkable act – is presented on the stage. A further compelling dynamic is family: all the main characters are related, the sons and the grandsons of a great king, long dead. Richard will be forced to abdicate by his cousin, Henry Bolingbroke, who has the backing of most of the country, but who must go against the strongly held belief that only God can remove an anointed king. The playwright is careful to balance sympathies so that audiences will side both with Bolingbroke and with Richard himself at different points in the story.

In order to perform the play, the actors playing Richard and Bolingbroke need to know which is the hero, who is in the right (perhaps not the same thing). However complex a reading a production aims for, credible characterisation must be arrived at, and a rounded presentation of this very particular world must be achieved. We do not know how Shakespeare's original company trod this tightrope.[3] However, when *Richard II* has been played in our own times, the openness of the script has led to some diverse performances.

Let us consider how a handful of productions from the last couple of decades have staged one pivotal moment when, outmanoeuvred, Richard is called before parliament, and faces Bolingbroke:

RICHARD   [*to an attendant*] Give me the crown.
                     Here, cousin, seize the crown. Here [*to Bolingbroke*] cousin –
                     On this side my hand, on that side thine.
                     Now is this golden crown like a deep well
                     That owes two buckets, filling one another,
                     The emptier ever dancing in the air,
                     The other down, unseen, and full of water.
                     That bucket down and full of tears am I,
                     Drinking my griefs, whilst you mount up on high.

BOLINGBROKE   I thought you had been willing to resign.

RICHARD   My crown I am, but still my griefs are mine.
                     You may my glories and my state depose,
                     But not my griefs. Still am I king of those.

BOLINGBROKE   Part of your cares you give me with your crown.

RICHARD   Your cares set up do not pluck my cares down.
                     My care is loss of care by old care done;
                     Your care is gain of care by new care won.
                     The cares I give, I have, though given away;
                     They 'tend the crown, yet still with me they stay.

BOLINGBROKE   Are you contented to resign the crown?

RICHARD   Ay, no; no, ay; for I must nothing be,
                     Therefore no no, for I resign to thee.

(*Richard II*, IV, i, lines 171–92; Greenblatt, 1997, p. 997)

Our extract is taken from the last minute or two before Richard is compelled to abdicate. The language is dense, evasive, confusing, as if Richard, despite having run out of alternatives, cannot bring himself to do it. His second line, inviting Bolingbroke to 'seize the crown' is both a stage direction and a challenge: will his cousin take the crown, or wait for it to be given? How will Richard give it? The dialogue is played out before the most powerful men in England, and what happens will have national significance. Richard's last speech is ambiguous and difficult, further complicated by the fact that the audience might hear 'I' for 'Ay'. After the extract finishes, Richard's next line will be 'Now mark me how I will undo myself', and he will invent and enact an anti-coronation ceremony, reversing his original crowning and anointing, and investing them in Bolingbroke. So our few lines represent the springboard for the shocking action at the heart of the play where Richard's love of self-dramatisation and the power and ambition of his enemies fatally meet.

In order to make discussion of performance material manageable I will concentrate on some specific areas: what happens to the crown (the central prop at this point, and mentioned seven times in our 21 lines), the relationship between the king and his usurper, and the delivery of some of the more obscure dialogue, dense when written four hundred years ago, which must now be received by a modern audience. While discussing the staging of each version in a general way, my detailed comments will relate to one specific, recorded performance in each case. Although the recording of a play may involve changes to artistic considerations in order to make filming possible, it is necessary to rely on a recording here because the fleeting nuances of live performance make each show, even in a long run, subtly different from all others: to discuss performance we must first pin it down.

In 1986–89 the English Shakespeare Company toured *Richard II* as part of their Wars of the Roses[4] cycle, directed by Michael Bogdanov. In 1989 a performance (essentially an edited recording of the stage production) was filmed for International TV Enterprises Ltd, in which Michael Cronin was a bearded, sober-suited, firm-voiced Henry Bolingbroke, keeping the serious business of Parliament on track. Michael Pennington's King Richard was by contrast a clean-shaven, curly-locked dandy, using his outstanding control of language as a last resort for his sense of himself and his kingship. In reaction to more traditional stagings of *Richard II,* this production avoided ornate, medieval sets or props, using quite a dark, bare stage with a backcloth painted as the flag of St George, red cross on white, which, in this scene, had just a chair and table in front of it to indicate state business being transacted. The action of our extract took place with the two cousins facing one another, crown between them, right in front of this English flag, the other players seated tensely on two sides of the stage.

The emotional focus was on Richard, attempting a last revenge on the plain-speaking Bolingbroke by being so much more clever, so much more at home with courtly language, than the man who is about to eclipse him. As our extract begins, Pennington's Richard narrows his eyes in ironic threat at 'seize the crown', holding out the coronet at eye level, so that when Cronin's Bolingbroke faces him their eyes meet, and remain locked, across that symbol of kingship. Richard holds the crown both close to his face, as if his by right, and high enough up to seem to be offering it – daring Bolingbroke to lay hands on it.[5] However, his cousin keeps his hands behind his back, maintains eye contact, and stands firm.

The metaphorical speech about well and buckets is spoken with defiance, and some sense of triumph that Richard, having lost all else, will at least continue to be king of his griefs. Bolingbroke replies with firm practicality and an unwavering gaze – a crushing response. Pennington/Richard now uses the shift of the text into rhyming verse to speed up his delivery. By 'The cares I give, I have ...' his meaning is much trickier to follow. They are facing one another still, and this almost sneering Richard derives a minor victory from dazzling his cousin with words – all he has left. But Bolingbroke is unmoved, and, aware of the public gravity of the situation, he asks with formal simplicity 'Are you contented to resign the crown?'

Finally Richard abandons the stand-off. Straightening his posture, bringing the crown to his heart and breaking the eye contact at last, he considers, then responds formally with 'Ay'. But he cannot bear this resignation, so clasping the crown with both hands he turns away from Bolingbroke and half-groans 'no, no', before turning back once more to his public role and saying with a forced smile 'Ay', still keeping both hands on the crown. The final lines, beginning with 'For I must nothing be' are an attempt to recover the initiative with more quibbling words, speeding his delivery up again to gather energy for the great scene of self-deposition he must immediately play, when he will at last formally give up the symbols of his authority.

A striking feature of this staging is the way that, with so few onstage distractions, the crown is invested with as much significance as possible: golden in the darkness, it draws our eyes. It cannot simply be handed over, despite Richard having been called to appear before his nobles for this precise purpose.[6] And the identification of the crown with Richard, as Michael Pennington keeps it in his hands and close to his body throughout, is a powerful visual signal to the audience that Richard, for all his faults, is the true king. Significantly, Bolingbroke resists the invitation to 'seize' the crown: the king must give it, so that no blame may be attached to Richard's enemies.

In this production neither Richard nor Bolingbroke was depicted entirely sympathetically. Bolingbroke had the weight of history on his side, but did not woo the audience; Richard was charismatic and intelligent, but also vindictive, narcissistic, and doomed.

Apart from the question of audience sympathy, the matter of Richard's effeminacy is regularly on the agenda when preparing *Richard II* for the stage. Deborah Warner's Royal National Theatre production of 1995 at the Cottesloe studio handled this neatly by casting a woman, Fiona Shaw, in the part. Shaw thus followed in a tradition of major actresses occasionally taking leading male Shakespearean roles.[7] The overall orientation of the production, perhaps arising from a more traditionally female paradigm, was to heighten the family drama, and to downplay the state politics. Particularly striking throughout was the suggestion of a bond between Richard and Bolingbroke, which accounted for Bolingbroke's indulgence of Richard in our chosen scene. The closeness of this bond at times produced tears from both actors. The production was re-staged for a 1995 BBC Performance broadcast, and my description is taken from this recording.

The set is suffused with a dim but golden candlelight, recalling perhaps the Wilton Diptych,[8] and Richard is dressed in white clothes, just grubby enough to suggest what he might have been through since giving himself up to his enemies. He appears exhausted. Bolingbroke, played by Richard Bremmer, stands isolated in the middle of the room, nobles and churchmen seated in pews on each side, with the throne dimly discerned at the back. Bolingbroke is dressed in dark clothes, and supports himself with a stick.

He keeps quite still for most of this scene, looking rather dazed by what is happening. Richard moves to, from, and around his hollow-eyed cousin.

Richard remains assertive in defeat. 'Here cousin', he says lightly, going to face Bolingbroke. He puts the crown on the floor at Bolingbroke's feet before sitting down among the other lords, saying 'seize the crown' with an exaggerated picking-up gesture on 'seize'. Bolingbroke will not do it. Going to stand face to face again, Richard continues cajolingly 'Here, cousin', his hands making movements from a children's grabbing game, inviting Bolingbroke to pick up the crown before Richard can retrieve it. Bolingbroke's face registers both pain at a childhood memory and weariness at Richard's insistence on playing at a time like this. 'On this side my hand, and on that side thine' is an instruction, and Richard repeats the playtime gestures. This proves irresistible: they reach down together quickly, their hands take the crown up simultaneously, and it is held between them.

Richard is now steering the scene: still as if playing a game, he leads his cousin. They revolve slowly as the crown becomes a well and the two holding it are the buckets: Richard speaks mesmerisingly, almost chanting as he takes back the crown, raising it as if about to crown his cousin, at 'mount up on high', before replacing it at Bolingbroke's feet. Bolingbroke's delivery reflects the way he has been de-centred: 'I thought you had been willing to resign' is said with a note of surprise and uncertainty. 'Part of your cares you give me with your crown' is offered as a comfort, but is received with anger as its hidden purpose – to regain control of events – is discerned. Shaw, as Richard, maintains the upper hand, slowing down her delivery to point up the meanings about lost and gained care in her next speech: even if Richard hands his crown over, the cares of the realm will never be divorced from the rightful king. Stung, Bolingbroke asks with more force 'Are you contented to resign the crown?' – the crown that remains between them on the floor.

Richard, standing still, nodding, as if having been told to pull himself together, must respond with 'Ay' – it is what he has come there to do. But then he turns away from Bolingbroke and the audience, moving to the back of the stage with a howl of 'no, no I', bent double and beating his chest with his fist at each word of 'I must nothing be', then forcing himself into a formal, singsong tone for the final weary line of resignation, delivered standing up straight, facing his peers, in front of the empty throne, where he will sit for his self-deposition one last time.

So this production gave us a more appealing Richard by foregrounding a childhood relationship with his cousin-usurper. It is also a version that took care to work with the nuances of the text, making speeches which were used to obscure and dazzle in the English Shakespeare Company production described above, explicit and full of loss. The move into rhymed verse, in this Royal National Theatre production, rather than being a cue for speed, invited complex thoughts to be explored more slowly, because the rhyme and regular metre could be trusted to keep the audience's attention focused on the words as they were spoken. The overriding impression was of a family grief, rather than a political coup.

While grief was still palpable in the Elizabethan staging of the play at the reconstructed Globe Theatre in 2003, it was handled rather differently. Mark Rylance, in white satin sixteenth-century costume, used Richard's star status and characteristic playfulness, combined with an intimate relationship with the audience,[9] to produce a scene where sympathetic laughter helped Richard face up to the inherent tragedy. The BBC 4 live outside broadcast on 7 September 2003 is the basis of the following description, and it should be noted that this open-ended recording is the closest of our examples to the original theatrical experience, in that the production was not re-shaped or edited for television.

The Globe's large thrust stage brings actors and audience very close together. Because of the resulting trust in the audience's complicity, the Globe actors allowed pauses for laughter to underscore the fact that Richard's emotional reluctance to abdicate, and the difficulty the nobles will have if he does not, is a source of great embarrassment and annoyance. Looking at the whole deposition scene on the page, Richard's speeches are long and poetic, and those of his enemies very short and awkwardly expedient. Between the lines, they would like him to get this awful business over with, but he refuses to throw away a moment of it – because of the importance of what is to be done, or because he cannot resist making or playing a scene – and this dynamic opens up opportunities for stage business that increase delay and, thereby, the tension: will he or won't he?

So when this Richard commands 'Give me the crown' it must be brought. Rylance, as Richard, registers the muddle with 'O', raising a laugh, which gives him time to make for the previously empty throne, settling into it with comic hesitancy and relish, twinkling conspiratorial glances at the audience. The crown arrives, borne on a cushion by a servant. 'Here, cousin, seize the crown', delivered from the throne to a tense, black-clad Bolingbroke, is immediately received as a joke in poor taste, bringing more laughter. Richard descends mock-apologetically to face Bolingbroke, repeating 'here, cousin' with encouragement. Taking up the crown, Richard holds it out, inviting Bolingbroke to join him before the throne. Bolingbroke expects to receive the crown and puts his hand on it, but Richard keeps holding on to his side. He makes his speech about crown, well and buckets a courtly amusement to cover the sorrow evident in his eyes, the sorrow which stops him from letting go. Bolingbroke, also still holding on to the crown, must wait. So 'I thought you had been willing to resign' is impatient, and to emphasise this impatience, cuts are made to the text, which speed up the scene:

BOLINGBROKE	I thought you had been willing to resign.
RICHARD	My crown I am, but still my griefs are mine.
BOLINGBROKE	Part of your cares you give me with your crown.
RICHARD	Your cares set up do not pluck my cares down.
BOLINGBROKE	Are you contented to resign the crown?

This stichomythic exchange builds the pace, bringing out Richard's underlying seriousness along with Bolingbroke's barely concealed irritation. The rhyme words (resign/mine; crown/down) are given added stress. The crown is still held between the two men when Richard must finally answer his cousin's question. As he says 'Ay', Bolingbroke pulls the crown towards himself. Richard tugs it back: 'No!' There is a pause as the audience laughs. Recovering, Richard speaks the rest of his lines with maddening smoothness, taking the crown away from Bolingbroke and moving up to the throne, where he will at last 'undo' himself. Bolingbroke's taut body language speaks of utter frustration, and his ally Northumberland moves swiftly between them, as if to prevent Bolingbroke laying angry hands on his cousin.

So in this Globe production the focus was less on the relationship between Richard and Bolingbroke, and more on the star and his audience. Critics have long regarded Shakespeare's Richard II as an actor-king, with his need to make beautiful speeches and manipulate moments of pageantry.[10] Liam Brennan, as Bolingbroke at the Globe, was in this scene not Richard's level-headed nemesis, nor his dearest relative, but very much the unwilling foil for a star performer.

At this point in the play, Richard has a captive audience of men uncertain whether it is even possible for a reigning king to resign, yet all, except a few cowed into silence, determined that it must happen. For Richard it will be the end of everything; it is insupportable. Ultimately, what helped Rylance's Richard to engineer his own downfall was the irresistibility of playing a scene nobody had ever played before, a scene guaranteed to be attended to with the greatest degree of tension and anticipation. He needed the audience to help him to do the unthinkable – all his teasing and delay designed to keep them with him in extremis.

While there is some common ground in these performances – for example, Richard's centrality, his playfulness, his need to delay the inevitable – we are given divergent interpretations of character and relationship: a political struggle between a plain man and a dazzling dandy; a heartrending scene in which one cousin must break another for state reasons; a showcase for the king of the stage. In examining these interpretations my contention is that the playing of texts on stage is perhaps the ideal way of investigating their richness, both in terms of their original purpose as performed scripts, and ultimately, in illuminating the range of meanings they might contain.

Notes

1   Six passages from *Richard II* appear in *England's Parnassus*, printed in 1600.

2   Many of the scene divisions, stage directions, not to mention the punctuation, in modern versions of Elizabethan and Jacobean plays are the result of four hundred years of editing, and there can be marked variation between contemporary editions of the same play. For all plays in this discussion I will be using Greenblatt, S. et al. (eds) (1997) *The Norton Shakespeare* text, based on the *Oxford* text (1986, 1988).

3 For a discussion of the original staging of Richard II, see Andrew Gurr's introduction to the New Cambridge Shakespeare edition: *King Richard II* (2003) ed. A. Gurr, Cambridge, Cambridge University Press.

4 The Wars of the Roses refers to the period of dynastic conflict which followed Richard II's deposition, covered by Shakespeare in a series of history plays about the reigns of Henry IV, Henry V, Henry VI and Richard III. The wars finally end with the defeat of Richard III by Elizabeth I's grandfather, Henry Tudor, at the battle of Bosworth Field.

5 In *The English Shakespeare Company: The Story of 'the Wars of the Roses'*, Bogdanov reflects on how much stage business was cut for the recording, describing Pennington as playing 'with Bolingbroke as a cat with a mouse. The crown was dangled like a carrot, it was held high, gently offered, snatched away... delaying the moment as long as possible. And the language to match. I wanted to keep it all, but time was to pare this sequence down to a spare minimum' (Bogdanov, M. and Pennington, M. (1990) London, Nick Hern Books).

6 *Richard II*, IV, i., lines 153–71.

7 For example, Sarah Bernhardt at London's Adelphi Theatre as Hamlet in 1899; Asta Nielsen in the same role on screen in 1920; Vanessa Redgrave as Prospero in *The Tempest* at the Globe in 2000.

8 The Wilton Diptych, on view in London at the National Gallery, was painted for Richard II and shows him kneeling with saints and angels, on a heavily gilded background.

9 In his introduction to the programme for the 2003 Globe season, Mark Rylance writes to his audience, 'It is the presence of your intelligent, humorous, and generous imagination in the Globe which inspires our creation.'

10 The very first scene of the play is a good example of this stage manipulation.

Source: commissioned for this volume.

READING C: It's not just the words ... : the arts and action of performance

Ruth Finnegan

> Hey! Attention you. Everyone come and listen. ... I'm Dauda, the son of Fanneh Konteh of Kamabai. I've come. Well now, a story for you oh! *Listen*, won't you! ...

The blind narrator's voice rang out through a West African village, a prelude to his story, while the audience gathered to join in the performance.

How should we understand such tales? One method has been to transcribe, translate and print them, conceptualising and analysing them essentially as written texts. Here I illustrate a different approach, one that foregrounds performance and context. Developed particularly by anthropologists and folklorists this sees meaning as actualised not just in entextualised words but in performances through a range of communicative channels, participants, settings, and events.

Tale of a snuff-taker in Sierra Leone

To explain this let me first return to the African story. Dauda's narration was one of many tales being told by Limba-speaking narrators in northern Sierra Leone in the 1960s[1]. As with any literary form the stories revolved around favourite themes – winning a wife, competitions, the antics of fools – or presented stock figures with new twists, like the obstinate young girl, powerful chief, or bombastic trickster spider. Some tellers were admired for their imaginative plots, characterisation and artful delivery but even by the less skilled each telling was new, original in its detailed wording, delivery, occasion, and audience.

Dauda was notable for his clever plots and performance skills. He would intersperse his narrations with asides like 'and I was there too, peeping at them' – striking indeed since everyone present knew he was blind. This time it was to be an uproarious tale about a ludicrous snuff addict and the audience was already agog for an entrancing and engaging occasion.

Dauda gets into his narrative in typical Limba style, his voice rising in pitch, volume and rapidity to convey his hero's absurdly extreme personality:

> Well then, a human once came out on earth. He was called Daba. *Daba*. **Daba**. He was a great great **great** taker of snuff, the **greatest taker of snuff on the earth**. ...

He shows Daba going round the local chiefs asking for snuff, causing great merriment as he irreverently conveys the chiefs' characters through voice and mien. Dauda enacts their dialogues as Daba scornfully rejects the housefuls(!) of snuff he's offered. The events and characterisation are vividly portrayed through Dauda's speed, repetitions, abrupt shouts or stops, intonation, exaggeration, gestures and facial expression, his voice and body dramatising the action whilst also slyly satirising the Limba formalities of greeting and begging. The audience is part of it all, co-creators of the performance, with exclamations, anticipation, laughter, repetition. They join lustily in a repeated song, half-dancing, leading up to the laughter-provoking sound of Daba's nostril sniffing up the snuff.

Finally Daba over-reaches himself – 'I stood behind and heard him' says Dauda – takes a huge sniff, and to the laughter of all falls down dead.

In print the plot looks simple, even stupid – apparent evidence, for those with such expectations, of the 'crudeness' of African tales. And yet – this was one of the liveliest narrations I encountered, subtle as well as hilarious. Why?

The answer of course lay in its performance. It was actualised in Dauda's creative marshalling of sound, sight and movement to exploit the genre's conventions, the sonic nuances, reduplications, mimicry, characterisation, gesture, direct speech, working of the audience, songs, atmosphere, and the bodily involvements of the participants, both teller and co-performing audience. What looks trite on the printed page was profound, allusive, and full of both sharply observed individuality and universal drama on the performed occasion.

Enclosing this multidimensional and multi-participant performance within the narrow one-voiced medium of writing is a kind of translation (an even more radical one perhaps than the more obvious linguistic translation from Limba into English). As with other attempts to capture the magic of live performance in the cage of linear print these transformations suppress so much of the art – one reason why collections of oral narratives, whether from Africa or elsewhere, often convey such a thin, even demeaning, impression of these rich genres. The univocal linear text – the element captured on the written page and the focus of many approaches to literature – can convey, at best, only one of its multiple dimensions.

The reason I started from this (non-English) example is that it illustrates so directly the kind of analysis that, like some others, I was first tussling with in the 1960s. It was part of what has been called the 'breakthrough into performance' that was then emerging, a radical break with earlier traditions in folklore and related disciplines where researchers had so often focused on *text*: transcriptions and translations as the base for studying content, structure or origins. Since then 'performance' approaches have been extending in various forms across a wide range of disciplines. Amidst many variants and newer developments, the basic thrust is still to draw attention to precisely the kinds of features illustrated in Limba storytelling: the performance as a communicative event in time, its multiple participants and their role (audience as well as lead speaker), its setting, the multiple channels it exploits, and the problematic processes by which such performance events have been transmuted into written text. It is a perspective which, starting largely through the study of non-western performances, has been extended to apply to analyses of events throughout the world, not least in English.[2]

Lillian Allen's dub poetry

The second example is very different in social and historical setting, participants, and generic conventions – dub poetry by the contemporary Jamaican–Canadian poet Lillian Allen. Start with her 'Birth Poem':

> An mi labour an mi labour an mi labour
> An mi labour an mi labour an mi labour:
> An mi bawl Whai
> An mi push an mi push an mi push
> An mi push an mi push an mi push
> AN MI PUSH
> An baps she born
> An it nice yu see
> an she sweet yu see
> This little girl mi call Anta
>
> (Extract, as printed in Habekost, 1993, p. 206)

The text doesn't seem to amount to much: a woman recalling being in labour, yelling 'whai', pushing, then *baps* her daughter is born, isn't she sweet. But so much is created in performance. It starts with a rhythmic musical beat, setting the scene then running through the whole, and a gentle chorus about 'this little girl mi call Anta'. Then comes the poet's voice portraying the length and suffering and intensity of the labour, words mingling with – formed through – groans, sighs, shouts, repetitions, crescendos … . As one admirer describes:

> Allen's breathtaking performance of 'Birth Poem' never fails to mesmerize her audiences. It is obvious what this piece means to its author. Pushing herself and her baby poetically towards birth, Allen shows what an accomplished performer she is: her face distorts in pain, her gestures provide staccato punctuation as she rants a fast, rolling wave-like rhythm culminating in the onomatopoeic 'baps.' [Then] … the poet relaxes into smiles, and, in a happy melodious Jamaican voice, celebrates her baby.
>
> (Habekost, 1993, p. 206)

Then back to the chorus, 'this little girl mi call Anta'. It is emphatically not just words-as-written but the intense, forceful, vehement, repeated and repeated and repeated 'an mi labour and mi labour and mi labour' as the meaning grows beyond the birth of one small baby into the labour and strength of the women whose cause Allen's poetry promotes and celebrates.

'Dub' poetry is rooted in the popular musical culture of Jamaica, presented in Creole and developing as a performance genre from the 1970s, initially linked to disc jockeys' 'dubbing' words in over recorded reggae rhythms: *riddim*, the Creole spelling, has strong associations with black identity, struggle, and resistance. Performance is paramount but dub poets sometimes also publish their poetry. It also came to be broadcast and

You met 'dub' in the work of Asian Dub Foundation, discussed in Alistair Pennycook's Reading D in Chapter 1.

performed in more commercial multicultural settings through audio, video and film to changing (and sometimes disapproving) audiences, disseminated not just in Jamaica but overseas, including the UK.[3]

Lillian Allen, Jamaican-born but now settled in Canada and renowned for her distinctive black feminist voice, exploits the fertile resources of this dub tradition in her own style. Her quasi-intoning delivery and caressed Creole pronunciations are intertwined with non-verbal voiced sounds, with interjections, cadences, mimicry and vocal startlements. She exploits gesture, facial expression and body language, deploying seen and heard movement and mood, with a pervading musical frame as drum and bass rhythms reverberate through the bodies of the participants.

In her powerful 'Riddim An' Hardtimes' for example the poetic impact comes though the beat, her embodied presence, and her creative use of pacing, silence and sound, not least her memorable swoop up of 'hardtimes' and, in performance, the echoic dying-away of the repeated 'hard, hard, hard, hard ...'.

> An' him chucks on some riddim
>   an' yu hear him say
>   riddim an' hardtimes
>   riddim an' hardtimes
>
> music a prance
> dance inna head
> drumbeat a roll
> hot like lead
>
> [...]
>
> drum beat drum beat
> pulse beat
> heart beat
> riddim an' hardtimes
> riddim an' hardtimes
>
> riddim an' hard
>   hard
>   hard
>
> (Allen, 1993, pp. 63–4 [extracts])

'Nellie belly swelly' is more verbally extended:

> Nellie was thirteen
> don't care 'bout no fellow
> growing in the garden
> among the wild flowers

she Mumma she dig & she plant
nurtures her sod
tends her rose bush
in the garden pod

lust leap the garden fence
pluck the rose bud
bruk it ina the stem

oh no please no
was no self defence
oh no please no
without pretence
offered no defence
to a little little girl
called Nellie

Nellie couldn't understand
Mr Thompson's hood
so harsh, so wrong
in such an offensive

Nellie plead, Nellie beg
Nellie plead, Nellie beg
but Mr. Thompson's hood
went right through her legs

knowing eyes blamed her

Nellie disappeared from sight
news spread wide
as the months went by
psst psst psst Nellie belly swelly
Nellie belly swelly Nellie belly swelly
children skipped to Nellie's shame

Nellie returned from the night
gave up her dolls
and the rose bush died
Nellie Momma cried Nellie Momma cried
little Nellie no more child again

No sentence was passed
on this menancing ass
who plundered Nellie's childhood

In her little tiny heart
Nellie understood war

She mustered an army within her
strengthened her defence
and mined the garden fence

No band made a roll
skies didn't part
for this new dawn
infact, nothing heralded it
when this feminist was born

(Allen, 1993, pp. 25–7)

This could certainly be approached as a poetic text primarily existent in its printed words. But it was created for and in performance. Its meaning also lies in its music, audience reactions, Nellie's begging, the (non-printed) repetitions, the unverbalised gossiping scorn over Nellie's condition, the beautiful Creole sounds with evocations far beyond the words-as-written, and the repeated and repeated chanting of the children's gleefully mocking 'Nellie belly swelly, Nellie belly swelly…'. The poem exists in all these, not just in writing.

Allen has also published recordings and printed versions of her poems. Unlike the African examples above these are not transformations by outsiders; but the process is not unproblematic either. As she prefaces her collection *Women Do This Every Day* (1993):

Because words don't (always) need pages, I have published extensively in the form of readings, performances and recordings. I have been reluctant to commit my poetry to the page over the years because, for the most part, these poems are not meant to lay still.

As I prepared poems for this collection, I was required to 'finalize' pieces I had never imagined as final. Like a jazz musician with the word as her instrument, reading and performing these poems is an extension of the creative and creation process for the work. In some ways, I had to reverse this process to 'finalize' these poems for print; finding their written essence; pages do need words.

(Allen, 1993, Preface)

Such publications also need to be set in the Jamaican context where 'standard' English had long been the 'proper' form, with Creole denigrated or ignored. In this struggle over language, publishing poetry in Creole was a political not just a literary act. Not that Caribbean writers have used Creole-indicative spellings in particularly systematic ways, nor do such spellings always appear throughout a poem even when its performance is unmistakably Creole. What they do however is provide hints of Creole speech and, equally important, symbolise and assert the rights of the 'non-standard' – an eye token, visually displayed, of the oral powers and traditions of Jamaican speech, 'making concrete a resistance to exclusion' (Casas, 1998, p. 7). Allen's evocation of Creole speech in 'Riddim An' Hardtimes' is 'a defiant gesture … [invoking] the sound of Caribbean Creole in the diaspora in the 1990s' (Casas, 1998, p. 19). Like other dub poets Allen cleverly uses spellings, creative typographical formats and crafted layout to visually signal and play on the emotive relations between orality and 'scriptism', Creole speech and 'standard' writing, 'high' and 'low', 'vulgar' and 'respectable'.

In one sense, her text now exists in its own right, with all its visual play and multimodal resonances, insisting on its right to appear in printed format, Creole-oral intermixtures and all. So yes, it *is* the words too and for Allen these are one important element – her performances are of *poems*. But they are complemented by the performed arts of both live delivery and broadcast or recorded presentations. And anyone with experience of her stunning performances would surely find it impossible to approach the printed text of, say, 'Riddim An' Hardtimes' without echoic resonances interwoven with the aural and visual overtones of spellings and printed format: the performance *in* the text.

Here again to take the text alone – however authoritatively verbalised on the printed page – would be to miss the many performance dimensions. Only by widening our focus to include performance can we fully appreciate the significance of occasion, context, the specificities of historical and ideological setting, the participants, the mode of delivery with its multimodal (not just verbal) channels and, once again, that problematic relation between textualisation and performance.

Going further

The examples so far have been from contexts which may be relatively unfamiliar to many readers. But let me correct any impression that this kind of approach applies only to cases with (in some way) African or non-western roots. It is true that scrutinising certain Limba or Jamaican genres can help to bring out the significance of performance. But it could equally have been other examples, and a performance perspective can illuminate genres ranging from the highest of high culture to the most familiar of everyday entertainment and experience.

Take for example the performances of joke tellers, after-dinner speakers, or stand-up comedians. Looking to the verbal text alone would miss much of the fun. A degree of improvisation and variability – of emergence *in* performance – is sometimes the expectation here, a pattern well-known throughout the world. Sometimes a script exists too, whether written down or in the head, and performance events sometimes go along with relatively stable and fixed written texts too: think of poetry readings, political oratory, sermons, reading aloud to children, poems performed on the web. Each genre and occasion may well have its own expected delivery conventions with varying deployment of, for example, facial and gestural expressions and movements, vocal effects both verbal and non-verbal, specific setting and appropriate deportment, costume and timing.

Or consider the many examples of sung art. Lyrics – poems-set-to-music – are a common format for the art of English, even if often conceptualised as essentially just their written words. Here too, as in previous examples, verbal language is indeed one dimension – but *not* necessarily the only or even the most salient one. You will certainly have some familiarity with some such forms – the songs of manifold kinds that throng the airways, ring through churches or precede sports encounters. Indeed English is nowadays perhaps even more widely known throughout the world in the framework of song than in its formulation on printed page, part of high art as well as popular display. From Elizabethan madrigals, Shakespeare's lyrics, George Herbert's hymns or the choruses and arias of Handel's *Messiah* to calypsos, nursery rhymes, Bruce Springsteen's lyrics, or the latest pop idol's songs, their reality does not just lie in entextualised words. It also exists in a range of multimodal dimensions such as (depending on genre and context) musical enactment, instrumentation, participants, chorus-leader interactions, visual components, and/or expression through dance, rhythm and bodily dynamic. These are often integral rather than peripheral to their existence.

The significance of these performance dimensions does not necessarily depend on how a particular formulation first originated. We do not always know the origins of particular lyric forms for example. In some cases, it seems, the words may in some sense have come first, in others the music; sometimes the two together. But however they arose we can still take account of their performance features, not excluding cases where the verbal texts are more or less fixed rather than variable. The words of the British national anthem, 'Jerusalem', 'Amazing grace', 'Hark the herald angels sing', 'Abide with me', or 'Auld Lang Syne' may indeed have started off – and continue – as crystallised written texts; but for vast numbers of people it is their musical, sung and sometimes somatic enactments that ring through memory and experience. To fail to take account of this would be to give the thinnest of impressions of their mode of existence – their ontology.

Every enactment of these or other performed genres is unique. Each performance has its own features, both expected and specific to the occasion: its mix of communicative channels; its particular place and timing; its participants with their own perspectives and perhaps struggles among themselves; the detailed performance arrangements, music, singing, colour – all the elements that enter into one given event. At the same time other enactments may colour the occasion. 'Performance, even in its dazzling physical immediacy, drifts between present and past, presence and absence, consciousness and memory', Elin Diamond writes, and 'embeds features of previous performances' (1996, p. 1). For those acquainted with these or other well-known songs it would be hard to participate in any rendering, even to read their words, without creatively entexturing the experience with a host of multimodal resonances.

This leads to one final point. Given the dominant role of written text in our western educational practices, it is scarcely surprising that when we are faced with any verbal text – printed book, manuscript note, transcript from performance – we too readily prioritise its *textual writable* qualities: these, it seems, are what defines it, the mode in which it exists. The perspective indicated here suggests that this sometimes needs querying. To approach a

Beatles lyric, oft-sung carol or Lillian Allen poem as essentially existent in verbalised textual form might be to appreciate one dimension but at the same time to miss much of their reality and richness.

It is useful to bear this possibility in mind for other texts too. When we read a poem the auditory resonances may be a real part of our experience – resonances which we have only too often been trained to suppress as if merely peripheral to the 'hard text'. So too with multimodal memories of experienced performances which can sometimes drench the text for us as we read, whether from Shakespeare play, audio read-aloud novel, dub poem, or childhood lullaby – all are part of their existence for us. Indeed performance of a kind is in a sense involved in any act of reading: the 'en-performancing' of text in the 'now' when the reader personally experiences and (re-)creates it, intershot as this is with evocations *beyond* the immediate moment. Even an unfamiliar text can call up personal or shared echoes from a multiplicity of situations and experiences, while for poetry we regularly create its sonic presence not just attend to its visual layout: the performance *in* the text. We may screen these multimodal dimensions out of our consciousness – but they are there in our lived experience.

To conclude

Though the details will differ, parallel approaches can be taken to other genres too, performed or performable, read or heard, past or present – including, no doubt, many that you may be more directly familiar with than the examples here. Each can be illuminated by taking account of the kinds of features illustrated in this discussion. In analysing some particular performance event and/or text and/or genre it can be useful to consider features such as the following [see boxed table overleaf] (the list is selective rather than comprehensive, and not all will apply in any given case).

(continues overleaf)

Some features of texts in performance: a selective checklist[4]

Setting	Time? place? cultural and historical specificity?
Participants	Performer(s): who? how many? if several how interacting?
	Others: who? taking what role? how far co-creating? relation/interaction/overlap/ contests between audience and performer(s)?
Mode of delivery	Spoken, sung, unison, instrumental, recorded, broadcast?
What channels?	Acoustic: use of voice, non-verbal sounds, music?
	Visual: stance, facial expression, gesture, movement, dance, bodily appearance, spatial patterning?
	Tactile: touching between performers? or audience? bodily presence? somatic interaction?
	Olfactory (if relevant).
	Material: accoutrements, costume, props?
Organisation and dynamics	'Framing' devices, changes during performance, temporal development?
Degree of textual/verbal crystallisation or stability	Generic conventions in relation to improvisation, textual repetition, representation in written medium (or not)?
Overtones/ echoes from previous performances or experiences	Sonic, multimodal?

'Performance' is not some simple opposite or 'add-on' to text but a range of multimodal dimensions and processes through which verbal art exists. Our grasp of the ontology and meaning of the many diverse genres which represent the art of English can be enriched by exploring their performance dimensions: among them the immediate or imagined settings; participants; diverse multimodal actualities and resonances; the situations and ideologies (perhaps contested or multiply interpreted); and the generic conventions creatively marshalled in both unique and recurrent ways.

Does all this sound too multidimensional to grasp? But, whether we consciously notice it or not, it is something people are in one way or another engaged in every day as they practise and experience the rich arts of English.

Notes

1   Recorded during anthropological fieldwork in the 1960s (see Finnegan 1967, 2002, esp. pp. 226ff).

2   This set of approaches was enunciated in anthropology and folklore (Hymes, 1975, 1977; Bauman, 1977, 1992; Bauman and Sherzer, 1989), but has since developed in transdisciplinary directions through linguistic and literary anthropology and performance studies more generally (Bauman and Briggs, 1990; Duranti, 1997), also to some extent in postcolonial writing and new approaches to literacy (Cooper, 1995; Cope and Kalantzis, 2000).

3   For more on dub poetry see Brown, 1987; Cooper and Devonish, 1995, Glaser and Pausch, 1994, Habekost, 1993, Morris, 1999.

4   For further elaboration, see Finnegan, 1992, pp. 94 ff. and Finnegan, 2002.

References

ALLEN, L. (1993) *Women Do This Every Day: Selected Poems of Lillian Allen*, Toronto, Women's Press.

BAUMAN, R. (1977) *Verbal Art as Performance*, Rowley MA., Newbury House.

BAUMAN, R. (1992) 'Performance', in R. BAUMAN (ed.) (1992) *Folklore, Cultural Performances, and Popular Entertainment*, New York, Oxford University Press.

BAUMAN, R. and BRIGGS, C.L. (1990) 'Poetics and performance as critical perspectives on language and social life', *Annual Review of Anthropology*, **19**, pp. 59–88.

BAUMAN, R. and SHERZER, J. (eds) (1989) *Explorations in the Ethnography of Speaking*, 2nd edn, London, Cambridge University Press.

BROWN, S. (1987) 'Dub poetry: selling out', *Poetry Wales*, **22**, pp. 51–4.

CASAS, M. DE LA CARIDAD (1998) 'Orality and literacy in a postcolonial world', *Social Semiotics*, **8**, pp. 5–24.

CASAS, M. DE LA CARIDAD (2002) 'Multimodality in the poetry of Lillian Allen and Dionne Brand: a social semiotic approach', doctoral thesis, Institute of Education, University of London.

COOPER, C. (1995) *Noises in the Blood. Orality, Gender, and the 'Vulgar' Body of Jamaican Popular Culture*, Durham, Duke University Press.

COOPER, C. and DEVONISH, H. (1995) 'A tale of two states: language, lit/orature and the two Jamaicas', in S. BROWN (ed.) *The Pressures of the Text: Orality, Texts and the Telling of Tales*, Birmingham: Birmingham University African Studies Series 4.

COPE, B. and KALANTZIS, M. (2000) (eds) *Multiliteracies*, London, Routledge.

DIAMOND, E. (ed.) (1996) *Performance and Cultural Politics*, London, Routledge.

DURANTI, A. (1997) *Linguistic Anthropology*, Cambridge, Cambridge University Press.

FINNEGAN, R. (1967) *Limba Stories and Story-Telling*, Oxford, Clarendon Press.

FINNEGAN, R. (1992) *Oral Traditions and the Verbal Arts*, London, Routledge.

FINNEGAN, R. (2002) *Communicating. The Multiple Modes of Human Interconnection*, London, Routledge.

GLASER, M. and PAUSCH, M. (eds) (1994) *Caribbean Writers: Between Orality and Writing*, Amsterdam-Atlanta GA., Rodopi.

HABEKOST, C. (1993) *Verbal Riddim. The Politics and Aesthetics of African-Caribbean Dub Poetry*, Amsterdam-Atlanta GA., Rodopi.

HYMES, D. (1975) 'Breakthrough into performance', in D. BEN-AMOS and K.S. GOLDSTEIN (eds) *Folklore: Performance and Communication*, The Hague, Mouton.

HYMES, D. (1977) *Foundations in Sociolinguistics: An Ethnographic Approach*, London, Tavistock.

MORRIS, M. (1999) *'Is English We Speaking' and Other Essays'*, Kingston, Randle.

Source: commissioned for this volume.

The art of translation

Anna Magyar

5.1 Introduction

> Such is our Pride, our Folly, or our Fate,
> That few but such as cannot write, Translate.

(Denham, cited in Steiner, 1975, p. 63)

The quotation above was written by Sir John Denham (1615–1659) as part of a poem addressed to Sir Richard Fanshawe, another English poet of the same period. It is often quoted in studies about translation. Lamenting the lack of good translators, Denham goes on to extol the virtues of a translation by Fanshawe.

ACTIVITY 1 **Preserving the flame**

Allow about
5 minutes

For the first activity, please read the longer extract from this poem (below). Then consider how Denham sees the role of a translator of poetry.

> That servile path thou nobly dost decline
> Of tracing word by word, and line by line
> Those are the labour'd births of slavish brains,
> Not the effect of Poetry, but pains;
> Cheap vulgar arts, whose narrowness affords
> No flight for thoughts, but poorly sticks at words.
> A new and nobler way thou dost pursue
> To make Translations and Translators too.
> They but preserve the Ashes, thou the Flame,
> True to his sense, but truer to his fame.

(Denham, cited in Steiner, 1975, pp. 63–4)

Comment

Denham sees the proper aim of translation as respecting both the 'fame' of the original author, and what was valuable in the original literary work.

His poem provokes a number of questions about what constitutes a good translation, and about the relationship between the original text and the translation. A central metaphor he uses is the contrast between the ashes and the flame of a literary work. A bad translation, his poem suggests, mechanically preserves the ashes.

This chapter will explore these issues, considering what perspectives the translation of literary texts from and into English can offer on creativity, and examining where and how different kinds of creativity can be located in the translation of literary texts. In Chapter 4, Reading B (by Maria Thomas) you looked at different productions of the same play, Shakespeare's *Richard II*. Here I will explore what happens to literature when it is translated, rather than adapted or interpreted within the same language. (For the purposes of this book I have assumed only knowledge of English.) I will start by giving a brief background to the practice of translation, and consider the role of creativity in original and translated texts, largely from an inherency perspective. I then move on to look at sociocultural issues around translation and creativity, including sociocultural aspects which can be considered 'ideological'. Finally, I consider how translation can be viewed as a participatory activity, and I look at texts where the reader (or audience in the case of the plays presented in the final reading) is instrumental in helping to create the text as it is read and/or performed.

5.2 Translating words, translating meanings

Translation is the realising of meanings and effects in one language that correspond in some way to the meanings and effects realised in another.

(Pope, 2002, p. 247)

Although translation as a defined field of academic inquiry is relatively young, it has been a central part of literary life within Anglo/European literary traditions, certainly since Roman times (Roman writers such as Cicero and Horace translated extensively). Translation goes back much further in time for languages such as Sanskrit, Persian and Arabic. Indeed, literary texts have always been translated or adapted, reworked and refashioned into other literary texts – often by authors and poets, already writers of their own creative texts. So, the British poet Ted Hughes' *Tales from Ovid*, for example, is based on a collection of Greek myths adapted by the Roman writer Ovid. *Pyramus and Thisbe*, the play within a play in Shakespeare's *A Midsummer Night's Dream*, is in fact the title of one of Ovid's retellings. Some sacred texts too, such as the Bible (whether one considers it 'literary' or not), are good examples of culturally valued texts that are translated many times over, and which exist in different versions within the same language, too.

The focus in this section is primarily textual, in that it explores linguistic aspects of translation from the **source text** (the original) and the **target text** (the translation into the new language). Two key terms used when comparing a target text with a source text are **fidelity** and **equivalence**. Fidelity is a value judgement used when discussing translations, and literary adaptations or performances: it has to do with our perceptions of 'faithfulness' to the original. The concept of equivalence is used in discussions of what the equivalent cultural concept, or the equivalent proverb, might be in another language. Unlike fidelity, equivalence does not involve a value judgement. However, both fidelity and equivalence are problematic notions. When a text is translated, it can be argued that it becomes a different text, so judgements about its fidelity to the original could be countered with the argument that we are not comparing like with like. Literary texts especially are often translated across cultures (as well as languages), and perhaps across historical periods too. Equivalence, too, has come under fire – recent work in translation studies has challenged the notion that there can be such a thing as 'equivalence'. A single word expressing a concept in one language may require a whole phrase to make it meaningful in another; even within a single language, there is rarely such a thing as a pure synonym:

> [...] a dictionary of so-called synonyms may give *perfect* as a synonym for *ideal* or *vehicle* as a synonym for *conveyance* but in neither case can there be said to be complete equivalence, since each unit contains within itself a set of non-transferable associations and connotations.
>
> (Bassnett, 2002, p. 22)

Moreover, translating idiomatic expressions or metaphors into other languages frequently involves finding a word or phrase that *functions* in an equivalent way, rather than being the linguistic 'equivalent' of the original. Bassnett (2002, p. 31) gives the example from Italian of the phrase *Giovanni sta menando il can per l'aia*. This translates literally in English as *John is leading his dog around the threshing floor* – the correct idiomatic equivalent is *John is beating around the bush*.

Translation has not always been viewed in the most positive light by readers familiar with, and affectionate towards, literature in the source language. Translations have been disparaged as imitations, a favoured metaphor casting the translator as a painter copying an 'original'. The recipient of Denham's poem, Fanshawe, wrote that a translation can only ever be at best 'a mock-Rainbow in the clouds, faintly imitating the true one' (Steiner, 1975, p. 19). In Fanshawe's view, loss is inevitable: 'this famous Dramatick Poem must have lost much of the life and quickness by being powred out of one vessell [...] into another' (Steiner, 1975, p. 19). Yet in some cases, translations can come to be valued as more aesthetically pleasing than the originals.

As well as being a respected translator himself, the English poet John Dryden (1631–1700) wrote more extensively about translation than any of his contemporaries, such that other translators tended to defer to his views.

The notion of fidelity (or faithfulness to an original text) also arises in Chapters 4 and 7 of this book, in relation to literary adaptation.

He drew up a set of 'rules' or guidelines for the translator of poetry. In his view, a good translator should:

1   Be a poet.

2   Be a master of both the language of the original and his own.

3   Understand the characteristics that individuate his author.

4   Conform his genius to that of the original.

5   Keep the sense 'sacred and inviolable' and be literal where gracefulness can be maintained.

6   Make his author appear as 'charming' as possible without violating his real character.

7   Be attentive to the verse qualities of both the original and the English poem.

8   Make the author speak the contemporary English he would have spoken.

9   Do not improve the original.

10 Do not follow it so closely that the spirit is lost.

(Cited in Hammond and Hopkins, 1995–2005, pp. 388–9)

In Dryden's view, then, to translate a poem, one must be a poet. The translator has a particular responsibility towards the author of the source text. The author is assumed to have created something of value: a particular charm and character that the text embodies and that the translator must somehow preserve.

The next activity begins to explore some questions in relation to creativity at the level of the text, and identify some features of the language of literary texts relevant to translation. To do this I consider the limitations of translation done by computer, in order to throw some light on what is creative about human translation. In particular, I want to raise the issue of whether a literary translation *is* mere imitation, and whether that precludes it being seen as creative; what kinds of losses might occur in the translation of creative texts; and what resources might be required in order to create a successful literary translation.

ACTIVITY 2   Machine versus human translation

Allow about 20 minutes

The following pairs of extracts are all translations of literary texts; but, in each case, one version was generated by typing the source text into a translation software program on the internet, while the other is translated by a person. Looking at each pair:

- decide which version was translated by machine;

- identify some characteristics of the texts that helped you decide.

Text 1a

Young lovers beginning
begin a new season,
fill streets with unreason,
ride around, spinning,

bright sparks on paving
like fires in the autumn:
young lovers behaving
like mares in their season.

I don't know if they're sinning
against Time, or erring:
but under Love's spurring
they're horses – and winning
young lovers beginning.

Text 1b

Young people in love new
In the springtide,
By the streets, without reason,
Pheasant the jumps overlap.

And make over the cobbles fire, like coal:
Young people in love new In the springtide.
I know not if their labours they employment well or not;
But spades of the hope Are as much as their horses,
Young people in love new

Text 2a

We were being studied, when the Headmaster entered, follow-up again
equipped as middle-class man and of a boy with class which portrait a
large desk. Those which slept awoke, and each one rose, as surprised in
its work.

Text 2b

We were in study hall when the headmaster walked in, followed by a
new boy not wearing a school uniform, and by a janitor carrying a large
desk. Those who were sleeping awoke, and we all stood up as though
interrupting our work.

Text 3a

Let us test I tested as I had seen in the court of the butcher the cows the
oxen the sheep lengthened in the court of the same butcher the small
calves.

Text 3b

Let's try I was trying like I'd seen in the butcher's yard the cows the cattle the sheep stretched out in the butcher's yard even the little calves

Comment

You probably found it easy to identify the texts generated by the translation software – 1b, 2a and 3a – but you may have found it more difficult to explain why.

Text 1 ('Jeunes amoureux nouveaulx' from *Poésies* by Charles d'Orléans.)

It is likely that you saw immediately that Text 1a (translated by Gavin Ewart, cited in Holmes, 1988, pp. 39–40) has a grammatical and semantic coherence lacking in Text 1b. Some words, such as *pheasant*, are entirely inappropriate lexically; in this case the machine has probably taken the verb form *faisans* from the original and read it as *faisan* which means *pheasant*. Other words are grammatically inappropriate such as the noun *employment* where the line requires a verb. The French verb *emploient* in the original poem actually means *they use*; the software used to generate Text 1b did not recognise the third-person plural of the verb. Some of the words in the original poem are no longer used by French speakers, or have changed in their spelling so that the contemporary dictionary used by the computer simply does not recognise them. The machine translator was unable to choose the appropriate lexical item.

Text 2 (From *Madame Bovary* by Gustave Flaubert, quoted in Raffel, 1994, p. 49).

In this case the human translation is Text 2b (by Lowell Bair, cited in Raffel, 1994, p. 49). You may have found Text 2 the easiest pair from which to identify the human and machine translations. This may be to do with the particular characteristics of prose as opposed to poetry. In poetry, we are more accustomed to deviation from the syntax of language (you will remember Mukařovský's notion of deviation from the standard, in Chapter 2). Therefore, if words or phrases seem unusual or surprising, we may think that it is intentional, for creative effect. In other words, as suggested in Chapter 1, our recognition of the text-type we are dealing with motivates the way that we approach the text. We are more likely to expect prose to conform to basic grammatical rules of English.

Neither does Text 2a comply with our lexico-grammatical expectations. Even where individual lexical items are used correctly and are recognisably English, the overall meaning often breaks down, as in *follow-up again equipped as middle class man*. The machine cannot recognise the different parts of speech and so uses nouns, for example *portrait*, when the phrase in fact requires a verb. A human being, even one who did not understand the exact meaning of the French *portant*, would know from the rest of the sentence that the word carried a verbal meaning.

Text 3 (From *Enfantillages* by Raymond Cousse).

Text 3b was translated by Singleton (cited in Findlay, 2000, p. 38). You may have found the Text 3 versions hardest to compare. This is because neither version complies with our lexico-grammatical expectations. *Butcher's yard* is less unexpected than *The court of the butcher* but then from a Formalist point of view, prototypical poetic language (as you have seen in previous chapters) revels in presenting us with unexpected juxtapositions and metaphors. It may be that the writer wanted to juxtapose *the court*, with its connotations of wealth and royalty, with the place where animals are killed. Each version presents us with a string of associated lexical items. *Trying* seems to make more sense than *tested*. The colloquial abbreviations, *I'd seen* and *Let's*, which evoke spoken rather than written English, seem more appropriate than *I had seen* and *Let us*. Because the text violates rules, you may have adjusted your expectations about how easily it would make sense.

To summarise, the machine translations are clumsy and 'over-literal'. In all three extracts, there are examples of deviations which are clearly not intentional but due to the fact that the computer, translating at word level, has been unable to interpret the function of the word within the phrase or overall meaning of the text. Much gets lost, especially perhaps the skilful way in which indirect meanings have been achieved by the writer. Translation requires a creative interpretation which relies on far more than knowledge of the language system. The machine translations appear to be somewhat similar to creative texts in that they (inevitably) break language rules and violate expectations. However, they do so without creative intent – intent which helps us, as readers, to recognise the creative choices made and thereby value a 'creative' text. A machine is unable to make creative choices.

Dryden noted that the authority of the author is important in a work of literature. No one would be concerned whether a translated brochure or advertisement was being faithful to its author. Creators of such texts are not, in the 'western' tradition of the canon, seen as relevant in the way that the author of a literary text might be. A literary text is seen as an expressive communication of a particular author. While it is true that the author's exact intentions – the meaning of the text – are difficult to pin down (especially if the author is dead or writing in a very different time and place to our own), this does not permit an 'anything goes' attitude to the nature of the source text. When the literary text is part of the canon, the communicative and aesthetic intentions of the author are likely to be held in high esteem and there may be strong feelings about translations that are seen to betray those intentions in some way.

Reading A provides an example of a 'literary canon' approach to literary translation. Here the translator Burton Raffel compares five published translations of *Madame Bovary,* the French author Gustave Flaubert's novel written in the nineteenth century. The plot involves Emma, a young woman who lives with her father in rural France. She is courted by and marries a young doctor, Charles Bovary. The novel follows her through disappointments, affairs, debts and, eventually, suicide.

ACTIVITY 3   Lexical choices in translation

Allow about 20 minutes

First, turn to Reading A and read the first two sets of translations from the source texts. The first set (1a–e) is on pp. 220–1, the second set (2a–e) on pp. 223–4.

- How did you respond to the two sets of extracts?

- What governs your preference?

- Are there particular words used which sound better than others?

Comment

You may have had difficulties understanding certain words like 'mufti'. 'The sleepers' in the version by May sounded awkward to me, as did 'school servant'. 'Prep-room' is associated with English public schools – perhaps this felt quaint or dated. Perhaps you found one version more 'literary' than another.

The second passage is about a young man in love. Raffel argues that the best translation is the one by Steegmuller, as it best recreates the lilting, dreamy state associated with being in love. In the next activity Raffel outlines the reasons for his preference.

ACTIVITY 4   Being faithful to syntax (Reading A)

In Reading A, Raffel criticises translators who, in his view, too often approach prose translation as a semantic exercise, a search for equivalence of meaning 'in its narrowest verbal sense – pretty much word-by-word' (Raffel, 1994, p. x). He argues that the aspect of prose too often overlooked is the way that words are combined – its syntax.

Read through the whole of Reading A, 'Famous and infamous translations', by Raffel. How do you respond to Raffel's argument about syntactical tracking?

Comment

Raffel's approach is an inherency one, tightly focused on the need to be faithful to the syntactical patterns of Flaubert's original prose. This may work where source and target languages and cultures are relatively close. It is questionable whether this evaluative criterion, presented by Raffel as a universal one, could be applied to translation between languages and cultures (English and Chinese, or English and Japanese, for example) which are very far apart.

Alongside this, Raffel gives consideration to the lexical choices made by the five translators, and the degree to which they succeed in translating the culturally specific connotations of the words used in the source text. It is worth remembering here that Raffel is speaking from a particular personal position. As was argued in Chapter 1, it is in the nature of our relationship with literary texts that their meaning changes subtly as our perspective and moral and aesthetic concerns change.

To be successful, a translation of a literary text has somehow to meet our expectations of literary texts. I have looked, in this section, at some of the textual elements of translation such as lexis and syntax. In the next section we broaden out from the text itself, moving on to consider sociocultural aspects of literature in translation. This opens up the question of the extent to which a translator translates the language (words), or must also engage with social, historical and cultural meanings. Translated texts are often seen by readers familiar with the source text as evidence of loss or betrayal, as inferior copies of a prioritized original (Bassnett, 2002, p. 7), an attitude which hints at the fact that there is more to translation than the elements focused on by Raffel.

5.3 From text to culture

In the previous section I introduced two key terms in translation, fidelity and equivalence, in relation to the text. This section looks at some of the creative possibilities open to translators. Of course, to enter into a debate about fidelity and equivalence, ideally we need access to both source and target text, which cannot be provided here. Instead, I will explore these terms further through looking at different translations of the same source text.

ACTIVITY 5   **The historical and cultural location of poems**

Allow about 20 minutes

This activity builds on Activity 2, which asked you to compare translations by humans and by machines. Here you are asked to compare different translations of the same poem, although the original source (in French) is not provided. It is the poem used in Text 1 in Activity 2, 'Jeunes amoureux nouveaulx', by Charles d'Orléans.

You will notice that there are differences in the language used in Texts 1–3 (overleaf). To help you compare them more systematically, focus on the sociocultural features, such as those relating to the time in which the poem is set – the 'world out there' of the poem. You may also like to think about contemporary possibilities for this poem.

Text 1

Lusty yonge bacheleres,
In the Spring sesoun,
Ryden the streets sans resoun,
Making to-lepen hir coursers.

And strykken al-over
Fyr fro everich stoon:
Lusty yonge bacheleres
In the Spring sesoun.

I noot nat yif hir labours
Been to gode or il chosen;
But prikke of spore felen
Even as doon hir coursers,
Lusty yonge bacheleres.

Text 2

Hot young lovers, season-sick,
Burning with the year's advance
Roam the restless streets of France;
As their stallions wheel and kick

The flinty cobbles sharp and quick
The sparks fly like a fiery lance.
Hot young lovers, season-sick,
Burning with the year's advance.

God knows what makes the youngsters tick
Or even if they like the dance ...
The spur's what makes the stallion prance:
They too are governed by the prick.
Hot young lovers, season-sick.

Text 3

Young rockers with a bird in tow,
Now the long evenings are here,
Revving their engines, changing gear,
Up and down the streets they go.

They do a ton-up, just for show
Along a stretch not far from here:
Young rockers with a bird in tow,
Now the long evenings are here.

Whether they're having it or no
I'm left to wonder, but it's clear
The engine's music in their ear
Speaks for the urge that works them so,
Young rockers with a bird in tow.

(Holmes, 1988, pp. 38, 40–1)

Comment

Despite significant differences, elements of these three poems are clearly similar. In terms of lexis, the protagonists are respectively *lusty young bachelors*, *hot young lovers* and *young rockers*, the common elements being that they are human, young and male. In each case, these young men are riding around town, whether the vehicles they ride are horses or motorbikes. In terms of form, the poems are all composed of three stanzas: two four-line stanzas followed by a five-line stanza.

Text 1 (translated by Adam Khan) is in fact written in Middle English (used between about 1100 and 1450), the language therefore that would have been used in Charles d'Orléans' lifetime (1394–1465). Text 2 (translated by Peter Rowlett) retains the stallions (*coursers* in Text 1), while Text 3 (by G.R. Nicholson) updates the poem by substituting motorbikes. Text 3's reference to *rockers* describes members of a youth culture in 1960s' America and the UK, and therefore locates the text in a very different time and place.

Text 1 could be seen as more 'faithful' to a fifteenth-century source text. It preserves the rondel form of the original (*rondel* meaning literally 'round' and referring to the repetition of the line *Lusty yonge bacheleres* moving through each verse). Yet literary history tells us that the language Charles d'Orléans used was in his time considered experimental, so is it appropriate to use an old form of English? Perhaps Text 2 could be argued to be more 'faithful' in that it uses current English usage. However, the source poem does not locate the action explicitly in 'France', as Text 2 does.

Denotation and connotation are developed further in Chapter 6.

The semiotic terms **denotation** and **connotation** are highly relevant to choices made by translators. Denotational meaning is concerned with the representation of an entity or concept. Connotative meaning is concerned with the speaker's or writer's feelings or attitude, or the meanings attached to a term by speakers of a language. Many seemingly similar terms, including synonyms in a single language, can be said to have different shades of connotative meaning. Thus, if we compare the difference between *don't complain* and *don't whinge* we can say that their denotational meaning is the same (they refer to broadly the same thing) while their connotational meaning is not. In the translations of the poem you have just considered, different lexical choices were made (*lusty yonge bacheleres, hot young lovers,* *young rockers*). In terms of denotation, these terms mean different things. But on the connotative level, they are more similar. Each poet has used lexical equivalences that reflect the historical period selected. 'Bachelors' hardly sounds very racy or dangerous in a modern context, so perhaps 'hot young lovers' is a good equivalent that conveys the connotations of 'bachelor'. The motorbikes 'revving their engines' seems a suitable modern equivalent of stallions wheeling and kicking. It's in the juxtaposition of several translations of the same poem that we can illuminate how problematic the notions of fidelity and equivalence are.

Of course, a key issue for translation is the fact that across languages we find words that are denotationally the same but have very different connotative meanings. One example might be the French *fameux* and the English *famous*, which both mean more or less 'well known'. In English, however, *famous* is connotatively neutral whilst the French *fameux* is derogatory, 'une femme fameuse' meaning roughly 'a woman of ill repute'. Therefore, we can see that the connotation of a word is complex, ambiguous and mutable: meaning changes over time, in combination with other words, and can be culturally, historically or socially specific. Since the meaning of a word is open to interpretation, this can make it hard to talk of accurate or inaccurate translations. There are subtle and not so subtle differences in the way that languages lexicalise experience.

In the box below, the translation scholar Mona Baker (1992) considers a number of linguistic features, and gives concrete examples of the role that culture plays in the way we create and communicate meaning. It is a useful breakdown of some aspects of language that a translator needs to consider when translating any text, whether literary or non-literary.

Culture and connotative meaning

Culture-specific concepts: a concept that is unknown in the target language. An example of an English abstract concept without an equivalent in some languages is *privacy*.

Differences in expressive meaning (connotations): words can acquire different cultural connotations and expressive meanings at different times. There is an example of this in the old English poem, 'Wulf and Eadwacer': The *fenne* in Anglo Saxon times was a boggy and dangerous tract of land where outlaws lived – thus it evoked a sense of the forbidden which is absent in the current usage of the term 'fen' which now refers to land that has been drained for farming and, more recently, used for leisure activities.

Non-lexicalised concepts: the source language word may express a concept that is known in the target culture but not lexicalised. An example of this is *savoury* which does not have equivalents in some other languages. The abstract use of *landslide* as in *landslide victory* is also not lexicalised in many languages, although the concept itself of *overwhelming majority* is easily understood.

Semantic complexity: languages can develop very concise words to describe complex concepts if they are important enough. One word, for example the Brazilian word *arruação*, can express a complex set of meanings – in this case, *clearing the ground under coffee trees of rubbish and piling it in the middle of the row in order to aid in the recovery of beans dropped during harvesting*. Consider the hapless translator of a text in which the poet wishes to invoke this social activity within the succinct lines of a poem.

Differences in form: languages add prefixes (placed at the beginning) and suffixes (added to the end) to root words in different ways to create meaning, and this often means that equivalences cannot be found. English has many couplets such as *employer-employee, payer-payee*. Speakers use the suffix *-ish* to create adjectives such as *boyish*, or the suffix *–ese* which adds an expressive dimension to certain words such as in *journalese*. Another suffix used to create new words is *-eria* as in *washeteria, carpeteria*. Aside from being succinct, such linguistic resources can be used in verbal play which does not have direct equivalences in other languages. The meanings can be conveyed in other ways (paraphrased) but where form is important – in verbal art for example – expressive and aesthetic meanings and their contribution to the overall meaning of the text can be lost.

Loan words: languages borrow from other languages for various reasons. Sometimes the word form is changed to resemble the target language, sometimes it remains in its source language form and in literary texts can be used in many different ways, giving information about a character's social background or the narrator's attitude to a character. Examples of loan words in English are *chic* (sophisticated/trendy) and *alfresco* (outdoors).

Idioms: fixed expressions that sometimes have similar expressions in the target language, using the same interplay of images, but sometimes not. Expressions that violate the truth, like *it's raining cats and dogs*, or *throw caution to the winds*, are easily recognisable. Idioms that play with everyday objects and concepts are easy to understand, even if different images are used in the target language to express the same meaning. Others may be based on long-forgotten events and people, and will have no meaning except to speakers within a culture: for example, *Murphy's law* (used in the UK and USA to mean 'if anything can go wrong, it will'). Idiomatic expressions may exist in the target language but have entirely different meanings. Thus to *sing a different tune* in English indicates a change in opinion, whereas in Chinese a similar expression has strong political connotations.

> **Metaphorical language**: this is strongly associated with literary language. Metaphors often play a crucial role in the coherence of a poem or novel; if the metaphor carries different connotations or has no equivalent in the target language, this can present a significant challenge to the translator.
>
> (Adapted from Baker, 1992)

Mona Baker is pointing here to the difficulties of equivalence in translation, from a sociocultural perspective. Burton Raffel, despite his insistence in Reading A that a good prose translation should preserve the original syntax as far as possible, also argues that in poetry, the formal aspects of language make equivalence from one language to another extremely hard to achieve:

1   No two languages having the same phonology, it is impossible to recreate the sounds of a work composed in one language in another language.

2   No two languages having the same syntactic structures, it is impossible to re-create the syntax of a work composed in one language in another language.

3   No two languages having the same vocabulary, it is impossible to re-create the vocabulary of a work composed in one language to another language.

4   No two languages having the same literary history, it is impossible to re-create the literary forms of one culture in the language and literary culture of another.

5   No two languages having the same prosody, it is impossible to re-create the prosody of a literary work composed in one language in another language.

(Raffel, 1994, p. ix)

Raffel seems to echo Denham when he says that attempts to be faithful to a poem's rhymes, meter and forms end up 'stifling poetic vitality'. He suggests re-creation and approximation instead as guiding principles. This seems to contradict the emphasis he places, in Reading A, on replicating syntactic structures as far as possible in the target text, although he was referring to prose translation in Reading A, not poetry as he is here. Looking back to the poems in Activity 5, the fact that they are derivative texts does not mean they are not creative in the way that they exploit the sounds, the look, the connotations of words in poetic ways. Perhaps, then, a translated literary text should be judged not in terms of what Bassnett (1998, p. 39) calls the 'moralising discourse of faithfulness and unfaithfulness' but on how well it stands as a creative text in its own right.

It could be argued that the most difficult aspects of any text to translate are its word play (or other forms of patterning) and its cultural references. These could involve the cultural connotations of particular words or concepts which, in turn, are connected to the social, historical and cultural knowledge a language group will share. Alternatively, they could be related to the **intertextual** dimension of texts – the way that the text draws explicitly or implicitly on other texts and textual traditions. It is to these aspects of translation that we now turn.

ACTIVITY 6   Finding creative equivalences (Reading B)

Reading B, by Alba Chaparro, discusses the Catalan translation of a text that is part of the canon of English children's literature: *Alice's Adventures in Wonderland*. Here, Chaparro focuses on sociocultural aspects of the translation – the search for creative equivalences made by the Catalan translator in order to make it comprehensible and culturally relevant for the new audience. She shows how the translator uses substitution and finds cultural references for the target text which make sense to Catalan culture.

Turn to Reading B, extracts from 'Translating the untranslatable: Carroll, Carner and *Alícia en Terra Catalana?*' by Alba Chaparro. As you read, note:

- the significant characteristics that Chaparro identifies in the source text.

- the creative equivalences the translator uses in the target text.

Comment

Chaparro discusses linguistic aspects of the story such as the use of rhyme patterns and repetition, and word play (puns and **homophones** – words that are pronounced the same but differ in meaning and sometimes spelling, such as *new* and *knew*). She shows how these are used to make the story semantically distinctive, and make it fit within the literary tradition of 'nonsense' – a tradition where surrealism and stylistic characteristics of humour and parody come to the fore.

She also discusses the intertextual dimensions of the story: the poems that are parodies of popular Victorian songs, and the cultural knowledge that is needed to appreciate the nuances of parody and humour. In fact, it is not just readers from other cultures but other historical contexts who may miss the layers of meaning that a Victorian reader would have been aware of.

Most striking are the ways in which the translator uses the cultural and linguistic resources of the target language to recreate the features of Carroll's writing that make it a valued text. In so doing, much of the denotational meaning is changed: the Dodo become an 'Ocell babau', a fantastical creature; the King and Queen of Hearts become the King and Queen of Spades, for example. But this is a long way from the notion of translation as imitation, and closer to the idea of translation as a creative activity. In a text like *Alice*, you will notice that a variety of text types mingle – prose, poetry, songs, nursery rhymes – and poetic devices such as deviation, repetition and parallelism abound.

Chaparro also reminds us of another dimension of literary texts – images – particularly in children's literature, which is traditionally illustrated. Texts that include images are the subject of Chapter 6, but you may be interested to see some of the original illustrations by John Tenniel, from the English (1929) edition of *Alice's Adventures in Wonderland*. Figures 5.1, 5.2 and 5.3 show Tenniel's drawings from Chapter 4 of *Alice* ('The Rabbit Sends in a Little Bill'). Alice is shown having grown in size after drinking from a bottle labelled 'DRINK ME'; the Rabbit falls into a cucumber frame beneath the window; and a lizard is ejected from the chimney after Alice kicks it hard. If you compare these to Figure 1 in Reading B, you can see how elements from the three original illustrations were redrawn and assembled into a composite image by Anglada for the Catalan translation.

Figure 5.1   Source: Carroll (1929), p. 44.

Figure 5.2   Source: Carroll (1929), p. 46.

Figure 5.3   Source: Carroll (1929), p. 48.

The King and Queen of Hearts in Tenniel's original text are shown in Figure 5.4, and the kitchen scene from Chapter 6 of *Alice*, was drawn by Tenniel as shown in Figure 5.5.

Figure 5.4   Source: Carroll (1929), p. 97.

In this section, I have moved from a focus on the language of the text alone, to a more sociocultural focus, and have shown how connotation and cultural meanings in the target language need to be accounted for by translators of literary texts. In the next section, I move further away from the creative *text*, to the sociopolitical issues that are often involved in translation. I also explore how literary texts – and the translators themselves – may come to be evaluated.

Figure 5.5   Source: Carroll (1929), p. 71.

5.4 Creative translation and cultural politics

I discussed some sociocultural aspects of creative texts and their translation in the previous section. Here I stay with those ideas, but move into the territory of 'ideology' and translation. In Reading B, Alba Chaparro pointed, albeit briefly, to this complex area. For example, the choice of a Castilian cat to stand for the Cheshire cat in *Alice in Wonderland* relies for its effect on Catalan readers' understanding of Spanish politics: the Castilian cat can be seen to stand for Madrid, reflecting historical tensions between the political centre of Spain and its autonomy-seeking regions such as Catalonia.

Literary texts draw on literary traditions, whether of content or form, and these traditions may not have the same value, carry the same meaning, or perform the same function across cultures. In other words, literary texts are not produced or received in a cultural or temporal vacuum, and this has clear implications for how they are dealt with in translation. A key debate in translation studies of recent years centres around what the translator does, or should do, with the 'culturalness' of literary texts.

One approach is **domestication** of the text – adapting it to suit the tastes of the target audience and suppressing cultural references and meanings which would be alien, unsettling or incomprehensible to this new audience.

An example of domestication occurs in May's translation of the opening paragraph of *Madame Bovary* (see 1b in Reading A by Raffel) which uses *in the prep-room* for the British reader. **Foreignisation** is another possibility: to leave the text rooted as far as possible in its original culture, and rely on the target language audience to make the effort to learn about this culture in order to understand the text. This debate draws attention to the political implications of translation and to the active role of the reader/audience in translation practices. Tymoczko (1999) summarises succinctly the dilemmas involved in domestication and foreignisation of literature:

> [...] translators [...] are caught in the dilemma of producing texts with large amounts of material that is opaque or unintelligible to international readers on the one hand or having large quantities of explanation and explicit information on the other hand. Either choice threatens to compromise the reception of the text as literature. A third alternative – suppressing the distinctive qualities of the writer's culture and language – compromises the writer's own affiliation with his or her culture and probably the very reasons for writing, just as a translation which is highly assimilated or adapted to the standards of the receiving culture raises questions of 'fidelity'.
>
> (Tymoczko, 1999, p. 29)

It goes without saying that any translator must consider his or her audience when preparing to translate a literary text. As approaches, domestication and foreignisation share a concern with cultural context and with writing itself. Those who favour domestication argue that, for a literary text to be well received in translation, it needs to be adapted to the sociocultural knowledge and understanding of the reader in the target culture. It should not read like a translation, and should create the illusion for the reader that they are reading an 'original' text (Venuti, 1998). It can be argued that in his translation of *Alice's Adventures in Wonderland*, Josep Carner has 'domesticated' the text. The translation is 'reader friendly' in that sociocultural aspects of the text have been replaced along with traces of the Victorian times in which it was written. Foreignisation, on the other hand, relies on the reader being willing to make the effort to understand what may be unfamiliar. Textually, the translation does not disguise itself, and footnotes or commentaries may be added by the translator.

Both domestication and foreignisation can be viewed as problematic: domestication because of its tendency to suppress any traces of the source culture from the text (particularly where the culture of the target text is in a position of dominance over the culture of the source text), and foreignisation because the result may be less accessible or acceptable to the target culture. The translator therefore faces a dilemma: eliminating the cultural distinctiveness of the source text deprives potential readers of some insight into other experiences and perspectives, might be viewed as 'imperialist', and suppresses the distinctive voice of the author. On the other hand, the text may be so 'foreign' in its cultural references that readers are unable to engage with it.

THE Sun

22p

Friday, November 25, 1994   22p   Audited daily sale for October 4,057,394

£5M LOTTERY JACKPOT

By LENNY LOTTERY

TOMORROW's second National Lottery jackpot is set to be a bumper £5million — £1million up on early forecasts.

By yesterday afternoon, 18 million tickets had sold. And by 7.30pm tomorrow sales should hit 35 million. Organisers Camelot expect between 500,000 and 600,000 will win something — but hope the jackpot goes to just one punter.

£100,000 REPLAY

SEE PAGE 17

I SAVED HURLEY FROM 4 BURLY GIRLIES

Hug for a hero . . . brave Sam with girlfriend Lorraine yesterday   Picture: HARRY PAGE

Sun EXCLUSIVE

By MARK WOOD

A HANDSOME hat seller last night revealed he was the have-a-go hero who saved lovely Liz Hurley from a gang of four girl muggers.

Fitness fan Sam Latifi, 30, chased the teenage gang after they held a knife to the terrified actress's throat and stole £10.

He was **SLASHED** on the hand and **PELTED** with bricks and bottles before cornering the girls with police. Grateful Liz — girlfriend of film heart-throb Hugh Grant — rewarded him with a big kiss.

As he got a "well done" hug from his pretty girlfriend Lorraine Lever last night, brave Sam said: "I'd have done the same for anyone."

Full story — Pages 2 and 3

Shaken . . . Liz yesterday

Figure 1

'I saved Hurley from 4 Burly Girlies', *The Sun*, 25 November, 1994

English Shakespeare Company,
1989; Michael Pennington as
Richard.

Royal National Theatre, 1995;
Fiona Shaw as Richard.

Globe Theatre, 2003;
Mark Rylance as Richard

Figure 2
Scenes from productions of *Richard II*

Figure 3
Baby McFry (Adbusters)

In Italy **Leonardo** had already constructed a fine pair of mechanical wings for Butterfly. She could move them simply by pulling the flap cords. Butterfly soon found herself gliding over the lovely countryside.

"How happy am I, at last I can fly!"

Figure 4
First Flight, Sarah Fanelli

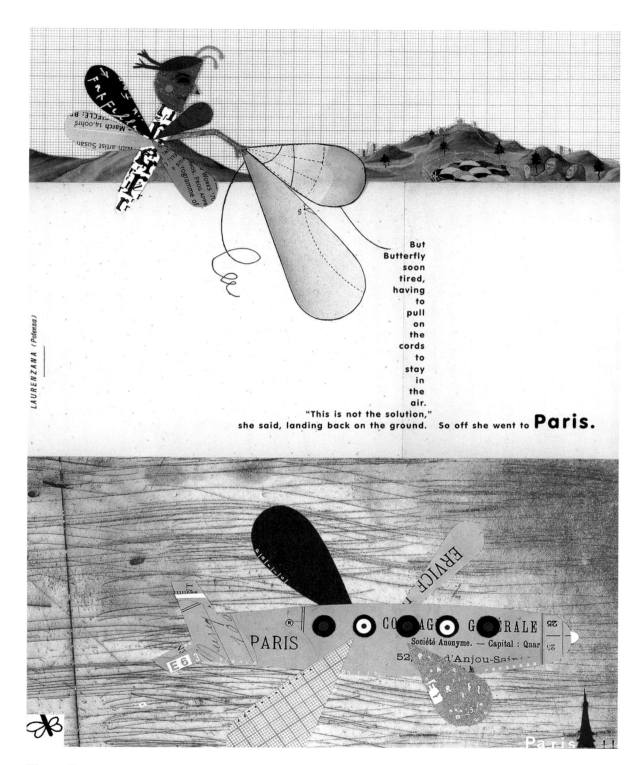

But
Butterfly
soon
tired,
having
to
pull
on
the
cords
to
stay
in
the
air.
"This is not the solution,"
she said, landing back on the ground. So off she went to **Paris.**

Figure 5
First Flight, Sarah Fanelli

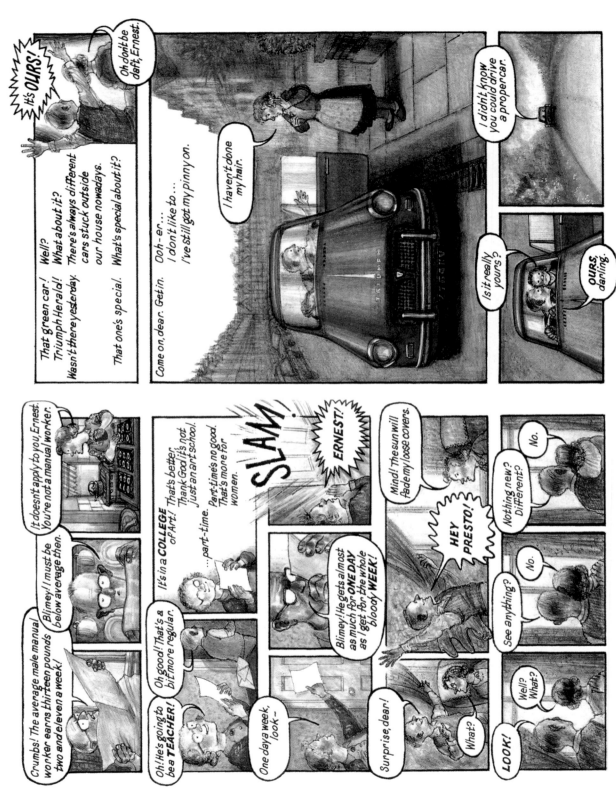

Figure 6
Ethel and Ernest, Raymond Briggs

She stops by the bridge to say goodnight to the gulls and the ducks on the canal.

Figure 7
Lily Takes a Walk, Satoshi Kitamura

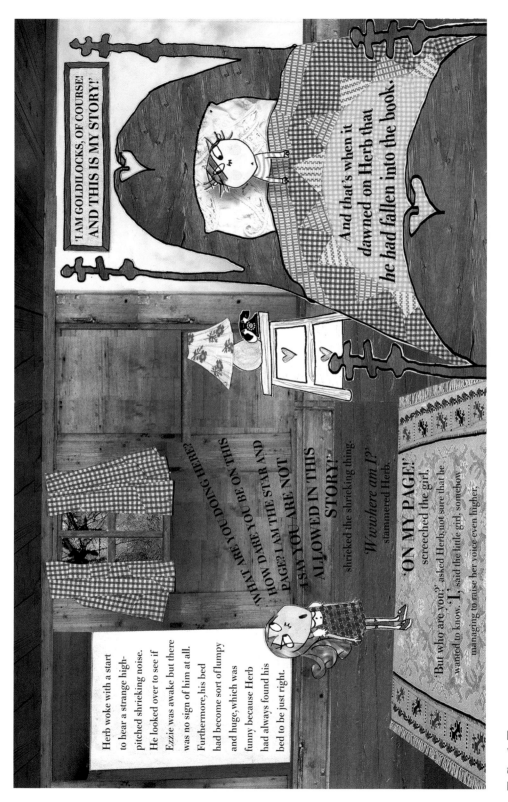

Figure 8

Who's Afraid of the Big Bad Book?, Lauren Child

"I have found a kernel of wheat," said the Little Red Hen. "Now who will help me plant this wheat? Where is that lazy dog? Where is that lazy cat? Where is that lazy mouse?"

"Wait a minute. Hold everything. You can't tell your story right here. This is the endpaper. The book hasn't even started yet."

"Who are you? Will you help me plant the wheat?"

"I'm Jack. I'm the narrator. And no, I can't help you plant the wheat. I'm a very busy guy trying to put a book together. Now why don't you just disappear for a few pages. I'll call when I need you."

"But who will help me tell my story? Who will help me draw a picture of the wheat? Who will help me spell 'the wheat'?"

"Listen Hen— forget the wheat. Here comes the Title Page!"

Title Page.

(for The Stinky Cheese Man & Other Fairly Stupid Tales)

PUFFIN BOOKS

Figure 9
Endpaper from *The Stinky Cheeseman and Other Fairly Stupid Tales*, Jon Scieszka and Lane Smith

Figure 10
Anansi the spider, by pupils of Newnham Croft Junior School, Cambridge, UK

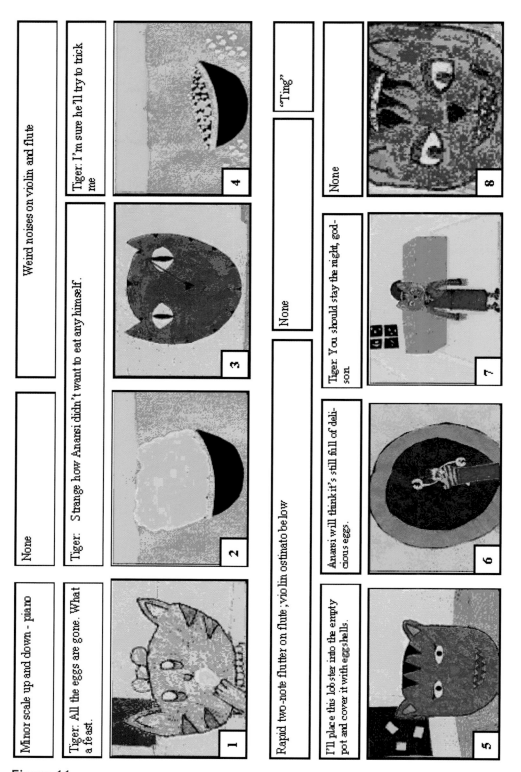

Figure 11

A short sequence from *Anansi and the Fire Fly*, by pupils of Newnham Croft Junior School, Cambridge, UK

Figure 12

The Tyger, William Blake, 1794

Figure 13
Landscape with the Fall of Icarus, Pieter Brueghel the Elder, c. 1558

A C T I V I T Y 7   Domestication as compromise? (Reading C)

Read Reading C, extracts from 'Translation, colonialism and poetics: Rabindranath Tagore in two worlds', Mahasweta Sengupta's account of the Indian poet Tagore's translations of his own poems from Bengali to English. Here, Sengupta looks at literary translation from a postcolonial theoretical perspective. She is concerned with the legacy of the British empire and the dominant role that English language and literature played in the way India was ruled by the British.

How far do you accept Sengupta's argument for the reasons behind the differences between the Bengali and English versions of Tagore's poems? Although Sengupta does not explicitly use the concepts of domestication or foreignisation, what do you think might be her position on this debate? Sengupta expresses strong views in this reading. To what extent do you feel these are supported by the evidence she provides?

Comment

Sengupta argues that Tagore changed the content, form and style of his poetry in order to suit the expectations and traditions of his target audience – to conform to the 'aesthetic ideology of the Romantic and Victorian periods'. She concludes that the innovative role that he played in the Bengali literary tradition is at odds with the way in which his translated poems were received in the target culture: they were valued not for their creativity but for shoring up cultural stereotypes of an exotic, 'other', East. She seems to portray Tagore as a victim of his own colonisation, and sees his being awarded the Nobel prize for literature as mere tokenism because it was not in recognition of the literary place he held in the Bengali literary canon. She provides her own translation, from Bengali of Tagore's *Gitanjali: Song Offering*, claiming that it is 'considerably different' from Tagore's own rendering into English. However, she does not go into detail about these differences – information that would have been helpful (especially to a non-Bengali speaking reader).

Unlike other examples in this chapter, here we have a target text written by the writer of the source text himself. Domestication as a choice and strategy, according to Sengupta's argument, appears to achieve a very different result to the 'domestication' that occurred in translating *Alice's Adventures in Wonderland* for a Catalan audience. Tagore's approach, Sengupta argues, means that he has compromised the distinctive qualities of his work and, although he gained recognition in the target culture, it was for the wrong reasons and was short-lived (although she is talking here of his reputation in the 'west' in the first half of the twentieth century, not his reputation in India nor his current status worldwide as a respected poet).

This is one example of how reader expectations (keeping in mind that both writers and translators are also readers) shape literary translation. How might the audience of Tagore's day have received Sengupta's own translation? Readers' sensibilities do change, which is why literature from the past can always be revisited, and fresh meanings found and retranslated, for a new readership in an ever-changing sociocultural context. In this respect, the views of the philosopher and cultural critic Walter Benjamin have been highly influential, as Susan Bassnett notes:

> Translation, it is argued, ensures the survival of a text. The translation effectively becomes the after-life of a text, a new 'original' in another language. This positive view of translation serves to reinforce the importance of translating as an act both of inter-cultural and inter-temporal communication.
>
> (Bassnett, 2002, p. 9)

So far in this chapter I have dealt primarily with translation of *printed* literature. But many works of literature are, of course, encountered as performances. What readers of novels and theatre audiences share is that both bring unique interpretations to text, whether written or performed. Nonetheless, reading a novel, for example, occurs predominantly in private and on one's own, whereas theatrical texts are more likely to be seen as a group and in public. An audience of a play is far more directly involved in its performance than a reader is in the unfolding of a novel. Audience and cast respond directly and react to each other, making each performance unique. I now move on to look at this key area of literary output, the particular issues it raises in relation to translation, and to where we can locate creativity.

5.5 Recreating literature through participation

In Section 5.2 you were introduced to John Dryden's set of guidelines for translators: you will recall that these included the exhortation to keep the sense of the text 'sacred and inviolable', and that they also conveyed a strong sense of deference to the original author. This focus on the translator-as-writer somewhat ignores, however, a key element in the literary 'game': the reader or audience of the text. Under the influence of postmodern conceptions of what a text is and where its boundaries are, translation has come to be seen as a continuum of 'interventions' into the source text (Steiner, 1998; Pope, 1995, 2002). Rather than being something 'fixed' in its meaning and status, which must be respected and preserved, the source text can be seen as providing opportunities for creative play. It is continually becoming something else through each reading, and through the accumulation of readings and performances. In this section I explore different ways in which an audience can have an impact on a translated literary text.

You will recall that you also examined the role of the audience in Chapter 4.

ACTIVITY 8   The creative audience? (Reading D)

In Reading D, extracts from 'Shakespearian transformations', Ania Loomba describes the translation, production and performance of Shakespeare's plays in India through the second half of the nineteenth century and the beginning of the twentieth century. She starts by explaining that, from the 1850s, travelling theatre companies were run by the Parsis, a community originally from Persia but long settled in India, which was distinguished by its religion, relative prosperity and supposed westernisation. The Bombay Theatre, established in 1849, produced English-language plays. Then came the 'Hindu Dramatic Corps' whose aim was to perform plays in Indian languages. Its first performance was given in Marathi; it went on to perform in Gujarati and Urdu. Loomba describes these theatres as embodying 'colonial negotiations, theatrical transformations and cross-cultural adaptations at their most complex and hilarious' (Loomba, 1997, p. 114).

Please turn to Reading D. As you read, note the changes made to the plays and your reaction to these changes, in light of the discussion of domestication and foreignisation in the preceding section.

Comment

Loomba says little about textual changes, aside from mentioning titles of several plays: *Othello* was translated as *Lionheart* in Urdu, *The Winter's Tale* was translated as *Dissolution of Doubt*, *Hamlet* became *Unjust Murder*.

Changes were made to domesticate the formal conventions of Shakespearian theatre, notably the addition of songs and dances, to the extent that *Unjust Murder* was a musical. Changes were also made to the plot where the source plot would have been incomprehensible or culturally inadmissible to the target audience: therefore, in *Cymbeline*, Cloten is the Queen's nephew and not her son.

In another change (one of plot), we are told that since tragedy as a genre is not part of theatre traditions in India, Shakespeare's tragedies have happy endings.

Religious references are also inserted into the script and the performance: in *Priyaradhana* (*All's Well that Ends Well*) Helena makes reference to her misdeeds in a past life and one performance is quoted as opening with a hymn to the god Narayan. The goddess Parvati is also given a role in the performance, and ideological appropriation is illustrated by a wish made for the 'uplifting of the Motherland'.

Although, as with Tagore's English translations, Shakespeare was 'rewritten' to meet the popular tastes of the audience, Loomba does not present the result as a compromise or an impoverishment of the source text. In fact, rather than compromise, she sees these performances as instances of rich cross-fertilisation.

The idea of an audience directly influencing the course of a theatre production, rather than being in thrall to the authority of a text simply because it is part of a canon of literature, may be an attractive one to some, because it can be seen as transgressive or slightly subversive. Perhaps because of the playwright's worldwide popularity and familiarity, we are used to Shakespeare being adapted for different audiences. Perhaps the recognised 'universal' appeal and relevance of the themes lend themselves to a kind of domestication which amply balances out any loss of meaning that arises from the translation. Or perhaps it is more to do with the nature of the genre. Drama is essentially collaborative and multi-voiced, created through the successive creative interpretations of translators, directors, actors, musical directors, costume designers. But is it still Shakespeare? When does a performance stray so far from its source text that it is not recognisable as a text by a particular author? One might come to see such intervention as the creation of a new play, rather than as a translation. Tymoczko (1999) argues that domestication is acceptable, even desirable, when the audience or 'translators' are appropriating a dominant poetics, rather than the other way round. Whether or not you agree that this is the case for Parsi theatre, the encounter between a source text and the receiving material conditions and aesthetic sensibilities of a culture and audience certainly holds the potential for creativity, in the sense of creating new texts and new ways of seeing. What it also suggests is that audiences domesticate and appropriate texts to their own sensibilities.

5.6 Conclusion

I have looked in this chapter at some of the ways in which translated literary texts – both English source and English target texts – use linguistic and cultural resources to make meaning. You have been introduced to some of the strategies that translators use, and the specific challenges and creative possibilities that different literary genres present. I have discussed the tension inherent in being faithful to the cultural meanings of a source text, on the one hand, and finding an audience in the target culture, on the other. A literary text – indeed any text – has many levels of meaning, and translators creatively play with the cultural and linguistic resources of the target language. I have looked at some of the aspects of translation which relate directly to creativity – in source and target texts themselves, and in the ways that texts are received and reworked by readers and audiences.

Literary texts are – always – created, received, and recreated within historical and social contexts. Translations can be seen as readings, interpretations and, ultimately, rewritings of the source text; therefore it is helpful to see both the source text and the target text as creative. Attridge (2004) sees translation as enriching the canon of literature in the target language:

> Translation in the sense of complete transference from one language to another is impossible [...] for the same reason that identical repetition of any work is impossible; but translation as a process of always incomplete transfer of what is literary in a work is part and parcel of the singularity of literature. Inventive singularity is what provokes translation (in all senses) as a creative response, rather than a mechanical rewording. To translate is, of course, to welcome the work as an other into the same, to transform it from the foreign to the familiar; but in so doing, if its otherness and singularity are respected – if, that is, the translation is inventive – the field into which it is welcomed is also transformed in the process.
>
> (Attridge, 2004, p. 74)

'Otherness' is discussed in Chapter 2 of this book.

Equally, it is hard to separate the linguistic meaning of a text from its social and cultural meaning. Therefore, when translating a literary text, one is to some degree translating a culture. Languages and cultures fertilise and cross-fertilise each other through the exchange of cultural products, including literary output. These are creative and enriching processes. At the same time, one cannot ignore the dominance of particular languages and cultures over others, which leads to the silencing or marginalising of so many voices and perspectives. Translation cannot occupy a neutral position.

READING A: Extracts from 'Famous and infamous translations'

Burton Raffel

[...] We can begin, as Flaubert had to, at the beginning:

> Nous étions à l'étude, quand le Proviseur entra, suivi d'un *nouveau*
> habillé en bourgeois et d'un garçon de classe qui portait un grand
> pupitre. Ceux qui dormaient se réveillèrent, et chacun se leva, comme
> surpris dans son travail.

The chiseled understatement of Flaubert's style [...] is packed into two
delicately balanced sentences. Each opens with a pair of short clauses,
pegged into place with a pair of commas, the first of each pair having, in
both cases, five words, the second of each pair having four. But where the
second sentence (and the paragraph) ends with yet another five-word phrase,
the first sentence eventuates in a slightly longer-breathed utterance, marked
by no signs of punctuation and consisting of a seven-word phrase linked by
the coordinating conjunction *et* (and) to a still longer ten-word phrase. The
weight of the paragraph thus falls, as also its sense turns, on these two longer
phrases, the key words of the first phrase being *nouveau* (newcomer) and
en bourgeois (in plain/civilian/common style), the key words of the second
phrase being *garçon de classe* (classroom servant) and *grand pupitre* (big/
bulky writing-desk). To be sure, such syntactic positioning does not, in and of
itself, carry the entire meaning of this incisive paragraph (again, this is the
novel's opening). But how the writer places and organizes the flow and
presentation of his paragraph's verbal elements clearly affects how the reader
apprehends and understands what has been written. Indeed, creating more or
less precise significances, and shadings of significances, in these and in other
ways, is in a sense virtually a definition of what literary style is supposed
to do.

The translator of Flaubert plainly faces enormous challenges, and to meet
those challenges must possess equally large skills.

> **1a** We were in class when the head-master came in, followed by a 'new
> fellow,' not wearing the school uniform, and a school servant carrying
> a large desk. Those who had been asleep woke up, and everyone
> rose as if just surprised at his work.[1]

In Eleanor Marx Aveling's century-old translation, Flaubert's carefully balanced
syntactic movement has quite simply been destroyed. The first sentence is
now divided into four approximately equal clauses, none having any greater
positional weight than any other; in addition, the parallelism between
sentences 1 and 2 has been eliminated. Without for the moment reaching

issues of lexicon, it must be noted that the Aveling rendition is in many ways the worst translation of *Madame Bovary* ever to see print: although as we shall see not so untrustworthy in matters strictly lexical, it so distorts Flaubert's style, and thus his stylistic 'meaning,' that those who know *Madame Bovary* only in this version are apt to seriously misunderstand the book.

> **1b** We were in the prep-room when the Head came in, followed by a new boy in 'mufti' and a beadle carrying a big desk. The sleepers aroused themselves, and we all stood up, putting on a startled look, as if we had been buried in our work.[2]

As this perhaps even more inept translation indicates, there are plainly many ways to ruin syntactic tracking and obfuscate literary style: this second version (still without any consideration of its lexicon) takes a very different but more or less equally devastating structural path. Mr May makes the sentences roughly equal in length (25 and then 23 words); he uses only one comma in the first sentence, and three in the second, instead of two in each. And once again there is no reason to expect this translation even to approximate the standards of Flaubert's painstakingly crafted prose. [...]

> **1c** We were studying when the headmaster came in, followed by a new boy, not yet wearing a school uniform, and a monitor carrying a large desk. Those of us who had been sleeping awoke, and we all stood up as if we had been interrupted in our work.[3]

Word counts do not match much differently here, but the pattern of movement does: remove the more or less optional third comma in sentence 1, and add an optional comma after 'stood up,' in sentence 2, and the syntactic flow becomes distinctly Flaubert-like.

> **1d** We were in study-hall when the headmaster entered, followed by a new boy not yet in school uniform and by the handyman carrying a large desk. Their arrival disturbed the slumbers of some of us, but we all stood up in our places as though rising from our work.[4]

Again, add optional commas after 'study-hall' in sentence 1, and after 'our places' in sentence 2, and Flaubert's syntactic movement is very nicely reflected; word count is again only roughly approximated. But as discussion of lexical matters will show, this version, by Francis Steegmuller, is arguably the best translation in print. Lowell Bair's version, finally, is in this passage not far behind:

> **1e** We were in study hall when the headmaster walked in, followed by a new boy not wearing a school uniform, and by a janitor carrying a large desk. Those who were sleeping awoke, and we all stood up as though interrupting our work.[5]

Indeed, adding the same optional commas, and deleting the equally optional comma after 'school uniform,' produces very Flaubert-like word-counts of 5–5–10–7 for sentence 1 and 5–4–5 for sentence 2. As I have insisted before, however, words are not identical phenomena in different languages, and translations that nicely track syntactic movement must also be evaluated on other scores, notably lexical choice.

To which we now turn. Aveling starts off as if to handle lexicon as freely as syntactic movement. The meaning of *à l'étude* is to 'be studying,' or as two of the translators render it, 'in study hall.' 'In class' means something very different; given the powers of teachers in those days, there were not likely to be boys actually sleeping during a class. 'In the prep-room' (May's rendering) is British slang and totally out of place: the rhetorical tone of *à l'étude* is neither slang nor in any way parochial. [...]. 'We were studying' (Marmur) is dead right, and both 'in study-hall' (Steegmuller) and 'in study hall' (Bair), though also limited usages (American, that is, rather than British), are in no way mistranslations.

En bourgeois is not a negative construction, but the translator must be allowed some linguistic rope, and the variations on 'not yet wearing the school uniform' are unexceptionable. However, May's 'in "mufti" [is] rhetorically inconsistent with the French, as the embarrassed quotation marks indicate. The fact that Flaubert uses a singular verb form (*se leva*) with *chacun* (each/all of us) need not bind the translator, so that all the versions, singular or plural, are satisfactory, as are the assorted renderings of the preceding phrase (plural in the French), 'ceux qui dormaient' ('those who were asleep/slept/were sleeping'), and the various translations of *se réveiller* (to wake up/be roused) and *se leva* (rose/stood up). 'Comme surpris dans son travail' ('as if surprised in his [*son* here refers back to *chacun*] work/labors') is also handled freely, but there is not much to choose from, as between and among 'as if just surprised at his work' (Aveling), 'as if we had been interrupted in our work' (Marmur), 'as though rising from our work' (Steegmuller), and 'as though interrupting our work' (Bair). 'Putting on a startled look, as if we had been buried in our work' (May) and 'with an air of being interrupted at work' (Russell) seem both too wordy and too presumptuous in their freedoms. [...]

Here is [a set of additional] evidence, chosen from near the end of chapter 8 of the novel's second part. I give first the French and immediately thereafter, without intervening comment, the five translations, in the same order as before:

> Rodolphe, le dos appuyé contre le calicot de la tente, pensait si fort
> à Emma, qu'il n'entendait rien. Derrière lui, sur le gazon, des domestiques
> empilaient des assiettes sales; ses voisins parlaient, il ne leur répondait
> pas; on lui emplissait son verre, et un silence s'établissait dans sa pensée,
> malgré les accroissements de la rumeur. Il rêvait à ce qu'elle avait dit et à
> la forme de ses lèvres; sa figure, comme en un miroir magique, brillait sur
> la plaque des shakos; les plis de sa robe descendaient le long des murs,
> et des journées d'amour se déroulaient à l'infini dans les perspectives
> de l'avenir.

A shako is a type of military dress helmet with a plaque on the front.

2a [*Aveling:*] Rodolphe, leaning against the calico of the tent, was thinking so earnestly of Emma that he heard nothing. Behind him on the grass the servants were piling up the dirty plates, his neighbors were talking; he did not answer them; they filled his glass, and there was silence in his thoughts in spite of the growing noise. He was dreaming of what she had said, of the line of her lips; her face, as in a magic mirror, shone on the plates of the shakos, the folds of her gown fell along the walls, and days of love unrolled before him in the vistas of the future.[6]

2b [*May:*] Rodolphe, leaning back against the canvas of the tent, was thinking so deeply of Emma that he heard nothing. Behind him on the grass the servants were piling up the dirty plates; his neighbors spoke, but he did not answer them; they filled up his glass, but silence reigned in his mind, despite the ever-growing clamour. He pondered on what she had said and on the shape of her lips. Her face shone as in a magic mirror in the badges of the shakos; the folds of her gown hung droopingly on the walls, and days of love stretched out in an endless line down the long vistas of the future.[7]

[...]

2c [*Marmur:*] Rodolphe, leaning back against the side of the tent, was concentrating so much on Emma that he heard nothing. Behind him, on the lawn, the servants were stacking the dirty dishes; his neighbors addressed him, but he did not answer. His glass was filled and, despite the increasing volume of the sound, in his mind there was silence. He was dreaming about what she had said and the shape of her lips; her face, as in a magic mirror, was shining on the badges of the military caps. The folds of her dress were draping the walls, and days of love unfurled into infinity in the perspective of the future.[8]

2d [*Steegmuller:*] Rodolphe, his back against the cloth side of the tent, was thinking so much about Emma that he was aware of nothing going on around him. Out on the grass behind him servants were stacking dirty plates; his tablemates spoke to him and he didn't answer; someone kept filling his glass, and his mind was filled with stillness despite the growing noise. He was thinking of the things she had said and of the shape of her lips; her face shone out from the plaques on the shakos as from so many magic mirrors; the folds of her dress hung down the walls; and days of love-making stretched endlessly ahead in the vistas of the future.[9]

2e [*Bair:*] Rodolphe, sitting with his back against the cotton tent, was thinking so hard about Emma that he heard nothing. Behind him, on the grass, servants were piling up dirty dishes; the people around him spoke to him but he did not answer; someone kept refilling his glass and there was silence in his mind, despite the growing clamor. He was thinking about the things she had said, and about the shape of her lips; her face shone in the plaque of each shako as in a magic mirror; the folds of her dress hung down the walls, and days of love-making stretched forth endlessly into the future.[10]

[...] Without analyzing the [five] translations in complete detail, we find the following:

Aveling this time tracks syntactic movement well, but does poorly with lexicon: 'calico' for *calicot* (used by none of the other versions) is strictly a British usage and distinctly something of a 'false friend'; 'of the tent' is very much a mechanical *la plume de ma tante* aping of the French structure, unacceptable in any variety of English; *fort* indicates 'strength, intensity,' not 'earnestness'; 'piling up' is not as idiomatic, for *empilaient*, as 'stacking' (used by Marmur and Steegmuller); '*they* filled his glass' (used by May) creates pronoun reference problems not present in the French; 'built up' or 'settled' would be a far stronger, as well as more accurate rendering of *s'établissait* than the limp rendering, 'was'; 'line' is similarly weak and unevocative for *la forme* (form, shape, appearance); and 'the plates of the shakos,' also used by Steegmuller and Bair, is truly ludicrous for 'la plaque des shakos' ('metal plates at the front of stiff military dress hats').

May uses four sentences instead of three and is generally inadequate both structurally and lexically; he handles *calicot* and *fort* better than Aveling does, but 'reigned' for *s'établissait* is archly out of place; 'pondered' for *rêvait* ('was dreaming, day-dreaming') is terribly wrong; 'the badges of the shakos' (also used by Marmur) is no better than 'the plates' (or 'the plaques') 'of the shakos'; and 'hung droopingly' for *descendaient* is totally out of place. (None of the translations picks up on the contrast of Rodolphe's mental 'unfolding,' *se déroulaient*, of the 'folds' [*plis*] of her dress.)

[...] Marmur, who came off well on the first round, unnecessarily adds two sentences to Flaubert's three [...]. Lexically there are some very good touches: 'concentrating,' 'stacking,' and 'his glass was filled' are good, and 'shining on the badges of the *military* caps' (emphasis added) is the best of all the translations in its handling of 'la plaque des shakos'; 'draping the walls' is ingenious; and 'unfurled into infinity' for *se déroulaient* is an extremely sensitive translation. But *parlaient* means 'spoke' not 'addressed,' and 'in his mind there was silence' is, again, singularly limp for *un silence s'établissait*.

Steegmuller, who also scored high on round one, tracks the syntactic movement very well indeed; only Bair does as well. There are some splendid lexical touches, especially 'thinking so much' for 'pensait si fort,' '*out* on the grass behind him' (emphasis added), which alone among these translations transmits something of the 'turf' meaning of *gazon*, and 'shone out' for *brillait*. Steegmuller's sensitivity, too, shines out both structurally and lexically (though 'the plaques of the shakos' remains a poor rendering).

Bair comes off second best on this round. Structurally he does well, but lexically he is a bit limp in places, notably with 'there was silence in his mind' (compare Steegmuller's 'his mind was filled with stillness') and 'stretched *forth*,' which is far too wordy for *se déroulaient*. [...]

   And what we can conclude from this consideration of [these] translations of *Madame Bovary* is [that] syntactic tracking is the key; lexical approximation comes a close second; and success in handling both of these factors largely determines success overall. [...] On balance, Steegmuller's is plainly the best of these [five] versions; Marmur's is next most reliable; then comes Bair's. The first [two] translations are [un]reliable representations of Flaubert's French original.

Notes

1   Trans. Eleanor Marx Aveling (New York: Pocket, n.d. [1886]), p. 3.

2   Trans. J. Lewis May (New York, Heritage, 1950), p. 1.

3   Trans. Mildred Marmur (New York, Signet, 1964), p. 27.

4   Trans. Francis Steegmuller (New York, Modern Library, 1957), p. 3.

5   Trans. Lowell Bair (New York, Bantam, 1959), p. 1.

6   Trans. Aveling, p. 161.

7   Trans. May, p. 150.

8   Trans. Marmur, p. 154.

9   Trans. Steegmuller, p. 171.

10   Trans. Bair, p. 131.

Source: RAFFEL, B. (1994) ***The Art of Translating Prose***, **Chapter 3, University Park, PA, Pennsylvania State University Press.**

READING B: Extracts from 'Translating the Untranslatable: Carroll, Carner and *Alícia en Terra Catalana?*'

Alba Chaparro

   Le plus sage, pour le traducteur, serait sans doute d'admettre qu'il ne peut faire que mal, et de s'efforcer pourtant de faire aussi bien que possible, ce qui signifie souvent faire autre chose.

   (Gérard Genette)

   ['The best thing for a translator is to admit that he can only do harm, yet to strive to do as well as possible, which often means doing something different' – Ed.]

Josep Carner's Catalan translation of *Alice's Adventures in Wonderland*, *Alícia en Terra de Meravelles*, first appeared in 1927, some 62 years after Lewis Carroll's original text. [...]

The international success of *Alice in Wonderland*, both during and especially after Carroll's life, suggests that it has a breadth of appeal endowed with the power to transcend linguistic and cultural divides. This is especially surprising when we consider the book's socio-cultural specificity, a fact which, one might think, would pose insurmountable problems for the translator.[1] Besides its plethora of culturally determined references in the form of poems, songs, nonsense verse, puns, and illustrations, the book flaunts itself as chronologically contingent: both in its proto-surrealist non-sequiturs and in its adaptation of contemporary songs and sayings, it is an archetypally Victorian narrative, unmistakably a product of its time and place. These factors might suggest that the original text would be impossible to translate into another language without losing either its comic features or its lexical idiosyncrasies. Bearing in mind the resistance to adaptation that these considerations imply, it is tempting to speculate to what extent this *Alícia en Terra de Meravelles* may be considered a translation at all, and whether it might be more appropriately thought of as a literary transposition into a quite different cultural setting.

A striking feature of *Alícia en Terra de Meravelles* is its 'Catalanization'. Carner's translation retains not only the broad characteristics of the original *Alice* – the plot, its [dreamlike] atmosphere, its mixture of fantastic characters and events in a conventional narrative framework – but also, to a large degree, the lexical and semantic richness of its songs, poems, puns and word-play. Curiously, a reading of the Catalan version is inevitably accompanied by the growing awareness that we are *not* entering a foreign land. This may be attributed in large part to Carner's awareness of the demands of translating between two quite different socio-linguistic spheres of reference; secondly, and just as crucially, we must consider the role of Lola Anglada's illustrations.

Even a cursory glance at the Catalan translation reveals the process of socio-linguistic transferral in the names of the characters, which vary from the perfunctory to the fanciful. In the simplest cases, they are rendered directly in Catalan, the Mouse and the Caterpillar becoming el Ratolí and l'Erugot respectively; where Carroll is more inventive, choosing names with popular or humorous connotations, Carner too is forced to find a less obvious equivalent: the King and Queen of Hearts, figures with no direct counterparts in the traditional Spanish pack of playing cards, become *el Rei i la Reina d'espases*. The Cheshire Cat, devoid of a Catalan counterpart, is transformed into 'un gat castellà', a transmutation which satisfies on artistic and political levels, conveying as it does both the nonsensical connotations of the English original and a degree of gentle inter-regional satire. Amusing though it may be to Catalan readers, the concept of a Castilian cat has none of the popular idiomatic associations conveyed to an English-speaking readership by its counterpart from Cheshire.

One of the most interesting examples of lexico-cultural transposition is the Dodo, whose name derives from the Portuguese *doudo* (simpleton, fool), and yet which has no direct equivalent in Catalan.[2] Carner's solution is to invent the *ocell babau*,[3] which works well on semantic, lexical and phonetic levels defined in the *Diccionari de la Llengua Catalana* simply as 'Ésser fantàstic amb què hom fa por als infants',[4] has connotations of *baboia* (a simpleton) and *babuí* (an anthropoid primate), and as such retains not only the quasi-mythical connotations of the English term, but also the physical characteristics of Carroll's talking, anthropomorphic beast.[5] Moreover, in its phonetic proximity to 'dodo', 'babau' echoes the childlike appeal of the word and alludes implicitly to Carroll's own stammer.[6]

Carner's translation relies to a necessarily large extent on the simple transferral of socio-cultural references from source to target language. Allusions to the English language or to particular aspects of English culture, unsurprisingly, become references to the Catalan language and culture:

[...] for the moment she quite forgot how to speak good English [...].

(Carroll, 1987, p. 16)

[...] en aquell moment, s'oblidà de parlar català fi [...].

(Carner, 1992, p. 15)

'Speak English!' said the Eaglet [...].

(Carroll, 1987, p. 25)

— Parleu clar i català — diguè l'Aguiló — [...].

(Carner, 1992, p. 28)

Carroll's text is peppered with verses of his own invention, many of which are parodies of popular Victorian poems and songs. He felt no need to attribute these, assuming that his reader would be familiar with them and would therefore require no further contextualisation in order to understand their humorous references. Carner, for his part, simply translates Carroll's verses, but places some of them in a more familiar socio-cultural context by attributing them to two well-known contemporary Catalan poets, Maragall (1992, p. 118) and Guimerà (1992, p. 119). Songs and poems are among the most difficult features of *Alice* to translate, due to their dependence, for comic effect, on the reader's shared cultural knowledge. To a large extent their humorous content is diminished or lost in translation, since no parody can be appreciated in them, although this has also become true of the original English version, whose parodies are lost on most modern-day readers without the benefit of footnotes. For all that the Catalan version loses the caricatural quality of Carroll's original, it does nonetheless retain the illogical character of its nonsense verse. Carner's imaginative use of vocabulary and his ability to imitate Carroll's rhyme pattern are quite impressive:

How doth the little crocodile	Com l'infantívol cocodril
Improve his shining tail.	l'esplendorosa cua entrena
And pour the waters of the Nile	i d'aigua plàcida del Nil
On every golden scale!	la seva escata emplena, emplena!
How cheerfully he seems to grin,	Com ganyoteja amb gai instint!,
How neatly spreads his claws,	que fi que estén les urpes feres,
And welcomes little fishes in,	i els peixetons es va encabint
With gently smiling jaws!	amb dolces barres rioleres!
(Carroll, 1987, p. 19)	(Carner, 1992, p. 19)

As the repetition of 'emplena, emplena!' demonstrates, Carner was at pains not only to achieve semantic accuracy (the repetition conveying the thoroughness of '*every* scale'), but also, and especially, to echo the rhythmic regularity which is so important to the sung verse.

Some of the most distinctive aspects of *Alice*, and amongst its most difficult features to translate, are its copious puns and instances of word-play. Carner's efforts here vary from the elegant to the pedestrian. In the following example, his choice of the word 'cua' [tail] and the expression 'portar cua' [to be long-winded] produces the same ambiguous effect as its English equivalents 'tale/tail', which means that the homophonic word-play, on which the entire passage depends, is preserved.

'Mine is a long and sad tale!,' said the Mouse [...] 'It is a long tail, certainly,' said Alice ...

(Carroll, 1987, p. 28)

'— La meva vida porta una llarga i trista cua!' — digué el Ratolí [...]
'És una cua *llarga*, segurament' — digué Alicia.

(Carner, 1992, p. 32)

In other instances comic effects deriving from homophones in the original text are recreated by analogous means in the translation. In the following example, the phonetic proximity of 'd'astrals' [stars] and 'destrals' [axes] echoes not only the comic effect of the original text but also the linguistic method of its production:

'You see the earth takes twenty-four hours to turn round on its axis —'

'Talking of axes,' said the Duchess, 'chop off her head!'

(Carroll, 1987, p. 54)

La terra necessita vint-i-quatre hores per a donar el tomb al voltant del seu eix, i és d'astral importància.

Parla de destrals — va dir la Duquessa —, doncs escapceu-la d'una vegada.

(Carner, 1992, p. 64)

[...] A discussion of this, or any translation of *Alice's Adventures in Wonderland*, would be incomplete without considering one of the most communicative, and yet frequently overlooked, aspects of *Alícia en Terra de Meravelles*: its illustrations. [...]

The relationship between illustrations and text is crucial in considering the reader's reaction to each medium. The number and style of illustrations, their point of insertion and the kind of information that they convey, can all determine whether the image may justifiably be considered an integral part of the text. In content and style, Lola Anglada's pictures in *Alícia en Terra de Meravelles* are inspired to a large extent by Tenniel's illustrations and in some cases by Carroll's drawings, which were originally chosen for the book; in some important respects however, Anglada asserts her status not as a mere imitator, but rather as a mediator between two quite different cultural and literary traditions. [...]

In other cases, Anglada fuses what appear in *Alice's Adventures in Wonderland* as several different illustrations into a single composite picture (see Figure 1). Here the effect is quite different from Tenniel's corresponding engraving. In the latter the reader's reconstruction of the scene in his imagination is less controlled, while Anglada's illustration imposes a much more concrete image upon the reader. Anglada's picture is a mixture of reality and fantasy. Its recognisable elements, such as the typically Catalan farmhouse or 'masia' surrounded by the exuberant Mediterranean vegetation and engulfed by the sun's bright rays, contrast uncomfortably with the anthropomorphic rabbit, the gigantically proportioned Alice and the 'flying' lizard which has been foregrounded by its disproportionate size.

For all its surreal distortions, the overall atmosphere created here is less ominous and threatening than is the case in Tenniel's corresponding illustration. The use of engravings to reproduce Tenniel's drawings, with their bold chiaroscuro, creates a far more sinister character than Anglada's airy watercolour and ink drawings. The air of menace in Tenniel's illustrations is further intensified by the surprising lack of expressivity in Alice's face: by portraying her as an almost impassive participant in the sequence of bizarre events, Tenniel suggests that the dream and waking experience have come so close as to be virtually confluent. This conjunction of two disparate realities helps to explain the fascination for Carroll's work felt by the Surrealists, and not least Max Ernst, whose collages took as their basis late nineteenth-century line-block illustrations. If Anglada's drawings depict a more expressive Alice, this greater emphasis on her rational, human responses means that she, and consequently, we, the readers, remain on the outside looking in, and not fully comprehending the scene before us.

Figure 1

Tenniel's practice of reducing the background of his pictures to a minimum of information reinforces the [dreamlike] character of the book in sharp contrast to Anglada's Mediterranean background. The influence of Anglada's Hispanic background is apparent in her choice of a different type of playing cards to embody the Gardeners, the King, the Queen and their Soldiers (see Figure 2). Perhaps one of the illustrations that most emblematically summarises Anglada's process of cultural transposition is the illustration of the kitchen in Chapter 6 (see Figure 3). Even a cursory glance at Anglada's drawing reveals that her realism contrasts with the grotesque and nightmarish style of Tenniel's drawing. The Catalan version seems more appropriate for children in that the atmosphere depicted is a more benign one. In it we recognise details instantly familiar to the Catalan reader. In the foreground, the vegetables, aubergines and the càntir (terracota drinking jug with a spout); in the background the typically Catalan plates on the mantelpiece, the 'setrill' (olive-oil bottle) and the 'botifarra' sausages suspended from the

Figure 2

beams. Such is the geophysical realism of the scene that even the cat has more in common with the skinny Iberian stray than with its overfed English cousin. It is a different atmosphere altogether, one which reminds the Catalan reader that, however unfamiliar Alice's dream-world may be, it is fundamentally, if perhaps only subliminally, close to home.

[...] If we take a close look at Anglada's illustrations, we realise that she, just as much as Josep Carner, transposes the English *Alice* into an unmistakably Catalan setting. Curiously, on reading the Catalan version, we are aware that we are *not* entering a foreign land. Carner's awareness that the simple word-for-word translation would have no impact whatsoever upon the Catalan readership led him to look for adequate substitutions in the Catalan language. And as we have seen, the high degree of semantic closure in the Catalan edition has as much to do with Anglada's images as with Carner's words. It might not be misplaced in this context to consider Carner's and Anglada's roles not only as those of translator and illustrator, but, to cite Gérard Genette's terms, as co-authors, or as the authors of the hypertext to which Carroll – and Tenniel – have provided the hypotext (Genette, 1982, pp. 19–27).[7]

Figure 3

Obviously, Carner and Anglada were aware of the cultural implications and stylistic and associative meanings contained in the original work, but they were also aware that they were, necessarily, creating another work of art destined to reach a different readership with its own literary traditions and socio-cultural expectations. An overly literal translation might simply have reinforced the idiosyncrasies of Victorian England without offering the Catalan reader the possibility of association and identification with its characters. Carner's and Anglada's version, on the other hand, succeeds in inviting us to jump into Carroll's dream world. Crucially, too, through the polygraphy of text and image, it also offers us a [...] looking glass to remind us that this *Terra de Meravelles* is, ultimately, a *terra catalana*.[8]

Notes

1   Carroll himself states in a letter date 24 October 1866 that 'friends seem to think that the book is untranslatable into either French or German [...]' (Weaver, 1964, p. 33).

2   Modern Spanish dictionaries translate dodo as 'dodó', but no related word is listed in the *Diccionari de la Llengua Catalana* (Barcelona, Enciclopèdia Catalana, 1994). It does, however, define 'baboia' as 'ximplet, beneit', which corresponds exactly to the etymological meaning of the dodo: 'simpleton, fool; applied to the bird because of its clumsy appearance' *Concise Dictionary of English Etymology* (Oxford, Oxford University Press, 1986). The word 'babui', defined as 'gènere de primates catarrins cinocèfals de la família dels cercopitècids, de musell llarg I glabre I de callositats isquiàtiques sovint de colors vius', conveys the primal character of the dodo, and is extremely well suited to Carroll's anthropomorphic beast.

3   Literally, 'silly bird'.

4   Literally, 'a fantastic being which children are afraid of'.

5   In Chapter 3, Carroll's narrator alludes ironically to the Dodo's intellectual capacity: 'This question the Dodo could not answer without a great deal of thought, and it stood for a long time with one finger pressed upon its forehead (the position in which you usually see Shakespeare, in the pictures of him)' (Carroll, 1987, p. 26). John Tenniel's illustration [...] depicts the Dodo with human hands.

6   Martin Gardner (1960, p. 44) cites Carroll's stammer as the key to the Dodo's autobiographical origins: 'Do-Do-Dodgson.'

7   In a sense, not only Carner's finished work, but also his procedure is analogous to that of Carroll, who often reworked familiar texts (popular songs, sayings and poems) which he inserted into his works of fiction. These parodies stand in hypertextual relation to their hypotextual precedents. In this respect the process of transformation implicit in the term translation is foregrounded (Genette, 1982, pp. 19–27).

8   I am grateful to Editorial Joventut for kindly granting me permission to reproduce the illustrations by Lola Anglada.

References

BARTHES, R. (1984) *Le bruissement de la langue, Essais critiques IV*, Paris, Seuil.

CARNER, J. (1992) *Alícia en Terra de Meravelles*, Barcelona, Editorial Joventut.

CARROLL, L. (1954) *The Diaries of Lewis Carroll*, Roger Lancelyn Green (ed.), London, Cassell.

CARROLL, L. (1986) *Alicia en el país de las maravillas*, trans. Luis Maristany, Barcelona, Plaza & Janés.

CARROLL, L. (1987) *Alice's Adventures in Wonderland*, Oxford, Oxford University Press.

CARROLL, L. (1989) *Alicia en el país de las maravillas*, trans. Jaime de Ojeda, Madrid, Alianz Editorial.

CARROLL, L. (1992) *Alícia en Terra de Meravelles,* trans. Josep Carner, Barcelona, Editorial Joventut.

ECO, U. (1968) *L'Oeuvre Ouverte*, Paris, Editions du Seuil.

GARDNER, M. (1960) *The Annotated Alice*, London, Penguin.

GENETTE, G. (1982) *Palimpsestes. La Littérature au second degré*, Paris, Editions du Seuil.

WEAVER, W. (1964) *Alice in Many Tongues*, Madison, University of Wisconsin Press.

Source: CHAPARRO, A (2000) *Journal of Iberian and Latin American Studies*, **6(1), pp. 19–28.**

READING C: Extracts from 'Translation, colonialism and poetics: Rabindranath Tagore in two worlds'

Mahasweta Sengupta

Let me begin by quoting a poem from Tagore's anthology *Gitanjali: Song Offering*, the collection of poems for which he was awarded the Nobel Prize for literature in 1913; it was the first time that the coveted prize was awarded to a non-European, a poet from Asia. In Tagore's own English prose rendering, poem No. 5 reads

I ask for a moment's indulgence to sit by thy side.
The works that I have in hand I will finish afterwards.
Away from the sight of thy face my heart knows no rest or respite, and my work becomes an endless toil in a shoreless sea of toil.
    To-day the summer has come at my window with its sighs and murmurs; and the bees are playing with their ministrelsy at the court of the flowering grove.

> Now it is time to sit quiet, face to face with thee, and
> to sing dedication of life in this silent and overflowing leisure.
>
> (Tagore, *Gitanjali*, pp. 4–5)

My literal translation from the original Bengali appears to be considerably different in several respects from this English version in Tagore's prose:

> Let me sit near you only for a little while
> The work I have in my hands,
> I will finish later.
> If I do not look at your face,
> My heart finds no peace;
> The more I plunge myself in work,
> I wander in a sea that has lost its shores.
> Spring with its ecstatic breath
> Has come to my window,
> The lazy bee comes humming
> And dwells in the garden.
> Today it is the time to sit in a nook,
> Look into each other's eyes
> Today the song of life-surrender
> I will sing in the quietness of leisure.

In this example, one can notice clearly that Tagore changes not only the style of the original, but also the imagery and tone of the lyric not to mention the register of language which is made to match the target language poetics of Edwardian English. These changes are conscious and deliberately adopted to suit the poetics of the target system, which Tagore does by altering tone, imagery and diction, and as a result, none of the lyrical qualities of the originals are carried over into the English translations.

Why this discrepancy in the form and style of the originals and the translations? Why did Tagore himself choose to render his own poems in a way that was remarkably different from what they were in their original form? These questions take us into the realm of cultural values and the forces that shape our attitudes regarding the 'other'. The case of Tagore clearly illustrates complex factors at work in translation, and proves the problematics of the process in which a translator remains primarily faithful to the audience of the target language culture. This discrepancy in his attitude towards poetry in two different languages has to be examined within the framework of cultural systems and their relationship.

My assumptions regarding the specifically unique nature of the auto-translations of Tagore are based on two distinct premises. The first is that I believe that his understanding of English language and literature was largely influenced by the aesthetic ideology of the Romantic and Victorian periods, the time when imperialism reached its high-water mark in the expansion of the British empire. Though Tagore himself did not have any formal education and heartily disliked the British educational system that was being imposed on India, he nevertheless imbibed the aesthetic ideology that was prevalent at the time of his growing up and learnt the language primarily through its literature. Largely self-taught, he read extensively both English and Sanskrit literatures and translated poems from both languages when he was young. In English, he preferred reading Shakespeare, the Romantics and the Victorians. Two remarks made on two different occasions illustrate his ideas and biases towards the English language and its literature.

> When we had proceeded well enough in our study of Bangla, we started learning English. Our instructor Aghorbabu was a medical student. He came to teach us in the evening. The discovery of fire is said to be mankind's most important invention, and I do not want to dispute that. But the birds cannot light their homes in the evening, and I cannot but feel how lucky their children are. The language they learn is learnt in the morning and learnt happily. But we should remember that they do not learn English.
>
> (Tagore, 1961, p. 22)

Tagore clearly had strong feelings about the imposition of English on youngsters whose minds reacted adversely to the foreign language, and thus early experiences might have shaped his attitude to the culture that this foreign language represented. In a conversation with Edward Thompson much later in his life, Tagore says: 'These new poets of yours speak a new language, and after Keats and Shelley, I cannot understand them. I can understand Blunt and Davies and De la Mare, that is about all'. (Thompson, 1926, p. 315).

[...] What is apparent is that Tagore deliberately chooses to write like these poets when he translates his own poems into English; he makes adjustments to suit the ideology of the dominating culture or system, and therefore his translations fit the target-language poetics quite easily. He fits perfectly into the stereotypical role that was familiar to the colonizer, a voice that not only spoke of the peace and tranquility of a distant world, but also of an escape from the materialism of the contemporary Western world. [...]

Tagore chose to translate only those poems from several anthologies of verses that were of a particular type – devotional or spiritual. But devotional poems in Bengal and also in India, particularly after the Vaisnava poets, were of a highly ambiguous kind. They talk of the devotee as a lover or a friend and not necessarily as a subject seeking the master. Anyone familiar with the Bengali tradition would have grasped their peculiar appeal: they were both love poems and religious or spiritual poems and derived their imagery largely from Vaisnava literature. This idea certainly did not conform to the orthodox Christian doctrine, and it puzzled Westerners who were unaware of the richness and vitality of that tradition but responded more in terms of the stereotypes that already existed [...]

What is striking as well as quite natural is that he approaches poetry in two different languages in two widely different manners. In fact, Tagore inhabits two different worlds when he translates from the originals; in his source language, he is independent and free of the trappings of an alien culture and vocabulary, and writes in the colloquial diction of the actually spoken word. When he translates, he enters another context, a context in which his colonial self finds expression. Tagore illustrates very clearly the validity of the Sapir hypothesis that language shapes reality and therefore, when one uses another language, one is entering a different reality (Sapir, 1956, p. 69).

[...] In November of 1913, Tagore was awarded the Nobel Prize for *Gitanjali.*

Perhaps the most fascinating piece of evidence regarding the colonial encounter comes from the citation of the Nobel Prize, where the Nobel Committee refers to *Gitanjali* as 'a collection of religious poems' (Frenz, 1969, p. 127). This document is a wonderful proof of the attitude of the West towards a poet from the East who was being judged for his ability to transmit wisdom and not because of his artistic abilities. My assumption is that this is the only way in which the colonizer was prepared to deal with the colonized, the only possible ground for admitting one from the subject race, who is accepted because he represents the wisdom and exoticism of the 'other' world. Tagore's mission in the West became something very different from that of an artist or poet, and his poetry in translation became a vehicle for his mission. [...]

The poem quoted in this paper proves that not all poems in *Gitanjali* were overtly spiritual or religious, and there are others which contain a wide variety of emotions and tones. The Nobel Citation, however, generalizes on the basis of the common assumptions about the wisdom of the East and says:

> Praise, prayer, and fervent devotion pervade the song-offerings that he lays at the feet of this nameless divinity of his. Ascetic and even ethic austerity would appear to be alien to this type of divinity worship, which may be characterized as a species of aesthetic theism. Piety of that description is in full concord with the whole of his poetry, and it has bestowed peace upon him. He proclaims the coming of that peace for weary and careworn souls even within the bounds of Christendom.
>
> (Frenz, 1969, p. 132)

Tagore, therefore, was valuable because he was capable of bestowing peace on weary and unhappy souls, even among the Christians. As a matter of fact, *Gitanjali* fell so easily into the Western stereotype of Eastern mysticism that other aspects of the work were completely ignored.

Tagore's reputation and immense popularity in the West in the first three decades of this century were not based on an intellectual appreciation of his works but on the emotional association of the East as an enigma, where saints and prophets brought deliverance to ordinary people. In other words, Tagore was supplying another basis for the already existing superstructure of orientalism; he became a representative of the alluring 'Other' to the Western world. He became a missionary with a difference, but a missionary none the less, through his translations. [...]

It is obvious that the West was prepared to accept the poet Tagore only on two distinct grounds, as a mystic or a religious prophet, and as a person who was following the Christian missionaries in their task of unshackling the natives from the bondage of tradition and history. The irony remains that Tagore himself had provided the basis for such an appraisal by translating his works in a manner that suited the psyche of the colonizer, a manner that was perfectly adjusted to the prevailing paradigms of the East. The poet and his poetry were lost in this politics of translation. Mysticism was a highly prized virtue during the first decades of the twentieth century, and Tagore was conveniently categorized as a type, a type that he helped create through his translations. [...]

It is quite natural and obvious that Tagore's reputation did not survive the onslaughts of time in the West. He was forgotten as fast as he was made famous; very soon, the West found him immensely boring and discarded him as a passing vogue. Western literati were now wary and intolerant of the same qualities for which they had exalted Tagore a few years earlier. The war and consequent happenings had changed the West's aesthetic ideology about poetry.

English poetics was becoming professedly modern, and the revolt against Romanticism, Victorianism and Edwardianism was the slogan of the avant-garde. Tagore's translations were the victim of this change in poetics and ideology, which was just a manifestation of the deep-rooted change in the life and time of the Western audience. Moreover, Tagore also proved to be very different from what the colonizer had thought him to be. He was vehemently lecturing against nationalism in its fierce forms, and in so doing created enemies both at home and abroad. He was growing out of the straitjacket the West had cut for a poet from the East.

Reviews and articles consequently started pouring out their unabashed criticism of his works – the exact opposite of the ovation they had offered him a few years before. Rabindranath Tagore lived until 1941, and he remained an innovator in his creative efforts throughout his life. His writings in Bengali changed the course of that literature and also influenced the life and literatures of the subcontinent. He is a vital influence even now in Bengal and in India and represents the cultural achievements of the people in many ways. In English translation, however, we get a very different Tagore, a writer who is epigonic and tied to an ideology associated with colonialism and cultural domination, where his poems speak in terms of the master–servant relationship. His overt faithfulness to the target-language audience has proved to be devastating for his works in translation.

References

BASSNETT-MCGUIRE, S. (1980) *Translation Studies*, London, Methuen.

FRENZ, H. (ed.) (1969) *Nobel Lectures on Literature*, London, Nobel Foundation.

SAPIR, E. (1956) *Culture, Language and Personality*, Berkeley and Los Angeles, University of California Press.

TAGORE, R. (1915) *Gitanjali*, New York, Macmillan.

TAGORE, R. (1961) 'Jeevansmriti' *Complete Works*, vol. 10, Calcutta, Govenment of West Bengal, 15 vols.

THOMPSON, E. (1926) *Rabindranath Tagore: Poet and Dramatist*, London, Oxford University Press.

Source: adapted from SENGUPTA, M. (1990) 'Translation, colonialism and poetics: Rabindranath Tagore in two worlds', in S. BASSNETT and A. LEFEVERE (eds) *Translation, History and Culture*, London, Pinter, pp. 56–63.

READING D: Extracts from 'Shakespearian transformations'

Ania Loomba

[...] Shakespeare was in constant repertory on the Parsi as well as the Marathi and Bengali stages. In the Marathi theatre, a distinct 'Shakespearian style' of acting has been identified, as opposed to a 'Sanskrit style'. Though both categories are rather imprecise, they nevertheless indicate the way in which a revival of ancient Indian plays co-existed, and sometimes meshed, with the staging of Western plays. In 1934 R.K. Yajnik listed over two hundred adaptations of Shakespeare in various languages, despite the fact that many play scripts were lost and surely many others were not known to him. In Urdu, Shakespeare has been the most translated foreign author – the first Urdu translation of Shakespeare was of *The Merchant of Venice* in 1884 called *Tajir-i-Venice*. Plays were often produced in a hurry, and adapted to suit the company's or the audience's needs. This was no simple case of imitation. Indian theatres certainly inherited Shakespeare from the British, but just as they used fancy Western theatrical devices to stage the exploits of local heroes and figures from Indian mythology, so in turn they transformed Shakespearian plays into Indian folk performances. [...]

[...] Whereas these accounts emphasise the psychic dislocations between black skins and white masks, and the mimicry of colonial culture by colonised subjects, the performances we are considering here were not conducted with attitudes of reverence towards Shakespeare or Western theatre, nor did they force the performers to abandon their own forms of acting.

Other changes were more deliberate, songs and dances being the most constant additions to most Shakespearian plays. Thus, *Sherdil* (*Lion-heart*), an Urdu version of *Othello* by Najar Dehivi, performed by the Parsi Alfred Company in 1918, opens with Brabantio entertaining Othello with dance and music. Desdemona and Othello's courtship is depicted through songs. Roderigo and Iago sing in duet to awaken Brabantio and his kinsmen with the news that the 'peacock is in the house of the thief' or that Desdemona and Othello have eloped. Most of the love-scenes lent themselves easily to the insertion of songs, but these were also used in less obviously conducive situations: in a popular Marathi version of *The Winter's Tale* (*Vikalpavimocana* or *Dissolution of Doubt*; translated by Nevalakar and performed by the Natyakala Company, Poona, 1894) Hermione asks Polixenes not to depart from the court in a song. Polixenes also sings what is called 'a philosophical song' at the end of Act I. Even more startlingly, *Hamlet* in Urdu (*Khune-nahaq* or *Unjust Murder* by Munshi Mehdi Hasan, Parsi Alfred Company, Bombay, 1898) was turned into a musical. *Junun-i-Vafa*, an Urdu adaptation of *Titus Andronicus* acted in 1910, incorporated an old favourite of the English music hall called 'Navaho'. In the Marathi *All's Well That Ends Well* (*Priyaradhana* or *Propitiation of a Lover*, adapted by V.S. Patvardhan, Natyakala Company, Poona, 1894), Helena bewails her lot in a song, and attributes her present misery to her misdeeds in a past life, holding herself responsible for the premature deaths of her mother and her father.

Favourite songs had to be sung thrice or even five times to please the audiences. In the midst of a serious play, says Yajnik, 'the action stops, and the other characters lose all interest in the performance while the favourites are charming the audiences as in a music hall'. Songs and dances were not the only demand of the Bombay audiences. During performances of *Macbeth*, which was one of the most popular productions on the Marathi stage, audiences literally could not have enough of the actor Balabhau Jog as Lady Macbeth in the sleep-walking scene [...]:

> When the troupe went to Bombay, on the night of its first production the tumultuous enthusiasm of the audience reached such a high pitch that they continued shouting 'Once more!' (meaning repeat the sleep walking scene), declaring that they would nor allow the play to continue until they were satisfied. Then the great Ganapatrao, who played Macbeth with distinction, came forward and lectured the audience: 'This is not a music-hall, where you can encore a song as many times as you like. If you still persist in your demand, realize that such a consummate piece of acting cannot be repeated devoid of its context. Yes, I shall start the whole play again, and will need three more hours to reach this point. It is already one in the morning; but I have no objection if you get the necessary police sanction'. The effect was instantaneous; the play proceeded.

No wonder plays carried on for many hours: a performance of *Cymbeline* at the festivities during the wedding of the Maharaja of Baroda in 1879 reportedly lasted nearly six hours from 9.10 pm till 2.55 am! This performance was put on by the Itehal Karanjikar Company in Marathi. The players here adapted to a non-urban stage, as indeed all the Parsi and other travelling companies had to do. A detailed contemporary account of this performance by a visiting Englishman tells us that the

> theatre was a temporary structure of bamboo poles and canvas. The stage, a whitewashed sandbank forming an oval about three feet in height, twenty feet in breadth, and forty feet in depth, was partly concealed behind a drop curtain, on which an elephant-and-tiger-fight was depicted, and by a proscenium of canvas, adorned with full-length portraits of three-headed gods and mythic heroes in strange attire. Three uprights – one of them a growing tree – on either side the stage, sustained the 'foot-lights' – some twenty kerosene lamps.

The performance itself was equally unorthodox for a Shakespeare play: it opened with the *sutradhar* (the leader of the chorus in Marathi theatre) and others presenting a hymn to the god Narayan, and then the curtain was raised to reveal the elephant-god Ganapati (Littledale calls him 'a vermilion-faced, elephant-trunked monster') who directed the manager to sing in praise of the goddess Saraswati (goddess of learning and the arts). Saraswati appeared to dance, and then another choral hymn to the gods was sung before the play proper began. In fact such proceedings would be less incongruous in a makeshift theatre which would be closer to traditional performative spaces than in formal Bombay theatres whose Western space they transformed as radically as they did Shakespeare. Littledale claims that Cymbeline itself was minimally changed from the original. Cloten, however, was the Queen's nephew instead of her son, since her having a child by a previous marriage was implausible in a society where widow remarriage was still largely forbidden. Also, 'the audience seemed rather horrified at the love scenes between Imogen and Posthumus, for the well-regulated Indian wife, so far from running to embrace her husband, usually veils her face at his approach'. The soothsayer in Act V was replaced by a Brahmin astrologer, who promised a victory to Iachimo's side if he took care to feed the Brahmins. The costumes were 'Indian' although this was not always the case, and it is said that for the greatly successful Urdu *Hamlet* 'the famous man[a]ger-actor, Khatau, tried his best to follow Henry Irving's model for dress and scenery'. The result usually was a strangely hybrid dress, sometimes more Indian than Victorian, sometimes the other way around, and a theatrical look that was common in early Indian cinema as well [...].

The plays were often far less respectful of the Shakespearian text than this version of *Cymbeline* was. For example, in the first scene of the Urdu *Twelfth Night* (*Bhula-bhuliaiyan* or *The Maze* acted by the New Alfred Dramatic Company, Bombay, 1905), Dilera, the princess of Baghdad (Viola) and Jafar (Sebastian) are seen escaping in a railway train from the invading army of Safdarajanga, King of Bokhara, who is in love with Dilera. The train is caught in a storm, a bridge crashes and the twins fall into the seawater below. They survive, however, and the rest of the play follows the original. The Marathi version of *Measure for Measure* dramatises the song, 'Take o take those lips away' by showing the lovelorn goddess Parvati pining for her Lord Shiva. And the play ends with not only the message of upright government, justice and chastity but a wish for the 'uplifting of the Motherland'. Thus Shakespeare is made to speak for anti-colonialism. Such a manoeuvre was not unusual, and elsewhere I have discussed the contradictions inherent in making Shakespeare speak for particular positions by subscribing to his universal appeal. In comparison with some others, this was not a self-consciously political theatre. But my point here is that it eluded categories such as 'élite' or 'Westernised' on the one hand and 'nationalist' or 'folk' on the other; rather it was both the product and the producer of a hybridity that was the hallmark of urban colonial India.

Such a hybridity permeated to the other theatres which were influenced by the Parsi stage. The enormously popular Gujarati version of *Othello* changed Shakespeare's play into a tragic-comedy in three acts with songs. Othello is a handsome young prince who does not know his own identity, an idea that is more profound than perhaps the adapter intended. In the first act:

> there is an echo from *Cymbeline*, for Cloten is pining for Desdemona at instigation of his stepmother. By the favourite Shakespearian device [*sic*] Desdemona, dressed as a boy, escapes with Othello, while his friend, dressed as a boy makes love to Cloten. The true lovers ultimately find their way to the kingdom of Othello's father. The King, not knowing his son, gives him permission to marry Desdemona and appoints him the Commander of the army by removing Iago from the post. Thus the motive for revenge is established ... A new complication is created by Iago's daughter, married to Othello's friend, who tries to save Cassio. Othello throws his innocent wife into a river after half strangling her. She is rescued in the last act by Othello's mother, who is leading a pious, retired life. Later on a farcical situation is developed by Iago's daughter trying to make love to Desdemona dressed as a boy ... In the final scene an effective curtain is secured by the sensational exposure of Iago by Desdemona, by the dramatic recognition of Othello and his mother by the King, by the installation of the hero, and the marriage of Iago's daughter and Othello's friend.[1]

It is worth noting that tragedy as a genre is not generally part of either classical or folk theatres in India – hence most adaptations of Shakespearian tragedies transform the endings to happy ones. [...]

Note

1   Yajnik, R.K. (1969) *The Indian Theatre*, Haskell House Pub. Ltd.

Source: LOOMBA, A. (1997) 'Shakesperian transformations', in J. JOUGHIN (ed.) *Shakespeare and National Culture*, Manchester, Manchester University Press, pp. 109–41.

Word and image

Sharon Goodman

6.1 Introduction

This chapter deals with a range of printed literary texts which use visual communication as a meaning-making resource. Different aspects of texts, such as typography and images – and the way they are combined – will be considered with a view to understanding how their analysis can illuminate aspects of literary creativity.

In Chapters 4 and 5 of this book, you encountered examples of creativity in texts which utilise communicative resources beyond the means of language alone, such as plays and other performance art, and the translated *Alice in Wonderland* which included images made culturally appropriate to a Catalan reader. Here I look more closely at printed texts to see what – and how – combinations of word and image communicate to us as readers. For this, I will be using three approaches: semiotics, a 'literary studies' approach, and a look at what postmodern theory can illuminate about visual playfulness in literature.

The use of different forms of communication in a single text is often known as **multimodality**. I am primarily concerned here with texts utilising image and words, from the genres of poetry and narrative. Texts from other genres, such as advertisements, and texts using other modes of communication, such as movement, are also included where they seem particularly salient and can be seen as literary, in the Formalist sense. It is important to look both at how individual modes can communicate meaning, and at their *interaction* in the text – how they can be combined to open up new possibilities for interpretation. Such combinations and juxtapositions of modes can be seen to enhance, reinforce or contradict each other, making meaning unstable and challenging the reader's attempts to make sense of the text.

Multimodality is researched in a range of academic disciplines, among them linguistics, art history, information technology, sociology, cultural studies and media studies. Multimodal texts tell us something about linguistic and artistic creativity, but also about the social and cultural spheres in which we live, and about ourselves as producers and consumers of texts. Close analysis opens up questions about how we make judgements about visual texts, about how we value or downplay their status. Creative multimodality also tells us something about how language works – it may force us to focus on a metaphor or a pun, for example. Or it may reveal something about how relationships between people and institutions are represented, or just cause us to reflect on something we had forgotten to notice for a while.

The impact of various kinds of technology on literary creativity is the subject of Chapter 7.

New technology has brought about a surge in multimodal creativity, as anyone with a reasonably up-to-date computer can now produce texts filled with images, sound and movement. But texts using visuals to make meaning are far from new.

A C T I V I T Y   1   **The Mouse's Tale**

Allow about
10 minutes

Start by considering the well-known example of 'The Mouse's Tale' from Lewis Carroll's *Alice's Adventures in Wonderland* (1865), shown in Figure 6.1 overleaf. First, what is this? A poem, a narrative, a picture?

Think about how the physical shape of the printed text influences your interpretation. It might be helpful to imagine it laid out differently. If the text were set out in the usual, left-aligned layout of prose or some other poems, would you 'read' it differently? Why?

C o m m e n t

'The Mouse's Tale' is an example of **concrete poetry**, where words are arranged on the page in a significant way. When read aloud, its rhyme and metre are easier to access, but the layout initially challenges our attempts to read it as a poem. We consider concrete poetry in more detail in the next section.

'The Mouse's Tale' can be considered as literary not only because it comes from a highly valued and canonical work of literature, but because it can be analysed in terms of **defamiliarisation** and creative **deviation** which you came across in Chapters 1 and 2, in the discussion of Russian Formalism. The poem is eye-catching ('made strange') due to its unusual shape and can thus be seen as deviating from 'normal' layout conventions of poetry – even though readers of poetry are familiar, of course, with a range of such conventions. The text is also poetic in Formalist terms because it contains an obvious pun – in this case between semiotic modes. The verbal 'tale' being told by the mouse is represented by the visual 'tail'.

Multimodality forces us as readers to focus on 'the message for its own sake' (Jakobson, 1960, p. 356) and pay fresh attention to departures from routinised conventions of literature or poetry. Victor Shklovsky believed that the purpose of art was exactly this – to counter our habitualised perceptions, to force us to notice:

> Habitualization devours works, clothes, furniture, one's wife, and the fear of war. 'If the whole complex lives of many people go on unconsciously, then such lives are as if they had never been.' And art exists that one may recover the sensation of life; it exists to make one feel things, to make the stone *stony*.
>
> (Shklovsky, 1965, p. 12)

'Fury said to a
mouse, That he
met in the
house,
"Let us
both go to
law: *I* will
prosecute
you. – Come,
I'll take no
denial; We
must have a
trial: For
really this
morning I've
nothing
to do."
Said the
mouse to the
cur, "Such
a trial,
dear Sir,
With
no jury
or judge,
would be
wasting
our
breath."
"I'll be
judge, I'll
be jury "
Said
cunning
old Fury:'
"I'll
try the
whole
cause,
and
condemn
you
to
death."

Figure 6.1 'The Mouse's Tale' (Lewis Carroll, 1865, p. 38).

In an analogous way, then, Carroll's poem can be seen as poetic because it makes the mouse *mousy*. I will revisit 'The Mouse's Tale' later in the chapter and consider its value as a poem, as well as looking again at some creative texts from earlier chapters to draw out their multimodal nature. First however, it's important to set out a definition of 'text' that is broad enough for the purposes of this chapter.

A note about 'text'

It will already be clear that to accept non-linguistic textual elements – such as layout and shape in 'The Mouse's Tale' – as meaningful and communicative, we will need to work with a definition of 'text' which will admit these as a valid focus for analysis. A simple and useful definition of 'text' for this purpose is the one provided by August Rubrecht:

> A text is ...
> - any **artifact**
> - **produced** or **modified**
> - to **communicate meaning**.
>
> (Rubrecht, 2001)

This definition allows us to consider how meaning can be conveyed via a range of textual elements, as long as these elements are meaningful. It is important to differentiate things we perceive or see, from things we take meaning from:

> A piece of driftwood on the beach is not an artifact, just a random object shaped and placed by natural forces. If a beachcomber takes it home, paints a face on it, and hangs it on a wall, it turns into a text communicating the beachcomber's ideas about what is interesting and beautiful. [...] A text is purposeful. A line of footprints taking the left fork at a junction on a snowy trail is not a text. An arrow drawn in the snow and pointing left is.
>
> A beautiful sunset is not a text. A painting or photograph of one is.
>
> (Rubrecht, 2001)

Later in the chapter I will return to problematise this definition of text, as not all texts which make a claim to be meaningful, or 'art', are necessarily interpreted as such. But I turn now to the field of semiotics and consider what it can offer us when we start to analyse multimodal texts.

6.2 Semiotics

Semiotics was introduced in Chapter 4.

The first reading in this chapter outlines some useful terms from semiotics, which will occur throughout this chapter. **Semiotics** is a well-established approach to the study of language and other forms of communication which are socially and culturally meaningful. Its fundamental premise is that we use **signs** – words (both spoken and written), images, clothing, gesture – to communicate meaning. Much of semiotics has its roots in Formalism, developed in the early twentieth century, which saw language not just in terms of its constituent parts but in terms of how its individual elements are related. Formalism focused on the form and structure of language, the message for its own sake, and evolved into structuralism in the 1920s and 1930s. A semiotic framework is applicable to language, images, photographs, diagrams – any aspect of the text which can be seen to carry meaning. Semiotics also helps to account for meaning created by letterforms, typeface and page layout – often highly creative elements of the text which lie outside what linguists often admit as 'language'.

ACTIVITY 2   Some semiotic concepts (Reading A)

Read 'Signs and myths' by Jonathan Bignell, which first outlines some basic concepts in semiotics: Ferdinand de Saussure's theory of semiology, and Charles Peirce's theory of semiotics (both theories are now usually conflated as 'semiotics'). Bignell then explains some of the main concepts you will need for the rest of this chapter.

Comment

In semiotics, the basic unit of communication is the sign, which for Saussure is made up of a **signifier** (for our purposes here, the linguistic or visual representation) and a **signified** (the concept it represents). Signs are always culturally situated – they *mean* to members of a language community or wider society – which is why Saussure calls them 'arbitrary'. For Peirce, the sign also comprises signifier and signified, but he divides signs themselves into three types. **Symbolic** signs are those where the signifier does not resemble the signified – meaning is arbitrary and culturally learnt and understood (such as the use of the colour red for a Stop sign, or a linguistic sign – the word 'cat' for the animal). **Iconic** signs are those where a resemblance can be perceived, such as a portrait of someone. **Indexical** signs often have some kind of causal relationship between signifier and signified: smoke is an index of fire.

In a moment I will move on to look at how these concepts and others from Bignell, such as denotation and connotation, may be applied to word and image in literature, but first we take a look at how these semiotic 'nuts and bolts' can be applied to an advertisement.

ACTIVITY 3 Signs in an advertisement

Allow about
20 minutes

Take a look at the image shown in Colour Figure 3, 'Baby McFry'. What signs seem meaningful to you, and how do you interpret the image?

Comment

As a single image, Baby McFry is iconic – a photograph of a toddler. On the level of **denotation**, then, we could say it denotes that particular child, wearing those particular clothes, at the particular time the photograph was taken. On the **connotative** level, though, the image is complex. It is made up of component signs. Connotations evoked by signs are not universal – different people may read any image in different ways. Images also require some interpretative *effort* on the part of the reader: the more time you spend looking at them, the more you will probably see. For example, you may look at Baby McFry and immediately recognise the McDonald's corporate logo (known as the 'Golden Arches', due to the shape of the letter M). It is one of the best known logos in the world. You might then decide that the bib and hat are significant – for you, these may connote pleasure, distaste, or neither, but quite possibly a feeling you associate with a trip to McDonald's.

Bignell also discusses **codes** in his reading, a discussion which relates to the principle of selection and combination you met in Chapter 2. Signs are selected from a **paradigm** – a set of possible signs in a given category, such as nouns, jackets, colours. Here we have a white (not Asian or Black, for example) child (not a man, not an adolescent, not a grandfather), with a McDonald's bib (not a different bib), and so on. These are combined along the **syntagm** – in a sentence, this would be the linear order of the words, but in an image it is the spatial arrangement. Because on the paradigmatic and syntagmatic axes elements have been selected and combined, it is often illuminating to consider what elements were *not* selected, and how a different combination would have changed the meaning.

All the advertisement actually shows (denotes) is a fairly plump-looking baby, probably between 12 and 18 months old, wearing a McDonald's bib and a paper hat with an image of chips printed on it. So it would be quite possible to read this as an advertisement for McDonald's itself, or as a children's party invitation, or a family snap.

But this image is an 'anti-advertisement' or 'subvertisement' produced by Adbusters, a network of artists and activists concerned about ecological and commercial issues. They are known for their anti-consumption campaigns such as Buy Nothing Day, and TV Turnoff Week, as well as for their parodies of advertisements by international corporations, such as this one. This multimodal text condenses into a single image current and ongoing concerns about the activities of large multinational corporations, and the amount of contextual information we need to read it is enormous.

Saussure's terms 'paradigm' and 'syntagm' were introduced in Chapter 2.

McDonald's is a global brand; many people know that it has been targeted by anti-capitalism activists, who raise concerns about the environmental damage they believe stems from the production of 'fast food'; by those who want to replace what have been termed 'McJobs' with better long-term career options and pay for young people; by health professionals concerned with the projected rise in obesity attributable, in part, to excessive consumption of fast food; and by those concerned that the global expansion of McDonald's rides roughshod over local cultural traditions. When viewing this advertisement, you may or may not have access to all of this background information. Your interpretation of this spoof advertisement therefore depends on your recognition (or not) of at least some of the current controversies, your attitudes towards them, and perhaps your attitudes to advertising in general. Your experience of such texts (and indeed any other text) is dependent also on your cultural context, and social and political factors: you may be fully aware of the opposition to McDonald's but think it entirely unreasonable. We return later to this point in Reading B, where the meanings of the words and images in postcolonial picturebooks are discussed.

I now turn to some ways in which semiotic analysis can illuminate the creative nature of visual elements of literature and poetry. The remainder of this section looks firstly at visual aspects such as letterforms, punctuation and layout, and secondly at concrete poetry. Section 6.3 broadens out to consider literary works of fiction which use illustrations and images to convey meaning, although there will be some overlap between the two sections.

Semiotics and paralanguage in literature

Linguists generally define **paralanguage** as features of language (particularly of speech) which are combined with words to create additional meaning, such as intonation, pitch, tempo and tone. In face-to-face conversation, or in a stage production, visual non-linguistic features such as gesture, facial expression or movement may also be included in paralanguage. You looked at some of these features in the performances discussed in Chapter 4.

It might be assumed that paralinguistic features do not occur in written texts. But literature and poetry are in fact perfectly capable of utilising paralinguistic signs, and semiotics gives us a way of analysing these. Some authors play very creatively with letterforms, layout of words on the page, and different typefaces to creative effect, and such play can be highly motivated and meaningful.

ACTIVITY 4   **Poetry and paralanguage**

Allow about
30 minutes

Read the poem below, by e e cummings, about the experience of driving
a new car, and think about:

- how spatial layout is used as a semiotic device;

- how punctuation and case (lower case versus capital letters) are used to
  create meaning (as signs);

- how deviations from convention are used creatively.

Do you see any difference between what appears to be denoted, and
connotations that are perhaps not immediately obvious?

    she being Brand

    -new;and you
    know consequently a
    little stiff i was
    careful of her and(having

    thoroughly oiled the universal
    joint tested my gas felt of
    her radiator made sure her springs were O.

    K.)i went right to it flooded-the-carburetor cranked her

    up,slipped the
    clutch(and then somehow got into reverse she
    kicked what
    the hell)next
    minute i was back in neutral tried and

    again slo-wly;bare,ly nudg.   ing (my

    lev-er Right-
    oh and her gears being in
    A 1 shape passed
    from low through
    second-in-to-high like
    greasedlightning)just as we turned the corner of Divinity

    avenue i touched the accelerator and give

    her the juice,good

                (it
    was the first ride and believe i we was
    happy to see how nice she acted right up to
    the last minute coming back down by the Public

Gardens i slammed on
the
internalexpanding
&
externalcontracting
brakes Bothatonce and

brought allof her tremB
-ling
to a:dead.

stand-
;Still)

(cummings, 1960, p. 15–16)

Comment

There are no right or wrong responses to this activity. You may have perceivec some of the following.

Firstly, the overall layout of the poem seems to be highly connotative. It conveys through its iconic shape the juddering first minutes of a man trying out his new car. The lines are arranged in short stanzas (apart from the stanza starting *it was the first ride*, which I took to be an indication that the car is actually running smoothly here, just before the brakes are slammed on). Words are split across both lines and stanzas, which disrupts a smooth reading and conveys the jerkiness of the driving experience.

The punctuation is, of course, highly non-standard and forces us to notice it, as it deviates from conventional grammatical functions. Punctuation here functions to slow us down and speed us up, interrupting us and jolting us about as we read. In that sense it puts us in the car to experience the jerky ride for ourselves. Words in this poem are also compressed into single units by the removal of spaces, to convey speed and abruptness (such as *Bothatonce*). In this way, the poem manages to simulate a third semiotic mode, movement.

A complete analysis would need to combine the stylistic tools outlined in preceding chapters, particularly Chapter 2, with an understanding of the contribution to the text's meaning(s) of the visual elements. Linguistically, we could note the instances of creative rule-breaking on the grammatical level (*believe i we was*) and the deliberate flouting of the rules of English capitalisation and punctuation, for example. The pronouns (*i* for the driver, *she* for the car), as well as the lexis, also hint at another possible interpretation of this poem – the driver's fumbling attempts at the seduction of a lover.

No two people are likely to have interpreted every element of the poem by cummings in exactly the same way, nor will everyone reading this book agree with my points above. I have already stated that meanings taken from a text vary culturally as well as individually. This points to a drawback of semiotic analysis, which is a risk when looking at verbal language but even more salient in the visual. The connotations of a sign are often multiple and unstable – as Cook puts it:

> Paramount among the techniques for extending denotational meaning is the exploitation of **connotation** – the vague association which a word may have for a whole speech community or for groups or individuals within it. Connotations are both variable and imprecise. The connotations of 'dog' might include such different qualities as loyalty, dirtiness, inferiority, sexual promiscuity, friendliness; of 'stallion' such qualities as sexual potency, freedom, nobility.

> (Cook, 2001, p. 105)

Semiotics is always influenced by subjective interpretation, so it must be remembered that like any analytical approach, it cannot provide answers to everything. Nor can semiotics escape the critique that it is impressionistic and non-verifiable. But it does give us a useful 'way in' to multimodal texts.

Playfulness with the visual possibilities of letters and words is not a new phenomenon, of course. I can **SHOUT AT YOU**, *whisper quietly*, or *pretend to be a friend*, even in this very straightforward (semiotically speaking) paragraph. These conventions – as well as innumerable icons and graphic devices for linking visual and verbal text – are widely exploited in cartoons and comic strips (Goodman, 1996) and logos and advertisements (Cook, 2001, van Leeuwen, 2005). They are also detectable in older forms of play with words and letterforms, such as the rebus – a visual/verbal word game traditionally written on paper, in which images are combined with words or morphemes, leaving the reader the task of deciphering the meaning.

Figure 6.2   Rebus in a letter from 'Brittania to her "daughter" America' (Darly, 1778).

In Figure 6.2, 'mother' is realised as a drawing of a moth, alongside the suffix –*er*. It is an example from an eighteenth-century historical document. These days we would be more likely to encounter the rebus in books of word games or on puzzle websites (Figure 6.3).

ARURMS
_____
IT

('you are up in arms over it')

(http://www.fun-with-words.com/rebus_puzzles_23.html [accessed 6.1.06])

TRAVEL
CCCCCCCC

('travel over C's = travel overseas)

(http://www.fun-with-words.com/rebus_puzzles_12.html [accessed 6.1.06])

(plant a tree)

(www.yourpage.org/planttree-rebus.html [accessed 6.1.06])

Figure 6.3   Rebus examples from puzzle websites.

The rebus frequently relies for its effect on a pun across modes. The visuals have to be read literally and the result transposed into words for the reader to make any sense of it. We can see a 'return to the rebus' evidenced in text messages on mobile phones, too, as in 'CUL8R' for 'see you later'.

Concrete poetry

We looked at 'The Mouse's Tale' in the first section of this chapter. Concrete poetry (also called 'pattern poetry') – where the lines are arranged in a specific shape on the page in a meaningful way – has been around for centuries. Mosaics are amongst the earliest examples of it (see Danet, 2001, pp. 197–202, for some of the history, and examples of poems). The cummings poem could be considered concrete, as the spatial layout is significant. The term 'concrete poetry' is usually used, however, for poems where the visual shape is paramount, 'so that they visually reinforce, or act as a counterpoint to, the verbal meaning' (Crystal, 1987, p. 75). The French poet Guillaume Apollinaire (1880–1918) is probably the most widely known producer of these artforms, which he entitled *Calligrammes*. The English poet George Herbert (1593–1633) also wrote concrete poetry, the best known of which is 'Easter Wings', published posthumously in 1633.

See Chapter 5 of the companion volume, **Maybin and Swann (2006)** for more on creative adaptation of texts due to the affordances and constraints of technology, and Reading D in Chapter 7 of this volume for more on creative abbreviation.

Concrete poetry is still very much alive as a literary artform. Figure 6.4 shows a poem from a more recent source, the NASA website. Start reading at the bottom left of the poem, as the aeroplane is taking off:

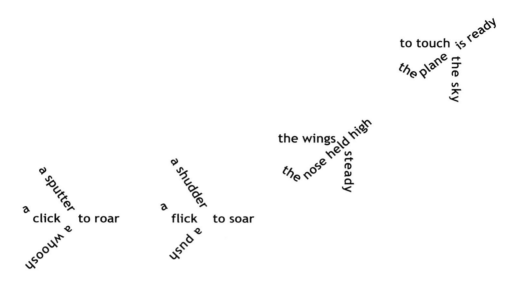

Figure 6.4   Untitled poem (NASA Quest 2005).

The verses of this poem follow that of the aeroplane, upwards and rightwards as it lifts into the sky. As well as the iconic shape of the four text-aeroplanes, the semiotic mode of movement, following the left-to-right reading path of the English language, is implied.

The NASA poem is fairly traditional in its form, and works just as well on paper as it does on a computer screen. The advent of computers, however, has revitalised the form by adding new modes, particularly sound, colour and movement. An example using movement is shown in Figure 6.5, in the series of stills from a visual poetry website. Dan Waber's 'argument' shows a rope moving from side to side forming the words *yes* and *no*, using movement to realise the visual metaphor of a tug-of-war. The obvious irony of attempting to represent this poem here in print was overridden by its usefulness – it seemed too interesting to leave out. At the time of writing, this poem is available on the internet (at http://www.vispo.com/guests/DanWaber/ argument.html), or you may be able to find it via a search engine.

There are many virtual art galleries displaying poems that make use of sound, image and text: an internet search of 'concrete poetry' should produce many examples of multimodal artwork on the web.

We have seen in this section how letterforms, punctuation, and their playful spatial arrangement can be seen as artful. The semiotic concepts introduced so far will be revisited, as I now turn to some multimodal works of fiction which employ these features and more.

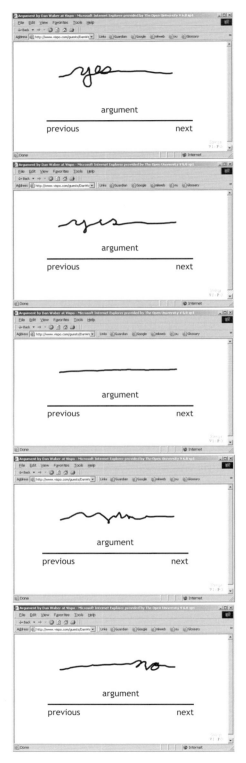

Figure 6.5   'argument' (Dan Waber, 1999).

6.3 Word and image in fiction

The rebus is created and enjoyed by both adults and children, but it is a common assumption in some cultures that while literature designed for children contains pictures, adult fiction does (or should) not. This view is not, of course, universal: there is a strong tradition in France, for example, of the *bande dessinée*, a comic-style format for fiction aimed at an adult readership. Here I consider fictional texts for both child and adult readerships which use images alongside words. The particular focus will be the creative juxtaposition of word and image, as this is often crucial to how readers interpret the text as a whole.

Books for both adults and children have been illustrated (and re-illustrated for different editions and audiences) for centuries, and there is a vast literature on the work of illustrators. Some of the examples in this section are fairly traditional literary works in which images are used to illustrate the story being told in words (with illustrations often separated in some way from the verbal text, printed above or below it, or even as separate plates). In such texts, the narrative is conveyed in words while the illustrations have a supporting role, reinforcing the narrative or perhaps illuminating a salient detail. Others, often more modern texts, employ paralanguage, images and words – in some cases blurring the boundaries between them to such an extent as to make the distinctions unidentifiable. These kinds of texts are the subject of an increasing academic interest in how words and pictures are used in books, particularly those for children (Nodelman, 1988; Unsworth and Wheeler, 2002; Watson and Styles, 1996; Arizpe and Styles, 2003; Nikolajeva and Scott, 2000; Wyile, 2001). In what follows I show you a small selection, to demonstrate how visual elements function in the text – what they do and how they might be seen to 'mean'.

Locating the reader in the fictional world

The concept of 'text world' occurs again in Chapter 8.

When we read a narrative, we create a 'text world' – described by Semino (1997, p. 1) as 'the context, scenario or type of reality that is evoked in our minds during reading and that (we conclude) is referred to by the text'. Werth (1999) states that this mental space, drawn for us by the author, is one which we usually willingly enter into. When reading, we piece together a mental map from the description of a location and the way elements are described in relation to each other. Sometimes, authors draw actual maps for us. Maps help us to 'find our feet' by physically locating the narrative in an imaginary space; they are a fairly common strategy in literary texts. The degree to which maps insist to us that 'this is where it all happened' can vary: some maps are very detailed and complex (and can be vital to the reader in navigating the narrative); others are more lighthearted, such as that of the Hundred Acre Wood in A.A. Milne's *Winnie the Pooh* (Figure 6.6).

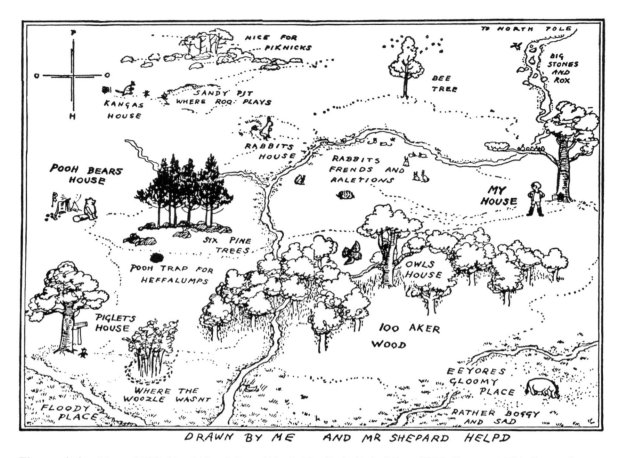

Figure 6.6   'Map of 100 Aker Wood' from *Winnie The Pooh* (A.A. Milne, 1989; illustrator E.H. Shepard).

This map is poetic, in Formalist terms, for several reasons. There is deviation from standard English spelling (*piknicks, 100 Aker Wood, drawn by Me and Mr Shepard helpd*) and an absence of apostrophes. Other renderings of childlike speech and writing are found in *floody place, sandy pit where Roo plays* and, of course, *heffalumps*. The map also includes an unusual version of the compass. You may be able to think of other examples of maps in fiction, such as Tolkien's *Lord of the Rings*, Swift's *Gulliver's Travels*, C.S. Lewis' 'Narnia' books and Lewis Grassic Gibbon's *Sunset Song*.

Sometimes the illustrations in older books seem to be less concerned with explanation or elucidation, than with with providing visual support for the narrative, or perhaps with making a claim to authenticity. Thomas Hughes' *Tom Brown's Schooldays* (1949) uses illustrations in this way. Figure 6.7 shows an image entitled 'A few parting words' – a phrase that occurs in the verbal text on the previous page.

that the Peacock arrangement would get him to Rugby by twelve o'clock in the day, whereas otherwise he wouldn't be there till the evening, all other plans melted away; his one absorbing aim being to become a public school-boy as fast as possible, and six hours sooner or later seeming to him of the most alarming importance.

Tom and his father had alighted at the Peacock, at about seven in the evening, and having heard with unfeigned joy the paternal order at the bar of steaks and oyster-sauce for supper in half an hour, and seen his father seated cosily by the bright fire in the coffee-room, with the paper in his hand, Tom had run out to see about him, had wondered at all the vehicles passing and repassing, and had fraternized with the boots and ostler, from whom he ascertained that the Tally-ho was a tip-top goer, ten miles an hour including stoppages, and so punctual, that all the road set their clocks by her.

Then being summoned to supper, he had regaled himself in one of the bright little boxes of the Peacock coffee-room, on the beef-steak and unlimited oyster-sauce, and brown stout (tasted then for the first time—a day to be marked for ever by Tom with a white stone); had at first attended to the excellent advice which his father was bestowing on him from over his glass of steaming brandy-and-water, and then begun nodding, from the united effects of the stout, the fire, and the lecture. Till the Squire observing Tom's state, and remembering that it was nearly nine o'clock, and that the Tally-ho left at three, sent the little fellow off to the chambermaid, with a shake of the hand (Tom having stipulated in the morning before starting, that kissing should now cease between them) and a few parting words.

'And now, Tom, my boy,' said the Squire, 'remember you are going, at your own earnest request, to be chucked

A few parting words

Figure 6.7   'A few parting words' (Thomas Hughes, 1949, p. 62–3; illustrator S. Van Abbé).

188   TOM BROWN'S SCHOOLDAYS

pleased them so much that they spent all their spare time there, scratching and cutting their names on the top of every tower; and at last, having exhausted all other places, finished up with inscribing H. EAST, T. BROWN on the minute-hand of the great clock.   In the doing of which they

Drawing of the old minute hand of the great clock, Rugby
(now in a case in the Temple Reading Room)

held the minute-hand, and disturbed the clock's economy. So next morning, when masters and boys came trooping down to prayers, and entered the quadrangle, the injured minute-hand was indicating three minutes to the hour.

Figure 6.8   Detail of object from a page of *Tom Brown's Schooldays* (Thomas Hughes, 1949, p. 188).

The function of this illustration is not to tell us anything new or explain something unclear from the verbal narrative, but appears to signify 'this is what happened, and this is exactly how it happened'. By showing us, rather than telling us, the author is appealing to what some see as our inherent trust of the visual (that 'seeing is believing'). The book is also filled with images of parts of the British public school, Rugby, which the author attended and where the story is set (see Figure 6.8).

One rationale for this use of an image is that the author supposes readers might be interested to visit the school, which still exists, and see the artefacts for themselves. But images can also make a claim to truthfulness or reality for the story: if the places and artefacts are real, then it might be easier to see the story in the same way. In linguistics this kind of claim to truthfulness would be termed 'high modality' – events or things are represented as if they were true and real. In semiotic terms, this image denotes a real-life artefact, but it also connotes 'truth', 'reality', perhaps 'honesty' – it asks us to accept its authenticity. We could therefore interpret such images as telling us something about the reliability of the narrator, or the judgement of a character, depending on what other information we have to hand as readers.

Conveying emotion

Other uses of images in fiction seem to function at the level of connotation rather than denotation: they add affective meaning but don't seem to have an explicitly narrative function. *The Coma,* by Alex Garland (2004), tells the story of a man who is beaten unconscious on a late-night train, and is hospitalised as a result. As he describes waking up from his comatose state in the hospital, talking to the doctors and returning home, it gradually becomes apparent that he has not recovered at all, but is 'dreaming', or at least only semi-conscious. He remembers very little about himself, and events are described in a disconnected, 'other-worldly' way. *The Coma* contains a series of woodcuts (see Figure 6.9) produced by the author's father, Nicholas Garland (a political cartoonist for the British newspaper, *The Daily Telegraph*).

The woodcuts in this book are instrumental in conveying a sense of the threatening, alienating world that the narrator inhabits. All the monochrome images are dark (in every sense); the large black shapes of the policemen and doctors loom over the man in hospital, but we never see their faces and nor does the comatose man. The result is a distancing, an ability only to see outlines and shadows, which take on the character of vague, unspecified threats. This is reflected in the story where we learn something of what is going on inside the man's head. He cannot grasp what has happened to him, nor whether he is dead or alive, asleep or awake. In an interview in the

British newspaper the *Observer*, the author Alex Garland commented on the links between the images and writing in this book:

> I think the way [my father] does woodcuts and linocuts very much influenced the way I write prose. I mean the heavy emphasis on craft with the aim of making things simple, hopefully deceptively so.

(Adams, 2004)

The connotations of such images affect us as readers and influence our reading experience. Their significance can sometimes be better understood by imagining the image differently: a different kind of image, perhaps also literally showing a different visual viewpoint, would produce a different meaning entirely.

2

Some time later, I sat in a wheelchair and talked to two policemen. The older of the two did most of the speaking. He wanted to know if prior to the attack I had laid a hand on the young men, or assaulted them in any way.

'Absolutely not,' I replied. 'I mean, I was trying to stop them from robbing the girl. But all I did was stand up. The next thing I knew, they were punching me. I wouldn't have had time to assault them, even if I had wanted to.'

The older policeman nodded. 'That's no different to the statement of the witness.'

'Was she hurt? The girl?'

'No.'

'I was afraid she might have been raped.'

'She wasn't hurt. They took her bag, but we recovered it when we arrested them.'

'You caught them?'

I must have sounded surprised, because the younger policeman seemed to take offence.

'We do catch people sometimes,' he said, with a little heat in his voice.

The older policeman continued. 'When they jumped off at the next station, they'd been captured five different times on CCTV before they even reached street level. In fact, two of them we were able to track on camera right to the doors of their homes. They won't be getting away with this; you can rest assured of that.'

'What about my bag?' I asked. 'I had a bag. Did you recover that too?'

The older policeman frowned. 'A bag?'

'Yes. With a brass clasp. It had papers inside.'

Figure 6.9   Woodcut from *The Coma* (Garland, 2004).

Characterisation and narrative

Many literary works use images as clues to characterisation, an important aspect of narrative which you looked at in Chapter 3. A good example is found in Mark Haddon's *The Curious Incident of the Dog in the Night-Time* (2003), a book widely read by both adults and children. Christopher, the central protagonist and narrator, is fifteen years old and has Asperger's syndrome. He has trouble understanding what people mean if they depart from the strictly literal – in particular he finds gestures, facial expressions and metaphors incomprehensible. In other words, he cannot read the semiotic codes on the connotative level:

> I find people confusing.
>
> This is for two main reasons.
>
> The first main reason is that people do a lot of talking without using any words. Siobhan says that if you raise one eyebrow it can mean lots of different things. It can mean 'I want to do sex with you' and it can also mean 'I think that what you just said was very stupid.'
>
> [...]
>
> The second main reason is that people often talk using metaphors. These are examples of metaphors:
>
> **I laughed my socks off.**
>
> **He was the apple of her eye.**
>
> **They had a skeleton in the cupboard.**
>
> **We had a real pig of a day.**
>
> **The dog was stone dead.**
>
> The word metaphor means carrying something from one place to another, and it comes from the Greek words μετα (which means *from one place to another*) and φερειν (which means *to carry*) and it is when you describe something by using a word for something that it isn't. This means that the word metaphor is a metaphor.
>
> I think it should be called a lie because a pig is not like a day and people do not have skeletons in their cupboards. And when I try and make a picture of the phrase in my head it just confuses me because imagining an apple in someone's eye doesn't have anything to do with liking someone a lot and it makes you forget what the person was talking about.
>
> (Haddon, 2003, pp. 19–20)

Highly intelligent and logical, Christopher documents these complexities throughout the book and details his rationale for telling his story in his own way (for example, by using prime numbers for the chapters of his story, complete with diagrams showing how prime numbers are identified). As you can see in Figure 6.10 below, he illustrates his writing when he feels the need to explain detail which to most people would seem superfluous, but which to Christopher is crucial.

restaurant or on a beach you couldn't understand what anyone was saying which was frightening.

It takes me a long time to get used to people I do not know. For example, when there is a new member of staff at school I do not talk to them for weeks and weeks. I just watch them until I know that they are safe. Then I ask them questions about themselves, like whether they have pets and what is their favourite colour and what do they know about the Apollo space missions and I get them to draw a plan of their house and I ask them what kind of car they drive, so I get to know them. Then I don't mind if I am in the same room as them and don't have to watch them all the time.

So talking to the other people in our street was brave. But if you are going to do detective work you have to be brave, so I had no choice.

First of all I made a plan of our part of the street which is called Randolph Street, like this

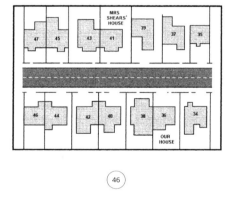

46

Then I made sure I had my Swiss Army Knife in my pocket and I went out and I knocked on the door of number 40 which is opposite Mrs Shears' house which means that they were most likely to have seen something. The people who live at number 40 are called Thompson.

Mr Thompson answered the door. He was wearing a T-shirt which said

Beer.
Helping ugly people
have sex for
2,000 years.

Mr Thompson said, 'Can I help you?'
I said, 'Do you know who killed Wellington?'
I did not look at his face. I do not like looking at people's faces, especially if they are strangers. He did not say anything for a few seconds.
Then he said, 'Who are you?'
I said, 'I'm Christopher Boone from number 36 and I know you. You're Mr Thompson.'
He said, 'I'm Mr Thompson's brother.'
I said, 'Do you know who killed Wellington?'
He said, 'Who the fuck is Wellington?'
I said, 'Mrs Shears' dog. Mrs Shears is from number 41.'
He said, 'Someone killed her dog?'
I said, 'With a fork.'

 47

Figure 6.10   Christopher's narrative style (Haddon, 2003, pp. 46–7).

In this book, many aspects of Christopher's character are accessible to the reader through the writing itself, but his somewhat obsessive attention to detail evidenced by the images sends the reader a strong message about how he thinks and how he sees the world. You may like to revisit the discussion of characterisation in 'Eveline', in Chapter 3, and compare the two texts. 'Eveline' is perhaps more subtly layered in terms of characterisation – it is possible to see the visuals in *The Curious Incident* as 'closing down' the range of interpretations potentially available to the reader, although you may not agree with this. I will return to this point in Section 6.5. I now move on to look at texts in which the images almost assume the role of the narrator.

Picturebooks and multimodality

There are many modern picturebooks where the images assume a central role in telling the story and creating the central meaning(s) of the narrative. This is achieved in a variety of ways. Images are often wholly integrated with the words, and layout, image and typography are inextricably intertwined. An example of this is shown in Colour Figures 4 and 5, taken from a children's story by Sarah Fanelli, about a butterfly who lacks the confidence to fly. She travels around asking the world's flying experts for help – in the extract, she has partial success in Italy, before leaving for Paris. Among the many meaningful visual and verbal elements here, you could consider the following. On the first page:

- the signs which connote Italy and 'Italianness': Italian words (*via aerea, farfalla* – on Butterfly's purple wing); the buff-coloured wings with geometric drawings, reminiscent of Leonardo da Vinci's diagrams;
- the layout showing Butterfly taking off towards the right (like the NASA aeroplane poem, shown on page 255).

On the second page:

- the signs connoting 'Frenchness': the red, white and blue of the French flag; the French words; the Eiffel Tower;
- the layout of the words, reflecting Butterfly's descent to the ground in Paris.

On both pages, note that Butterfly's body is constructed of letterforms. A variety of backgrounds are used, most notably the 'graph paper' done in blue, perhaps connoting 'design' or 'technology' to echo the design of her mechanical wings by Leonardo in Italy.

Another visual device for narration is the cartoon format. Usually, cartoons use the left-to-right reading path of English prose (although this directionality can be violated to particular effect).

ACTIVITY 5 The cartoon format as narrative device

Allow about 30 minutes

Look at the double page spread taken from Raymond Briggs' story of the life of his parents, *Ethel and Ernest* (Colour Figure 6). The book – written primarily for an adult audience due to its subject matter – is an affectionate narration of the lives of the author's parents, from their early adulthood in the late 1920s when they met, through the birth of their son, the trials of living through the Second World War and their later life. The book ends with their deaths, within a year of one another, in the early 1970s. As you read, consider the following questions:

- Why do you think the author chose the cartoon format for his story?
- What elements of the visual and verbal text seem to you significant, and why? In other words, what are the signs and what do they connote?

Comment

The multiple signs – and therefore the possible range of interpretations – are complex. The text uses a fairly conventional cartoon format in some ways – scenes are depicted in a series of frames which are read from left to right, speech bubbles are connected graphically to the speaker or laid out in columns, so that the reader can attribute one part of the conversation to the man and the other to the woman. Emphasis and intonation are conveyed through large, bold type and capitalisation (and of course exclamation marks and 'spiky' speech bubbles). The fact that this cartoon is so carefully hand-drawn made me wonder if this has semiotic significance – the care and attention to detail evident in its production seem to add to the overall meaning of the book, as a 'homage' to the author's parents. The writing, too, seems genuinely handwritten rather than produced with a computer-generated cursive font. You may well, in your reading, have found other details more salient, such as the use of colour, perspective, and the details of the couple's clothing and car.

Image, words: which mode for which job?

I've already mentioned the use of maps in books to help the reader 'see' where the action 'happened' in order to fully enter into the narrative and take part in it. It can be worthwhile looking at which semiotic mode is used for which parts of a narrative, and why this might be the case.

Nikolajeva and Scott (2000) describe a variety of ways in which words and pictures can be combined:

[I]n *symmetrical* interaction, words and pictures tell the same story, essentially repeating information in different forms of communication. In *enhancing* interaction, pictures amplify more fully the meaning of the words, or the words expand the picture so that different information in the two modes of communication produces a more complex dynamic. When enhancing interaction becomes very significant, the dynamic becomes truly *complementary*. Dependent on the degree of different information presented, a *counterpointing* dynamic may develop where words and images collaborate to communicate meanings beyond the scope of either one alone. An extreme form of counterpointing is *contradictory* interaction, where words and pictures seem to be in opposition to one another. This ambiguity challenges the reader to mediate between the words and pictures to establish a true understanding of what is being depicted.

(Nikolajeva and Scott, 2000, pp. 225–6)

The next reading, by Clare Bradford, looks at combinations of word and image in postcolonial literature. Bradford is a researcher in children's literature at Deakin University, Australia. She is concerned here with representations, both linguistic and visual, of racial politics in children's books, and in this reading shows how these social tensions surface in texts from New Zealand and Canada. She shows how the images, as well as the verbal text, creatively disrupt expectations, taking traditional narratives and playing around with them.

In the first part of this reading, Bradford looks at Gavin Bishop's reworking of a traditional rhyme, 'The House that Jack Built'. In case you are not familiar with the rhyme he uses, it makes extensive use of parallelism, and goes like this:

This is the house that Jack built.

This is the malt
That lay in the house that Jack built.

This is the rat
That ate the malt
That lay in the house that Jack built.

And so on. The last stanza is:

This is the farmer sowing the corn,
That kept the cock that crowed in the morn,
That waked the priest all shaven and shorn,
That married the man all tattered and torn,
That kissed the maiden all forlorn,
That milked the cow with the crumpled horn,
That tossed the dog,
That worried the cat,
That killed the rat,
That ate the malt
That lay in the house that Jack built.

Bradford then moves on to another text, *A Coyote Columbus Story*. Coyote is a mystical creature, part-human, part-canine, who occurs in many oral folktales around the world, but is particularly associated with indigenous North American Indians. Coyote is a devious trickster, not unlike Anansi from African folk tales (whom you will meet in Chapter 7).

A C T I V I T Y   6   Picturebook politics (Reading B)

Please read Clare Bradford's discussion of postcolonial politics in children's picturebooks, in Reading B. As you read, look out for:

- what Bradford points to as evidence of the instability of signs;

- how the interaction of words and images invites you to interpret these stories;

- the different connotations of visual signs when stories are re-told in new contexts for new audiences.

C o m m e n t

Bradford uses terms from semiotics in this reading, although her work is probably better located within a literary criticism approach rather than a semiotic or linguistic one. And although she picks out for analysis many semiotic signs in the texts, her focus is not strictly a Formalist one. For Bradford, the sociocultural significance of what she sees in these stories is at least as important as the textual elements themselves.

Bradford shows how analysis of visual representation illuminates the meanings in what appear at first to be simple narratives for children. The texts encode, through their words and pictures, conflicting messages and symbolism which convey hybrid, ambiguous or overtly political messages. Oppositional meanings are implied in both modes which destabilise the interpretation of the whole. Such texts are powerful as they call into question cultural narratives – stories we tell ourselves and each other about who we are – and can create unease. There are links here with the notion of 'hybridity' which you met in Chapter 1 (exemplified in relation to Asian Dub Foundation's rap music and Zadie Smith's novel *White Teeth*, in Alistair Pennycook's reading). In Chapter 1, Maybin and Pearce point to new, creative, hybrid cultural practices emerging from migration and the resulting mixing of traditions. Clare Bradford's texts provide further evidence of such texts emerging from postcolonial contexts.

In 'The House that Jack Built', signifiers are interpreted by Bradford as having different connotations in New Zealand than they did in the original British rhyme. How convincing did you find her interpretations? Did you agree, for example, that the copybook page in Figure 2 represented the imposition of English on the Maori people and the ascendancy of literacy over orality?

The example from Canada, *A Coyote Columbus Story*, demonstrates how mockery and cartoon-like parody can be used to undermine established narratives of colonial heroism. Although the language clearly pokes fun at Christopher Columbus, it is in the visuals that the real story takes place and readers are invited to take up a questioning and oppositional viewpoint to the verbal narrative.

'The House that Jack Built' and *A Coyote Columbus Story* are examples of texts in which the images carried a large part of the meaning, and introduced an ideological/politicised spin to the story represented in words. In Nikolajeva and Scott's terms then, we could see these texts as examples of a *counterpointing* dynamic, where additional meanings are generated by the interaction of words and images. Further along this cline is their *contradictory* interaction, an example of which is shown in Colour Figure 7. It is taken from Satoshi Kitamura's *Lily Takes a Walk* (1987), widely cited in the literature on picturebooks (e.g. Arizpe and Styles, 2003; Watson and Styles, 1996; Bromley, 2001). Here words and images struggle hard against each other in the text as they tell their contradictory stories.

Lily Takes a Walk tells the story of a little girl, Lily, who takes her dog Nicky for a walk. The words tell the story from Lily's point of view and describe where she goes and what she sees on her very pleasant walk. Nicky's experience is entirely different: he sees monsters around every corner and threatening faces in the forms of lamp posts, pillar boxes, and so on. The catalogue of horrors he experiences is represented entirely in the visual mode. Lily, whose experience is represented verbally, is oblivious.

Lily Takes a Walk is not, of course, an 'ideological' text in the way that those shown in Reading B were, although it could be interpreted as rejecting any notion that allowing a young child to walk the city streets unaccompanied by an adult is potentially dangerous. Crucial to a semiotic reading of any text is an understanding of the culture, context and prevailing concerns of the society in which it was produced, and the purpose and significance of the text. The importance of this knowledge for interpretation has been demonstrated in the examples so far in this chapter, but I want to outline the concept of **semiotic domains** (Gee, 2003). It provides a useful broadening of semiotics, describing the kinds of knowledge that readers need to have in order to engage in all sorts of social practices, including reading. Gee's work has, generally, an educational focus, but his recognition of the importance of being able to 'read' further than the literal meaning of words on a page is what makes it useful here.

Semiotic domains

By a semiotic domain I mean any set of practices that recruits one or more modalities (e.g. oral or written language, images, equations, symbols, sounds, gestures, graphs, artifacts, etc.) to communicate distinctive types of meanings. Here are some examples of semiotic domains: cellular biology, postmodern literary criticism, first-person-shooter video games, high-fashion advertisements, Roman Catholic theology, modernist painting, midwifery, rap music, wine connoisseurship. [...]

[Take a sentence] about basketball – "The guard dribbled down court, held up two fingers, and passed to the open man" – is a sentence from the semiotic domain of basketball. It might seem odd to call basketball a semiotic domain. However, in basketball, particular words, actions, objects, and images take on distinctive meanings. In basketball, 'dribble' does not mean drool; a pick (an action where an offensive player positions him or herself so as to block a defensive player guarding one of his or her teammates) means that some defensive player must quickly switch to guard the now-unguarded offensive player; and the wide circle on each end of the court means that players who shoot from beyond it get three points instead of two if they score a basket.

If you don't know these meanings – cannot read these signs – then you can't 'read' (understand) basketball. The matter seems fairly inconsequential when we are talking about basketball. However, it quickly seems more consequential when we are talking about the semiotic domain of some type of science being studied in school. [...]

In the modern world, print literacy is not enough. People need to be literate in a great variety of different semiotic domains. If these domains involve print, people often need the print bits, of course. However, the vast majority of domains involve semiotic (symbolic, representational) resources besides print and some don't involve print as a resource at all.

(Gee, 2003, pp. 18–19)

As readers or viewers, our recognition of semiotic domains will vary according to our social and cultural background. In Reading B we could, for example, identify the semiotic domains of colonial history and postcolonial resistance to that history, as well as canonical English children's literature and nursery rhymes. These domains are particularly salient in the visual mode.

The next section in this chapter continues the focus on sociocultural aspects of multimodality, and contains the final reading (Reading C), on the subject of postmodern literature. I look at some possibilities for analysing multimodal texts in terms of the wider literary and social trend of postmodernism, seeing if and how multimodal texts can be seen to fit within this trend.

6.4 Postmodern multimodal literature

In the next reading, Lewis starts by outlining some key features of postmodernity.

Postmodernity and postmodernism are notoriously difficult to define, but for our purposes here it is enough to understand postmodernity as a cultural condition ('the state we find ourselves in'), of living in an increasingly technologically orientated society, with lower levels of trust in authority and 'truth' than previously, where the meaning of things is unstable and open to interpretation. Postmodernism, as it relates to literature, can be understood to refer to texts that can be seen to represent such instability and unreliability. A key feature of postmodern texts is the intrusion of the author. Postmodern texts are often playful, opening up alternative interpretations for the reader in a variety of creative ways:

> Postmodern literature and art often challenge conventions of representation, particularly any straightforward notions of unity of meaning, emphasising instead the possibility of consciously playing with meaning in any text or art form.
>
> (Swann, et al., 2004, p. 246)

The next reading is about postmodernism in children's literature.

ACTIVITY 7   **Postmodernism in fiction (Reading C)**

Read Reading C, 'Postmodernism and the picturebook', by David Lewis. Lewis provides a useful framework for thinking about the links between trends in sociology and cultural studies, adult literature and picturebooks. He starts by outlining some of the main aspects of postmodernity – indeterminacy, fragmentation, decanonisation, irony and hybridisation. These are not, of course, exclusive properties of postmodern texts: indeterminacy and irony are, for example, features of many novels and poems. At issue perhaps is the degree to which such features seem salient to the reader: the extent to which they invite us to see them as 'postmodern'. You have already considered the idea of the literary canon and the notion of hybridity, in Chapter 1, and some of these concepts may be familiar to you from literary studies. What may be new is Lewis' analysis of how these are represented visually in texts for children. Activity 8 then offers some examples of texts (both children's and adult) which demonstrate his points.

ACTIVITY 8   **Postmodern picturebooks**

Allow 30–40 minutes

Look at Colour Figures 8 and 9. They are examples of what could be termed postmodern picturebooks (Child, 2003; Scieszka and Smith, 1993). What evidence can you find of the 'markers' of postmodernism that Lewis outlines?

Comment

In Colour Figure 8, *Who's Afraid of the Big Bad Book?* by Lauren Child, the main character, Herb, has found himself inadvertently in somebody else's story. The 'story', or what we initially assume to be the narrator's voice, is on the left

(*Herb woke with a start* ...). You may like to think about the significance of this position on the page, and whether or not this part of text is on a wall, a blackboard, a separate book? The girl's speech is printed in capitals and gets progressively bigger (suggestive of rising tone and volume?). It emerges at an angle from her mouth, and appears to be so forceful as to buffet the curtains at the window. Other visual and typographical pointers are the depiction of Herb's stammering, the girl's aggressive facial expression and the use of the (similarly aggressive?) angle of the girl's speech to draw us on to the next page.

The reader is obliged to interpret the words and pictures as a whole in this text – indeed it is arguable here whether the words are not actually more meaningful if interpreted as images. Even the boxed text on the left carries potential meanings unrelated to the words themselves, due to its positioning, its difference to the rest of the page, and its plain background, set apart from the other elements. In postmodern terms, the text is unstable and hybrid, positioning the reader uncomfortably. The text is **polysemous** – that is, open to multiple interpretations. We are left unsure of the identity of the narrator, our relationship with the shrieking girl, and even which (whose) story we are reading. It posits a complex reading position where we have to accept instability and uncertain meanings as part of the experience.

The second example, Colour Figure 9, is similarly unsettling and equally fun. Here the narrator explicitly breaks into the story being told by the Little Red Hen and starts arguing about the proper place in the book for its non-narrative elements (endpapers, title pages and so on). This intrusion forces the reader back to reality: we are pulled back with a jolt from 'storyland' into the real world. We are 'knowing' in all sorts of ways: we know that books are produced as commercial and cultural artefacts; we also know that to read a book is to enter an imaginary world. Here our expectations are undermined and we have no choice but to play along with this fragmentation of identity and roles. (Who is the narrator? Jack? The Little Red Hen? The authors? The reader? All of us?) Texts such as these make demands on the reader, who is forced to construct some kind of narrative sense out of a multitude of possibilities.

These are just a few preliminary reflections linking the examples to the points in Lewis' reading – you will probably think of many more questions yourself and link them to issues he raises. The example in Figure 6.11 serves to illustrate that adult fiction can also be playful, and creatively disrespectful of boundaries and conventions. The endpaper from Dave Eggers' *A Heartbreaking Work of Staggering Genius* (2000) shows the author intervening in the space conventionally reserved for legal and copyright information. There's a good chance that most readers would merely glance at this. Unless you were a writer intending to cite from the book, or had

First published 2000 by Simon & Schuster, New York, a division of a larger and
more powerful company called Viacom Inc., which is wealthier and more populous than
eighteen of the fifty states of America, all of Central America, and all of the former Soviet Republics
combined and tripled. That said, no matter how big such companies are, and how many things they
own, or how much money they have or make or control, their influence over the daily lives and hearts
of individuals, and thus, like ninety-nine percent of what is done by official people in cities like
Washington, or Moscow, or São Paulo or Auckland, their effect on the short, fraught lives of
human beings who limp around and sleep and dream of flying through bloodstreams, who
love the smell of rubber cement and think of space travel while having intercourse,
is very very small, and so hardly worth worrying about.

This edition published 2000 by Picador
an imprint of Macmillan Publishers Ltd
25 Eccleston Place, London SW1W 9NF
Basingstoke and Oxford
Associated companies throughout the world
www.macmillan.co.uk

ISBN 0 330 48454 0

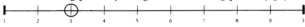

A portion of this book appeared in *The New Yorker* in a somewhat different form.

NOTE: This is a work of fiction, only in that in many cases, the author could not remember
the exact words said by certain people, and exact descriptions of certain things, so had to fill in
gaps as best he could. Otherwise, all characters and incidents and dialogue are real, are not products
of the author's imagination, because at the time of this writing, the author had no imagination
whatsoever for those sorts of things, and could not conceive of *making up* a story or characters—it
felt like driving a car in a clown suit—especially when there was so much to say about his own, true,
sorry, and inspirational story, the actual people that he has known, and of course the many twists and
turns of his own thrilling and complex mind. Any resemblance to persons living or dead should be
plainly apparent to them and those who know them, especially if the author has been kind enough to
have provided their real names and, in some cases, their phone numbers. All events described herein
actually happened, though on occasion the author has taken certain, very small, liberties with
chronology, because that is his right as an American.

7 9 8

A CIP catalogue record for this book is available from the British Library.

Printed and bound in Great Britain by Mackays of Chatham plc, Chatham, Kent

Figure 6.11   *A Heartbreaking Work of Staggering Genius* (Dave Eggers, 2000).

a pressing need for the address of the publisher, you would normally have no reason to look at an endpaper.

There is a kind of comedy double act going on here, this time with the visual layout playing the 'straight man'. The combination of conventional print size, shape, location and general appearance of the endpapers – and, of course, the reader's expectations – makes this look conventional and unexceptional. The joke – the creative intervention into both the text and our expectations – takes place in the verbal mode.

More visible traces of postmodernism in adult literature are the creative uses of typography and layout to signify different voices in the text. There are many examples of these: one is Mark Danielewski's *House of Leaves* (2000), which has a different typeface for each 'voice', and different characters intruding on each other's prose, inserting footnotes, poems, citations, contradictions and corrections, musical notation and images.

In Reading C, Lewis referred to the 'flattening out of differences between high and low', and postmodernism's tendency towards hybridisation of styles. This 'mixing and matching' can be seen in many of the texts discussed in this chapter: rules and conventions are cheerfully disregarded, the narrator interrupts the reader, and grammatical rules are violated to creative effect.

I now return briefly to an issue raised in the introduction to this chapter, which is how we decide which multimodal texts are creative, and also how we decide which have 'literary value'.

6.5 Valuing multimodal texts

In this chapter I have explored a number of ways of looking at and analysing multimodal texts. The examples shown can be said to display creativity or 'artistry' in some way, but not all multimodal texts are necessarily creative, even some of those which can be analysed as 'literary' via Formalism. There are dangers in assigning the 'creative' label to any text purely on the basis of its visual nature. Multimodal texts are ubiquitous in everyday life (shop and traffic signs, labels and packaging, telephone directories). But although these are often analysable in terms of poetic structures such as deviation or parallelism, some, like dead metaphors, are now so routinised that they deliver little by way of illumination of creativity, even if they might be interesting for other reasons. Not everything that is created is creative, perhaps – some texts and artefacts are simply 'made' or 'produced' (Pope, 2005).

So on what basis do we as readers judge multimodal literature as 'good' or 'bad'? These are necessarily subjective judgements. Perhaps we learn to ascribe value to multimodal literary texts depending on the same (albeit even less specific) notions of 'good' and 'bad', or 'high' and 'low', discussed in earlier chapters. In a sense, then, our aesthetic judgements depend at least in part on what we have learned to value in our society and culture. Tenniel's illustrations in *Alice's Adventures in Wonderland*, or E.H. Shepard's in *Winnie the Pooh,* tend be accorded high value, but it is very difficult to disentangle them from the value accorded to the whole text, both being widely accepted as part of the canon of English literature. Viewed in isolation, for example, 'The Mouse's Tale' could be said to be quite superficial in terms of the range of interpretations and layers of meaning it potentially offers to the reader. It is a successful, quick pun between visual and verbal modes, but there is no real complexity in the poem in terms of the relationship between the actual words used, the overall shape it takes, and the meanings. In Reading C of Chapter 2, Richard Bradford argued that 'good literature' is distinguished from 'bad literature' by the extent to which form and meaning are held in balance – a complex interplay that allows a poem to resist closure. 'The Mouse's Tale' is fun, but it seems to me that here meaning is rather unrelated to form, apart from the tale/tail pun. The poem 'she being Brand', on the other hand, by e e cummings, can be seen as having a clearer relationship between typographical form, and at least two possible interpretations of the meaning of the poem – a drive in a new car, or a sexual experience. Re-readings of this poem can easily trigger new associations and semantic connections: it resists closure, leaving us slightly unsure as to what is its central topic.

The context in which we encounter a text can also influence the value we ascribe to it. Chapter 1 contained the example of 'The Unknown', a 'poem' constructed – by setting it out in a 'poem-like' way – from a political speech by Donald Rumsfeld, at a US Department of Defense news briefing in February 2002. It has been taken from the mode of speech into the mode of writing, and laid out on the page in a way which suggests (visually) 'this is poetry'. We can of course analyse it as a poem, even without knowing its provenance, and find that it 'counts' as poetry because of its textual features. But one of the main signifiers in Hart Seely's reappropriation of the words as a poem is the visual layout. The change from oral to visual mode enacts a re-evaluation of the text – Seely decided that it 'counted' as poetry, set it out as such, and in doing so asks us to accept his claim.

But the visual appearance of a poem can also lead us to devalue its worth. Figure 6.12 is an example that, for me at least, does not 'count' as poetry.

This 'found poem' is part of a collection of texts encountered at random by Kenneth Goldsmith, posted up on billboards or taped onto lamp posts in New York City. There are at least 75 'found' texts on the UbuWeb website, all varying considerably in their style and purpose. Some are home-made adverts, some are appeals for information about lost dogs, and so on, and some, like this one, claim to be poetry. In some respects it succeeds, for me, in its claim to be a poem – a Formalist analysis would find that it rhymes, it scans, it has repetition and parallelism. But despite the claim to be accepted as a poem evidenced in its title ('Poems For All'), I find it particularly hard to divorce the *words* of the poem itself from the *look* of it and the fact that it was found in the street. I find this poem interesting because of its scrawled,

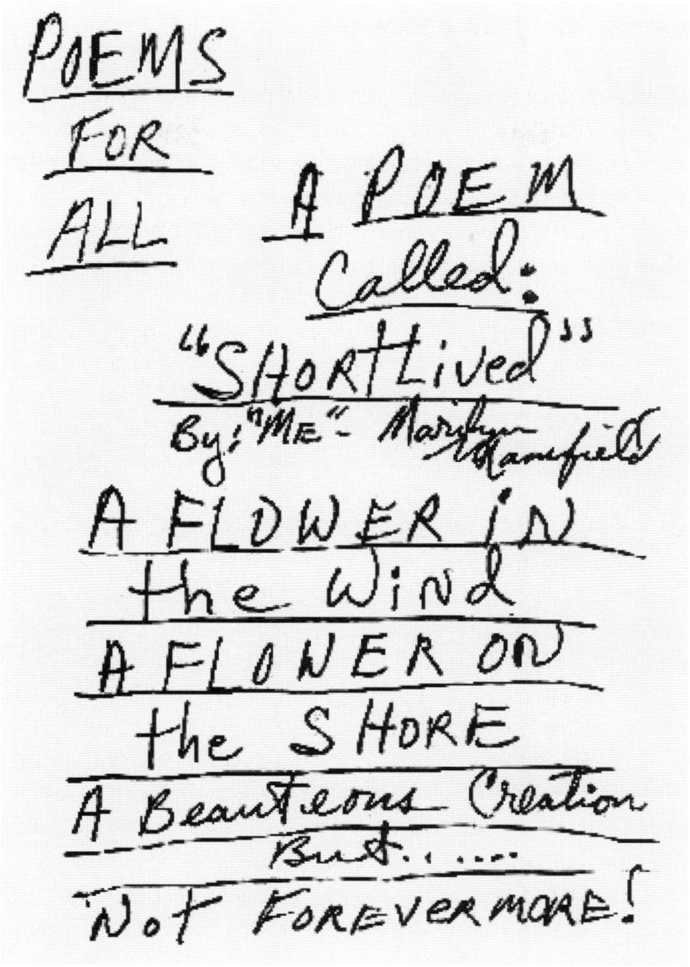

Figure 6.12   Poem collected from a public space in New York City (Kenneth Goldsmith).

handwritten letters (and the erratic mix of lower and upper case), the underlining, and the tatty paper it is written on.

Materials are imbued with semiotic significance – a hasty, handwritten note pinned to an office door has a different meaning to an engraved plaque, even if the words themselves are identical. We take meaning from texts depending on what they are made of (pen on notepaper, graffiti on a wall) and on where we encounter them. 'The Mouse's Tale' could *mean* differently if it were subway graffiti, or scrawled on a torn piece of notepaper like 'Poems For All'. 'Materiality' – the stuff that texts are made of – can be seen as significant in terms of literary value.

ACTIVITY 9   Context, material and value

Allow 10 minutes

Figure 6.13 shows a poem carved along the length of an underpass wall at Waterloo station in London. The two photographs are of the same poem – it starts at the underpass entrance as shown in the first, then continues down the pedestrian walkway as shown in the second. Do you accept it as poetry? Would you change your mind if you found it spray-painted rather than carved, or printed in a book rather than created on a wall?

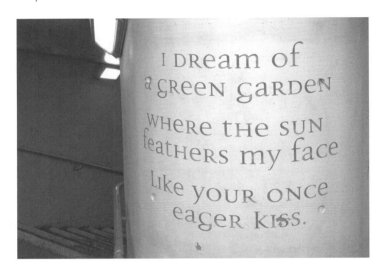

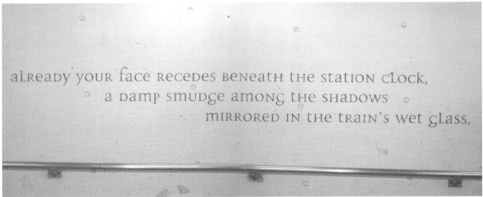

Figure 6.13   Verses from 'Eurydice' (Sue Hubbard).

Comment

Like 'Poems For All', this is a poem encountered in a public space. I would accept this as poetry, and accord it literary value. Its meaning and form seem to connect quite directly with each other, and with the context of the poem's encounter. There are references such as *damp city streets* and *rush-hour headlights* which the weary commuter passing through the subway would find easy to relate to. You may well disagree.

6.6 Conclusion

This chapter has shown some of the many ways in which authors and illustrators can use visual communication in their work. There is a huge range of possible signifiers, from non-standard punctuation (as in the cummings poem), to concrete poetry, to whole multimodal books where an understanding of the visual meaning is just as important, if not more so, than the words.

I have introduced different ways of approaching multimodal literature, from the Formalist or inherency-based to the more sociocultural. Inevitably, we tend to use a combination of approaches when faced with a multimodal text, as they provide us with different tools. Semiotics, for example, relies on an understanding of social and cultural connotations to find the meaning of the linguistic or visual sign in the text. Similarly, as Clare Bradford showed in Reading B, the meanings of individual signs in the text and their shifting meanings in different cultures are crucial to understanding the oppositional narrative presented by writers in postcolonial contexts.

What such texts mean to us as readers is due in no small part to our previous experience of literary texts and our culture, and to what we have been taught to value. As with language, visual elements of a text are often intertextual. These may be allusions to other visual texts, or deliberate connections made across semiotic modes such as in punning. In terms of Russian Formalism, writers and illustrators can be seen as creating and re-creating poetic structures, making the textual world strange and forcing us to consider it afresh.

I have looked in this chapter at some texts that use (or ask the reader to infer) a further semiotic mode – movement. The next chapter takes this further, introducing multimodal texts such as film and the internet. As well as considering further semiotic *modes* in literary texts, Chapter 7 looks in more detail at readers and producers of such texts. So, as well as continuing with analysis of multimodal texts, Chapter 7 considers what readers/viewers do when engaging with and interpreting literary texts, and how the wider adoption of technology has the potential to turn us all into film producers or internet authors.

READING A: Extracts from 'Signs and myths'

Jonathan Bignell

Semiotics originates mainly in the work of two people, Ferdinand de Saussure, and Charles Peirce. Their ideas are quite closely related, but exhibit some differences. [...] Saussure showed that language is made up of signs (like words) which communicate meanings, and he expected that all kinds of other things which communicate meanings could potentially be studied in the same way as linguistic signs, using the same methods of analysis.

Semiotics or semiology, then, is the study of signs in society, and while the study of linguistic signs is one branch of it, it encompasses every use of a system where something (the sign) carries a meaning for someone. [...] Since language is the most fundamental and pervasive medium for human communication, semiotics takes the way that language works as the model for all other media of communication, all other sign systems. [...]

Sign systems

Saussure's first move was to set limits to the variety of tasks which his study of language might involve. Instead of considering language from a psychological, sociological, or physiological point of view, he decided to focus on a clearly defined object of study: the linguistic sign. He showed that the linguistic sign is arbitrary. The linguistic sign 'cat' is arbitrary in that it has no connection either in its sound, or its visual shape, with what cats are really like. In another language, the sign for cat will be different from the linguistic sign in English (e.g. French uses *chat*). Clearly, there must be a kind of agreement among the users of our language that the sign 'cat' shall refer to a particular group of furry four-legged animals. But this agreement about signs is not consciously entered into, since we learn how to use language so early in our lives that there can be no deliberate choice available to us. Language has always been there before we arrived on the scene. Even if I perversely decided to adopt another sign for what we call a cat, like 'yarup' for instance, this sign would be entirely useless since no-one else would understand me. The capacity of linguistic signs to be meaningful depends on their existence in a social context, and on their conventionally accepted use in that social context.

[...] The systems in which signs are organised into groups are called codes. This is a familiar term, for instance in the phrase 'dress codes'. In our society, the dress code that governs what men should wear when going to a formal wedding includes items like a top hat and a tail jacket. [...] By contrast, a man might select jogging shorts, training shoes and a baseball cap to go to the local gym. These clothing signs belong to a different dress code, and communicate a message of 'informality'. In the case of dress codes, it is possible to select the clothing signs which we use in order to communicate particular messages about ourselves. Even when clothes perform practical functions (like the loose and light clothes worn to play sports) codes still give social meanings to our choices, like codes of fashionableness and codes governing what men may wear versus what women may wear. [...]

Components of the sign

[...] In his analysis of linguistic signs, Saussure showed that there are two components to every sign. One is the vehicle which expresses the sign, like a pattern of sound which makes up a word, or the marks on paper which we read as words, or the pattern of shapes and colours which photographs use to represent an object or person. This vehicle which exists in the material world is called the 'signifier'. The other part of the sign is called the 'signified'. The signified is the concept which the signifier calls forth when we perceive it. So when you perceive the sign 'cat' written on this page, you perceive a group of marks, the letters c, a, and t, which are the signifier. This signifier is the vehicle which immediately calls up the signified or concept of cat in your mind. The sign is the inseparable unity of the signifier with the signified, since in fact we never have one without the other. [...]

Sequences of linguistic signs

[...] When signs are spread out in a sequence over time, or have an order in their spatial arrangement, their order is obviously important. In a sentence like 'The dog bites the man', meaning unfolds from left to right along the line of the sentence, as we read the words in sequence one after another. This horizontal movement is called the 'syntagmatic' aspect of the sentence. If we reverse the order into 'The man bites the dog', the meaning is obviously different. Each linguistic sign in the syntagm could also be replaced by another sign which is related to it, having perhaps the same grammatical function, a similar sound, or relating to a similar signified. It is as if there are vertical lists of signs intersecting the horizontal line of the sentence, where our sentence has used one of the signs in each vertical list.

See also the discussion of syntagm and paradigm in Chapter 2.

These lists of signs are called 'paradigms'. We could replace 'dog' with 'cat' or 'tiger', and replace 'bites' with 'licks' or 'kicks' or 'chews'. Each different selection from these paradigms would alter the meaning of the syntagm, our horizontal sentence of words.

[...] As a general principle, every sign that is present must be considered in relation to other signs present in the structure of the articulation, and every sign present has meaning by virtue of the other signs which have been excluded and are not present in the text.

Visual signs

Most of the account of linguistic signs above comes directly from Saussure, but some of the principles and terms [...] derive from the semiotic work of the American philosopher Charles S. Peirce (1958). In particular, the semiotic analysis of images and other nonverbal signs is made much more effective by some of Peirce's distinctions. Although language is the most striking form of human sign production, the whole of our social world is pervaded by messages which contain visual as well as linguistic signs, or which are exclusively visual. Gestures, dress codes, traffic signs, advertising images, newspapers, television programmes and so on are all kinds of media which use visual signs. The same principles underlie the semiotic study of visual signs and linguistic signs. In each case, there is a material signifier, which expresses the sign, and a mental concept, a signified, which immediately accompanies it. Visual signs also belong to codes, are arranged in syntagms, and selected from paradigms. [...]

We have already seen how linguistic signs are arbitrary, since there is no necessary connection between the signifier 'cat' on this page and the signified concept of cat in our minds. [...] The relationship of signifier to signified, and of sign to referent, is entirely a matter of the conventions established [...] in this case by the English language in particular. This type of sign, characterised by arbitrariness, Peirce calls the 'symbolic' sign.

But a photograph of a cat looks recognisably like a specific cat. The arrangement of shape and colour in the photograph, the signifier which expresses the signified 'cat', has a close resemblance to its referent, the real cat which the photograph represents. In a photograph, the signifier is the colour and shape on the flat surface of the picture. The signified is the concept of a cat which this signifier immediately calls up. The referent is the cat which was photographed. Just as my cat is white with some black and orange patches, so a photograph of my cat will faithfully record these different shapes and colours. This kind of sign, where the signifier resembles the referent, Peirce calls an 'iconic' sign. [...] Unlike the case of linguistic signs, iconic signs have the property of merging the signifier, signified and referent together. It is much more difficult to realise that the two components of the photographic sign plus their referent are three different things. It is for this reason that photographic media seem to be more realistic than linguistic media [...].

When a cat is hungry and miaows to gain our attention, the sound made by the cat is pointing to its presence nearby, asking us to notice it, and this kind of sign Peirce calls 'indexical'. Indexical signs have a concrete and often causal relationship to their signified. The shadow cast on a sundial tells us the time, it is an indexical sign which is directly caused by the position of the sun, and similarly smoke is an index of fire, a sign caused by the thing which it signifies. Certain signs have mixed symbolic, indexical and iconic features. For instance, a traffic light showing red has both indexical and symbolic components. It is an indexical sign pointing to a traffic situation (that cars here must wait), and using an arbitrary symbolic system to do this (red arbitrarily signifies danger and prohibition in this context).

Connotation and myth

[...] Because we use signs to describe and interpret the world, it often seems that their function is simply to 'denote' something, to label it. The linguistic sign 'Rolls-Royce' denotes a particular make of car, or a photographic sign showing Buckingham Palace denotes a building in London. But along with the denotative, or labelling function of these signs to communicate a fact, come some extra associations which are called 'connotations'. Because Rolls-Royce cars are expensive and luxurious, they can be used to connote signifieds of wealth and luxury. The linguistic sign 'Rolls-Royce' is no longer simply denoting a particular type of car, but generating a whole set of connotations which come from our social experience. The photograph of Buckingham Palace not only denotes a particular building, but also connotes signifieds of royalty, tradition, wealth and power.

When we consider advertising, news, and TV or film texts, it will become clear that linguistic, visual, and other kinds of sign are used not simply to denote something, but also to trigger a range of connotations attached to the sign. [The French critic, Roland] Barthes calls this social phenomenon, the bringing-together of signs and their connotations to shape a particular message, the making of 'myth'. Myth here does not refer to mythology in the usual sense of traditional stories, but to ways of thinking about people, products, places, or ideas which are structured to send particular messages to the reader or viewer of the text. So an advertisement for shoes which contains a photograph of someone stepping out of a Rolls Royce is not only denoting the shoes and a car, but attaching the connotations of luxury which are available through the sign 'Rolls-Royce' to the shoes, suggesting a mythic meaning in which the shoes are part of a privileged way of life. [...]

Myth takes hold of an existing sign, and makes it function as a signifier on another level. The sign 'Rolls-Royce' becomes the signifier attached to the signified 'luxury', for example. It is as if myth were a special form of language, which takes up existing signs and makes a new sign system out of them. [...M]yth is not an innocent language, but one that picks up existing signs and their connotations, and orders them purposefully to play a particular social role.

Reference

PEIRCE, C.S. (1958) *Selected Writings (Values in a Universe of Chance)*, ed. P. WIENER, New York, Dover Press.

Source: BIGNELL, J. (2002) *Media Semiotics: An Introduction,* 2nd edn, Chapter 1, Manchester/New York, Manchester University Press.

READING B: Extract from 'Narratives of identity and history in settler colony texts'

Clare Bradford

I [consider here] picture books which engage in the postcolonial strategy of revisioning history, representing colonial events from the point of view of indigenous peoples: [...] a New Zealand text, Gavin Bishop's *The House that Jack Built* (1999), and a Canadian text, Thomas King's *A Coyote Columbus Story* (1992), with illustrations by William Kent Monkman. Bishop is a Maori author-illustrator; King is a Native author of Cherokee descent; and Kent Monkman belongs to the Swampy Kree band [a group of native communities in Canada]. [...]

The House that Jack Built

Gavin Bishop's *The House that Jack Built* concerns itself with colonial history and its effect upon the land and its indigenous people. The narrative is focused through the story of Jack Bull, who departs London in 1798 and whose progress from trader to wealthy merchant is ended in the Land Wars of the 1860s. Bishop draws upon three quite distinct sets of visual imagery: Western styles of representational art; folk art characterised by stylised figures and forms; and symbols from Maori mythology. These three strands comment ironically on one another as well as producing a composite portrait of a nation where British and Maori traditions and ideologies jostle and struggle for ascendancy. [...]

The nursery rhyme that comprises the book's verbal text is, like Jack Bull, of British stock, and is imbued with signifiers (cow, dog, cat, rat, malt, priest, soldier)[1] which, in the new country, no longer bear stable relations to systems of meaning. Such instability is crucial to Bishop's postcolonial strategy of defamiliarising aspects of European culture by representing them through Maori perspectives, an effective example of which occurs in the double-spread in which a Maori man encounters the 'cow with the crumpled horn', depicted following its act of tossing the dog that worried the cat [see Figure 1].

The elaborate borders on the spread enclose a narrative about the *taniwha*, a shape-changing trickster who 'could look like a log floating in the water or he could look like an eel'. The Maori is a man of status — he wears a nephrite ear-pendant and ornamental feathers in his hair, bears the *moko* (tattoo) of a warrior and holds a wooden club with a carved edge. He does not, however, wear a traditional cloak made of flax fibre, but a length of red flannel from Jack Bull's store, which in itself is suggestive of a shift in signification: a length of cloth within British culture comprises the raw materials for a garment, whereas for this Maori warrior it functions as a cloak. However, as is clear from the folds at his neck and the necessity of holding the fabric with one hand, it departs from traditions of Maori garment-making,

Figure 1   Gavin Bishop, *The House that Jack Built,* pp. 8–9.

which through complex techniques of weaving produced cloaks designed to fit the body, and which were finished with ties, borders and sometimes collars (Pendergrast, 1996, pp. 126–43). Throughout Polynesia the colour red was 'the colour of rank and sacred value' (Neich, 1996, pp. 74–5), worn only by those of the highest status, whereas Jack Bull's red flannel allows anyone to appropriate such a position. The length of red cloth worn by the warrior is therefore a sign of indeterminacy – neither British nor Maori in its form and function, and metonymic of the shifting meanings of colonialism and its destabilisation of traditional life.

Bishop's strategy of placing this moment of encounter within a frame alluding to Maori traditions filters figures and events through a perspective that accepts the existence of a host of supernatural beings, deities, spirits and ancestors intimately involved in the lives of humans (Te Awekotuku, 1996, pp. 26–30). The spirals incorporated into the frame, and the face with protruding tongue and rolling eyes seen at top left, encode this supernatural world, while in the background beyond the cow and the man, the eyes of the gods can be seen. These eyes, staring out of the page and ungrounded in bodily forms, position readers to imagine a watching presence, just as the wary, knowing eyes of the cat at the bottom right of the picture seem to observe and judge from the perspective of a creature introduced to the land. The encounter between the cow and the warrior, which on the face of it has a ludic quality, in fact conveys a much more serious interplay between cultures with opposing and incompatible epistemologies and systems of valuing and belief.

The book's visual narrative represents colonisation as a process in which Maori people experience alienation and degradation: Jack Bull cuts down trees to build his house without appeasing Tane, the god of the forests; Maori use shellfish to barter for goods instead of as food for their people; and rifles, alcohol and tobacco become the principal objects of trade. Along with this narrative goes another, which involves the courtship of 'the man all tattered and torn' and 'the maiden all forlorn'. The man in question is European and the maiden Maori, and their interracial relationship is blessed by 'the priest all shaven and shorn' who stands before the pair at their wedding [see Figure 2].

This is the **priest** all **shaven** and **shorn**,
That **married** the man all tattered and torn,
That kissed the maiden all forlorn,
That milked the cow with the crumpled horn,
That tossed the dog,
That worried the cat,
That killed the rat,
That ate the malt,
That lay in the house that Jack built.

Figure 2   Gavin Bishop, *The House that Jack Built*, pp. 21–2.

The woman wears a nephrite *tiki*, which is traditionally associated with fruitfulness, while the man smiles out of the page, his *pohutukawa* buttonhole echoing the flowers with which the woman is adorned. Behind the pair the eyes of the gods observe, while in the facing page a complex set of signifiers appears. The copybook page which serves as background encodes the imposition of English upon indigenous people and the ascendancy of literacy over orality, while the framed, folk-art picture beneath the rhyme identifies colonisation with Christianity and Maori culture with devil worship. These signifiers of constraint and prohibition are taken up in the carving that ushers in the scene of the wedding. and relate specifically to sexuality, for the genitalia of the two ancestor figures are covered by the Christian symbol of the cross. Bishop's representation of the happy couple and the possibility of interracial harmony, read in the light of these images, is thus loaded with doubt and premonition.

From this point, the narrative tends towards conflict as the land is engulfed by buildings; the native birds are driven out by the 'cock that crowed in the morn'; and the farmer sows his corn on land formerly covered by trees. The poem's reference to the 'soldier all weary and worn' leads to a page whose border describes how Tumatauenga, the war god, 'called to the people of the land. "*E Tu!*" he cried "Stand up! Protect the earth mother! Rise up! Fight for the spirit of Papatuanuku." The people took up their weapons and the terrible dance of war was heard over the land.'[2] Bishop's note, 'About this book', also appears on this spread, explaining that 'on the last pages the conflict is recorded for future generations on the wall of a meeting house in a folk-art style blending traditional Maori and European artforms. Both cultures are now intertwined in the rich history of Aotearoa.' But the impact of the book's endpapers ironises Bishop's explanation, especially his final sentence concerning racial harmony. For these *tukutuku* panels[3] comprise three images: *te pakeha*, the Pakeha; *Tumatauenga*, the god of war; and *te tangata whenua*, the people of the land [see Figure 3].

Figure 3   Gavin Bishop, *The House that Jack Built*, endpapers.

Not only are Maori and Pakeha separated by Tumatauenga, so interrogating the notion that the two cultures are 'now intertwined', but the nature of the images – the static, warlike poses – fixes them in a state of conflict. The central image of Tumatauenga, which adheres to the stylised figure of the *manaia*,[4] has a forcefulness which makes it the focus of the panel, producing the inference that conflict is inevitably present in interactions between Pakeha and Maori.

A Coyote Columbus Story

Thomas King and William Kent Monkman's *A Coyote Columbus Story* deploys a different strategy for rereading colonialism, one involving the parodic undermining of the high seriousness with which stories of colonial exploration have traditionally been told, and of the trope of explorer as hero. The trickster figure of Coyote (represented in Kent Monkman's illustrations dressed in shorts, shocking pink tanktop and sneakers) creates turtles, beavers, moose and turtles expressly to join in the game of ball which she desires above everything else. When these creatures evince little enthusiasm for the game, she 'sings her song and dances her dance and thinks so hard her nose falls off', and so creates Native people, who enjoy playing ball until they grow weary of Coyote's propensity for changing the rules in order to win. It is at this point, when Coyote is bored, that she makes a foolish mistake – she 'doesn't watch what she is making up out of her head', and Christopher Columbus and his men arrive:

> Hello, says one of the men in silly clothes with red hair all over his head. I am Christopher Columbus. I am sailing the ocean blue looking for India. Have you seen it?
>
> Forget India, says Coyote. Let's play ball.

In a playful mix of periods and cultures, verbal and visual texts interrogate colonial discourses. Columbus is a cartoon figure, using words from a playground chant ('sailing the ocean blue') to describe his mission. Represented as a visual cliché, he is surrounded by characters who include an Elvis look-alike wearing red stilettos and carrying a bundle of firearms [see Figure 4]. With their golf clubs and suitcases, the explorers look like

Figure 4   Thomas King and William Kent Monkman, *A Coyote Columbus Story*, p. 15.

shady entrepreneurs and they prove themselves to be concerned solely with material gain as they search the New World for gold, chocolate cake, computer games and music videos. Within this scheme, native animals are no more than commodities:

> I see a four-dollar beaver, says one.
> I see a fifteen-dollar moose, says another.
> I see a two-dollar turtle, says a third.
> Those things aren't worth poop, says Christopher Columbus.
> We can't sell those things in Spain. Look harder.

When Columbus conceives the idea of transporting Indians to sell in Europe, Coyote laughs: 'Who would buy human beings, she says'. The frame of this coyote story does not allow for explicit moral commentary, since Coyote's concern is with the balance of humans with the natural environment, and not with individual humans. Rather, it is Kent Monkman's illustration that uncovers colonial meanings, showing 'a big bunch of men and women and children', tied together like so many pieces of firewood, transported from the shore to the Spanish frigates [see Figure 5].

Figure 5 Thomas King and William Kent Monkman, p. 23.

Readers are positioned to look from Columbus's gleeful smile as he stands at the foreground of the frame, to the Spanish sailor who gives him a thumbs-up sign; and from the sailor to the Native people as they stand in the dinghy, bound together. These are stereotypes of Indians – the unemotionality projected onto them within colonial discourses constructs them as Other, as impervious to the 'normal' range of emotions and as somewhat less than 'us'.

King's strategy of collapsing historical periods allows for a connection between colonial and neo-colonial practices: when Columbus returns to Spain, he sells the Indians to 'rich people like baseball players and dentists and babysitters and parents', figures representative of those who benefit from the labour migrations that feed the accelerating demands of contemporary capitalism. Meanwhile, emerging from their hiding places, the remaining Native people challenge Coyote: 'you better watch out or this world is going to get bent'. The narrative concludes with another wave of colonisers when Jacques Cartier reaches the New World. As the beavers, moose, turtles and human beings 'catch the first train to Penticton', Coyote continues to hope for another chance to play ball; however, the untrustworthy smiles of the colonisers, and their accoutrements of golfclubs and cameras, promise only the continuation of colonialism under a new guise.

The [two] picture books I have discussed are alike in their refusal of consolatory closures: [...] *The House that Jack Built* projects a future of cultural conflict; and *A Coyote Columbus Story* builds into its ending the expectation of new waves and forms of colonial subjection. These texts thus refuse to induct readers into the fantasy that colonialism is finished, its effects blunted and ameliorated by time. Rather, their revisionings of stories of colonial engagement insist on how the past is present to indigenous peoples and national cultures and remind readers to read against the grain of colonial and neo-colonial narratives.

Notes

1   Polynesian dogs (*kuri*) came to New Zealand with the ancestors of the Maori, but with the advent of European breeds of dog, the *kuri* was bred out. A species of small rat was also introduced by the Maori immigrants.

2   Papatuanuku is the earth goddess.

3   *Tututuku* are knotted latticework panels which feature in meeting houses. They are often used for narrative purposes.

4   *Manaia* are highly significant figures normally shown in profile and characterised by avian and reptilian features such as forked tongues and lizard-like feet; in ancient carvings, a hand with three fingers is common.

References

BISHOP, G. (1999) *The House that Jack Built*, Auckland and Sydney, Scholastic.

KING, T. and MONKMAN, W.K. (1992) *A Coyote Columbus Story*, Toronto, Douglas and McIntyre.

NEICH, R. (1996) 'Wood carving' in D.C. STARZECKA (ed.) *Maori Art and Culture*, pp. 69–113, London, British Museum Press.

PENDERGRAST, M. (1996) 'The Fibre Arts' in D.C. STARZECKA (ed.) *Maori Art and Culture*, London, British Museum Press.

TE AWEKOTUKU, N. (1996) 'Maori: People and Culture' in D.C. STARZECKA (ed.) *Maori Art and Culture*, pp. 114–46, London, British Museum Press.

Source: Adapted from BRADFORD, C. (2001), *Reading Race: Aboriginality in Australian Children's Literature*, Chapter 8, Melbourne University Press.

READING C: Extracts from 'Postmodernism and the picturebook'

David Lewis

> WARNING: This book appears to contain a number of stories that do not necessarily occur at the same time. Then again, it may contain only one story. In any event, careful inspection of both words and pictures is recommended.
>
> (from *Black and White* by David Macaulay)

Introduction

Although young readers of picturebooks might be said to be relatively unsophisticated and unworldly, the same could hardly be said of their writers and illustrators. Those who write, illustrate, design and publish picturebooks live and have their being in the complex contemporary world that we all share; it has been suggested that the makers of picturebooks [...] are doing no more than responding to the tenor of the times and either consciously or unconsciously importing the approaches, techniques and sensibilities of postmodernism into their work.[1] This shift from playfulness to postmodernism is important for a number of reasons. It not only introduces a technical vocabulary into the discussion but explicitly connects picturebooks with larger social and cultural developments. However, despite the fact that the influence of postmodernism on the picturebook is a phenomenon that has been observed and commented upon a number of times in recent years, I believe it remains poorly understood. [...] In what follows, therefore, I describe some of postmodernity's defining features and provide some examples of how these features have influenced writing for adults before returning us to the children's picturebook with an account of the ways in which some picturebooks might be considered to qualify as postmodern. [...]

The key features of postmodernity

Indeterminacy

In the postmodern world we are a lot less sure about the nature of objective reality, our own selves and the products of our hands and minds than we used to be. The more we know about the world the less stable and certain it seems. Instead of our knowledge and understanding growing steadily in a cumulative way, science and philosophy, along with many other disciplines, seem to be telling us that we will never be able to be sure of anything, once and for all, ever again. [...] The human universe too has become a far less stable place. The more we know about other societies and cultures, the more we become attuned to difference and the less confident we become in our judgements of what constitutes normal human behaviour. Literature has responded to such developments by placing an increased emphasis upon undecideable outcomes and irresolvable dilemmas. In place of the obscurities of the modernist text – the difficulties of Joyce, Eliot and Pound – we now have the indeterminacies of the postmodern text. As we shall see, it is not uncommon for readers of the postmodern to be left not knowing which way to turn.

Fragmentation

Postmodernism suspects totalization, attempts to unify and synthesize being considered the imposition of an ideological, and thus spurious, order. According to Ihab Hassan, postmoderns prefer the 'openness of brokenness, unjustified margins' (Hassan, 1986, p. 505) to the tendentious unity brought about by the various forms of artistic closure. The metaphor of 'unjustified margins' is a useful one for it suggests graphically the refusal to tidy up loose ends. Rather than attempt to pull everything into shape at the last minute, and thus create an illusion of order where none in fact exists, the postmodern artist or writer is likely to let the ends remain loose and visible: indeed they may well be moved to the foreground to emphasize the fact that wholeness and completeness are not honestly achievable. Collage, with its juxtaposition of disparate elements, is thus a favourite postmodern method.

Decanonization

Perhaps the most widely disseminated tenet of postmodernism is that the governing narratives of our culture – *les grands récits* – have broken down (Lyotard, 1984). We are less likely now to trust blindly in authority than were the citizens of previous ages. Fewer and fewer people believe wholeheartedly the overarching stories we tell ourselves about ultimate values, truth, progress and reason because the authorities that underwrote such stories – the church, rationality, science – are no longer viable. Jean-Franois Lyotard, in his seminal work *The Postmodern Condition*, defined postmodernism, loosely, as, ' ... incredulity towards metanarratives'. The very fact that it is possible to speak of the most fundamental belief as 'stories' suggests the extent to which the unquestioning acceptance of them as revealed truths has atrophied. [...] With the grand narratives in ruins at our feet all we have left are *les petits récits*, stories that do not aspire to global significance, but operate at the level of discrete language games. Such stories work insofar as we can invest in them and turn them to our ends but there is little left now in which the postmodernist can put absolute trust.

A further effect of decanonization is the ironing out of differences in value between cultural artefacts and images. The more our lives are invaded by relativism, the harder it becomes to feel confident about absolute standards in art and life and the boundaries separating pop and high culture become blurred. [...]

Irony

Indeterminacy, fragmentation and decanonization inevitably lead to irony. Whether we like it or not, modern life and culture is massively 'double-coded', images and ideas coming to us ready equipped with an ironic spin that tells us not only what we are looking at but also how to look at it. High Street and television advertisements are today so much more 'knowing' than they were and the consumer at whom they are aimed is expected to understand the allusions and get the jokes in the act of reading the text. [...]

Hybridization

The dissolving of boundaries, the fragmentation of wholes, the flattening out of differences between high and low are all held to be characteristic of our postmodern condition, and they have all contributed to the rise of bizarre hybrid genres and artefacts. Skyscrapers capped with motifs borrowed from Chippendale furniture are now possible, the non-fiction novel emerges from the blending of journalism and imaginative literature and on television docu-soaps import the conventions and expectations of cheap, serial melodrama into the real lives of hospital or airport staff. Nothing is sacred any more for the canons have faded that told us of the great and the good and that kept high culture and low in separate compartments. [...]

Performance and participation

The more that authorities dissolve and the more authors and artists abrogate responsibility for leading readers and viewers towards sense and meaning, then the more readers have to write the text they read. Much art is now conceived in terms of performance and participation, the role of the onlooker or participant in the process being deemed as important as any product. In such a climate the craft element in art, the idea that the artist possesses superior manipulative and creative abilities, has withered away [...].

Postmodernism in literature

How, then, have these trends within the larger culture affected the writing of fiction? The main influence has been upon the structures and conventions that have traditionally been shared between writer and reader. We expect a well-constructed, well-told story to have – to put it crudely – a beginning, a middle and an end. We expect to find more or less convincing characters interacting in an imaginary world according to the dictates of a plot which the author usually takes the trouble to resolve in some more or less satisfying way. Stories seem to follow rules and although the rules might differ for different kinds of stories – fairy tales, school stories, thrillers, romances, etc. – we do not usually expect the rules to be broken or abandoned. We expect something like a decorum, a sense of fittingness, to prevail within the fictions that we read and we very soon notice when incongruities intrude.

For example, we would not normally expect an author to step out onto the stage of his ongoing fiction to inform the reader about exactly what it is he is up to, but such interruptions are commonplace in postmodern writing. Take for example the following passage from the novel *How Far Can You Go?* by David Lodge (Lodge, 1980). Lodge would not consider himself to be a postmodern writer, but his academic interest in the subject has prompted him time and again to employ postmodern devices within his otherwise realistic novels. Here, a group of old friends who have not met for some time raise the subject of the accidental death of the daughter of some other, absent friends.

> 'Yes,' said Edward, shaking his head, and looking at his toecaps, 'that was too bad.'
>
> Adrian and Dorothy had not followed this and had to have it explained to them, as you will, gentle reader. Two years after Nicole was born, Dennis and Angela's next youngest child, Anne, was knocked down by a van outside their house and died in hospital a few hours later. I have avoided a direct presentation of this incident because frankly I find it too painful to contemplate. Of course, Dennis and Angela and Anne are fictional characters, they cannot bleed or weep, but they stand here for all the real people to whom such disasters happen with no apparent reason or justice. One does not kill off characters lightly, I assure you, even ones like Anne, evoked solely for that purpose.
>
> 'Of course, they blame themselves for the accident, one always does,' said Miriam ...
>
> (Lodge, 1980, p. 125)

The kind of intrusion of the author's voice into the fictional conversation of the characters is rather different from the traditional author strategy of appealing to the 'gentle reader', despite the fact that Lodge makes such an appeal at the beginning of the passage. What we experience here is a deliberate interruption of the drama that throws the fictional nature of that drama into high relief. We are suddenly aware that the story is precisely that, a story.

Consider a further, related example. In a short story by the Latin American author Julio Cortázar entitled 'Continuity of Parks', a man is described as reading a novel in a high-backed, green velvet armchair in his study. The novel he is reading tells of a desperate but resolute murderer who follows an avenue of trees that leads to a house; he climbs the stairs and locates the study, ' ... and then, the knife in hand, the light from the great windows, the high back of an armchair covered in green velvet, the head of the man in the chair reading a novel.' Thus is someone murdered by a character in the story that he is reading (Cortázar, 1968).

What is it that these two examples have in common? In one the author steps out from behind the curtain to address his audience, his readers, and in the other an 'unreal', fictional character is made to commit a 'real' murder. In both examples, figures involved in the creation of a fiction or belonging to the fiction refuse to stay in their assigned places and, like Anthony Browne's little bear in *Bear Hunt*, cross boundaries to take upon themselves roles they would not normally occupy. The effect is to disturb the expectations of the reader and once again to push into the foreground the fictional nature of the story. [...]

Postmodernism and metafiction

Postmodern fictions are usually unsettling, sometimes very funny and occasionally completely bewildering, but what is the justification for considering them to be specifically postmodern? How do these fictions display postmodernity? The most obvious connection between these examples and the list of characteristics discussed above lies in their authors' unwillingness to permit the reader to enjoy an uninterrupted illusion of a secondary world. Amongst other things they are concerned to remind the reader that literary fiction is not a window onto, or a mirror of, the real world but a fabrication that temporarily deludes us into believing that 'real' people are engaged in 'real' events. Furthermore, such stories often imply that the everyday-life-world itself will not withstand too much scrutiny, and that our own lives, with all their randomness and chaos, are only endowed with sense and meaning through out persistent liking for and belief in stories. [...]

The postmodern picturebook

The claim that certain picturebooks may be considered to be postmodern rests largely upon some very compelling parallels between the picturebooks in question and the kinds of prose fiction for adults discussed above. [...] As picturebooks possess some features that prose fictions do not, rather than attempt to squeeze my examples into a typology derived from novels and short stories, I have grouped them into five rather loose categories of my own devising into which both prose and picturebooks can fit.

Boundary breaking

Boundary breaking occurs when characters within a story are allowed by their author to wander beyond the narrative level to which they properly belong. [...]

In *The Story of a Little Mouse Trapped in a Book* by Monique Felix a mouse appears to be confined within the page upon which she is represented. She pushes at the sides in her attempts to get free, then nibbles around the edges to cut out a square of paper from the page, folds the square into an aeroplane and flies down to safety 'out' of the book and into the 'real world' depicted beyond the ragged edges that are left. *Simon's Book* (Henrik Drescher), *Benjamin's Book* (Alan Baker), and *The Book Mice* (Tony Knowles) all rely upon similar effects. Benjamin, for example, is a rather clumsy hamster who gets into scrapes through such tricks as walking across the page upon which he is represented leaving a trail of muddy paw prints behind him. In attempting to wipe the page clean he only makes matters worse. John Burningham's *Where's Julius?* manages the curious feat of having one character trespass upon the inner fantasies of another.

Excess

Excess [...] may take the form of any kind of gigantism that upsets our expectations. Interestingly, picturebooks often have an 'over the top' quality. They frequently involve a stretching and testing of norms – linguistic, literary, social, conceptual and ethical as well as narrative. [...] The unthinkable or the unmentionable appears with startling regularity in picturebooks. Alarming, disturbing or exciting possibilities are put to the test in *Would You Rather ...* by John Burningham. In this book narrative is abandoned altogether and the reader is invited to choose between extraordinary, exciting or disgusting possibilities. Many of the options on display are grotesquely humorous in the manner familiar from children's comics and cartoon strips while others put social norms to the test. Indeed, the book can cause embarrassment in children as they recognize the enormity of some of Burningham's suggestions.

Angry Arthur by Hiawyn Oram and Satoshi Kitamura takes a different form of excess as its theme: the extravagant results of a temper tantrum. Once again there is an accumulation that goes well beyond the bounds of realism, but in this instance there is a clear metaphorical purpose to the depicted events. The eponymous anti-hero is so angry at being prevented from watching late night TV that his rage brings on typhoons and earthquakes. In the real world the actual results of bad temper are rather more localized but the images of chaos in the book serve as the perfect objective correlate for the sense of boundless outrage experienced by angry infants. The dissolution of one's personality in blind rage is well portrayed in the loss of a universe.

Indeterminacy

Indeterminacy is the opposite of excess. In the latter case readers are offered an accumulation of one sort or another way beyond the normal for realistic stories; in the former, they are left with very little information. The contrast between these two extremes reminds us of the fact that a sense of the real in stories depends upon what Susan Stewart calls 'an economy of significance' that is governed by generic conventions (Stewart, 1984): writers (or in the case of picturebooks, writers and illustrators) must neither say too much nor too little or they risk losing the reader.

All stories are built upon gaps – writers and picturebook makers cannot describe, explain or show everything – but some picturebooks expose those gaps for us and thus reveal the comic absurdity of the situation we are left in when textual props are missing. For example, *How Tom Beat Captain Najork and His Hired Sportsmen* by Russell Hoban and Quentin Blake has at its heart a series of three testing games that are simultaneously present and absent. Womble, Muck and Sneedball are named and (partially) illustrated but we are never allowed to learn their precise nature. Blake's illustrations hint at their complexity, and Hoban offers one or two clues about scoring and procedures, but the three games remain a pungent lack throughout the story.

Time to Get Out of the Bath, Shirley also relies upon an absence, but here it takes the form of a withholding of information about how two sequences of images are related. The pictures and words on the left-hand pages clearly relate to the images on the right but we are left to make up our own minds about the precise nature of the relationship. [...]

Another book that leaves relationships and outcomes obscure is *Black and White* by David Macaulay. The four stories told in the four quarters of each page-opening are depicted in four separate styles, one of them entirely wordless, another packed with the kinds of visual puns that some picturebook illustrators delight in. There are hints and suggestions embedded in the picture that the four stories might be connected but Macaulay makes no efforts to explain how, or indeed if, this is so. In fact, he prints a warning label on the title page: 'This book appears to contain a number of stories that do not necessarily occur at the same time. Then again, it may contain only one story. In any event, careful inspection of both words and pictures is recommended.'

Parody

Parody is inherently metafictive as it involves a refusal to accept as natural and given that which is culturally determined and conventional. As a literary device it is usually associated with satire and ridicule and may thus seem an unlikely trait to find in children's picturebooks, but in fact picturebook makers often lean towards this particular mode. The aim of parody in the picturebook, however, is not to ridicule any particular author or style but to poke fun at the conventions, manners and affectations of a particular genre.

The Worm Book by Janet and Allan Ahlberg is an excellent example of how a relatively rigid form – the child's 'information book' – can be undone by placing straight-faced captions beneath silly pictures: 'All good worms have a beginning, a middle and an end ... Worms with two beginnings, a middle and no end are apt to injure themselves ... Worms with two ends, a middle and no beginning get bored.'

A more sophisticated parody of a non-fiction, information text can be found in *How Dogs Really Work* by Alan Snow. This book comes complete with table of contents, index, cut-away pictures with keys, labels with arrows, inset diagrams and so on. The target of the parody is clearly the glamorous books that have proliferated in recent years showing the insides of everything from skyscrapers to ocean liners. Snow's book, however, shows caricature dogs opened up to reveal pulleys, levers and valves and the text purports to explain how doggy behaviour can be explained in terms of the rudimentary, Heath Robinson-like machinery shown in the pictures. Thus, in the section headed, 'Legs and Getting About' we read:

> Legs are organs of support and locomotion in animals (and humans). In dogs, the legs are fixed at the four corners of the main body, (see diagram 1). Nearly all dogs have four legs, even the short funny ones that sometimes look like they may not, (see diagram 2). Legs are powered by energy generated from the food the dog eats.

As befits this kind of manual everything is shown in the greatest possible detail, and there are lots of handy hints for the prospective dog owner ('Make sure you are running your dog on the right fuel. If you are not it may affect the dog's performance.') [...]

Performance

Many picturebooks are constructed to be deliberately interactive and participatory. Picturebooks with tabs to pull, flaps to lift, wheels to rotate, pages to unfold, holes to peep through and, most recently, buttons to push and sounds to listen to, are now quite commonplace. Notable examples include: the popular *Spot* books; the elaborately engineered works by Jan Pienkowski such as *Haunted House* and *Robot*; the books of Eric Carle and Ron Maris with their cut and shaped pages; much of the work of the Ahlbergs, in particular *Peepo*, *The Jolly Postman*, *Yum Yum* and *Playmates*. [...]

Books such as these are not particularly concerned with undermining, or resisting the creation of, a secondary fictive world through manipulation of the text. Instead they foreground the nature of the book as an object, an artefact to be handled and manipulated as well as read. They are thus metafictive to the extent that they tempt readers to withdraw attention from the story (which, it must be said, is often pretty slender) in order to look at, play with and admire the paper engineering. One of the characteristics of a well-told tale is that as we read it our awareness of the book in which it is written tends to fade away, but when the material fabric of the book has been doctored in such a way as to draw attention to itself, it is less easy to withdraw into that fictive, secondary world.

Pop-ups and movables tend to produce a degree of unease amongst children's book critics and scholars for they often do not seem to offer much in the way of a reading experience at all. For this reason they are sometimes considered to be more like toys than books, objects to play with rather than to read. There is some justice in this view, but it is far too simplistic for it tidies up too neatly something that, if we are honest, rather resists pigeonholing. We might better understand the movable if we view it as a hybrid, a merging of two, otherwise incompatible artefacts: the toy and the picturebook. Under this description, movables are both books that can be played with and toys that can be read.

Picturebooks: postmodern or playful?

Boundary breaking, excess, indeterminacy, parody and performance are all strategies or devices that authors and illustrators can use to push what can be done with the picturebook to its limits, but they are also frequently used by writers of fiction for adults to unsettle readerly expectations. The view that some picturebooks can be considered to be postmodern arises out of this parallel between the picturebooks in question and certain kinds of novels and stories for adults. [...]

The question of why many picturebook makers feel free to abandon settled modes of storytelling may best be answered by taking a good close look at the nature of the form within which they are working and the audience to whom that work is addressed.

Notes

1   My own first attempt to write about this subject was published in *Signal* as 'The constructedness of texts: picture books and the metafictive' (also collected in Egoff, Stubbs, Ashley and Sutton 1996). Other relevant texts include: Moss, G. (1992) ' "My Teddy Bear Can Fly": postmodernizing the picture book'; Styles, M. (1996) 'Inside the tunnel: a radical kind of reading – picture books, pupils and postmodernism'.

References

CORTÁZAR, J. (1968) *End of the Game and Other Stories*, trans. P. BLACKBURN, London, Collins and Harvill Press.

HASSAN, I. (1986) 'Pluralism in postmodern perspective', *Critical Inquiry*, **12**(3), pp. 503–20.

LODGE, D. (1980) *How Far Can You Go?*, Harmondsworth, Penguin.

LYOTARD, J. (1984) *The Postmodern Condition: A Report on Knowledge*, trans. G. BENNINGTON and B. MASSUMI, Manchester, Manchester University Press.

STEWART, S. (1984) *On Longing: Narratives of the Miniature, the Gigantic, the Souvenir, the Collection*, Baltimore, Johns Hopkins University Press.

Source: LEWIS, D. (2001) *Reading Contemporary Picturebooks: Picturing Text*, Chapter 6, London, RoutledgeFalmer.

Literature and technology

Sharon Goodman

7.1 Introduction

The focus of this chapter is the impact of technology on literature. I will be looking at examples of reworkings of some canonical literary texts, along with some newer ones, and considering how technology may afford new possibilities for literary creativity.

We stay with the theme of multimodality which has been considered in several chapters of this book so far. Chapter 4 contained examples of performances, where the meanings of the verbal text are influenced by sets, props, and of course the movements, gestures and facial expressions of the actors/performers. In Chapter 5 you saw how a traditional illustrated book was reworked for a Catalan audience, and how theatre audiences in India influenced the performance and meaning of Shakespearean plays. Chapter 6 looked in detail at textual aspects of printed multimodal literature, and at some sociocultural factors which affect the production and interpretation of such texts. This chapter broadens out the discussion and analysis. It moves further away from the Formalists' focus on textual features, because newer technologies force us to look at creativity as much in the *process* of text production as in the finished product. I will also be considering texts using a wider selection of semiotic modes, because technology makes such texts possible.

The term 'technology' is used in this chapter to mean relatively recent technologies such as film and the internet. It therefore moves on from Chapter 6 where most examples were drawn from the medium of printed books. It's important to recognise that books – indeed writing of any sort – are a form of technology (Ong, 1982), even pencil on paper. But the technologies discussed here have brought to literature a different range of resources and increased creative potential for authors and readers.

I start by considering a television advert which uses poetry.

7.2 Poetry on screen

While advertisements frequently contain linguistic features such as parallelism that can be seen as 'literary' in the Formalist sense, they would not normally fit many people's definition of 'literature'. Sometimes, however, advertisements make use of actual poems. The advertisement in the first activity was made by a financial services company, The Prudential, and was shown on British television in 2003. A man takes a walk though a dreary, rain-soaked tunnel at night, making a plea for some clarity from the financial services sector. As he walks he recites a poem (commissioned by The Prudential from the poet Ralph Rochester), and words from the poem appear superimposed on walls of the tunnel.

ACTIVITY 1   Poetry in an advertisement

Allow about
10 minutes

Look at the still images and poem from the Prudential advertisement shown below. What semiotic modes can you identify?

Gobble us no gook, man
And poppy us no cock!
Mumbo us no jumbo
And jabber us no wock!

Spare us all the twaddle
Cut the gibble-gabble
Stow the fiddle-faddle
And lose the bibble-babble

Hocus us no pocus
Roll away the mist
Sharpen up the focus, man!
Just tell it like it is!

Figure 7.1   Stills from the Prudential television advertisement, and the poem, 'Tell it like it is', by Ralph Rochester, which accompanies them.

Comment

In terms of semiotic modes, this advert contains images, speech, writing and movement (the movement obviously can't be shown here, but it is easy enough to imagine). There is colour (also not shown here), which may, or may not, be significant to the television viewers.

Formalism could be used to approach the words of the poem itself. There is creative deviation evident in almost every line – words such as *gobbledegook* and *poppycock* (both meaning, roughly, *rubbish* or *nonsense*) are split and reformulated; there is plenty of evidence of rhyme and parallelism.

In semiotic terms, we could note that we are presented with a large number of signs here. The man is one of the most salient – he is an iconic sign as this is clearly an image of a real person, the actor. He is a certain type of man (40-something, perhaps), wearing a certain kind of clothing. So from the paradigms of, say, 'people' and 'clothing', certain choices have been made and other alternatives rejected. On the syntagm, this man-as-sign has been combined with other signs: the tunnel, the words of the poem, his movement towards the viewer rather than away from us, and so on.

A wider range of meanings can be seen at the level of connotation. We could note:

- The dark colours seem to signify more than 'night-time': Is the man depressed? tired? does the sombreness stand for the 'fog' of financial information he is struggling to work through?

- The man himself (appealing to rather broad social stereotypes): What sort of man is he? Is he a manual worker or a professional? Is his clothing (dark, thick overcoat and boots) significant? Is it late? Cold? Winter? His accent (Scottish) might mean something, as accent is frequently used in advertising as a signifier of certain qualities the advertiser wishes to associate with the product – here, does it connote 'straightforwardness', 'honesty', 'down-to-earth-ness'? His gaze (focused on the viewer) supports the verbal mode of direct address.

- Movement: The man is walking, and quite fast. Is he in a hurry to get home after a long day at work? Or frustrated and desperate for some financial help?

- The man's location in a tunnel is significant in terms of the meanings open to us as viewers. The tunnel is dark, wet and gloomy, as tunnels often are in metaphors in English. Does this represent the dark tunnel of financial confusion he feels himself to be in, and will he find the inevitable light at the end of it when he telephones Prudential?

There is clearly some mileage in semiotics as an approach to this advertisement. But this means thinking about the choices that were made in each mode (and those potential choices which were rejected) and the possible meanings of each choice. To do this, we have to split the poem into separate modes – sound, image, movement. This is worth doing, but the modes are actually used in combination. When it comes to the syntagm (the axis of combination) we make meaning not only out of how each individual semiotic mode combines things, but how the modes themselves are combined. This is very difficult to analyse, although some researchers (Thibault, 2000) are now conducting frame-by-frame analysis of such texts, using computer technology to build up a corpus for considering multimodal texts like this.

It is in the articulation of modes as a whole – in the constellation of meanings – that we make sense of such texts. Separating the dialogue from the sound, from the movement, from the images actually doesn't explain why a text engages the reader or viewer in particular ways.

Advertisements have, of course, been around for centuries. But the shift from printed billboard advertisements to television (and now, of course, internet advertising) complicates the task of interpretation. More semiotic modes are now available to such texts, which can widen the possibilities for interpretation.

You may, or may not, accept the poem used in the Prudential advertisement as literature. But this text was selected to start the chapter because it provides an illuminating but concise example of the complexities of interpreting texts on screen. The move from print to screen (like the move from page to performance in Chapter 4) means that as well as being complex in terms of interpretation, both advertisements and literature made or adapted for film are complex in terms of their production. The Prudential advert was produced by a large team of people that included designers, editors, technical and marketing staff. So the combination of our increasing engagement with multimodal texts produced with technology, and the collaborative nature of their production, means that there are limitations with seeing 'creativity' as text intrinsic, as the Formalists did. We'll need to broaden out the framework in order to locate creativity in the production and reception of such texts in wider social processes.

The limitations of Formalism and some alternatives to it have been discussed in Chapters 2, 3 and 4.

In this chapter I look at texts which display the potential to change us from reader/viewers to designer/producers. I consider novels adapted for CD-ROM and film, an oral narrative made into a film by a group of schoolchildren, literature created as electronic hyperfiction, and Shakespeare's *Hamlet* recreated as a live performance on the internet. In all, I consider how and where the creativity resides – in some ways it can be seen in the text itself (the product) but in others it is more usefully located in the process (the production) and/or the reading/viewing (the reception).

In the next section I come to the first example of a canonical work of literature adapted from print to new media. A huge number of novels, both 'classic' and contemporary, has been adapted for the screen, and adaptation is the subject of wide academic literature (Reynolds, 1993; McFarlane, 1996; Cardwell, 2002, 2003; Naremore, 2000; Cartmell and Whelehan, 1999). I start by looking at the adaptation of John Steinbeck's *Of Mice and Men*.

7.3 Adapting literature for technology

Adaptation from one medium to another is fundamentally the art of making choices. To do it, you first need to make some decisions as to what to show, and how to show it. Different semiotic modes, such as word, image and sound, are capable of representing different things, or representing things in different ways, as we saw in many of the examples in Chapter 6. Following

Kress' framework (2003) we can note that semiotic modes afford different possibilities of meaning:

> The point is that whether I want to or not I have to use the possibilities given to me by a mode of representation to make my meaning. Whatever is represented in speech (or to some lesser extent in writing) inevitably has to bow to the logic of time and of sequence in time. [...] Whatever is represented in image has to bow, equally, to the logic of space, and to the simultaneity of elements in spatial arrangements.
>
> (Kress, 2003, p. 2)

If you think back to the Baby McFry example in Chapter 6 (Colour Figure 3) this will become clearer. Because visual signs are necessarily arranged spatially, they 'mean' differently than they would if the same ideas were conveyed in writing. You might like to think about trying to describe your interpretation of that image in words. However you might formulate it, it would be linear, with one word after another. In an image we can be shown many meanings simultaneously.

To show you how this might work in a longer text, we now turn to look at how a novel may be adapted for new media.

ACTIVITY 2 Thinking about adaptation

Allow about 30 minutes

Below is a section from Chapter 1 of John Steinbeck's 1937 novel, *Of Mice and Men*. The novel tells the story of two migrant labourers, George and Lennie. Lennie, despite his great strength, has the mind of a child, and the story tells of his friendship with George, on whom he is dependent. In the opening pages of the novel, we learn that Lennie's innocence has got them both into trouble, that Lennie's memory is unreliable and that George's affection for Lennie is punctuated by outbursts of frustration with him.

Read this passage to familiarise yourself with this excerpt from the novel.

'There's enough beans for four men,' George said.

Lennie watched him from over the fire. He said patiently, 'I like 'em with ketchup.'

'Well, we ain't got any,' George exploded. 'Whatever we ain't got, that's what you want. God a'mighty, if I was alone I could live so easy. I could go get a job an' work, an' no trouble. No mess at all, and when the end of the month come I could take my fifty bucks and go into town and get whatever I want. Why, I could stay in a cat-house all night. I could eat any place I want, hotel or any place, and order any damn thing I could think of. An' I could do all that every damn month. Get a gallon of whisky, or set in a pool-room and play cards or shoot pool.' Lennie knelt and looked over the fire at the angry George.

And Lennie's face was drawn with terror. 'An' whatta I got?' George went on furiously. 'I got you! You can't keep a job and you lose me ever' job I get. Jus' keep me shovin' all over the country all the time. An' that ain't the worst. You get in trouble. You do bad things and I got to get you out.' His voice rose nearly to a shout. 'You crazy son-of-a-bitch. You keep me in hot water all the time.' He took on the elaborate manner of little girls when they are mimicking one another. 'Jus' wanted to feel that little girl's dress – jus' wanted to pet it like it was a mouse – Well, how the hell did she know you jus' wanted to feel her dress? She jerks back and you hold on like it was a mouse. She yells and we got to hide in an irrigation ditch all day with guys lookin' for us, and we got to sneak out in the dark and get outta the country. All the time somethin' like that – all the time. I wisht I could put you in a cage with about a million mice and let you have fun.' His anger left him suddenly. He looked across the fire at Lennie's anguished face, and then he looked ashamedly at the flames.

It was quite dark now, but the fire lighted the trunks of the trees and the curving branches overhead. Lennie crawled slowly and cautiously around the fire until he was close to George. He sat back on his heels. George turned the bean-cans so that another side faced the fire. He pretended to be unaware of Lennie so close beside him.

'George!' very softly. No answer. 'George!'

(Steinbeck, 1937, pp. 11–12)

Now think about what sorts of choices you would have to make in adapting this for a different medium, such as television. You will have available to you the semiotic modes of speech, other sound, image and movement – although you don't have to use all of them. Which modes would you choose to use? How would you arrange them, and how might you connect them?

Comment

There are of course many possible ways of 'carving up' this passage into semiotic modes, to make it work as an adaptation for television. There's no right or wrong way to do this – there are options – what to show, and how to show it.

You will have imagined Lennie and George as having particular physical characteristics, and as interacting with one another in various ways, both verbally and non-verbally, such as in the use of gaze. You will probably have positioned your two characters in some kind of outdoor setting, near a fire – although you may have transposed them to a different setting entirely. You may – or may not – have taken your cues from the text regarding how your characters move in this extract (*Lennie knelt; George turned the bean-cans*). You may even have decided that the recounting of the incident where Lennie had held onto the little girl's dress was best shown as a flashback.

Whatever you chose to do with this excerpt, your choices would have been affected by what you wanted to show or foreground. Your choices would have also affected the meanings taken from your story by readers or viewers.

Gunther Kress's thesis is that 'the world told' is different to 'the world shown'. He sees profound shifts occurring to the ways we engage with texts, both receptively and productively – and the advent of communications technology is having a major role to play in these shifts. To understand this, and the first reading, we'll need some more focused terminology.

Modes, media and affordances

See Chapter 5 of the companion volume, **Maybin and Swann (2006)**, for more on modes, media and affordances.

It is important to distinguish the terms 'mode' and 'medium'. The texts in Chapter 6 primarily used the semiotic **modes** of writing and image; some contained additional modes such as colour, or implied other modes such as movement. Chapter 7 looks at literary texts which contain the modes of movement and sound.

The texts in this chapter are also created in different **media**. The term 'medium' is used here to mean the medium of dissemination of the text (Kress and van Leeuwen, 2001; Jewitt, 2004) – book, website, film and so on. We are therefore moving on from the medium of printed books in Chapter 6 into other media such as CD-ROM, film and the internet.

Affordances are properties of the relationship between an organism and the material environment. Objects afford possibilities to humans (and animals: a tree affords shade to a lion and perching to an eagle, for example, as well as climbing to a child). In terms of computer technology, different software and hardware afford different possibilities to readers and writers, whether or not we avail ourselves of all of them.

The next reading exemplifies the terms mode, medium and affordance, through looking at the choices made for one particular CD-ROM.

A basic CD-ROM is usually presented as a series of sequential screens, which the viewer navigates through by pressing a button to see the next part of the text. Choices have to be made about which mode will be used for which aspect of the story, and how these will be combined. For *Of Mice and Men*, you could, for example, have images of the two men at the top, with the text underneath, like some traditional illustrated books. The text could be a series of static screens, or scrolling text. The words or images could contain clickable links to, say, descriptions of their characters, or reminders of past events in the narrative, or other books by the same author, or location maps to show the wider scene.

ACTIVITY 3   **From print to CD-ROM (Reading A)**

Please now read Carey Jewitt's discussion of the presentation of John Steinbeck's novel, *Of Mice and Men*, on CD-ROM.

As you read, consider the following questions:

- What are the different ways readers can interact with this text on CD-ROM?
- What does Jewitt say about the affordances of mode and medium in this text?
- How does Jewitt see the choice of semiotic mode as portraying narrative action and characterisation?

Comment

Jewitt compares two versions of the novel presented on the same CD-ROM – one as more traditional written text, the other as a visual version containing video and drawings. She looks at the use of this CD-ROM by secondary school students, noting that it can be engaged with in different ways. The reader can choose to read it as written text, or as illustrated text. It is also possible to click through links in the text to obtain further information about the characters in the novel, or some background on the sociocultural context Steinbeck drew from when he wrote the novel. Jewitt is interested in the way different semiotic modes are used to present the novel, and in how readers engage with the text in different ways.

Jewitt highlights what she sees as the affordances of mode, and the affordances of medium in her analysis. She shows how choices of mode are used to portray narrative action. The way the modes of writing and image interact focuses attention on Lennie or George. The different semiotic modes also differentiate the two characters: George is verbally represented, as having 'thoughts, worries and dreams', whereas Lennie is visually represented as 'doing things'. This is a strategy for portraying aspects of characterisation unavailable to printed literary texts such as 'Eveline', which you considered in Chapter 3. In 'Eveline', characterisation is portrayed in a variety of ways, but it is achieved linguistically rather than by using different semiotic modes *per se* (although authors do, of course, cue or simulate other semiotic modes, creating a variety of literary effects. For example, in line 141 of 'Eveline' (p. 123) sound is cued by the 'long mournful whistle' of the boat, and in e e cummings' poem 'she being Brand' shown on p. 251–2, movement is cued by techniques of punctuation and layout).

In terms of medium, the CD-ROM exploits the potential for interactivity. Because a reading path is not totally prescribed, the reader is freer to move around the text in a different order, and become a producer of alternative meaning. Jewitt notes that some students of this text used the affordances of the technology to view the story as a set of video clips – almost making it into a film. Others transformed it into a 'cartoon', and yet another group into 'music'

The reader of these texts is, for Jewitt, doing a different job than the reader of a book. She or he takes responsibility for deciding what is meaningful and for how the elements are to be ordered and engaged with. Although these decisions are necessarily constrained by the options for action embedded in the text by the designer, the CD-ROM is far more open in this respect than a traditional book. Jewitt links this to the notion of 'design', which means that the text can be at least partially constructed by the decisions and actions taken by the reader. We will be returning to the notion of design in Section 7.5.

You may like to borrow a novel on CD-ROM from a local library (choosing a novel you know well will be easier) and see how it divides information into semiotic modes for the reader. What choices and constraints does it give you in navigating the narrative? How does it represent the characters?

We have looked briefly in this section at the presentation of a small excerpt of a novel adapted for new technology, and started to consider the role of the reader in constructing meaning while interacting with the text. I move on now to consider a wider range of texts, adapted from written originals into other media, and at the creative work that viewers need to do to engage with them.

7.4 Adapting narrative elements across semiotic modes

Among the choices the adapter or creator of a text must make are those relating to the presentation of narrative elements. Carey Jewitt in Reading A noted the use of semiotic modes to convey character in *Of Mice and Men*. What strategies can a film producer deploy to give the audience enough information about a character without the resources of lengthy description and presentation of thought available to novelists?

ACTIVITY 4   Adapting literature for film (Reading B)

Please read 'Adaptation across media' by H. Porter Abbott. Porter Abbott describes the process of adaptation as 'creative destruction'. The film producer has to make ruthless decisions in order to create, or recreate, a coherent narrative for the new medium.

Porter Abbott notes some important aspects of novels which have to be recreated in new ways for moving images such as films – duration, characterisation, metaphor, and gaps.

As you read, consider:

The term fidelity is discussed in Chapters 4 and 5, referring to how 'faithful' we feel a text is when compared to the original.

- what the author says about the 'fidelity' of the text when reproduced in a different medium;

- some of the ways in which adaptations into plays or film deal with narrative elements such as characterisation and metaphor;

- what the author says about the engagement of the reader in constructing meaning from the text.

Comment

Fidelity, for Porter Abbott, is an even more slippery concept for adaptation than it is for translation. Because adaptation crosses media boundaries, the original is only loosely connected to the new production, and his reading shows us some of the reasons why. Plays and films necessarily compress time, for example, whereas a novel does not have to constrain itself to conventional performance lengths, nor to the attention span of the audience. Aspects of character can be slowly revealed in a novel, but in film the visual representation can appear more fixed and less open to interpretation. Metaphors also have to be handled differently in the visual mode.

This reading further highlights the role of the reader/viewer in constructing meaning from the text. When viewing film sequences we infer considerable amounts of meaning from the way different shots are combined in sequences. Porter Abbott exemplified the same technique in comic strips with a visual quotation, the excerpt from Scott McCloud's *Understanding Comics* (the two frames showing the scene just before and just after a murder). Although comics and films are different media, they juxtapose images in much the same way. In his book, McCloud says that because this murder is not actually shown in the text we, as readers, are 'responsible' for the crime (McCloud, 1993, p. 68). In film, this kind of juxtaposition is part of 'film grammar' (Arijon, 1976; Bordwell and Thompson, 1993; Stewart et al., 2001, among others).

Gaps are also, of course, present in traditional printed literature (Iser, 1978, pp. 165–9) and because the reader is forced to take action and interpret them, we become more involved and implicated in the story. We are, then, in whatever medium or mode, active producers of the text. This is a long way from the Formalists' insistence on the primacy of the text itself as the location of meaning.

So far in this chapter, we have looked at some of the creative choices text producers make – and the effects these have – when they adapt literary narratives for different media and semiotic modes. In the rest of this chapter, we look further at the interpretative work readers and viewers do, and consider how access to new communications technologies has the potential to turn us all into producers of literature.

7.5 Creative involvement in the text

What does a reader/viewer do?

The notions of 'reader' in this chapter are necessarily idealised models. See Chapters 8 and 9 for further discussion of the reader.

We have seen that reading (or viewing) requires engagement – creative action – from us in some way. In reading a novel, we enter into the world of the characters, we piece together 'mind maps' of locations from the author's descriptions, we decode metaphors, we form opinions about characters and predict events. In other words, readers are involved in meaning making. Stanley Fish's influential critique of stylistics and what he saw as its practitioners' avoidance of the role of the reader in meaning-making is relevant here. Fish (1980, p. 89) rejects the notion that meaning resides in the text, insisting upon its location in the process of reading: 'meaning is not the property of a timeless formalism but something acquired in the context of an activity'. Of poetry, he states 'Interpretation is not the art of construing but the art of constructing. Interpreters do not decode poems; they make them' (1980, p. 327). It's not a difficult task to draw broad analogies here with points made by Jewitt and Porter Abbott, about the roles played by readers and viewers of CD-ROM and film texts respectively. Readers must infer or create connections which are not actually seen, fill in the gaps and construct a coherent narrative path through the story.

If we accept that readers are always active and creative, and that interpreting a metaphor in a printed novel, or watching a film, or interacting with hypertext fiction (see Section 7.6) are all creative acts, it is nonetheless debateable which act is the *most* creative. In Table 1, I outline some of the many different ways the role of the reader has been described.

There are several unclear boundaries in Table 1, both implicit and explicit:

- between the creative processes of reading and writing.
- between creative texts: is a film more or less creative than a novel, and on what basis can we decide?
- between creative agents: readers and authors, or film producers and viewers.

These tensions run throughout this chapter. The last point in the table – the perceived shift from interpretation to design – needs some expansion.

Table 1 What do we do with texts?

The reader/ viewer/ producer as …	engaged in reading, viewing, changing, producing …	… which involves action (mental and/or physical) …	… which is creative because …
Active	Reading a novel, watching a film at the cinema or a play at the theatre.	… actively making connections and seeking/ creating meaning from a text – whether in a traditional novel or a multimodal text. We can also, if we wish, exercise a degree of control over how we read a book. We can choose to read the chapters of a book in non-standard order, we may interrupt our reading to turn to an index or bibliography, we may stop reading altogether. We can walk out of a cinema or theatre. But we can't actually do anything to the text (although it is true that some stage plays involve audience participation). Even writing on the pages of a book doesn't change the original text, and has no effect on it or the author.	… our response is interpretative, and to different degrees individual, even if aspects of it might be predictable within a specific cultural or social context. We seek and infer meaning from what is in the text, as well as from what is absent. In addition we bring to the process our societal and cultural knowledge, and our knowledge of textual conventions.
Interactive	Watching a film on DVD, reading a novel on CD-ROM.	… making decisions, choosing elements from the selection made available. Action also involves actually changing channels, pressing buttons, etc.	… compared to film or print, we are more in control of how we receive the narrative, even though we still do not actually intervene in the text itself. Texts can be liberating or constraining of our pathways through them – some CD-ROMs have strictly prescribed navigational pathways which affect what we can do with them (and therefore the range of possible meanings we can construct). Others are more open, and their creators may be unable to predict the multiple pathways that the reader might choose.

Agentive or selective	Using websites, interactive television.	... making choices as to what to read/view, and in what order (including the possibility of backtracking and making alternative choices, creating a different pathway through the text).	... depending on the text's design, we have greater physical control of the text(s) we read. In principle, the combinations of hypertext links we can make in reading websites is inexhaustible.
Interventive or transformative	Editing email, contributing to internet chatroom discussions, collaboratively writing hypertext fiction.	... intervening: here the reader is more clearly involved in the text's production. The reader indisputably becomes a writer. Depending on how text is designed, hypertext allows you to write back, intervene and change the text. Email can be edited and sent back. Internet chatrooms engage readers/writers in dialogue.	... the boundaries between readers and writers break down – all can be involved in a text's creation and recreation.
The designer/ producer	Making a film or hypertext narrative ourselves.	... producing: in all sorts of ways. Writing is only one aspect of text design.	Obviously, in common-sense parlance, anyone involved in 'design' is 'creative'. It's probably not controversial to call a film producer 'creative', for example. But some theorists (Kress, 2003; Kress and van Leeuwen, 2001) argue that multimodality turns us all into designers, even when we are reading. Reading itself moves from *interpretation* to *design*.

From interpretation to design

Following on from the notion that meaning is created during the process of reading or viewing (and does not reside solely in the text) it will be helpful to add the notion of design. **Design** is currently important in multimodality theory, and, while it encompasses interpretation, it goes further. Design suggests that we are all designers of meaning: faced with an increasing number of multimodal texts in all aspects of our lives, we are called upon to construct meaning from all semiotic modes *and from the ways these modes are articulated and combined*. This may be a letter containing a visual corporate logo, a television advertisement using sound, image and words, or a website where the pathways through the text are open, flexible and unpredictable. Constructing meaning from such texts is what it means to talk of a shift from 'reading as interpretation' to 'reading as design'. (This is what Carey Jewitt refers to in Reading A, where she notes that reading a CD-ROM involves precisely this shift.)

Alongside this, because of wider dissemination of and access to technology – the tools of multimodal text production – we are all potential producers (designers) of multimodal texts as well as consumers of them. Although we have always written and drawn, technology means that we are able to deploy and organise a wider range of semiotic resources than ever before, according to what we want to mean and how we want to mean it (our 'interest', in Kress' terms).

Kress and van Leeuwen (2001) see a decline in traditional spheres of expertise when it comes to text production, and a concomitant rise in multimodality. We can all, given equal access to the technology, produce and disseminate our own texts. This leads to a decline in authorship and authority – a levelling of hierarchies:

> [T]he former boundaries between certain sets of professions and trades have become weakened, permeable, or have, in many cases, disappeared under the pressure of quite new representational arrangements. Formerly, professions established themselves in relation to *one mode*, or around what was seen as one mode, and developed their practices around that. The issue of choice did not arise in this context. Instead of choice there was competence, and competent practice in relation to one mode – whether that was the mode of writing, as in the production of a film script for instance; of image production, as in cinematography; or acting, or of musical composition [...] In the case of industrial modes of semiotic production such as film production, one person then integrated the various practices of a group of professionals into one coherent performance – the conductor of the orchestra [...], or the editor (and the editorial team) of the newspaper, or the director of the film. Digital

technology, however, has now made it possible for one person to manage all these modes, and to implement the multimodal production single-handedly.

(Kress and van Leeuwen, 2001, p. 47)

Design very much implies engagement with creative processes as well as creative texts. The degree, and location of activity and creative intervention may be difficult to pin down, but the point is that it is difficult to see creativity as solely, or mainly, located in the text. Nor is it primarily located in the reader/receiver, as Fish (1980) suggested. Design implies that we need to locate creativity at least partially in the text-production process. Living in a social and cultural environment where reading (and writing) can mean intervening in an existing text, both in our heads and on the page/screen, we can all become producers – or designers – of literary works.

We now look in more detail at the redesign of one particular narrative. The third reading in this chapter looks at a film produced by children, adapted from a traditional folktale. In Reading C, Andrew Burn and David Parker analyse the semiotic modes used to redesign an oral narrative, a Ghanaian Anansi story.

Anansi is a trickster spider, common in oral folktales in many different African countries and the Caribbean. He is usually considered deceitful, although not malicious, and his actions and their consequences always have a moral lesson to teach the audience.

Burn and Parker are particularly interested in how modes are combined in the film, terming this 'mode of combination' the *kineikonic* mode. Burn and Parker's rationale for analysing media texts in this way is to restore what they see as a loss of balance in semiotic analysis, particularly in cultural studies, between the processes of production and reception:

> Our kineikonic mode [...] refers to how all the elements of the moving image are assembled, but includes the particular conventions afforded by the practices of filming and editing. This mode uses a range of semiotic resources to make the moving image, integrating them into the spatiotemporal flow by (re)designing and producing them within the spatial frame and the temporal sequence of the film.

(Burn and Parker, 2003, p. 59)

Martin Montgomery's reading in Chapter 3 looked at transitivity, an aspect of Halliday's ideational function.

The authors analyse a short section of the film in terms of the overall 'communicative metafunctions', *ideational*, *interpersonal* and *textual* (derived from the functional linguistic model of Michael Halliday (1985). The box below gives a brief summary of Halliday's terms.

Halliday's communicative metafunctions

1   **Ideational**: Every semiotic mode will have resources for constructing representations of (aspects of) the world.

2   **Interpersonal**: Every semiotic mode will have resources for constructing (a) relations between the communicating parties (between writers and readers, painters and viewers, speakers and listeners); and (b) relations between these communicating parties and what they are representing, in other words, attitudes to the subject they are communicating about.

3   **Textual**: Every semiotic mode will have resources for combining and integrating ideational and interpersonal meanings into the kinds of wholes we call 'texts' or 'communicative events' and recognize as news articles, paintings, jokes, conversations, lectures, and so on.

(Goodman, 1996, p. 53)

ACTIVITY 5   **Redesigning an oral folktale (Reading C)**

Please read 'Tiger's big plan: multimodality and the moving image' by Andrew Burn and David Parker.

This reading is a detailed look at a short extract from the film the authors studied. As you read, consider:

*   what Burn and Parker say about the choices made by the children in terms of visual representations of the characters in the story;

*   how gaps were created, making the viewer work at interpretation;

*   what choices were made to convey narrative time in the sequence?

Comment

Burn and Parker look first at some of the choices made in the visual mode by the children. They note the mixing of cultural frames and intertextual references to other texts the children are familiar with, such as *Spiderman* and *The Simpsons*.

In their discussion of the ideational function they point out that the viewer is required to make some interpretative effort to make connections between shots – and the meanings of individual semiotic modes – to grasp the meaning. You'll be able to make links here with Porter Abbott's discussion of 'gaps' in novel and film narratives in Reading B. The interpersonal function has to do with relationships between the viewer and the text, and this is evidenced by the choices of camera shots and angles, the music and the quality of Tiger's voice. Burn and Parker's discussion of the textual function will remind you of the discussion in Chapter 6 of the distribution of information between modes. Just as in multimodal printed texts, the fact that some information appears in one mode but not another can be significant – it can be due to the affordances of a particular mode, or say something about what the text producer was trying to communicate.

Burn and Parker are interested in how each mode deals differently, and in combination, with the passing of time. The mode of speech uses past, present and future tenses, whereas the moving image uses cuts and conjunctions as conventions which the viewer is expected to interpret successfully.

So far, then, we've considered literary texts which have been adapted (redesigned) across modes and media in a range of creative ways. We now turn to literature that utilises the technological capabilities of new media to engage in serious play.

7.6 Interactive creative play

IRC, play and intertextuality in everyday chat on the internet are discussed in Chapter 5 of the companion volume, **Maybin and Swann (2006)**.

The examples in this section are of literature created on the internet – in hypertext and in internet relay chat (IRC). **Hypertext** refers to the 'chunks' of text or images used in electronic text such as websites. These chunks are not connected sequentially, but are accessed by readers clicking on links between them, known as **hyperlinks**. **IRC** is an internet chat system that allows users to have live discussions with one another. These definitions will become clearer as you read through the examples given in this section.

Both hypertext and IRC allow texts to be created by multiple authors. Like other texts in this chapter, hypertext literature and IRC literature are created collaboratively. But in IRC, participants are separated in space (they may have never even met) and in hypertext participants are separated in both space and time (they create the text asynchronously, interacting with the text and other participants at different times, sometimes over a long period). Both media can be seen to encourage playfulness. Bolter (1991, p. 130) says of hypertext fiction that:

> Playfulness is a defining quality of this new medium. Electronic literature will remain a game, just as all computer programming is a game. [...] By contrast, there is a solemnity at the center of printed literature – even comedy, romance, and satire – because of the immutability of the printed page.

Danet (2001, p. 100) notes that 'the digital medium is inherently playful and dramatic because of its interactivity and immersive quality, the release from physicality, and the rich array of easy-to-use possibilities at the user's disposal'. In producing literature for hypertext and IRC, every act of authorship can be potentially seen as an act of play.

Hypertext, the author and playfulness

Hypertext shows us more clearly than some other texts how the boundaries between author and reader can be seen as shifting. All websites are based on hypertext – electronic blocks of text and images, and their connecting hyperlinks which allow users to click through them to reach another part of the world wide web. The pathways through the networks of hyperlinks are potentially infinite and unpredictable, depending as they do on the user's interests and decisions. The web itself can be seen as a vast hypertext, constructed by millions of individual authors – authors who not only have little control on how readers will access their websites, but who also link to many other websites, which in turn link to others. The traditional distinction between 'author' and 'reader', therefore, is challenged as readers construct their own experience of the text, reading in unpredictable ways:

> Hypertext differs from printed text by offering readers multiple paths through a body of information: it allows them to make their own connections, incorporate their own links, and produce their own meanings. Hypertext consequently blurs the boundaries between readers and writers [...] The extent of hypertext is unknowable because it lacks clear boundaries and is often multi-authored.
>
> (Snyder, 1998, p. 127)

To read these texts is, in a sense, to 'author' them. But although hypertext theorists all see a shift in the balance of power between author and reader, they vary in terms of how much control they see residing in this 'reader-as-author' (Johnson-Eilola, 1994).

Hypertext readers or hypertext authors?

The reader of hypertext can be seen, for example:

- **as active**: as the embodiment of poststructuralist notions of the 'death of the author', an influential idea put forward by Roland Barthes in 1977 (Landow, 1997).

- **as a writer**: 'In the electronic medium readers cannot avoid writing the text itself, since every choice they make is an act of writing' (Bolter, 1991, p. 144).

- **as an author (perhaps), but not a writer**: Montfort (2003) says that in much interactive fiction, the reader at most types a couple of commands, or simply clicks on the mouse. This is not writing, although it might be authoring.

- **as an interactor, rather than an author**: Murray (1997, p. 152–3) sees the (originating) author of hypertext as a kind of choreographer, supplying the possibilities for a *performance*, which are then enacted by the reader/interactor:

'There is a distinction between playing a creative role within an authored environment and having authorship of the environment itself [...] The interactor is not the author of the digital narrative, although the interactor can experience one of the most exciting aspects of artistic creation – the thrill of exerting power over enticing and plastic materials. This is not authorship but agency.'

Whatever the terminological disagreements and differing conceptualisations of what the reader does, it's clear that some interesting uses of hypertext are emerging in the sphere of fiction. Literature created in this way is often known as **hyperfiction** or **digital fiction**, and exists in a range of genres, from role playing and games, to narrative fiction and poetry. One of the best ways to understand hypertext fiction is to experience it – which can't be reproduced here – but it is available from electronic literary publishers on the world wide web, some of which host a huge number of such texts. Below is a description of how it works, followed by a description of one of the best-known and most widely cited works of hyperfiction, *Afternoon*, by Michael Joyce (1987). *Afternoon* was one of the first to be created and is still widely read. The hypertext theorist and co-creator of *Afternoon*, Jay David Bolter, describes hyperfiction as follows:

Hyperfiction

The author can create a fictional space of great flexibility. Readers may be allowed to examine a story in chronological order, in reverse chronology, or in a complicated sequence of flashbacks and returns. They may follow one character through the story, and then return to follow another. A reader might play the role of the detective trying to solve a murder, a role familiar from the computerized adventure games. A reader might be asked to influence events in a novel by choosing episodes that promise to bring two characters together or to punish an evil character for his or her deeds: each choice would define a new course for the story. Such multiple plots, however, are only one possibility for interactive fiction. The electronic writing space can accommodate many other literary strategies. It could offer the reader several different perspectives on a fixed set of events. In this case the reader would not be able to affect the course of the story, but the reader could switch back and forth among narrators, each with his or her own point of view.

(Bolter, 1991, p. 122)

The choices made by readers of hyperfiction vary according to the amount of control retained or relinquished by the originating author. In terms of creativity, Bolter sees both author and reader as creative and active, although the balance shifts depending on how a particular work is designed. Hyperfiction that gives more control and more choices to the reader will obviously give them greater opportunities for creativity. An example from *Afternoon* is shown below. The visually simple opening screen is shown as Figure 7.2.

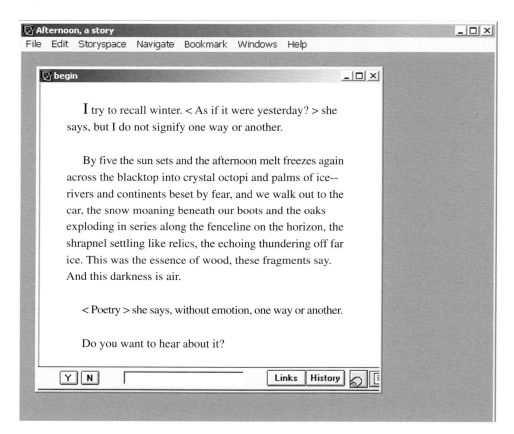

Figure 7.2   Opening screen from *Afternoon.*

At the bottom left of the screen, there are 'Y' and 'N' buttons for 'yes' and 'no'. Here (Figure 7.3) is what you would see by pressing 'yes':

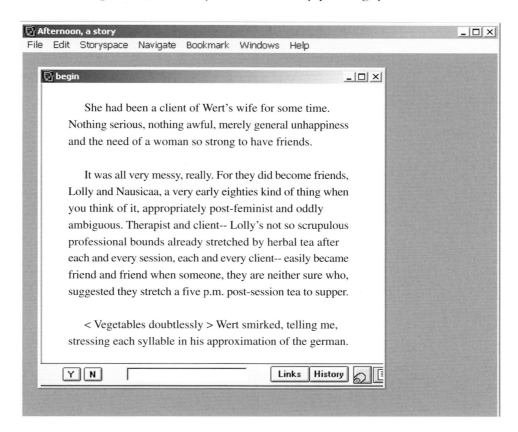

Figure 7.3   'Yes' option from opening screen of *Afternoon*.

Pressing 'no', however, would move you on to the screen shown in Figure 7.4:

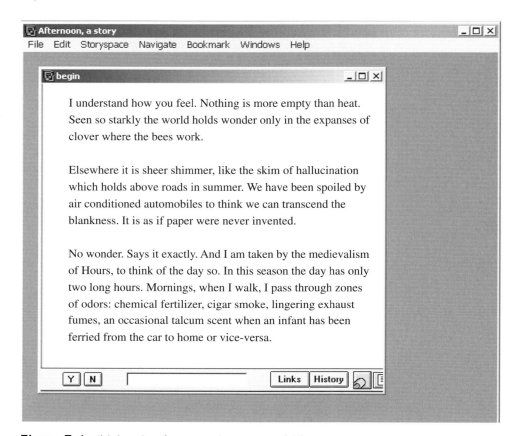

Figure 7.4 'No' option from opening screen of *Afternoon*.

You'll see that selecting 'no' does not stop the narrative, nor does it take 'no' for an answer – it simply takes you to a different place. Other branches are built in, too: the reader can select particular words in the text or press 'Return' to access another part of the story. Bolter comments on this:

> There is no single story of which each reading is a version, because each reading determines the story as it goes. We could say that there is no story at all: there are only readings. Or if we say that the story of 'Afternoon' is the sum of all its readings, then we must understand the story as a structure that can embrace contradictory outcomes. Each reading is a different turning within a universe of paths set up by the author. Reading 'Afternoon' several times is like exploring a vast house or castle [...] – as in a computer game in which the descent down a stairway reveals a whole new level of the dungeon.

(Bolter, 1991, pp. 124–5)

Hyperfictional narratives seriously disturb our sense of narrative time (Douglas, 1994; Landow, 1997; Eskelinen, 2000; Sloane, 2000; and Montfort, 2003). Often they have no beginning (they may notionally create one in the form of a 'starting point' for the reader – but this is not necessarily the beginning of the story); they have no end; they have a range of middles, and the plot – the sequence of events – is constructed by (although not always under the control of) the reader, who creates a different sequence at every reading. Even returning to the same point another day and clicking on the same links does not guarantee the same sequence of events, as the programmers often design this option out. The reader may be taken to a different scene, a different event or a different character's point of view.

Hypertext poetry

Computer technology is also used to create interactive hypertext poetry, and readers/viewers are again called to act upon, 'author', or create the text as they read it. Like hyperfiction, hyperpoetry can be seen as blurring the boundaries between readers and authors, and between texts and readers. Such texts appear to bear out Fish's view (1980) that meaning is created in the process of reading – at the moment of the reader's encounter with the text. But unlike a traditional printed novel, hyperpoetry does not really exist outside of that encounter. Of course the computer code with its options and instructions is there, but the text and its meaning are actualised at the moment of reading. Prior to that, it is only a set of possibilities.

Here are just a couple of examples. The first, 'Mountain rumbles', by Deena Larsen (Figure 7.5), allows the reader to move the mouse over the text, and click through links, to read a different part of the poem.

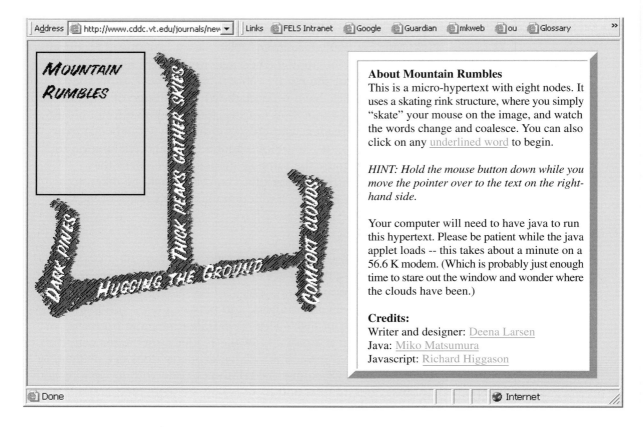

Figure 7.5(a)   (Here and opposite) Screenshots of hypertext poem 'Mountain rumbles', by Deena Larsen.

The black rectangle at the top left shows the position of the mouse. By moving it around, different text appears in the white window on the right. (The reader can also click through the underlined hyperlinks in the white window for more of the poem.) The shape taken by the poem is the Chinese character *shān*, meaning 'mountain'.

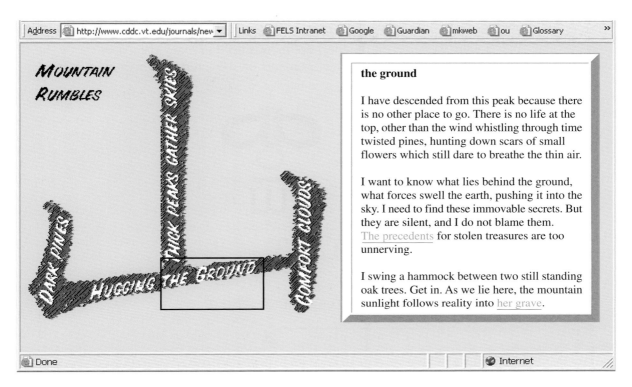

Figure 7.5(b)

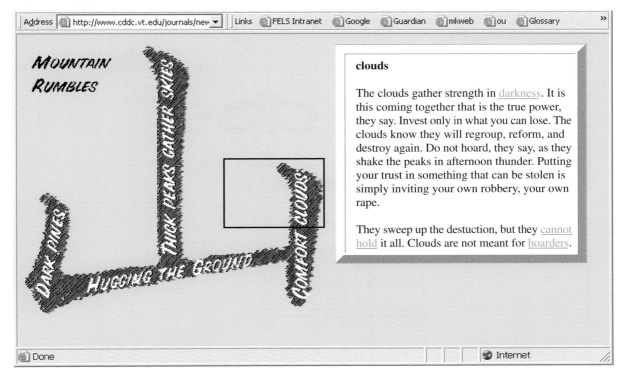

Figure 7.5(c)

The next example, 'Yes, I'm a pop-up poem' by Jim Andrews (Figure 7.6), is a witty variation on the 'pop-up' menus used in many databases (not to be confused with pop-up advertisements on the internet, which work in a different way):

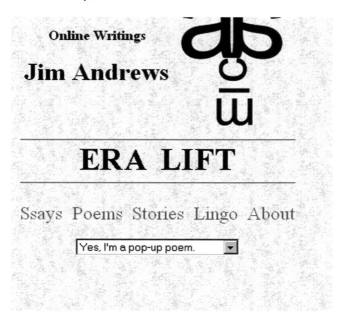

Figure 7.6   Screenshots (above and below) of pop-up poem by Jim Andrews.

By clicking on the down arrow, to the right of the words *Yes, I'm a pop-up poem*, the whole poem then pops up and can be scrolled through:

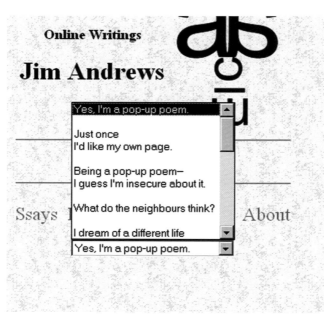

What these examples of hyperfiction and hyperpoetry share is that they make creative demands on the reader, who can alter the text and their encounter with the text in many ways. Both author and reader are involved in the construction of meaning.

In the final example in this chapter, we look at a Shakespeare play redesigned in an internet chatroom. Here authorship is more visible and attributable (although still complex), as the contributions of the 'actors' in this performance of Hamlet leave a visible trace on the screen.

Performance on the internet

The last reading is about online theatre, and is taken from Brenda Danet's book *Cyberpl@y*. It has been chosen because it highlights the aspects of creativity in texts produced with newer technology outlined so far in this chapter (design, the utilisation of modes and affordances to creative effect, and the collaborative nature of such creativity). It also encompasses some of the points made in Chapter 6, particularly about paralanguage in writing, and in Chapter 2 on poetic language and creative deviation.

See Chapter 9 for more on re-reading and re-writing.

The actors in this 1993 online performance of Shakespeare played with, intervened into and deformed almost every possible aspect of *Hamlet* to create their own version of the play. They played with the affordances of writing, image, layout and punctuation, and they played with the medium of computer communication, and its sub-medium, IRC.

Like hypertext, this adaptation (or transformation) is a collaborative endeavour. Unlike hypertext, *Hamnet* was produced synchronously, in real time. The actors were online simultaneously, and could therefore use the creative affordances of time as a semiotic mode. Danet shows how IRC provides extensive opportunities for playful and creative uses of language.

ACTIVITY 6   Playing with Shakespeare online (Reading D)

Please read Danet, 'Shakespeare "live" online: the Hamnet Players'. As you read, consider:

- how Hamnet can be seen as performance (you may wish to revisit Chapter 4);

- what Danet says about the cultural and social knowledge required to make sense of the text that was created;

- which semiotic modes were used by the actors, and what possibilities for creative play these modes afforded to the participants.

Comment

Danet defines *Hamnet* as a performance because the actors are co-present in time, although not in space. The actors experienced a sense of close community and participated in all kinds of (virtual) activities associated with performing a play on a stage – emailing theatre programmes to each other, expressing congratulations and drinking champagne.

In terms of the kinds of knowledge the actors drew upon, and played intertextually with, Danet describes some of what Gee (2003) calls 'semiotic domains': that experience and knowledge needed to understand, or read, the text. We need to know the semiotic domain of the internet, and of IRC, as well as that of Shakespeare, and of more conventional versions on stage or film of his work. To participate fully in the playfulness of *Hamnet*, we need prior experience of 'straight' Shakespeare, as well as of parody and pastiche. Danet identifies the different elements being played with in this text and discusses them in some detail. It should be apparent that a vast amount of knowledge – of all sorts of conventions and semiotic domains – is called for by both the actors and by us, as readers after the event.

Semiotic domains are introduced in Chapter 6.

The primary semiotic mode used for *Hamnet* was writing, as this is the main mode in IRC. But it draws on representations of direct speech, like novels do, and this opens up further opportunities. Danet says elsewhere that:

> Two features of IRC enhance its dramatic potential: its inherent script-like quality and the fact that it employs direct speech as its main mode of communication. In ordinary chat, participants' contributions are listed on screen in sequence, as registered by the IRC servers. With players' nicknames shown at the left of their contributions, their words look like lines in the script of a play [...] typed 'talk' on IRC is rendered in the first and second person. In addition, the software guarantees orderly turns at talking. Unlike [real life] conversations, where obtaining the floor is a potential issue and people often talk at once, there is no struggle to be 'heard' in IRC chat, no overlap in the contributions of various players. Each individual's contributions automatically appear on screen exactly in the order received by the server. It becomes possible, then, to perform a prepared script.
>
> (Danet, 2001, pp. 100–1)

The actors played with the conventions of speech and writing, typing informal (and occasionally obscene) contributions which would normally not be written – the position of IRC as a mode located somewhere between speech and writing afforded them this flexibility. Punctuation was also used to creative effect, both in the lines of the script and the souvenir programme, where it was combined with letterforms to create an image of Elsinore Castle. Modes which could not be present due to the constraints of the medium, such as sound, were represented graphically, with conventionalised onomatopoeia, as in the Drum in line 75: *Like, rat-a-tat, man.*

There are also, of course, the numerous instances of defamiliarisation and poetic language evident in the use of puns, violation of spelling conventions, abbreviation (*2b or not 2b ...*) which shares features with text messaging, and paralanguage such as the use of 'smilies' to indicate facial expression, such as :-(*Bummer ...* in line 19.

7.7 Conclusion

We've looked in this chapter at a range of literary works produced with newer technology, considering them in terms of how they create their meanings out of different semiotic modes and different media. Often, meaning is created through the interaction and articulation of modes and media – what Burn and Parker call the 'kineikonic mode', or the mode of combination.

Chapter 9 also deals with the blurring of the terms 'reader' and 'writer'.

A major focus, however, has been the complication of traditionally understood notions of authors and readers, and the implications of this for understanding the locus and nature of creativity. The traditional notion of a (single) creative literary author, producing great works of literature, dissolves when we have technology which allows us to interact and redesign texts, and even more so when we can do this collaboratively. The advent of computers and their dissemination into many workplaces and homes means that more people than ever before have been handed the tools of text production. And all of our acts of interpretation and production are creative acts and processes, just as the texts we read and produce are creative texts.

To end this chapter, a brief note on the notion of 'aesthetic value' or quality in literary texts, which recurs throughout the chapters in this book.

Adaptations of texts such as popular novels into film are perhaps particularly susceptible to not living up to our expectations, because in reading we have created impressions and mental images which are our own – and seeing them portrayed differently on screen can be distressing. Murray notes, however, that this complaint tradition goes back a long way:

> We often assume that stories told in one medium are intrinsically inferior to those told in another. Shakespeare and Jane Austen were once considered to be working in less legitimate formats than those used by Aeschylus and Homer.
>
> (Murray, 1997, p. 273)

She goes on, explaining why she thinks this feeling is misplaced:

> [N]arrative beauty is independent of medium. Oral tales, pictorial stories, plays, novels, movies, and television shows can all range from the lame and sensationalist to the heartbreaking and illuminating [...] The real literary hierarchy is not of medium but of meaning [...] Commercial forces favor simplistic stories over more authentic engagement with the world. [...]

> People who get great pleasure from books and film are often hostile to the very idea of digital narrative because they expect it to be disappointing [...] With familiarity we will come to realize that the procedural author can shape a juxtaposition or a branch point in a multiform story as artfully as a traditional author shapes a speech in a play or a chapter in a novel.

(Murray, 1997, pp. 273–5)

Porter Abbott argues that to compare a story told in different media is to miss the point, as they are not (and are not intended to be) the same:

> Reviewers who complain that a film or play is a poor 'translation' of the original, may miss the fact that adaptation across media is not translation in anything but the loosest sense.'

(Porter Abbott, 2002, p. 105)

Chapter 5, on translation, introduced the terms 'fidelity' and 'equivalence' with regard to translated text. These are useful concepts here too, analogously. The most useful way of evaluating adaptations – whether across languages, modes or media – may be to evaluate them in their own terms (looking at *what* they mean and *how* they mean), rather than in comparison with each other. Many of the readings in this chapter have suggested that different versions of a literary text are in fact not the same text in different modes, but different texts. If you accept this (and you may not), it becomes almost impossible to say whether one is better than the other (subjective preference aside), as you are not comparing like with like. *Hamlet* and *Hamnet* are a good example of this – they are not the same text, and were never intended to be. But that doesn't necessarily make one 'better' than the other – it depends what you think each text *is*.

READING A: Extracts from 'Multimodality and new communication technologies

Carey Jewitt

The discussion of the impact of new communication technologies on social interaction and discourse is increasingly accompanied by the discussion of multimodality (and vice versa). Through these discussions medium and mode have become woven together like two threads in a cloth. In order to understand the impact on social interactions and discourses themselves that these technologies have, [I argue] that the complex relationship between new communication technologies and multimodality needs to be explored. [...]

Medium refers to how texts are disseminated, such as printed book, CD-ROM, or computer application. Mode refers [to] any organized, regular means of representation and communication, such as still image, gesture, posture, speech, music, writing, or new configurations of the elements of these (Kress *et al*. 2001). [Here I examine] this relationship to explore the affordances of technologies of dissemination (media) and the affordances of the technologies of representation (modes). [I focus] on the transformation of the John Steinbeck novel *Of Mice and Men* (1937) from print technology to digital technology, that is, from the medium of the book to the medium of the CD-ROM (1996). This move from one medium to another enables the designer of a CD-ROM (and the reader of it) to engage with the affordances of a range of representational modes in ways that can both reshape entities ('things to think about and things to think with'), such as character, and the practices of reading. [...]

[My contention] is that research on new communication technologies tends to foreground the affordances of medium at the cost of neglecting the affordances of representational modes. The point I want to make is this: the meaning of a text is realized by people's engagement with both the medium of dissemination *and* the representational affordances (whether social or material) of the modes that are used.

Mode as technology of representation: the move from page to screen

The CD-ROM as a medium of dissemination has the potential to bring together the mode-aspects of gesture, movement, sound-effect, speech, writing, and image into one multimodal ensemble. Writing remains within the space of new technology in all its forms, but with specialized tasks. The question of what affordances this new space has, and what are the representational modes which are most apt in relation to it, remains (Lanham 2001).

Reading the CD-ROM version of the novel *Of Mice and Men*, the reader is required to select their preferred version of the text: the 'written' version of the book or the 'visual' version of the book, which includes video clips and drawings alongside the writing. The novel as CD-ROM includes hyperlinks to definitions of colloquial words used in the novel and to a map of the area the story is set in, and it, in its turn includes hyperlinks to information on the population and industry of the towns.

The potential of the medium to link texts via visual hyperlinks enables the reader to move between the [...] character in the 'fictional domain' of the novel and the [...] character in a 'factual domain' beyond the novel – the historical-social context of the novel. The two domains of fact and fiction provide the potential for a complex notion of character and text to be realized. [...]

The two versions of the novel as CD-ROM offer the designer and the reader of the CD-ROM different resources for meaning-making. The move from page to screen realizes a changed compositional relationship between image and writing. Image dominates the space in the majority of the screens. The relationship between image and writing is newly configured and is itself a visual meaning-making resource. In the context of the screen the writing has become a visual element, a block of 'space,' which makes textual meaning beyond its written content. The blocks of writing are positioned in different places on the screen (the left or right side, along the bottom or top length of the screen). Depending both on the size and position of the block of writing different parts of the image layered 'beneath it' are revealed or concealed. In this way a block of writing (and its movement across screens) can change the screen image fundamentally, as is the case in these three screens shown in Figure 1. These three screens are taken from Chapter 1 of the novel as CD-ROM. They depict the two main characters in the story, George and Lennie, having an argument as they are traveling to start a new job together at a ranch.

In the first screen, the block of writing is positioned above George's head as he talks to Lennie about what he could do if he left him. In the second, Lennie is visually obliterated and George visually foregrounded by the block of text that 'contains' George's angry talk of leaving. In the third, the block of writing is placed on the screen in a way that makes both George and Lennie visible as George's anger subsides. The interaction of the blocks of writing and the still image on the screens serve to foreground or background the two characters, and to visually mark the intensity of a moment through the persistence of an image on screen.

The modes of writing and image are also used differently in realizing the characters. For example, writing focuses on the thoughts, worries, and dreams of George, while Lennie is more frequently visually represented as expressing himself actionally. Writing is used to indicate reflection, and image is used to indicate action, and through this specialized use of mode these different qualities are associated with the characters George and Lennie. [...]

Hyperlinks are links within an electronic document to other information, and are usually represented by highlighted words or images. Clicking on a hyperlink switches to the document or part of it referenced by the hyperlink.

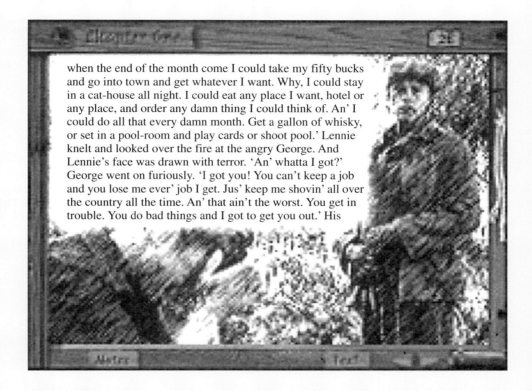

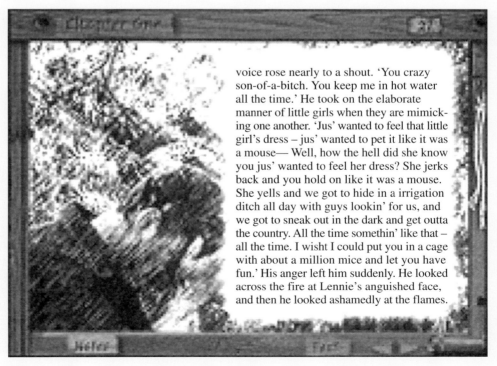

Figure 1   An extract from Chapter 1 of the CD-ROM version of *Of Mice and Men*.

It was quite dark now, but the fire lighted the trunks of the trees and the curving branches over head. Lennie crawled slowly and cautiously around the fire until he was close to George. He sat back on his heels. George turned the bean-cans so that another side faced the fire. He pretended to be unaware of Lennie so close beside him.

'George,' very softly. No answer. 'George!'

Technologies of dissemination: the move from page to screen

The transformation from book to CD-ROM brings with it the affordances of a different technology of dissemination. A central point is the potentials for interaction that the medium (the book or the CD-ROM) makes available to the 'reader'. In reading a book, the reader is given a clear reading path – from the top left corner of the page, to the bottom right and so on, from page one to the end. She or he might move to a footnote, to the index, return to the contents page, or abandon the book altogether: but the reading path is nonetheless there. [...] The CD-ROM makes possible, brings forth, a different kind of activity from that of the book [...]. This enables the reader to some significant extent, to determine their own route through materials (Andrews 2000).

One of the affordances of the technology of dissemination is that it is also a technology of production, and as such it enables [readers] to produce their interaction through different genres, through different forms of engagement. The openness of the 'novel as CD-ROM' not only extends but also alters the traditional notion of reading from a matter of interpretation to design (Kress and van Leeuwen 2001). Students (aged 14–15) were observed using the Steinbeck CD-ROM over a series of five school English lessons in an Inner London secondary school (for a fuller discussion see Jewitt 2002). Two of these students used the Chapter Menu Bar as a navigational tool to move almost seamlessly through the 'novel as CD-ROM' as a series of video clips.

Another pair of students 'flicked' through the still images of the chapter in a way that 'animated' the text like a cartoon. While two other students selected characters with audio clips of songs, they learned some of the words, sang, and tapped along – they momentarily transformed the novel into 'music'. The students' genre of interaction with the text reshaped the entity character through a shift from the literary genre of 'novel' to the popular textual genre of comic, film, and song. That is, their engagement introduced a shift from the literary aesthetic to the popular, and from the world of fiction to the students' everyday lifeworlds.

The CD-ROM brings forth a different kind of reading that requires a different kind of imaginative work. The reader of the novel as CD-ROM has to choose from the elements available on screen, to decide what elements and modes to take and make meaningful, and then to order them into a text. [...]

Conclusion

This example illustrates the relationship between mode and medium and the potential for the reshaping of meaning and of practices in the move from the medium of book to the medium of CD-ROM. [It demonstrates] that the semiotic potentials made available via a multimodal text, whatever its technology of dissemination, contribute to the shaping of what can be 'done with it' – how meaning can be designed. [In] order to understand the practices of people engaged with new (and old) technologies we need to understand *what it is* that they are working with. Understanding the semiotic affordances of medium and mode is one way of seeing how technologies shape the learner, and the learning environment, and what it is that is to be learned.

The relative newness of new communication technologies still shines, making digital and computer technologies appear to stand apart from older technologies, such as pen and paper – naturalized everyday technologies that no longer glitter. Nonetheless, the question of how technologies of dissemination shape meaning is always present.

The representational shifts that are so often associated with new communication technologies go well beyond it. The increased intensity of the use of image, the increased visualization of writing is present on screen, page, and elsewhere. The assertion that 'we are entering a historical epoch in which the image will take over from the written word' (Gombrich 1996, p. 41) appears to have some value. History shows that modes of representation and technologies of dissemination are and always have been inextricably linked. Understanding new communicational technologies as the differently configured combinations of the affordances of representational modal resources and technologies of dissemination offers one way to understand how multimodal representations between or across technologies reshape knowledge.

References

ANDREWS, R. (2000) 'Framing and design in ICT in English', in A. GOODWYN (ed.) *English in the Digital Age*, London, Cassell.

GOMBRICH, E.H. (1996) 'The visual image: its place in communication', in R. WOODFIELD (ed.) *The Essential Gombrich: Selected Writings on Art and Culture*, London, Phaidon.

JEWITT, C. (2002) 'The move from page to screen: the multimodal reshaping of school English', *Visual Communication*, **1**(2), pp. 171–96.

KRESS, G. and VAN LEEUWEN, T. (2001) *Multimodal Discourse*, London, Arnold.

KRESS, G., JEWITT, C., OGBORN, J. and TSATSARELIS, C. (2001) *Multimodal Teaching and Learning: The Rhetorics of the Science Classroom*, London, Continuum.

LANHAM, R. (2001) 'What's next for text?', *Education, Communication, and Information*, **1**(1), pp. 15–36.

STEINBECK, J. (1937) *Of Mice and Men*, London, Penguin.

STEINBECK, J. (1996) *Of Mice and Men*, CD-ROM version, New York, Penguin Electronic.

Source: LEVINE, P. and SCOLLON, R. (eds) (2004) *Discourse and Technology: Multimodal Discourse Analysis*, pp. 184–195, Washington, DC, Georgetown University Press.

READING B: Extracts from 'Adaptation across media'

H. Porter Abbott

Adaptation as creative destruction

If the creative leeway between script and performance is wide in the production of plays, it is enormous when adaptation crosses media boundaries. This is necessarily the case. Reviewers who complain that a film or play is a poor 'translation' of the original, may miss the fact that adaptation across media is not translation in anything but the loosest sense. In fact, it can sometimes be the attempt to make a strict translation that winds up in failure. George Bluestone formulated the strong 'destructivist' position on this issue over forty years ago:

> What happens ... when the filmist undertakes the adaptation of a novel ... is that he does not convert the novel at all. What he adapts is a kind of paraphrase of the novel – the novel viewed as raw material ... it has

always been easy to recognize how a poor film 'destroys' a superior novel. What has not been sufficiently recognized is that such destruction is inevitable. In the fullest sense of the word, the filmist becomes not a translator for an established author, but a new author in his own right.

(Bluestone, 1957, p. 62)

[...] In this [reading] I discuss a few of the reasons why there should be such great differences when you adapt across media.

Duration and pace

A work of prose fiction, like a novel, can take any amount of time to read. [...] In the theater, plays and movies are neither portable nor interruptible. Given the expense and logistics of production, plus the limits of audience endurance, the outside limit for narrative length in these media is usually two hours. [...] Early in the development of cinema, the length of feature films became standard across the industry and today, despite the portability and viewing flexibility of VCRs and DVDs, it holds steady. In addition, the primary venue for the cinematic narrative event is still the theater, and the continuous, unbreakable experience that theater demands exerts control not only over the length of the narrative but its pacing. This also holds for films made for TV, which, despite the private intimacy of the performance venue, are not (yet) designed to be taped and played under the control of the viewer.

The difference in duration alone has major implications for adaptation. Longer prose narratives, like novels, [...] create a world that you can freely enter and leave, and that can include a multitude of characters involved in a number of concurrent threads of action. [...] Adaptation to the shorter, continuous forms of stage and screen is, then, a surgical art. [...] *Wuthering Heights* at four hundred pages is a short nineteenth-century novel, yet William Wyler's award-winning 1939 film version amputated the original halfway through the narrative at the point where Catherine dies. Except for the death of Heathcliff, the whole second half of the novel with its diversity of character and incident is missing. This necessary economy alone would have made Wyler's film a fundamentally different narrative from the book. The same is true for nineteenth-century stage adaptations of *Wuthering Heights*, which stopped at the same point.

But Wyler had to reduce even further, not only to squeeze four hundred pages into 104 minutes, but also to insure that the audience would not get lost. Ironically, it is theater's absolute control over the pacing of the narrative experience, keeping the audience prisoners in their seats, that gives audiences enormous power of their own over the content of that experience. The result is a kind of tyranny of the story line, which must be kept clear enough to be grasped in one continuous experience. Conversely, novel readers tolerate a great deal of material unrelated or only peripherally related to the story lines. Anecdotes, mediations, conversations, descriptions can all be piled on to the narrative platform of a novel without necessarily cutting into its appeal (and market value). There have been in fact highly successful novels with wide audiences, like *The Life and Opinions of Tristram Shandy* (1759–67), in which the central story is so encumbered by extraneous material that it barely comes alive. This rarely works in plays or films [...] However, what the film in its finished form does bring out clearly is what readers of the novel often find themselves struggling to understand: the story's *constituent events*. We see much more clearly than in the novel how one event leads to the next, and this is a direct result of the time constraint that filmmakers have to deal with. [...]

Character

[...]

> Mr Heathcliff forms a singular contrast to his abode and style of living. He is a dark skinned gypsy in aspect, in dress and manners a gentleman; that is, as much a gentleman as many a country squire: rather slovenly, perhaps, yet not looking amiss with his negligence, because he has an erect and handsome figure, and rather morose.
>
> (Emily Brontë, *Wuthering Heights*, p. 3–4)

This is one of the earliest descriptions we have of Heathcliff in *Wuthering Heights*. What do we see and understand from this passage? It provides what seem to be contradictions of nineteenth-century type: a 'dark skinned gypsy,' yet a gentleman; slovenly in dress, yet 'erect and handsome.' If we are not seriously underreading, we must deploy some kind of mental flexibility that allows us to hold these traits loosely together in our minds. Moreover, this description is transmitted through Mr Lockwood, who proves himself elsewhere to be an *unreliable narrator*. A silly and shallow man, Lockwood goes on astonishingly to see his own traits of modesty and reserve in Heathcliff. Realizing this, we must be additionally wary, keeping our sense of Heathcliff open, rejecting selectively some of what Lockwood says (for example: 'his reserve springs from an aversion to showy displays of feeling'). As the story progresses, we cobble together from these and other descriptions, combined with Heathcliff's words and actions, a fascinatingly complex entity – highly intelligent, passionate, articulate, avaricious, haunted, murderous and cruel – who somehow seems to hold together as a character. But when we see the character on stage, or see Olivier play him on the screen, *much of this flexible indeterminacy is foreclosed*. The character is to a considerable degree fixed for us, both visually and aurally. This kind of fixing of a character through image, of course, happens when written narratives are illustrated, either in hard copy or hypertext.

It is also much harder to get inside a character on stage or on screen. Actors' soliloquies can approximate the associative flow of private thoughts, and dream sequences can represent an internal struggle, but they rarely match the kind of extensive explorations in depth that can unfold over many

Figure 1   Laurence Olivier, *Wuthering Heights,* United Artists, 1939, courtesy of
the Academy of Motional Picture Arts and Sciences.

pages of confessional fiction, letter-fiction, diary fiction, or stream of
consciousness fiction. Tied to the dominance of visual and aural sensation,
audiences of stage and film must apprehend human interiors by inference,
much as we do in the course of our lives. For the dramatist and filmmaker,
this constraint, like all constraints in art, can be the source of discipline and
inspiration. Francois Truffaut's decision to end *The Four Hundred Blows* with
the face of the child was a brilliant stroke in this regard. The view is external,
but the face becomes a screen in which the audience reads the child's
abandonment and what must be, at some level, his despair. [...]

Figurative language

Quite similar to this difference between media in the representation of
characters is the difference that verbal narration has when it draws on
figurative language, particularly on metaphors. Often on the page what is
internal to a character comes out in metaphorical language. [...]

It is a mistake, however, to think that stage and screen are entirely without this resource. As long as there are characters in a narrative, they can in their turn become describers and even narrators who use words. They have in fact given us some of the most powerful figurative language ever employed in narrative. In Shakespeare's *Antony and Cleopatra*, here is how Enobarbus begins to describe Antony's first view of Cleopatra:

> The barge she sat in, like a burnished throne,
> Burned on the water. The poop was beaten gold,
> Purple the sails, and so perfumèd that
> The winds were lovesick with them. The oars were silver,
> Which to the tune of flutes kept stroke and made
> The water which they beat to follow faster,
> As amorous of their strokes.

(William Shakespeare, *The Tragedy of Antony and Cleopatra*, II, ii, lines 196–202)

This is not what anyone would call detached, objective reporting. Enobarbus draws on a diverse arsenal of figurative tropes – personification, hyperbole, metaphor, catachresis – to saturate the wind and water with the feelings of the 'amorous' and 'lovesick' Antony. But to appreciate it in the theater, we must to some degree detach ourselves from what we see before us on stage (Enobarbus and Agrippa in a house in Rome) and engage in the same sort of mental theater that we do all the time with verbal narrative. And as with the case of characters like Heathcliff, brought to earth photographically in film, the filming of Cleopatra's 'barge' cannot hope to compete with Enobarbus's words.

Figure 2   Cleopatra, Twentieth Century Fox, 1963, courtesy of the Academy of Motion Picture Arts and Sciences.

Drama and screen can also deploy their visual resources in an effective counterpoint to language like this. In the scene above, a sturdy, domestic this-worldly Roman set can put Enorbarbus's language into sharp relief, making the imagined African river scene it describes seem to belong to a different world, exotic and mythological. Such contrasts can give wonderful energy to a scene. When Romeo spies Juliet on the balcony, he cries,

> But, soft! What light through yonder window breaks?
> It is the east, and Juliet is the sun!
> Arise, fair sun, and kill the envious moon,
> Who is already sick and pale with grief
> That thou her maid are far more fair than she.
>
> (William Shakespeare, *The Tragedy of Romeo and Juliet*, II, ii, lines 2–6)

Personification again, hyperbole, metaphor, but all of them deployed while the object of description is right there before our eyes. It can even help if Juliet is not exceptionally beautiful, since the difference between her quite mortal beauty and the romantic excess of her lover's words can say a great deal about the power of love.

Gaps

[Gaps] are everywhere in prose narrative. There is no way that a narrator can avoid calling on listeners or readers to help bridge one gap after another. But what if we had the *characters* in the story actually before us, alive, and the *action* unfolding with no difference between the time it takes and clock time? What happens is that many of these narrational gaps disappear. This is what happens on stage. The difference in effect is great, and it makes you see why some narratologists would rather not include staged action as a type of narrative, but instead fall back on categories like 'mimesis' or 'the presentation of events' to categorize what they are. It is important to bear in mind, though, that most prose narratives also include stretches of dialogue, some of them quite long. At these moments, prose narrative approaches the kind of gaplessness in staged narrative. There usually are, of course, a few major gaps in plays. Scene breaks and act breaks sometimes separate installments of the action by great swathes of time. There have also been quite fluid stagings of time shifts in any number of twentieth-century productions. With a modest set, John Guare's play *Six Degrees of Separation* can easily slide from one time and place to another with no breaks over 120 pages of script. But despite devices like this that have given some playwrights considerable flexibility, the unit of drama is still the scene. And scenes take place in real time. So, by and large, adaptation of a novel to the stage requires finding and shaping the scenes that carry action and intensity. Again, it is a highly selective process.

[...] Much of the art of film is an art of gap management that Eisenstein called '*montage*.' In French, montage literally means 'assembly.' In film, it is the art of assembling a multitude of different lengths of film to make the continuous narrative we see. Eisenstein argued that the effect of moving from one image to the next was not the sum of the two images but something quite new. In this way, an entire car chase through a city can be conveyed by a few selected moments. Conveying continuous events like a car chase, a climb upstairs, a fall from a window, a sudden embrace, or a conversation through the use of montage makes for great efficiency in the deployment of a film's 90 to 120 minutes. But suggesting the continuity of events is only one aspect of the art of montage. Putting disparate shots next to each other can also convey meaning, and often with considerable power. In *Apocalypse Now* (1979), the onrush of helicopter gunships flying to the strains of Wagner's *Die Walküre*, suddenly gives way to the sight and sound of Vietnamese schoolchildren in a village compound. The contrast not only conveys the continuous action of an assault on the village but also suggests a moral discrepancy between the invaders and the invaded. In sum, the ease of narrative movement that montage permits approximates the freedom of movement novelists enjoy as they jump ahead, fall back, speed up, slow down, or drift from character to character. And though the voice of the narrator can still take us many places the camera cannot go, it cannot match film's immediacy of sound and sight.

A narrative art form that draws, like hypertext fiction, on both film's visuals and prose's narrative flexibility is the comic strip. Long neglected as a 'legitimate' art, comics are only now beginning to be theorized as they gain a certain level of respect through the innovative work of artists like Scott McCloud, Frank Miller, and Neil Gaimon. At the center of this theory is, once again, the principle of the gap. McCloud, in his *Understanding Comics*, vividly demonstrated this centrality of the gap in his explication of the 'gutter' – the necessary gap that regularly falls between succeeding images [see Figure 3].

Moving pictures don't really move. All the motion that we think we see on the screen is in fact a succession of still pictures. Its appearance as motion relies on the principle of 'persistence of vision.' Images persist on the retina for roughly one tenth of a second after their initial impact. This is enough to carry over from one frame of a film to the next, tricking us into seeing motion where, were it not for this persistence of vision, we would see only a jerky succession of still pictures. In other words, even here, at this molecular level of cinematic narrative, we are engaged in bridging gaps.

Figure 3   From *Understanding Comics* by Scott McCloud, p.66.

References

BLUESTONE, G. (1957) *Novels into Film*, Berkeley, University of California Press.

BRONTE, E. (1981[1847]) *Wuthering Heights*, Oxford, Oxford University Press.

McCLOUD, S. (1993) *Understanding Comics*, New York, HarperCollins.

SHAKESPEARE, W. *The Tragedy of Antony and Cleopatra*.

SHAKESPEARE, W. *The Tragedy of Romeo and Juliet*.

Source: PORTER ABBOTT, H. (2002) *The Cambridge Introduction to Narrative*, Chapter 9, Cambridge, Cambridge University Press.

READING C: Extracts from 'Tiger's big plan: multimodality and the moving image'

Andrew Burn and David Parker

Here is an image of Anansi the Spider [see Colour Figure 10] from one of the cycle of African folk-tales about the spider-man trickster. It is a single frame from a short [...] animated film made by 10- and 11-year-old children and their teacher in a primary school in Cambridge, United Kingdom. [...]

[The] architects of the project and the children working on it are imagining a final production in which speech, music and animated film blend. Our purpose [...] is to explore how this blending works, both in terms of the social and technological processes of design and production, and in the final film and how we might read it. [...] We will develop the idea of the moving image as a specific mode – the *kineikonic* – and identify some of the principles through which it integrates other communicative modes through the design of time and space, and the use of a wide variety of media and tools. We will use this theory to analyse a short section of the film of *Anansi and the Firefly*. [...]

The film is a transformation of a Ghanaian folk-tale. It tells the story of how Anansi, the trickster spider, goes out with Firefly to collect eggs. While Firefly lights the way, Anansi takes all the eggs for himself, leaving Firefly to return home with none. However, Anansi now cannot see to find his way home, and has to stop for help at Tiger's house. In order to convince Tiger to take him in, he gives him the eggs for dinner. To present himself as unselfish, Anansi refuses any eggs at dinner, secretly planning to steal any remaining eggs and eat them during the night. Tiger's suspicions are aroused, and he conceals a live lobster in the pot of eggs, covering it with eggshells. When Anansi goes to steal the eggs during the night, the lobster pinches him. Tiger shouts out, hearing Anansi's cry of pain; Anansi pretends it is only dog-fleas biting him. Tiger pretends to be outraged; and Anansi is driven from the house, disgraced and devoid of eggs. [...]

[The] child recreating Anansi here must make quite specific decisions about what he looks like. What resources have been used to make these decisions? We want to suggest three important factors. Firstly, the child could reach for images of 'Africanness', garnered from film or television, perhaps. The visual composition, however, suggests nothing of this. Though this is an African story, it is easier to stick with familiar images, which may duck the representational issue, rendering the Africanness of the story invisible; but may on the other hand avoid an embarrassingly stereotypical image of Africa. Already, the image has a complex relation to the provenance of the narrative on the one hand, and of the visual resources used to present it on the other.

Secondly the child who drew the picture has made some decisions about colours. It may be no coincidence that the red and blue of the spider along with the enormous web, are elements of the design of Marvel's comic strip superhero, Spiderman [...]

Thirdly, if the colours are those of Spiderman, the bulbous eyes with pinpoint pupils and the rotund body are reminiscent of the *Simpsons* and *South Park*, and the humorous characterisation associated with them, as well as the discourse of mischief and irreverence in which Anansi is rooted.

This image of Anansi, then, is on the one hand completely original – it exists absolutely for the first time. On the other hand, all the decisions in its making are framed by the discourses within which the children are working, and the genres that most typically express these discourses in their experience: the folk-tale, the comic strip, and the animated cartoon. [...]

Design: The kineikonic mode

The moving image is an integrative, combinatorial assemblage of modes [...] Our kineikonic mode [...] refers to how all the elements of the moving image are assembled, but includes the particular conventions afforded by the practices of filming and editing. This mode uses a range of semiotic resources to make the moving image, integrating them into the spatiotemporal flow by (re)designing and producing them within the spatial frame and the temporal sequence of the film. [...]

What does the choice of the kineikonic mode mean for [...] this project? We need to look back at the beginning of the process: like many moving image projects, this one began with storyboarding. Two points are clear in this practice: firstly, that the modes of written language and still visual design are employed as notations for the moving image that is to be; and secondly, that the eventual moving image has to be imagined by the child-designers in order for them to make any sense of this notation. [...] Two particular difficulties children have experienced [...] at the stage of storyboard design are in framing the shot in each drawing. They showed a tendency to draw everything in long shot, as if needing to see whole figures against backgrounds all the time. The convention of the close-up, with its selective indicators of salient detail and its implications of social proximity, needed to be explicitly taught. The other difficulty, not overcome in this film, is that of

Storyboarding is the process of making a series of drawings, to plan key shots in a film.

drawing low-angle shots, because of the technical difficulty of drawing foreshortened images. As we shall see, this difficulty with visual design can be overcome by saying something similar in another mode.

At the storyboard stage, the other key mode in play was writing, as a way of notating the dialogue and voiceover. For the children, the writing of the script involves cutting it up into groups of words, clauses or sentences, the decision hinging on which groups of words will go with which shot. Already then, *design* means to articulate image and word.

The notation of movement on a storyboard is – can only be – minimal. Though movement and duration are criterial to the kineikonic mode, in the early stages of design they remain largely in the heads of the designers. The next stage of this animation moves more decisively towards the design of movement. It involves making drawn bits to be animated. The decision facing the children here is: which bits will move, and therefore need to be drawn separately? [...] This movement from design into production is a new multimodal inflection of art – the mode of visual design orientated towards the kineikonic mode. [...]

We want to look at the film in terms of three overarching functions of any form of communication (Kress et al., 2001, p. 13): *ideational* (how some aspect of the world is represented); *interpersonal* (how the film constructs imagined relationships between text and spectator); and *textual* (how the text is composed as coherent message).

Ideational function

In this first part of the sequence [in Colour Figure 11], who is doing what? The answer is complex. As far as the overall sequence is concerned, Tiger is talking, and we infer his image, perhaps, from the sound of his voice, which we recognise. The sound of his voice, in other words, only works if the spectator's act of interpretation produces a new sign, combining the speech with the memory of Tiger's appearance from earlier shots. At the same time, this is a double narrative – Tiger as part of the larger story, and Tiger as narrator of this section, which is both a memory and a plan for the future. The first shot, then, in terms of the image track, represents the cub eating eggs: a single action, grouped into a sequence of three – the eating movement is repeated three times.

In the speech track, the voiceover has two groups for the three in the image track. The two groups do not represent the cub at all, but make the eggs the subject of the first clause: 'All the eggs are gone'. Clearly it is the disappearance of the eggs that is important rather than who has eaten them, teaching us that the cub is simply an exemplary instance of egg-eating. Shots 2 and 4 reinforce this emphasis, presenting a visual equivalent of the deleted agency of Tiger's first clause: it is the disappearance of the eggs that is important, rather than who has eaten them.

The second group tells us Tiger's feelings about the egg-supper: 'What a feast!'

The unworried enthusiasm in Tiger's voice (partly achieved by the words themselves, partly by the material signifier of the mildly excited tone of voice of the child doing the voice characterisation) is significant because of its contrast with the dawning suspicion in the next clause/shot group. This contrastive structure, which works to heighten the suspicious tone of the next section, is also related to the music track. The initial shot/sound group has coinciding boundaries for the speech, image and music tracks. While the image shows the cub enjoying the eggs, and the speech shows Tiger innocently enthusing over the meal, the musical phrase consists of a rising and falling minor scale on a piano. Its function is to introduce a sinister note of warning, *anticipating* the suspicion in the following speech, and *contradicting* the image and speech groups with which it is conjoined.

The other images in the sequence represent the other projections of Tiger's mental act. If the cub represents the immediate past – the delicious dinner – the lobster (shot 6) represents the future – Tiger's plan to place the lobster in the pot to punish Anansi. However the complex temporal design of this sequence – Tiger's voiceover in the 'present' tense of the overall story, the dinner in the past, and the lobster in the future – is constructed through a complex multimodal interweaving of speech, image and music.

Temporality is constructed in all moving image narrative sequences using five possible time relations which have been categorised and used within film semiotics (Chatman, 1978):

1   Summary duration: the discourse takes less time than the events depicted.
2   Ellipsis duration: the discourse stops but we infer from the subsequent shots that some time has passed.
3   Scene duration: story and discourse are of approximately equal lengths.
4   Stretch duration: here discourse time is over-cranked, taking more time than the story events.
5   Pause duration: where discourse time continues but story time stops.

In the sequence of shots listed above, the discourse time is easily established; the sequence lasts about 20 seconds. However, the events depicted in that relatively short time take place over a much longer durative span: we might suggest about one hour. So one of the main functions of time, as it is designed here, is to condense a series of narrative events into a much shorter timespan than they would normally take. What design choices are made in order to make this happen?

Shot 1 begins a flashback sequence that serves as an example of summary duration, as the eggs disappear (shots 2 and 4) and a clock face made in Tiger's image depicts time passing (shot 3). Although this use of literal symbols is a common way of depicting the passage of story time in a succinct way (many films have resorted to pages of a calendar peeling off or dates and times written as the legend on-screen) the children have made an effective design choice. Not only have they passed over moments of marginal interest in terms of plot to reach the moment in the story on which the narrative pivots (Tiger's trick on Anansi), but they have visually depicted in a clear way that this is very much 'Tiger's time', both in terms of his importance as a plot device at this moment, and in the sense that he will get revenge for Anansi's past tricks and at the same time punish the spider's greed in giving no eggs to Firefly.

As the image groups and the sharp boundaries between them emphasise this temporal summary, the speech track is accomplishing a quite different, but complementary, representation of time. Over the two images in shots 2 and 3, the speech track continues in one single sentence, composed of three clause groups. The first is a compressed clause consisting of one word – 'Strange' – which implies the missing verb structure 'It is'. This omission emphasises the strangeness as the theme for this utterance, aligned with disappearing eggs: and both of these imply Tiger's suspicion, the causal hinge of his revenge trick. This is immediately followed by 'how Anansi didn't want to eat any himself'. Ideationally, this has two main functions. It introduces Anansi's agency: his refusal to eat the eggs; and it locates it in the past, continuing the established temporal status of this and the previous shot as flashbacks. However, the temporality constructed by the two modes is mobile and syncopated: as the speech track utters the past tense 'didn't', the clock face shows time hurrying by on the clock, already moving on to the present tense of the story.

Shots 4, 5 and 6 reinforce our burgeoning sense of Tiger's importance. Shot 4 begins with the eggs disappearing, marking both the 'dinner we did not see' and the passing of time generally. Again, the speech track staggers the temporal design – as shot 4 represents the past dinner, the speech track introduces a flash forward for the first time – 'I'm sure he'll try to trick me'. This is a future event entirely made by the voiceover – it has no visual equivalent on the image track. Again, Anansi's agency is confined to the speech mode, and absent from the Tiger-dominated image track; and again, his agency is relegated to the secondary clause in the structure, the bracketing clause representing Tiger's controlling mental act: 'I'm sure...'.

We cut to the next shot (5) in which the disembodied head of Tiger talks to us in a theatrical soliloquy. This is an example of *scene* duration – the speech equalling the discourse time: it brings us back to the present, anchoring Tiger's voiceover in image and lip-synched mouth movements. At the same time, the future tense in the speech track again constructs a flash forward, this time anticipating the visual event in the next shot, as well as preparing us for the fact that this is a future event.

Indeed, when we cut to shot 6 and see the empty pot and Tiger's hand placing the lobster inside, we recognise that this is a resumption of the summary mode, this time as flash forward. The voiceover continues to run ahead of time represented in the visual track, this time indicating a future time in which Anansi, again only present in word, not image, will be fooled by the pot full of empty eggshells.

Shot 7 marks a cut to Tiger in medium shot, implicitly talking directly to Anansi (though again Anansi is absent visually) – 'You should stay the night, godson'. It takes us back to 'real-time', the story and discourse times merging as Tiger speaks.

We have left out an account of the music track, apart from pointing out the effect of rising and falling minor scale in shot 1. Over shots 3 and 4, the sounds suggest no clear melody, but rather an ostinato (a persistent, repetitive pattern) of agitated notes on the violin and a rapid repeating two-note sequence on the flute. This suggests something disturbing and hard to resolve; and this music grows through the next two shots. Unlike the minor scale, which suggests closure (perhaps the finishing of the eggs, with which it coincides) the ostinati suggest lack of closure, and coincide with Tiger's plan to put a lobster in the pot. The modality created by the lack of either closure, clear rhythm or clear melody is one of uncertainty. In tandem with the future tense in Tiger's voiceover ('...he'll try to trick me... I'll place this lobster into the empty pot and cover it with eggshells. Anansi will think it's still full of delicious eggs'.), the sense of uncertainty is reinforced.

Clearly, this sequence is a complex marriage of dialogue and visuals that combine to create an impression of a great deal of time passing quickly. This is common during plot-rich moments in moving image narratives and that is certainly a likely reason for this sophisticated use of summary duration.

[...] Time is signified in speech by past, present and future verb forms. This is an explicit representation of narrative time, formed by the grouping of a clause around the verb structure. In the image track, by contrast, time is signified entirely by boundary – the abrupt cut of one moment in time and conjunction – the juxtaposition of a different moment in time. Here, temporal shifts are, as is common in film, implicit rather than explicit – they are conventions that the spectator learns and will construct as part of the process of internal sign production [...]

Interpersonal function

[...] The text works to establish a particular relationship with the audience: that of confidant. This sequence is directly addressed to the audience, evoking the genre of the theatrical aside, which in the moving image is characterised by a direct gaze at the camera; by a closeup of the character's face, which augments the social proximity of the theatrical aside with actual proximity; and by a voiceover, which indicates in various ways that it represents the character's thoughts, spoken aloud to the audience. We can see that they are spoken aloud in shot 5, which is clearly not addressed to anyone in the story, but in which Tiger's lips move, and speech and image are grouped in one of the most common multimodal groupings of the moving image, lipsynching. The entire voiceover's interpersonal function is affected by this – it is the visual equivalent of the words 'Dear Spectator', and we hear the words as dialogue with the audience. At the same time, our speculation about Tiger's trick and our sense of certainty about how these future events will pan out is coloured by modality created by the music: anxiety, uncertainty, lack of closure.

The different modes offer other aspects of spectator position. We appear, for instance, to be on an equal level with Tiger, as the horizontal angle of the frame is level. However, this may be a question of what semiotic resources were readily available to the children. They drew the characters from front, side and back – drawing them from different angles may have been beyond the resources of the students – and drawing a human figure from below requires a sophisticated ability to represent foreshortening, which is not easy. That the children's intentions may have been to make Tiger a powerful character, at least to a child audience, is perhaps shown in the choice of material quality of Tiger's voice – a simulation of gruff adulthood, which is a sound signifier in some ways equivalent to a low angle camera shot. These principles operate in different modes to construct the relation between text and spectator around spatial principles, placing us higher or lower (through angle), and further or closer (through shot distance – or through sounds that suggest distance, or through signifiers of social hierarchy, such as the gruff voice of Tiger, or his patriarchal location in the family group shown in the visual design of the animation). In the sequence immediately before the one upon which we focus, Tiger is shown in a family group, almost like a family portrait – he is central in the group, and taller than his wife, who in turn is taller than the child/cub.

Textual function

The distribution of information throughout the sequence sees a similar interplay between the modes. In the voiceover (shot 5), which anticipates the lobster shot, there are two clauses: 'I'll place this LOBster into the empty pot/ and cover it with the EGGshells.' The information marked as new by its tonic prominence is 'lobster' in first clause and 'eggshells' in the second. By the time we see the lobster in the following shot, then, it's not new; though its appearance is. What's new is its comic appearance, with one claw waving over its head. The marked aspect, then, is this comical quality. Simultaneously, the voiceover is saying 'Anansi will think it is full of deLICIOUS eggs'. Here, the tonic prominence is placed on the second and third syllables of 'delicious'. Eggs are old news – we've been told about those in the previous section of the voiceover; the emphasis on 'delicious' implies the potency of the snare being laid for Anansi.

Anansi, as agent of the presumed conspiracy to eat the eggs in the night, is represented not in the image track at all, but purely in the spoken sequence. His visual absence both suggests the negative action that triggers Tiger's suspicion – he didn't eat the eggs at dinner – and allows Tiger to be foregrounded in the image track as the dominant character of this sequence. The spoken voiceover sometimes anticipates the information in the image track, as in the introduction of the lobster; and in the emphasising, again through tonic prominence, that ALL the eggs are gone in the voice-track for shot 1, whereas the eggs do not finally disappear on the image track till shot 4. Sometimes information is offered in one mode which contradicts that in another mode, for purposes of ambiguity (as in the uncertainty expressed in the music while Tiger is spelling out his plan); or for dramatic irony, as when the tooth glint and the 'Ting!' contradict the apparent hospitality of Tiger's offer of a bed in the final shot, suggesting a much more sinister intention. [...]

Conclusion

[...] The design of an animated film by 10-year-old children is a collaborative and creative venture that embraces a range of processes, each deploying particular tools and other resources in different ways at different stages. We have attempted to show how the creation of a moving image text is simultaneously multimodal and yet governed by a single overarching mode that we call kineikonic. In the sequence of shots analysed above we have attempted to show how this kineikonic mode acts as a kind of mixing board through which different combinations of image, music, sound and speech can create a narrative experience, like spun colours blurring into white, in the synthesised narrative perceived by the spectator. In design, however, as in the disaggregative work of analysis, the significations of character, locations and event are revealed as transformatively shuttled between the modes. [...]

References

CHATMAN, S. (1978) *Story and Discourse: Narrative Structure in Fiction and Film*, Ithaca, Cornell University Press.

KRESS, G.R. and VAN LEEUWEN, T. (2001) *Multimodal Discourses*, London, Arnold.

Source: JEWITT, C. and KRESS, G. (eds) (2003) *Multimodal Literacy*, Chapter 4, New York, Peter Lang.

READING D: Shakespeare 'Live' Online: the Hamnet Players

Brenda Danet

[This] study is of a group called the Hamnet Players, who experimented with the idea of virtual theater in 1993–94, in partially scripted, partially improvised performances of parodies of Shakespeare's *Hamlet* and *Macbeth*. [...]

It asks: what forms does playful performance take when the performance is typed, not spoken? [...] What accounts for the fact that artful, stylized communication – occasionally, even brilliant improvisation – can flourish in a context in which the participants have never met, cannot see one another, and can only participate by typing? [...]

Who were the Hamnet Players?

The Hamnet Players were founded in 1993 by Stuart Harris, an Englishman living in San Diego, California, a former actor, a computer professional and author of computer manuals, including one on IRC (Harris, 1995a). Harris brought to the Hamnet Players five years' experience in theater in England, three as a semi-professional actor on the festival circuit, and two more as a professional in London and in provincial repertory theater. In addition, he had further experience as a director in television. His unique background and combination of talents led him to recognize the dramatic potential of IRC.

> ... since all participants in an irc conversation may choose whatever nickname they wish to be known by ... and since an irc channel may contain many people who contribute nothing, but merely watch, the elements of theater are there: a cast of characters with names like Hamlet, Ophelia, Polonius etc. can be convened and an audience invited to watch.
>
> (Harris, 1995b, p. 500)

Harris's irreverent spirit and love of wordplay strongly influenced all Hamnet activities. Consider his email address:

sirrah@cg57.esnet.com

A userid (User Identification) is a unique name chosen by a user for participation in various online activities.

The userid 'sirrah' is a sly anagram: 'Harris' spelled backwards! According to the Oxford English Dictionary, 'sirrah' is an archaic term of address to an inferior, 'expressing contempt, reprimand, or the assumption of authority on the part of the speaker.' It was used in Shakespeare's time and even by Shakespeare himself, as in *Macbeth* IV.ii.30. [...] Sometimes, another expression appeared alongside his email address:

sirrah@cg57.esnet.com (irco_ergo_sum).

This is a playful reworking of *cogito ergo sum*. Instead of Descartes' famous 'I think, therefore I am,' he wrote, 'I IRC, therefore I am.'

The name 'Hamnet Players' is rich in cultural resonances. A 'ham' is 'an ineffective or overemphatic actor, one who rants or overacts' (Oxford English Dictionary). Thus, besides being an obvious pun on 'Hamlet,' the expression invites association to 'hamming it up on the Net.' Another association is to amateur ham radio. Ham radio culture shares with hacker culture, as well as with Net culture more generally, something of its subversive, 'alternative' nature. It also so happens that Shakespeare actually had a son called 'Hamnet,' one of a pair of twins, who died at the age of 11 on August 11, 1596 (Muir, 1971).

The case for virtual theater

An ostensible oxymoron, a contradiction in terms, the expression 'virtual theater' is actually quite on the mark. Until recently, many people believed that what makes theater unique is 'the fact that it's live and unmediated, that it can put us in the presence of other living, breathing human beings' (Copeland, 1990 p. 30). In conventional thinking about the performing arts, 'these arts require the physical presence of trained or skilled human beings whose demonstration of their skills is the performance' (Carlson, 1996, p. 3). In Jerzy Grotowski's hard-line stand against technological mediation, he argued that we could do without makeup, costume, scenography, the stage, lighting and sound effects, but we could not do without 'the actor-spectator relationship of perceptual, direct, live, communion' (Grotowski, 1968, p. 19; cited in Copeland, 1990, p. 32).

Hamnet performances were a form of virtual theater, first of all, because they were focused gatherings, just like face-to-face encounters (Goffman, 1963). Although participants could not see one another, and their bodies were not co-present to one another, they cooperated to sustain a single focus of attention, taking turns at talking (Goffman, 1963, p. 24).

Discussions of 'live' vs. mediated performance generally assume that the latter is 'taped,' 'canned', broadcast or experienced at a later time than that of the original performance, or, at best, that a live event happening 'somewhere else' is being relayed in real time, e.g., by satellite. These assumptions strongly colored an online debate about theater and performance in an era of mediatization which took place on the PERFORM-L discussion list in May–June, 1995. In one posting, Richard Schechner, a prominent practitioner as well as theoretician in the field of theater,[1] listed a number of reasons why live performance is prized in areas where media are also widely available. Of these, four are pertinent to the idea of virtual theater: (1) contingency, accident, unexpectability; (2) direct competition among known individuals; (3) interaction and participation by the audience; (4) a sense of control, in the here-and-now, not present when performance is not 'live'.[2]

Hamnet activities are of theoretical importance because this group was one of the first to challenge the conventional dichotomy between the 'live' and the 'mediated'. Hamnet performances shared most of the characteristics Schechner ascribes to 'live,' unmediated performance, as is attested by this public relations statement prepared by Stuart Harris:

> True to the concept of theater, the production is presented in real time with live performers and audience, with all the opportunities for spontaneous genius and imminent disaster that entails. The debut performance of 'Hamnet' was interrupted by a thunderstorm which cut the producers' online access; the play had to be restarted after the producers logged back on via Taiwan. The second performance was enlivened by a 'bot'[3] which accidentally killed Hamlet halfway through the production.

As is evident from Harris's comments, Hamnet performances were characterized by contingency and suspense. The challenge to maintain the focus online may be greater than in a conventional theater space, but perhaps not more so than in outdoor theater. Two main factors foster this sense of contingency, the vulnerability of the technology to breakdown, evident in Harris's comments, and the distraction of other conversations – of people 'coming and going'. [...]

Artful performance and competition among individuals

Hamnet activities were performances in two distinct but complementary senses. First, as we have seen, they were scheduled, programmed events, whose centerpiece was the theater-like performance of a script. There were roles, cues, 'sets', a plot to be realized from beginning to end, and a producer, director and stage manager to keep things in hand, all components we associate with conventional theater. Strictly speaking, players did not so much 'act' as collectively put the pieces of a textual puzzle together on screen.

This collective enterprise was embedded in a wider performance frame, both a social performance in Erving Goffman's sense – 'all the activity of an individual which occurs during a period marked by his continuous presence before a particular set of observers and which has some influence on the observers' (Goffman, 1959, p. 22) – and, of course, an artful one. [...]

Many kinds of zany improvisation enlivened the time before and after performances of the script, as well as realization of the script itself. 'Audience' was scripted as a role to be played during performances. At least one person had to change his/her nickname to <audience> and to type 'Clap clap clap'. But the dozens of people who attended needed no prodding to simulate audience behaviour spontaneously. Some of the best improvisation was by people in the audience. [...]

Because they took place over a period of months, and required a good deal of behind-the-scenes coordinated activity, Hamnet productions also engendered a strong sense of community, even if fairly short-lived. An exuberant sense of 'collaborative expectancy' (Bauman, 1977, p. 16) and a festive 'sense of occasion', shared by audience and performers, permeated all performances. Thus, at the first performance of 'Hamnet', one person declared, 'We are making cyber-history,' and a young participant gushed, 'I want my MOM to see me!!!' Many participants were eager to receive logs of performances or to make one themselves. In the belief that he was making history, Harris also prepared mock souvenir 'programs' which people could receive by email. [...]

Hamnet scripts: a closer look

[...] [The] scripts themselves are a form of play with digital writing – the unique form of writing that is IRC style, as well as with language more generally, and with the commands of the IRC software and Shakespearean texts.

[They] outrageously and incongruously juxtaposed Shakespeare's canonical plot and archaic literary register with contemporary low register, outright slang, and even the slurred speech of drunks, as well as with content taken from contemporary popular and computer culture.

The complete script of 'Hamnet,' authored by Harris himself and including a miniature ASCII set of Elsinore Castle, is shown in Figure 1. [...]

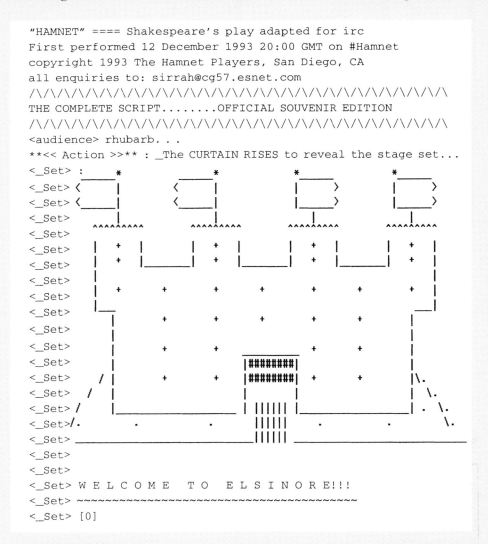

Figure 1   'Hamnet,' the script, by Stuart Harris (continues until page 356).

```
<audience> Clap,clap,clap.... etc.... [1]
     =====PROLOGUE /TOPIC World_Premiere _irc_Hamlet_in_Progress
[2]
*** PROLOGUE has changed the topic on channel #Hamnet to
"World_Premiere _irc_Hamlet_in_Progress"<PROLOGUE> All the world's
a Unix term.... [3]
<PROLOGUE> . . .and all the men & women merely irc addicts. . . .
[4]
<PROLOGUE> This show is Copyright 1993 The Hamnet Players [5]
<PROLOGUE> Enjoy our show + no heckling plz [6]
<PROLOGUE> Script should not be re-staged w/out permish [7]
**<< Action >>** : SCENE 1: THE BATTLEMENTS [8]
**<< Action >>** : _Enter Hamlet [9]
**<< Action >>** : _Enter Ghost [10]
<Hamlet> re, Ghost. Zup? [11]
<Ghost> Yr uncle's fucking yr mum. I'm counting on u to /KICK the
bastard. [12]
     ======== GHOST /MODE * +o Hamlet [13]
*** Mode change "+o Hamlet" on channel #Hamnet by Ghost
<Hamlet> Holy shit!!!! Don't op me, man!!!! I've gotta think abt
this, + I've got chem lab in 1/2 hr. :-(((( [14]
**<< Action >>** : _Exit Hamlet [15]

**<< Action >>** : SCENE 2: AFTER HAMLET'S CHEM LAB [16]
<Hamlet> 2b or not 2b. . . [17]
<Hamlet> Hmmmmmm. . . [18]
<Hamlet> :-( Bummer. . . [19]
<Hamlet> Ooops, here comes Ophelia [20]
**<< Action >>** : _Enter Ophelia [21]
<Ophelia> Here's yr stuff back [22]
<Hamlet> Not mine, love. Hehehehehe ;-D [23]
<Ophelia> O heavenly powers: restore him! [24]
**<< Action >>** Ophelia thinks Hamlet's nuts [25]
<Hamlet> Make that "sanity-deprived", pls. . . . [26]
<Hamlet> Oph: suggest u /JOIN #nunnery [27]
<Ophelia> :-( [28]
*** Signoff: Ophelia (drowning) [29]

**<< Action >>** : SCENE 3: INTERIOR [30]
**<< Action >>** : _Enter R_krantz [31]
**<< Action >>** : _Enter G_stern [32]
<R_krantz> re [33]
<G_stern> re [34]
<Hamlet> re, guys... :-\ [35]
```

Re, as in lines 33, 34 and 35, signifies *hello again* (it derives from *Re: hi* when electronic messages are responded to).

```
<R_krantz> zup? [36]
<Hamlet> Fucked if i know. brb. . . [37]
**<< Action >>** : _Exit Hamlet in a sulk. [38]
<G_stern> fuckza matter w/him? [39]
<R_krantz> Guess he must be lagged. Let's lurk [40]
**<< Action >>** : R_krantz lurks [41]
**<< Action >>** : G_stern lurks [42]
**<< Action >>** : SCENE 4: THE QUEEN'S CLOSET [43]
<Hamlet> Ma: what the fuck's going on? [44]
<Queen> Don't flame me, i'm yr Ma! [45]
<Queen> Er. . . . [46]
<Prompter> Psst! Thou hast thy father much offended.. [47]
<Queen> Oh, right.. . . . Yr dad's pissed at u [48]
**<< Action >>** : Hamlet slashes at the arras [49]
<Polonius> Arrrghhhh!!! [50]
     ========= HAMLET /KICK * Polonius [51]
*** Polonius has been kicked off channel #Hamnet by Hamlet
<Queen> Now look what u've done u little nerd. :-( [52]
<Hamlet> Wrong man...... Bummer... [53]

**<< Action >>** : SCENE 5: GRUESOME FINALE [54]
     ========= QUEEN /TOPIC DEATH [55]
*** Queen has changed the topic on channel #Hamnet to "DEATH"
**<< Action >>** : _Enter Hamlet, Queen, King, Laertes, R_krantz,
G_stern [56]
**<< Action >>** : Queen takes a drink [57]
**<< Action >>** : King gives Ham & Laer swords [58]
<King> Go for it, lads! [59]
**<< Action >>** : Laertes stabs Hamlet [60]
**<< Action >>** : Hamlet stabs Laertes [61]
**<< Action >>** : Hamlet stabs King [62]
<Queen> Holy shit this Danish vodka is like poison :-@
[63]
<Hamlet> and u always thought i was just wasting my time in chem
lab, hehehe [64]
**<< Action >>** : Queen dies in agony [65]
<King> Aaaaaarrgghhh! [66]
**<< Action >>** : King dies [67]
<Laertes> AAaaaaarrrrrhhhhh!!!! [68]
**<< Action >>** : Laertes dies [69]
<Hamlet> AAAAaaaaaarrrrrhhhhhhhh!!!!!!!!!!!!!!!!!!!!!!!!!!
!!!!!!!! [70]
**<< Action >>** : Hamlet dies [71]
**<< Action >>** : R_krantz + G_stern GULP!!!!!! [72]
```

```
**<< Action >>** : _Enter Fortinbras + drum + colours + attendants
[73]
<Fort_bras> EEEEEEuuuuuucchhhhhh!!!!!! What's been hpng here?
[74]
<Drum> Like, rat-a-tat, man [75]
<Colours> Hmmmmmmmm...... [76]
<Attndts> Holy sheeeeet!!!!! [77]
     ============ FORT_BRAS /NICK _King [78]
** Fort_bras is now knwn as _King
**<< Action >>** : _The CURTAIN SLOWLY FALLS. {{{{{{—THE END—
}}}}}}} [79]
<audience> hmmmmmmmmm..... [80]
```

Play with Shakespeare

Harris and [his companion] Gayle Kidder made 'mincemeat' of the characters, plots and texts of the originals. [...] Gross reduction of the length of the text and caricaturization of plot and action, along with transformation of Renaissance poetry into late 20th century colloquial prose and even lowly slang turn the play into a kind of typed Punch and Judy show. The number of named characters in *Hamlet* is slashed from 17 to 9. A five-act script that ordinarily takes hours to perform is impertinently reduced to a mere 80 lines. Some characters barely have one or two lines. The part of Polonius, poor man, is reduced to his one-line death cry:

```
<Polonius> Arrrghhhhh! [50]
```

Play with the conventions of script-writing

The 'Hamnet' script contained parts not only for Ophelia, Hamlet, the King and Queen, etc. but also for 'Enter', 'Exit,' 'Prologue,' 'Scene,' and even inanimate objects like 'Drums' and 'Colors.' Among these 'textual' roles, that of 'Prologue,' at least, was not entirely Harris's invention. One of the characters in the play-within-the play in the original *Hamlet* is also called 'Prologue.' At the opening of the play-within-the-play, he steps forward to declare:

Prologue. For us, and for our tragedy, Here stooping to your clemency, We beg your hearing patiently.

(*Hamlet*, Act III, Scene 2, lines 159–161)

Inanimate objects also have to be realized textually, as in

```
<Drum> Like, rat-a-tat, man [75]
```

The scripts included these 'roles' because the players actually perform not the play but the text. When all actors perform their lines, they recreate the text online. But they also improvise on it, as will be shown below.

Play with language

The most obvious contrast in the 'Hamnet' scripts was between the now-archaic literary language of the Renaissance English original and the colloquial, often slang, register of contemporary Anglo-American English. Only two of the 80 lines of 'Hamnet' cited Shakespeare's own words, intact; the rest was in 'IRC-ese.' Thus, in Scene 2, when Hamlet and Ophelia meet, the original line 'O heavenly powers: restore him!' (Act III, Scene 1, line 147) is embedded in an otherwise later 20th-century rendering of their encounter, part colloquial ('stuff'; 'nuts'), part digital chat style ('yr' for 'your'; the comics-like 'hehehehehe,' the 'smiley' ;-D).

```
<Ophelia> Here's yr stuff back[22]
<Hamlet> Not mine, love. Hehehehehe ;-D[23]
<Ophelia> O heavenly powers: restore him![24]
**<<Action>>** Ophelia thinks Hamlet's nuts[25]
<Hamlet> Make that 'sanity-deprived', pls ...[26]
```

Note also the politically correct 'sanity-deprived.' [...]

Obscenity was rampant in 'Hamnet' [...]. The profusion of profane language mocked the canonical status afforded to Shakespeare's works and language in the 20th century. At the same time, the obscenity should not be taken as standing in too strong a contrast. Even in Shakespeare's language – though not necessarily in Hamlet specifically – there is a very wide range of registers and styles, and, indeed, much has been written about colloquial and even bawdy language in his plays. In general, IRCers took particular delight in writing what ordinarily might only be spoken, or at best scrawled behind the closed door of a public toilet wall. In the pre-digital era, socialization to the norms of literate culture worked to suppress the use of foul language in writing.

Play with IRC and email conventions and practices

[Hamnet] relentlessly spoofed IRC, email and other internet conventions and practices. A striking example was the line:

```
<Hamlet> Oph: suggest u /JOIN #nunnery[27]
```

Instead of 'get thee to a nunnery,' Hamlet is made to tell Ophelia to join an IRC channel named *#nunnery*. The script cites the IRC command */join*. Ordinarily, the slash is necessary to activate the command online; here, of course its only function is to make us laugh. [...]

Textual freezing of online style

The very idea of freezing ephemeral IRC chat style in a solo-authored, quasi-literary text is amusing. The script nicely captured the mix of speech-like, writing-like and digital features that characterized online writing in the 1990s, as one can see even in just these three short lines from 'Hamnet':

```
<Hamlet> 2b or not 2b ... [17]
<Hamlet> Hmmmmm. [18]
<Hamlet> :- ( Bummer ... [19]
```

These lines contain the speech-like 'Hmmm' and 'bummer,' speedwriting ('2b or not 2b'), and a frowning smiley, a uniquely digital phenomenon. When one character after another dies, Harris has a field day with multiple exclamation points and the comics-like representation of sounds, so common in ordinary IRC chat:

```
<Polonius> Arrrghhh!!! [50]
<King> Aaaaarrgghhh! [66]
**<<Action>>** : King dies [67]
<Laertes> AAaaaaaarrrrrhhhh!!!! [68]
**<<Action>>** : Laertes dies [69]
<Hamlet> AAAAaaaaaarrrrrhhhhhh!!!!!!!!!!!!!!!!!!!!
!!!!!!!! [70]
**<<Action>>** : Hamlet dies [71]
```

Hamnet performances: some highlights

Performers did not simply recreate the text on screen, although it is true that they performed the text, not the play. Indeed, if they had only performed the text, word for word, I would not be able to speak of artful performance. Harris was all for improvisation. He told me, 'If irc actors ever got so skilled, and the irc audience so tame, that the entire script came out exactly as written, the performance would be a failure by definition.' [...] Here are some highlights. [...]

Play with Shakespeare

[...] One of the best extended examples of an individual playing with Shakespearean texts occurred in the waning moments of an ill-fated November 1993 first attempt to perform 'Hamnet'. The performance was already in shambles, as a result of an electricity outage in California. Harris himself was about to log off when someone from Israel's Technion began to spout clever parodies of Hamlet and Macbeth (a short extract of which can be seen in Figure 2). Changing his nick to <Hamlet>, he produced a brilliant improvisation of the famous 'To be or not to be' soliloquy. 'To be or not to be' was rendered in even more condensed form than in Harris's script: '2B | !2B' is mathematicians' formal way of expressing 'is/is not.' He substituted 'splits' and 'lags' for 'slings and arrows,' an appropriate choice both semantically and phonetically: all are single-syllable words and the first word in both expressions begins with /s/ and contains /l/ as well. Moreover, fortuitously, 'splits' and 'slings' even contain the same vowel sound.

HAMLET, Act III, Scene 1.

Line 56   To be, or not to be, that is the question:
          Whether 'tis nobler in the mind to suffer
          The **slings and arrows** of outrageous fortune
          Or to take arms against a sea of troubles
      60 And by opposing end them. **To die: to sleep**.
          No more; and by a sleep to say we end
          The heart-ache and the thousand natural shocks
          That flesh is heir to; 'tis a consummation
          Devoutly to be wish'd. To die: to sleep.

The Improvisation

Line 1   *** RosenKRNZ is now known as Hamlet
          <Producer> . . . . but u'd hv been great
          <Hamlet> **2B | !2B. . .** the question
          <Producer> Welcome lobber. . . the perf is
                 cancelled
      5   <Hamlet> Whether tis nobler to the mind
          <tyree> So pls keep me posted on retry huh
                 Producerf?
                 <Hamlet> To suffer the *splits and lags*
                 <Hamlet> That *net is hair* to
                 <Producer> tyree:u bet
      10 <Hamlet> Tis a **logoffing** devoutly to be
                 wished
          <lobber> was wondering where everybody
                 was
          <Producer> Hamlet:u hv definitely got the
                 idea
          <Hamlet> **To lag, to split** no more

Figure 2   Parody of Hamlet's soliloquy, aborted performance of 'Hamnet,' November 1993

Note especially the transformation of 'the heart-ache and the thousand natural shocks/That flesh is heir to' into 'the splits and lags/The net is hair to.' Not only does he substitute one pair of troubles for another, he substitutes the near-homophone 'hair' for 'heir', because of his association to 'net' as 'hair net' (in 'hair' the 'h' is aspirated; in 'heir' it is not).

He substitutes 'logoffing' for 'consummation,' implying that to log off is a kind of 'Net-death.' 'To lag, to split/No more' is a clever adaptation of 'To die, to sleep no more.' [...]

Play with the theater game

The players devised verbal equivalents of actors' onstage and backstage behaviour. They textually tried their costumes on, and took them off:

```
* G_Stern tries his costume on
* Ophelia slips out of her costume and tosses it aside. "I
hate stage clothes!"
```

('Hamnet' performance, December, 1993)

The actors peeked out at the audience, sent virtual roses, and took bows:

```
* The_King looks out between the curatins[sic] - whoah-big
corwd[sic]
* laertes orders roses for Ophelia. Hopes they will be
delivered after +performance
* exKing finishes strongly, then takes a *bow* to rapturous
applause
```

('Hamnet' performance, December, 1993)

Still another game was to invent lines having to do with one's 'occupation' as a professional actor, as in

```
<GeekChrus> is thre[sic] a rep of actor's guild in the
house ...
*The_King thinks this wait wasn't in his contract.
```

('Hamnet' performance, December, 1993)

[...] Some of the players gushed about the performance. After the February 1994 performance of 'Hamnet,' <Hamlet> was especially effusive:

```
Darlings you were wonderful!!!!
```

Play with language

[...] The most impressive, most extended sequence of punning occurred during the first performance of 'Hamnet,' as part of ongoing flirtation between the <King> and <Queen> (see Figure 3). In this striking instance of 'ping-pong punning' (Chiaro, 1992, p. 114), participants exploited the ambiguity of words used, and tried to outdo each other [...]

```
* King wonders if queen wishes to produce Any litle heirs?...
<King> Queen?
* QuEeN re evaluates the King//...says..'with that
little thig' [sic] ???
<King> Melady?...
<King> Queen - but, you ain't got me excited yet!...
<QuEeN> King...what..so then I won't need the
tweezers???...
<King> Queen - no ... calipers, maybe...
<DRUM> PLease keep it in the royal Chamber, you too [sic].
<QuEeN> Microinches??...
* ophelia thinks that the king and queen should be
BANISHED... (or at least thrown in the dungeon *evil
laugh*)...
* King sits on his thone, unabashed...
* King unfolds his full manhood ... better?
* ophelia chucks the king twards [sic] and [sic] audience member
eheheh...
<G_Stern> give king his /PART
<King> heh heh
* King has a HUGE part...
* QuEeN chuckles ... at her witless mate...
<King> Queen - no wits maybe, but a very nice ****...
* King enters Queen
* TheGhost exits right...
<SCENE> Is this going to be logged?...
<Recorder> SCENE: I am logging it....
<DRUM> I am logging
* Recorder is logging this session....
* ThE_QuEeN would like a log file sent to her...
* The_King gives the Queen his log...
* ThE_QuEeN examines said log.... and puts it toflame
[sic]...
* KaiKul warms his hands on the burning Log
```

Figure 3   'Ping-pong' punning during the December 1993 performance of 'Hamnet'

Play with norms of decorum

Finally, there was play with the norms of decorum. The players simulated all kinds of inappropriate behaviour on stage and in public, gleefully doing things textually which they would never have done in public (at least not intentionally) in real life. Thus, when the audience in the first 'Hamnet' performance got restless, waiting for the show to begin, it began to 'throw popcorn and fruit' around:

```
<jeffrey68> I think the audience is hgtting[sic] restless ...
<jeffrey68> theater owner should have passed out free drinks ...
<fan> more popcorn please. and could someone tell that lady in
        the third row to take hat off ...
<AUDIENCE>  throws fruit at javalima ...
*KaiKul has  eaten all his popcorn and started on the box ...
<AUDIENCE>  mild clapping and shouts of 'this better be good! We
        have fruit!'
```

('Hamnet' performance, December 1993)

[...]

The flowering of verbal art online

A vast research literature in folklore and the ethnography of communication has long documented playfulness and stylization in many oral genres of communication, in societies without writing and in certain sub-cultures within literate societies, e.g., Afro-American culture.[4] [Here I have documented] the flowering of artful uses of language and typography in interactive writing – a new phenomenon in the history of human communication. The analysis adds strength to the argument [...] that online group communication can afford a sense of presence not so very different from that in face-to-face encounters. We saw that, contrary to common sense expectations, hearing the sounds of words is not essential for extensive interactive punning to take place. The punning and other forms of wordplay in Hamnet productions were very much in the spirit of Shakespeare himself. [...] We can see that digitization invites us once again, as in oral cultures, to pay attention to the form of messages. [...]

Notes

1   See e.g. Schechner, 1985, 1993.

2   These categories appeared in a posting by Schechner to PERFORM-L on 3 June 1995.

3   A bot is a small program; bots on IRC are additions to the basic program which perform specific functions. The term 'robot' contains the word 'bot'.

4   See, e.g. Hymes (1964); Kirshenblatt-Gimblett (1976); Edwards and Sienkewicz (1990); Bauman (1977). I do not mean to suggest that stylization and playfulness necessarily go together. Indeed, in many settings they do not.

References

BAUMAN, R. (1977) *Verbal Art as Performance*, Prospect Heights, IL., Waveland Press.

CARLSON, M. (1996) *Performance: A Critical Introduction*, New York and London, Routledge.

CHIARO, D. (1992) *The Language of Jokes: Analyzing Verbal Play*, London, Routledge.

COPELAND, R. (1990) 'The presence of mediation', *TDR: The Drama Review*, **34**, pp. 28–44.

GOFFMAN, E. (1959) *Presentation of Self in Everyday Life*, Garden City, Anchor.

GOFFMAN, E. (1963) *Behavior in Public Places*, Glencoe, IL., Free Press.

GROTOWSKI, J. (1968) *Towards a Poor Theatre*, New York, Simon & Schuster.

HARRIS, S. (1995a) *The IRC Survival Guide; Talk to the World on Internet Relay Chat*, Reading, MA., Addison-Wesley.

HARRIS, S. (1995b) 'Virtual reality drama', *Cyberlife!* pp. 497–520, Indianapolis, IN, Sams.

MUIR, K. (1971) *A New Companion to Shakespeare Studies*, Cambridge, NY., Cambridge University Press.

SCHECHNER, R. (1985) *Between Theater and Anthropology*, Philadelphia, University of Pennsylvania Press.

SCHECHNER, R. (1993) *The Future of Ritual: Writings on Culture and Performance*, New York and London, Routledge.

Source: DANET, B., (2001) *Cyberpl@y: Communicating Online*, extracts from Chapter 3, Oxford, Berg.

8 The literary mind

Kieran O'Halloran

8.1 Introduction

Imagine you are on an underground train in London. Your eyes drift upwards towards a selection of texts. Here is one that you focus on:

> When my daddy was ill
> for a long time mummy said
> there wouldn't be enough money
> for us to live on. But daddy
> told mummy not to worry because
> he had a special plan with
> the AA.
>
> eleanor age 7

AA = (British) Automobile Association.

Figure 8.1   AA advert.

But why is it using a 'child's voice'? Next to it is another text:

Street Song

Pink Lane, Strawberry Lane, Pudding Chare:
someone is waiting, I don't know where;
hiding among the nursery names,
he wants to play peculiar games.

Child's voice again perhaps? A London underground carriage usually displays several adverts and sometimes amongst the adverts is a single poem. Despite the fact that a single poem can be surrounded by several adverts, what is it about how you would read the 'Street Song' text above that enables you to decide it is poetry rather than an advert?

The main focus of Chapters 2, 3 and 6 was on exploring literariness *in* the text. In other words, these chapters worked from an inherency perspective. So you have looked, for example, at how creative exploitation of English can lead readers to generate meanings about how a character in a story is feeling. But these meanings are also effects on *readers*. Since this is the case, perhaps by also addressing the effects on readers of engaging with literary texts, further illumination can be provided about what literariness is. What is happening in our heads in literary reading? Is it different from what happens in non-literary reading? If so, what is it about literary reading which make this reading different, if at all? This chapter will address these questions, and explore the notion of reader cognition in relation to literary and non-literary works. By 'cognition', I mean a reader's mental processes. To deal with these issues, then, this chapter will develop discussion of a perspective you were introduced to in Chapter 1 – the cognitive perspective. I will also continue to draw on the inherency perspective.

Like Chapters 4 and 7, where there was some focus on the audience/reader, this chapter looks at 'idealised subjects' – that is, readers imagined and modelled by an analyst, not actual flesh and blood readers. Where Chapter 8 is different is that it uses cognitive theory to model the processes involved in reading literature. The branch of linguistics which deals with such modelling is known as cognitive poetics (see Stockwell, 2002; Gavins and Steen, 2003), and the cognitive theories that I draw on here are **relevance theory** and schema theory. Relevance theory is a development from Grice's 'cooperative principle' that you met in Chapter 1. Schema theory was also introduced in Chapter 1 and you will look at it in more detail here.

8.2 Relevance theory

In Chapter 1 (Section 1.4), you were introduced to the work of the influential theorist of language communication, Paul Grice (1975). You will recall that, for Grice, in communication we operate on a cooperative principle, observing four basic maxims (*quantity*: give as much information as is required and no more; *quality*: be truthful; *relation*: be relevant; *manner*: be clear). A significant development of Grice's work is the work of Dan Sperber and Deirdre Wilson (Sperber and Wilson, 1995). In contrast to Grice, they argue that only one maxim is necessary – that of *relevance*. They contend that the human brain is genetically geared to seek relevance in any form of communication and through human evolution has become very efficient at doing so. Therefore, for Sperber and Wilson, there is in fact no 'cooperative principle' to follow.

Within the perspective of Sperber and Wilson's relevance theory, a piece of language has an in-built guarantee that it is relevant. It comes with a presumption that it is the most relevant way for the author or speaker to communicate a set of assumptions. The advert in the introduction (Figure 8.1) is one for AA health insurance. From a relevance theory perspective, its multimodality, i.e. its simulation of a child's handwriting, must be relevant to its communicative intentions. The author of the AA advert presumably wants the target reader to think about the effects of their being ill for their children. Creating a 'child's voice' to imply the effects of poverty through illness may be an effective spur for a parent to buy health insurance or increase their cover, because the parent could mingle the voice of the advert with the voice of their own child. An advert without the 'child's voice' which just stated: 'No health insurance? Don't get ill 'cos your children might starve!' does not take as much effort to process, but would it be as effective as the AA advert?

For an exploration of the concept of multimodality see Chapter 6.

For Sperber and Wilson (1995), a text has **optimal relevance** if for *minimum* effort in reading it, its processing leads to *maximum* cognitive effects. So, the alternative advert just mentioned is optimally relevant since we get the message without too much difficulty. However, if a reader needs to invest more than minimum effort (i.e. the text is not optimally relevant), then on the principle of relevance extra effort needs to be balanced by extra cognitive effects. For the AA advert to be successful, it will require effort from a parent relating it to their own children and their own specific circumstances. But this effort might be worth it if the parent becomes aware of the potential vulnerability of their children if they are ill and not financially protected.

In this section, we will look at how relevance theory might help to illuminate the nature of literary reading and whether or not this is different from non-literary reading.

ACTIVITY 1   **Relevance and literature (Reading A)**

In Reading A, 'Relevance and literature', Tony Bex draws on relevance theory in an attempt to show how literary texts are different to non-literary texts, such as the AA advert, because of how they are read. Part of his case involves arguing that literary texts have no necessary practical consequences for the reader.

Please now turn to Reading A. How convincing do you find Bex's argument?

Comment

Bex argues that, with an advert, readers would expect practical consequences to follow. Moreover, readers seek relevance from the text in line with such consequences, e.g. how much a product is going to cost. Given this, for minimum effort, readers are unlikely to be closely drawn to the form of the text. A literary text, on the other hand, for him has no necessary practical consequences and does not directly refer to the actual world. This is why, for Bex, and in an argument similar to Widdowson's (Chapter 1, Reading B), readers view 'Musée des Beaux Arts' as a poem in seeking significance in its patterns. Bex takes this argument a little further than Widdowson, though. He argues that because there are no necessary practical consequences from a literary text, the reader only has the imaginary world they generate to attach relevance to. In cognitive poetics, this imaginary world is known as the 'text world' (mentioned first in Chapter 6).

On the principle of relevance, minimum effort is invested for maximum cognitive effects. Any additional processing effort in a reader's search for optimal relevance needs to be balanced by a suitable set of effects. So, for Bex, readers assume that the additional processing involved in finding relevance in the text world they create will lead to the following: cognitive effects of enjoyment, stimulation, mental enrichment in being able to use an imaginary world to reflect on, judge or escape from the actual world, etc.

One might, though, take issue with aspects of Bex's position. There are certain texts with direct reference, such as autobiographies, which have attained a valued literary status, for example, St Augustine's *Confessions* or Jean-Jacques Rousseau's *The Confessions*. Indeed, Thomas Keneally's *Schindler's Ark* won the Booker prize for literature in 1982 though it was based on real events and characters in a Nazi concentration camp. And so on. So it is probably more prudent to say that literary texts have indirect reference prototypically speaking. Moreover, there may be circularity in how Bex makes his case. For him, literature is recognisable because it has no necessary practical consequences. But one might argue that one has to read something as literature in the first place to recognise that it has no necessary practical consequences. Bex also says that societies choose to classify literary texts for ideological reasons but he does not mention that the educational institutional use of literature has a set of practical consequences which may seem necessarily bound up with a literary work for educators at a particular time. Recall, for example, from Eagleton's argument (Chapter 1, Reading A) that the teaching of literature in the nineteenth century was designed to inculcate a set of moral values.

Eagleton is right that institutions have put literature to all sorts of uses. Having said this, such institutional practical consequences may not be the ones private, recreational readers derive from the text worlds they seek relevance in. Indeed, it could be argued, in line with Bex, that a key difference between literary and non-literary texts is as follows: if practical consequences do follow on from private, recreational literary reading, this could well be because readers invent these consequences.

The issue of designating a text as literary in relation to reference and practical consequences can be tricky, it would seem. The next activity asks you to test out some of the ideas in Bex's argument on texts presented as literary and non-literary.

ACTIVITY 2   The relevance of a poem versus that of an advert

Allow about 20 minutes

We return to the AA advert and the whole of 'Street Song', a poem written by the New Zealand poet, Fleur Adcock. (You met another of her poems, 'Against Coupling', in Chapter 2.)

With regard to the concepts of 'relevance' and 'practical consequences', consider why 'Street Song' works as a poem and whether this is different to the way the AA text works as an advert.

Street Song

Pink Lane, Strawberry Lane, Pudding Chare:
someone is waiting, I don't know where;
hiding among the nursery names,
he wants to play peculiar games.

In Leazes Terrace or Leazes Park
someone is loitering in the dark,
feeling the giggles rise in his throat
and fingering something under his coat.

He could be sidling along Forth Lane
to stop some girl from catching her train
or stalking the grounds of the RVI
to see if a student nurse goes by.

In Belle Grove Terrace or Fountain Row
or Hunter's Road he's raring to go–
unless he's the quiet shape you'll meet
on the cobbles in Back Stowell Street.

Monk Street, Friars Street, Gallowgate
are better avoided when it's late.
Even in Sandhill and the Side
there are shadows where a man could hide.

So don't go lightly along Darn Crook
because the Ripper's been brought to book.
Wear flat shoes, and be ready to run:
remember, sisters, there's more than one.

Comment

Here is my analysis of why 'Street Song' functions as a poem and why the AA text functions as an advert. How far do you agree or disagree?

In the AA advert, the simulation of the child's voice is done almost entirely at the graphological level – the jagged writing, its sloping in different directions, etc. An adult voice is reflected in the standard English correctness of the grammar and punctuation, apart from the deliberate lower case initial 'e' in *eleanor*. On a relevance theory account, because a reader will seek relevance in line with (for them) obvious practical consequences of the advert, they may well not readily notice the mixing of voices. Naturally, it is in the interests of AA insurance for them not to. Advertisers ultimately want the target reader to mull over the consequences for their children of not being insured. Evidently, they want this more than a sense of delight in the creativity of the advert being excited.

In Adcock's poem, since I do not know the streets and other places mentioned, I do not treat them as directly referential; moreover, I do not derive practical consequences from the poem. So I only have the text world

The simple rhythm is more precisely referred to as iambic tetrameter. See Short (1996).

Mixing of voices is referred to by the Russian linguist, Mikhail Bakhtin, as **heteroglossia**. See Chapter 9 in our companion volume, **Maybin and Swann (2006)**.

I create to assign relevance to; I thus pay close attention to the substance of the text. The poem uses a simple rhythm redolent for me of children's songs and the patterned language of certain children's games. The semiotic mode of sound is thus cued, which I take as simulating a child's voice in the first verse. But simultaneously, dark content is suggested through the poem in a way in which I would not expect from a child. In contrast with the advert, because 'Street Song' has no practical consequences for me, I attach more significance to this mixing of voices than in the advert. I start to seek relevance in the tensions in voices (child versus adult) which the poem cues me to generate in my text world. In seeming to posit a ubiquitous threat from men, could it be argued the poem is parodying alarmism about the dangers of men?

Alternatively, does the poem not have practical consequences, consequences for women readers in warning them of the dangers of walking alone at night in cities? For it to function effectively as a warning text and be processed with optimal relevance, an argument could be made that women readers need (i) referential details for specific places that are relevant to their lives (ii) to be convinced of the evidence of the warning, e.g. there have been assaults in the places they are being warned about. But, all the same, what if some women do choose to read it as a warning text? As justification, they might make their focus the imperatives in the last verse to argue that the practical consequences of being on guard late at night in a city are *necessarily* bound up with the text.

The above difficulty of whether or not 'Street Song' could function as an effective warning text may seem to create difficulties for Bex's account when people do derive practical consequences from reading literary texts which they regard as necessary ones. It might help to use another example here. There was a fashion amongst young men of the time to read Goethe's epistolary novel, *The Sorrows of Young Werther* (1774) as a kind of suicide manual, killing themselves in the fashion of love-sick 'Werther'. Committing suicide after reading a book clearly does not allow the reader to seek alternative practical consequences. These readers, one would imagine, felt this was the only response to Goethe's book and thus one necessarily bound up with it. But actually, these consequences were bound up with the then Romantic socioculture. This example helps us to see that though practical consequences from the reading of literature may seem necessary ones to readers of a particular time and place, they are not a necessary *function* in the same way that recipes necessarily function to provide information on how to prepare a meal. So, returning to the poem 'Street Song', some women may see it in functional terms – a (poetic) warning text – and may indeed be hailed by the 70s feminist term of address 'sisters'. But others may not feel hailed in this way and thus not read the poem in functional terms.

It might be a good idea to pause here and take stock of preceding ideas. Prototypically speaking, literary texts have indirect reference and do not presuppose necessary practical consequences for the solitary recreational reader, divorced from an institutional practice. Prototypically, such readers only have the text world they generate in which to seek relevance, and if practical consequences ensue it is because they actively generate them (as an individual act or in line with a fashion). But setting out these conditions for literary reading to take place does not get us yet to the issue of literary value. Sperber and Wilson (1995), and literary scholars who have drawn on relevance theory such as Adrian Pilkington (Pilkington, 1991; 2000), use the term **poetic effects** to describe the meanings that can be generated in the reading of literary work. For you, is 'Street Song' really only a 'poetic warning text'? Or could the poem support a range of very different poetic effects? For Pilkington (1991, p. 60), 'a poem is successful and has value to the extent that it communicates poetic effects'. How good then is 'Street Song' in terms of the range of possible poetic effects that can be generated from it? What does the poem mean to you? Think also about the range of possible poetic effects it might have for different types of readers. Ask different people to read the poem and see what poetic effects emerge in their readings. If the overall range of poetic effects is large does that lead you to see 'Street Song' as having high literary value? If the range is not so great, does that lead you to the opposite conclusion?

You have looked at the issue of literary value in previous chapters but mostly from an inherency perspective (e.g. Reading C in Chapter 2). It is difficult to assess the value of a literary work in terms of its effects on readers when the focus is on idealised ones as it is in this chapter. To find out, I would need to talk to actual readers as I just suggested you did. Nevertheless, from an idealised reader perspective, some assessment can be made of the value of 'Street Song' in terms of its capacity to generate poetic effects. To enable such assessment, as well as to further explore issues of literariness with regard to reader cognition, this chapter will continue to build up a cognitive vocabulary. In Reading C, Chapter 1, you read stylistician Elena Semino on schema theory and literature, where she mentions Guy Cook's concept of discourse deviation in relation to schema refreshment. In Section 8.3, you will encounter a reading by Cook where the notion of schema and his argument about the relationship between schemata and literariness are examined in more detail.

8.3 Schema theory

In Chapter 1 you learned that schemata (plural of schema) are packets of knowledge of the world which are drawn upon, either consciously or unconsciously, in helping us to make sense of the world and communicate about it.

Schema theory

The concept of schema was first used by the German philosopher, Kant, in the eighteenth century but in the twentieth century was initially associated with the work of the psychologist, Bartlett (1932). In the 1970s, schema theory was seized upon in artificial intelligence work. Attempts to generate computer models of human text processing led to the realisation that this involves not only knowledge of language but also organised knowledge of the world. Guy Cook, in Reading B, derives his schema framework from Schank and Abselson (1977), who put forward one of the most complete and influential models in the artificial intelligence revival of schema theory in the 1970s.

ACTIVITY 3   Activating schemata to make sense of a text

Allow about
10 minutes

To see how we regularly draw upon schemata in making sense of language, consider the following text. What kinds of knowledge are being activated in your mind to help you make sense of the text?

John put his foot down on the accelerator and was now hurtling along the roads. He was way out of the city and the country roads were empty. Such a beautiful pastoral scene. The only thing that spoiled it though was the excruciating noise from his faulty exhaust which spewed huge plumes of smoke. But in being so absorbed in the pastoral scene, John soon became lost. Two hours went by without him seeing a single person and he was beginning to get very worried. Why didn't he bring a map? When he finally with some relief saw a woman walking along the road, he began to apply the brakes. As he got closer to her, he could see the walker was unlikely to be a tourist and figured she must be a local. John became more convinced she would be able to help.

Comment

That John is lost is not made explicit above. So if you understood readily what was happening here, it is because you have a set of schemata for what happens when people get lost while out driving. In modern, industrialised cultures at least, such schemata would be regarded as fairly stereotypical.

There are in fact different types of schemata being activated when you read the text above. I will outline four main types of schemata, which all feature in Reading B:

- script
- plan
- goal
- theme

One that you most probably activated is called a **script**. A script refers to knowledge of a stereotypical situation or activity. While there is no explicit mention of a vehicle such as a car in the above text, this gap can be filled in with information about the 'faulty exhaust' and 'brakes'. That is, many of us have a stored script that drivers sit in the front of a car and apply brakes with their feet, etc.

A second schema that was likely generated is known as a **goal** and this relates to stereotypical *purposes*. When we are lost, stereotypically our goal is to find out where we are. Sense can be made of the text by recognising the goal that John wants to find out where he is. But in order for John to achieve this goal, he needs to do something first: he would need to *ask* the walker where he was. To understand the goal, you would need to have activated another schema. This other type of stereotypical schema is known as a **plan** and is often activated in advance of a goal schema. A plan is something that needs to happen so that a goal can be achieved.

Now go back to the text above. You should see that there are no explicit references to the plan, goal and script. But these schemata needed to be activated to understand the text. Finally, other more abstract and evaluative schemata may have been activated in your reading. For example, you might have disapproved of the faulty exhaust and thought about its noise and chemical pollution of the environment. Such schemata which are less tied to specific situations but derive from our evaluations of our experience are known as **themes**. Themes thus carry much more of an element of subjectivity in contrast to scripts, plans and goals, which are more stereotypical. So some people may not have had an ecological response to the faulty exhaust. Some people may (also) have had a theme activated for the pleasure and freedom that driving in the country can afford. Others may not.

Let me return to the poem, 'Street Song' and look at it in relation to schema theory. Since Reading B will use the concepts of script, plan, goal and theme in relation to analysis of a literary text, the purpose of the following is to help you become more comfortable with these concepts with regard to literary reading. Stylistician Roger Fowler (1996, pp. 201–4) outlines what is triggered in his mind while reading the poem (which he finds 'dynamic and disturbing'). So although Fowler does not draw explicitly on schema theory in his analysis, I have separated some of what is activated in his reading (a, b, c, d, e below) into scripts, plans, goals, themes. As you will see, there is overlap between the different types of schemata:

(a) loitering – 'from the register of police observation; people can only
    "loiter with bad intent"'
    (verse 2, line 2)

(b) 'vernacular, colloquial mode ... as if some local people are talking about
    a voyeur'
    (verse 3)

(c) 'Better-class residential area' suggested by the street names: 'Belle Grove Terrace', 'Fountain Row'.
(verse 4, line 1)

(d) "Monk' and 'Friars' are sinister or medieval in their connotation; Chaucer's readers know about the bad morals of the monks of olden times'
(verse 5, line 1)

(e) 'someone addressing a local support or self-defence group'
(verse 6)

- Script   (a), (b), (e)
- Plan   (a), (e)
- Goal   (a), (e)
- Theme   (a), (c), (d)

I placed (a), (c) and (d) into the category of theme because of the evaluation (*bad* and *better-class*); (b) and (e) are script-like in that they refer to human activities that are fairly stereotypical. So, for example, with (b), it is very human for sinister events to bring complete strangers together into conversation. For (e), we can imagine a script for a self-defence group, e.g. where people meet in the evening at a community centre. Fowler's plan schema here is presumably activated by the warning about wearing flat shoes, etc.; the goal schema here is the self-defence group helping women escape attack. Loitering with (bad) intent (a) also involves scripts for such behaviour (e.g. a lone man in a park looking shifty), as well as both plans (e.g. loitering with an attractor such as a puppy) and goal (what his deviant purpose is).

Separating schemata into scripts, plans, goals and themes can sometimes be tricky because boundaries are not always so clear-cut. This is why Cook (1994) uses the expression 'interpretative schemata' rather than just 'schemata'. However, the latitude for interpreting schemata as scripts or plans or goals or even themes is not enormous if interpreters are from the same culture and what is being talked about is stereotypical experience. You may want to think about how you would analyse and interpret Fowler's schemata: how far does your interpretation agree or disagree with mine?

You are now going to read how Guy Cook uses the above schema vocabulary to try to account for the effects of a poem on readers and why these are likely to be different for a non-literary text such as an advert. In so doing, he points up limits with using only a Jakobsonian (see Chapters 1 and 2) approach to accounting for literariness.

ACTIVITY 4   Schema theory and literariness (Reading B)

Please read Reading B and consider the following questions:

- What, for Cook, is the relationship between schemata and literariness?

- Do you agree that his analyses indicate limits in using only a Jakobsonian approach to accounting for literariness?

- Do you see any problems with Cook's argument?

Comment

The advert analysed by Cook has much formal patterning and deviation. But as Cook argues, this will not bring it into the 'literary canon'. For him, this is because the linguistic deviation of the advert does not translate into deviation at the level of background knowledge; the advert for Cook confirms stereotypical assumptions about people and the world. The advert then results in **schema reinforcement**. The poem, on the other hand, is not as dense with linguistic patterning and deviation, yet could still be regarded as literary. This is, for Cook, because the poem leads to **schema refreshment**, in leading to cognitive change. While indicating problems with using a purely Jakobsonian inherency approach, Cook all the same favours supplementing this Formalist approach with a focus on cognitive change or otherwise in relation to trying to gauge literariness.

It is true that readers prize certain literary works because they have changed their attitudes and perspectives in some way – perhaps even changed their life! However, whether a poem leads to schema refreshment ultimately depends on a reader's willingness for this to happen. Cook mentions a colleague who was disgusted by the Bond poem. Clearly, his colleague did not allow schema refreshment to take place though he recognised the provocative content of the poem, i.e. he recognised its potential for schema refreshment. By the same token, if a reader finds something problematic with the content of a poem, this too is likely to impede the prospect of schema refreshment. For example, one might argue the following. The British First World War poets, such as Sassoon and Owen, were officers, not working class. Why then would generals, unsympathetic to the socio-economic problems of the working-class, send Sassoon and Owen to die as the poem seems to imply in line 18? This could be a stumbling block for a reader, leading them to dismiss the poem.

More on Cook's theory

Semino (1997) and Jeffries (2001) have made criticisms of Cook's perspective on literariness and schema refreshment. We will come to these shortly. Before we do, in order that you can appreciate Cook's theory in more detail, and how it relates to literary value, I will outline more of it. Cook goes on to propose in his book a theory of literariness:

> [...] as a dynamic interaction between linguistic and text-structural form on the one hand, and schematic representations of the world on the other, whose overall result is to bring about a change in the schemata of the reader.

(Cook, 1994, p. 182)

The concept of 'discourse deviation' was first introduced in Chapter 1.

He uses the term 'discourse deviation' for the phenomenon where linguistic or text-structural deviation 'interacts with the reader's existing schemata to cause schema refreshment'. In other words, literature works in the way it does because of the interaction between formal deviation in the text and what the reader *brings* to the text. Cook points out that the experience of discourse deviation can never lead to assigning the quality of 'literariness' once and for all to a given text, but only to a given discourse: to a text, in other words, in interaction with a particular reader. ('Discourse' for Cook is the product of text and reader.) Cook is then arguing that literariness exists somewhere *between* the literary text and the reader. This is different to Formalists such as Jakobson (see Chapter 2) who saw literariness as inherent in the text only.

Another key idea in Cook (1994) in the discussion of schema refreshment is that of **novel linking of schemata**. For Cook, literary texts typically evoke conflicting and open-ended schemata and establish complex and novel relationships between them. In his reading of William Blake's poem, 'The Tyger', the following script schemata are activated: TIGER, FORESTS, NIGHT, BLACKSMITH, ARTISTS, GOD, SPEAR, THROWER, TEARS. Read the poem in Colour Figure 12 to see cues for these schemata (e.g. *anvil*, *furnace* for BLACKSMITH). For Cook, these usually unrelated schemata (e.g. TIGER and BLACKSMITH) are brought together in reading. Likewise, with the Edward Bond poem, various schemata are linked together in a novel way: the conventions of poetry and the conventions of war for example. Where 'The Tyger' is different to 'First World War Poets', though, is in its greater amount of patterning, deviation and ambiguity. For example, *in* in the second line, *in the forests of the night* may mean either 'within/as an integral part of' (as in 'there is hydrogen in water') or 'contained in but not part of' (as in 'there are fish in water). It is ambiguities such as this one which, Cook argues, allow for hierarchical connections between schemata:

> Thus, if we read 'in' as 'within' (i.e., an integral part of) we may regard the tiger as part of a FORESTS schema or a NIGHT schema; if we read it as 'in, but not part of' ('among') we may treat it as a separate schema. The two readings of 'forests of the night' will allow night to be a part of FORESTS or forests to be part of NIGHT.

(Cook, 1994, p. 221)

Multimodal poetry was discussed in Chapter 6.

It is the capacity of a poem to lead to multifariously novel linking of schemata, and in turn schema refreshment, which gives a poem value for Cook. Having said this, Colour Figure 12, one multimodal version of the poem by Blake, would seem to make the text more 'closed' to interpretation in cueing the 'integral' reading as the preferred one; the tiger and the tree share the same colour and 'stripes' and the poem itself is entwined by branches of the forest.

Cook does not assert, however, that only literature can result in schema refreshment. Naturally many genres lead us to create and/or refresh schemata. I think I know a little about the physics of black holes in outer space but I am sure even a popular book on this subject would lead to schema refreshment of my probably misleading ideas. While the ideas in such a book and thus my capacity to create schemata for them will challenge me, the conventional arrangements of words on the pages in a popular book on black holes is unlikely to. In other words, such schema refreshment would not take place through discourse deviation because the latter requires deviation at linguistic and/or text-structural levels.

In Bex's (1996) conception of literariness, he includes jokes since, like prototypical literary texts, they do not usually refer directly to the actual world. In contrast, Cook (1994) does not regard this genre as literary. This is partly because jokes do not lead to schema refreshment:

Cook makes a similar point about adverts in Chapter 1 of the companion volume, **Maybin and Swann (2006)** 'contributing to group formation'.

> Firstly, though they share many features with literary discourse, they often have a dominant function considered alien to literature, for example to establish group identity or to give voice to taboos. Secondly, they are often concerned with communal rather than individual creative identity, and the former, in a literate culture, is often regarded as inferior.

(Cook, 1994, p. 193)

Cook (1994) points out also that though jokes might be patterned at the linguistic and text-structural levels, they nevertheless preserve schemata.

Criticism of Cook's theory

I now examine some criticism of Cook's theory. The first critic I mention is Lesley Jeffries. While Cook has a focus on the literary experience in the individual, Jeffries argues that literary experience is likely to be communal for readers if they do not have schemata 'which are culturally dominant' (Jeffries, 2001, p. 340). To illustrate this point, Jeffries uses another Fleur Adcock poem, 'Against Coupling', which you have met in Chapter 2, a poem seemingly about female masturbation. For Jeffries, in reinforcing schemata that might get repressed culturally, a literary work such as 'Against Coupling' has communal impact in normalising an experience which may not have been previously discussed. In other words, for Jeffries, and in contrast with Cook, a poem such as 'Against Coupling' actually functions in the same way as jokes in 'giving voice to taboos'.

Another critic is Elena Semino (1997, p. 154), who, drawing on Cook's work, suggests that discourse deviation and thus schema refreshment may only be a property of prototypically literary texts. She argues that, in practice, texts that are regarded as literary range on a continuum from schema reinforcement at one end to schema refreshment at the other. She seeks to demonstrate this through an analysis of a Seamus Heaney poem, 'A Pillowed Head', a poem on the birth of a child. Heaney links a schema for DAWN and a schema for BIRTH of a child. This can be seen especially in the last three verses:

And then later on I half-fainted
When the little slapped palpable girl
Was handed to me; but as usual

Came to in two wide-open eyes
That had been dawned into farther
Than ever, and had outseen the last

Of all those mornings of waiting
When your domed brow was one long held silence
And the dawn chorus anything but.

This is hardly a novel linking of schemata and so is not likely to lead to schema refreshment but to schema reinforcement. From Cook's perspective, this would mean the poem is not prototypically literary. Do you agree that if a poem leads to schema reinforcement, this means it is not prototypically literary?

Again, the issues are tricky. But perhaps by bringing relevance theory into a schema theory account of literariness, we can come to better clarity on what is prototypically literary, at least for the reading of poetry. This is one of the purposes of the next section, where *both* relevance and schema theory are drawn upon.

8.4 Relevance theory and schema theory

Relevance theory and schema theory are from different scholarly traditions. Relevance theory is part of a branch of linguistics known as 'pragmatics' which has its roots in philosophy. (Grice, whose work Sperber and Wilson start from, was a philosopher.) Schema theory, on the other hand, derives from work in psychology and artificial intelligence. Despite this, for Semino (1997, p. 159) 'Relevance theory is not in fact incompatible with schema theory'. Here is Semino (1997, p. 170) on the connection:

Sperber and Wilson claim that in comprehension we always aim to balance the effort involved in searching and activating background knowledge with the resulting cognitive effects. In schema-theory terms, this is equivalent to saying that we activate a schema when its contribution to interpretation counter-balances the effort expended in activating it.

Indeed, Sperber and Wilson (1995, pp. 190, 236) themselves make use of the term 'schema'. On a different but related point, Guy Cook says that literature is able to lead to schema refreshment because 'it is removed from immediate practical and social functions' (Cook, 1994, p. 183). Given that Bex, in his relevance theory-inspired Reading A, also argues that literary works do not have necessary practical consequences, again there would seem to be some scope for aligning relevance theory and schema theory.

We return to the poem, 'A Pillowed Head', a poem which from Cook's perspective would not be prototypically literary since it does not result in novel linking of schemata. Readers are guided by its patterns, through its linguistic and/or text-structural deviations, to choose certain linkages of schemata, choices which are relevant for them. In line with relevance theory and thus with Bex's argument, in the absence of conventionally associated practical consequences, the patterning of a poem creates a certain resistance for the reader. On the principle of relevance, extra effort needs to be balanced by poetic effects – i.e. the seeking of relevance in how a poem has led the reader to link schemata together. With 'A Pillowed Head', the reader thus needs to *work* to seek relevance for the linking of DAWN and BIRTH schemata but crucially via these patterns. From this cognitive work, poetic effects ensue. Some of these poetic effects may be schema refreshment or schema reinforcement.

In contrast, consider a cringe-worthy e-circular by new parents to their friends which includes the following: *last Tuesday was the dawn of our little Jimmy*. With such an announcement, the linking of DAWN and BIRTH schemata by a reader is done via maximisation of relevance around conventional practical consequences (e.g. the need to buy a present). The linking of DAWN and BIRTH schemata on reading the announcement is thus much less labour intensive. As a result, relevance which is separate from obvious practical consequences is unlikely to be sought in the text world generated from this announcement.

I would argue that by introducing relevance theory into the schema theory account of literariness, it becomes possible to see that prototypical literary reading, at least for poems, is not defined by either schema refreshment or reinforcement. The difference is that in prototypical reading of poetry, schema refreshment and schema reinforcement are *by-products* of a unique cognitive process where:

1   guided by textual patterns in the poem, and in the absence of necessary practical consequences, the reader expends effort to link schemata together, whether the linking is novel or not;

2   the reader then seeks relevance in the text world they generate.

It is this cognitive process which I would contend primarily marks the prototypical experience of reading poetry. And it is this cognitive process which is necessary for the generation of *literary* poetic effects. The generation of poetic effects in the reading of poetry is very much dependent on 2 following 1. In contrast, *non-literary* poetic effects, such as a delight in the word play in an advert, are not dependent on 2 following 1. You might want to spend a few moments thinking about the extent to which you agree.

The chapter so far has only been looking at schema theory and relevance theory accounts of literariness in relation to the genre of poetry. It would be useful to broaden things out to another genre – narrative fiction – to see whether similar issues apply.

ACTIVITY 5   The prologue in *Bilgewater* by Jane Gardam

Allow about
30 minutes

Reading C starts with a prologue from Jane Gardam's novel, *Bilgewater*. In the prologue, a young woman is being interviewed for a place at Cambridge University. Read the prologue in the box below (sentences are numbered) and answer the following questions:

- In what ways, if any, do you think the prologue is skilfully written so as to establish sympathy for the candidate and suspense at the end?
- Do you think the candidate will take up a university place if she is offered one?
- In trying to answer these questions, think about the kinds of schemata activated in your reading that help you to understand what is happening. Are the concepts of schema refreshment or schema reinforcement relevant for your reading experience?

Prologue from *Bilgewater* by Jane Gardam

(1) The interview seemed over. (2) The Principal of the college sat looking at the candidate. (3) The Principal's back was to the light and her stout, short outline was solid again the window, softened only by the fuzz of her ageing but rather pretty hair. (4) Outside the bleak and brutal Cambridge afternoon – December and raining.

(5) The candidate sat opposite wondering what to do. (6) The chair had a soft seat but wooden arms. (7) She crossed her legs first one way and then the other – then wondered about crossing her legs at all. (8) She wondered whether to get up. (9) There was a cigarette box beside her. (10) She wondered whether she would be offered a cigarette. (11) There was a decanter of sherry on the bookcase. (12) It had a neglected air.

(13) This was the third interview of the day. (14) The first had been as she had expected – carping, snappish, harsh, watchful – unfriendly even before you had your hand off the door handle. (15) Seeing how much you could take. (16) Typical Cambridge. (17) A sign of the times. (18) An hour later and then the second interview – five of them this time behind a table – four women, one man, all in old clothes. (19) That had been a long one. (20) Polite though. (21) Not so bad.

(22) 'Is there anything that you would like to ask us?'

(23) ('Yes please, why I'm here'. (24) Whether I really want to come even if you invite me. (25) What you're all like. (26) Have you ever run mad for love? (27) Considered suicide? (28) Cried in the cinema? (29) Clung to somebody in bed'?)

(30) 'No thank you. (31) I think Miss Blenkinsop-Briggs has already answered my questions in the interview this morning.' (32) They move their pens about, purse their lips, turn to one another from the waist, put together the tips of their fingers. (33) I look alert. (34) I sit up-right. (35) I survey them coolly but not without respect. (36) I might get in on this one. (37) But don't think it is a good sign when they're nice to you, said old Miss Bex.

(38) And now, here we are. (39) The third interview. (40) Meeting the Principal. (41) An interview with the Principal means I'm in for a Scholarship. (42) How ridiculous!

(43) I can't see her face against the light. (44) She's got a brooding shape. (45) She is a mass. (46) Beneath the fuzz a mass. (47) A massive intelligence clicking and ticking away – observing, assessing, sifting, pigeonholing. (48) Not a feeling, not an emotion, not a dizzy thought. (49) A formidable woman.

(50) She's getting up. (51) It has been delightful. (52) She hopes that we may meet again. (53) (Does that mean I'm in?) (54) What a long way I have to come for an interview. (55) The far far north (56) She hopes that I was comfortable last night.

(57) We shake hands in quite a northern way. (58) Then she puts on a coat – very nice coat, too. (59) Fur. (60) Nice fur. (61) Something human then about her somewhere. (62) She walks with me to the door and down the stairs and we pause again on the college steps.

(63) There is a cold white mist swirling about, rising from the river. (64) The trees lean, swinging long, black ropes at the water. (65) A courtyard, frosty, of lovely proportions. (66) A fountain, a gateway. (67) In the windows round the courtyard the lights are coming on one by one. (68) But it is damp, old, cold, cold, cold. (69) Cold as home.

(70) Shall I come here?

(71) Would I like it after all?

You will now be able to compare your reading with an analysis and interpretation of the *Bilgewater* prologue by Mick Short, Jonathan Culpeper and Elena Semino. In Reading C, these authors try to capture how a reader will understand the opening of the prologue. To do this, they trace its creative narration and schema activation.

ACTIVITY 6   **Narrative skill in *Bilgewater*'s prologue (Reading C)**

Please read Reading C. Does the analysis of Short et al. capture your experience of reading the prologue? Do you agree with their assessment of narrative skill? Do you agree with their use of relevance theory in relation to the chronological order of interviews?

Comment

Short et al. argue that the prologue very carefully adjusts to the 'focalizer' – the candidate – and, in activating appropriate schemata, positions the reader to sympathise with the candidate. I agree, on the whole, that the narrative is able to achieve sympathy with the candidate and a degree of suspense at the end by invoking relevant schemata as well as through its careful shifts in narration, tense and co-text. Where I am less convinced is in the assumption that the lack of chronological order has to translate into relevant effects – i.e. the reader understands the candidate is confused. For a start, it is not clear whether, as Short et al. suggest, sentence 38 and after indicate the *beginning* of the third interview. The candidate could be thinking about the Principal and the third interview – in the *middle* or possibly at the *end* of it. Moreover, a large function of the prologue is to set up questions in the reader's mind as to whether the candidate will go to Cambridge University or not. Making the last interview the focus from the start seems to me to be the most effective way of achieving this.

The prologue relies on the reader activating a stereotypical script schema about interviews and a theme schema about how young interviewees might feel. Furthermore, the linguistic patterns of the text are not leading the reader to work to link schemata in a specific way. So the concepts of schema refreshment and reinforcement do not seem so relevant here.

Having said this, the focus so far has only been on the prologue. Might the concepts of schema refreshment/reinforcement relate to the novel as a whole? The prologue is followed in *Bilgewater* by a first-person narration from a young woman, Marigold Green, who describes the period from her sixth-form studies up to the point where she goes to Cambridge University. The title of the novel is her nickname, Bilgewater, given to her by the boys of a local school where she lives with her father and headmaster, Bill. (She is 'Bill's daughter' which following some teasing word play by the boys becomes, 'Bilgewater'.) So the reader is likely to retrospect that the candidate in the prologue is Marigold Green/Bilgewater. The main narration ends at the point when Marigold Green/Bilgewater is about to go to Cambridge University. But the novel has a 'twist-in-the-tale', an epilogue which forces the reader to re-interpret the prologue. The epilogue takes us back to the original interview scene. But now the Principal refers to the candidate as

'Miss Terrapin' and not 'Miss Green' as we might have expected. Short et al. explain what is going on here in a section which was not in your extract:

> ... we know from the main narration that Bilgewater had a relationship with a boy called Terrapin before she fell in love with another young man called Boakes. All this effectively blocks the assumption that Bilgewater is the candidate in the epilogue. Indeed, the Principal is also referred to as Lady Boakes, and, as we know from the end of the main narration that she was in love with a young man called Boakes, who went 'up' to Cambridge at the same time as her, we infer that they must have married and that they have both had very successful careers. Indeed, it transpires that Lady Boakes is the first woman principal of Caius college.
>
> The effect of the parallels between the prologue and the epilogue, and the 'blockings' referred to above, effectively make the identity of the two main characters in the prologue ambiguous, and thus provides an explanation of the author's avoidance of naming the candidate and Principal in the prologue. Effectively, the epilogue constitutes a recontextualisation of the prologue, so that the candidate could be Bilgewater or Miss Terrapin and the Principal could be Lady Boakes (Bilgewater) or a previous incumbent. The chronological effect of the overall novel pushes us towards the assumption that the original candidate was probably Bilgewater, but the ambiguity leads to a vision of circularity and repetition, through the generations, of similar experiences.
>
> (Short et al., 2000, p. 150–51)

So is the reinterpretation of the prologue a case of schema refreshment? The answer would have to be no because it is not a refreshment of world knowledge. It is instead a case of **text world refreshment**. Once readers suspect changes have occurred in the text world they generate in reading, then on a relevance theory account, they will seek to attach relevance to this. In searching for optimal relevance, there will be an expectation, whether unconscious or conscious, that additional processing costs will be met by cognitive reward. In the case of *Bilgewater*, one possible reward for text world refreshment is that the reader experiences surprise and possibly delight in being transported from the particularities of the novel to a more universal appreciation of human life cycles. This narrative technique of getting us to construct a text world and then to refresh it is not just used in novels. Other narrative genres such as films also use such a device, for example exhilaratingly near the end of Bryan Singer's *The Usual Suspects* (1995). This is not, though, to say that this is how all narratives work. When Eveline, in the Joyce short story in Chapter 3, did not go with Frank to Argentina, this was not so obviously a 'twist-in-the-tale' since there were clues before the ending that she had difficulties in taking a decisive course of action. And in line with what I said above, while fictional narratives can lead to text world refreshment, this does not necessarily translate into refreshment of world knowledge, i.e. schema refreshment. For instance, in the case of *Bilgewater*, readers get transported to a perspective many already understand – life is cyclical. *Bilgewater*, in this sense, would be schema reinforcing for many.

Consonant with Semino's (1997) argument, then, fictional narratives just like poems do not necessarily lead to refreshment of schemata. However, narratives through use of focaliser techniques are able to position readers to sympathise with or even identify with a character or set of characters. Once readers have begun sympathising with characters in a novel, they are then in a 'vulnerable' position from the perspective of the author. That is, the genre of narrative fiction is well placed to 'play with' readers through refreshing text worlds.

This chapter has shown how having a cognitive vocabulary can be used to help illuminate how literary works function for readers. A problem, though, with using schema theory to try to take account of the literary experience is that we cannot actually *observe* schemata. As Carter (1999: 214) argues, ultimately schemata remain speculative and relative to the interpreter. For example, we saw Cook in Reading B saying, with regard to his interpretative schemata in his analysis of the Elizabeth Taylor advert: 'I can only appeal to my intuition and cultural knowledge, though this is likely to be shared by other readers'. How schemata can be more empirically accounted for is the focus of the last substantive section. In doing so, I also look at how the literary value of 'Street Song', in its capacity to be 'dynamic and disturbing' not just for one reader such as Roger Fowler but more generally, can be given some substantiation from corpus analysis.

8.5 Using a corpus to substantiate analysis of literary vagueness

Some schemata are very 'local', schemata which only a few people may have, e.g. where members of a particular family habitually sit at the dining table. But by inhabiting the same society and culture or by speaking the same language, there are other schemata which can be taken as more generally shared.

By interviewing many users of English I could obtain a sense of people's expectations with regard to English usage in a literary text and in turn reveal common schemata which are likely to be activated in reading. To achieve a reasonable representativeness, I would need to elicit responses from many people and for different variables (age, culture, gender, level of education, etc). Clearly, such an exercise is going to be very time consuming and is really only achievable in a large-scale research project. When this ideal is infeasible, a more indirect but at least convenient way would be to make use of large corpora of English. Regularities as revealed by a concordancer can provide some evidence for our habitual expectations with regard to particular English usage. Since this is the case, regularities which show up in a corpus could provide partial evidence for common schemata about language use (our 'language schemata').

Let me give an example with *is waiting* from the first verse of 'Street Song', 'someone is waiting, I don't know where'. My intuition tells me that habitual language use around *waiting* would indicate the purpose of the waiting.

Ideas from corpus
linguistics were
introduced in
Chapters 2 and 3.

To see if my intuition could be corroborated, I employed the 450-million word corpus (The Bank of English) which was used in Chapter 2. This corpus consists mostly of journalism (e.g. newspapers) though it also contains several million words of spoken English, both British and American. I found that *is waiting* habitually occurs with *for* (*+ something / somebody*) or *to* (*+ do something*). When grammar and lexis regularly co-occur like this, they are known as **phraseologies** (see Figures 8.2 and 8.3).

```
      time as studying the SAB bid, he  is waiting for  the go-ahead from the European
                    wing. Parliament  is waiting for  its expensive new home to be
        season closed. The 28-year-old  is waiting for  international clearance but
           fell 2p to 38.5 p. The market  is waiting for  an update on existing and
        sides claim that each carrier  is waiting for  a response from the other.
   The Indonesian business community  is waiting for  a Supreme Court decision on
             I am God." "I think this person  is waiting for  an opportune moment," said
     arrive at the big event everyone  is waiting for. Which, as we all know, is the
          ROW SOCCEROO Mark Viduka  is waiting for  Celtic and Croatia Zagreb to
        from feeling how baldly Timer  is waiting for  some comment about her, some
         nothing had happened. " Diego  is waiting for  us." He led her down the
              after his lay-off." Dixon  is waiting for  a late fitness check on stand-
    1.9 million for the frontman and  is waiting for  a reply from Old Trafford
       play-off glory. The Icelander  is waiting for  the club's owners to talk over
   lounge, or bar, don't assume she  is waiting for  another guest to buy her a
        Smith, Minister for Culture,  is waiting for  me in a roped-off, private
           sex god. Titchmarsh, 53,  is waiting for  me on the terrace at the Royal
                  s right. said The world  is waiting for  sun rise on his bed springs.
   Angolan government says that it  is waiting for  the former rebel movement,
   Saisse demanded. 'Monsieur Jannoc  is waiting for  you.' Whitlock followed Saisse
          without being asked. But he  is waiting for  her to start asking for
                  1.45 pm Mrs Jackson  is waiting for  a lumpectomy. Her tumour,
     glass removed from is eye and  is waiting for  a medical verdict on how long
```

Figure 8.2   Random sample concordance lines of the phraseology *is + waiting + for*.

```
  in case a lurking photographer  is waiting to  snap them. The book is
      old Derek Jacobs from Florida  is waiting to  have the centimetre-long
   of the Metronet consortium, which  is waiting to  pop the champagne on two of the
      which another son, Johnson,  is waiting to  plunder with your help. Perhaps
         that the hardest part now  is waiting to  see the finished version of
   speaks barely a word of Chinese,  is waiting to  hear if FIFA will allow his
    does anything about it. Forestyer  is waiting to  hear what the grand jury has to
       sporting events. Maybe everyone  is waiting to  see if things will be better
        pulls up at her home, a friend  is waiting to  drop off bottles of salt that
   who pledged $4.5 billion in aid –  is waiting to  see if the nation begins the
      they exchanged gifts. Mr Gusmao  is waiting to  be moved to a house owned by
        job very seriously. 'My crew  is waiting to  strike the set," Garrett
           injury in July. And Fowler  is waiting to  see if he requires a second
     heavyweight showdown Britain  is waiting to  see. But they will not be
           Spurs boss Glenn Hoddle  is waiting to  see if striker Les Ferdinand
      ball. The West Ham midfielder  is waiting to  see whether Durkin reports him
   risk to other children if a child  is waiting to  go back to the doctor for
      airport. There, a BAC Express  is waiting to  fly my letter to Bristol, where
   for the market is that everybody  is waiting to  hear more details about the
        rice to feed the population  is waiting to  be shipped from neighbouring
        to spare?' 'No.' 'But Jehovah  is waiting to  welcome you into his glorious
      mistake. A pile of letters  is waiting to  be opened and more, no doubt,
              s blue/grey quarry  is waiting to  be 'dressed", or cut to size,
```

Figure 8.3   Random sample concordance lines of the phraseology *is + waiting + to*.

Corpus phraseology evidence corroborates the intuition that it is common in language use to indicate purpose around 'waiting', i.e. to make linguistically explicit *plan* and *goal* schemata. If corpora can provide information on regularities of usage, one useful role they can play is in the following: helping us to sift more personal and thus 'local' schemata activated in reading a literary text from schemata that are more likely to be activated by readers generally. Fowler (1996) finds 'Street Song' 'dynamic and disturbing' and other people I have shown this poem to agree. What I want to show is how corpus analysis can help to substantiate why the poem can be 'dynamic and disturbing' for readers more generally.

Recall from Section 8.3 that *loitering* triggered in Fowler a plan schema for the crime of 'loitering with intent'. For Fowler, *loitering* involves intention to act and 'people can only loiter with bad intent'. A concordance search of *loitering* in the 450-million word corpus tells us that there is evidence for this, for example:

> Mrs de Rosnay told the Old Bailey that she had seen a well-built man in a dark suit loitering near Miss Dando's house two hours before the killing.

But the corpus search also tells that usage of *loitering* is more complicated. People can also loiter in the sense of just 'hanging about' with no clear and specific intention to act (or so it would seem just from just the textual record). For example, in one co-text for *loitering* we have:

> Should you be loitering around Hyde Park Corner over the next three weeks, pop into Pizza on the Park for a comical crash course in the lost art of cabaret.

Alternatively, people may loiter with an intention to act but an action that does not necessarily have criminal 'bad intent':

> When he arrived he had to make his way through a loitering group of journalists. They regarded him with brief interest, until they concluded he was neither a doctor not a policeman, and they ignored him.

Around 40 per cent of instances of *loitering* in the Bank of English occur without obvious intentions being indicated or being readily inferable.

In analysing corpus evidence though we must be careful to distinguish *quantitative* frequency evidence from *qualitative* evidence about the salience of a phenomenon in a culture. The crime 'loitering with intent' may be salient across a culture without it necessarily being talked or written about very much. Just because a phenomenon is not reflected by frequency of instances in a corpus does not mean it is not salient. So the corpus evidence does not tell us that Fowler's generation of a plan schema for *loitering* is wrong. But it does tell us that *loitering* is not always associated with plan schemata. In turn, this tells us that readers generally speaking may not always associate 'loitering' with intention, let alone criminal intention. In Reading C, Short et al. use the expression 'semantic prosody' in relation to collocations around *frosty*. In other words, *frosty* usually carries negative meanings in collocation, e.g. 'frosty relations'. The corpus evidence tells us that 'loitering' really only carries a negative semantic prosody in relation to crime.

As we have seen in this chapter, Cook and Semino are mostly concerned with the outcome of our engagement with a literary work – schema refreshment or schema reinforcement. They are much less concerned with what makes readers in the first place invest processing effort. In one place, though, Cook (1994, p. 222) does talk of the suggestive power of the poem, 'The Tyger'. He highlights the suggestiveness of a link between a *script* for a BLACKSMITH and a *script* for GOD in the verse:

> What the hammer? what the chain?
> In what furnace was thy brain?
> What the anvil? what dread grasp
> Dare its deadly terrors clasp?

These are evoked, as he argues, not by a lexical item referring to them but by reference to elements of the schemata. So, for example, he argues that *dread* cues a script for GOD in the above verse and *hammer* and *furnace* cue a script for BLACKSMITH. Thus, in the same verse, a script for BLACKSMITH and GOD are linked, leading Cook to conjure up Thor (a god who was a blacksmith) and in relation to the idea of creation and its wonder. Cook (1994, p. 222) stresses that these schematic evocations are highly indirect and that 'their presence through implication makes them both more powerful and more mysterious; this evocation of parts of schemata without reference to their unifying concept, this vagueness gives the poem the power to yield many interpretations'. In a similar vein, Widdowson (Reading B, Chapter 1), argues that a literary text creates 'a referential vacuum which the reader is drawn into to give imaginative substance to'.

Extrapolating from the above, it could be argued that the reason many poems work, in the first instance, for a large number of readers is because they have the quality of 'optimum literary vagueness' which draws readers in to 'fill the vacuum', to project schemata into them in their generation of a text world. Too much obscurity might be seen by many as not worth the effort; too little indirectness would mean very little effort would be needed. If very little effort is needed, then the reader is likely not to seek much relevance in the slight text world they would construct. In relevance theory terms, the range of poetic effects generated would be limited.

Let me return to 'Street Song' using corpus evidence to help assess its literary vagueness for readers more generally. You will notice in verse 1 that there is no sentence which directly represents someone (an AGENT) acting on another person (an AFFECTED), e.g. the man assaulted the woman. So, in the absence of such explicit linguistic representation, *plan* and *goal* schemata about assaults on women or children are indirectly evoked. In line with what Cook says, indirect evocation is more mysterious. Focus now on the second line of verse 1, *someone is waiting, I don't know where.* As you saw above, on the basis that regular phraseologies might tell us something about commonly

Short et al. (2000) talk, too, of the vaguely named characters, 'the candidate' and 'the principal' in *Bilgewater*. This leads the reader to project assumptions into the prologue.

See Chapter 3 for an explanation of these functional labels, AGENT and AFFECTED.

Phraseological deviation is a different form of deviation to that which Mukařovský worked on (see Chapter 2) since deviation from phraseological norms, as revealed in large corpora searches, may not be immediately obvious, unlike say grammatical deviation, e.g. 'someone are waiting'.

shared language schemata, the corpus evidence for *is waiting* would seem to suggest that habitually people make explicit the purpose of 'waiting' in their language use. This means that in the line in the poem, *someone is waiting, I don't know where*, there is a **phraseological deviation**.

It could be argued, of course, that *someone is waiting* is an instance of ellipsis with an implicit 'to do something or other' or 'for something'. But if this was the case, I would expect on the basis of corpus evidence a follow-up such as 'I don't know why' or 'I don't know what for' rather than *I don't know where*. Indeed, in the poem the *where* would seem to have been already communicated in the first line with *Pink Lane, Strawberry Lane, Pudding Chare*. So with this line *someone is waiting, I don't know where*, intention would seem not to be obviously present. But in line 4 of verse 1, *he wants to play peculiar games*, intention *is* expressed. There is then a tension in the first verse: the intention of the *someone* is vague, ambiguous. This tension, I would argue, adds to the mystery of verse 1. Corpus evidence thus helps to explain why the verse is 'dynamic and disturbing' and likely to be for readers more generally.

ACTIVITY 7   Assessing literary vagueness via corpus analysis

Allow about 30 minutes

A further search of the 450-million word Bank of English corpus found that *sidle* (as used in the line *he could be sidling along Forth lane*) is used much more with *up* or *over* rather than *along* and with humans than with a place (e.g. *he sidled up to her*). When the crime of *stalking* is being written or talked about, corpus evidence suggests that it is related strongly to human AFFECTED participant roles (e.g. *a psychopathic serial killer stalking a pretty woman*) which contrasts with the lack of a human AFFECTED in the line *or stalking the grounds of the RVI*. Lastly, recall also the results of the corpus investigation above of *loitering*.

- What light might all this corpus evidence throw on the capacity of verses 2 and 3 to continue to set up literary vagueness/suggestiveness?

- In what ways, though, should we be cautious in making deductions from corpus evidence?

Comment

Here is my analysis. How far do you agree or disagree?

On the basis of corpus evidence, it is ambiguous whether *someone is loitering* is associated with intention (whether that intention is bad or not) and thus with a plan schema. Sometimes *loitering* is associated with bad intention, sometimes with a neutral intention and sometimes with no intention at all. The corpus evidence helps substantiate vagueness and ambiguity.

Interestingly, in verse 3 plan schemata are indicated explicitly via the infinitives *to stop some girl* and *to see if a student nurse*. If the argument is made that literary value is connected with a certain optimum vagueness, then I might say the poem falls down here. This is because intention to act on another human being is being expressed more explicitly with the *to stop* infinitive. Suggestiveness is seemingly reduced. Yet corpus analysis suggests that *sidling along* is an instance of **non-core phraseology** because schemata for language usage with *sidle* is more likely to relate to human beings than places. Moreover, corpus evidence for *stalking* in regard to criminal activity also relates much more to humans than places. Taking the corpus evidence for *sidling* and *stalking* together, tension is engendered between action in a place as communicated in verse 3 and what readers might more generally expect as action around human beings.

An advantage of using corpus evidence with 'Street Song' is that it assists explanation of why the poem is likely to be 'dynamic and disturbing' for readers more generally. It suggests that a reader might not always be sure whether to project plan schemata into the poem or not. The effect is an unsettling one, a little like walking down quiet streets at night and not knowing whether the footsteps behind you are those of someone who is just walking or someone who may have malign intentions towards you.

There are, though, a number of issues to bear in mind when using corpora. The empirical evidence that corpora can provide is limited by the extent to which the sampling is representative. As mentioned earlier, the Bank of English corpus is heavily skewed towards journalism. To try to check a potential imbalance, it is advisable to draw on other corpora if possible, corpora which are skewed towards other genres as well as those more equally proportioned in terms of their genre content. Finally, the tension about salience and frequency mentioned earlier always needs to be borne in mind when using corpus evidence. Nevertheless, use of corpora in the way shown offers a method for developing constrained hypotheses, i.e. ones worth empirically testing, when the ideal of a large-scale reader response study (see, for example, Reading B, Chapter 9) is practicable.

Another usefully large corpus (100 million words) is the British National Corpus.

I have provided evidence that much of 'Street Song' could well have a certain literary vagueness for readers generally which explains its capacity to disturb. In this respect, the poem would seem to have a certain literary value (though the whole poem would need to be analysed in relation to a corpus/corpora). This is not to say that non-literary texts such as newspaper headlines and adverts are never deliberately vague and ambiguous in an attempt to draw readers in. The difference with such texts is that they prototypically have direct reference and conventionally associated practical consequences which in the end will lead readers to close down on meanings relevant to such consequences. Finally, there is a difference, though, between assessing the value of a literary work in its capacity to disturb readers generally, as compared with its capacity to lead readers to generate rich and divergent poetic effects. That is, the above analysis is *not* an interpretation of what the poem means to individual readers. You might want to pause here and consider again what 'Street Song' means to you in how its patterning and text structure guide novel (or unnovel) linking of schemata and, in doing so, lead you to seek relevance for the text world you generate.

8.6 Conclusion

This chapter has gone beyond the idea that literariness only resides *in* the text, a perspective that was dealt with particularly in Chapters 2, 3 and 6. It has done this by discussing the kinds of cognitive processes involved in literary reading and whether literariness can be defined in terms of cognitive effects. Though this chapter has explored the relationship between literariness and the reader's cognitive processes, the reader has been an idealised one. There have been no flesh and blood readers of literary works other than the analysts themselves. In Chapter 9, however, you will be able to see how readers who are not literary analysts respond to literary texts, in terms of their cognitive processes, and also in relation to their sociocultural circumstances.

Appendix: 'The Tyger' by William Blake

Here is the text of the poem that appears in original form in Colour Figure 12.

Tyger! Tyger! burning bright
In the forests of the night,
What immortal hand or eye,
Could frame thy fearful symmetry?

In what distant deeps or skies,
Burnt the fire of thine eyes?
On what wings dare he aspire?
What the hand dare sieze the fire?

And what shoulder, & what art,
Could twist the sinews of thy heart?
And when thy heart began to beat,
What dread hand? & what dread feet?

What the hammer? what the chain?
In what furnace was thy brain?
What the anvil? what dread grasp,
Dare its deadly terrors clasp?

When the stars threw down their spears,
And watered heaven with their tears,
Did he smile his work to see?
Did he who made the Lamb make thee?

Tyger! Tyger! burning bright,
In the forests of the night;
What immortal hand or eye,
Dare frame thy fearful symmetry?

READING A: Relevance and literature

Tony Bex

Introduction

The ultimate communicative success of any individual text must depend on the uses to which it is put. If we read a set of instructions such as a recipe, recognise them as instructions and then choose to ignore them, it is likely that the task they describe will be performed badly. Such texts, then, are intended to have immediate practical consequences. Such texts make direct reference to the real world in some way.

This raises a number of interesting problems in the case of a particular set of texts which do *not* seem to have the same kind of referential and practical effects. Traditionally, such texts are referred to as literary texts and the fact that they are identified by a generic name suggests that they are recognised as performing some kind of function. However, the precise nature of this function is not immediately apparent.

The super-genre of literature

One way into this discussion would be to consider Jakobson (1960). He identifies a set of functions that language typically performs, and then singles out the poetic function as 'the dominant, determining function' in verbal art (1960, p. 37). A way of dealing with Jakobson's characterisation is to recognise that all language use manifests a poetic function to some degree (cf. Werth, 1976) and that the classification of some texts as literature is undertaken for purely institutional reasons. Roger Fowler (1996) adopts this strategy and argues that the use of language in literature is co-extensive with other uses of language and can therefore be analysed in the same ways. In so far as literature is considered to be unique (and therefore in some sense better) than other kinds of texts, it is because societies choose to classify them in this way for particular ideological reasons. Fowler's argument chimes with that of Eagleton (1996) [see also Reading A, Chapter 1]. But there is something uncomfortable about this claim. Although it seems to account for why some rhyming texts are treated as advertisements while others are treated as poems, it fails to capture the distinctive ways in which literature is used, and recognised, by *individuals* within a society. It is just not enough to say that one text is an advertisement and another a poem simply because society has decreed this to be the case. The texts operate differently because they are perceived both by their writers and their readers as performing different functions.

Fowler and Eagleton's argument is close to Fish's (1980) view that the identification of literary value is the function of an 'interpretative community'. For Fish, it is the norms of communities of literary scholars, literary journalists, etc. which dictate whether a particular text is classified as having any literary value. Of course, the identification of aesthetic value is not quite the same thing as the identification of a text as literary *per se*, but the way in which Fish has constructed his argument certainly suggests a significant overlap between the two concepts. Fish refers to an experiment he conducted in which he invited his students to discuss a random list of names left on the board by a previous lecturer as though it were a poem:

> Jacobs-Rosenbaum
> Levin
> Thorne
> Hayes
> Ohman

He comments that they were all prepared to engage in an analysis of the displayed text using the techniques appropriate to literary criticism, thus demonstrating that there is nothing intrinsic to any text which declares it to be a work of literature. This leads him to claim that:

> Skilled reading is usually thought to be a matter of discerning what is there, but if the experience of my students can be generalised, it is a matter of knowing how to *produce* what can thereafter be said to be there.
>
> (Fish, 1980, p. 327)

There are certain deeply flawed assumptions at play here. In the first place, we have to acknowledge that Fish was in a position of authority, and there is nothing unreasonable in a literature class assuming that the given text was literary if their teacher had asserted it was so. Perhaps, more importantly, acknowledging with Jakobson that the poetic function is present in all texts, it is not surprising that students, asked to find such features, should strive to identify them. However, this is not proof that literature is solely in the eye of the beholder, although it may be evidence to suggest that the analytic techniques appropriate to literary study are the possession of an interpretative community and can be applied by that community to other kinds of texts. Also, we still have to establish why a given range of texts are considered by a significantly large proportion of the reading public to be examples of literature while other texts are not. Simply appealing to some form of institutional authority, whether conceived in broad terms as with Fowler or Eagleton or in the narrower sense used by Fish, seems deeply unsatisfactory if only because readers, under normal circumstances, seem able to make such classifications on their first acquaintance with a given text.

This might seem to suggest that there is something intrinsic in the text which signals that it is to be read 'as literature' in which case we have come full circle to the original followers of Jakobson. An attempt to square this circle has been made by Ronald Carter [see Reading B, Chapter 2 of this volume] who believes that there may be a cline of 'literariness', and that different texts will be more or less literary. This certainly has the merit of accounting for why it is that we view certain (non-literary) works as being more like literature rather than other works and it acknowledges that all texts demonstrate some degree of 'literariness'. But by tending to resituate the element of 'literariness' as to do with the choice of language rather than the *use* of the text as a communicative act, it leaves open the question as to how 'literary' a text has to be to count as literature.

Literature and relevance theory

What we need to consider is how readers read, and what it is in the work that they are reading *regardless of its form* that persuades them that they are reading literature. From there, we can construct a possible theory as to what functions literature performs within society. To illuminate the issue I start with non-literary texts. Consider someone reading a recipe. Following Sperber and Wilson's (1995) principle of relevance, I would understand the recipe in terms of maximum effects (e.g. how to prepare the ingredients) for minimum effort invested in reading. But suppose I were to find that the recipe's instructions were flawed in some way. I would still be likely to consider it as a recipe rather than as belonging to some other genre since I would assume that its function (although flawed) was to instruct me how to prepare a meal. If, on a careful re-reading, I notice some element that seems incommensurate with my experience of previous recipes, then I might be inclined to view it as a parody. But such re-classification also depends on my recognition that the use of texts as recipes has specific effects which, in this case, are not taking place. Moreover, if I read a work of history, or a news report in the paper and am not convinced by the information offered, I have ways of confirming or denying what I believe to be the case. I can seek out another history book and search for an alternative interpretation of the event, or I can make contact with the people whose story has been reported and confirm its veracity. My claim, then, is that in most of our interactions with the written word we expect practical consequences to follow on our interpretation and that this expectation will be bound up with our seeking of optimal relevance. So, with an advert that I read completely, the effort invested is more likely to be directed towards relevant effects – practical consequences I readily associate with adverts such as 'where shall I buy this product?' – rather than non-relevant ones – becoming excessively entranced by the typography of the advert. Because I know the genre of advertising, am used to seeing many adverts, it does not take very much processing effort for me to link my reading of an advert to such relevant practical consequences. Analysis of the typography of the advert, which for a consumer is not a relevant practical consequence, will take much more effort.

All of the above texts mentioned relate to the real world and the consequence of a particular interpretation can be tested empirically against this real world. In the case of literary texts this is just not the case. When I open a novel, I cannot question the characters in it to discover whether they really did perform the actions that have been described. When I read a poem, I cannot directly question the accuracy of the feelings expressed in quite the same way as I can question whether the events in an autobiography actually occurred simply because the emotions are those of the writer and therefore unknowable except in the linguistic form offered. My central claim, then, is that literature is recognisable precisely because its propositions are not propositions about the real world and belief (or disbelief) in them has no necessary practical consequences for the reader.

I can best illustrate this by considering a poem which, on the face of it, appears to be firmly rooted in the world that we typically experience in making mention of an actual museum and specifically to a painting. Auden's (1940) 'Musée des Beaux Arts':

> About suffering they were never wrong,
> The Old Masters; how well, they understood
> Its human position; how it takes place
> While someone else is eating or opening a window or just walking
> dully along;
> How, when the aged are reverently, passionately waiting
> For the miraculous birth, there always must be
> Children who did not specially want it to happen, skating
> On a pond at the edge of the wood:
> They never forgot
> That even the dreadful martyrdom must run its course
> Anyhow in a corner, some untidy spot
> Where the dogs go on with their doggy life and the torturer's horse
> Scratches its innocent behind on a tree.
>
> In Brueghel's Icarus, for instance: how everything turns away
> Quite leisurely from the disaster; the ploughman may
> Have heard the splash, the forsaken cry,
> But for him it was not an important failure; the sun shone
> As it had to on the white legs disappearing into the green
> Water; and the expensive delicate ship that must have seen
> Something amazing, a boy falling out of the sky,
> had somewhere to get to and sailed calmly on.

The poem seems to be a description of a set of paintings with special emphasis on Brueghel's *The Fall of Icarus* [Colour Figure 1]. The poem, then, could be considered to be a form of reportage or art criticism and could therefore be treated in exactly the same way as any other art criticism. One might argue that the practical consequences of reading the text in this way would be to enable a visitor to the museum to look at the paintings with new perceptions. Although such an outcome is likely to be the case, readers are left with certain puzzles. The first, and most obvious, is why Auden should have chosen to construct his art criticism using rhyme. This is not an insoluble problem, and can be treated as a textual feature which is of minimal significance in identifying this as a work of literature. Related to the use of rhyme is the unusual typographical layout but this, again, is not in itself sufficient to assign it to literature (cf. the layout of certain advertisements). Another noticeable feature is the somewhat contorted syntax. The opening lines:

> About suffering they were never wrong,
> The Old Masters

are unusual in that the use of the pronoun 'they', in referring forward, may well be more associated with speech than writing. A close reading is likely to identify a number of unusual collocations: e.g. 'the torturer's horse / Scratches its *innocent* behind on a tree'; while a still closer reading will pick out a higher than statistically likely number of rhymes and half-rhymes. However, if we use these features as a means of identifying the work as literary, we run the risk of assuming that literature can be distinguished by the use of a particular selection of 'literary' language.

But if we consider Auden's description of the pictures themselves, it slowly becomes apparent that we are being offered an interpretation rather than a description. It is quite clear that looking at the pictures themselves in the Musée des Beaux Arts will not enable us to establish the truth of what Auden appears to be claiming. There is nothing directly present in Brueghel's *Icarus* to confirm his observation that:

> ... everything turns away
> Quite leisurely from the disaster; the ploughman may
> Have heard the splash, the forsaken cry,
> But for him it was not an important failure ...

because Auden is extrapolating from a visual experience to an entirely fictional world. While we can identify the ploughman in the picture, and may be inclined to agree with Auden's attribution of insouciance, we have no way of questioning the figure to find out whether it actually occurred. Further, of course, we may notice that the painting itself is not of an historical event and that at least one representation in the picture is of a mythical person. Thus, the world created in the poem is at two removes from the world we experience with our senses.

The social function of literature

Although it is true that literature does not refer directly to the actual world, this is not to say that it does not refer indirectly. The concepts and propositions which are evoked by reading a literary text may not have specific correlations with items and relationships in the non-fictional world, but they enable us to create relatively rich imaginary worlds which mimic the external world. However, given that these worlds are constructed of words rather than things, the choice of words takes on added significance. If language is not referring conventionally, then we as readers are likely to pay

Collocation – words which co-occur with one another. For example, 'heavy' regularly collocates with 'rain' but 'big' does not.

The Musée des Beaux Arts referred to is in Belgium.

more attention to the materiality of language and recognise it for itself as well as for what it does. And this does, indeed, seem to occur in certain literary reading processes. With poetry, for example, we pay attention to the rhythms and rhymes and treat them as meaningful. In narrative, we pay attention to features such as the method of characterisation, the ways narrative has been constructed, and treat these as meaningful. Thus we engage in literary reading strategies, which is why we know how to apply them to non-literary texts should we so desire.

This brings us to the social function of literature as a super-genre. It offers us an alternative world against which we can judge the actual world. This possibility seems to be confirmed by the application of relevance theory. If readers initially approach written texts using the same cognitive interpretive processes, when they are faced with a text that clearly does not refer to the real world they will assign some relevance to the imaginary world they have created (Bex, 1992). Initially it is not entirely clear what kinds of cognitive effects might be derived from the creation of a fictional world, and it is likely that these will vary from reader to reader. Some readers may well use the fictional world as a pleasant escape from the real world, but other readers are likely to assess its potentiality for existence and in that way use it as a means of criticising the external world. On the principle of relevance, additional processing effort in a reader's search for optimal relevance needs to be offset by a suitable set of effects. So readers make the assumption that this effort in reading a poem will transfer into mental stimulation, delight, etc. Readers make the assumption that the effort is worth it.

References

BEX, A.R. (1992) 'Genre as context', *Journal of Literary Semantics*, **21**(1), pp. 1–16.

EAGLETON, T. (1996) *Literary Theory: An Introduction*, 2nd edn, Oxford, Blackwell.

FISH, S. (1980) *Is There a Text in this Class?: The Authority of Interpretative Communities*, Cambridge, Harvard University Press.

FOWLER (1996) *Linguistic Criticism*, 2nd edn, Oxford, Oxford University Press.

JAKOBSON, R. (1960) 'Closing statement: linguistics and poetics' in T.A. SEBEOK (ed.) *Style in Language*, Cambridge, Mass., The MIT Press.

SPERBER, D. and WILSON, D. (1995) *Relevance: Communication and Cognition*, 2nd edn, Oxford, Blackwell.

WERTH, P. (1976) 'Roman Jakobson's verbal analysis of poetry', *Journal of Linguistics,* **12**(1), pp. 21–73.

Source: adapted from BEX, T. (1996) *Variety in Written English: Texts in Society – Society in Texts*, Chapter 8, London, Routledge.

READING B: Schema theory and literariness

Guy Cook

Introduction

In the analyses which follow, I shall first apply the Jakobsonian methodology to two texts: the first an advertisement, the second a poem. I then contrast these stylistic analyses with descriptions in terms of interpretative schemata. By so doing, I hope to illustrate some of the strengths and weaknesses of the two approaches and also ways in which they interact in understanding the nature of literariness.

Elizabeth Taylor's passion

The nine-word text in the advertisement below (Figure 1) contains an extraordinarily concentrated exploitation of every linguistic level, in a way which reinforces and represents the message. It is a gift to formal stylistic analysis, and, if such matters were simply quantifiable – a ratio of stylistic points to words – would be a great lyric poem.

Graphology

On a graphic level, the varying lengths of the four lines allow the text to reproduce iconically the hexagonal shape of the perfume bottle which is pictured below it.

For discussion of the semiotic concept of 'icon', refer back to Chapter 6.

Phonology

In a Jakobsonian view, the patterning of stressed and unstressed syllables to create rhythm, and of phonemes to create rhyme, alliteration, consonance, assonance, and the other sound effects of verse, is at once both a deviation from the code and an imposition of order upon it. Assuming that phonic regularity is unusual, literary, and a feature of text, the stress patterns of the advertisement are as follows:

. / .	. / .	. / .	. / .
Be touched by	the fragrance	that touches	the woman

Key

/ = stressed syllable

. = unstressed syllable

The rhythm, in other words, is absolutely regular. It consists of four amphibrachs: a metrical unit comprising a single stressed syllable between two unstressed syllables. And as an amphibrach has the quality of being the same backwards and forwards, it follows that a succession of an equal number of amphibrachs can be divided into two halves, of which the second half is a reversal, an exact mirror image, of the first. The name:

./ . | . / .
Eliza | beth Taylor

moreover, is amphibrachic, and the rhythm of the advertisement thus mimics the name of the product, in much the same way as its shape reproduces the shape of the bottle.

Figure 1   Advertisement for Elizabeth Taylor's 'Passion'.

Lexis

The advertisement exploits lexical ambiguity, both at the relatively fixed semantic level of denotation, and at the discoursal level of meaning in context. Thus, at the semantic level, 'touches' means both 'to bring or be brought into physical contact with' and also 'to arouse positive emotion'.

'Woman' means both 'adult, female, human being' and also 'femininity' (as it does in a sentence like 'It brings out the woman in you'). Both of these lexical items, when taken in the context of the pictorial part of the advertisement, and in the context of its function of persuading a reader to buy a product, take on further meaning. The noun phrase 'the woman', with its definite article assuming a specific identifiable referent, can now mean either 'the woman in the picture' (i.e. Elizabeth Taylor) or 'the woman reading the advertisement' (i.e. you, the reader), and in fact invites the reader to identify with Elizabeth Taylor, presumably on the assumption that readers will wish to take on certain of her qualities.

Grammar

Grammatically, as well as phonically, the text is both deviant and patterned. Deviance is found in the use of the passive imperative, an exceedingly rare form. ('Be seated' is an exception, but 'be kissed', 'be killed', 'be seen', 'be amused', would be similarly odd.) The advert is addressed to a woman reader. In other words, the 'woman' in 'Woman be touched' has been ellipted. The usual function of a relative clause ('that touches the woman'), as of any modifier, is to add information which will help identify the referent of the head word ('fragrance'). Here the relative clause simply repeats the meaning of the full main clause, 'Woman, be touched by the fragrance'. This creates a grammatical mirror image which becomes clearer if we replace the relative pronoun 'that' by the noun it stands for 'fragrance':

woman	be touched	by the fragrance
[the fragrance]	touches	the woman

The relative clause 'that touches the woman' reflects the main clause 'woman, be touched'. We thus have a grammatical parallelism.

The break between the two clauses coincides with the half-way point in the rhythm which is also reversed after the half-way point. The grammar is mimed by the sound which mimes the grammar – (to use the same device myself). The woman is touched by the perfume which touches the woman.

The language of this advertisement, then, reveals regularities, similarities, ambiguities, and polysemies of the kind revealed by classic Jakobsonian analyses. The specific linguistic choices of the advertisement may be seen as creating a unique meaning which cannot be separated from its form. The reader is invited to become like Elizabeth Taylor through the use of a bottle of perfume.

Schemata

So far, following Jakobson, I have analysed the formal features of the advertisement. Yet, for the advertisement to function as a coherent communicative act rather than to be merely a superfluous and meaningless (if grammatical) bit of text, certain schemata must be recognized by the reader, if only subconsciously. At this level there is even less certainty than there can be concerning norms of language and significant deviations. Allowing for the usual fuzziness in distinguishing plans, goals and scripts, I interpret relevant reader schemata (male and female) to be as follows:

Script	(FEMALE)	WEARING PERFUME
Plan	(FEMALE)	BE ATTRACTIVE
Plan	(FEMALE)	BE FEMININE
Plan	(FEMALE)	IMITATE ATTRACTIVE WOMEN (Like LIZ TAYLOR)
Goal	(FEMALE)	OBTAIN SEXUAL SATISFACTION
Plan	(MALE)	TOUCH WOMAN
Plan	(MALE)	BUY PERFUME
Plan	(MALE)	GIVE PERFUME
Goal	(MALE)	OBTAIN SEXUAL SATISFACTION

No explicit mention of these schemata is made in the text, and in asserting them I can appeal only to my own intuition and cultural knowledge, though this is likely to be shared by other readers. It is the advertiser's assumption that receivers share and recognize these plans and are susceptible to the suggestion that they may be fulfilled by buying the perfume, which enables them to go unsaid. They are – in every sense – schematic, stereotypical, and predictable. As a result, in reading, the advert results in what I call, schema reinforcement.

The concept of defamiliarisation was introduced in Chapters 1 and 2.

I hope to have shown that, in this text, the Formalist notion of defamiliarisation operates only at the linguistic level, not at the schematic and discoursal level. In so far as this text is classified as an advertisement and not as a work of literature, that classification appears to view the schematic level as more important. This judgement, however, will vary with the schemata of the reader.

'First World War poets' by Edward Bond

1   You went to the front like sheep

     And bleated at the pity of it

     In academies that smell of abattoirs

     Your poems are still studied

5   You turned the earth to mud

     Yet complain you drowned in it

Your generals were dug in at the rear

Degenerates drunk on brandy and prayer

You saw the front – and only bleated

10   The pity!

You survived

Did you burn your general's houses

Loot the new millionaires?

No, you found new excuses

15   You'd lost an arm or your legs

You sat by the empty fire

And hummed music hall songs

Why did your generals send you away to die?

They saw a Great War coming

20   Between masters and workers

In their own land

So they herded you over the cliffs to be rid of you

How they hated you while you lived!

How they wept for you once you were dead!

25   What did you fight for?

A new world?

No – an old world already in ruins!

Your children?

Millions of your children died

30   Because you fought for your enemies

And not against them!

We will not forget!

We will not forgive!

To many readers who value and admire both the lives and the poetry of the First World War poets, this poem is likely, and no doubt calculated, to cause offence and outrage, and this reaction in turn will lead to a strong rejection of any claim that it is literary. Indeed, a colleague whom I consulted over this analysis felt moved, on every occasion we discussed it, to voice his deeply-felt disgust with it, and deny its status as a poem. Yet these feelings (with which, to some extent, I am in sympathy) may aid my purpose here. It is precisely as a text whose literary status is in doubt that this poem, like the perfume advertisement, is of particular interest. If the appellation 'literary' functions largely to indicate approval, then the reader's agreement or disagreement with the views expressed are likely to be crucial. If, on the other hand, as the Formalists claimed, 'literary' is a term for texts which defamiliarise through the manipulation of form, then the case may remain open. Certainly, by violently contradicting views which are deeply ingrained and treasured by many readers, it sets out to disturb. But then so does mere abuse which focuses on what is most valued by the abused. It is the manner rather than the fact of the challenge which is my concern.

Yet the form of this poem seems also markedly 'unliterary'. Arguably, it is, both linguistically and schematically, the polar opposite of the perfume advertisement analysed above. Linguistically conformist and unoriginal, it is innovative and disruptive at both the text-structural and schematic levels. (Again, these judgements are those of one reader but assumed to hold for some other readers, on the assumption that certain schemata are shared.) My argument is that this text is literary without being linguistically deviant or patterned, while the previous text is not literary, despite a significant concentration of both linguistic patterning and deviation. As such, my argument can be instantly demolished by the claim that this is 'not literary' or 'not a poem'. Against this I can say only that it is presented as a poem by writer and publisher (in the 'poems' section of a book entitled *Theatre Poems and Songs*) and that this classification is accepted by bookshops and literature courses. It is also graphologically set out as a poem in that line breaks are an intrinsic part of the text and do not depend on the width of the page, and lines are grouped into stanzas. There is also an absence of conventional punctuation, fairly common in twentieth-century poetry. Thus, though there may well be readers who reject its pretensions to be poetry, I shall proceed as though (and indeed I believe that) it is.

Graphology and phonology

On the graphological level, the only features of note are those already mentioned above: the conventional lineation and stanza divisions of poetry, and the absence of conventional punctuation. On the phonic level, there is little regularity. Line by line, the syllable count is as follows: 7, 9, 11, 7; 6, 7, 9, 10, 9, 3; 3, 8, 6, 7, 7, 7, 6; 11, 7, 7, 4, 14, 8, 9; 5, 3, 10, 3, 6, 9, 5; 5, 5. Although there is a tendency towards six- and seven-syllable lines, there are many other lengths too. Similarly, though there are lines which fall into metrical patterns reminiscent of more conventional poetry:

> .   /   .   /   .   /
> You turned the earth to mud

> .   .   /   .   /   . .
> Yet complain you drowned in it

the effect is immediately broken:

> .   / . .   .   / /   .   .   /
> Your generals were dug in at the rear

> . / . .   /   .   /   .   .   /
> Degenerates drunk on brandy and prayer

There is no rhyme except the (possibly accidental) half rhyme in lines 7 and 8 between 'rear' and 'prayer', perhaps in lines 12 and 14 between 'houses' and 'excuses', and the internal echo between 'generals' and 'degenerates' in lines 7 and 8.

The overall effect is thus of language whose phonic regularity is no greater than that of genres (for example bureaucratic prose) where attention is traditionally supposed to be on meaning rather than sound, and less than that of other genres excluded from the literary canon such as advertisements, prayers, football chants, etc. Arguably, however, there is just enough patterning – in syllables, prosody, and rhyme – for expectations to be set up and immediately dashed: a feature which is reinforced by the contrast between the traditionally 'poetic' graphology and the lack of 'poetic' phonology. That, at least, is how it seems to me.

Grammar

The grammar of the poem, like its phonology, seems pointedly 'unpoetic'. Occasional glimpses of patterning or 'poetic' syntax serve only to highlight their absence elsewhere. For example there is a degree of parallelism between sentences beginning with the subject 'you'. There is also grammatical parallelism in the two lines:

> How they hated you while you lived!
> How they wept for you once you were dead!

The adjective 'dead', though it has no syntactic parallel with the preceding line, is semantically linked to 'lived'. Such parallelism is, however, often found in political rhetoric, a genre with which this polemical diatribe, by virtue of its subject matter, has much in common. Consider also lines 3 and 4:

> In academies that smell of abattoirs
> Your poems are still studied

Here there is a fronting of information contained in a prepositional phrase ('In academies that smell of abattoirs'). This is a construction much favoured in poetry. Interestingly, this comes, like the syllabic and prosodic patterning referred to above, near the beginning of the poem, and thus establishes a hint of convention, making its later absence more marked.

Given the length of the poem (186 words), however, syntactic patterning and deviation are not intense, especially when compared with that in the advertisement (nine words).

Lexis and metaphor

The lexis is 'ordinary' rather than 'poetic'. Almost the only lexical cohesion of note is the lexical chain created by the sustained metaphor of sheep: 'like sheep', 'bleated', 'abattoirs', 'bleated', 'herded'. But this comparison is a cliché: a fact which, paradoxically, makes it deviant in poetry, where, traditionally, clichés are avoided. The only other metaphor in Bond's poem is another standard one that of drowning in mud about which I have more to say below.

Intertextuality

Poor in prosodic, grammatical, lexical, and metaphorical innovation, the poem is rich in intertextual meanings. These, like schemata, must be described with a specified reader or group of readers in mind. At this point, it is necessary to become personal, especially as this is a poem written by, and perhaps primarily for, members of the post-war generation in Britain. I am such a reader myself, and I assume that there are several allusions which will be shared by others like me. The intertextual allusions which I have noticed are listed in Table 1. For other readers there may well be more or less, and the effect of the poem may be quite different.

Evoked reference	'Trigger' in poem
'My subject is war and the pity of war,' (Wilfred Owen [1920] 1931, p. 40)	'bleated at the pity of it' (line 2) 'only bleated! The pity!' (lines 9–10)
'He was brought as a lamb to the slaughter. (Isaiah 53:7)	'like sheep ... abattoirs' (lines 1, 3)
'Guttering choking drowning' (Wilfred Owen: 'Dulce et Decorum Est')	'You turned the earth to mud! Yet complain you drowned in it' (lines 5–6)
'The whole herd rushed down the steep bank into the lake and died in the water.' (Matthew 8:28–32)	'they herded you over the cliffs to be rid of you' (line 22)
'We will remember them.' (Laurence Binyon: 'For the Fallen')	'We will not forget!' (line 32)
'Then Jesus said, Father forgive them for they know not what they do.' (Luke 23:34)	'We will not forgive!' (line 33)
'Father forgive.' 'Lest we forget.' (On war memorials)	

Table 1   Intertextuality in the poem 'First World War Poets' by Edward Bond

Schemata

Here again, hypotheses must relate to particular readers. Let us specify, then, British readers who received a Christian education during the twenty-five years following the Second World War. For these readers, a good deal of time and emotional intensity was devoted to:

- study of the First World War poets (especially Wilfred Owen)
- study of the New Testament (in the Authorized or Revised Standard version)
- an annual Remembrance Service
- study of nineteenth- and early twentieth-century poetry.

We can therefore hypothesize that, for such readers, the intertextual references listed above will evoke the following schemata. In fact, it was the intention of the educators of that time to inculcate such schemata. For each schema, I give only a selection of default elements.

Theme /

Goal: MAKE LIFE BETTER

Script: FIRST WORLD WAR

      In execution of: Plan BRITAIN DEFEND EMPIRE;

      Events: Slaughter of young men; maiming of young men.

      Results: Sympathy for veterans/invalids; war poetry (see Script
      WAR POETRY); Second World War; Goal AVOID REPETITION of
      another large scale war.

Script: WAR POETRY

      version 1: 'patriotic' poets: Rupert Brooke, Laurence Binyon,
      and others

      version 2: 'anti-war' poets: Wilfred Owen, Siegfried Sassoon,
      and others

      ARE sensitive, brave, good, wasted.

      Events: writing poetry about Script FIRST WORLD WAR.

      Results: Sympathy for soldiers, 'Anti-war' feelings.

Plan: STUDY 'ANTI-WAR' POETRY

Goal: HELP PREVENT WAR

Plan: REMEMBER WAR DEAD

Goal: HELP PREVENT WAR

Plan: FORGIVE ENEMIES

Goal: BRINGS REWARD, MAKES LIFE BETTER

Script: POETRY

      Poetry HAS rhythm, rhyme, and other sound effects, elevated
      language, figurative language, original language.

The poem challenges every element in the schemata (as I have described
them), its poets and their poetry, and the efficacy of remembrance. In
challenging and thus refreshing, the poem leads to what I call schema
refreshment. It refreshes by effecting novel links between schemata for the
conventions of poetry, the conventional philosophy of proponents of war,
and conventional anti-war views. It acts out, in its own poetic form
(or lack of it), the revolution which it advocates in the political sphere.

Yet, paradoxically, it also very obviously, and presumably self-consciously, does what it criticizes – 'bleats' and does not act.

However, the defamiliarisation of ideas about the First World War, etc. does not come especially from patterned or deviant language. In other words, the literariness of this poem cannot then be described in simple Jakobsonian terms. In fact in purely textual terms it is singularly lacking in linguistic interest. Only with reference to schemata, can an argument be made for its literariness at all. Interestingly, one of the schemata it breaks is precisely that which demands that literary language be innovative.

Conclusion: incorporating the reader

The two analyses in this reading attempted to demonstrate the weaknesses of the Jakobsonian approach in isolation, and the greater power of a linguistic description working in concert with a description related to certain reader-specific schemata. The Jakobsonian approach in other words should not be abandoned, but supplemented by some description of the reader.

The reader-dependency of literariness was overlooked by Jakobson, despite the fact that the terms in which he chose to express his theory imply very strongly the presence of the reader. If language has a poetic 'function' then it must do something to somebody – the reader – and if that function reflects a 'set towards the message', then it must be a 'set' by somebody – again the reader. The analyses of the advert and poem point clearly to the limitations of Jakobson's attempt to identify and characterize literariness at the linguistic level in isolation. The density of formal patterning and deviation in the advertisement will not raise it, in most people's estimation, into the literary canon. The poem, by contrast, lacks linguistic patterning and deviation, yet may still be regarded as literary. Whether it is so regarded will depend upon the reader, and it is precisely the kind of poem which, because of its viewpoint and technique, will arouse very different judgements. Such judgements will vary with the political outlook and schemata of the reader, and the degree to which the attempted disruption of them is valued. On the other hand, both the advertisement and the poem are vulnerable to reclassification as audiences change. It is not difficult, in the contemporary world, to imagine a readership which might reclassify both.

Reference

BOND, E. (1978) 'First World War Poets' in *Theatre Poems and Songs*. London, Methuen.

Source: adapted from COOK, G. (1994) *Discourse and Literature*, Oxford, Chapter 6, Oxford University Press.

READING C: Narrative skill in *Bilgewater*'s prologue

Mick Short, Jonathan Culpeper and Elena Semino

Preliminary narratological observations and different notions of 'context'

In narratological terms, it would appear that the **focalizer** of the prologue is the candidate. By focalizer we mean the character whose perspective the majority of the passage is seen from (Bal, 1997). We would be very surprised if you, the reader, had come to any other conclusion and we will spell out in some detail why we think this is the case.

But first let us focus on the sequence in which the three interviews are presented. The novel opens with the end of an interview, which turns out to be the third one for the candidate that day. Then there is a flashback to the first and second interviews (sentences 14–17 and 18–37 respectively). After the flashback we do not immediately return to the point at which the main narrative had been interrupted but to the *beginning* of the third interview. It is not until sentence 50 that the narrative returns to the point where the flashback started after sentence 12.

Within the perspective of Sperber and Wilson's (1995) relevance theory, the opening of the novel comes with a presumption of its own optimal relevance. The lack of chronological sequencing in the presentation of the three interviews can be seen as a source of processing effort (as compared with a chronological presentation). In the reader's search for optimal relevance, this additional processing effort needs to be offset by a suitable set of effects: additional assumptions which could not have been derived from a chronological presentation of events. The communicating of assumptions to do with the candidate's confused state of mind can be seen as a possible effect of the cognitively 'expensive' way in which the interviews are introduced.

Crucial to this whole process of establishing relevance is the reader's selection of a 'context' within which the processing of each segment of a text leads to the greatest cognitive effects with the smallest cognitive effort. Sperber and Wilson describe 'context', in purely cognitive terms, as the subset of the reader's existing assumptions against which information is processed in order to arrive at new assumptions. They stress that the context against which a text is processed is not fixed, but is a dynamic construct which evolves during processing, as new assumptions are incorporated, old assumptions are weakened or cancelled, and different sections of world knowledge are applied to the interpretation of new information.

Other theories of cognition would see the different types of assumptions in Sperber and Wilson's broad notion of 'context' as belonging to different types of 'context'. Generally speaking, it is possible to draw distinctions between at least four types of 'context' relevant to text processing, which are outlined below. It needs to be stressed that we do not aim at a complete typology of different types of context, but rather seek to identify types of context which (1) are involved in making sense of a text, and (2) can add clarity and precision in textual analysis.

1   *The context that one segment of text provides for another*. This is frequently referred to as the co-text. The notion of co-text might be divided into two sub-types. The first relates to surface form. Foregrounding strategies may attract the reader's attention to the surface form. An example from the prologue is the parallelism 'cold, cold, cold', where the form 'cold' unexpectedly acts as co-text to the same form. We will briefly return to this example later. The second aspect of the notion of co-text relates to semantic structure. This could include the semantic colouring one word lends another, a phenomenon that has been referred to as **semantic prosody** (Louw, 1993). We will discuss this below in relation to the prologue's words 'cold' and 'frosty'.

2   *The context that is projected by the text itself or, in other words, the scenario that the reader constructs in processing the text*. This is known as the text world. In the case of the prologue to Bilgewater, the context projected by the text itself is that where a female candidate is going through a set of interviews for a place at the University of Cambridge.

3   *The context of the reader's prior knowledge of the world, i.e. the schemata that the reader applies to the processing of the text*.

4   *The extra-linguistic context in which communication takes place*. This can be variously approached as a physical, social or cognitive entity. Strictly speaking, this type of context is not highly relevant to the current analysis, since the writer and the reader do not share a physical environment in which communication takes place. Nevertheless, the particular context of reception in which the reader processes the text may well affect processing in significant ways. For example, if you had encountered *Bilgewater* in the context of an examination and had you known that your tutor favoured particular interpretative strategies, you may well have read the text with a rather different set of goals and assumptions from those of someone simply reading the novel for pleasure.

The relationship between sociocultural context and the reading process is explored in Chapter 9.

In the case of *Bilgewater*, the reader needs to activate schemata about (university) interviews, Cambridge, young people, and so on, in order to make sense of the text, and indeed to be able to construct context (2) above, the text world. Different understandings of the text will result from differences in the nature and amount of schematic knowledge the reader possesses about the places and experiences described in the novel. While it can be expected that any reader of the novel will have a schema for INTERVIEWS as gate-keeping encounters, only readers familiar with a university system like the

British one will have a version of the schema where the aim of the interview is to verify the interviewee's suitability to study towards a particular degree at a particular university.

How the prologue establishes sympathy

In this and the next section, we will illustrate how the first three types of context identified in the previous section are involved in an understanding and appreciation of *Bilgewater* and thus skilfully engage the reader to sympathise with the candidate. However, our main focus will be on the projected text world, and how textual features and prior knowledge are involved in its creation. In this section, we will pay particular attention to the creation of perspective or point of view in the text world, and, then, we will pay particular attention to the creation of *character* in the text world.

One aspect of the creation of a context of situation can be seen in the *in media res* beginning of the novel. The definite reference of 'the interview' in sentence 1 leads us to presuppose that we must be being given a perspective which assumes that the identity of the interview being referred to is already known. The use of the cognitive verb 'seemed' also helps us to infer that the perspective involved is probably that of a character in the story, and particularly of a character who is not in control of when the interview ends (in other words, someone other than the interviewer). Sentence 2 is, however, indeterminate with respect to viewpoint. It is perhaps most likely to be seen as a statement by a third-person narrator, external to both of the characters, but it could conceivably also be anchored within the perspective of either of the characters.

Sentence 3, however, is clearly anchored within the viewpoint of the candidate. We are presented with an outline of the Principal against the background of a window from a position in front of her, in which we would expect the candidate to be placed. Given schematic assumptions which readers have about interviews and how they are normally conducted, we expect the interviewer and interviewee to be seated facing one another. In other words, lexical items like 'interview', 'Principal' and 'candidate' have led us to make reference to a pre-existing schema, or more specifically a script, which we have for interviews in general and interviews for university places in particular. The activation of this script in turn helps us to establish the viewpoint from which most of the things presented are being described (the viewpoint of focalizer).

So far, in beginning to establish the linguistic bases for the observation that the candidate is the focalizer for most of the prologue, we have used three different kinds of trigger, which Short has outlined in his checklist of viewpoint indicators: given vs. new information, cognitive verbs and linguistic triggers for schema-activation (Short, 1996). These mechanisms all help locate the candidate as the focalizer, and they are used a number of times in the passage. There are, however, a large number of other ways in which the focalized viewpoint is established and maintained. In sentence 4, for example, the evaluative lexis in the phrase 'bleak and brutal' can be seen as indicating the candidate's attitude to the weather, and 'soft seat but wooden arms' in sentence 6 represents the candidate's contrasting tactile experience of the chair she is sitting in.

Another significant viewpoint indicator is the use of thought presentation (Leech and Short, 1981) exclusively for the candidate, thus allowing us access to her mind, but no-one else's. In the second paragraph, she is subject of the verb 'wondered' in sentences 5, 7, 8 and 10. This is, though, a report of the candidate's thought. It is a necessarily indirect expression of what the candidate is thinking herself. As the passage unfolds, the thought presentation becomes more direct and vivid, as in the presentation of the candidate's direct thought stream in sentences 23–9 marked off by brackets. Direct thought presentation for the candidate then becomes fairly prevalent in the rest of the passage. For example sentences 38–49 and the final two sentences of the passage are all arguably in this format. The move from indirect to direct thought presentation, is likely, other things being equal, to lead the reader to sympathise with the candidate. Given that most people will have schematic knowledge (or more specifically, in Cook's 1994 vocabulary, a theme schema) of the feelings of uncertainty and lack of power induced by being interviewed (e.g. for a university place or a job), that push towards sympathy appears to have no reason to be resisted. The Principal, on the other hand, appears more distant from us. It is not just that we do not see into her thoughts. When she speaks, in sentences 51–2 and 54–6, her speech is represented via the thought of the candidate.

See Chapter 3, Section 3.2, on first-person narrators and third-person narrators.

This effect of moving closer to the candidate as focalizer is achieved in other ways. The first two paragraphs have only third-person references to the characters and the narrative tense is past. This configuration of third-person reference and past tense is that normally associated with a third-person narrator. But by the time we get to sentence 33, in the middle of paragraph 6, we have been moved to a very different narratorial format, namely that of a first-person present-tense narrator. As it is the candidate who produces the narration, we have clearly been moved closer to her in viewpoint and sympathy terms. These changes do not all take place at the same time however, and so the reader is moved gradually to the new narrator-viewpoint position. The first narration sentence in the present tense is sentence 32 in paragraph 6. But the previous two narratorial sentences (20–21) were elliptical and tenseless, and in any case were separated from sentence 32 by 56 words (10 sentences) of thought and speech presentation. The change from third- to first-person narratorial format is finally achieved in sentence 33, but again the change does not appear to be sudden. Firstly, the last third-person reference to the candidate is in sentence 14 (paragraph 3). Then, in the second half of that sentence, and the following one, the candidate is referred to through a generalizing version of the second-person pronoun 'you'. From then on, until sentence 33, no narratorial reference is made to the candidate directly. This is achieved by the prevalence of grammatically elliptical sentences which avoid specifying both tense and person-reference. The consequence of this strategy is that the form of the narration changes quite quickly but in a way that is unlikely to be noticed on first reading by many readers, thus achieving within a short stretch of text a subtle intensification in our feelings of closeness with the candidate.

The projected text world, characterisation and suspense

Having spent some time establishing how the events are represented to us through the viewpoint of the candidate, we now examine how suspense is effected in the prologue leaving the reader to ask whether the candidate will accept the offer of a place.

If the issue as to whether the candidate has been offered a place is to be solved by indirect methods, this is even more the case for the question of whether or not the candidate will accept the place. The fact that she asks the questions 'Shall I come here?' and 'Would I like it after all?' suggests that at the very least she must be unsure as to what to do, and there have been a number of sentences where her discomfort has been made clear in connotative terms. In addition to 'the bleak and brutal Cambridge afternoon' of sentence 4, we also have the unpleasant characterization of the first interview in sentence 14 ('... carping, snappish, harsh, watchful – unfriendly even before you had your hand off the door handle'), the comment that this is 'typical' of Cambridge in sentence 16, the depersonalized way in which the Principal is referred to in sentences 45–9 ('She is a mass. Beneath the fuzz a mass. A massive intelligence clicking and ticking away – observing, assessing, sifting, pigeonholing. Not a feeling, not an emotion, not a dizzy thought. A formidable woman.') and, finally, the candidate's feeling of damp and cold in the courtyard after the interview ('But it is damp, old, cold, cold, cold') (68).

But balanced against those negative evaluations there are more positive ones. The second interview was 'Polite though. Not so bad' (20–21), the Principal has a 'very nice coat, too. Fur. Nice fur. Something human then about her somewhere' 58–61) and the courtyard is 'frosty, of lovely proportions' (65).

The positive characterization of the cold in the courtyard (sentence 65), as opposed to the negative one of sentence 68, relates to a type of context we have referred to as co-text. At the level of the word, co-text relates to the study of collocation, or, put simply, 'the company words keep.' The words 'cold' and 'frosty' gain their typical semantic associations from the lexical contexts in which they usually occur. A cursory look at examples from the British National Corpus reveals that 'cold' is frequently coordinated with words like 'lonely', 'afraid', 'dirty', 'hungry', and 'depressing'. 'Frosty', on the other hand, has fairly neutral connotations when it is used literally, but is frequently used metaphorically in contexts of social discomfort: 'Britain and China's sometimes frosty relations', 'has been given a frosty reception', 'cool to the point of frosty formality', 'frosty stare', 'the atmosphere is decidedly frosty as Charles and Diana begin their tour of Korea.' In sentence 68 of the prologue, 'cold' is part of the normal pattern in that it is grammatically paralleled with 'damp' and 'old' (but see immediately below). 'Frosty', however, is paralleled by 'of lovely proportions', a positive evaluation.

In addition to the opposing lexical characterizations above, we can point to a series of paralleled contrastive phrases, clauses and sentences using 'but' which have the same effect:

> her ageing **but** rather pretty hair (3)
> a soft seat **but** wooden arms (5)
> I survey them coolly **but** not without respect (35)
> I might get in on this one. **But** don't think it is a good sign (36–7)
> lights are coming on one by one. **But** it is damp, old, cold, cold, cold. (67–8)

In all of these examples, positive and negative characterizations of the same phenomenon are contrasted through grammatical parallelism. Not surprisingly, it appears that the candidate's decision as to whether to go to Cambridge or not is fairly finely balanced. This is also suggested by sentences 68–9, which occur very near the end of the prologue: 'But it is damp, old, cold, cold, cold. Cold as home' (68–9). The repetition of 'cold' three times in the context of 'damp' and 'cold' in 68 makes the negative evaluation seem very final, but then the following elliptical sentence (69) appears to 'latch on' to the syntax of 68 and adds a simile which involves the positive connotations of 'home', a word which connects both with where she comes from ('the far far north' (55) so that cold is associated with home), and also with the Principal, who shakes her hand in 'quite a northern way' (57). The fact that the positive co-textual associations come at the end and are linked back to the Principal lead us to infer that she probably will go to Cambridge after all, in spite of her reservations.

Conclusion

We hope to have laid bare some of the factors involved in Jane Gardam's skilful writing. She rapidly induces our sympathy for the prototypically young, vulnerable and confused prospective student, by invoking relevant schemata and moving us, via carefully orchestrated shifts in style of narration, tense, viewpoint markers and speech and thought presentation, from a relatively externalized, dispassionate perspective to one where we sympathise strongly with the candidate and look forward to her story in the rest of the novel. All this is achieved through Gardam's careful manipulation of language and her sensitivity to how readers respond to co-textual linguistic patterning, invoke stored schematic knowledge on the basis of textual stimulus and infer appropriate contexts in constructing the fictional world of the novel as they read.

References

BAL, M. (1997) *Narratology, Introduction to the Theory of Narrative*, 2nd edn, Toronto, Toronto University Press.

GARDAM, J. (1978) *Bilgewater*, London, Abacus.

LOUW, B. (1993) 'Irony in the text or sincerity in the writer?: The diagnostic potential of semantic prosodies', in M. BAKER, G. FRANCIS and E. TOGNINI-BONELLI (eds) *Text and Technology: In Honour of John Sinclair*, Amsterdam, John Benjamins.

SHORT, M. (1996) *Exploring the Language of Poems, Plays and Prose*, London, Longman.

Source: adapted from SHORT, M., CULPEPER, J. and SEMINO, E. (2000) 'Language and context: Jane Gardam's *Bilgewater*' in T. BEX, M. BURKE and P. STOCKWELL, *Contextualised Stylistics*, pp. 131–151, Rodopi, Amsterdam, which contains a much fuller analysis of *Bilgewater's* prologue.

Readers and writers

Theresa Lillis

9.1 Introduction

Literariness and sociocultural practice

Allow about
20 minutes

Read the two texts below. Drawing on your reading of earlier chapters, consider the following questions:

*   To what extent would you describe these as literary texts? Which linguistic and other semiotic features in the texts are influencing your judgements?

*   What factors – such as your educational, social or linguistic background (or even your reading of earlier chapters in this book) – do you think may be influencing your judgements?

Text A

> We quail, money makes us quail.
> It has got us down, we grovel before it in strange terror.
> And no wonder, for money has a fearful cruel power among men.
>
> But it is not money we are so terrified of,
> it is the collective money-madness of mankind.
> For mankind says with one voice: How much is he worth?
> Has he no money? Then let him eat dirt, and go cold —
>
> (Lawrence, 1972, p. 486)

Text B

> *Gate*, he thought as he walked out of the gate. *Gate. Road. Stones. Sky. Rain.*
> > *Gate.*
> > *Road.*
> > *Stones.*
> > *Sky.*
> > *Rain.*
>
> The rain on his skin was warm. The laterite rock under his feet jagged. He knew where he was going. He noticed everything. Each leaf. Each tree. Each cloud in the starless sky. Each step he took.

Koo-koo kookum theevandi
Kooki paadum theevandi
Rapakal odum theevandi
Thalannu nilkum theevandi

That was the first lesson he had learned in school. A poem about a train.

(Roy, 1997, pp. 284–5)

Comment

You may have identified Text A as a poem because of linguistic features such as repetition (*quail*) and alliteration (*money-madness of mankind*) and other semiotic features such as its layout and punctuation. But you may have resisted identifying it as a poem because some of the language may seem ordinary or the subject matter too prosaic. You may have identified Text B as a narrative because of the layout and specific features such as the material action processes (see Chapter 3) in *he walked*, *he was going*, *each step he took*. But there may be features in Text B which surprised you, such as the different genres within the same extract or the use of a language in addition to English.

At this point, it is worth considering how your own reading and judgement of these texts may have been influenced by a whole range of factors. I am sure, for example, that conventional notions I learned about poetry at school will have helped inform my judgement that Text A is a 'poem'. However, my readings of a much wider variety of texts as an adult – in many forms and in several languages – means that I was more willing to suspend judgement about Text B and concentrate instead on simply making sense of it and enjoying it. We will return to both texts later in the chapter.

In this chapter I will draw on a sociocultural approach to readers and writers, which I am using to encompass two things:

- To indicate that my interest is in real readers and writers.
- To acknowledge the importance of context for understanding what real readers and writers do in, and with, literary texts. The different ways in which context is understood – cultural, psychological, social, linguistic – and the extent to which context shapes what readers and writers do will be a point of debate in the chapter.

9.2 From 'idealised' to 'real' readers

Throughout this book, there have been many references to how readers engage with creative texts and judge literary quality. In Chapter 7, Sharon Goodman mapped out the different ways in which idealised readers (alongside viewers of film and users of multimedia technology) can be conceptualised in relation to the different kinds of multimodal texts with which they are engaging. In Chapter 8, Kieran O'Halloran explored how idealised readers engage with texts, by drawing on relevance theory and schema theory. This interest in how readers respond to and engage with texts stands in contrast to a Formalist tradition in literary studies (reflected in Chapters 2 and 3 for example), where the focus is on textual properties. Key early writers who shifted their focus away from the formal properties of texts to a focus on how readers 'received' texts are Jauss (1982) and Iser (1974). In focusing on the reader, Jauss in particular was interested in not only bringing the reader, rather than the text, to the centre of literary studies but in historicising judgements of aesthetic and literary quality (see discussions in Holub, 1984). This interest is echoed in Reading B which I will discuss later in this chapter.

In order to foreground the importance of the reader in any interpretation of the workings of texts, Iser (1974) introduced the influential notion of the 'implied reader': which is close to the notion of the 'idealised reader' discussed in Chapter 8. A range of terms have since been used to refer to the 'reader', some of these are listed and briefly explained below.

Different ways of theorising the reader

Example	Key writers	Description
Implied (idealised) reader	Iser (1974)	There is a particular reading implied in any given text which the reader is likely to take up.
Informed reader	Fish (1980)	The way readers read texts is based on their understanding of particular reading conventions. We all learn to read in particular ways depending on our membership of particular communities.
De-centred/free reader and readings	Barthes (1975) Derrida (1978)	No one reading position inheres in any text. Barthes (1975) points to the many readings possible, whereas Derrida (1978) stresses the complete freedom of the reader to construe meanings in a text.
Resistant readers	Kristeva (1986) Said (1993)	The text sets up particular ways for the reader to respond to the text but the reader (consciously or unconsciously) reads against the intended/implied meanings and reading positions.

However, whilst an interest in readers has been prominent for some time, this interest has been theoretical in nature, with comparatively little empirical research exploring what real readers do. In Chapter 8, Kieran O'Halloran illustrated how one kind of empirical research – the use of language data in large corpora – can help ground claims made about readers on the basis of theory or intuition. I continue with this empirical interest in the following sections where I discuss different ways in which researchers are setting out to explore how real readers engage with literary texts.

9.3 Expert readers

I will begin by focusing on perhaps the largest source of data available to us about how a particular category of real readers – 'expert readers' – read literary texts: the body of work known as 'literary criticism'. The sheer number of readings by academics and literary and cultural commentators, available to us in written form, exceeds in many cases the number of literary texts being written about. But what kind of readings are these? And what do they tell us about what gets counted and valued as literary creativity?

ACTIVITY 2   **Expert readings**

Allow about
45 minutes

Read through the expert readings below on the work of three canonical British writers. For my purposes here, it is not important whether you are familiar with the text that the expert reader is commenting on (although if you have read the text you may wish to consider the extent to which your perspective matches that of the expert). As you read, consider the following questions:

- What do the expert readers focus on? To what extent do they focus on the literariness or literary value of the texts?

- Are you surprised by any of their comments? Which ones?

- What, if any, similarities can you see between the experts' readings?

Don't worry if you cannot fully understand what the experts are saying – they are after all very specialised kinds of writings. You may find it helpful to make a note of any key terms or phrases that the writers use which seem to you symptomatic of the kind of focus, or judgements, being made.

Expert Reading 1: Sandra Gilbert and Susan Gubar (1979) on *Wuthering Heights* by Emily Brontë

As we have seen, Catherine has no meaningful choices. Driven from Wuthering Heights to Thrushcross Grange by her brother's marriage, seized by Thrushcross Grange and held fast in the jaws of reason, education, decorum, she cannot do otherwise than as she does, must marry Edgar because there is no one else for her to marry and a lady must marry. Indeed, her self-justifying description of her love for Edgar – 'I love the ground under his feet, and the air over his head, and everything he touches, and every word he says' (chap. 9) – is a bitter parody of a genteel romantic declaration which shows how effective her education has been in indoctrinating her with the literary romanticism deemed suitable for young ladies, the swooning 'feminity' that identifies all energies with the charisma of fathers/lovers/husbands. Her concomitant explanation that it would 'degrade' her to marry Heathcliff is an equally inevitable product of her education, for her fall into ladyhood has been accompanied by Heathcliff's reduction to an equivalent position of female powerlessness, and Catherine has learned, correctly, that if it is degrading to be a woman it is even more degrading to be *like* a woman. Just as Milton's Eve, therefore, being already fallen, had no meaningful choice despite Milton's best efforts to prove otherwise, so Catherine has no real choice. Given the patriarchal nature of culture, women must fall – that is, they are already fallen because doomed to fall.

(Gilbert and Gubar, 1979, p. 277)

Expert Reading 2: Edward Said (1993) on *Mansfield Park* by Jane Austen

In too small a space, you cannot see clearly, you cannot think clearly, you cannot have regulation or attention of the proper sort. The fineness of Austen's detail ('the solitary candle was held between himself and the paper, without any reference to her possible convenience') renders very precisely the dangers of unsociability, of lonely insularity, of diminished awareness that are rectified in larger and better administered spaces.

That such spaces are not available to Fanny by direct inheritance, legal title, by propinquity, contiguity, or adjacence (Mansfield Park and Portsmouth are separated by many hours' journey) is precisely Austen's point. To earn the right to Mansfield Park you must first leave home as a kind of indentured servant or, to put the case in extreme terms, as a kind of transported commodity – this, clearly, is the fate of Fanny and her brother William – but then you have the promise of future wealth. I think Austen sees what Fanny does as a domestic or small-scale movement in space that corresponds to Sir Thomas, her mentor, the man whose estate she inherits. The two movements depend on each other. [...]

My contention is that by that very odd combination of casualness and stress, Austen reveals herself to be *assuming* (just as Fanny assumes, in both senses of the word) the importance of an empire to the situation at home.

(Said, 1993, pp. 105–6)

Expert Reading 3: Roger Simmonds (2003) 'Money madness' in a collection of poems, *Pansies* by D.H. Lawrence

Language is not 'deformed' or made 'strange' as the Russian Formalists insisted it must be in order to be alienating. Perversely however, the poem is alienating (to which the critical response over the years surely testifies), not merely in its abandonment of the conventionally 'strange' techniques of poetry, but in its unique use of 'ordinary' language. The poem develops out of its initial direct, generalising assertion, 'Money is our madness, our vast collective madness', expressing ideas that are not normally voiced by either the poet or the man in the street. Any reader familiar with poetry in the slightest would certainly not expect this directness of expression adopted by the speaker (phrases such as 'of course', 'I doubt', 'no wonder', 'it is') without any form of irony; such matter-of-fact language is disconcertingly 'unpoetic'. However, this ordinariness (an ordinariness inherent in the poem's personal quality – the speaker does not appear to conceal his feelings and the reader feels that he is being addressed directly and even incorporated into a collective identity with the speaker 'We') is counterpoised by clear yet unusual images such as 'grain of insanity' and 'we grovel before it in strange terror'. [...]

[T]he multiplicity of discourses which invade 'Money-Madness' and their 'dialogic' 'interillumination' of each other, in fact immediately deter any attempt at reading the poem as a self-contained and autonomous entity.

(Simmonds, 2003, pp. 126, 138)

Comment

Expert Reading 1

Sandra Gilbert and Susan Gubar focus on the constraints under which Catherine, the female protagonist in the novel, has to live and act. They illustrate how the character is forced to act in accordance with the expectations surrounding what it means to be a woman in nineteenth-century England. As a woman living in a patriarchal society she is ultimately 'doomed to fall' should she step outside of the dominant conventions. A similar fate awaits male characters – in this case, Heathcliff – as both female and male protagonists who step outside of dominant gendered conventions must suffer fatal consequences.

This kind of commentary illustrates some key strands of feminist literary criticism: (a) an interest in exploring the ways in which female characters are portrayed; (b) an interest in exploring binary constructions of gender – male/female, masculine/feminine – and the values attached to these; (c) a focus on patriarchy and of power relations. The extract here is an example of a tradition that grew up particularly in the 1970s and 1980s in the UK and US, involving re-reading classic texts through the lens of feminist perspectives (see Belsey and Moore, 1997; Mills, 1995).

Expert Reading 2

In this brief extract from a longer discussion, you have glimpsed what is often referred to as a **postcolonialist** expert reading. Some clues to Said's particular reading of *Mansfield Park* can be found in a number of key phrases and words: most obviously in the final phrase *the importance of an empire*, but also, *better administered spaces* at the end of the first paragraph, and *indentured servant* and *transported commodity* in the second paragraph. Said situates the production of this specific novel within a broader historical context, in particular in the context of Britain's imperialist expansion. Focusing on the way in which space is dealt with in the novel – here linking the experiences of the main character Fanny in her small family home with her new home, the large Mansfield Park – he argues that larger spaces (empire) are being represented as necessary and desirable for the stability and efficiency of smaller spaces (Britain). Said goes on to argue that such texts not only reflected the historical context of their production, Britain's imperialist expansion, but contributed to normalising expectations surrounding the Britain–empire relationship. The kind of commentary that Said makes here is part of a larger tradition, which Said himself helped to forge, often referred to as postcolonialist criticism, where the relationship between Britain and the empire, as played out in literary texts, is made the object of analysis and explored critically (for example, Ashcroft et al., 2002).

Interestingly, neither Expert Reading 1 or 2 seeks to define the literary value of the texts by making close reference to their formal features. (Could this be because the texts they discuss have achieved canonical status and therefore their literary value does not need establishing?) Rather, they offer specific kinds of readings drawing on particular theoretical and critical frameworks. To what extent do you think such readings seem to reflect the notion of the 'resistant reader' referred to in Section 9.2?

Expert Reading 3

In contrast, Roger Simmonds focuses on a text whose literary value is under some dispute. His focus, and indeed his aim, in discussing these texts seems to be to claim a literariness for the texts and, in so doing, argue that they have literary value. The texts are a collection of poems by D.H. Lawrence, *Pansies*, which have been criticised by some commentators for being 'weak', indeed for being 'bad poetry'. You have read an extract from the specific poem Simmonds is talking about, *Money-madness*, at the beginning of this chapter in Text A, and may have already made a judgement about its value. In his comments on this poem, Simmonds argues that it does not conform to Formalist notions of literariness since it does not 'make strange' through the use of any typical poetic techniques. Instead, Lawrence's use of ordinary language constitutes a strangeness in itself. Simmonds' key argument is that Lawrence's texts should not be evaluated against any straightforward notion of poetry as a specific genre. Drawing on the work of Bakhtin (1981, 1986), as indicated in the extract by his use of terms such as 'dialogic' and 'interillumination', he goes on to argue that the texts should be viewed as an 'interplay of languages' and forms.

There are several points I wish to draw from this focus on experts' readings. Reading from a sociocultural perspective is understood not (primarily) as an individual phenomenon but rather as a situated activity, that is, as taking place and being shaped by the context of a particular time and place, and as involving the following:

1   Traditions of reading emerge from specific communities.

2   Readings are embedded in particular theoretical traditions.

3   Texts can be read and valued differently.

I shall look at these in more detail now.

Traditions of reading emerge from specific communities

See also discussion of Fish (1980) in Chapter 7, as well as in Reading A of Chapter 8.

Together, the three expert readings here illustrate a particular way of engaging with literary texts which are associated with a particular community: the 'academic' or 'intellectual' community. They seem to reflect Fish's notion of the 'informed reader', reading from the position of a particular 'interpretive community' (Fish, 1980) that engages with texts in rather specialised ways. These readers, predominantly academics working at universities, devote considerable time and energy to developing specialist readings. Within this broad community, subcommunities or specialist subfields are also identifiable, depending on the tradition the academics are working within.

Readings are embedded in particular theoretical traditions

In order to make sense of literary texts, readers draw (explicitly or implicitly) on theoretical traditions of reading. This is particularly evident in expert readings of literature since the 1960s where theory itself became explicitly valued as a tool for making sense of literary texts. These theories can have something in common with more Formalist traditions – staying close to issues of texts and language – such as Simmond's use of a particular philosophy of language, Bakhtin's – or broader critical traditions, such as feminism and postcolonialism, as illustrated in Expert Readings 1 and 2 above. (You will recall that you met critical-ideological approaches in Chapter 6).

For a more detailed discussion of Bakhtin, see Chapter 9 of the companion volume, **Maybin and Swann (2006)**.

The prominence of different theories in academic fields at specific historical moments influences experts' interpretations of texts and assumptions about their value. A good example here is that the work of the Russian philosopher Mikhail Bakhtin has become prominent in recent years in the Western academy and his concepts are influencing the ways in which expert readers are making sense of and valuing texts. This is illustrated in Simmonds' use of the Bakhtinian terms 'dialogic', 'interillumination' – which he uses to add authority to his claim that Lawrence's texts should be valued rather than dismissed.

Texts can be read and valued differently

Whilst context is central to a sociocultural approach, context does not rigidly determine how any text will be read. This is illustrated in the debate referred to above amongst one specific community of readers – expert readers – as to whether Lawrence's collection of poems *Pansies* has any literary merit. Of course, such differences and debates about the value of any text may be even greater when we consider views from a range of communities. Whether familiar or not with the original texts discussed above, you may have found some of the experts' comments unusual or surprising. For example, as someone who has read quite a lot of feminist theory, I found Gilbert and Gubar's comments quite familiar. But as someone less familiar with postcolonial critique, I was surprised by Said's emphasis on the significance of space in *Mansfield Park*. We each – whether expert or non-expert – bring our own specific history to the reading of texts. The extent to which a range of readings is possible or desirable is a theme I will return to in this chapter.

Expert readers, whilst a small proportion of readers overall, often function as 'professional valuers' (Bourdieu, 1984), mediating the readings of others directly and indirectly: through the teaching of English literature in formal education contexts and through the production of secondary texts (such as cultural commentary in the media for instance), which may exert an influence on the wider public.

The importance attributed to expert readings is a debated topic and controversial in a number of ways. For example, it may be argued that:

1   Such readings bear no relation to what other real or 'ordinary' readers do.
2   Such approaches exert too powerful an influence over the discipline of literary studies itself.

In the next section, I want to begin to explore the first of these two issues.

9.4 Ordinary readers: a psycho-formalist approach

A relatively recent focus in the study of literature is what is often referred to as the 'empirical study of literature' or the 'science of literature'. It involves psychologists and linguists taking account of how people actually engage with literary texts, as a way of learning more about the workings of the human mind (see for example László and Cupchik, 2003). So though this approach takes account of empirical data, it is actually only focused on the psychology of reading literary texts with an emphasis on how textual forms lead to meanings in readers' heads. Hence, the approach is also known as **psycho-formalism**.

This approach includes a wide range of interests such as: the relationship between personality types and reading and writing; 'processing' patterns, such as the effect of the speed of reading on how people read; comprehension strategies (see, for example, Zwaan, 1993; Schram and Steen, 2001). A significant strand involves research into how ordinary readers respond to literary texts, and, in particular, how they recognise and respond to features typically viewed as 'literary', such as rhyme, alliteration, and different forms of linguistic deviation. This kind of research can also involve empirical investigation of modelling of cognitive processes, the kind of modelling that you saw in Chapter 8. Psycho-formalism can indeed be seen as part of cognitive poetics (see Chapters 1 and 8). Also, to some extent, this approach represents a continuity with the Formalist approach outlined in Chapters 1 and 2. However, in contrast to Formalist approaches which focus solely (or primarily) on the features in literary texts, psycho-formalism aims to explore whether there are particular textual features that are recognised as 'literary' by all readers and what it is about the features of texts that the reader notices. Psycho-formalism thus combines an inherency approach to literariness with a cognitive approach to readers' engagement with literary texts.

ACTIVITY 3   **What is poetic?**

Allow about
20 minutes

Before you read more about this kind of approach to the study of literature and literariness, read part II of James Joyce's poem, *Chamber Music*. Make a note of any features of the text which you consider to be 'poetic'.

CHAMBER MUSIC

(II)

The twilight turns from amethyst
  To deep and deeper blue,
The lamp fills with a pale green glow
  The trees of the avenue.

The old piano plays an air,
  Sedate and slow and gay;
She bends upon the yellow keys,
  Her head inclines this way.

Shy thoughts and grave wide eyes and hands
  That wander as they list –
The twilight turns to darker blue
  With lights of amethyst.

(James Joyce, *Poems and Shorter Writings*, Faber and Faber, London 1991 and 2001 p. 14)

Comment

What kinds of features did you identify? You may have commented on the line layout and division into three verses or stanzas, rhyme (e.g. blue/avenue, gay/way, list/amethyst) and half-rhyme (e.g. glow/avenue), alliteration (piano/plays, sedate/slow), metaphor (twilight turns from amethyst).

Hanauer (1996) sought to manipulate what he considered to be the 'poetic' features of extracts of this poem by Joyce, which he termed *graphic* and *phonetic*, in order to explore whether these influence how readers read them. 'Graphic' manipulation involved changing punctuation, spacing, capitalisation; and phonetic manipulations involved changing alliteration, consonance, assonance and rhyme. Readers were presented with manipulated versions classified as high, medium, low: high (the original version), medium (where some changes were made), low where a greater number of changes were made. The manipulations are illustrated below. It was anticipated that a 'high' version would result in a reader categorising the text as 'clearly a poem', in contrast to a low version which would result in a classification such as 'not a poem at all'. Readers were asked to categorise the extent to which the text was a poem along a rating scale. Hanauer was particularly interested to see whether there were different responses from two groups of readers; 'expert', that is students with a degree in literature, and 'novice' readers, that is entry-degree level students of literary texts (note that those readers defined as 'expert' here are not the professional experts discussed in Section 9.3). His findings reflect a midway position between an inherency position (textual features of literariness do appear objectively to exist) and what is known as the **conventionalist** position, i.e., where readers are influenced by the conventions they associate with literariness.

Hanauer's manipulation of some 'poetic features' in James Joyce's poem 'Chamber Music II'

Examples of stimulus items

1   High phonetic/high graphic
The twilight turns from amethyst
To deep and deeper blue,
The lamp fills with a pale green glow
The trees of the avenue.

The old piano plays an air,
Sedate and slow and gay;

2   High phonetics/low graphics
The twilight turns from amethyst to deep and deeper blue, the lamp fills with a pale green glow the trees of the avenue. The old piano plays an air, sedate and slow and gay;

3   Low phonetic/high graphic
The twilight changes from purple
To deep and darker blue,
The lamp fills with a faint glow
The trees of the street.
The aged piano creates an air,
Quiet and slow and joyful;

4   Low phonetic/low graphic
The twilight changes from purple   to deep and darker blue,   the lamp fills with a faint glow   the trees of the street. The aged piano creates an air,   quiet and slow and joyful;

(Adapted from Hanauer, 1996, pp. 376–8)

ACTIVITY 4   **The form of reading (Reading A)**

You can find out more about Hanauer's findings and similar studies in
Reading A, 'The form of reading: Empirical studies of literariness' by Miall and
Kuiken. Please turn to this now.

- As you read, notice how Miall and Kuiken are arguing in part for a return
  to a Formalist approach to the text alongside a focus on ordinary readers'
  judgements of literariness.

- Pay attention too to their criticisms of literary theory, as exemplified in the
  kind of 'expert readings' I discussed in Section 9.3 above.

- What criticisms do Miall and Kuiken make of literary theory? In their view,
  what does an 'empirical' approach offer that a traditional literary theory
  approach does not?

Comment

The principal criticisms that Miall and Kuiken make against much literary theory
are as follows:

- Particular, elite ways of talking about literature have developed which are
  known only by literary theorists and are actually very different from the
  way ordinary readers talk about and engage with real texts.

- Claims made in expert readings are not based on any empirical
  (observable) evidence, but rather on theory and furthermore on experts'
  use of a particular theory.

- Literary theorists do not focus on real readers but rather only make claims
  about what real readers do, or in some instances, even dismiss the value
  of considering what real readers do.

- In many expert readings, the text and its textual features have become
  largely irrelevant as part of a wider backlash against 'Formalism'.

- 'Literariness' as a textual phenomenon is ignored.

- Undue importance is often given to the social context of readings and the
  ways in which socially shaped reading conventions determine individual
  readers' engagement with texts.

Miall and Kuiken argue that there is a need to focus both on the text –
dismissed in anti-Formalist approaches – and the ordinary or actual reader –
dismissed in particular by those emphasising the sociocultural, or the
'conventionalist position' – and to explore the interrelationship between text
and reader empirically. An important starting point in their empirical approach
is to work with a notion of literariness as a textual phenomenon identifiable in
features associated with 'foregrounding' and to explore whether and how

readers' engagement with texts are driven by such features. However, their approach should not be viewed as simply a return to Russian and Prague school Formalism but rather as an attempt to maintain an inherency focus whilst adopting a cognitive perspective on reader processing – what the reader does while reading the text. This is similar to Guy Cook's perspective (see Chapter 8, Reading B) though Cook performs no empirical investigation. Miall and Kuiken set out to explore the extent to which literariness can be said to be both a property of texts and also, crucially, of reader 'processing'. They review the work by Hanauer (1996), discussed above, but re-interpret the study to argue for a greater significance of formal features of the text (Zwann, 1991, also argues for this midway position). Miall and Kuiken argue that although novice readers recognise fewer poetic features than expert readers, they do in fact recognise certain features as poetic and the distribution of features recognised as poetic is similar across both groups. Furthermore, Miall and Kuiken argue that their own previous studies offer support for their argument that literariness can be identified as a textual feature by all readers, regardless of previous education or experience (see Miall and Kuiken, 1994).

ACTIVITY 5   How useful is Miall and Kuiken's approach?

Allow about
15 minutes

You may find it useful at this point to consider the usefulness of Miall and Kuiken's approach. Consider the extent to which you think their work is successful in meeting their aim of focusing on ordinary readers' identification of, and responses to, the literariness of texts.

Comment

Miall and Kuiken's work is clearly important in illustrating the need to revisit dominant positions within literary debate and in offering a way in which this can be done, drawing on a specific psychological tradition. Despite this, my own view is that there are shortcomings in their approach. Firstly, it seems to me that through their references to 'ordinary person', 'ordinary reader', 'actual reader', they fall into a similar trap to those theorists they set out to criticise: whilst literary theory can be accused of dealing with the reader in abstraction, Miall and Kuiken's work might be seen as suffering from generalisation. Who is the 'reader' they are talking about? In all studies mentioned, the readers are university students, albeit from different disciplines and at different stages in their studies – viewed along a continuum from novice to experts. To what extent can these readers be considered 'ordinary' or representative of other groups of readers? This is a concern raised by those working within the same tradition as Miall and Kuiken and clearly needs to be addressed (for example, Schram and Steen, 2001, p. 9). A second and related concern I have is the focus on the reader and the text with only minimal reference to the social context in which reading takes place. I think Miall and Kuiken may be missing important sociocultural dimensions to the relationship between readers and texts. You may wish to spend some time here thinking about the extent to which you agree or disagree.

9.5 Real readers: a social practices approach

The focus in Section 9.4 was on readers' responses to the literariness of literary texts, as identifiable by particular textual features. In this section, I want to turn to a contrasting approach to the ways readers engage with literary texts that emphasises the importance of social, cultural and historical context.

ACTIVITY 6   **Literature as social practice (Reading B)**

Now read Reading B, 'Literature as social practice', by Geoff Hall. As you read, consider the following questions:

- Which groups of readers does Hall focus on, and why?

- What kinds of research methods are used to explore how ordinary readers engage with literary texts? In what ways do these differ from those reported by Miall and Kuiken?

- What do readers seem to value in literary texts? In what ways does this contrast with the focus of 'professional valuers'– the 'expert readers' – in Section 9.3?

Comment

There are strong connections between the work of Hall and the work of Miall and Kuiken, notably: (a) the criticism of the lack of interest in literary studies in how real readers engage with literary texts and (b) in the call for more research on what actual readers do. Albeit in very different ways, both readings indicate the human interest in literary and creative texts, whether this is construed as the universal human impulse to literariness (as in Miall and Kuiken) or as a socially variable and valuable dimension to human existence (as in Hall). Both readings also illustrate the difficulties surrounding research into what real readers do. Miall and Kuiken resolve this by setting up experimental conditions as a way of controlling both the nature of the texts (texts are pre-selected) and readers' possible responses to them (specific questions are asked). Hall, in contrast, provides an overview of ethnographic research which seeks to document in different ways (survey, archive, observation or interview) how ordinary readers engage with literary texts in their everyday lives. The key elements of ethnography or an ethnographic approach are summarised below.

> ## Key features of ethnography
>
> - It is concerned with analysis of empirical data that is systematically selected for the purpose.
> - Those data come from 'real-world' contexts, rather than being produced under experimental conditions created by the researcher.
> - Data is gathered from a range of sources including observation, interviews and documentation.
> - The focus is a single setting or group, of relatively small scale, or a small number of these. In life-history research the focus may even be a single individual.
> - Much ethnography seeks to explore participants' perspectives.
> - The analysis of the data involves interpretation of the meanings and functions of human actions and mainly takes the form of verbal descriptions and explanations, with quantification and statistical analysis playing a subordinate role at most.
>
> (Adapted from Lillis and McKinney, 2003, p. 139, after Hammersley 1994)

In one sense, the psycho-formalist and social practices approaches are not incompatible: rather, the findings they generate can be treated as simply providing different answers to very different questions about 'real' readers.

All the same, there is a fundamental distinction between the two approaches related to the disciplinary positions and traditions from which each are writing and their consequent research interests. Miall and Kuiken draw on cognitive psychology and Formalist traditions to place the individual reader's response to pre-selected texts – whose literariness is taken as a given – at the centre of their lens. In contrast, Hall draws on ethnographic approaches from anthropology and sociolinguistic traditions to focus on readers as socially, culturally and historically located beings whose engagement with and valuing of literary texts is shaped (albeit in unpredictable ways) by the contexts in which they live. The rather different premises upon which their different research is based leads them to contrasting perspectives on the notion of the 'value' of literary texts. Miall and Kuiken look in towards the text to locate 'value': the value of the text resides in its literariness which can be identified in specific textual features as recognised by readers. Hall in contrast tends to look outwards beyond the text, to consider how readers value texts as they relate to their lives: for example, the value of the *Iliad* to the working class male reader is that it transports him to a more beautiful world; the value of reading a particular text in the reading club lies not so much in the text itself but in its capacity to generate discussion amongst members (often university graduates) – its 'discussability'.

9.6 Expert writers

Writing and social context

I began this chapter by focusing on expert readers and some of the specific ways in which they engage with literary texts. I now want to turn to expert creative writers and to consider how a sociocultural approach can illuminate some aspects of their literary and creative activity. I focus in particular on three dimensions:

1   The social contexts in which creative writers develop their relationships with language;

2   The ways in which writers draw on specific linguistic and other semiotic resources in different linguistic and cultural contexts;

3   The significance of different kinds of readers for writers at different moments in time.

ACTIVITY 7   Writing and social background

Allow about
15 minutes

Read the extract below by Ian McEwan, the English writer whose short stories and novels have earned him many awards since the 1970s. Consider how he locates his own creative use of language in his childhood and social background.

Mother tongue

I don't write like my mother, Rose, but for many years I spoke like her, and her particular, timorous relationship with language has shaped my own. There are people who move confidently within their own horizons of speech [...] My mother was never like that. She never owned the language that she spoke. Her displacement within the intricacies of English class, and the uncertainty that went with it, taught her to regard language as something that might go off in her face, like a letter bomb. A word bomb. I've inherited her wariness, or more accurately, I learned it as a child. I used to think I would have to spend a lifetime shaking it off. Now I know that's impossible, and unnecessary, and that you have got to work with what you've got. [...]

During my early teens, as my education progressed, I was purged of my mother's more obvious traits, usually by a kind of literary osmosis — when I was 14 I was an entranced reader of the handful of novels Iris Murdoch had published. I was also reading Graham Greene. Slowly, *nothink* [nothing], *somethink* [something], *cestificate* [certificate], *skelington* [skeleton], *chimley* [chimney] all went, as well as the double negatives and mismatched plurals. [...]

When I started writing seriously, in 1970, I may have dropped all or most of my mother's ways with words, but I still had her attitudes, her wariness, her unsureness of touch. Many writers let their sentences unfold experimentally on the page in order to find out what they are, where they are going, and how they can be shaped. I would sit without a pen in my hand, framing a sentence in my mind, often losing the beginning as I reached the end, and only when the thing was secure and complete would I set it down. I would stare at it suspiciously. Did it really say what I meant? Did it contain an error or ambiguity that I could not see? Was it making a fool of me? Hours of effort produced very little, and very little satisfaction? From the outside, this slowness and hesitancy may have looked like artistic scrupulousness, and I was happy to present it that way, or let others do it for me. [...] In fact, my method represented an uncertainty that was partly social: I was joining the great conversation of literature which generally was not conducted in the language of Rose or my not-so-distant younger self. The voices of giants were rumbling over my head as I piped up to begin, as it were, my own conversation on the train.

(McEwan, 2002, pp. 34–8)

Comment

McEwan describes his journey as a developing creative writer from the close community of his childhood towards the rather more abstract and diffuse community of writers of literature. In this journey, his first community – mother, home, English working and lower middle class – powerfully shapes the particular kind of relationship he has with the resources of the creative writer-language. He learns to treat language carefully and cautiously rather than as something to be taken for granted. It is this treatment of language as an object to hold, to manipulate, to struggle with and against which helps him, perhaps surprisingly given his sense of being an outsider, to join 'the great conversation of literature'.

I am struck by the way in which McEwan's account of his journey seems to reflect the development of a 'poetic relationship' with language. This signals a shift away from Jakobson's emphasis on the poetic function of language-as-text (as discussed in Chapter 1) towards a recognition of the importance of poetic relations *with* language-as-text. McEwan's comments suggest that the creative writer has to develop a sensitivity whereby language as a whole is 'made strange', that is, it becomes visible as an object to be consciously forged by the writer.

English as a global writing resource

ACTIVITY 8   **Interview with Arundhati Roy (Reading C)**

Now read Reading C, which is an extract from an interview with the writer Arundhati Roy, whose first fictional book *The God of Small Things* was published to worldwide acclaim in 1997. As you read, consider:

- the extent to which she considers context has shaped her creative writing;
- her own creative writing processes, and how these differ from McEwan's.

Note: Before you read the interview you may like to re-read the brief extract from Roy's book, which is Text B at the beginning of this chapter.

Comment

The significance of Roy's particular sociocultural context for writing initially seems obvious: her writings reflect her Indian background in terms of focus and language; the setting, characters, themes of *The God of Small Things* are closely bound up with India, and in particular Kerala, the state where she grew up and where the novel is set; the language used by Roy reflects the use of Indian Englishes as well as multilingualism – Malayalam the official language of Kerala is used, as illustrated in the poem in Text B at the beginning of the chapter where Malayalam is represented in the Roman alphabet. However, as her response to the interviewer's first question indicates, Roy resists the call to define her book, and indeed her self, in any simple geographical and cultural terms; and, more specifically, she challenges the assumption that it is possible to offer one overarching definition of what it means to talk of 'India' and being 'Indian'. Roy instead emphasises a less nationally bound notion of context as being important for herself development and interests as a creative writer, notably the rural environment and landscape she inhabits. As such, she sees a stronger rationale for linking herself with writers of the American South, such as Mark Twain and Harper Lee who likewise deal with rural contexts, than with Indian writers such as Salman Rushdie. She also points to the importance of context in terms of her previous training as an architect, which influences how she views the creative process.

Unlike McEwan who describes the extreme caution with which he approaches language and crafts his sentences, Roy says that she doesn't think about language at all and gives an impression of writing freely and without effort, 'I don't rewrite'. However, she also indicates a more deliberate and conscious approach to the construction of her texts overall.

As a trained architect, she approaches her writing in terms of patterns and motifs. She also states that she is 'creative with the design of words', graphically and rhythmically (later = *Lay. Ter*, an owl = *A Nowl*). Punctuation and layout, in addition to words, are all central to her creative acts of design. She also points to her sheer pleasure in the use of repetition which makes her feel safe because it has a 'rocking feeling'. In general, she emphasises pleasure as a central dimension to her creative writing, which contrasts with the struggle emphasised by McEwan.

Roy's comments in the interview alongside her own writings reflect the nature of English as a global semiotic resource and three specific ways in which such a resource is being used by creative writers. Firstly, English involves multiple varieties because of its use across many different geographical and linguistic contexts, reflected in more recent specific geographical labels, such as 'Indian English' (for example, McArthur, 2002, pp. 317–26) or using 'small initial letter english(es)' to distinguish between the many varieties and a Standard (UK or US) English. The Nigerian writer, Chinua Achebe, commenting on the colonial legacy of English, points to the desirability of this varied nature: 'So my answer to the question *Can an African ever learn English well enough to be able to use it effectively in creative writing?* is certainly yes. If on the other hand you ask: *Can he ever learn to use it like a native speaker?* I should say, I hope not' (Achebe, 1975, p. 100).

Secondly, a common feature of texts written out of multilingual contexts is the juxtaposition of English with other languages, which you saw illustrated at the beginning of the chapter in Text B, where a poem in Malayalam is included. Including an untranslated section of text, as Roy does here, is one of many ways in which writers in multilingual contexts are bringing other languages into a primarily English medium text. Ashcroft et al. (2002) refer to the use of new forms of english(es) and the juxtaposition of englishes with other languages as 'strategies of appropriation': that is, remaking resources for meaning making in accordance with writers' desires and contexts for meaning.

Thirdly, as indicated by Roy's use of *Lay. Ter*, writers – whether monolingual or multilingual users of English – do not simply use words from existing varieties of languages, but also invent their own usages. This is a long standing tradition which was most famously evident in the work of James Joyce, particularly in his most linguistically complex novel, *Finnegan's Wake*. Consider below the explanations Joyce gave of the meanings of just some of the vocabulary he invented.

Language used in *Finnegan's Wake* by James Joyce

The following are a selection of glosses from a letter from James Joyce to Harriett Shaw Weaver, dated 13 May 1927:

Mickelmassed (Michael, his conqueror = much heaped up)

Norronesen = Old Norse, warrior

Irenean = Irish born, peace (eirene)

secrest = superlative of most secret

soorcelossness = the source is not to be found any more than that of the Nile

Wolken = woollen cap of clouds (wolking – welkin)

Frowned = He is crowned with the frown of the deaf

bottles (battles) = the vintner's dream of Satan & Michael

far ear = far east

mous at hand = close at hand

Hairfluke (Herrfluch = the curse of the Lord on you for not talking louder, he tries to grab her hair which he hopes to catch by a fluke

If he could bad twig her
        twig = Anglo-Irish = understand
        twig = beat with a twig.

(Cited in Ellman, 1975, pp. 321–2)

As indicated by McEwan's comments and in Joyce's inventions above, in many ways the key issue faced by all creative writers (whatever their social, cultural and linguistic context) is the same: how to take control over the 'stuff' of writing – the range of linguistic and other semiotic resources – and to create these anew adopting a range of stylistic strategies, many of which have been discussed in several chapters in this book.

However, a focus on what multilingual writers are doing with English/es alongside other languages expands what constitutes 'new' or creative uses of language beyond existing or conventional stylistic devices and the ways in which we think about such devices. More fundamentally, the use of real and invented languages serves to problematise any straightforward notions about what constitutes literariness. Consider the multilingual graphic/phonemic playfulness of Roy: where would these fit into the framework of features manipulated in Hanauer's experiment? How might a multilingual stylistic lens extend what is understood by 'foregrounding' and 'deviation', discussed in Chapters 1 and 2? My feeling is that in any attempt to explore empirically how real readers respond to specific features of texts, there is a need: (a) to extend the range of features (for example to include varieties of Englishes) and representations of these feature; (b) to include a greater diversity of readers in any attempt to explore what constitutes any particular poetic practice, for example, 'deviation'.

A writer's readers

I want to conclude this section by focusing for a moment on the relationship between the creative writer, the reader and the text. In Reading C, Roy seems to signal not one but several kinds of relationships with her readers. The first is one of handing over control to the reader: she refers to her writing as a 'gift' to readers who will 'do with it what they want', echoing the idea of the 'free reader' discussed in Section 9.2. But she also expresses frustration with readers who want to classify her in any straightforward way, such as 'magical realist' and talks of such categorisations leading to 'mis-readings' of her text. Roy's reference to categorisation suggests to me that the latter group of readers are those 'expert' readers, discussed in Section 9.3, whereas the former group seems to be the lay or ordinary reader. The ways in which writers and readers negotiate the meaning and values of any one text is clearly complex. Doris Lessing for example was clearly disappointed with the (mis)readings of her book *The Golden Notebook*. From her perspective the key theme was one of personal breakdown as a process of healing:

> But nobody so much as noticed this central theme, because the book was instantly belittled, by friendly reviewers as well as by hostile ones, as being about the sex war, or was claimed by women as a useful weapon in the sex war.
>
> (Lessing, 1974, p. viii)

But Lessing offered an explanation for such misreadings, pointing to the significance of historical context:

> Some books are not read in the right way because they have skipped a stage of opinion, [and] assume a crystallisation of information in society which has not yet taken place. This book was written as if the attitudes that have been created by the Women's Liberation movements already existed. It came out first ten years ago, in 1962. If it were coming out now for the first time it might be read, and not merely reacted to.
>
> (Lessing, 1974, p. ix)

Lessing thus offers a sociocultural dimension to the abstract notion of the 'implied reader' referred to in Section 9.2: whilst a writer may consider that her text affords the opportunity for a particular reading, readers may only be able to take up such a reading at a particular cultural and historical moment. Reflecting on her experience of grappling with the apparent disjunction between her desire to have her book read in a particular way and readers' real responses to it, Lessing reaches the following conclusion:

> And from this kind of thought has emerged a new conclusion: which is that it is not only childish of a writer to want readers to see what he sees, to understand the shape and aim of a novel as he sees it – his wanting this means that he has not understood a most fundamental point. Which is that the book is alive and potent and fructifying and able to promote thought and discussion *only* when its plan and shape and intention are not understood, because that moment of seeing the shape and plan and intention is also the moment when there isn't anything more to be got out of it.

(Lessing, 1974, p. xx)

9.7 Ordinary readers and writers: creative relations around texts

For the main part of this chapter, we have focused on readers and writers as distinct groups of people who engage in different kinds of activities, notably writers writing and readers reading. But of course this relationship is much more fluid in a number of ways. Readers are not simply recipients of a writer's meanings but rather engage creatively with texts, often according to contexts and interests. Moreover, the act of reading plays a powerful part in shaping the resources and practices of creative writers, as indicated by McEwan: writers are readers too. A writer's writing is always informed by readings, and in part re-writings of others words. 'Writing back' and 'talking back', as mentioned in Reading B, are phrases which explicitly signal this in the context of feminist and postcolonial writing, and are used to describe a particular kind of response – challenging, responding, resisting – to traditionally conceived notions, products and practices of 'English literature'. In this chapter, I have briefly considered how both expert readers and some expert writers engage in this re-writing 'English literature' (see also Hooks, 1994; Rushdie, 1982). The interrelationship between writer/reader is stressed in Bakhtin's theory of language and captured in his notion of **addressivity**.

Addressivity and meaning making

An essential (constitutive) marker of the utterance is its quality of being directed to someone, its *addressivity*. As distinct from the signifying units of a language – words and sentences – that are impersonal, belonging to nobody and addressed to nobody, the utterance has both an author [...] and an addressee. This addressee can be an immediate participant-interlocutor in an everyday dialogue, a differentiated collective of specialists in some particular area of cultural communication, a more or less differentiated public, ethnic group, contemporaries, like-minded people, opponents and enemies, a subordinate, a superior, someone who is lower, higher, familiar, foreign, and so forth. And it can also be an indefinite, unconcretized *other* ... All these varieties and conceptions of the addressee are determined by that area of human activity and everyday life to which the given utterance is related. Both the composition and, particularly, the style of the utterance depend on those to whom the utterance is addressed, how the speaker (or writer) senses and imagines his addressees, and the force of their effect on the utterance.

(Bakhtin, 1986, p. 95)

Bakhtin's emphasis on the powerfully interactive relationship between writers, readers and texts has increasingly been taken up in recent times in approaches to literature and literary activity. I briefly considered in Section 9.3 the way in which Simmonds was using some notions from Bakhtin. Rob Pope, a UK-based academic, has set out a Bakhtinian-inspired 'manifesto' which challenges any presumed dichotomies between writing and reading.

Pope's manifesto for re-writing

1   In reading texts we re-write them.

2   Interpretation *of* texts always entails interaction *with* texts.

3   Interaction *with* texts always entails intervention *in* text.

4   One text leads to another and another and another – so we had better grasp texts *intertextually*, through comparison and contrast.

5   One's own words and worlds are necessarily implicated in those of others – so we had better grasp our selves *interpersonally*, through dialogue, voicing conflict as well as consensus.

6   De-construction is best realized through *re*-construction – taking apart to put back together differently. Just as *critique* is always, in a radical sense, about *re-creation*.

7   For *interpretation* can be done through acts of creative performance no less than of critical commentary. And we are all in various ways both performers *and* commentators, critics *and* creators.

8   In sum, *textual changes* always involve *social exchanges*. You can't have the one without ... the other ... and one another ...

(Pope, 2003, p. 108)

Pope argues that this manifesto should be at the centre of English literature education. Such education should encourage students, the 'ordinary readers and writers', in this context, to explore the complexity, tensions and dynamism evident in the creative and diverse practices of 'expert writers' and 'expert readers': they should not be passive consumers of traditional or dominant conceptions of what counts as literature, literariness and creativity. Rather they should be allowed and encouraged to 'intervene', that is, actively engage in a range of activities which allow them to 'play' with texts at the same time as critically explore them. Through such activity, they become more aware of the tensions surrounding what counts as the study of English literature itself.

ACTIVITY 9   Rewriting a poem

Allow about
45 minutes

In order to find out what Pope means by encouraging students to 'play' with texts, read the two tasks below that he devised. After you have read the tasks, *either* try out one of the tasks *or* read examples of other students' attempts at such tasks. Consider how engaging in such activities may encourage students to reflect on the nature of literariness and literary creativity.

Note: If you have never tried 'rewriting' before, this may seem a strange activity; but just have a go.

Task 1

Re-write Text A so as to produce an alternative which is different yet recognizably related. (Restrict your changes to word choice and combination: deleting words, substituting with different words, changing the word order, changing the sequence of lines, adding new words, etc.).

Task 2

Combine and adapt Text A with Text B so as to produce a single text suitable as a script for use in TV, film, stage or other performance, or print (e.g. as part of a novel, educational textbook, and so on).

Text A

I'm Nobody! Who are you?
Are you – Nobody – Too?
Then there's a pair of us?
Don't tell! They'd advertise – you know!

How dreary to be Somebody!
How public – like a Frog –
To tell one's name – the livelong June
To an admiring Bog!

(Emily Dickinson, c.1861)

Text B

Emily Dickinson (1830–1886) lived all her life in Amherst, Massachusetts. By the age of 30 she had become an almost total recluse, never leaving her father's house and garden, dressing completely in white, receiving very few visitors, and carrying on most of her many friendships almost solely by means of correspondence. She wrote well over a thousand poems; but only seven were published during her lifetime. The above poem was not one of them. It was found after her death, with the rest, carefully parcelled up in a chest. Since their first publication in the 1890s (when many of Dickinson's distinctive features of punctuation, meter and idiom were 'standardized' or simply changed by the editors), her poems have steadily increased in readership and reputation. Indeed, since the 1970s 'Emily Dickinson' (as both poet and personality) has become something of an enigmatic cult figure – especially amongst feminists. The above text (ed. Thomas Johnson *The Complete Poems of Emily Dickinson*, London, Faber, 1970, no. 288. p. 133) restores Dickinson's word choice, punctuation and meter to that in what appears to be the final draft. It is generally agreed to be a preferable text to that produced by Todd and Higginson in 1890.

(Adapted from Pope, 2003, pp. 117–18)

Below are examples of some responses to Tasks 1 and 2 that Pope gives.

Responses to Task 1

1

> I was somebody! But who were you?
> Couldn't you have been some body too?
> Then there were two of us. Oh well … !
> We should've welcomed her – no?
> How dreary to be a nobody
> How private like a toad
> Croaking her name the dark night through
> Under a stone by the road.

2

> He's nobody! Who's she?
> Is she nobody, too?
> They they are a pair, aren't they?
> We'd banish them, wouldn't we?
>
> How dreary to be nobody!
> How private, like a fish
> Never telling its name the livelong day
> To the scorning pond!

Responses to Task 2

1

This was read aloud by two voices: a woman for the text of the letter; a man for the narrative commentary in brackets.

Amherst Mass

April 1, c. 1861

Dear Nobody,

> I'm Emily – Who are you?
> I know you are – not Emily – too
> (She said, putting on her white dress)
> There's only one of me. You as well.
> (She said, not answering the door)
> Don't tell – or pull the bell.
> (She said, in a letter to a friend
> which was not posted
> till much later
> then advertised and published and read
> by EVERYBODY!)

Yours

E.D.

2

from: e.d.@FROPG
to: x.h.@BOG

Who are you, dear Mr Higginson?
I'm NOBODY!
Are you – Nobody – too?

But do not advertise there's a pair of us. You know how dreary it is to be Somebody! During your life time and become something of an enigma, a cult figure – especially amongst feminists. To become public and to tell my name and use my word choice punctuation and metre. It is generally agreed to be a preferable text to an admiring bog.

(From Pope, 2003, pp. 118–21)

Comment

Students both created text (as exemplified above) and reflected on the text in written commentaries. In these commentaries, Pope's students drew attention to different aspects of text creation. As Pope had anticipated, commentaries on the rewriting activity of Task A tended to be inherency based, that is focusing inwards to the text and the impact of changing specific textual elements such as use of pronouns, punctuation, rhyme, alliteration. In contrast, commentaries on Task B looked outwards towards relations between text and context and the extent to which decisions about creating texts were influenced by notions of particular literary conventions (Todd and Higginson clearly had their own) and also assumptions about readers/viewers. Pope's aim was to draw students into debates at the heart of English literature – most obviously here Formalist or inherency notions as compared with conventionalist or sociocultural approaches: in so doing, the aim is not only to make visible the nature of the discipline and study of 'literature' itself but to involve students in discussing what the focus should be, why and how.

ACTIVITY 10   You as reader and writer

Allow about
20 minutes

Pope emphasises that creativity is something that everyone can engage in, echoing views of linguists such as Ronald Carter (2004, p. 13) who states that 'linguistic creativity is not simply a property of exceptional people but an exceptional property of all people'. As we come to the end of this chapter, I suggest you take a few moments to reflect on your ideas about literary creativity and how they relate to you as a reader and writer.

- *You as reader* – Return to the extracts A and B at the beginning of the chapter. Having worked through this chapter, are you reading them any differently now? Does thinking of them as 'gifts from the author' (Roy) change your reading in any way? If so, how?

- *You as writer* – Do you normally think of yourself as a writer, a creative writer? Has your view of yourself changed in any way after reading this chapter? If so, how?

9.8 Conclusion

Throughout this chapter I have explored some different ways of considering how real readers and writers engage with literary texts. It is always tempting to see different perspectives as antagonistic. However, you may like to consider what the different perspectives in this chapter offer. Here I summarise some of my own responses below. To what extent are they similar to or different from yours?

What do I learn from a focus on expert readings?

I don't need to see expert readings as offering the definitive reading of a particular text. Rather I see them as windows onto possible worlds of the writer, the text and readers. They offer me ways of reading and re-reading texts which I might not have considered on my own.

What do I learn from the psycho-formalist perspective?

I appreciate the commitment to exploring what real readers do. And I take away a curiosity to know more about the human impulse to literariness and creativity.

How does a sociohistorical approach help me understand literariness?

For me this offers a way of thinking about reading and writing at a particular historical moment which in turn usefully opens up debates about what we mean by literariness. I am also left with more questions to explore. What is the nature of the association between literariness and print forms in different contexts? And in relation to psycho-formalism, what is the relation between a human impulse to literariness and specific sociohistorical contexts?

What can I learn about writing from 'real writers'?

It reminds me that at the heart of the study of literature are writers and writing ... not critics or theory.

And as for the participants in the study of literature?

That these are many and varied ... that the processes and practices surrounding the world of literary activity, however defined, need to be brought to the heart of the institutional study of literature.

In this book, you have been a participant in the study of literary creativity. In engaging with many different authorial and conceptual perspectives, as well as a range of contexts, genres and tasks, you have been actively exploring the nature of literariness and how this relates, or does not, to literary value. You may find it interesting now to reflect on the ways in which your participation in this book has altered, or confirmed, your previous understanding of literary creativity.

READING A: Extracts from 'The form of reading: Empirical studies of literariness'

David S. Miall and Don Kuiken

Challenging the dismissal of Formalism

Literary theory in recent decades has dissolved one form of elitism and replaced it with another. One specialized ideology, according to which immersion in a timeless literary canon fostered personal sensibility and cultural refinement, has been found more historically constrained than its advocates cared to realize. That doctrine has been replaced by an equally specialized ideology of 'postmodernism' where [...] the examination of literary diversity, from high to low art, from privileged to underprivileged cultures, promises an egalitarian appreciation of the extent to which readers are 'thrown' into socio-historical contexts that embody particular conventions for identifying literariness and guiding reading.

As proponents of this new 'sensibility', literary scholars continue to produce readings of texts and elaborations of literary theory in an institutional culture that is inhabited almost exclusively by fellow scholars and senior students. While this transformed elite 'lives' its specialized ideology, almost no attention is given to the ordinary reader, who, outside of that institutional culture, continues to read for the pleasure of understanding the world of the text. [...] The concerns that an ordinary person revisits while exploring a literary text, such as its style or narrative structure, its author's relation to the reader, or its impact on the reader's understanding or feelings – such concerns now seem of little interest.

[...] If the gap is to be narrowed, it may come from focusing once again on the formal aspects of the literary text through which, we will argue, the ordinary reader's concerns primarily can be located. However, in contrast to earlier, now discredited versions of formalism that explicitly forbade interest in readers, we argue that the formalist dimension of reading can be examined effectively only in cooperation with actual readers. By studying the experience of literary reading and its outcomes, we will begin to map the interaction between reader and text and discover what formal structures created within that interaction warrant reference to such reading as 'literary'. From this perspective, too, we will develop a more ecologically valid approach to understanding the role and functions of literature in general. Why have all cultures, as far as we know, developed a literary culture, whether oral or print? Why do people seek out and read novels and poems, or go to watch plays?

[...] Of course, it may be the case that the vision of today's theorists will become the standard wisdom of tomorrow, just as we all (or almost all) now live within a world view shaped by Darwin and Einstein. However, modern arguments about literary meaning lack one dimension that, in the end, made the arguments of Darwin and Einstein compelling: today's theorists produce no evidence to back up their claims other than their own experience and assumptions and their appeals to other theorists. The empirical dimension, in other words, is absent: naturalistic investigation is considered futile. While Darwin's views were supported, for example, by his observations on a series of finches, [...] studies of literary meaning are carried out within a purely theoretical framework [...]. The study of [...] actual readers is ruled out of order by theorists such as Culler (1981, p. 121): what is of interest, he argues, are the conventions that determine reading, not the experience of real readers; what these conventions might be is, of course, decided *a priori* by Culler and his colleagues. This refusal to check theoretical presuppositions against the reading practices of actual readers calls into question the recent, almost universal dismissal of formalism. Yet *the claims of formalism,* as proposed, for example, by critics from Coleridge to Wimsatt, *have not been falsified by any empirical investigation of whether formalist dynamics underlie the literary reading of ordinary readers.*

[...] At the heart of the formalist proposal, which we elaborate more fully later, is the constructive and transformative nature of the interaction between reader and text. This engagement is driven by textual features that include distinctive and systematic language forms; the resulting interpretive processes in the reader are distinctive to the literary domain. Perhaps the central issue of formalism is that of 'literariness': the claim that literary texts possess certain distinctive forms and features not found in other types of text. It has been common, for example, to attribute 'foregrounding' to literary texts, following Mukařovský's well-known formulation (1964/1932). From this perspective, literary texts are distinguished by the systematic use of figurative and stylistic devices at the phonetic, grammatical, and semantic levels (Van Peer, 1986; Miall and Kuiken, 1994). But if this claim can be invalidated, then other concomitant claims asserted by formalism become untenable. Thus, it is this position that we will now examine in more detail, by reviewing several theoretical and empirical studies, including our own. After that review we will suggest some of the wider implications of the concept of 'literariness' for the function of reading in culture.

See coverage of Mukařovský in Chapter 2.

Literariness

[...]

See also a related argument by Eagleton in Chapter 1, Reading A.

> Anything can be literature, and anything which is regarded as unalterably and unquestionably literature – Shakespeare, for example – can cease to be literature. Any belief that the study of literature is the study of a stable, well-definable entity, as entomology is the study of insects, can be abandoned as a chimera.

(Eagleton, 1983, pp. 10–11)

Eagleton, like Fish [1980], sees literariness as an institutional construct, an artifact defined by the current purposes of a specific 'interpretive community'. At the same time, his statement indicates one source of the confusion that surrounds the issue. A literary experience is created through the interaction of a reader and a text; the object of study is not objectively given as insects are to entomology. By assuming that formal accounts of literariness require a 'stable, well-definable entity' Eagleton essentializes the object in order to dismiss it. Formal properties can be shown, by linguistic or narrative analysis, to inhere in texts, but these do not constitute 'literariness' until they incur a certain quality of attention from a reader. The question at issue is [...] whether readers pay attention only within certain institutional contexts, or whether our psychobiological and psychological organization predispose us to bestow such features with the kind of attention we then recognize as characteristically literary.

Literature, of course, does not function in a social vacuum. Like language itself, for which our brains are pre-programmed before birth, actualization of the response we recognize as literary depends upon the shaping influence of experiences within a human community. But to speak of the social contexts within which art is recognized does not preclude pointing to the 'natural' foundation of its effects, as though the agencies of nature and culture were mutually exclusive (cf. Storey, 1993, p. 62). Thus, Mukařovský, who shows that the borderline of the 'aesthetic' shifts across time according to social conditions, also appeals to the bodily rhythms of the blood and of breathing in understanding music, or to the physics of colour that underlie painting. Such 'constitutive' principles, he argues, provide an essential context against which changes in aesthetic norms are perceived (Mukařovský, 1970, pp. 29–31).

[...] We will focus on whether textual features, rather than readers' expectations, are responsible for initiating literary processing of a particular text. Specifically we will discuss those textual features known as foregrounding, which have been described by Mukařovský (1964/1932) and examined empirically by Van Peer (1986) and Miall and Kuiken (1994). We will critically reconsider [one study (Hanauer, 1996)] that tested whether 'literariness' is a convention and then review evidence from our own research indicating that 'literariness' resides in foregrounded textual features. Although foregrounding is only one component of literariness, [...] we propose that the processes specific to foregrounding offer principles capable of generalization to other distinctive components of literary response.

Empirical studies

[...] In Hanauer's [1996] paper, he describes two main views on how judgements are made of what is poetic: the 'traditional', which gives a central place to formal features of a text, and the 'conventionalist', which emphasizes the conventions that are applied during reading [...]. Hanauer sets out to test the conventionalist and formalist positions against empirical evidence, and for this purpose he sees the text categorization judgement as critical. [...]

Hanauer used two texts. Each was a poem in which Hanauer manipulated 'poetic' features in two ways. First, the phonetic features were altered to produce versions that were low, middle, or high (original version) in such features. For example, in the Joyce poem used, the first line of the 'low' version is 'The twilight changes from purple'; its original version reads 'The twilight turns from amethyst'. Secondly, the graphic form was manipulated by removing initial capitalization, and then by rewriting the lines as prose. Participants were presented with nine versions of the poem that varied these dimensions in every combination. The readers were then asked to rate each version on a continuous scale running from 'clearly a poem' at one end to 'clearly not a poem' at the other. Readers were of two kinds, novice (entry-level literature students) and experienced (holding a degree in literature). The study was replicated with both poems and with both types of reader, with generally similar results.

The ratings of the novice group, especially at the lower end of the ratings scale, were lower than those of the experienced group: as in Hoffstaedter's study (1987) and our own studies, the less experienced readers seem less committed to the act of reading. Hanauer takes this as support for the conventionalist position. It should be noted, however, that to the extent that more of the poetic features are present the closer are the judgements of the two groups of readers. Our own graph based on Hanauer's data for the first poem [see Figure 1] shows this more clearly than Hanauer's report: the more poetic the text, the more judgements of it are independent of literary experience, an argument for the formalist view.

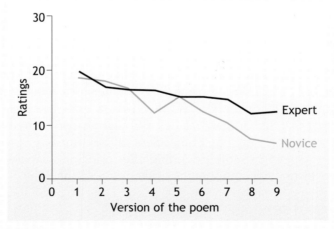

Figure 1   Mean poetic text categorization ratings – a horizontal scale of 'more poetic' to 'less poetic' (derived from Hanauer, 1996).

More striking, however, is the fact that the distribution of judgements across the different texts was largely the same in both groups, as our graph, as well as Hanauer's own [see Figures 2a and 2b], show: in other words, novice readers were as competent as experienced readers in placing texts on a poetic scale according to the degree to which they possessed graphic or phonetic features. [As in Hoffstaedter's study (1987),] the judgements of the novice readers occur at a lower level than those of the experienced readers, a finding that appears to support the conventionalist view. But the close correspondence of the judgements clearly speaks for the formalist view, as the high correlation between them [evident in Figures 2a and 2b] shows [...]. As Hanauer notes: 'both novice and expert literary readers were found to be sensitive to the use of graphic and phonetic information in making poetry categorization judgements and ... these information sources were integrated in a similar way' (Hanauer, 1996, p. 371).

Hanauer concludes that formal features play an important role in categorizing texts. However, 'While sensitivity to formal textual features and the way to integrate this information may stay constant, the value assigned to these textual features was seen to change according to literary educational background' (Hanauer, 1996, p. 374). This last comment seems apt: literary education, among other things, enables a reader to build interpretive strategies upon the observed textual features, that is, to assign them a value within the larger unfolding sense of meaning of the text as a whole. But this is not a strong argument for the conventionalist position. If we take the formalist position to argue for the initiation of poetic processing through readers' recognition of poetic features, then the weight of evidence in Hanauer's study is largely in favour of it.

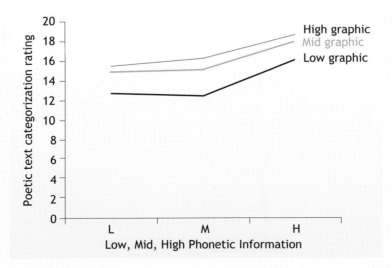

Figure 2a   Mean poetic text categorization rating – **expert** readers (from Hanauer, 1996, reproduced from Poetics **23**, with permission).

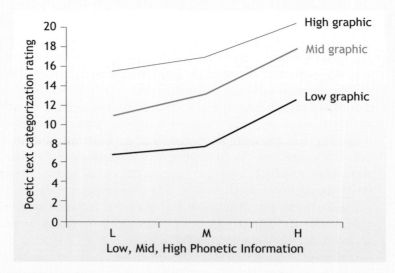

Figure 2b   Mean poetic text categorization ratings – **novice** readers (from Hanauer, 1996, reproduced from Poetics **23**, with permission).

Our own research, particularly the set of studies we reported [...] in *Poetics* (Miall and Kuiken, 1994), can also be seen as evidence for the formalist view, although our main purpose in conducting the studies was not to arbitrate between the two opposing views, as in Hanauer's work. We set out, rather, to ask the question, 'What is the purpose of poetic features?' Or, more precisely, 'What is distinctive about readers' responses to foregrounding? [...]

We took [literary short stories by] Woolf and Mansfield, and coded each segment (roughly one sentence) for foregrounded features at the phonetic, grammatical, and semantic levels. We then elicited several measures from readers, such as reading times per segment and ratings for affect and strikingness. We also employed two types of readers: experienced students of literature, most in their third or fourth year of studies, and introductory psychology students, who had little experience of literature. [...] Both groups read the Woolf and Mansfield stories, and it is notable that the level of correlations with foregrounding is almost the same in both groups. This finding lends support to the hypothesis that all readers appear sensitive to foregrounding, regardless of literary training.

It was also noteworthy that the overall means of the ratings provided by the two groups differed consistently: our experienced readers gave higher affect and strikingness ratings than the psychology students. This suggests that the inexperienced readers were less committed to the reading or less interested in it. Yet, both groups appear to have been almost equally responsive to the presence of foregrounding [...].

In addition, the foregrounding measure correlated significantly with ratings for uncertainty, which we also collected for several stories. This has led us to propose that foregrounding initiates interpretive activity in the reader, first by defamiliarizing the referent of the text (the strikingness rating provides one measure of this) and by arousing feeling; then, the resulting uncertainty causes the reader to search for a context in which the new material can be understood, a process in which feeling plays a key role. Feeling may be the route to relevant concepts, memories, or experiences that the reader has not yet applied to understanding the text. A study of Andringa (1990) seems to support this proposal: examining [responses to a literary text while she was present], she found that expressions of emotion in response to a literary text tended to be followed by evaluations and arguments. This sequence of events provided the main impetus to the development of an interpretation.

Here, we would suggest, lies one of the natural bases of literary response. If the defamiliarization induced during literary reading disturbs the automatic assignment of meaning, then, as Reuven Tsur has argued, disturbing the categorization process 'makes lowly categorized information, as well as rich pre-categorical sensuous information, available to consciousness' (Tsur, 1983, p. 8). This, Tsur adds, 'gives the organism great flexibility, adaptability to ever-changing physical or mental environments'. In other words, the moments of feeling initiated by defamiliarization provide the context within which recategorization can unfold. Elsewhere (Miall, 1995) we have presented neuropsychological evidence for this view of feeling. [...]

Conclusion

In conclusion, we believe that the empirical evidence available on the issue tends to support the formalist hypothesis rather more strongly than the opposing positions. Moreover, we agree with Van Peer, who argues that the theory of literariness 'describes and explains a number of fundamental issues of literature in a powerful and elegant way' (Van Peer, 1995, p. 315). As we remarked at the outset, however, to adopt this position is not to return to dogmatic formalism (e.g. Wimsatt and Beardsley, 1954), but to move forward to more fruitful ground – that of research with actual readers. This research will address the possibility that certain components of reader response, such as the defamiliarization and feeling response to foregrounded text, are 'natural'. Far more general than literary conventions, these components of response may be based on psychobiological, cognitive, and psycholinguistic processes that do as much to shape institutional conventions as they are shaped by them. [...]

References

ANDRINGA, E. (1990) 'Verbal data on literary understanding: a proposal for protocol analysis on two levels', *Poetics*, **19**, pp. 231–57.

CULLER, J. (1981) *The Pursuit of Signs*, London, Routledge and Kegan Paul.

EAGLETON, T. (1983) *Literary Theory: An Introduction*, London, Routledge.

FISH, S. (1980) *Is There a Text in this Class? The Authority of Interpretive Communities*, Cambridge, MA., Harvard University Press.

HANAUER, D. (1996) 'Integrations of phonetic and graphic features in poetic text categorization judgements', *Poetics*, **23**, pp. 363–80.

HOFFSTAEDTER, P. (1987.) 'Poetic text processing and its empirical investigation', *Poetics*, **16**, pp. 75–91.

MIALL, D.S. (1995) 'Anticipation and feeling in literary response: a neuropsychological perspective', *Poetics*, **23**, pp. 275–98.

MIALL, D.S. and KUIKEN, D. (1994) 'Foregrounding, defamiliarization, and affect: response to literary stories', *Poetics*, **22**, pp. 389–407.

MUKAŘOVSKÝ, J. (1964[1932]) 'Standard language and poetic language' in P. GARVIN (ed. and trans.) *A Prague School Reader on Esthetics, Literary Structure, and Style,* Washington, DC., Georgetown University Press.

MUKAŘOVSKÝ, J. (1970) *Aesthetic Function, Norm and Value as Social Facts* (trans. M.E. SUINO) Ann Arbor, MI, University of Michigan Press.

STOREY, R. (1993) ' "I am because my little dog knows me": Prolegomenon to a theory of mimesis' in N. EASTERLIN and B. RIEBLING (eds) *After Poststructuralism: Interdisciplinarity and Literary Theory*, Evanston, IL, Northwestern University Press.

TSUR, R. (1983) *What is Cognitive Poetics?* Papers in Cognitive Poetics, **1**, Tel Aviv, The Katz Research Institute for Hebrew Literature, Tel Aviv University.

VAN PEER, W. (1986) *Stylistics and Psychology: Investigations of Foregrounding*, London, Croom Helm.

VAN PEER, W. (1995) 'The empirical study of (literary) texts', in G. RUSCH (ed.) *Empirical Approaches to Literature: Proceedings of the Fourth Biannual Conference of the International Society for the Empirical Study of Literature* IGEL, Siegen: LUMIS-Publications, Siegen University.

WIMSATT, W.K. and BEARDSLEY, M. (1954) 'The affective fallacy', in W.K. WIMSATT (ed.) *The Verbal Icon*, London, Methuen.

Source: D.S. MIALL and D. KUIKEN (1998) *Poetics*, 25, pp. 327–41.

READING B: Literature as social practice

Geoff Hall

The idea of literature as a social practice (LASP) is that we need to study people's reading and writing activities in the broader contexts of their lives and social interactions. The empirical investigation of what people do with texts and how they find value in literature within the constraints of their own social contexts has been neglected. Suggestive studies are beginning to appear, however, and are highlighted in what follows. In such studies, individuals are seen as social agents, who turn to literature to help them pursue larger purposes in life, such as developing friendships and partnerships, reflecting on their own lives and identities, and the possibilities for future personal intellectual, moral and emotional development. A 'social practice' perspective on literature reading, informed by the work of Street (1993) and others seeks answers to questions like:

* Why do people read and write literature?
* What is their understanding of 'literature'?
* Which people?
* Under what conditions?
* What do people do with and through their literature reading?
* How does this literature reading (and writing) relate to their wider lives?

Research discussed here shows that literary reading means different things to different people according to their life circumstances. It is valued highly by some and often in ways which have tended to be overlooked by literary scholars.

Contradictory perspectives on literature reading

My view is that there are two apparently contradictory perspectives about how ordinary readers read literature:

* Story 1: Literature serves the interest of elites or those more powerful in society
* Story 2: Literature serves the interests of ordinary individuals

The first is the story of the exploitation of literature in the interests of the ruling class or those more powerful in society. For example, literature was introduced in public institutions in Britain as a subject to be examined from the 19th century (Eagleton, 1996) and was designed to meet various demands: the need for literate clerks both in Britain and across the British Empire; to amuse bourgeois women with time on their hands; to respond to the thirst for knowledge of some members of the working classes. Lists of approved works of poetry (primarily), fiction and 'great' writing were presented to the less socially powerful so that predetermined moral lessons would be assimilated (Richardson, 1994).

But the second story, told insistently through a wide range of sources, such as memoirs, diaries, and interviews, reports the value of literature in everyday life and the significance of the epiphanic, that is, 'life changing' text. These are stories of pleasure, resistance, engagement or self-education, a world away from any class, gender or colonial conspiracy to maintain unequal power relations. A frequent consonant story is of an opposition between the stultifyingly, boring experience of reading in school, as compared with the more highly valued private and pleasurable uses of reading.

LASP studies show that both stories have elements of truth for different readers in different times, places and circumstances. Two key themes seem to emerge:

- The works valued and/or what is valued about particular literary works, is often not what academics or critics identify or predict.

- Readers emerge as capable and conscious exploiters of their own reading for their own purposes, even if what they read and how they read can be shown to be influenced by the professional discourses of expert reviewers and professors of literature.

A historical perspective: British working class readers

I have understanding as well as you; I am not inferior to you ...

(Job 12: 3; chalked on the college walls of Christminster by Hardy's working class hero, Jude Fawley, after the University has excluded him. Quoted in Rose, 2001, p. 7)

See also Chapter 8 in **Maybin and Swann (2006)** on the reading practices of British working-class men in the nineteenth century.

Rose's *Intellectual Life of the British Working Classes* (2001) uses a range of anecdotal and statistical sources to tell the story of how British working class men (mainly), in the 19th and 20th centuries, educated themselves through their reading.

Library and institute records, unpublished memoirs, autobiographies and diaries are used as well as Mass Observation surveys (see http://www.massobs.org.uk) and interviews to give a voice to the voiceless. What emerge from this research are preferences for realistic and optimistic literature, and voracious but 'indiscriminate' and opportunistic reading by the self-taught on limited resources. In contrast to Eagleton's claim that literature reading teaches fatalism (Eagleton 1996) ideas of alternative, better lives – were often drawn from 'indiscriminate' reading. Will Crooks, later a Labour member of parliament growing up in the 1890s in extreme poverty in East London, bought a second hand *Iliad* for 2d:

> What a revelation it was to me! Pictures of romance and beauty I had never dreamed of suddenly opened up before my eyes. I was transported from the East End to an enchanted land.
>
> (quoted in Rose, 2001, pp. 4–5)

In an age largely before the radio and cinema, when national newspapers were only slowly replacing local sheets, and many working people could not expect to travel far or often from their own town or village, the thrill of the exotic, of far-off places and utterly alien experiences and ways of life attracted greatly. 'Things that went beyond the small utilities of our lives ... Here in books was a limitless world that I could have for my own' (Northampton cowman's son, born c.1900, quoted in Rose 2001, p. 127). Undoubtedly there is an element of escapism, but also of aspiration in this, as in most, literary reading: 'so reading is the quickest way out of Glasgow' (Scottish postman, 1944, quoted in Rose, 2001, p. 8).

Whilst Rose's study focuses on a particular social group – skilled working class men – the sheer quantity of the evidence and its internal consistency with what we learn from other studies, is impressive. People can read for themselves.

Literature reading as a gendered activity

Reading of literature is numerically dominated by women, whether in formal (literature courses in higher or extension education) or informal (private or in reading groups) contexts. A consistent finding of reading group studies in the UK and the US is that 60% or more are women only, and less than 10% men only. Reading seems a less important activity for most men, and perhaps more solitary too, though this is an area of relative ignorance.

'Reading the romance'

A highly influential first study to argue the value of romance reading to women, was Radway's (1984) ethnography, *Reading the Romance*. For the women in her study, romances offered a respite from a demanding social world where they could find a temporary escape and refuge, and sometimes a space to reflect on their hopes and desires. One woman commented: 'The heroine makes me feel it's a lovely world, people are good, one can face anything and we are lucky to be alive ... if it wasn't for Harlequin [publisher of romances], I'd never know this uplift' (quoted in Radway, 1984, p. 3). Radway's study contradicts notions of romance as a necessarily retrograde form which condones non-progressive images of women and their place in society. For, while textually the 'Pride and Prejudice' plots can be argued to reinforce patriarchal ideologies, they also provide a vital resource for their readers in surviving the stresses of everyday life, while admittedly not doing much to change the social order. Husbands typically criticise women's reading of literature as a waste of time and money (compare Zubair 2003 a, b for contemporary Pakistan, Flint 1993 for 19th century Britain, or Rockhill 1993 for Los Angeles). Yet the women nevertheless go on reading, particularly admiring 'spunky' heroines who are not afraid to stand up for themselves.

Early teenage readers

Cherland (1994) is another important ethnography, this time of teenage girls reading romance serials (for example, *Sweet Valley High*) in a Canadian suburb. Literature reading for girls is part of a larger concern with relationships. Cherland reports the importance of sharing books, using stories as sources for conversation in the maintenance of the girls' own everyday relationships, recommending good reads, and identifying themselves into groups who like or dislike certain genres and writers. Where Cherland's boys (like in Sarland, 1991) read adventure and action genres, the girls read about people, and write diaries recording their feelings. Indeed the development of a whole discourse of feelings is another common reason for valuing reading.

I loved it. I cried so much. It was excellent.

(quoted in Cherland, 1994, p. 102)

Girls read to forget their troubles, in the privacy of suburban bedrooms, where boys are more likely go out and play. The girls explore what they can learn of the performance of gender in a wider world (relationships, marriage, friendship especially), not uncritically but with real interest.

Book clubs

There has been a significant growth in 'book clubs' in the US and the UK in recent times: people organise themselves to meet on a regular basis to discuss books they have collectively decided to read. Hartley (2001) reports a widespread British book club view of schooling as an unfortunate intermission in the pleasures of reading, which begin pre-school and continue outside of school, and are then picked up again after university by working and retired adults, mostly female.

Long has carried out a large ethnographic and survey study of book club practices in Texas, US (Long, 1987, 2003). Long argues that readers in such clubs read to clarify values and beliefs, sometimes at critical junctures in their lives: 'You will never know what a difference it made in my life' (quoted in Long, 2003, p. ix). 'Life experience' is at the centre of literature use. There is awareness of cultural 'authorities' such as reviews in literary magazines or university course reading lists. But there is clear resistance to 'high' literature, postmodernist fiction and poetry. Realism, with coherent plots, and believable characters – especially females – is preferred. Indeed, the centrality of character to literary reading is notable in the search for personal significance. There is a distinct lack of interest in broader cultural analysis or precise textual work, even though many members are aware that this is how literature is read in colleges and universities. 'Discussibility' is a key criterion for selection and is expected to enhance the likely success of book group meetings. The picture is not all rosy however. Long notes that reading groups exclude as well as include: less educated women, who do not find it natural or pleasurable to discuss literature will leave or never join such groups. 'It is a rare group that includes even one participant who has not attended college' (Long, 2003, p. 62); 75% of women in the U.S. have not graduated from college.

Reading canonical texts

Zubair writes of how young women reading English literature on a Masters course in Pakistan, explore marriage concerns and their own identities. Constrained by a conservative English literature syllabus which requires them to read the high canonical 'classics' of English literature, Zubair and her largely female 18–22-year-old students nevertheless find relevance through feminist readings of texts of Chaucer, Shakespeare, or Austen that were unlikely to have been intended or desired by the authorities or families of the young women. English language and literature seem to be a potential, if problematic, site for resistance which would be difficult for these young women to find elsewhere in their lives.

Students reading *Hamlet* were asked, 'Is Ophelia a good and obedient daughter?' because this is a pressing question for many women in Pakistan today:

> [T]his is what is being implanted in our minds through the media ... we are being trained from the very beginning to please men, either a father or a brother or a husband or a son ... I mean what I want to do for myself I can't, father won't like it, son would think what my mum is up to ... Why? This is the training. I'm talking about the training we're given from the very beginning ... look at the media advertisements ... from every side family life, social set-up ... this is the training:

> (Female student in class discussion in Zubair, 2003a, p. 169)

Another student reflected on her experience of literature reading:

> I like Tess [of the D'Urbervilles – Hardy novel] ... that girl ... that girl sacrificed so much all her life ... It is a wonderful novel. I mean ... like I haven't read anything else as powerful as that ... she is portrayed as a typical Eastern woman she was ... her husband has rejected her in spite of that she is constant and above all what I like about it is the scene which I like most in the entire novel is that of their wedding night ... she talks to her husband about her past and a similar incident has occurred in his life too and he admits that he has had relationships ... she forgives him but when she tells her story her husband leaves her there and then ...

> (Zubair, 2003b, p. 26)

Zubair notes uneasiness with English as a colonial language and literature. Nevertheless it seems to allow these young Pakistani women some space to discuss and reflect on their identities, positions in society and aspirations. The values of this language and literature are not uncritically swallowed nor are western practices uncritically assimilated – but rather they are used to think and talk through new, rather unconventional, positions. One 23-year-old woman commented:

> A few days ago I made an effort to read Islamic books because I felt distanced from Islam after studying English literature that's why I read Islamic books (laughs) to clarify the concepts.

> (23-year-old female, choosing to speak in Urdu, Zubair, 2003b, p. 24)

English at university is seen in the larger society as a kind of safe 'finishing school' for girls who want more education before settling down to marry. But we may remember *Madame Bovary*, *Don Quixote* or Rose's readers too. Literary reading can have unforeseen consequences, which is why parents and other powerholders are right to be suspicious.

Colonial and postcolonial readers and writers in India

Joshi (2002) critiques simple determinist views of literary activity through a stimulating study of the popularity of English fiction in colonial India. Using 19th and early 20th century library records, publishers' archives and other writings, Joshi charts the unpredictable and creative transformations of colonial subjects into the producers of a newly prestigious literary canon. Joshi points to the preferences for romance and melodrama rather than realism, explainable perhaps, because of their echoes of Indian epic and oral traditions. But, Joshi suggests, the appeal of such literature to a population under foreign occupation was in its attention to the miraculous intervention of the gods, coincidences, and heroes triumphing against injustice.

By the end of the 19th century the Indian market was a key concern for British publishers like Macmillan, although Indian best-sellers were not quite those of the domestic market. G.M.W. Reynolds, barely a footnote to Dickens for literature students today, was often read for different values in west and east. The meticulous descriptions central to classic realist technique since Defoe, were less important in India than melodramatic plots, including the recurrent eventual triumph of virtue over adversity:

> I read English novels as the plain man reads *Paradise Lost*, skipping over the classical allusions. ...

> I hurry over graphic descriptions of scenes which to me are outlandish; inventories of articles of furniture which it will never fall to my lot even to dream of buying; vivid pictures of costumes which I scarcely expect to see; and portraitures equally realistic of drawing-rooms in which I should probably feel myself and be felt to be a fish out of water ...

[He nevertheless found scenes] which lifted me above my own self, and stirred up all that was good within me.

(R.C. Bose, review of Robert Elsmere, in *Madras Christian College Magazine*, 7, pp. 287, 288, 287; quoted in Joshi, p. 129)

Ultimately, those readers and their sons and daughters were to respond to their diet of English novels by 'writing back' in original creative ways (see Ashcroft *et al.*, 2002). This includes, for example, the 'magic realism' and native oral and epic features of Rushdie's *Midnight's Children* which is a nationalist-inflected rewriting of imported English realist novels, highlighting absurdity and improbability as the new 'real'. Furthermore, literature thought likely to support assimilation to the Empire from the end of the 19th century, promoted writings and debate on identity, social relations and increasingly turned against the colonialists. (e.g. Satthianadhan, *Saguna* [1887-8], *Kamala* [1894], Ahmed Ali, *Twilight in Delhi* 1940).

Conclusion

I began with a set of questions an LASP approach might ask about how real readers engage with literary texts. Some emerging answers have been suggested:

- Much literature reading takes place outside the academy, though higher educational institutions remain influential in shaping tastes and habits of reading, just as institutions like publishing, cultural reviews and bookseller distribution impact on reading choices.

- How and what readers will take from their literary reading cannot be predicted – readers have their own agendas.

- Reading takes place as an activity in wider social contexts serving complex personal and social functions for participants, including reflection on and development of their own life goals and achievements and relations to significant others.

- Numbers of reading groups have grown, perhaps at a previously unappreciated rate in recent years; typically in such groups, predominantly working married women with some higher education, discuss modern realist novels for the relevance of characters and their actions to the readers' own life circumstances, 'remaking themselves in dialogue with others and with literary texts' (Long, 2003, p. 22).

Acknowledgment

Sincere thanks to Theresa Lillis for her constructive reading practices and rewriting activities.

References

ASHCROFT, B., GRIFFITHS, G. and TIFFIN, H. (2002) *The Empire Writes Back*, 2nd edn, London, Routledge.

BOURDIEU, P. (1984[1979]) *Distinction. A Social Critique of the Judgement of Taste*, London, Routledge.

CHERLAND, M.R. (1994) *Private Practices. Girls Reading Fiction and Constructing Identity*, London and Bristol, PA, Taylor and Francis.

DAI, S. (2002) *Balzac and the Little Chinese Seamstress*, trans. I. Rilke, London, Virago.

EAGLETON, T. (1996) *Literary Theory*, 2nd edn, Oxford, Blackwell.

FLINT, K. (1993) *The Woman Reader 1837–1914*, Oxford, Clarendon Press.

FOWLER, K.J. (2004) *The Jane Austen Book Club*, London, Penguin.

HARTLEY, J. (2001) *Reading Groups*, Oxford, Oxford University Press.

JOSHI, P. (2002) *In Another Country. Colonialism, Culture, and the English Novel in India*, New York, Columbia University Press.

LONG, E. (1987) 'Reading groups and the postmodern crisis of cultural authority', *Cultural Studies*, **1**, pp. 306–27.

LONG, E. (2003) *Book Clubs. Women and the Uses of Reading in Everyday Life*, Chicago and London, University of Chicago Press.

NAFISI, A. (2004) *Reading Lolita in Tehran. A Memoir in Books*, London, HarperCollins.

NOBLE, E. (2004) *The Reading Group*, London, Hodder and Stoughton.

RADWAY, J.A. (1984) *Reading the Romance. Women, Patriarchy and Popular Literature*, Chapel Hill and London, University of North Carolina Press.

RICHARDSON, A. (1994) *Literature, Education and Romanticism. Reading as Social Practice, 1780–1832*, Cambridge, Cambridge University Press.

ROCKHILL, K. (1993) 'Gender, language and the politics of literacy' in B. Street, *Cross-cultural Approaches to Literacy*, Cambridge, Cambridge University Press.

ROSE, J. (2001) *The Intellectual Life of the British Working Classes*, New Haven and London, Yale University Press.

SARLAND, C. (1991) *Young People Reading. Culture and Response*, Buckingham, Open University Press.

STREET, B. (ed.) (1993) *Cross-cultural Approaches to Literacy*, Cambridge, Cambridge University Press.

ZUBAIR, S. (2003a) 'Women's critical literacies in a Pakistani classroom', *Changing English*, **10**(2), pp. 163–73.

ZUBAIR, S. (2003b) *Women's identities and English in Pakistan* unpublished manuscript.

Source: commissioned for this volume.

READING C: Extracts from 'Interview with Arundhati Roy'

Reena Jana

[The interviewer's questions are in bold text and Arundhati Roy's responses are in normal text.]

[...] People around the world are asking, 'What does it mean to be an Indian novelist today? What does it mean to be Indian?' Will readers find the answers to these questions in 'The God of Small Things'?

You know, I think that a story is like the surface of water. And you can take what you want from it. Its volubility is its strength. But I feel irritated by this idea, this search. What do we mean when we ask, 'What is Indian? What is India? Who is Indian?' Do we ask, 'What does it mean to be American? What does it mean to be British?' as often? I don't think that it's a question that needs to be asked, necessarily. I don't think along those lines, anyway. I think perhaps that the question we should ask is, 'What does it mean to be human?'

I don't even feel comfortable with this need to define our country. Because it's bigger than that! How can one define India? There is no one language, there is no one culture. There is no one religion, there is no one way of life. There is absolutely no way one could draw a line around it and say, 'This is India' or, 'This is what it means to be Indian.' The whole world is seeking simplification. It's not that easy. I don't believe that one clever movie or one clever book can begin to convey what it means to be Indian. Of course, every writer of fiction tries to make sense of their world. Which is what I do. There are some things that I don't do, though. Like try to make claims of what influenced my book. And I will never 'defend' my book either. When I write, I lay down my weapons and give the book to the reader.

Speaking of influences and defenses, your work has been compared to Salman Rushdie's. And now, in India, you face charges of obscenity in India for the erotic ending of 'The God of Small Things' – a controversy reminiscent of (but not as severe as) Rushdie's *fatwa* (death sentence).

I think that the comparison to Salman has been just a lazy response. When in doubt, if it's an Indian writer, compare them to Salman, because he's the best-known Indian writer! When I say this, I feel bad, because I think it sounds like I don't think very highly of him, because I do. He's a brilliant writer. I think critics have a problem when a new writer comes along, because they want to peg an identity on them. And Salman is the most obvious one for me. But then readers begin to assume the influence, and this isn't fair.

The comparisons emerge from the need to create an analogy, a metaphor for readers to understand the unknown writer's work ...

I understand that need. But then I don't understand when readers assume that Indian writers are 'magical realists' and suddenly I'm a 'magical realist,' just because Salman Rushdie or other Indian writers are 'magical realists.' Sometimes people can misread because of such pegging. For example, when Baby Kochamma is fantasizing or Rahel is observing something as a child or Ammu is dreaming in my book, it is not me, the writer, creating the 'magical realism.' No, what I am writing is what the characters are experiencing. What the reader is reading is the character's own perceptions. Those images are driven by the characters. It is never me invoking magic! This is realism, actually, that I am writing.

Actually, it's not just Rushdie I'm compared to. There's García-Márquez, Joyce ... and Faulkner, always Faulkner. Yes, I'm compared to Faulkner the most. But I've never read Faulkner before! So I can't say anything about him. I have, however, read some other writers from the American South – Mark Twain, Harper S. Lee – and I think that perhaps there's an infusion or intrusion of landscape in their literature that might be similar to mine. This comparison is not that lazy, because it's natural that writers from outside urban areas share an environment that is not man-made and is changed by winds and rivers and rain. I think that human relationships and the divisions between human beings are more brutal and straightforward than those in cities, where everything is hidden behind walls and a veneer of urban sophistication.

[...] When I started to read 'The God of Small Things,' it took me some time to figure out who the protagonist was – and then I started to feel it was the place: India, Kerala.

That quest is interesting – that quest for one main character. There is no reason for there to be one. In fact, I think the center is everyone, Ammu, Baby Kochamma, Velutha, Estha, Rahel ... they all are the core.

Another 'core' of the book is the lyricism of your prose. The Indian-American writer [...] Chitra Banerjee Divakaruni has confessed to writing to the rhythms of Indian music; sometimes she reads her work out loud in public with the music playing in the background to enhance the musicality. Do you have a similar approach?

I don't listen to music when I write. It's about design to me. I'm trained as an architect; writing is like architecture. In buildings, there are design motifs that occur again and again, that repeat – patterns, curves. These motifs help us feel comfortable in a physical space. And the same works in writing, I've found. For me, the way words, punctuation and paragraphs fall on the page is important as well – the graphic design of the language. That was why the words and thoughts of Estha and Rahel, the twins, were so playful on the page. ... I was being creative with their design. Words were broken apart, and then sometimes fused together. 'Later' became 'Lay. Ter.' 'An owl' became 'A Nowl.' 'Sour metal smell' became 'sourmetal smell.'

Repetition I love, and used because it made me feel safe. Repeated words and phrases have a rocking feeling, like a lullaby. They help take away the shock of the plot – death, lives destroyed or the horror of the settings – a crazy, chaotic, emotional house, the sinister movie theater.

How do you react to reviews that analyze your wordplays as 'writerly' or self-conscious?

Language is something I don't think about. At all. In fact, the truth is that my writing isn't self-conscious at all. I don't rewrite. In this whole book, I changed only about two pages. I rarely rewrite a sentence. That's the way I think. Writing this novel was a very intuitive process for me. And pleasurable. So much more pleasurable than writing screenplays. I get so much more pleasure from describing a river than writing 'CUT TO A RIVER'.

You know, I always believe that even among the best writers, there are selfish writers and there are generous ones. Selfish writers leave you with the memory of their book. Generous writers leave you with the memory of the world they evoked. To evoke a world, to communicate it to someone, is like writing a letter to someone that you love. It's a very thin line. For me, books are gifts. When I read a book, I accept it as a gift from an author. When I wrote this book, I presented if as a gift. The reader will do with it what they want.

This is your first novel. How did you start writing it? What was your process? How did you guide yourself through it?

If someone told me this was how I was going to write a novel before I started writing it, I wouldn't believe them. I wrote it out of sequence. I didn't start with the first chapter or end with the last chapter. I actually started writing with a single image in my head: the sky blue Plymouth with two twins inside it, a Marxist procession surrounding it. And it just developed from there. The language just started weaving together, sentence by sentence.

How did you arrive at the final sequence that became the novel in its finished form?

It just worked. For instance, I didn't know, when I started writing, that this book would take place in exactly one day. I kept moving back and forth in time. And then, somehow, I realized that in some of the scenes, the kids were grown up, and sometimes they weren't. I wound up looking at the scenes as different moments, moments that were refracted through time. Reconstituted moments. Moments when Estha is readjusting his Elvis puff of hair. When Estha and Rahel blow spitballs. When Ammu and Velutha make love. These moments, and moments like these in life, I realized, mean something more than what they are, than how they are experienced as mere minutes. They are the substance of human happiness.

Your biography on the book's dust jacket says you are 'trained as an architect and the author of two screenplays.' By other published accounts you are an aerobics instructor. Why and how did you decide to write a novel?

From the time I was a very young child, I knew in my heart that I wanted to be a writer. I never thought I would be able to become one – I didn't have the financial opportunities to be a writer. But then I started writing for film, and this started my writing career. Still, when I was studying architecture, or teaching aerobics, these were things I really wanted to do, things I focused on completely. No matter what I did or what I do, I become absorbed in it. And that was what happened when I started writing 'The God of Small Things.' I worked for a long time, and finally, when I saved enough money to take time off and take the risk of writing a novel – which took me four and a half years of my life, once again I was able to focus on it completely and really enjoy writing it. I was as involved in being an architect as I was writing this novel, and vice versa. I never spent time just dreaming of becoming a writer and resenting my present state. No, my secret was to live my life refusing to be a victim. Failure – no, I shouldn't say 'failure,' rather, the 'lack of success' never frightened me. Even if this book never sold or caught any attention, it would still be the same book. This book is this book. At every point in my life, I decided what I could do and then did it.

There is no way for any publisher or writer to know what will sell and why, even though they are all looking for formula. People are asking me if I am feeling pressure now, and they ask me if I will repeat what I achieved in 'The God of Small Things.' How I hope I do not! I want to keep changing, growing. I don't accept the pressure. I don't believe I must write another book just because now I'm a 'writer.' I don't believe anyone should write unless they have a book to write. Otherwise they should just shut up. [...]

Source: JANA, R. (1997) 'Winds, rivers and rain', The Salon Interview: Arundhati Roy [online] http://www.salon.com/sept97/00roy.html (accessed 11 January 2005).

References

ACHEBE, C. (1975) *Morning Yet on Creation Day*, New York, Anchor Press.

ACHEBE, C. (1988) *Hopes and Impediments: Selected Essays 1965-1987*, London, Heinemann.

ADAMS, T. (2004) 'Coma chameleon', *Observer*, 27 June, [online], http://observer.guardian.co.uk/review/story/0,6903,1248127,00.html (accessed 8.12.2005).

ARIJON, D. (1976) *Grammar of the Film Language*, Hollywood, Silman-James Press.

ARIZPE, E. and STYLES, M. (2003) *Children Reading Pictures: interpreting visual texts*, London, Routledge.

ASHCROFT, B., GRIFFITHS, G. and TIFFIN, H. (2002) *The Empire Writes Back Theory and Practice in Post-colonial Literatures*, 2nd edn, London, Routledge.

ASIAN DUB FOUNDATION (2000) *Community Music*, London Records.

ASTON, E. and SAVONA, G. (1991) *Theatre as Sign System*, London/New York, Routledge.

ATTRIDGE, D. (2004a) *The Singularity of Literature*, London, Routledge.

ATTRIDGE, D. (2004b) 'Reading Joyce', in ATTRIDGE, D. (ed.) *The Cambridge Companion to James Joyce*, 2nd edn, Cambridge, Cambridge University Press.

BACON, F. (1625) *The Essayes or Covnsels, Civill and Morall*, London, John Haviland for Hanna Barret, [online version] www.library.utoronto.ca/utel/criticism/baconf_ess/ess_titlepage.html (accessed 17.2.06).

BAER, A. (2004) 'Call me e-mail', *New York Times*, 15 April, [online] www.nytimes.com/2004/04/15/technology/circuits/15nove.html

BAILEY, R.W. (1992) *Images of English*, Cambridge, Cambridge University Press.

BAKER, M. (1992) *In Other Words: a Coursebook on Translation*, London, Routledge.

BAKHTIN, M. ([1935]1981) 'Discourse in the novel', in M. HOLQUIST (ed.) *The Dialogic Imagination. Four Essays by M. Bakhtin*, trans. C. EMERSON and M. HOLQUIST. Austin, University of Texas Press.

BAKHTIN, M.M. ([1953]1986) 'The problem of speech genres', in C. EMERSON and M. HOLQUIST (eds) *Speech Genres and other Late Essays*, trans. V.W. McGEE, Austin, TX, University of Texas Press.

BARTHES, R. ([1970]1975) *S/Z.*, trans. R. MILLER (as *Extensive Interpretation of Balzac's Sarrasine, using Five 'coides'. Reading Viewed as Production of Text*), New York, Hill and Wang.

BARTHES, R. (1977) 'Introduction to the structural analysis of narratives', in *Image, Music, Text*, London, Fontana.

BARTLETT, F.C. (1932) *Remembering*, Cambridge, Cambridge University Press.

BASSNETT, S. (1998) 'When is a translation not a translation?', in S. BASSNETT and A. LEFEVERE *Constructing cultures*, Clevedon, Multilingual Matters.

BASSNETT, S. (2002) *Translation Studies*, 3rd edn, Routledge, London.

BAUMAN, R. (1986) *Story, Performance and Event*, Cambridge, Cambridge University Press.

BELSEY, C. and MOORE, J. (eds) (1997) *The Feminist Reader: Essays in Gender and the Politics of Literary Criticism*, 2nd edn, London, Macmillan.

BENNETT, A. and ROYLE, N. (2004) *Introduction to Literature, Criticism and Theory,* 3rd edn, Harlow, Pearson Education Ltd.

BEX, T. (1996) *Variety in Written English: Texts in Society – Society in Texts*, London, Routledge.

BIBER, D., JOHANSSON, S., LEECH, G., CONRAD, S., FINEGAN, E. (1999) *Longman Grammar of Spoken and Written English*, Harlow, Pearson.

BIGNELL, J. (2002) *Media Semiotics: An Introduction*, Manchester, Manchester University Press.

BIRCH, D. (1992) 'Gender and genre', in F. BONNER, L. GOODMAN, R. ALLEN, L. JANES and C. KING (eds) *Imagining Women*, Cambridge, Polity in association with Blackwell/The Open University.

BOLTER, J.D. (1991) *Writing Space: The Computer, Hypertext, and the History of Writing*, New Jersey, Lawrence Erlbaum.

BORDWELL, D. and THOMPSON, K. (1993) *Film Art: An Introduction*, New York, McGraw-Hill.

BOURDIEU, P. (1984) *Distinction: A Social Critique of the Judgement of Taste*, Cambridge, MA, Harvard University Press.

BOWERS, F. (1974) *Japanese Theatre*, Rutland VE, Tuttle.

BRADFORD, C. (2001) *Reading Race: Aboriginality in Australian children's literature*, Victoria, Melbourne University Press.

BRADFORD, R. (1997) *Stylistics*, London, Routledge.

BRATHWAITE, K. (1981) 'English in the Caribbean: notes on nation language and poetry, an electronic culture', in L.A. FIEDLER and J.R.BAKER (eds) *English Literature: Opening Up the Canon*, Baltimore and London, John Hopkins University Press.

BRIGGS, R. (1998) *Ethel and Ernest*, London, Jonathan Cape.

BROMLEY, H. (2001) 'A question of talk: young children reading pictures', *Reading*, **35**(2), pp. 62–6.

BURN, A. and PARKER, D. (2003) 'Tiger's big plan: multimodality and the moving image', in G. KRESS and C. JEWITT (eds) *Multimodal Literacy*, New York, Peter Lang.

BURROWAY, J. (2002) *Writing Fiction: A Guide to Narrative Craft*, 6th edn, New York, Addison Wesley Longman.

CARDWELL, S. (2002) *Adaptation Revisited: Television and the Classic Novel*, Manchester, Manchester University Press.

CARDWELL, S. (2003) 'About time: theorizing adaptation, temporality, and tense', *Literature Film Quarterly*, **31**(2).

CAREY, P. (2000) *True History of the Kelly Gang*, London, Faber and Faber.

CARROLL, J. (1999) 'The deep structure of literary representations', *Evolution and Human Behavior*, **20**, pp. 159–73.

CARROLL, L. ([1865]1929) *Alice's Adventures in Wonderland*, Everyman's Library Children's Classics, London, David Campbell.

CARTER, R. (1997) *Investigating English Discourse: Language, Literacy and Literature*, London, Routledge.

CARTER, R. (1999) 'Common language: corpus, creativity and cognition', *Language and Literature*, **8**(3), pp. 195–216.

CARTER, R. (2004) *Language and Creativity: The Art of Common Talk*, New York/London, Routledge.

CARTMELL, D. and WHELEHAN, I. (eds) (1999) *Adaptations: From Text to Screen, Screen to Text*, London, Routledge.

CHAPARRO, A. (2000) 'Translating the Untranslatable: Carroll, Carner and Alícia en Terra Catalana?', *Journal of Iberian and Latin American Studies*, **6**(1), pp. 19–28.

CHATMAN, S. (1969) 'New ways of analysing narrative structure, with an example from Joyce's *Dubliners*', *Language and Style*, **2**(1), pp. 3–36.

CHILD, L. (2002) *Who's Afraid of the Big Bad Book?*, London, Hodder.

CLEESE, J. and BOOTH, C. (1998) *The Complete 'Fawlty Towers'*, London, Methuen.

COOK, G. (1994) *Discourse and Literature: The Interplay of Form and Mind*, Oxford, Oxford University Press.

COOK, G. (2001) *The Discourse of Advertising*, 2nd edn, London, Routledge.

CRYSTAL, D. (1987) *The Cambridge Encyclopedia of Language*, Cambridge, Cambridge University Press.

CULLER, J. (1975a) 'Defining narrative units', in R. FOWLER (ed.) *Style and Structure in Literature*, Oxford, Blackwell.

CULLER, J. (1975b) *Structuralist Poetics*, London, Routledge.

CULPEPER, J. (2001) *Language and Characterisation: People in Plays and other Texts*, Harlow, Longman.

cummings, e e (1960) *Selected poems 1923-1958*, London, Faber and Faber.

DANET, B. (2001) *Cyberpl@y: communicating online*, Oxford, Berg.

DANIELEWSKI, M. (2000) *House of Leaves*, London, Anchor.

DARLY, M. (1778) 'Brittania to America; and America to her mistaken mother' (letter written in London), from the James Ford Bell Library, University of Minnesota.

DENSELOW, T. 'Asian Dub Foundation: the opera', *Guardian Unlimited*, 24 June, [online] http://www.guardian.co.uk/arts/news/story/0,,1246185,00.html (accessed 17.2.06).

DERRIDA, J. (1978) *Writing and difference*, trans. A. BASS, Chicago, Chicago University Press.

DOUGLAS, J. YELLOWLEES (1994) ' "How do I stop this thing?" Closure and indeterminacy in interactive narratives', in G.P. LANDOW (ed.) *Hyper/Text/Theory*, Baltimore, John Hopkins University Press.

EAGLETON, T. (1983) *Literary Theory: An Introduction*, Oxford, Blackwell.

EAGLETON, T. (1996) *Literary Theory*, 2nd edn, Oxford, Blackwell.

ECO, U. (1979) 'Narrative structures in Fleming' in *The Role of the Reader: Explorations in the Semiotics of Texts*, London, Hutchinson.

EGGERS, D. (2000) *A Heartbreaking Work of Staggering Genius*, London, Picador.

ELAM, K. (2002) *The Semiotics of Theatre and Drama*, 2nd edn, London/New York, Routledge.

ELLMAN, R. (1975) *Selected Letters of James Joyce*, London, Faber and Faber.

ESKELINEN, M. (2000) '(Introduction to) Cybertext narratology', in M. ESKELINEN and R. KOSKIMAA (eds) *Cybertext Yearbook 2000*, Finland, University of Jvyäskylä.

FAIRCLOUGH, N. (1995) *Media Discourse*, London, Arnold.

FANELLI, S. (2002) *First Flight*, London, Jonathan Cape.

FINDLAY, B. (2000) 'Translating standard into dialect: missing the target', in C. UPTON (ed.) *Moving Target: Theatre Translation and Cultural Relocation*, Manchester, St Jerome Publishing.

FINE, E.C. (1984) *The Folklore Text: From Performance to Print*, Bloomington and Indianapolis, Indiana University Press.

FISH, S. (1970) 'Literature in the reader: affective stylistics', *New Literary History*, **2**, pp. 123–62.

FISH, S. (1980) *Is There a Text in this Class? The Authority of Interpretive Communities*, Cambridge, MA, Harvard University Press.

FLANAGAN, R. (2001) *Gould's Book of Fish*, London, Atlantic Books.

FOWLER, R. (1996) *Linguistic Criticism*, 2nd edn, Oxford, Oxford University Press.

GARLAND, A. (2004) The Coma, London, Faber and Faber.

GAVINS, J. AND STEEN, G. (eds.) (2003) *Cognitive Poetics in Practice*, London: Routledge.

GEE, J.P. (2003) *What Video Games Have to Teach Us about Learning and Literacy*, New York, Palgrave Macmillan.

GILBERT, S. and GUBAR, S. (1979) *The Madwoman in the Attic: The Woman writer and the Nineteenth-Century Literary Imagination*, New Haven, Yale University Press.

GOLDSMITH, K. 'Poems for all', found poem, UbuWeb, [online] http://www.ubu.com/outsiders/ass.html (accessed 12.12.05).

GOODMAN, S. (1996) 'Visual English', in S. GOODMAN and D. GRADDOL (eds.) *Redesigning Texts: New Texts, New Identities*, London, Routledge.

GREIMAS, A.J. ([1968]1983) *Structural Semantics: An Attempt at a Method*, trans. D. McDOWELL, R. SCHLEIFER and A. VELIE, Lincoln, Nebraska, University of Nebraska Press.

GRICE, H.P. (1975) 'Logic and conversation', in P. COLE and J. MORGAN (eds) *Syntax and Semantics, 3: Speech Acts*, New York, Academic Press.

HADDON, M. (2003) *The Curious Incident of the Dog in the Night-Time*, London, Jonathan Cape.

HALLIDAY, M. (1985) *An Introduction to Functional Grammar*, London, Edward Arnold.

HAMMERSLEY, M. (1994) 'Introducing ethnography', in D. GRADDOL, J. MAYBIN and B. STIERER (eds) *Researching Language and Literacy in Social Context*, Clevedon/Milton Keynes, Multilingual Matters/Open University Press.

HAMMOND, P. and HOPKINS, D. (eds) (1995–2005) *The Poems of John Dryden, Vol. I*, Longman, London.

HANAUER, D. (1996) 'Integration of phonetic and graphic features in poetic text categorization judgements', *Poetics,* **23**, pp. 363–80.

HART, C. (1969) 'Eveline', in C. HART *James Joyce's 'Dubliners'*, London, Faber and Faber.

HAWKES, T. (1977) *Structuralism and Semiotics*, London, Methuen.

HERMAN, V. (1998) 'Turn management in drama' in J. CULPEPER, M. SHORT and P. VERDONK (eds) *Exploring the Language of Drama*, London, Routledge.

HIGGINS, C. (2004) 'Nauman's rehashed sounds reverberate around the Tate's emptiness', *The Guardian*, 12 October, Guardian Unlimited, [online] www.guardian.co.uk/arts/news/story/0,11711,1325065,00.html (accessed 17.2.06).

HODGART, M. (1978) *James Joyce: A Student's Guide*, London, Routledge and Kegan Paul.

HOLMES, J. (1988) *Translated!*, Amsterdam, Rodopi.

HOLUB, R.C. (1984) *Reception Theory. A Critical Introduction*, London/ New York, Methuen.

HOOKS, B. (1994) *Teaching to Transgress*, London/New York, Routledge.

HUGHES, T. ([1857]1949) *Tom Brown's Schooldays*, London, Dent and Sons.

HYMES, D. (1975) 'Breakthrough into performance', in D. BEN-AMOS and K. GOLDSTEIN (eds) *Folklore: Communication and Performance*, The Hague, Mouton.

ISER, W. (1974) *The Implied Reader: Patterns of Communication in Prose Fiction from Bunyan to Beckett*, Baltimore and London: John Hopkins University Press.

ISER, W. (1978) *The Act of Reading: A Theory of Aesthetic Response,* London, Routledge and Kegan Paul.

JAKOBSON, R. (1960) 'Closing statement, linguistics and poetics', in T. SEBEOK (ed.) *Style in Language*, Cambridge MA, MIT Press.

JAKOBSON, R. (1968) 'Poetry of grammar and grammar of poetry', *Lingua*, **21**, pp. 597–609.

JAMES, H. ([1888]1948) 'The art of fiction', in *The Art of Fiction and Other Essays*, New York, Oxford University Press.

JAUSS, H. R. (1982) *Toward an Aesthetic of Reception*, trans. T. BAHTI, Minneapolis, University of Minnesota Press.

JEFFRIES, L. (2001) 'Schema affirmation and White Asparagus: cultural multilingualism among readers of texts', *Language and Literature*, **10**(4), pp. 325–43.

JEWITT, C. (2004) 'Multimodality and new communication technologies', in P. LEVINE and R. SCOLLON (eds) *Discourse and Technology: Multimodal Discourse Analysis*, Washington, Georgetown University Press, pp. 184–195.

JEWITT, C. and KRESS, G. (2003) 'A multimodal approach to research in education', in S. GOODMAN, T. LILLIS, J. MAYBIN and N. MERCER (eds) *Language, Literacy and Education: A Reader*, Stoke-on-Trent, Trentham Books.

JOHNSON-EILOLA, J. (1994) 'Reading and writing in hypertext: vertigo and euphoria', in C.L. SELFE and S. HILLIGOSS (eds) *Literacy and Computers: The Complications of Teaching and Learning with Technology*, New York, MLA.

JOYCE, J. ([1922]1986) *Ulysses,* Harmondsworth, Penguin.

JOYCE, J. ([1914]2000) *Dubliners*, New York/Oxford, Oxford University Press.

JOYCE, J. ([1927]1991,2001) *Poems and Shorter Writings*, London, Faber and Faber.

JOYCE, M. (1987) *Afternoon: A Story*, [online] www.eastgate.com

KITAMURA, S. (1987) *Lily Takes a Walk*, London, Happy Cat.

KOWZAN, T. (1968) 'The sign in the theatre', *Diogenes*, **61**, pp. 52–80.

KRESS, G. (2003) *Literacy in the Media Age*, London, Routledge.

KRESS, G. and VAN LEEUWEN, T. (2001) *Multimodal Discourse: The Modes and Media of Contemporary Communication*, London, Arnold.

KRISTEVA, J. (1986) 'Word, dialogue and the novel', in T. MOI (ed.) *The Kristeva Reader*, Oxford, Basil Blackwell.

LANDOW, G.P. (1997) *Hypertext 2.0: The Convergence of Contemporary Critical Theory and Technology*, Baltimore, John Hopkins University Press.

LÁSZLÓ, J. and CUPCHIK, G.C. (2003) 'Psychology of literary narratives: studies of identity and conflict', *Empirical Studies of the Arts*, **21**(1), pp. 1–4.

LAWRENCE, D.H. (1972) *The Complete Poems of D.H. Lawrence*, in V. DE SOLA PINTO and F. WARREN ROBERTS (eds), London, Heinemann.

LEECH, G.N. and SHORT, M.H. (1981) *Style in Fiction: a linguistic introduction to English fictional prose*, London, Longman.

LEITH, D. and GRADDOL, D. (1996) 'Modernity and English as a national language', in D. GRADDOL, D. LEITH and J. SWANN (eds) (1996) *English: History, Diversity and Change*, London, Routledge.

LEONARD, G. (2004) 'Dubliners' in Attridge, D. (ed.) *The Cambridge Companion to James Joyce*, 2nd edn, Cambridge, Cambridge University Press.

LESSING, D. (1974) *The Golden Notebook,* Michael Joseph, London.

LEWIS, D. (2001) *Reading Contemporary Picturebooks: Picturing Text*, London, Routledge.

LILLIS, T. and McKINNEY, C. (2003) *Analysing Language in Context: A Student Workbook*, Stoke on Trent, Trentham Books.

LOOMBA, A, (1997) 'Shakespearean transformations', in J. JOUGHIN (ed.) *Shakespeare and National Culture*, Manchester, Manchester University Press.

LOUW, B. (1993) 'Irony in the text or sincerity in the writer?: the diagnostic potential of semantic prosodies', in M. BAKER, G. FRANCIS and E. TOGNINI-BONELLI (eds) *Text and Technology: In Honour of John Sinclair*, Amsterdam, John Benjamins.

MAYBIN, J. and SWANN, J. (eds) (2006) *The art of English: everyday texts and practices*.

McARTHUR, T. (2002) *Oxford Guide to World English*, Oxford, Oxford University Press.

McEWAN. I. (2002) 'Mother tongue: a memoir' in Z. LEADER (ed.) *On modern British Fiction*, Oxford, Oxford University Press.

McCLOUD, S. (1993) *Understanding Comics: The Invisible Art*, New York, Kitchen Sink Press, HarperCollins.

McFARLANE, B. (1996) *Novel to Film: An Introduction to the Theory of Adaptation*, Oxford, Clarendon.

McINTYRE, D. (2003) 'Using foregrounding theory as a teaching methodology in a stylistics course', *Style*, **37**(1), pp. 1–13.

MIALL, D.S. and KUIKEN, D. (1994) 'Foregrounding, defamiliarization and affect: response to literary stories', *Poetics*, **22**, pp. 389–407.

MIALL, D.S. and KUIKEN, D. (1998) 'The form of reading: Empirical studies of literariness', *Poetics*, **25**, pp. 327–41.

MILLS, S. (1995) *Feminist Stylistics*, London, Routledge.

MILNE, A.A. ([1926]1989) *The Complete Winnie-the-Pooh*, London, Chancellor Press/Methuen.

MONTFORT, N. (2003) *Toward a Theory of Interactive Fiction*, available online at http://nickm.com/if/toward.html.

MONTGOMERY, M. (1993) 'Language, character and action: a linguistic approach to the analysis of character in a Hemingway short story', in J. SINCLAIR, M. HOEY and G. FOX (eds) *Techniques of Description: Spoken and Written Discourse*, London, Routledge.

MUKAŘOVSKÝ, J. ([1932]1964) 'Standard language and poetic language', in P.L. GARVIN (ed. and trans.) *A Prague School Reader on Esthetics, Literary Structure and Style*, Georgetown, Georgetown University Press.

MUKAŘOVSKÝ, J. ([1932]1970) 'Standard language and poetic language', in D. FREEMAN (ed.) *Linguistics and Literary Style*, New York, Holt, Rinehart and Winston.

MURRAY, J.H. (1997) *Hamlet on the Holodeck: The Future of Narrative in Cyberspace*, Cambridge, Massachusetts, MIT Press.

NARAYAN, R.K. ([1945]1999) *The English Teacher* in *A Malgudi Omnibus*, London, Vintage, Random House.

NAREMORE, J. (ed.) (2000) *Film Adaptation*, London, Athlone Press.

NASA Quest (2005) Untitled poem, Writing Experience: writing concrete poetry, [online] http://quest.arc.nasa.gov/aero/events/regimes/poet.html (accessed 7.12.05).

NASH, W. (1993) 'The lyrical game: C. Day Lewis's "Last words"', in P. VERDONK (ed.) *Twentieth Century Poetry: From Text to Context*, London, Routledge.

NGUGI WA THIONG'O (1986) *Decolonising the Mind: The Politics of Language in African Literature*, London, James Curry.

NIKOLAJEVA, M. and SCOTT, C. (2000) 'The dynamics of picturebook communication', *Children's Literature in Education*, **31**(4), pp. 225–39.

NISSAN (2003) 'Shift expectations', [online] www.alphaleasing.co.uk/brochures/micra.pdf

NODELMAN, P. (1988) *Words about Pictures: The Narrative Art of Children's Picture Books*, Athens, GA, University of Georgia Press.

ONG, W. (1982) *Orality and Literacy: The Technologizing of the Word*, London, Methuen.

ORWELL ([1949]1989) *Nineteen Eighty-Four*, London, Penguin.

PAVIS, P. (1985) 'Theatre analysis: some questions and a questionnaire', *New Theatre Quarterly*, **1**(2), pp. 208–12.

PAVIS, P. (1992) *Theatre at the Crossroads of Culture*, trans. L. KRUGER, London and New York, Routledge.

PENNYCOOK, A. (1994) *The Politics of English as an International Language*, London, Longman.

PENNYCOOK, A. (2003) 'Beyond homogeny and heterogeny: English as a global and worldy language', in C. MAIR (ed.) *The Politics of English as a World Language*, Amsterdam, Rodopi.

PILKINGTON, A. (1991) 'Poetic effects: a relevance theory perspective', in ROGER D. SELL *Literary Pragmatics*, London, Routledge.

PILKINGTON, A. (2000) *Poetic Effects: A Relevance Theory Perspective*, Amsterdam, John Benjamins.

PLENZDORF, U. ([1973]1979) *Die Neuen Leiden des Jungen W.*, Surrey, Thomas Nelson.

POPE, R. (1995) *Textual Intervention: Critical and Creative Strategies for Literary Studies*, London, Routledge.

POPE, R. (2002) *The English Studies Book*, London, Routledge.

POPE, R. (2003) 'Re-writing texts, re-constructing the subject: work as play on the critical-creative interface', in T. AGATHOCLEOUS and A. DEAN (eds) *Teaching Literature: A Companion*, London, Palgrave.

POPE, R. (2005) *Creativity: Theory, History, Practice*, London, Routledge.

PORTER ABBOTT, H. (2002) *The Cambridge Introduction to Narrative*, Cambridge, Cambridge University Press.

PROPP, V. ([1928]1968) *Morphology of The Folk Tale*, trans. L. SCOTT, University of Texas Press.

RAFFEL, B. (1994) *The Art of Translating Prose*, Pennsylvania, Pennsylvania State University Press.

REYNOLDS, P. (ed.) (1993) *Novel Images: Literature in Performance*, London, Routledge.

ROSENBERG, D. (1994) *World Mythology: An Anthology of Great Myths and Epics*, 2nd edn, Lincolnwood IL, NTC Publishing Group.

ROY, A. (1997) *The God of Small Things,* Flamingo, London.

RUBRECHT, A. (2001) 'What is a text?', *Rubrecht on Texts* [online] www.uwec.edu/english/Library/Rubrecht/Text.htm (accessed 20.2.06).

RUMSFELD, D. (2002) US Department of Defense News Briefing [online] www.defenselink.mil/transcripts/2002/t02122002_t212sdv2.html (accessed 17.2.06).

RUSHDIE, S. (1982) 'The Empire writes back with a vengeance', *The Times,* 3 July.

SAID, E. (1993) *Culture and Imperialism,* Vintage, London.

SAUSSURE, F. de (1974) *Course in General Linguistics,* trans. W. BASKIN, London, Fontana. (Original French version 1915.)

SCHANK, R. and ABELSON, R. (1977) *Scripts, Plans, Goals and Understanding,* Hillsdale, NJ, Lawrence Erlbaum.

SCHRAM, D. and STEEN, G. (2001) (eds) *The Psychology and Sociology of Literature. In Honor of Elrud Ibsch,* Amsterdam, John Benjamins.

SCHRAM, D. and STEEN, G. (2001) 'The empirical study of literature: psychology, sociology and other disciplines', in D. SCHRAM and G. STEEN (eds) op. cit.

SCIESZKA, J. and SMITH, L. (1992) *The Stinky Cheeseman and Other Fairly Stupid Tales,* London, Penguin Books.

SEELY, H. (2003) 'The poetry of D.H. Rumsfeld', *Slate,* [online] http://slate.msn.com/id/2081042 (accessed 17.2.06).

SEMINO, E. (1997) *Language and World Creation in Poems and Other Texts,* London, Longman.

SENGUPTA, M. (1990) 'Translation, colonialism and poetics: Rabindranath Tagore in two worlds' in S. BASSNETT and A. LEFEVERE (eds) *Translation, History and Culture,* London, Pinter.

SHAKESPEARE, W. ([1623] 1902) *Mr William Shakespeares Comedies, Tragedies, & Tragedies,* London, Isaac Jaggard and Ed Blount (Facsimile edn: Oxford, Clarendon Press).

SHKLOVSKY, V. (1965) 'Art as technique', in L.T. LEMON and M.J. REIS (eds) *Russian Formalist Criticism: Four Essays,* Lincoln, NB, University of Nebraska Press.

SHORT, M. (1996) *Exploring the Language of Poems, Plays and Prose,* Harlow, Longman.

SHORT, M. (1998) 'From dramatic text to dramatic performance', in J. CULPEPER, M. SHORT and P. VERDONK (eds) *Exploring the Language of Drama,* London and New York, Routledge.

SHORT, M., CULPEPER, J. and SEMINO, E. (2000) 'Language and context: Jane Gardham's *Bilgewater*', in T. BEX, M. BURKE and P. STOCKWELL, *Contextualised Stylistics,* Amsterdam, Rodopi.

SHORT, M., SEMINO, E. and CULPEPER, J. (1996) 'Using a corpus for stylistics research: speech and thought presentation,' in J. THOMAS and M. SHORT (eds) *Using Corpora for Language Research: studies in the honour of Geoffrey Leech*, London and New York, Longman.

SHOWALTER, E. (1986) *The New Feminist Criticism: Essays on Women, Literature and Theory*, London, Virago.

SIMMONDS, R. (2003) 'The poem as novel: Lawrence's *Pansies* and Bakhtin's theory of the novel', *English Studies,* **2**, pp. 119–44.

SLOANE, S. (2000) *Digital Fictions: Storytelling in the Material World*, Connecticut, Ablex.

SMITH, Z. (2000) *White Teeth*, London, Hamish Hamilton.

SNYDER, I. (1998) 'Beyond the hype: reassessing hypertext', in I. SNYDER (ed.) *Page to Screen: Taking Literacy into the Electronic Age*, London, Routledge.

SPERBER, D. and WILSON, D. (1995) *Relevance: Communication and Cognition*, 2nd edn, Oxford, Blackwell.

STEEN, G. and GAVINS. J. (2003) 'Contextualising cognitive poetics', in J. GAVINS and G. STEEN (eds) *Cognitive Poetics in Practice*, London, Routledge.

STEINBECK, J. (1937) *Of Mice and Men*, Oxford, Heinemann.

STEINER, G. (1998) *After Babel: Aspects of Language and Translation*, Oxford, Oxford University Press.

STEINER, T.R. (1975) *English Translation Theory 1650-1800*, Assen/Amsterdam, Van Gorcum.

STEWART, C., LAVELLE, M. and KOWALTZKE, A. (2001) *Media and Meaning: An Introduction*, London, British Film Institute.

STOCKWELL, P. (2002) *Cognitive Poetics: An Introduction*, London, Routledge.

STUBBS, M. (2001) *Words and Phrases: Corpus Studies of Lexical Semantics*, Oxford, Blackwell.

SWANN, J. (2002) 'The intersection of verbal, visual and vocal elements in an oral narrative', in I. BLAYER and M. SANCHEZ (eds) *Storytelling: interdisciplinary and intercultural perspectives*, New York, Peter Lang.

SWANN, J., DEUMERT, A., LILLIS, T. and MESTHRIE, R. (2004) *A Dictionary of Sociolinguistics*, Edinburgh, Edinburgh University Press.

THIBAULT, P.J. (2000) 'The multimodal transcription of a television advertisement: theory and practice', in A. BALDRY (ed.) *Multimodality and Multimediality in the Distance Learning Age*, Campobasso, Italy, Palladino Editore.

TOOLAN, M. (2001) *Narrative: A Critical Linguistic Introduction*, 2nd edn, London, Routledge.

TYMOCZKO, M. (1999) 'Post-colonial writing and literary translation', in S. BASSNETT and H. TRIVEDI (eds) *Postcolonial Translation: Theory and Practice*, London, Routledge.

UNSWORTH, L. and WHEELER, J. (2002) 'Re-valuing the role of images in reviewing picture books', *Reading: Literacy and Language*, **36**(2), pp. 68–74.

VAN LEEUWEN, T. (2005) *Introducing Social Semiotics*, London, Routledge.

VENUTI, L. (1998) *The Scandals of Translation: Towards an Ethics of Difference*, London, Routledge.

VISWANATHAN, G. (1990) *Masks of Conquest: Literary Study and British Rule in India*, London, Faber and Faber.

VOLOSINOV, V.N. (1986) *Marxism and the Philosophy of Language* (trans. L. MATEJKA and I.R. TITUNIK), Cambridge, Cambridge University Press.

WABER, D. (1999) 'argument', *strings*, a Flash project, [online] http://vispo.com/ghosts/DanWaber/argument.html (accessed 7.12.05).

WATSON, V. and STYLES, M. (eds) (1996) *Talking Pictures: Pictorial Texts and Young Readers*, London, Hodder and Stoughton.

WERTH, P. (1999) *Text Worlds: Representing Conceptual Space in Discourse*, London, Longman.

WIDDOWSON, H. (2000) 'Critical practices: on representation and the interpretation of text', in S. SARANGI and M. COULTHARD (eds) *Discourse and Social Life*, Harlow, Pearson.

WOOD, M. (1994) 'I saved Hurley from 4 Burly Girlies' *The Sun*, 25 November, p. 1.

WOOD, M. and LOWRIE, H. (1994) 'That was real Top Crumpet!' *The Sun*, 25 November, p. 2.

WYILE, A.S. (2001) 'First-person engaging narration in the picture book: verbal and pictorial variations', *Children's Literature in Education*, **32**(3), pp. 191–202.

ZWAAN, R.A. (1991) 'Some parameters of literary and news comprehension: effects of discourse-type perspective on reading rate and surface structure representation', *Poetics*, **20**, pp. 139–56.

ZWAAN, R.A. (1993) *Aspects of Literary Comprehension. A Cognitive Approach*, Benjamins, Amsterdam.

Acknowledgements

Grateful acknowledgement is made to the following sources for permission to reproduce material in this book.

Text

Page 4 (text 1): By permission of The British Library. Any further reproduction outside of this use is prohibited; *(text 3)*: Rumsfeld, D. H. (2002) 'The Unknown', February 12 2002, Department of Defence News Briefing, from http://slate.msn.com/id/2081042/; *(text 6)*: By permission of The British Library. Any further reproduction outside of this use is prohibited; *(text 7)*: Asian Dub Foundation (2000) *Community Music* (CD), London: London Records 90. Warner Chappell Music; *page 23*: numerous extracts from the Tate Website: www.tate.org.uk/modern, Tate Modern; *pages 25–30*: Eagleton, T. (1996) 'The Rise of English', *Literary Theory: An Introduction*, Blackwell Publishing Ltd; *pages 30–37*: Widdowson, H. (2000) 'Critical practices: on representation and the interpretation of text', in Sarangi, S. and Coulthard, M., *Discourse and Social Life*, pp. 157–164, © Pearson Education Limited 2000; *page 38*: All lines from 'Tulips' from *Ariel* by Sylvia Plath. Copyright © 1962 by Ted Hughes. Reprinted by permission of HarperCollins Publishers, Faber and Faber Ltd. Edwards Fuglewicz; *pages 45–48*: Editions Rodopi BV; *page 49*: Leonard, T. (1984) 'Bunnit Huslin (A Summer's Day)', *Intimate Voices: Selected Work 1965–1983*, Copyright © Tom Leonard; *page 55*: By Dylan Thomas, from *The Poems of Dylan Thomas*, Copyright © 1939 by New Directions Publishing Corp. Reprinted by permission of New Directions Publishing Corp.; *pages 57–58*: Day Lewis, C. (1957) 'Last Words', *The Complete Poems*, Sinclair-Stevenson, 1992; *page 61*: 'she being Brand' is reprinted from *Complete Poems 1904–1962*, by e e cummings, edited by George J. Firmage, by permission of W.W. Norton & Company and Liveright Publishing Corporation. Copyright © 1991 by the Trustees for the E.E. Cummings Trust and George James Firmage; *page 68*: reproduced from The Bank of English ® part of Collins Word Web with the permission of HarperCollins Publishers Ltd; *pages 72 and 75–79*: Nash, W. (1993) 'The lyrical game: C. Day Lewis's "Last Words" ', in Verdonk, P. (ed.), *Twentieth-Century Poetry: From Text to Context*, pp. 46–56, Routledge, www.tandf.co.uk and www.eBookstore.tandf.co.uk; *pages 80–86*: Carter, R. (1997) 'Is there a literary language?', *Investigating English Discourse*, Taylor and Francis Books Ltd; *pages 86–93*: Bradford, R. (1997) 'Evaluative stylistics', *Stylistics*, Routledge, pp. 188–198, Taylor and Francis Ltd, www.tandf.co.uk and www.eBookstore.tandf.co.uk; *page 87*: Adcock, F. (2000) 'Against Coupling', *Poems 1960–2000*, Bloodaxe Books; *pages 120–123*: *Dubliners*/James Joyce. Text © Copyright 1967 by the Estate of James Joyce; *pages 124–127*: adapted from Toolan, M. (1988, 2001) 'Basic story structure', *Narrative: A Critical Linguistic Introduction*, pp. 31–37, Routledge, Taylor and Francis Books Ltd. © Michael Toolan; *pages 128–137*: adapted from Montgomery, M. (1993)

Picturebooks, pp. 87–100, Routledge, Taylor and Francis Books Ltd, www.tandf.co.uk and www.eBookstore.tandf.co.uk; *pages 318–320*: Eastgate Systems Inc.; *pages 322–323*: Deena Larsen; *page 324*: Jim Andrews; *pages 329–334*: Carey Jewitt; *pages 334–342*: Porter Abbott, H. 'Adaptation across media', *The Cambridge Introduction to Narrative*, 2002 © Cambridge University Press, reproduced with permission of the author and publisher; *pages 342–349*: Burn, A. and Parker, D. (2003) 'Tiger's big plan: multimodality and the moving image', in Jewitt, C. and Kress, G., *Multimodal Literacy*, pp. 57–72, Peter Lang Publishing Inc.; *pages 349–363*: Danet, B. (2001) *Cyberpl@y: Communicating Online*, Berg Publishers Ltd; *pages 364 and 368*: Anne Stevenson, *Poems 1966–2000*, Bloodaxe Books, 2000; *page 377*: 'A Pillowed Head' from *Seeing Things* by Seamus Heaney. Copyright © 1991 by Seamus Heaney. Reprinted by permission of Farrar, Straus and Giroux, LLC. And Faber and Faber Ltd; *page 384*: reproduced from The Bank of English ® part of Collins Word Web with the permission of HarperCollins Publishers Ltd; *page 389 (and Colour Illustration)*: 'The Tyger' from *Songs of Experience* by William Blake, 1927. Reference (shelfmark) 17078 d 391. Bodleian Library, University of Oxford; *pages 390–395*: adapted from Bex, T. (1996) *Variety in Written English: Texts in Society – Society in Texts*, Chapter 8, London, Routledge, Taylor and Francis Books Ltd, © Copyright Tony Bex; *page 393*: 'Musée des Beaux Arts', Copyright 1940 and renewed 1968 by W.H. Auden, from *Collected Poems* by W.H. Auden. Used by permission of Random House, Inc., Faber and Faber Ltd and Copyright © 1939 by W.H. Auden. Reprinted by permission of Curtis Brown, Ltd.; *pages 396–406*: adapted from Cook, G. (1994) *Discourse and Literature*, Oxford, Chapter 6, Oxford University Press, © Copyright Guy Cook; *pages 399–400*: Bond, E. (1978) *Theatre Poems and Songs*, Methuen Publishing Ltd and Casarotto Ramsay & Associates Limited; *pages 407–413*: adapted from Short, M., Culpeper, J. and Semino, E. (2000) 'Language and context: Jane Gardam's Bilgewater' in T. Bex, M. Burke and P. Stockwell, *Contextualised Stylistics*, pp. 131–151, Editions Rodopi, Amsterdam; *page 427*: Reproduced with permission, Estate of James Joyce. Copyright © Estate of James Joyce; *page 428*: based on an extract from *Chamber Music*, Copyright © Estate of James Joyce; *pages 446–453*: Miall, D.S. and Kuiken, D. (1998) Extracts from *Poetics*, pp. 327–341, Elsevier Science B.V.; *pages 462–465*: Jana, R. (1997) 'Interview with Arundhati Roy' (The Salon Interview, Sept. 1997) from www.salon.com.

Illustrations

Page 4 (item 5): Newsflash Scotland Ltd; *page 148*: BBC Motion Gallery; *page 253*: excerpt from personal letter M. Darly to her daughter, 1778, from the James Ford Bell Library, Minnesota; *page 254 (bottom)*: from www.yourpage.org/planttree-rebus.html; *page 258*: line illustration copyright E.H. Shepard, colouring © 1970, 1973 by E.H. Shepard & Egmont Books Ltd., reproduced by permission of Curtis Brown London; *page 261*: Garland, A. (2004) *The Coma*. Text © Alex Garland 2004. Images © Nicholas Garland 2004.